Eleventh Edition

ESSENTIALS OF
ORGANIZATIONAL BEHAVIOR

Eleventh Edition

ESSENTIALS OF ORGANIZATIONAL BEHAVIOR

Stephen P. Robbins
San Diego State University

Timothy A. Judge
University of Notre Dame

Prentice Hall
Boston Columbus Indianapolis New York San Francisco Upper Saddle River
Amsterdam Cape Town Dubai London Madrid Milan Munich Paris Montreal Toronto
Delhi Mexico City Sao Paulo Sydney Hong Kong Seoul Singapore Taipei Tokyo

Editorial Director: Sally Yagan
Editor in Chief: Eric Svendsen
Director of Editorial Services: Ashley Santora
Editorial Project Manager: Meg O'Rourke
Editorial Assistant: Carter Anderson
Director of Marketing: Patrice Lumumba Jones
Marketing Manager: Nikki Ayana Jones
Marketing Assistant: Ian Gold
Senior Managing Editor: Judy Leale
Project Manager: Becca Richter
Senior Operations Supervisor: Arnold Vila
Operations Specialist: Cathleen Petersen
Creative Director: Christy Mahon

Senior Art Director: Kenny Beck
Cover Designer: Ray Cruz
Cover Art: Michael Clutson/SPL/Photo Researchers, Inc.
Manager, Rights and Permissions: Hessa Albader
Media Project Manager, Editorial: Denise Vaughn
Media Project Manager, Production: Lisa Rinaldi
Full-Service Project Management: Christian Holdener,
  S4Carlisle Publishing Services
Composition: S4Carlisle Publishing Services
Printer/Binder: Edwards Brothers
Cover Printer: Lehigh-Phoenix Color/Hagerstown
Text Font: Times 10/12

Credits and acknowledgments borrowed from other sources and reproduced, with permission, in this textbook appear on appropriate page within text.

Library of Congress Cataloging-in-Publication Data
Judge, Tim.
   Essentials of organizational behavior / Timothy A. Judge, Stephen P. Robbins.—11th ed.
      p. cm.
   Rev. ed. of: Essentials of organizational behavior / Stephen P. Robbins, Timothy A. Judge. 10th ed.
   In earlier eds., Stephen P. Robbins name appeared first.
   Includes bibliographical references and index.
   ISBN 978-0-13-254530-3 (alk. paper)
 1. Organizational behavior.   I. Robbins, Stephen P., 1943– Essentials of organizational behavior.
II. Title.
   HD58.7.R6 2012
   658.3—dc22   2010031990
10 9 8 7 6 5 4 3 2 1

Prentice Hall
is an imprint of

www.pearsonhighered.com

ISBN 10:   0-13-254530-6
ISBN 13: 978-0-13-254530-3

This book is dedicated to our friends and colleagues in
The Organizational Behavior Teaching Society
who, through their teaching, research and commitment
to the leading process, have significantly
improved the ability of students
to understand and apply OB concepts.

BRIEF CONTENTS

PART 1 **Prologue**   1

    Chapter 1   Introduction to Organizational Behavior   1

PART 2 **The Individual in the Organization**   13

    Chapter 2   Attitudes and Job Satisfaction   13
    Chapter 3   Emotions and Moods   26
    Chapter 4   Personality and Values   41
    Chapter 5   Perception and Individual Decision Making   57
    Chapter 6   Motivation Concepts   72
    Chapter 7   Motivation: From Concepts to Applications   90

PART 3 **Groups in the Organization**   106

    Chapter 8   Foundations of Group Behavior   106
    Chapter 9   Understanding Work Teams   122
    Chapter 10 Communication   135
    Chapter 11 Leadership   150
    Chapter 12 Power and Politics   170
    Chapter 13 Conflict and Negotiation   186

PART 4 **The Organization System**   202

    Chapter 14 Foundations of Organization Structure   202
    Chapter 15 Organizational Culture   218
    Chapter 16 Organizational Change and Stress Management   234

CONTENTS

Preface xix
Acknowledgments xxiv
About the Authors xxv

Part 1 Prologue 1

Chapter 1 Introduction to Organizational Behavior 1
Enter Organizational Behavior 2
Complementing Intuition with Systematic Study 2
Disciplines That Contribute to the OB Field 3
  Psychology 3
  Social Psychology 4
  Sociology 5
  Anthropology 5
There Are Few Absolutes in OB 5
Challenges and Opportunities for OB 5
  Responding to Economic Pressures 6
  Responding to Globalization 6
  Managing Workforce Diversity 7
  Improving Customer Service 7
  Improving People Skills 9
  Stimulating Innovation and Change 9
  Coping with "Temporariness" 9
  Working in Networked Organizations 10
  Helping Employees Balance Work–Life Conflicts 10
  Improving Ethical Behavior 11
The Plan of This Book 11
  ■ Implications for Managers 12

Part 2 The Individual in the Organization 13

Chapter 2 Attitudes and Job Satisfaction 13
Attitudes 13
  What Are the Main Components of Attitudes? 14
  Does Behavior Always Follow from Attitudes? 15
  What Are the Major Job Attitudes? 16

Job Satisfaction 19

Measuring Job Satisfaction 19

How Satisfied Are People in Their Jobs? 19

What Causes Job Satisfaction? 20

The Impact of Satisfied and Dissatisfied Employees on the Workplace 21

■ Global Implications 24

■ Implications for Managers 25

Chapter 3 Emotions and Moods 26

What Are Emotions and Moods? 27

The Basic Emotions 28

The Basic Moods: Positive and Negative Affect 28

The Function of Emotions 29

Sources of Emotions and Moods 30

Emotional Labor 32

Emotional Intelligence 34

The Case for EI 34

The Case Against EI 34

OB Applications of Emotions and Moods 35

Selection 35

Decision Making 36

Creativity 36

Motivation 36

Leadership 37

Negotiation 37

Customer Service 37

Job Attitudes 38

Deviant Workplace Behaviors 38

Safety and Injury at Work 38

How Managers Can Influence Moods 39

■ Global Implications 39

■ Implications for Managers 40

Chapter 4 Personality and Values 41

Personality 41

What Is Personality? 41

The Myers-Briggs Type Indicator 43

The Big Five Personality Model 44

Other Personality Traits Relevant to OB 46

Values   49

The Importance of Values   50

Terminal Versus Instrumental Values   50

Linking an Individual's Personality and Values to the Workplace   51

Person–Job Fit   51

Person–Organization Fit   52

■ Global Implications   53

■ Implications for Managers   56

Chapter 5   Perception and Individual Decision Making   57

What Is Perception?   57

Factors That Influence Perception   57

Person Perception: Making Judgments About Others   58

Attribution Theory   58

Common Shortcuts in Judging Others   60

The Link Between Perception and Individual Decision Making   61

Decision Making in Organizations   61

The Rational Model, Bounded Rationality, and Intuition   62

Common Biases and Errors in Decision Making   63

Organizational Constraints on Decision Making   66

What About Ethics and Creativity in Decision Making?   66

Three Ethical Decision Criteria   66

Improving Creativity in Decision Making   67

■ Global Implications   69

■ Implications for Managers   70

Chapter 6   Motivation Concepts   72

Defining Motivation   72

Early Theories of Motivation   73

Hierarchy of Needs Theory   73

Theory X and Theory Y   74

Two-Factor Theory   74

McClelland's Theory of Needs   76

Contemporary Theories of Motivation   77

Self-Determination Theory   77

Goal-Setting Theory   78

Self-Efficacy Theory   81

Equity Theory/Organizational Justice   83
Expectancy Theory   86
■ Global Implications   88
■ Implications for Managers   88

Chapter 7 **Motivation: From Concepts to Applications   90**
Motivating by Changing the Nature of the Work Environment   90
The Job Characteristics Model   90
How Can Jobs Be Redesigned?   92
Alternative Work Arrangements   94
The Social and Physical Context of Work   97
Employee Involvement   98
Examples of Employee Involvement Programs   98
Linking Employee Involvement Programs and Motivation Theories   99
Using Rewards to Motivate Employees   99
What to Pay: Establishing a Pay Structure   99
How to Pay: Rewarding Individual Employees Through Variable-Pay Programs   100
Flexible Benefits: Developing a Benefits Package   103
Intrinsic Rewards: Employee Recognition Programs   103
■ Global Implications   104
■ Implications for Managers   105

Part 3 **Groups in the Organization   106**

Chapter 8 **Foundations of Group Behavior   106**
Defining and Classifying Groups   106
Stages of Group Development   108
The Five-Stage Model   108
Group Properties: Roles, Norms, Status, Size, and Cohesiveness   109
Group Property 1: Roles   109
Group Property 2 : Norms   110
Group Property 3: Status   113
Group Property 4: Size   114
Group Property 5: Cohesiveness   115
Group Decision Making   116
Groups Versus the Individual   116

Groupthink and Groupshift   117

Group Decision-Making Techniques   119

■ Global Implications   120

■ Implications for Managers   121

Chapter 9   Understanding Work Teams   122

Why Have Teams Become So Popular?   122

Differences Between Groups and Teams   123

Types of Teams   123

Problem-Solving Teams   124

Self-Managed Work Teams   124

Cross-Functional Teams   124

Virtual Teams   125

Creating Effective Teams   125

Context: What Factors Determine Whether Teams
Are Successful?   126

Team Composition   127

Team Processes   130

Turning Individuals into Team Players   131

Selecting: Hiring Team Players   132

Training: Creating Team Players   132

Rewarding: Providing Incentives to Be a Good
Team Player   132

Beware! Teams Aren't Always the Answer   133

■ Global Implications   133

■ Implications for Managers   134

Chapter 10   Communication   135

The Communication Process   135

Direction of Communication   136

Downward Communication   136

Upward Communication   137

Lateral Communication   137

Interpersonal Communication   137

Oral Communication   137

Written Communication   138

Nonverbal Communication   138

Organizational Communication   140

Formal Small-Group Networks   140

The Grapevine   140

Electronic Communications   142

Managing Information   144

Barriers to Effective Communication   145

Filtering   145

Selective Perception   145

Information Overload   146

Emotions   146

Language   146

Silence   146

Communication Apprehension   147

■ Global Implications   147

■ Implications for Managers   149

Chapter 11 Leadership   150

What Is Leadership?   150

Trait Theories   151

Behavioral Theories   152

Summary of Trait Theories and Behavioral Theories   153

Contingency Theories   153

The Fiedler Model   154

Leader–Member Exchange (LMX) Theory   156

Charismatic Leadership and Transformational Leadership   157

Charismatic Leadership   157

Transformational Leadership   160

Authentic Leadership: Ethics and Trust Are the Foundation of Leadership   163

What Is Authentic Leadership?   163

Ethics and Leadership   163

Trust and Leadership   164

What Are the Consequences of Trust?   165

Challenges to the Leadership Construct   165

Leadership as an Attribution   165

Substitutes for and Neutralizers of Leadership   166

Online Leadership   167

■ Global Implications   168

■ Implications for Managers   169

Chapter 12 Power and Politics   170

A Definition of *Power*   170

Contrasting Leadership and Power   171

Bases of Power   171
Formal Power   171
Personal Power   172
Which Bases of Power Are Most Effective?   172
Power Tactics   173
Politics: Power in Action   175
Definition of *Organizational Politics*   175
The Reality of Politics   175
Causes and Consequences of Political Behavior   176
Factors Contributing to Political Behavior   176
How Do People Respond to Organizational Politics?   178
Impression Management   180
The Ethics of Behaving Politically   183
■ Global Implications   184
■ Implications for Managers   184

Chapter 13   Conflict and Negotiation   186
A Definition of *Conflict*   186
Transitions in Conflict Thought   186
The Traditional View of Conflict   187
The Interactionist View of Conflict   187
Resolution Focused View of Conflict   188
The Conflict Process   188
Stage I: Potential Opposition or Incompatibility   189
Stage II: Cognition and Personalization   189
Stage III: Intentions   190
Stage IV: Behavior   191
Stage V: Outcomes   191
Negotiation   193
Bargaining Strategies   193
The Negotiation Process   196
Individual Differences in Negotiation Effectiveness   198
■ Global Implications   199
■ Implications for Managers   200

Part 4   The Organization System   202

Chapter 14   Foundations of Organization Structure   202
What Is Organizational Structure?   202
Work Specialization   203

Departmentalization   204
Chain of Command   205
Span of Control   205
Centralization and Decentralization   206
Formalization   206

Common Organizational Designs   207
The Simple Structure   207
The Bureaucracy   208
The Matrix Structure   208

New Design Options   209
The Virtual Organization   209
The Boundaryless Organization   211
The Leaner Organization: Organization
Downsizing   212

Why Do Structures Differ?   212
Strategy   213
Organization Size   214
Technology   214
Environment   214

Organizational Designs and Employee Behavior   215
■ Global Implications   216
■ Implications for Managers   217

Chapter 15 Organizational Culture   218
What Is Organizational Culture?   218
A Definition of *Organizational Culture*   219
Culture Is a Descriptive Term   219
Do Organizations Have Uniform Cultures?   219
Strong Versus Weak Cultures   220
Culture Versus Formalization   220

What Do Cultures Do?   220
Culture's Functions   220
Culture Creates Climate   221
Culture as a Liability   222

Creating and Sustaining Culture   223
How a Culture Begins   223
Keeping a Culture Alive   223
Summary: How Cultures Form   227

How Employees Learn Culture   227

Stories   227

Rituals   228

Material Symbols   228

Language   228

Creating an Ethical Organizational Culture   228

Creating a Positive Organizational Culture   230

■ Global Implications   232

■ Implications for Managers   233

Chapter 16   Organizational Change and Stress Management   234

Forces for Change   234

Resistance to Change   235

Overcoming Resistance to Change   236

Approaches to Managing Organizational Change   238

Lewin's Three-Step Model   238

Kotter's Eight-Step Plan for Implementing Change   239

Organizational Development   239

Creating a Culture for Change   241

Stimulating a Culture of Innovation   241

Work Stress and Its Management   243

What Is Stress?   243

Consequences of Stress   244

Managing Stress   245

■ Global Implications   247

■ Implications for Managers   248

Epilogue   249

Endnotes   251

Glindex   293

PREFACE

This book was created as an alternative to the 600- or 700-page comprehensive textbook in organizational behavior (OB). It attempts to provide balanced coverage of all the key elements comprising the discipline of OB in a style that readers will find both informative and interesting. We're pleased to say that this text has achieved a wide following in short courses and executive programs as well as in traditional courses as a companion volume with experiential, skill development, case, and readings books. It is currently used at more than 500 colleges and universities in the United States, Canada, Latin America, Europe, Australia, and Asia. It's also been translated into Spanish, Portuguese, Japanese, Chinese, Dutch, Polish, Turkish, Danish, and Bahasa Indonesian.

KEY CHANGES TO THE ELEVENTH EDITION

- Expanded and updated coverage of international issues in management covering such topics as cohesiveness in cross-cultural settings and cross-cultural differences in attributions
- New section on how to minimize intrusion of e-mails and the management of information
- New and updated information dealing with job enrichment, bonuses, effective feedback, and alternative work arrangements
- Expanded coverage of social relationships at work, including the importance of social relationships for job satisfaction and motivation
- Coverage of emerging literature on functional conflict, dysfunctional conflict, and conflict management
- New sections on safety and emotions at work, risk aversion, self-determination theory, managing information, and downsizing

RETAINED FROM THE PREVIOUS EDITION

What do people like about this book? Surveys of users have found general agreement about the following features. Needless to say, they've all been retained in this edition.

- *Length.* Since its inception in 1984, we've tried diligently to keep this book in the range of 325 to 350 pages. Users tell us this length allows them considerable flexibility in assigning supporting materials and projects.
- *Balanced topic coverage.* Although short in length, this book continues to provide balanced coverage of all the key concepts in OB. This includes not only traditional topics, such as personality, motivation, and leadership, but also cutting-edge issues such as emotions, diversity, negotiation, and teamwork.
- *Writing style.* This book is frequently singled out for its fluid writing style and extensive use of examples. Users regularly tell us that they find this book "conversational," "interesting," "student friendly," and "very clear and understandable."
- *Practicality.* This book has never been solely about theory. It's about *using* theory to better explain and predict the behavior of people in organizations. In each edition of this book, we have focused on making sure that readers see the link between OB theories, research, and implications for practice.

- *Absence of pedagogy.* Part of the reason we've been able to keep this book short in length is that it doesn't include review questions, cases, exercises, or similar teaching/learning aids. It continues to provide only the basic core of OB knowledge, allowing instructors the maximum flexibility in designing and shaping their courses.
- *Integration of globalization, diversity, and ethics.* As shown in Exhibit A, the topics of globalization and cross-cultural differences, diversity, and ethics are discussed throughout this book. Rather than being presented in stand-alone chapters, these topics have been woven into the context of relevant issues. Users tell us they find that this integrative approach makes these topics more fully part of OB and reinforces their importance.
- *Comprehensive supplements.* Although this book may be short in length, it's not short on supplements. It comes with a complete, high-tech support package for both faculty and students. This includes a comprehensive Instructor's Manual and Test Item File; a dedicated Web site (www .prenhall.com/robbins); an Instructor's Resource CD-ROM, including the computerized Test Item File, Instructor's Manual, and PowerPoint slides; and the Self-Assessment Library, which provides students with insights into their skills, abilities, and interests. These supplements are described in detail later in this Preface.

CHAPTER-BY-CHAPTER CHANGES

Chapter 1 (What Is Organizational Behavior?)

- Updated material on evidence-based management
- New section, "Responding to Economic Pressures," to lead off *Challenges and Opportunities for OB* section
- Revised and updated material on *Challenges to OB: Responding to Globalization*
- Revised and updated material on *Challenges to OB: Improving Customer Service*
- Revised and updated material on *Challenges to OB: Improving Ethical Behavior*

Chapter 2 (Attitudes and Job Satisfaction)

- Describes how the social relationships one has at work contribute to job satisfaction
- Updated material on the relationship between satisfaction and performance
- Includes new research on satisfaction and citizenship

Chapter 3 (Emotions and Moods)

- Updated information on emotional labor
- Updated coverage on emotional intelligence
- Description of new research on creativity and performance
- Review of the latest research on emotions and leadership, negotiation, and deviance
- New section on safety and emotions at work

Chapter 4 (Personality and Values)

- Updated information on faking in personality tests
- New research on how personality changes with age
- Includes new research on satisfaction and citizenship

- Includes new research on personality and leadership
- Includes new information on cross-cultural research designs

Chapter 5 (Perception and Individual Decision Making)

- New section: "Risk Aversion" (and its implications for organizations)
- New coverage of the role of mental ability in decision-making errors
- Updated example on anchoring bias
- Updated example on availability bias
- Updated material and examples on hindsight bias
- Expanded discussion of the limits of the rational decision-making model
- Updated discussion of the relationships among moods and creativity
- Updated discussion of cross-cultural differences in attributions
- Updated material on intuition

Chapter 6 (Motivation Concepts)

- New section: "Self-Determination Theory"
- Review of new research on culture and motivation

Chapter 7 (Motivation: From Concepts to Applications)

- New, updated job enrichment example (University of New Mexico)
- Updated material on bonuses
- New section about social context as an important job characteristic
- Updates on how to provide effective feedback at work
- Outlines new findings on how the meaningfulness of work can be enhanced
- New information about flextime and alternative work arrangements

Chapter 8 (Foundations of Group Behavior)

- Updated research on role conflict
- Update on a major replication of Zimbardo's famous prison experiment
- Updated research on workplace deviance in groups
- Updated material on groupshift or group polarization
- Expanded discussion on cohesiveness in cross-cultural settings

Chapter 9 (Understanding Work Teams)

- Update to research on demographic diversity and team performance
- Expanded description of how to effectively manage teams with diverse knowledge
- Increased attention to the importance of assigning members to roles in teams
- Discussion of the latest research on team processes

Chapter 10 (Communication)

- Extensive updating of e-mail communication and video conferencing
- New section on how to minimize intrusion of e-mails
- New section: "Managing Information"
- Updated information on potentially divisive issues in cross-cultural communication
- New sections on noncommunication and silence in organizations
- Discussion of emotion in electronic communications

Chapter 11 (Leadership)

- Updated discussion of the functions and processes underlying transformational and charismatic leadership
- Major revision of the discussion of trust and leadership

Chapter 12 (Power and Politics)

- Updated research on legitimate power
- Several updates to material on influence tactics
- Revised introduction to "The Reality of Politics"
- Extensive updates to "Impression Management" section
- Revision of Exhibit 12-4 (Impression Management [IM] Techniques)

Chapter 13 (Conflict and Negotiation)

- Extensive updates to "Functional View of Conflict" section
- Updates to personality and negotiation and moods/emotions and negotiation sections
- Extensive updates to "Dysfunctional View of Conflict" section
- Updates to "Transitions in Conflict Thought" section
- New material on managing functional conflict
- Extensive updates to "Global Implications" section
- Revision to definition of negotiation and accompanying material
- New material in "Negotiation: Preparation and Planning" section
- New section, "Resolution Focused View of Conflict," which focuses on latest research on this emerging topic

Chapter 14 (Foundations of Organization Structure)

- Major new section: "The Leaner Organization: Downsizing"

Chapter 15 (Organizational Culture)

- New example of effect of top management on culture formation (Wegman's)
- New example on dark side of socialization (Siemens)

Chapter 16 (Organizational Change and Stress Management)

- Updated material in "Forces for Change" section

SUPPLEMENTS PACKAGE

Essentials of Organizational Behavior continues to be supported with an extensive supplement package for both students and faculty.

FACULTY RESOURCES

Instructor's Resource Center

www.pearsonhighered.com/educator is where instructors can access a variety of print, media, and presentation resources available with this text in downloadable, digital format.

Once you register, you will not have additional forms to fill out, or multiple usernames and passwords to remember to access new titles and/or editions. As a registered faculty member, you can log in directly to download resource files, and receive immediate access and instructions for installing Course Management content to your campus server.

Our dedicated Technical Support team is ready to assist instructors with questions about the media supplements that accompany this text. Visit http://247pearsoned.custhelp.com for answers to frequently asked questions and toll-free user support phone numbers.

> **To download the supplements available with this text, please visit www.pearsonhighered.com/educator**
>
>> Instructor's Manual
>> Test Item File
>> TestGen test generating software
>> PowerPoints

Videos on DVD

Video segments illustrate the most pertinent topics in management today and highlight relevant issues that demonstrate how people lead, manage, and work effectively. Contact your Pearson representative for the DVD. Additional videos are available to mymanagementlab users at www.mymanagementlab.com

STUDENT RESOURCES

Prentice Hall's Self-Assessment Library (SAL)

The Self-Assessment Library is available with this text in print, CD-ROM, and online. It contains more than 60 self-scoring exercises that provide insights into your skills, abilities, and interests. To order *Essentials of Organizational Behavior* with the Self-Assessment Library, please use ISBN 0132616270.

mymanagementlab.com

mymanagementlab (www.mymanagementlab.com) is an easy-to-use online tool that personalizes course content and provides robust assessment and reporting to measure individual and class performance. All of the resources students need for course success are in one place—flexible and easily adapted for your students course experience. Some of the resources include a Pearson eText version of all chapters, quizzes, video clips, simulations, assessments, interactive lectures, and PowerPoint presentations that engage your students while helping them study independently.

CourseSmart eTextbooks

CourseSmart is an exciting new choice for students looking to save money. As an alternative to purchasing the print textbook, students can purchase an electronic version of the same content for less than the suggested list price of the print text. With a CourseSmart eTextbook, students can search the text, make notes online, print out reading assignments that incorporate lecture notes, and bookmark important passages for later review. For more information, or to purchase access to the CourseSmart eTextbook, visit www.coursesmart.com.

ACKNOWLEDGMENTS

We owe a debt of gratitude to all those at Prentice Hall who have supported this text over the past 25 years and who have worked so hard on the development of this latest edition. On the editorial side, we want to thank Editor-in-Chief Eric Svendsen, Director of Editorial Services Ashley Santora, Editorial Project Manager Meg O'Rourke, Editorial Assistant Carter Anderson, and Editorial Director Sally Yagan. On the production side, Project Manager Becca Richter did an outstanding job. Last but not least, we would like to thank Marketing Manager Nikki Ayana Jones and Director of Marketing Patrice Lumumba Jones and their sales staff who have been selling this book over its many editions. Thank you for the attention you've given this book.

ABOUT THE AUTHORS

Stephen P. Robbins

Ph.D. University of Arizona

Stephen P. Robbins is professor emeritus of management at San Diego State University and the world's best-selling textbook author in the areas of both management and organizational behavior. His books are used at more than a thousand U.S. colleges and universities, have been translated into 19 languages, and have adapted editions for Canada, Australia, South Africa, and India. Dr. Robbins is also the author of the best-selling books *The Truth About Managing People*, 2nd ed. (Financial Times/Prentice Hall, 2008) and *Decide & Conquer* (Financial Times/Prentice Hall, 2004).

In his "other life," Dr. Robbins actively participates in masters' track competitions. Since turning 50 in 1993, he's won 18 national championships; 12 world titles; and set numerous U.S. and world age-group records at 60, 100, 200, and 400 meters. In 2005, Dr. Robbins was elected into the USA Masters' Track & Field Hall of Fame.

Timothy A. Judge

Ph.D. University of Illinois at Urbana-Champaign

Timothy A. Judge is currently the Franklin D. Schurz Professor of Management at the Mendoza College of Business, University of Notre Dame. He has held academic positions at the University of Florida, University of Iowa, Cornell University, Charles University in the Czech Republic, Comenius University in Slovakia, and University of Illinois at Urbana-Champaign. Dr. Judge's primary research interests are in (1) personality, moods, and emotions; (2) job attitudes; (3) leadership and influence behaviors; and (4) careers (person–organization fit, career success). Dr. Judge published more than 120 articles in these and other major topics in journals such as the *Academy of Management Journal* and the *Journal of Applied Psychology*. He is a fellow of several organizations, including the American Psychological Association and the Academy of Management. In 1995, Dr. Judge received the Distinguished Early Career Contributions Award from the Society for Industrial and Organizational Psychology, and in 2001, he received the Larry L. Cummings Award for midcareer contributions from the Organizational Behavior Division of the Academy of Management. He is a co-author of *Organizational Behavior*, 13th ed., with Stephen P. Robbins and *Staffing Organizations*, 6th ed., with Herbert G. Heneman III. He is married and has three children, who range in age from a 22-year-old daughter who is in graduate school at Florida State University to an 8-year-old son.

CHAPTER **1**

Introduction to Organizational Behavior

After studying this chapter, you should be able to:

- Define *organizational behavior (OB)*.
- Show the value to OB of systematic study.
- Identify the major behavioral science disciplines that contribute to OB.
- Demonstrate why few absolutes apply to OB.
- Identify the challenges and opportunities managers have in applying OB concepts.
- Identify the three levels of analysis in OB.

If you ask managers to describe their most frequent or troublesome problems, the answers you get tend to exhibit a common theme. The managers most often describe people problems. They talk about their bosses' poor communication skills, employees' lack of motivation, conflicts between team members, overcoming employee resistance to a company reorganization, and similar concerns. It may surprise you to learn, therefore, that it's only recently that courses in people skills have become an important part of business school programs.

Until the late 1980s, business school curricula emphasized the technical aspects of management, focusing on economics, accounting, finance, and quantitative techniques. Course work in human behavior and people skills received relatively less attention. Over the past three decades, however, business faculty have come to realize the role that understanding human behavior plays in determining a manager's effectiveness, and required courses on people skills have been added to many curricula.

Developing managers' interpersonal skills also helps organizations attract and keep high-performing employees. Regardless of labor market conditions, outstanding employees are always in short supply. Companies known as good places to work have a big advantage. A recent survey of hundreds of workplaces, and more than 200,000 respondents, showed the social relationships among co-workers and supervisors were strongly related to overall job satisfaction. Positive social relationships also were associated with lower stress at work and lower intentions to quit.[1] So having managers with good interpersonal skills is likely to make the workplace more pleasant, which in turn makes it easier to hire and keep qualified people. Creating a pleasant workplace also appears to make good economic sense. Companies with reputations as good places to work (such as the "100 Best Companies to Work for in America") have been found to generate superior financial performance.[2]

We have come to understand that in today's competitive and demanding workplace, managers can't succeed on their technical skills alone. They also have to have good people skills. This book has been written to help both managers and potential managers develop those people skills.

ENTER ORGANIZATIONAL BEHAVIOR

OB's goal is to understand and predict human behavior in organizations; the complexities of human behavior are not easy to predict, but neither are they random—certain fundamental consistencies underlie the behavior of all individuals.

We've made the case for the importance of people skills. But neither this book nor the discipline on which it is based is called "people skills." The term that is widely used to describe the discipline is *organizational behavior.*

Organizational behavior (often abbreviated OB) is a field of study that investigates the impact that individuals, groups, and structure have on behavior within organizations, for the purpose of applying such knowledge toward improving an organization's effectiveness. That's a mouthful, so let's break it down.

Organizational behavior is a field of study, meaning that it is a distinct area of expertise with a common body of knowledge. What does it study? It studies three determinants of behavior in organizations: individuals, groups, and structure. In addition, OB applies the knowledge gained about individuals, groups, and the effect of structure on behavior in order to make organizations work more effectively.

To sum up our definition, OB is the study of what people do in an organization and how their behavior affects the organization's performance. And because OB is concerned specifically with employment-related situations, you should not be surprised that it emphasizes behavior as related to concerns such as jobs, work, absenteeism, employment turnover, productivity, human performance, and management. Although debate exists about the relative importance of each, OB includes the following core topics:

- Motivation
- Leader behavior and power
- Interpersonal communication
- Group structure and processes
- Personality, emotions, and values
- Attitude development and perception
- Change processes
- Conflict and negotiation
- Work design[3]

COMPLEMENTING INTUITION WITH SYSTEMATIC STUDY

Each of us is a student of behavior. Whether you've explicitly thought about it before, you've been "reading" people almost all your life, watching their actions and trying to interpret what you see or predict what people might do under different conditions.

Unfortunately, the casual or commonsense approach to reading others can often lead to erroneous predictions. However, you can improve your predictive ability by supplementing intuition with a more systematic approach.

The systematic approach in this book will uncover important facts and relationships and provide a base from which to make more accurate predictions of behavior. Underlying this systematic approach is the belief that behavior is not random. Rather, we can identify fundamental consistencies underlying the behavior of all individuals and modify them to reflect individual differences.

These fundamental consistencies are very important. Why? Because they allow predictability. Behavior is generally predictable, and the *systematic study* of behavior is a means to making reasonably accurate predictions. When we use the term **systematic study,** we mean looking at relationships, attempting to attribute causes and effects, and basing our conclusions on scientific evidence—that is, on data gathered under controlled conditions and measured and interpreted in a reasonably rigorous manner.

Evidence-based management (EBM) complements systematic study by basing managerial decisions on the best available scientific evidence. For example, we want doctors to make decisions about patient care based on the latest available evidence, and EBM argues that managers should do the same, becoming more scientific in how they think about management problems. A manager might pose a managerial question, search for the best available evidence, and apply the relevant information to the question or case at hand. You might think it difficult to argue against this (what manager would say decisions shouldn't be based on evidence?), but the vast majority of management decisions are still made "on the fly," with little or systematic study of available evidence.[4]

Systematic study and EBM add to **intuition,** or those "gut feelings" about what makes others (and ourselves) "tick." Of course, the things you have come to believe in an unsystematic way are not necessarily incorrect. Jack Welch (former chief executive officer [CEO] of General Electric [GE]) noted, "The trick, of course, is to know when to go with your gut." But if we make *all* decisions with intuition or gut instinct, we're likely working with incomplete information—like making an investment decision with only half the data.

DISCIPLINES THAT CONTRIBUTE TO THE OB FIELD

Organizational behavior is an applied behavioral science built on contributions from a number of behavioral disciplines, mainly psychology and social psychology, sociology, and anthropology. Psychology's contributions have been mainly at the individual or micro level of analysis, whereas the other disciplines have contributed to our understanding of macro concepts such as group processes and organization. Exhibit 1.1 is an overview of the major contributions to the study of organizational behavior.

There are several social science disciplines that contribute to OB, but none are more important than psychology.

Psychology

Psychology seeks to measure, explain, and sometimes change the behavior of humans and other animals. Those who have contributed and continue to add to the knowledge of OB are learning theorists, personality theorists, counseling psychologists, and, most important, industrial and organizational psychologists.

Early industrial/organizational psychologists studied the problems of fatigue, boredom, and other working conditions that could impede efficient work performance. More recently, their contributions have expanded to include learning, perception,

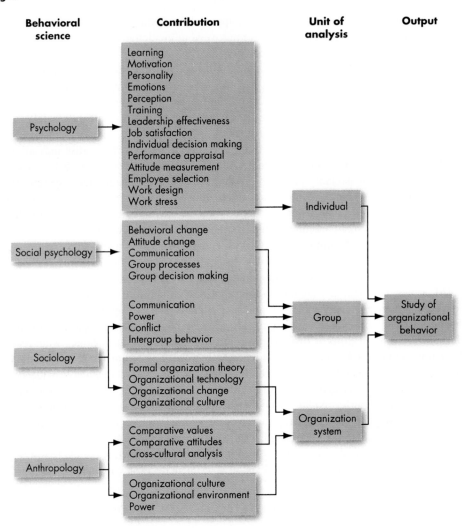

EXHIBIT 1.1
Toward an OB Discipline

Behavioral science	Contribution	Unit of analysis	Output
Psychology	Learning, Motivation, Personality, Emotions, Perception, Training, Leadership effectiveness, Job satisfaction, Individual decision making, Performance appraisal, Attitude measurement, Employee selection, Work design, Work stress	Individual	Study of organizational behavior
Social psychology	Behavioral change, Attitude change, Communication, Group processes, Group decision making		
Sociology	Communication, Power, Conflict, Intergroup behavior	Group	
	Formal organization theory, Organizational technology, Organizational change, Organizational culture	Organization system	
Anthropology	Comparative values, Comparative attitudes, Cross-cultural analysis		
	Organizational culture, Organizational environment, Power		

personality, emotions, training, leadership effectiveness, needs and motivational forces, job satisfaction, decision-making processes, performance appraisals, attitude measurement, employee-selection techniques, work design, and job stress.

Social Psychology

Social psychology, generally considered a branch of psychology, blends concepts from both psychology and sociology to focus on people's influence on one another. One major study area is *change*—how to implement it and how to reduce barriers to its acceptance. Social psychologists also contribute to measuring, understanding, and changing attitudes; identifying communication patterns; and building trust. Finally, they have made important contributions to our study of group behavior, power, and conflict.

Sociology

Whereas psychology focuses on the individual, **sociology** studies people in relation to their social environment or culture. Sociologists have contributed to OB through their study of group behavior in organizations, particularly formal and complex organizations. Perhaps most important, sociologists have studied organizational culture, formal organization theory and structure, organizational technology, communications, power, and conflict.

Anthropology

Anthropology is the study of societies to learn about human beings and their activities. Anthropologists' work on cultures and environments has helped us understand differences in fundamental values, attitudes, and behavior between people in different countries and within different organizations. Much of our current understanding of organizational culture, organizational environments, and differences among national cultures is a result of the work of anthropologists or those using their methods.

THERE ARE FEW ABSOLUTES IN OB

Laws in the physical sciences—chemistry, astronomy, physics—are consistent and apply in a wide range of situations. They allow scientists to generalize about the pull of gravity or to be confident about sending astronauts into space to repair satellites. But as a noted behavioral researcher observed, "God gave all the easy problems to the physicists." Human beings are complex, and few, if any, simple and universal principles explain organizational behavior. Because we are not alike, our ability to make simple, accurate, and sweeping generalizations is limited. Two people often act very differently in the same situation, and the same person's behavior changes in different situations. Not everyone is motivated by money, and people may behave differently at a religious service than they do at a party.

That doesn't mean, of course, that we can't offer reasonably accurate explanations of human behavior or make valid predictions. It does mean that OB concepts must reflect situational, or contingency, conditions. We can say x leads to y, but only under conditions specified in z—the **contingency variables.** The science of OB was developed by applying general concepts to a particular situation, person, or group. For example, OB scholars would avoid stating that everyone likes complex and challenging work (the general concept). Why? Because not everyone wants a challenging job. Some people prefer routine over varied, or simple over complex. A job attractive to one person may not be to another; its appeal is contingent on the person who holds it.

As you proceed through this book, you'll encounter a wealth of research-based theories about how people behave in organizations. But don't expect to find a lot of straightforward cause-and-effect relationships. There aren't many! Organizational behavior theories mirror the subject matter with which they deal, and people are complex and complicated.

CHALLENGES AND OPPORTUNITIES FOR OB

Understanding organizational behavior has never been more important for managers. Take a quick look at the dramatic changes in organizations. The typical employee is getting older; more women and people of color are in the workplace; corporate downsizing

There are many reasons why it is more important than ever to learn OB concepts.

and the heavy use of temporary workers are severing the bonds of loyalty that tied many employees to their employers; and global competition requires employees to become more flexible and cope with rapid change. The global recession has brought to the forefront the challenges of working with and managing people during uncertain times.

In short, today's challenges bring opportunities for managers to use OB concepts. In this section, we review some of the most critical issues confronting managers for which OB offers solutions—or at least meaningful insights toward solutions.

Responding to Economic Pressures

When the U.S. economy plunged into a deep and prolonged recession in 2008, virtually all other large economies around the world followed suit. Layoffs and job losses were widespread, and those who survived the ax were often asked to accept pay cuts.

During difficult economic times, effective management is often at a premium. Anybody can run a company when business is booming because the difference between good and bad management reflects the difference between making a lot of money and making a lot more money. When times are bad, though, managers are on the front lines with employees who must be fired, who are asked to make due with less, and who worry about their futures. The difference between good and bad management can be the difference between profit and loss or, ultimately, between survival and failure.

Managing employees well when times are tough is just as hard as when times are good—if not more so. But the OB approaches sometimes differ. In good times, understanding how to reward, satisfy, and retain employees is at a premium. In bad times, issues like stress, decision making, and coping come to the fore.

Responding to Globalization

Organizations are no longer constrained by national borders. Burger King is owned by a British firm, and McDonald's sells hamburgers in Moscow. ExxonMobil, a so-called U.S. company, receives almost 75 percent of its revenues from sales outside the United States. New employees at Finland-based phone maker Nokia are increasingly being recruited from India, China, and other developing countries—non-Finns now outnumber Finns at Nokia's renowned research center in Helsinki. And all major automobile makers now manufacture cars outside their borders; Honda builds cars in Ohio, Ford in Brazil, Volkswagen in Mexico, and both Mercedes and BMW in South Africa.

The world has become a global village. In the process, the manager's job has changed.

INCREASED FOREIGN ASSIGNMENTS   If you're a manager, you are increasingly likely to find yourself in a foreign assignment—transferred to your employer's operating division or subsidiary in another country. Once there, you'll have to manage a workforce very different in needs, aspirations, and attitudes from those you are used to back home.

WORKING WITH PEOPLE FROM DIFFERENT CULTURES   Even in your own country, you'll find yourself working with bosses, peers, and other employees born and raised in different cultures. What motivates you may not motivate them. Or your communication style may be straightforward and open, which others may find uncomfortable and threatening. To work effectively with people from different cultures, you need to understand how their culture, geography, and religion have shaped them and how to adapt your management style to their differences.

OVERSEEING MOVEMENT OF JOBS TO COUNTRIES WITH LOW-COST LABOR   It's increasingly difficult for managers in advanced nations, where minimum wages are typically $6 or more an hour, to compete against firms that rely on workers from China and other developing nations where labor is available for 30 cents an hour. It's not by chance that many in the United States wear clothes made in China, work on computers whose microchips came from Taiwan, and watch movies filmed in Canada. In a global economy, jobs tend to flow where lower costs give businesses a comparative advantage, though labor groups, politicians, and local community leaders see the exporting of jobs as undermining the job market at home. Managers face the difficult task of balancing the interests of their organization with their responsibilities to the communities in which they operate.

Managing Workforce Diversity

One of the most important challenges for organizations is adapting to people who are different. We describe this challenge as *workforce diversity*. Whereas globalization focuses on differences among people *from* different countries, workforce diversity addresses differences among people *within* given countries.

Workforce diversity acknowledges a workforce of women and men, many racial and ethnic groups, individuals with a variety of physical or psychological abilities, and people who differ in age and sexual orientation. Managing this diversity is a global concern. Most European countries have experienced dramatic growth in immigration from the Middle East, Argentina and Venezuela host a significant number of migrants from other South American countries, and nations from India to Iraq to Indonesia find great cultural diversity within their borders.

The most significant change in the U.S. labor force during the last half of the twentieth century was the rapid increase in the number of female workers. In 1950, for instance, only 29.6 percent of the workforce was female. By 2008, it was 46.5 percent. The first half of the twenty-first century will be notable for changes in racial and ethnic composition and an aging baby boom generation. By 2050, Hispanics will grow from today's 11 percent of the workforce to 24 percent, blacks will increase from 12 to 14 percent, and Asians will increase from 5 to 11 percent. Meanwhile, in the near term the labor force will be aging. The 55-and-older age group, currently 13 percent of the labor force, will increase to 20 percent by 2014.

Though we have more to say about workforce diversity in the next chapter, suffice it to say here that it presents great opportunities and poses challenging questions for managers and employees in all countries. How can we leverage differences within groups for competitive advantage? Should we treat all employees alike? Should we recognize individual and cultural differences? How can we foster cultural awareness in employees without lapsing into political correctness? What are the legal requirements in each country? As shown in Exhibit 1.2, there are many ways in which diversity can be conceptualized in contemporary organizations.

Improving Customer Service

Today, the majority of employees in developed countries work in service jobs, including 80 percent in the United States. In Australia, 73 percent work in service industries. In the United Kingdom, Germany, and Japan, the percentages are 69, 68, and 65, respectively. Service jobs

EXHIBIT 1.2
Major Workforce
Diversity
Categories

Gender

Nearly half of the U.S. workforce is now made up of women, and women are a growing percentage of the workforce in most countries throughout the world. Organizations need to ensure that hiring and employment policies create equal access and opportunities to individuals, regardless of gender.

Race

The percentage of Hispanics, blacks, and Asians in the U.S. workforce continues to increase. Organizations need to ensure that policies provide equal access and opportunities, regardless of race.

National Origin

A growing percentage of U.S. workers are immigrants or come from homes where English is not the primary language spoken. Because employers in the United States have the right to demand that English be spoken at the workplace during job-related activities, communication problems can occur when employees' English-language skills are weak.

Age

The U.S. workforce is aging, and recent polls indicate that an increasing percentage of employees expect to work past the traditional retirement age of 65. Organizations cannot discriminate on the basis of age and need to make accommodations to the needs of older workers.

Disability

Organizations need to ensure that jobs and workplaces are accessible to the mentally, physically, and health challenged.

Domestic Partners

An increasing number of gay and lesbian employees, as well as employees with live-in partners of the opposite sex, are demanding the same rights and benefits for their partners that organizations have provided for traditional married couples.

Religion

Organizations need to be sensitive to the customs, rituals, and holidays, as well as the appearance and attire, of individuals of non-Christian faiths such as Judaism, Islam, Hinduism, Buddhism, and Sikhism, and ensure that these individuals suffer no adverse impact as a result of their appearance or practices.

include technical support representatives, fast-food counter workers, sales clerks, waiters and waitresses, nurses, automobile repair technicians, consultants, credit representatives, financial planners, and flight attendants. The common characteristic of these jobs is substantial interaction with an organization's customers. Many an organization has failed because its employees failed to please customers. Management needs to create a customer-responsive culture. OB can provide considerable guidance in helping managers create such cultures—in which employees are friendly and courteous, accessible, knowledgeable, prompt in responding to customer needs, and willing to do what's necessary to please the customer.[5]

Improving People Skills

As you proceed through the chapters of this book, we'll present relevant concepts and theories that can help you explain and predict the behavior of people at work. In addition, you'll gain insights into specific people skills that you can use on the job. For instance, you'll learn ways to design motivating jobs, techniques for improving your listening skills, and how to create more effective teams.

Stimulating Innovation and Change

Whatever happened to Montgomery Ward, Woolworth, Smith Corona, TWA, Bethlehem Steel, and WorldCom? All these giants went bust. Why have other giants, such as General Motors, Sears, Boeing, and Lucent Technologies, implemented huge cost-cutting programs and eliminated thousands of jobs? The answer is to avoid going broke.

Today's successful organizations must foster innovation and master the art of change, or they'll become candidates for extinction. Victory will go to the organizations that maintain their flexibility, continually improve their quality, and beat their competition to the marketplace with a constant stream of innovative products and services. Domino's single-handedly brought on the demise of small pizza parlors whose managers thought they could continue doing what they had been doing for years. Amazon.com is putting a lot of independent bookstores out of business as it proves you can successfully sell books (and most anything else) from a Web site. After years of lackluster performance, Boeing realized it needed to change its business model. The result was its 787 Dreamliner and a return to being the world's largest airplane manufacturer.

An organization's employees can be the impetus for innovation and change, or they can be a major stumbling block. The challenge for managers is to stimulate their employees' creativity and tolerance for change. The field of OB provides a wealth of ideas and techniques to aid in realizing these goals.

Coping with "Temporariness"

Globalization, expanded capacity, and advances in technology have required organizations to be fast and flexible if they are to survive. The result is that most managers and employees today work in a climate best characterized as "temporary."

Workers must continually update their knowledge and skills to perform new job requirements. Production employees at companies such as Caterpillar, Ford, and Alcoa now need to operate computerized production equipment. That was not part of their job descriptions 20 years ago. In the past, employees were assigned to a specific work group, gaining a considerable amount of security working with the same people day in and day out. That predictability has been replaced by temporary work groups, with members from different departments, and the increased use of employee rotation to fill constantly changing work assignments. Finally, organizations themselves are in a state of flux. They continually reorganize their various divisions, sell off poorly performing businesses, downsize operations, subcontract noncritical services and operations to other organizations, and replace permanent employees with temporary workers.

Today's managers and employees must learn to cope with temporariness, flexibility, spontaneity, and unpredictability. The study of OB can help you better understand a work world of continual change, overcome resistance to change, and create an organizational culture that thrives on change.

Working in Networked Organizations

Networked organizations allow people to communicate and work together even though they may be thousands of miles apart. Independent contractors can telecommute via computer to workplaces around the globe and change employers as the demand for their services changes. Software programmers, graphic designers, systems analysts, technical writers, photo researchers, book and media editors, and medical transcribers are just a few examples of people who can work from home or other non-office locations.

The manager's job is different in a networked organization. Motivating and leading people and making collaborative decisions online requires different techniques than when individuals are physically present in a single location. As more employees do their jobs by linking to others through networks, managers must develop new skills. OB can provide valuable insights to help with honing those skills.

Helping Employees Balance Work–Life Conflicts

The typical employee in the 1960s or 1970s showed up at a specified workplace Monday through Friday and worked for clearly defined 8- or 9-hour chunks of time. That's no longer true for a large segment of today's workforce. Employees are increasingly complaining that the line between work and nonwork time has become blurred, creating personal conflicts and stress.[6] At the same time, today's workplace presents opportunities for workers to create and structure their roles.

How do work–life conflicts come about? First, the creation of global organizations means the world never sleeps. At any time on any day, thousands of General Electric employees are working somewhere. The need to consult with colleagues or customers eight or ten time zones away means many employees of global firms are "on call" 24 hours a day. Second, communication technology allows many technical and professional employees to do their work at home, in their cars, or on the beach in Tahiti—but it also means many feel like they never really get away from the office. Third, organizations are asking employees to put in longer hours. Over a recent 10-year period, the average U.S. work-week increased from 43 to 47 hours, and the number of people working 50 or more hours a week jumped from 24 to 37 percent. Finally, the rise of the dual-career couple makes it difficult for married employees to find time to fulfill commitments to home, spouse, children, parents, and friends. Millions of single-parent households and employees with dependent parents have even more significant challenges in balancing work and family responsibilities.

Employees increasingly recognize that work infringes on their personal lives, and they're not happy about it. Recent studies suggest employees want jobs that give them flexibility in their work schedules so they can better manage work–life conflicts.[7] In fact, balancing work and life demands now surpasses job security as an employee priority.[8] The next generation of employees is likely to show similar concerns.[9] Most college and university students say attaining a balance between personal life and work is a primary career goal; they want "a life" as well as a job. Organizations that don't help their people achieve work–life balance will find it increasingly difficult to attract and retain the most capable and motivated employees.

As you'll see in later chapters, the field of OB offers a number of suggestions to guide managers in designing workplaces and jobs that can help employees deal with work–life conflicts.

Improving Ethical Behavior

In an organizational world characterized by cutbacks, expectations of increasing productivity, and tough competition, it's not surprising many employees feel pressured to cut corners, break rules, and engage in other questionable practices.

Increasingly they face **ethical dilemmas** and **ethical choices,** in which they are required to identify right and wrong conduct. What constitutes good ethical behavior has never been clearly defined, and, in recent years, the line differentiating right from wrong has blurred. Employees see people all around them engaging in unethical practices—elected officials pad expense accounts or take bribes, corporate executives inflate profits so they can cash in lucrative stock options, and university administrators look the other way when winning coaches encourage scholarship athletes to take easy courses. When caught, these people give excuses such as "Everyone does it" or "You have to seize every advantage nowadays." Determining the ethically correct way to behave is especially difficult in a global economy because different cultures have different perspectives on certain ethical issues.[10] Fair treatment of employees in an economic downturn varies considerably across cultures, for instance. Is it any wonder employees are expressing decreased confidence in management and increasing uncertainty about what is appropriate ethical behavior in their organizations?[11]

Managers and their organizations are responding to the problem of unethical behavior in a number of ways.[12] They're writing and distributing codes of ethics to guide employees through ethical dilemmas. They're offering seminars, workshops, and other training programs to try to improve ethical behaviors. They're providing in-house advisors who can be contacted, in many cases anonymously, for assistance in dealing with ethical issues, and they're creating protection mechanisms for employees who reveal internal unethical practices.

Today's manager must create an ethically healthy climate for his or her employees, where they can do their work productively with minimal ambiguity about what right and wrong behaviors are. Companies that promote a strong ethical mission, encourage employees to behave with integrity, and provide strong ethical leadership can influence employee decisions to behave ethically.[13] In upcoming chapters, we'll discuss the actions managers can take to create an ethically healthy climate and help employees sort through ethically ambiguous situations.

THE PLAN OF THIS BOOK

How is this book going to help you better explain, predict, and control behavior? Our approach uses a building-block process. As illustrated in Exhibit 1.3, OB is characterized by three levels of analysis. As we move from the individual level to the organization system level, we increase in an additive fashion our understanding of behavior in organizations.

Chapters 2 through 7 deal with the individual in the organization. We begin by looking at such foundations of individual behavior as personality and values. Then we consider perceptions, decision making, and attitudes. Next, we focus on the fundamental role of motivational states to individual behavior. We conclude this section with a discussion of moods and emotions.

The behavior of people in groups is something more than the sum total of each individual acting in his or her own way. People's behavior in groups is different from their behavior when they are alone. Chapters 8 through 13 address group behavior. We introduce basic group concepts, discuss ways to make teams more effective, consider

EXHIBIT 1.3
Levels of OB
Analysis

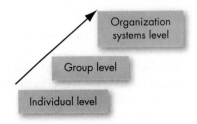

Organization
systems level

Group level

Individual level

communication issues and group decision making, and then investigate the important topics of leadership, power, politics, conflict, and negotiation.

OB reaches its highest level of sophistication when we add the formal organization system to our knowledge of individual and group behavior. Just as groups are more than the sum of their individual members, organizations are not necessarily merely the summation of the behavior of a number of groups. In Chapters 14 through 16, we discuss how an organization's structure affects behavior, how each organization has its own culture that acts to shape the behavior of its members, and the various organizational change and development techniques that managers can use to affect behavior for the organization's benefit.

Implications for Managers

Managers need to develop their interpersonal, or people, skills to be effective in their jobs. Organizational behavior (OB) investigates the impact that individuals, groups, and structure have on behavior within an organization, and it applies that knowledge to make organizations work more effectively. Specifically, OB focuses on how to improve productivity; reduce absenteeism, turnover, and deviant workplace behavior; and increase organizational citizenship behavior and job satisfaction.

Some generalizations provide valid insights into human behavior, but many are erroneous. Organizational behavior uses systematic study to improve predictions of behavior over intuition alone. But because people are different, we need to look at OB in a contingency framework, using situational variables to explain cause-and-effect relationships.

Organizational behavior offers specific insights to improve a manager's people skills. It helps managers to see the value of workforce diversity and practices that may need to be changed in different countries. It can improve quality and employee productivity by showing managers how to empower their people, design and implement change programs, improve customer service, and help employees balance work–life conflicts. It provides suggestions for helping managers meet chronic labor shortages. It can help managers cope in a world of temporariness and learn how to stimulate innovation. Finally, OB can guide managers in creating an ethically healthy work climate.

CHAPTER **2**

Attitudes and Job Satisfaction

After studying this chapter, you should be able to:

- Contrast the three components of an attitude.
- Summarize the relationship between attitudes and behavior.
- Compare and contrast the major job attitudes.
- Define *job satisfaction* and show how we can measure it.
- Summarize the main causes of job satisfaction.
- Show whether job satisfaction is a relevant concept in countries other than the United States.

We seem to have attitudes toward everything, whether it's about our leaders, our college or university, our families, or ourselves. In this chapter, we look at attitudes, their link to behavior, and how employees' satisfaction or dissatisfaction with their jobs affects the workplace.

ATTITUDES

Attitudes are evaluative statements—either favorable or unfavorable—about objects, people, or events. They reflect how we feel about something. When I say "I like my job," I am expressing my attitude about work.

Attitudes are complex. If you ask people about their attitude toward religion, Lindsay Lohan, or the organization they work for, you may get a simple response, but the reasons underlying the response are probably complex. In order to fully understand attitudes, we must consider their fundamental properties or components.

What Are the Main Components of Attitudes?

Typically, researchers have assumed that attitudes have three components: cognition, affect, and behavior.[1] Let's look at each.

The statement "My pay is low" is the **cognitive component** of an attitude—a description of or belief in the way things are. It sets the stage for the more critical part of an attitude—its **affective component.** Affect is the emotional or feeling segment of an attitude and is reflected in the statement "I am angry over how little I'm paid." Finally, affect can lead to behavioral outcomes. The **behavioral component** of an attitude describes an intention to behave in a certain way toward someone or something—to continue the example, "I'm going to look for another job that pays better."

Viewing attitudes as having three components—cognition, affect, and behavior—is helpful in understanding their complexity and the potential relationship between attitudes and behavior. Keep in mind that these components are closely related, and cognition and affect in particular are inseparable in many ways. For example, imagine you concluded that someone had just treated you unfairly. Aren't you likely to have feelings about that, occurring virtually instantaneously with the thought? Thus, cognition and affect are intertwined.

Exhibit 2.1 illustrates how the three components of an attitude are related. In this example, an employee didn't get a promotion he thought he deserved; a co-worker got it instead. The employee's attitude toward his supervisor is illustrated as follows: The employee thought he deserved the promotion (cognition), he strongly dislikes his supervisor (affect), and he is looking for another job (behavior). As we've noted, although we often think cognition causes affect, which then causes behavior, in reality these components are often difficult to separate.

In organizations, attitudes are important for their behavioral component. If workers believe, for example, that supervisors, auditors, bosses, and time-and-motion engineers are all in conspiracy to make employees work harder for the same or less money, it makes sense to try to understand how these attitudes formed, their relationship to actual job behavior, and how they might be changed.

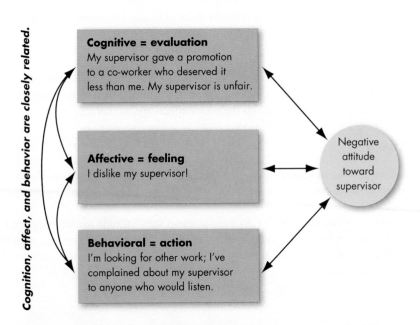

EXHIBIT 2.1 The Components of an Attitude

Does Behavior Always Follow from Attitudes?

Early research on attitudes assumed they were causally related to behavior—that is, the attitudes people hold determine what they do. Common sense, too, suggests a relationship. Isn't it logical that people watch television programs they like, or that employees try to avoid assignments they find distasteful?

However, in the late 1960s, a review of the research challenged this assumed effect of attitudes on behavior. One researcher—Leon Festinger—argued that attitudes *follow* behavior. Did you ever notice how people change what they say so it doesn't contradict what they do? Perhaps a friend of yours has consistently argued that the quality of U.S. cars isn't up to that of imports and that he'd never own anything but a Japanese or German car. But his dad gives him a late-model Ford Mustang, and suddenly he says U.S. cars aren't so bad. Festinger proposed that cases of attitude following behavior illustrate the effects of **cognitive dissonance,**[2] any incompatibility an individual might perceive between two or more attitudes or between behavior and attitudes. Festinger argued that any form of inconsistency is uncomfortable and that individuals will therefore attempt to reduce it. They will seek a stable state, which is a minimum of dissonance.

Research has generally concluded that people do seek consistency among their attitudes and between their attitudes and their behavior.[3] They either alter the attitudes or the behavior, or they develop a rationalization for the discrepancy. Tobacco executives provide an example.[4] How, you might wonder, do these people cope with the continuing revelations about the health dangers of smoking? They can deny any clear causation be-tween smoking and cancer. They can brainwash themselves by continually articulating the benefits of tobacco. They can acknowledge the negative consequences of smoking but rationalize that people are going to smoke and that tobacco companies merely promote freedom of choice. They can accept the evidence and make cigarettes less dangerous or reduce their availability to more vulnerable groups, such as teenagers. Or they can quit their job because the dissonance is too great.

No individual, of course, can completely avoid dissonance. You know cheating on your income tax is wrong, but you fudge the numbers a bit every year and hope you're not audited. Or you tell your children to floss their teeth, but you don't do it yourself. Festinger proposed that the desire to reduce dissonance depends on moderating factors, including the *importance* of the elements creating it and the degree of *influence* we believe we have over them. Individuals will be more motivated to reduce dissonance when the attitudes or behavior are important or when they believe the dissonance is due to something they can control. A third factor is the *rewards* of dissonance; high rewards accompanying high dissonance tend to reduce the tension inherent in the dissonance.

Although Festinger argued that attitudes follow behavior, other researchers asked whether there was any relationship at all. More recent research shows that attitudes predict future behavior and confirmed Festinger's idea that "moderating variables" can strengthen the link.[5]

MODERATING VARIABLES   The most powerful moderators of the attitudes relationship are the *importance* of the attitude, its *correspondence to behavior,* its *accessibility,* the pres-ence of *social pressures,* and whether a person has *direct experience* with the attitude.[6]

Important attitudes reflect our fundamental values, self-interest, or identification with individuals or groups we value. These attitudes tend to show a strong relationship to our behavior.

Specific attitudes tend to predict specific behaviors, whereas general attitudes tend to best predict general behaviors. For instance, asking someone about her intention to stay with an organization for the next 6 months is likely to better predict turnover for that person than asking her how satisfied she is with her job overall. On the other hand, overall job satisfaction would better predict a general behavior, such as whether the individual was engaged in her work or motivated to contribute to her organization.[7]

Attitudes that our memories can easily access are more likely to predict our behavior. Interestingly, you're more likely to remember attitudes you frequently express. So the more you talk about your attitude on a subject, the more likely you are to remember it, and the more likely it is to shape your behavior.

Discrepancies between attitudes and behavior tend to occur when social pressures to behave in certain ways hold exceptional power, as in most organizations. This may explain why an employee who holds strong anti-union attitudes attends pro-union organizing meetings, or why tobacco executives, who are not smokers themselves and who tend to believe the research linking smoking and cancer, don't actively discourage others from smoking in their offices.

Finally, the attitude–behavior relationship is likely to be much stronger if an attitude refers to something with which we have direct personal experience. Asking college students with no significant work experience how they would respond to working for an authoritarian supervisor is far less likely to predict actual behavior than asking that same question of employees who have actually worked for such an individual.

What Are the Major Job Attitudes?

Individuals have many kinds of attitudes about their job. Of the main job attitudes, organizational commitment and job satisfaction are the most widely studied.

We each have thousands of attitudes, but OB focuses our attention on a very limited number of work-related attitudes. These tap positive or negative evaluations that employees hold about aspects of their work environment. Most of the research in OB has looked at three attitudes: job satisfaction, job involvement, and organizational commitment.[8] A few other important attitudes are perceived organizational support and employee engagement; we'll also briefly discuss these.

JOB SATISFACTION   When people speak of employee attitudes, they usually mean **job satisfaction,** which describes a positive feeling about a job, resulting from an evaluation of its characteristics. A person with a high level of job satisfaction holds positive feelings about his or her job, whereas a person with a low level holds negative feelings. Because OB researchers give job satisfaction high importance, we'll review this attitude in detail later in the chapter.

JOB INVOLVEMENT   Related to job satisfaction is **job involvement,**[9] which measures the degree to which people identify psychologically with their job and consider their perceived performance level important to self-worth. Employees with a high level of job involvement strongly identify with and really care about the kind of work they do. Another closely related concept is **psychological empowerment,** employees' beliefs in the degree to which they influence their work environment, their competence, the meaningfulness of their job, and their perceived autonomy.[10] One study of nursing managers in Singapore found that good leaders empower their employees by involving them in decisions, making them feel their work is important, and giving them discretion to "do their own thing."[11]

High levels of both job involvement and psychological empowerment are positively related to organizational citizenship and job performance.[12] High job involvement is also related to reduced absences and lower resignation rates.[13]

ORGANIZATIONAL COMMITMENT   In **organizational commitment,** an employee identifies with a particular organization and its goals and wishes to remain a member.

There are three separate dimensions to organizational commitment:[14]

1. *Affective commitment* is an emotional attachment to the organization and a belief in its values. For example, a Petco employee may be affectively committed to the company because of its involvement with animals.
2. *Continuance commitment* is the perceived economic value of remaining with an organization. An employee may be committed to an employer because she is paid well and feels it would hurt her family to quit.
3. *Normative commitment* is an obligation to remain with the organization for moral or ethical reasons. An employee spearheading a new initiative may remain with an employer because he feels he would "leave the employer in the lurch" if he left.

A positive relationship appears to exist between organizational commitment and job productivity, but it is a modest one. A review of 27 studies suggested the relationship between commitment and performance is strongest for new employees, and considerably weaker for more experienced employees.[15] And, as with job involvement, the research evidence demonstrates negative relationships between organizational commitment and both absenteeism and turnover.[16]

Different forms of commitment have different effects on behavior. One study found managerial affective commitment more strongly related to organizational performance than was continuance commitment.[17] Another study showed that continuance commitment was related to a lower intention to quit but an increased tendency to be absent and lower job performance. These results make sense in that continuance commitment really isn't a commitment at all. Rather than an allegiance (affective commitment) or an obligation (normative commitment) to an employer, a continuance commitment describes an employee "tethered" to an employer simply because there isn't anything better available.[18]

PERCEIVED ORGANIZATIONAL SUPPORT   Perceived organizational support (POS) is the degree to which employees believe the organization values their contribution and cares about their well-being (for example, an employee believes his organization would accommodate him if he had a child-care problem or would forgive an honest mistake on his part). Research shows that people perceive their organization as supportive when rewards are deemed fair, when employees have a voice in decisions, and when they see their supervisors as supportive.[19] Research suggests employees with strong POS perceptions are more likely to have higher levels of organizational citizenship behaviors, lower levels of tardiness, and better customer service.[20] Though little cross-cultural research has been done, one study found POS predicted only the job performance and citizenship behaviors of untraditional or low power-distance Chinese employees—in short, those more likely to think of work as an exchange rather than a moral obligation.[21]

EMPLOYEE ENGAGEMENT   A new concept is **employee engagement,** an individual's involvement with, satisfaction with, and enthusiasm for, the work she does. We might ask employees about the availability of resources and the opportunities to learn new skills,

Source: Based on J. P. Meyer, N. J. Allen, and C. A. Smith, "Commitment to Organizations and Occupations: Extension and Test of a Three-Component Conceptualization," Journal of Applied Psychology 78, no. 4 (1993), pp. 538–551.

whether they feel their work is important and meaningful, and whether their interactions with co-workers and supervisors are rewarding.[22] Highly engaged employees have a passion for their work and feel a deep connection to their company; disengaged employees have essentially checked out—putting time but not energy or attention into their work. A study of nearly 8,000 business units in 36 companies found that those whose employees had high-average levels of engagement had higher levels of customer satisfaction, were more productive, had higher profits, and had lower levels of turnover and accidents than at other companies.[23] Molson Coors found engaged employees were five times less likely to have safety incidents, and when one did occur it was much less serious and less costly for the engaged employee than for a disengaged one ($63 per incident versus $392). Engagement becomes a real concern for most organizations because surveys indicate that few employees—between 17 percent and 29 percent—are highly engaged by their work. Caterpillar set out to increase employee engagement and recorded a resulting 80 percent drop in grievances and a 34 percent increase in highly satisfied customers.[24]

Such promising findings have earned employee engagement a following in many business organizations and management consulting firms. However, the concept is relatively new and still generates active debate about its usefulness. One review of the literature concluded, "The meaning of employee engagement is ambiguous among both academic researchers and among practitioners who use it in conversations with clients." Another reviewer called engagement "an umbrella term for whatever one wants it to be."[25]

Organizations will likely continue using employee engagement, and it will remain a subject of research. The ambiguity surrounding it arises from its newness and may also, ironically, reflect its popularity: Engagement is a very general concept, perhaps broad enough to capture the intersection of the other variables we've discussed. In other words, it may be what these attitudes have in common.

ARE THESE JOB ATTITUDES REALLY ALL THAT DISTINCT?   You might wonder whether these job attitudes are really distinct. If people feel deeply engaged by their job (high job involvement), isn't it probable they like it (high job satisfaction)? Won't people who think their organization is supportive (high perceived organizational support) also feel committed to it (strong organizational commitment)?

Evidence suggests these attitudes *are* highly related, perhaps to a troubling degree. For example, the correlation between perceived organizational support and affective commitment is very strong.[26] That means the variables may be redundant—if you know someone's affective commitment, you know her perceived organizational support. Why is redundancy troubling? Because it is inefficient and confusing. Why have two steering wheels on a car when you need only one? Why have two concepts—going by different labels—when you need only one?

Although we OB researchers like proposing new attitudes, often we haven't been good at showing how they compare and contrast with each other. There is some distinctiveness among them, but they overlap greatly, for various reasons including the employee's personality. Some people are predisposed to be positive or negative about almost everything. If someone tells you she loves her company, it may not mean a lot if she is positive about everything else in her life. Or the overlap may mean some organizations are just all-around better places to work than others. Then if you as a manager know someone's level of job satisfaction, you know most of what you need to know about how that person sees the organization.

JOB SATISFACTION

We have already discussed job satisfaction briefly. Now let's dissect the concept more carefully. How do we measure job satisfaction? What causes an employee to have a high level of job satisfaction? How do dissatisfied and satisfied employees affect an organization?

Measuring Job Satisfaction

Our definition of job satisfaction—a positive feeling about a job resulting from an evaluation of its characteristics—is clearly broad.[27] Yet that breadth is appropriate. A job is more than just shuffling papers, writing programming code, waiting on customers, or driving a truck. Jobs require interacting with co-workers and bosses, following organizational rules and policies, meeting performance standards, living with less than ideal working conditions, and the like.[28] An employee's assessment of his satisfaction with the job is thus a complex summation of many discrete elements. How, then, do we measure it?

Two approaches are popular. The single global rating is a response to one question, such as "All things considered, how satisfied are you with your job?" Respondents circle a number between 1 and 5 on a scale from "highly satisfied" to "highly dissatisfied." The second method, the summation of job facets, is more sophisticated. It identifies key elements in a job such as the nature of the work, supervision, present pay, promotion opportunities, and relations with co-workers.[29] Respondents rate these on a standardized scale, and researchers add the ratings to create an overall job satisfaction score.

Is one of these approaches superior? Intuitively, summing up responses to a number of job factors seems likely to achieve a more accurate evaluation of job satisfaction. Research, however, doesn't support the intuition.[30] This is one of those rare instances in which simplicity seems to work as well as complexity, making one method essentially as valid as the other. The best explanation is that the concept of job satisfaction is so broad a single question captures its essence. The summation of job facets may also leave out some important data. Both methods are helpful. The single global rating method isn't very time consuming, thus freeing time for other tasks, and the summation of job facets helps managers zero in on problems and deal with them faster and more accurately.

How Satisfied Are People in Their Jobs?

Are most people satisfied with their jobs? The answer seems to be a qualified "yes" in the United States and most other developed countries. Independent studies conducted among U.S. workers over the past 30 years generally indicate more workers are satisfied with their jobs than not.[31] But a caution is in order.

Research shows satisfaction levels vary a lot, depending on which facet of job satisfaction you're talking about. As shown in Exhibit 2.2, people are, on average, satisfied with their jobs overall, with the work itself, and with their supervisors and co-workers. However, they tend to be less satisfied with their pay and with promotion opportunities. It's not really clear why people dislike their pay and promotion possibilities more than other aspects of their jobs.

EXHIBIT 2.2
**Average Job
Satisfaction
Levels by Facet**

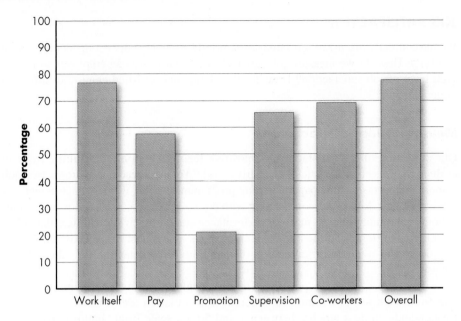

What Causes Job Satisfaction?

Think about the best job you've ever had. What made it so? Chances are you liked the work you did and the people with whom you worked. Interesting jobs that provide training, variety, independence, and control satisfy most employees.[32] There is also a strong correspondence between how well people enjoy the social context of their workplace and how satisfied they are overall. Interdependence, feedback, social support, and interaction with co-workers outside the workplace are strongly related to job satisfaction, even after accounting for characteristics of the work itself.[33]

You've probably noticed that pay comes up often when people discuss job satisfaction. For people who are poor or who live in poor countries, pay does correlate with job satisfaction and overall happiness. But once an individual reaches a level of comfortable living (in the United States, that occurs at about $40,000 a year, depending on the region and family size), the relationship between pay and job satisfaction virtually disappears. People who earn $80,000 are, on average, no happier with their jobs than those who earn closer to $40,000. Take a look at Exhibit 2.3. It shows the relationship between the average pay for a job and the average level of job satisfaction. As you can see, there isn't much of a relationship there. Handsomely compensated jobs have average satisfaction levels no higher than those that pay much less. One researcher even found no significant difference when he compared the overall well-being of the richest people on the Forbes 400 list with that of Maasai herders in East Africa.[34]

Money does motivate people, as we will discover in Chapter 6. But what motivates us is not necessarily the same as what makes us happy. A recent poll by the University of California at Los Angeles (UCLA) and the American Council on Education found that entering college freshmen rated becoming "very well off financially" first on a list of 19 goals, ahead of choices such as helping others, raising a family, or becoming proficient

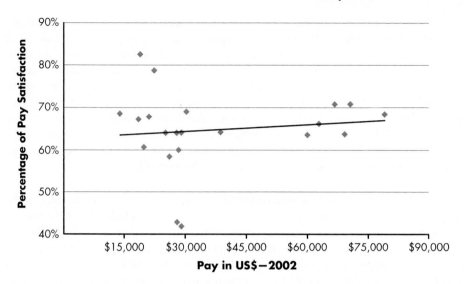

EXHIBIT 2.3
Relationship between Average Pay in a Job and Job Satisfaction of Employees in That Job

in an academic pursuit. Maybe your goal isn't to be happy. But if it is, money's probably not going to do much to get you there.[35]

Job satisfaction is not just about job conditions. Personality also plays a role. Research has shown that people who have positive **core self-evaluations**—who believe in their inner worth and basic competence—are more satisfied with their jobs than those with negative core self-evaluations. Not only do they see their work as more fulfilling and challenging, they are more likely to gravitate toward challenging jobs in the first place. Those with negative core self-evaluations set less ambitious goals and are more likely to give up when confronting difficulties. Thus, they're more likely to be stuck in boring, repetitive jobs than those with positive core self-evaluations.[36]

The Impact of Satisfied and Dissatisfied Employees on the Workplace

What happens when employees like their jobs, and when they dislike their jobs? One theoretical model—the *exit–voice–loyalty–neglect framework*—is helpful in understanding the consequences of dissatisfaction. The framework's four responses differ along two dimensions: constructive/destructive and active/passive. The responses are as follows:[37]

Most employees are satisfied with their jobs; when they're not, however, a host of actions in response to the dissatisfaction might be expected.

- *Exit.* The **exit** response directs behavior toward leaving the organization, including looking for a new position as well as resigning.
- *Voice.* The **voice** response includes actively and constructively attempting to improve conditions, including suggesting improvements, discussing problems with superiors, and undertaking some forms of union activity.
- *Loyalty.* The **loyalty** response means passively but optimistically waiting for conditions to improve, including speaking up for the organization in the face of external criticism and trusting the organization and its management to "do the right thing."
- *Neglect.* The **neglect** response passively allows conditions to worsen and includes chronic absenteeism or lateness, reduced effort, and increased error rate.

Exit and neglect behaviors encompass our performance variables—productivity, absenteeism, and turnover. But this model expands employee response to include voice and loyalty—constructive behaviors that allow individuals to tolerate unpleasant situations or revive satisfactory working conditions. It helps us understand situations, such as we sometimes find among unionized workers, for whom low job satisfaction is coupled with low turnover.[38] Union members often express dissatisfaction through the grievance procedure or formal contract negotiations. These voice mechanisms allow them to continue in their jobs while convincing themselves they are acting to improve the situation.

As helpful as this framework is, it's quite general. We now discuss more specific outcomes of job satisfaction and dissatisfaction in the workplace.

JOB SATISFACTION AND JOB PERFORMANCE   Happy workers are more likely to be productive workers. Some researchers used to believe the relationship between job satisfaction and job performance was a myth. But a review of 300 studies suggested the correlation is pretty strong.[39] As we move from the individual to the organizational level, we also find support for the satisfaction–performance relationship.[40] When we gather satisfaction and productivity data for the organization as a whole, we find organizations with more satisfied employees tend to be more effective than organizations with fewer.

JOB SATISFACTION AND OCB   It seems logical to assume job satisfaction should be a major determinant of an employee's organizational citizenship behavior (OCB).[41] Satisfied employees would seem more likely to talk positively about the organization, help others, and go beyond the normal expectations in their job. They might go beyond the call of duty because they want to reciprocate their positive experiences. Consistent with this thinking, evidence suggests job satisfaction is moderately correlated with OCBs; people who are more satisfied with their jobs are more likely to engage in OCBs.[42] Why? Fairness perceptions help explain the relationship.[43] Those who feel their co-workers support them are more likely to engage in helpful behaviors, whereas those who have antagonistic relationships with co-workers are less likely to do so.[44]

JOB SATISFACTION AND CUSTOMER SATISFACTION   As we noted in Chapter 1, employees in service jobs often interact with customers. Because service organization managers should be concerned with pleasing those customers, it is reasonable to ask, Is employee satisfaction related to positive customer outcomes? For frontline employees who have regular customer contact, the answer is "yes." Satisfied employees increase customer satisfaction and loyalty.[45]

A number of companies are acting on this evidence. The first core value of shoe retailer Zappos, "Deliver WOW through service," seems fairly obvious, but the way in which it does it is not. Employees are encouraged to "create fun and a little weirdness" and are given unusual discretion in making customers satisfied; they are encouraged to use their imaginations, including sending flowers to disgruntled customers, and Zappos even offers a $2,000 bribe to quit the company after training (to weed out the half-hearted).[46] Other organizations seem to work the other end of the spectrum. Two independent reports—one on the Transportation Security Administration (TSA) and the other on airline passenger complaints—argue that low employee morale was a major factor undermining passenger satisfaction. At US Airways, employees have posted comments on blogs such as "Our plans (sic) smell filthy" and, from another, "How can I take pride in this product?"[47]

JOB SATISFACTION AND ABSENTEEISM   We find a consistent negative relationship be-tween satisfaction and absenteeism, but it is moderate to weak.[48] Although it certainly makes sense that dissatisfied employees are more likely to miss work, other factors affect the relationship. Organizations that provide liberal sick leave benefits are encouraging all their employees—including those who are highly satisfied—to take days off. You can find work satisfying yet still want to enjoy a 3-day weekend if those days come free with no penalties. When numerous alternative jobs are available, dissatisfied employees have high absence rates, but when there are few they have the same (low) rate of absence as satisfied employees.[49]

JOB SATISFACTION AND TURNOVER   The relationship between job satisfaction and turnover is stronger than between satisfaction and absenteeism.[50] The satisfaction–turnover relationship also is affected by alternative job prospects. If an employee is presented with an unsolicited job offer, job dissatisfaction is less predictive of turnover because the employee is more likely leaving because of "pull" (the lure of the other job) than "push" (the unattractiveness of the current job). Similarly, job dissatisfac-tion is more likely to translate into turnover when employment opportunities are plentiful because employees perceive it is easy to move. Finally, when employees have high "human capital" (high education, high ability), job dissatisfaction is more likely to translate into turnover because they have, or perceive, many available alternatives.[51]

JOB SATISFACTION AND WORKPLACE DEVIANCE   Job dissatisfaction and antagonistic relationships with co-workers predict a variety of behaviors organizations find undesirable, including unionization attempts, substance abuse, stealing at work, undue socializing, and tardiness. Researchers argue these behaviors are indicators of a broader syndrome called *deviant behavior in the workplace* (or *counterproductive behavior* or *employee with-drawal*).[52] If employees don't like their work environment, they'll respond somehow, though it is not always easy to forecast exactly *how*. One worker might quit. Another might use work time to surf the Internet or take work supplies home for personal use. In short, workers who don't like their jobs "get even" in various ways—and because those ways can be quite creative, controlling only one behavior, such as with an absence control policy, leaves the root cause untouched. To effectively control the undesirable consequences of job dissatisfaction, employers should attack the source of the problem—the dissatisfaction—rather than try to control the different responses.

MANAGERS OFTEN "DON'T GET IT"   Given the evidence we've just reviewed, it should come as no surprise that job satisfaction can affect the bottom line. One study by a management consulting firm separated large organizations into high morale (more than 70 percent of employees expressed overall job satisfaction) and medium or low morale (fewer than 70 percent). The stock prices of companies in the high morale group grew 19.4 percent, compared with 10 percent for the medium or low morale group. Despite these results, many managers are unconcerned about employee job satisfaction. Still others overestimate how satisfied employees are with their jobs, so they don't think there's a problem when there is. In one study of 262 large employers, 86 percent of sen-ior managers believed their organization treated its employees well, but only 55 percent of employees agreed. Another study found 55 percent of managers thought morale was good in their organization, compared to only 38 percent of employees.[53]

Regular surveys can reduce gaps between what managers *think* employees feel and what they *really* feel. Jonathan McDaniel, manager of a KFC restaurant in Houston,

Job satisfaction is related to organizational effectiveness—a large study found that business units whose employees had high-average levels of engagement had higher levels of customer satisfaction and lower levels of turnover and accidents. All else equal, it clearly behooves organizations to have a satisfied workforce.

surveys his employees every 3 months. Some results led him to make changes, such as giving employees greater say about which workdays they have off. However, McDaniel believes the process itself is valuable. "They really love giving their opinions," he says. "That's the most important part of it—that they have a voice and that they're heard." Surveys are no panacea, but if job attitudes are as important as we believe, organizations need to find out where they can be improved.[54]

Global Implications

Is Job Satisfaction a U.S. Concept?

Most of the research on job satisfaction has been conducted in the United States. Is job satisfaction a U.S. concept? The evidence strongly suggests it is *not;* people in other cultures can and do form judgments of job satisfaction. Moreover, similar factors seem to cause, and result from, job satisfaction across cultures: We noted earlier that pay is positively, but relatively weakly, related to job satisfaction. This relationship appears to hold in other industrialized nations as well as in the United States.

Are Employees in Western Cultures More Satisfied with Their Jobs?

Although job satisfaction appears relevant across cultures, that doesn't mean there are no cultural differences in job satisfaction. Evidence suggests employees in Western cultures have higher levels of job satisfaction than those in Eastern cultures.[55] Exhibit 2.4 provides the results of a global study of job satisfaction levels of workers in 15 countries. (This study included 23 countries, but for presentation purposes we report the results for only the largest.) As the exhibit shows, the highest levels appear in the United States and western Europe. Do employees in Western cultures have better jobs? Or are they simply more positive (and less self-critical)? Although both factors are probably at play, evidence suggests that individuals in Eastern cultures find negative emotions less aversive more than do individuals in Western cultures, who tend to emphasize positive emotions and individual happiness.[56] That may be why employees in Western cultures such as the United States and Scandinavia are more likely to have higher levels of satisfaction.

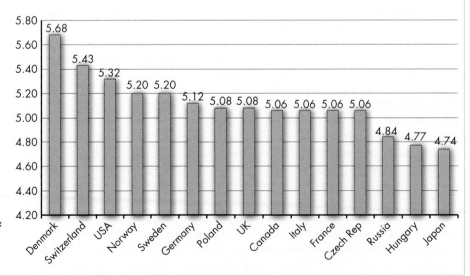

EXHIBIT 2.4 Average Levels of Job Satisfaction by Country

Implications for Managers

Managers should be interested in their employees' attitudes because attitudes give warnings of potential problems and influence behavior. Satisfied and committed employees, for instance, have lower rates of turnover, absenteeism, and withdrawal behaviors. They also perform better on the job. Given that managers want to keep resignations and absences down—especially among their most productive employees—they'll want to do things that generate positive job attitudes. As one review put it, "A sound measurement of overall job attitude is one of the most useful pieces of information an organization can have about its employees."[57]

The most important thing managers can do to raise employee satisfaction is focus on the intrinsic parts of the job, such as making the work challenging and interesting. Although paying employees poorly will likely not attract high-quality employees to the organization, or keep high performers, managers should realize that high pay alone is unlikely to create a satisfying work environment. Creating a satisfied workforce is hardly a guarantee of successful organizational performance, but evidence strongly suggests that whatever managers can do to improve employee attitudes will likely result in heightened organizational effectiveness.

CHAPTER 3

Emotions and Moods

After studying this chapter, you should be able to:

▪ Differentiate emotions from moods and list the basic emotions and moods.

▪ Identify the sources of emotions and moods.

▪ Show the impact emotional labor has on employees.

▪ Contrast the evidence for and against the existence of emotional intelligence.

▪ Apply concepts about emotions and moods to specific OB issues.

▪ Contrast the experience, interpretation, and expression of emotions across cultures.

Given the obvious role that emotions play in our work and everyday lives, it might surprise you to learn that, until recently, the field of OB has given the topic of emotions little or no attention. How could this be? We can offer two possible explanations.

The first is the myth of rationality. From the late nineteenth century and the rise of scientific management until very recently, the protocol of the work world was to keep a damper on emotions. A well-run organization didn't allow employees to express frustration, fear, anger, love, hate, joy, grief, and similar feelings. The prevailing thought was that such emotions were the antithesis of rationality. Even though researchers and managers knew that emotions were an inseparable part of everyday life, they tried to create organizations that were emotion free. That, of course, wasn't possible.

The second explanation is that many believed that emotions of any kind are disruptive. When researchers considered emotions, they looked at strong negative emotions—especially anger—that interfered with an employee's ability to work effectively. They rarely viewed emotions as constructive or contributing to enhanced performance.

Certainly some emotions, particularly when exhibited at the wrong time, can hinder employee performance. But this doesn't change the fact that employees bring their emotional sides with them to work every day and that no study of OB would be comprehensive without considering the role of emotions in workplace behavior.

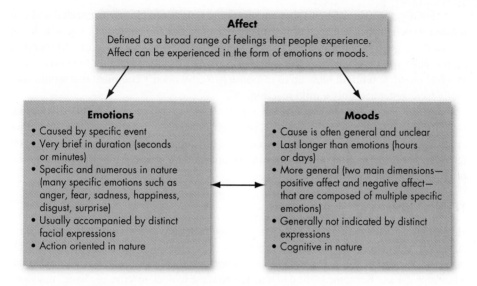

EXHIBIT 3.1
Affect, Emotions, and Moods

WHAT ARE EMOTIONS AND MOODS?

In our analysis, we'll need three terms that are closely intertwined: *affect, emotions,* and *moods.*

Affect is a generic term that covers a broad range of feelings people experience, including both emotions and moods.[1] **Emotions** are intense feelings directed at someone or something.[2] **Moods** are less intense feelings than emotions and often (though not always) lack a contextual stimulus.[3]

Most experts believe emotions are more fleeting than moods.[4] For example, if someone is rude to you, you'll feel angry. That intense feeling probably comes and goes fairly quickly, maybe even in a matter of seconds. When you're in a bad mood, though, you can feel bad for several hours.

Emotions are reactions to a person (seeing a friend at work may make you feel glad) or an event (dealing with a rude client may make you feel angry). You show your emotions when you're "happy about something, angry at someone, afraid of something."[5] Moods, in contrast, aren't usually directed at a person or an event. But emotions can turn into moods when you lose focus on the event or object that started the feeling. And, by the same token, good or bad moods can make you more emotional in response to an event. So when a colleague criticizes how you spoke to a client, you might show emotion (anger) toward a specific object (your colleague). But as the specific emotion dissipates, you might just feel generally dispirited. You can't attribute this feeling to any single event; you're just not your normal self. You might then overreact to other events. This affect state describes a mood. Exhibit 3.1 shows the relationships among affect, emotions, and mood.

First, as the exhibit shows, *affect* is a broad term that encompasses emotions and moods. Second, there are differences between emotions and moods. Some of these differences—that emotions are more likely to be caused by a specific event, and emotions are more fleeting than moods—we just discussed. Other differences are subtler. For example, unlike moods, emotions like anger and disgust tend to be more clearly revealed by facial expressions. Also, some researchers speculate that emotions may be more action oriented—they may lead us to some immediate action—whereas moods may be more cognitive, meaning they may cause us to think or brood for a while.[6]

Finally, the exhibit shows that emotions and moods are closely connected and can influence each other. Getting your dream job may generate the emotion of joy, which can put you in a good mood for several days. Similarly, if you're in a good or bad mood, it might make you experience a more intense positive or negative emotion than otherwise. In a bad mood, you might blow up in response to a co-worker's comment that would normally have generated only a mild reaction.

Affect, emotions, and moods are separable in theory; in practice the distinction isn't always crystal clear. In some areas, researchers have studied mostly moods, in other areas mainly emotions. So, when we review the OB topics on emotions and moods, you may see more information on emotions in one area and on moods in another. This is simply the state of the research.

The Basic Emotions

How many emotions are there? There are dozens, including anger, contempt, enthusiasm, envy, fear, frustration, disappointment, embarrassment, disgust, happiness, hate, hope, jealousy, joy, love, pride, surprise, and sadness. Numerous researchers have tried to limit them to a fundamental set.[7] But some argue that it makes no sense to think in terms of "basic" emotions because even emotions we rarely experience, such as shock, can have a powerful effect on us.[8]

It's unlikely psychologists or philosophers will ever completely agree on a set of basic emotions, or even on whether there is such a thing. Still, many researchers have agreed on six essentially universal emotions—anger, fear, sadness, happiness, disgust, and surprise.[9] Some even plot them along a continuum: happiness—surprise—fear—sadness—anger—disgust.[10] The closer two emotions are to each other on this continuum, the more likely people will confuse them. We sometimes mistake happiness for surprise, but rarely do we confuse happiness and disgust. In addition, as we'll see later on, cultural factors can also influence interpretations.

The Basic Moods: Positive and Negative Affect

One way to classify emotions is by whether they are positive or negative.[11] Positive emotions—such as joy and gratitude—express a favorable evaluation or feeling.

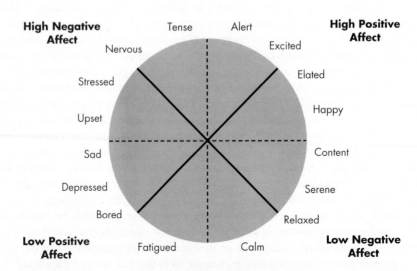

EXHIBIT 3.2
The Structure of Mood

Negative emotions—such as anger or guilt—express the opposite. Keep in mind that emotions can't be neutral. Being neutral is being nonemotional.

When we group emotions into positive and negative categories, they become mood states because we are now looking at them more generally instead of isolating one particular emotion. In Exhibit 3.2, excited is a pure marker of high positive affect, whereas boredom is a pure marker of low positive affect. Nervous is a pure marker of high negative affect; relaxed is a pure marker of low negative affect. Finally, some emotions—such as contentment (a mixture of high positive affect and low negative affect) and sadness (a mixture of low positive affect and high negative affect)—are in between. You'll notice this model does not include all emotions. Some, such as surprise, don't fit well because they're not as clearly positive or negative.

So, we can think of **positive affect** as a mood dimension consisting of positive emotions such as excitement, self-assurance, and cheerfulness at the high end and boredom, sluggishness, and tiredness at the low end. **Negative affect** is a mood dimension consisting of nervousness, stress, and anxiety at the high end and relaxation, tranquility, and poise at the low end. (*Note:* Positive and negative affect *are* moods. We're using these labels, rather than *positive mood* and *negative mood* because that's how researchers label them.)

Negative emotions are likely to translate into negative moods. People think about events that created strong negative emotions longer than they do about events that created strong positive ones. So, we should expect people to recall negative experiences more readily than positive ones. Perhaps one reason is that, for most of us, they're also more unusual. Indeed, research finds a **positivity offset,** meaning that at zero input (when nothing in particular is going on), most individuals experience a mildly positive mood.[12] So, for most people, positive moods are somewhat more common than negative moods.

The Function of Emotions

DO EMOTIONS MAKE US IRRATIONAL?   How often have you heard someone say "Oh, you're just being emotional"? You might have been offended. The famous astronomer Carl Sagan once wrote, "Where we have strong emotions, we're liable to fool ourselves." These observations suggest rationality and emotion are in conflict, and that if you exhibit emotion you are likely to act irrationally. One team of authors argues that displaying emotions such as sadness to the point of crying is so toxic to a career that we should leave the room rather than allow others to witness it.[13] These perspectives suggest the demonstration or even experience of emotions can make us seem weak, brittle, or irrational. However, research is increasingly showing that emotions are actually critical to rational thinking.[14] There has been evidence of such a link for a long time.

Consider Phineas Gage, a railroad worker in Vermont. One September day in 1848, while Gage was setting an explosive charge at work, a 3-foot 7-inch iron bar flew into his lower-left jaw and out through the top of his skull. Remarkably, Gage survived his injury. He was still able to read and speak, and he performed well above average on cognitive ability tests. However, it became clear he had lost his ability to experience emotion; he was emotionless at even the saddest misfortunes or the happiest occasions. Gage's inability to express emotion eventually took away his ability to reason. He started making irrational choices about his life, often behaving erratically and against his self-interests. Despite being an intelligent man whose intellectual abilities were unharmed by the accident, Gage drifted from job to job, eventually taking up with a circus. In commenting on Gage's condition, one expert noted, "Reason may not be as pure as most of us think it is or wish it were . . . emotions and feelings may not be intruders in the bastion of reason at all: they may be enmeshed in its networks, for worse *and* for better."[15]

The example of Phineas Gage and many other brain injury studies show emotions are critical to rational thinking. We must have the ability to experience emotions to be rational. Why? Because our emotions provide important information about how we understand the world around us. Would we really want a manager to make a decision about firing an employee without regarding either his or the employee's emotions? The key to good decision making is to employ both thinking *and* feeling in our decisions.

Sources of Emotions and Moods

Have you ever said, "I got up on the wrong side of the bed today"? Have you ever snapped at a co-worker or family member for no particular reason? If you have, it probably makes you wonder where emotions and moods come from. Here we discuss some of the primary influences.

PERSONALITY   Moods and emotions have a trait component: most people have built-in tendencies to experience certain moods and emotions more frequently than others do. People also experience the same emotions with different intensities. Contrast former Texas Tech basketball coach Bobby Knight to Microsoft CEO Bill Gates. One is easily moved to anger, whereas the other is relatively distant and unemotional. Knight and Gates probably differ in **affect intensity,** or how strongly they experience their emotions.[16] Affectively intense people experience both positive and negative emotions more deeply: when they're sad, they're really sad, and when they're happy, they're really happy.

DAY OF THE WEEK AND TIME OF THE DAY   Are people in their best moods on the weekends? As Exhibit 3.3 shows, people tend to be in their worst moods (highest negative

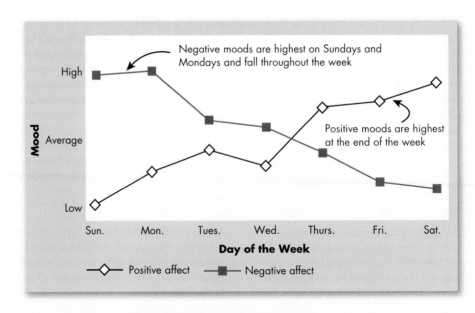

EXHIBIT 3.3
Our Moods Are Affected by the Days of the Week
Source: D. Watson, *Mood and Temperament* (New York: Guilford Press, 2000). Reprinted by permission.

affect and lowest positive affect) early in the week, and in their best moods (highest positive affect and lowest negative affect) late in the week.[17]

What about time of the day? (See Exhibit 3.4.) We often think we are either "morning" or "evening" people. However, most of us actually follow the same pattern. Regardless of what time we go to bed at night or get up in the morning, levels of positive affect tend to peak at around the halfway point between waking and sleeping. Negative affect, however, shows little fluctuation throughout the day.

What does this mean for organizational behavior? Monday morning is probably not the best time to ask someone for a favor or convey bad news. Our workplace interactions will probably be more positive from midmorning onward and also later in the week.

WEATHER   When do you think you would be in a better mood—when it's 70 degrees and sunny or on a gloomy, cold, rainy day? Many people believe their mood is tied to the weather. However, a fairly large and detailed body of evidence conducted by multiple researchers suggests weather has little effect on mood.[18] One expert concluded, "Contrary to the prevailing cultural view, these data indicate that people do not report a better mood on bright and sunny days (or, conversely, a worse mood on dark and rainy days)."[19] **Illusory correlation** explains why people tend to *think* nice weather improves their mood. It occurs when people associate two events that in reality have no connection.

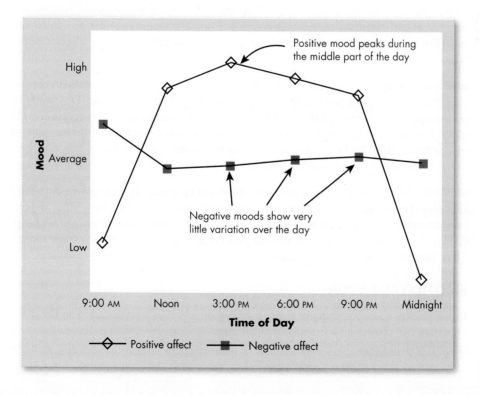

EXHIBIT 3.4
Our Moods Are Affected by the Time of the Day
Source: D. Watson, *Mood and Temperament* (New York: Guilford Press, 2000). Reprinted by permission.

STRESS   As you might imagine, stressful daily events at work (a nasty e-mail, an impending deadline, the loss of a big sale, a reprimand from the boss) negatively affect moods. The effects of stress also build over time. As the authors of one study note, "a constant diet of even low-level stressful events has the potential to cause workers to experience gradually increasing levels of strain over time."[20] Mounting levels of stress can worsen our moods, and we experience more negative emotions. Although sometimes we thrive on stress, most of us find stress takes a toll on our mood.

SOCIAL ACTIVITIES   Do you tend to be happiest when out with friends? For most people, social activities increase positive mood and have little effect on negative mood. But do people in positive moods seek out social interactions, or do social interactions cause people to be in good moods? It seems both are true.[21] Does the *type* of social activity matter? Indeed it does. Research suggests activities that are physical (skiing or hiking with friends), informal (going to a party), or epicurean (eating with others) are more strongly associated with increases in positive mood than events that are formal (attending a meeting) or sedentary (watching TV with friends).[22]

SLEEP   Does lack of sleep make people grumpier? Sleep quality does affect mood. Undergraduates and adult workers who are sleep deprived report greater feelings of fatigue, anger, and hostility.[23] One reason is that poor or reduced sleep impairs decision making and makes it difficult to control emotions.[24] A recent study suggests poor sleep also impairs job satisfaction because people feel fatigued, irritable, and less alert.[25]

EXERCISE   You often hear people should exercise to improve their mood. Does "sweat therapy" really work? It appears so. Research consistently shows exercise enhances people's positive mood.[26] Although not terribly strong overall, the effects are strongest for those who are depressed. So, exercise may help put you in a better mood, but don't expect miracles.

AGE   Do young people experience more extreme positive emotions (so-called youthful exuberance) than older people? If you answered "yes," you were wrong. One study of people ages 18 to 94 revealed that negative emotions seem to occur less as people get older. Periods of highly positive moods lasted longer for older individuals, and bad moods faded more quickly.[27] The study implies emotional experience improves with age; as we get older, we experience fewer negative emotions.

GENDER   Many believe women are more emotional than men. Is there any truth to this? Evidence does confirm women are more emotionally expressive than men;[28] they experience emotions more intensely, they tend to "hold onto" emotions longer than men, and they display more frequent expressions of both positive and negative emotions, except anger.[29] Thus, there are some gender differences in the experience and expression of emotions.

EMOTIONAL LABOR

If you've ever had a job in retail sales or waited on tables in a restaurant, you know the importance of projecting a friendly demeanor and smiling. Even though there were days when you didn't feel cheerful, you knew management expected you to be upbeat when dealing with customers. So you faked it. Every employee expends physical and mental labor by putting body and mind, respectively, into the job. But jobs also require **emotional labor** an employee's expression of organizationally desired emotions during interpersonal transactions at work.

The concept of emotional labor emerged from studies of service jobs. Airlines expect their flight attendants to be cheerful; we expect funeral directors to be sad and doctors emotionally neutral. But emotional labor is relevant to almost every job. At the least your managers expect you to be courteous, not hostile, in interactions with co-workers. The true challenge arises when employees have to project one emotion while feeling another.[30] This disparity is **emotional dissonance,** and it can take a heavy toll. Bottled-up feelings of frustration, anger, and resentment can eventually lead to emotional exhaustion and burnout.[31] It's from the increasing importance of emotional labor as a key component of effective job performance that we have come to understand the relevance of emotion within the field of OB.

Emotional labor creates dilemmas for employees. There are people with whom you have to work that you just plain don't like. Maybe you consider their personality abrasive. Maybe you know they've said negative things about you behind your back. Regardless, your job requires you to interact with these people on a regular basis. So you're forced to feign friendliness.

It can help you, on the job especially, if you separate emotions into *felt* or *displayed emotions.*[32] **Felt emotions** are an individual's actual emotions. In contrast, **displayed emotions** are those that the organization requires workers to show and considers appropriate in a given job. They're not innate; they're learned. "The ritual look of delight on the face of the first runner-up as the new Miss America is announced is a product of the display rule that losers should mask their sadness with an expression of joy for the winner."[33] Similarly, most of us know we're expected to act sad at funerals, regardless of whether we consider the person's death a loss, and to appear happy at weddings even if we don't feel like celebrating.

Effective managers have learned to be serious when giving an employee a negative performance evaluation and to hide their anger when they've been passed over for promotion. A salesperson who hasn't learned to smile and appear friendly, despite his or her true feelings at the moment, typically won't last long in the job. How we *experience* an emotion isn't always the same as how we *show* it.

Displaying fake emotions requires us to suppress real ones. **Surface acting** is hiding inner feelings and forgoing emotional expressions in response to display rules. A worker who smiles at a customer even when he doesn't feel like it is surface acting. **Deep acting** is trying to modify our true inner feelings based on display rules. A health care provider trying to genuinely feel more empathy for her patients is deep acting.[34] Surface acting deals with *displayed* emotions, and deep acting deals with *felt* emotions. Research shows surface acting is more stressful to employees because it entails feigning their true emotions.[35] Displaying emotions we don't really feel is exhausting, so it is important to give employees who engage in surface displays a chance to relax and recharge. A study that looked at how cheerleading instructors spent their breaks from teaching found those who used their breaks to rest and relax were more effective instructors after their breaks.[36] Instructors who did chores during their breaks were only about as effective after their break as they were before.

EMOTIONAL INTELLIGENCE

People who know their own emotions and are good at reading others' emotions may be more effective in their jobs.

Diane Marshall is an office manager. Her awareness of her own and others' emotions is almost nil. She's moody and unable to generate much enthusiasm or interest in her employees. She doesn't understand why employees get upset with her. She often overreacts to problems and chooses the most ineffectual responses to emotional situations. Diane has low emotional intelligence.

Emotional intelligence (EI) is a person's ability to (1) be self-aware (to recognize her own emotions when she experiences them), (2) detect emotions in others, and (3) manage emotional cues and information. People who know their own emotions and are good at reading emotion cues—for instance, knowing why they're angry and how to express themselves without violating norms—are most likely to be effective.[37] One simulation study showed that students who were good at identifying and distinguishing among their feelings were able to make more profitable investment decisions.[38]

EI has been a controversial concept in OB, with supporters and detractors. In the following sections, we review the arguments for and against its viability.

The Case for EI

The arguments in favor of EI include its intuitive appeal, the fact that it predicts criteria that matter, and the idea that it is biologically based.

INTUITIVE APPEAL   Almost everyone would agree it is good to possess street smarts and social intelligence. Intuition suggests people who can detect emotions in others, control their own emotions, and handle social interactions well have a powerful leg up in the business world. Partners in a multinational consulting firm who scored above the median on an EI measure delivered $1.2 million more in business than did the other partners.[39]

EI PREDICTS CRITERIA THAT MATTER   Evidence suggests a high level of EI means a person will perform well on the job. One study found EI predicted the performance of employees in a cigarette factory in China.[40] Another study found the ability to recognize emotions in others' facial expressions and to emotionally "eavesdrop" (pick up subtle signals about people's emotions) predicted peer ratings of how valuable people were to their organization.[41] Finally, a review of 59 studies indicated that, overall, EI correlated moderately with job performance.[42]

EI IS BIOLOGICALLY BASED   In one study, people with damage to the brain area that governs emotional processing (part of the prefrontal cortex) scored no lower on standard measures of intelligence than people without similar damage. But they scored significantly lower on EI tests and were impaired in normal decision making, as demonstrated by their poor performance in a card game with monetary rewards. This study suggests EI is neurologically based in a way that's unrelated to standard measures of intelligence.[43] There is also evidence EI is genetically influenced, further supporting the idea that it measures a real underlying biological factor.[44]

The Case Against EI

For all its supporters, EI has just as many critics who say it is vague and impossible to measure, and they question its validity.

EI IS TOO VAGUE A CONCEPT   To many researchers, it's not clear what EI is. Is it a form of intelligence? Most of us wouldn't think being self-aware or self-motivated or having empathy is a matter of intellect. Is EI a misnomer? Moreover, different researchers often focus on different skills, making it difficult to define EI. One researcher may study self-discipline, another empathy, another self-awareness. As one reviewer noted, "The concept of EI has now become so broad and the components so variegated that . . . it is no longer even an intelligible concept."[45]

EI CAN'T BE MEASURED   Many critics have raised questions about measuring EI. Because EI is a form of intelligence, they argue, there must be right and wrong answers for it on tests. Some tests do have right and wrong answers, although the validity of some questions is doubtful. One measure asks you to associate feelings with colors, as if purple always makes us feel cool and not warm. Other measures are self reported, such as "I'm good at 'reading' other people," and have no right or wrong answers. The measures of EI are diverse, and researchers have not subjected them to as much rigorous study as they have measures of personality and general intelligence.[46]

THE VALIDITY OF EI IS SUSPECT   Some critics argue that because EI is so closely related to intelligence and personality, once you control for these factors, it has nothing unique to offer. There is some foundation to this argument. EI appears to be highly correlated with measures of personality, especially emotional stability.[47] If this is true, then the evidence for a biological component to EI is spurious, and biological markers like brain activity and heritability are attributable to other well known and much more researched psychological constructs. But there hasn't been enough research on whether EI adds insight beyond measures of personality and general intelligence in predicting job performance. Still, EI is wildly popular among consulting firms and in the popular press. One company's promotional materials for an EI measure claimed, "EI accounts for more than 85 percent of star performance in top leaders."[48] To say the least, it's difficult to validate this statement with the research literature.

Weighing the arguments for and against EI, it's still too early to tell whether the concept is useful. It *is* clear, though, that it's here to stay.

OB APPLICATIONS OF EMOTIONS AND MOODS

In this section, we assess how an understanding of emotions and moods can improve our ability to explain and predict the selection process in organizations, decision making, creativity, motivation, leadership, interpersonal conflict, negotiation, customer service, job attitudes, and deviant workplace behaviors. We also look at how managers can influence our moods.

Positive emotions can increase problem-solving skills and help us understand and analyze new information.

Selection

One implication from the evidence on EI to date is that employers should consider it a factor in hiring employees, especially in jobs that demand a high degree of social interaction. In fact, more employers *are* starting to use EI measures to hire people. A study of U.S. Air Force recruiters showed that top-performing recruiters exhibited high levels of EI. Using these findings, the air force revamped its selection criteria. A follow-up investigation found future hires who had high EI scores were 2.6 times more successful than those who didn't.

Decision Making

As you will see in Chapter 5, traditional approaches to the study of decision making in organizations have emphasized rationality. But OB researchers are increasingly finding that moods and emotions have important effects on decision making.

Positive moods and emotions seem to help. People in good moods or experiencing positive emotions are more likely than others to use heuristics, or rules of thumb,[49] to help make good decisions quickly. Positive emotions also enhance problem-solving skills, so positive people find better solutions to problems.[50]

OB researchers continue to debate the role of negative emotions and moods in decision making. Although one often-cited study suggested depressed people reach more accurate judgments,[51] more recent evidence hints they make poorer decisions. Why? Because depressed people are slower at processing information and tend to weigh all possible options rather than the most likely ones.[52] They search for the perfect solution, when there rarely is one.

Creativity

People in good moods tend to be more creative than people in bad moods.[53] They produce more ideas and more options, and others think their ideas are original.[54] It seems people experiencing positive moods or emotions are more flexible and open in their thinking, which may explain why they're more creative.[55] Supervisors should actively try to keep employees happy because doing so creates more good moods (employees like their leaders to encourage them and provide positive feedback on a job well done), which in turn leads people to be more creative.

Some researchers, however, do not believe a positive mood makes people more creative. They argue that when people are in positive moods, they may relax ("If I'm in a good mood, things must be going okay, and I must not need to think of new ideas") and not engage in the critical thinking necessary for some forms of creativity.[56] The answer may lie in thinking of moods somewhat differently. Rather than looking at positive or negative affect, it's possible to conceptualize moods as active feelings like anger, fear, or elation and contrast these with deactivating moods like sorrow, depression, or serenity. All the activating moods, whether positive *or* negative, seem to lead to more creativity, whereas deactivating moods lead to less.[57]

Motivation

Several studies have highlighted the importance of moods and emotions on motivation. One study set two groups of people to solving word puzzles. The first group saw a funny video clip, intended to put the subjects in a good mood first. The other group was not shown the clip and started working on the puzzles right away. The results? The positive-mood group reported higher expectations of being able to solve the puzzles, worked harder at them, and solved more puzzles as a result.[58]

The second study found that giving people performance feedback—whether real or fake—influenced their mood, which then influenced their motivation.[59] Thus, a cycle can exist in which positive moods cause people to be more creative, which leads to positive feedback from those observing their work. This positive feedback further reinforces their positive mood, which may make them perform even better, and so on.

Another study looked at the moods of insurance sales agents in Taiwan.[60] Agents in a good mood were more helpful toward their co-workers and also felt better about themselves. These factors in turn led to superior performance in the form of higher sales and better supervisor reports of performance.

Leadership

Effective leaders rely on emotional appeals to help convey their messages.[61] In fact, the expression of emotions in speeches is often the critical element that makes us accept or reject a leader's message. Politicians, as a case in point, have learned to show enthusiasm when talking about their chances of winning an election, even when polls suggest otherwise.

Corporate executives know emotional content is critical if employees are to buy into their vision of the company's future and accept change. When higher-ups offer new visions, especially with vague or distant goals, it is often difficult for employees to accept the changes they'll bring. By arousing emotions and linking them to an appealing vision, leaders increase the likelihood that managers and employees alike will accept change.[62] Leaders who focus on inspirational goals also generate greater optimism and enthusiasm in employees, leading to more positive social interactions with co-workers and customers.[63]

Negotiation

Negotiation is an emotional process; however, we often say a skilled negotiator has a "poker face." Several studies have shown that a negotiator who feigns anger has an advantage over the opponent. Why? Because when a negotiator shows anger, the opponent concludes the negotiator has conceded all she can and so gives in.[64] Anger should be used selectively in negotiation: angry negotiators who have less information or less power than their opponents have significantly worse outcomes.[65] It appears that a powerful, better-informed individual will be less willing to share information or meet an angry opponent halfway.

Displaying a negative emotion (such as anger) can be effective, but feeling bad about your performance appears to impair future negotiations. Individuals who do poorly in a negotiation experience negative emotions, develop negative perceptions of their counterpart, and are less willing to share information or be cooperative in future negotiations.[66] Interestingly, then, although moods and emotions have benefits at work, in negotiation—unless we're putting up a false front like feigning anger—emotions may impair negotiator performance. A 2005 study found people who suffered damage to the emotional centers of their brains (the same part that was injured in Phineas Gage) may be the *best* negotiators, because they're not likely to overcorrect when faced with negative outcomes.[67]

Customer Service

A worker's emotional state influences customer service, which influences levels of repeat business and of customer satisfaction.[68] Providing quality customer service makes demands on employees because it often puts them in a state of emotional dissonance. Over time, this state can lead to job burnout, declines in job performance, and lower job satisfaction.[69]

Employees' emotions can transfer to the customer. Studies indicate a matching effect between employee and customer emotions called **emotional contagion**—the "catching" of emotions from others.[70] How does it work? The primary explanation is that when someone experiences positive emotions and laughs and smiles at you, you tend to respond positively. Emotional contagion is important because customers who catch the positive moods or emotions of employees shop longer. But are negative emotions and moods contagious, too? Absolutely. When an employee feels unfairly treated by a customer, for example, it's harder for him to display the positive emotions his organization expects of him.[71]

Job Attitudes

Ever hear the advice "Never take your work home with you," meaning you should forget about work once you go home? That's easier said than done. Several studies have shown people who had a good day at work tend to be in a better mood at home that evening, and vice versa.[72] People who have a stressful day at work also have trouble relaxing after they get off work.[73] One study had married couples describing their moods when responding to timed cell-phone surveys throughout the course of the day. As most married readers might suspect, if one member of the couple was in a negative mood during the workday, that mood spilled over to the spouse at night.[74] In other words, if you've had a bad day at work, your spouse is likely to have an unpleasant evening. Even though people do emotionally take their work home with them, however, by the next day the effect is usually gone.[75]

Deviant Workplace Behaviors

Anyone who has spent much time in an organization realizes people often behave in ways that violate established norms and threaten the organization, its members, or both. As we saw in Chapter 1, these actions are called *workplace deviant behaviors*. Many can be traced to negative emotions.

For instance, envy is an emotion that occurs when you resent someone for having something you don't have but strongly desire—such as a better work assignment, larger office, or higher salary.[76] It can lead to malicious deviant behaviors. An envious employee could backstab another employee, negatively distort others' successes, and positively distort his own accomplishments.[77] Angry people look for other people to blame for their bad mood, interpret other people's behavior as hostile, and have trouble considering others' point of view.[78] It's not hard to see how these thought processes, too, can lead directly to verbal or physical aggression.

Evidence suggests people who feel negative emotions, particularly anger or hostility, are more likely than others to engage in deviant behavior at work.[79] Once aggression starts, it's likely that other people will become angry and aggressive, so the stage is set for a serious escalation of negative behavior.

Safety and Injury at Work

Research relating negative affectivity to increased injuries at work suggests employers might improve health and safety (and reduce costs) by ensuring workers aren't engaged in potentially dangerous activities when they're in a bad mood. Bad moods can contribute to injury at work in several ways.[80] Individuals in negative moods tend to be more anxious, which can make them less able to cope effectively with hazards.

A person who is always scared will be more pessimistic about the effectiveness of safety precautions because she feels she'll just get hurt anyway, or she might panic or freeze up when confronted with a threatening situation. Negative moods also make people more distractable, and distractions can obviously lead to careless behaviors.

How Managers Can Influence Moods

You can usually improve a friend's mood by sharing a funny video clip, giving the person a small bag of candy, or even offering a pleasant beverage.[81] But what can companies do to improve employees' moods? Managers can use humor and give their employees small tokens of appreciation for work well done. Also, when leaders are in good moods, group members are more positive, and as a result they cooperate more.[82]

Finally, selecting positive team members can have a contagion effect as positive moods transmit from team member to team member. One study of professional cricket teams found players' happy moods affected the moods of their team members and positively influenced their performance.[83] It makes sense, then, for managers to select team members predisposed to experience positive moods.

> Managers need to know the emotional norms in each culture they do business in so they don't send unintended signals or misread the reactions of locals.

Global Implications

Does the degree to which people *experience* emotions vary across cultures? Do people's *interpretations* of emotions vary across cultures? Finally, do the norms for the *expression* of emotions differ across cultures? Let's tackle each question.

Does the Degree to Which People Experience Emotions Vary Across Cultures?

Yes. In China, people report experiencing fewer positive and negative emotions than people in other cultures, and the emotions they experience are less intense. Compared with Mainland Chinese, Taiwanese are more like U.S. workers in their experience of emotions: on average, they report more positive and fewer negative emotions than their Chinese counterparts.[84] People in most cultures appear to experience certain positive and negative emotions, but the frequency and intensity varies to some degree.[85]

Do People's Interpretations of Emotions Vary Across Cultures?

People from all over the world interpret negative and positive emotions in much the same way. We all view negative emotions, such as hate, terror, and rage, as dangerous and destructive, and we desire positive emotions, such as joy, love, and happiness. However, some cultures value certain emotions more than others.

U.S. culture values enthusiasm, whereas the Chinese consider negative emotions more useful and constructive than do people in the United States. Pride is generally a positive emotion in Western individualistic cultures such as the United States, but Eastern cultures such as China and Japan view pride as undesirable.[86]

Do the Norms for the Expression of Emotions Differ Across Cultures?

Absolutely. People in the United States and the Middle East recognize a smile as indicating happiness, but in the Middle East a smile is more likely to be seen as a sign of sexual attraction, so women have learned not to smile at men.[87] In collectivist countries people are more likely to believe another's emotional displays have something to do with the relationship between them, whereas people in individualistic cultures don't think others' emotional expressions are directed at them. In the United States, there's a bias against expressing emotions, especially intense negative ones. French retail clerks, in contrast, are infamous for being surly toward customers (as a report from the French government itself confirmed). Serious German shoppers have reportedly been turned off by Walmart's friendly greeters and helpful staff.[88]

In general, and not surprisingly, it's easier for people to accurately recognize emotions within their own culture than in others. A Chinese businessperson

(continued)

is more likely to accurately label the emotions underlying the facial expressions of a Chinese colleague than those of a U.S. colleague.[89]

Our discussion illustrates that cultural factors influence what managers think is emotionally appropriate.[90] What's acceptable in one culture may seem unusual or even dysfunctional in another. Managers need to know the emotional norms in each culture they do business in or with so they don't send unintended signals or misread the reactions of others. A U.S. manager in Japan, for instance, should know that although U.S. culture tends to view smiling positively, the Japanese attribute frequent smiling to a lack of intelligence.

Implications for Managers

Emotions and moods are similar in that both are affective in nature. But they're also different—moods are more general and less contextual than emotions. And events do matter. The time of day and day of the week, stressful events, social activities, and sleep patterns are some of the factors that influence emotions and moods.

Emotions and moods have proven relevant for virtually every OB topic we study. Increasingly, organizations are selecting employees they believe have high levels of emotional intelligence. Emotions and positive moods appear to facilitate effective decision making and creativity. Recent research suggests mood is linked to motivation, especially through feedback, and that leaders rely on emotions to increase their effectiveness. The display of emotions is important to negotiation and customer service, and the experience of emotions is closely linked to job attitudes and behaviors that follow from attitudes, such as deviant workplace behavior.

Can managers control colleagues' and employees' emotions and moods? Certainly there are limits, practical and ethical. Emotions and moods are a natural part of an individual's makeup. Where managers err is in ignoring co-workers' and employees' emotions and assessing others' behavior as if it were completely rational. As one consultant aptly put it, "You can't divorce emotions from the workplace because you can't divorce emotions from people."[91] Managers who understand the role of emotions and moods will significantly improve their ability to explain and predict their co-workers' and employees' behavior.

CHAPTER 4

Personality and Values

After studying this chapter, you should be able to:

- Define *personality,* describe how it is measured, and explain the factors that determine an individual's personality.
- Describe the Myers-Briggs Type Indicator personality framework and assess its strengths and weaknesses.
- Identify the key traits in the Big Five personality model and demonstrate how the Big Five traits predict behavior at work.
- Identify other personality traits relevant to OB.
- Define *values,* demonstrate the importance of values, and contrast terminal and instrumental values.
- Identify Hofstede's five value dimensions of national culture.

PERSONALITY

Why are some people quiet and passive, whereas others are loud and aggressive? Are certain personality types better adapted than others for certain job types? Before we can answer these questions, we need to address a more basic one: What is personality?

What Is Personality?

When we talk of personality, we don't mean a person has charm, a positive attitude toward life, a smiling face, or a place as a finalist for "Happiest and Friendliest" in this year's Miss America contest. When psychologists talk of personality, they mean a dynamic concept describing the growth and development of a person's whole psychological system.

DEFINING PERSONALITY   The definition of *personality* we most frequently use was produced by Gordon Allport nearly 70 years ago. He said personality is "the dynamic organization within the individual of those psychophysical systems that determine his unique adjustments to his environment."[1] For our purposes, you should think of **personality** as the sum total of ways in which an individual reacts to and interacts with others. We most often describe it in terms of the measurable traits a person exhibits.

MEASURING PERSONALITY   The most important reason managers need to know how to measure personality is that research has shown personality tests are useful in hiring decisions and help managers forecast who is best for a job.[2] Some managers use personality test scores to better understand and more effectively manage the people who work for them. The most common means of measuring personality is through self-report surveys, with which individuals evaluate themselves on a series of factors, such as "I worry a lot about the future." Though self-report measures work well when well constructed, one weakness is that the respondent might lie or practice impression management—that is, "fake good" on the test to create a good impression. Evidence shows that when people know that their personality scores are going to be used for hiring decisions, they rate themselves as about half a standard deviation more conscientious and emotionally stable than if they are taking the test just to learn more about themselves.[3] Another problem is accuracy. A perfectly good candidate could have just been in a bad mood when the survey was taken and that will make the test scores less accurate.

Personality—the sum total of ways in which an individual reacts to and interacts with others—is partly genetic in origins; yet, personality can be easily measured by various methods, including self-report surveys.

PERSONALITY DETERMINANTS   An early debate in personality research centered on whether an individual's personality was the result of heredity or of environment. Clearly, there's no simple black-and-white answer. Personality appears to be a result of both hereditary and environmental factors. However, it might surprise you that research has tended to support the importance of heredity over the environment.

Heredity refers to factors determined at conception. Physical stature, facial attractiveness, gender, temperament, muscle composition and reflexes, energy level, and biological rhythms are generally considered to be either completely or substantially influenced by who your parents are—that is, by their biological, physiological, and inherent psychological makeup. The heredity approach argues that the ultimate explanation of an individual's personality is the molecular structure of the genes, located in the chromosomes.

Researchers in many different countries have studied thousands of sets of identical twins who were separated at birth and raised separately.[4] If heredity played little or no part in determining personality, you would expect to find few similarities between the separated twins. But twins raised apart have much in common. For almost every behavioral trait, a significant part of the similarity between them turns out to be associated with genetic factors. One set of twins separated for 39 years and raised 45 miles apart were found to drive the same model and color car. They chain-smoked the same brand of cigarette, owned dogs with the same name, and regularly vacationed within three blocks of each other in a beach community 1,500 miles away. Researchers have found that genetics accounts for about 50 percent of the personality similarities between twins and more than 30 percent of the similarities in occupational and leisure interests.

Interestingly, twin studies have suggested parents don't add much to our personality development. The personalities of identical twins raised in different households are more similar to each other than to the personalities of siblings with whom the twins were raised. Ironically, the most important contribution our parents may make to our personalities is giving us their genes!

This is not to suggest that personality never changes. People's scores on measures of dependability tend to increase over time, as when young adults take on roles like starting a family and establishing a career that require great responsibility. However, despite this increase, strong individual differences in dependability remain; everyone tends to change by about the same amount, so their rank order stays roughly the same.[5] An analogy to intelligence may make this clearer. Children become smarter as they age, so nearly everyone is smarter at age 20 than at age 10. Still, if Madison is smarter than Blake at age 10, she is likely to be so at age 20, too. Consistent with the notion that the teenage years are periods of great exploration and change, research has shown that personality is more changeable in adolescence and more stable among adults.[6]

Early work on the structure of personality tried to identify and label enduring characteristics that describe an individual's behavior, including shy, aggressive, submissive, lazy, ambitious, loyal, and timid. When someone exhibits these characteristics in a large number of situations, we call them **personality traits** of that person. The more consistent the characteristic over time, and the more frequently it occurs in diverse situations, the more important that trait is in describing the individual.

Early efforts to identify the primary traits that govern behavior often resulted in long lists that were difficult to generalize from and provided little practical guidance to organizational decision makers. Two exceptions are the Myers-Briggs Type Indicator and the Big Five Model, now the dominant frameworks for identifying and classifying traits.

The Myers-Briggs Type Indicator

The **Myers-Briggs Type Indicator (MBTI)** is the most widely used personality-assessment instrument in the world.[7] It is a 100-question personality test that asks people how they usually feel or act in particular situations. On the basis of their answers, individuals are classified as extraverted or introverted (E or I), sensing or intuitive (S or N), thinking or feeling (T or F), and judging or perceiving (J or P). These terms are defined as follows:

- *Extraverted (E) versus Introverted (I).* Extraverted individuals are outgoing, sociable, and assertive. Introverts are quiet and shy.
- *Sensing (S) versus Intuitive (N).* Sensing types are practical and prefer routine and order. They focus on details. Intuitives rely on unconscious processes and look at the "big picture."
- *Thinking (T) versus Feeling (F).* Thinking types use reason and logic to handle problems. Feeling types rely on their personal values and emotions.
- *Judging (J) versus Perceiving (P).* Judging types want control and prefer their world to be ordered and structured. Perceiving types are flexible and spontaneous.

These classifications together describe 16 personality types, with every person identified with one of the items in each of the four pairs. Let's explore several examples. Introverted/Intuitive/Thinking/Judging people (INTJs) are visionaries. They usually have original minds and great drive for their own ideas and purposes. They are skeptical, critical, independent, determined, and often stubborn. ESTJs are organizers. They are realistic, logical, analytical, and decisive and have a natural head for business or mechanics. They like to organize and run activities. The ENTP type is a conceptualizer, innovative, individualistic, versatile, and attracted to entrepreneurial ideas. This person tends to be resourceful in solving challenging problems but may neglect routine assignments.

The MBTI is widely used by organizations including Apple Computer, AT&T, Citigroup, GE, 3M Co., many hospitals and educational institutions, and even the U.S. Armed Forces. In spite of its popularity, evidence is mixed about the MBTI's validity as a measure of personality—with most of the evidence suggesting it isn't.[8] One problem is that it forces a person into either one type or another (that is, you're either introverted or extraverted). There is no in-between, though people can be both extraverted and introverted to some degree. The best we can say is that the MBTI can be a valuable tool for increasing self-awareness and providing career guidance. But because results tend to be unrelated to job performance, managers probably shouldn't use it as a selection test for job candidates.

The Big Five Personality Model

The Big Five personality traits are related to many OB criteria; each of the five traits has proven its usefulness to understanding individual behavior in organizations.

The MBTI may lack strong supporting evidence, but the same can't be said for the **Big Five Model.** An impressive body of research supports its thesis that five basic dimensions underlie all others and encompass most of the significant variation in human personality.[9] The following are the Big Five factors:

- *Extraversion.* The **extraversion** dimension captures our comfort level with relationships. Extraverts tend to be gregarious, assertive, and sociable. Introverts tend to be reserved, timid, and quiet.
- *Agreeableness.* The **agreeableness** dimension refers to an individual's propensity to defer to others. Highly agreeable people are cooperative, warm, and trusting. People who score low on agreeableness are cold, disagreeable, and antagonistic.
- *Conscientiousness.* The **conscientiousness** dimension is a measure of reliability. A highly conscientious person is responsible, organized, dependable, and persistent. Those who score low on this dimension are easily distracted, disorganized, and unreliable.
- *Emotional stability.* The **emotional stability** dimension—often labeled by its converse, neuroticism—taps a person's ability to withstand stress. People with positive emotional stability tend to be calm, self-confident, and secure. Those with high negative scores tend to be nervous, anxious, depressed, and insecure.
- *Openness to experience.* The **openness to experience** dimension addresses range of interests and fascination with novelty. Extremely open people are creative, curious, and artistically sensitive. Those at the other end of the openness category are conventional and find comfort in the familiar.

HOW DO THE BIG FIVE TRAITS PREDICT BEHAVIOR AT WORK?   Research on the Big Five has found relationships between these personality dimensions and job performance.[10] As the authors of the most-cited review put it, "The preponderance of evidence shows that individuals who are dependable, reliable, careful, thorough, able to plan, organized, hardworking, persistent, and achievement-oriented tend to have higher job performance in most if not all occupations."[11] In addition, employees who score higher in conscientiousness develop higher levels of job knowledge, probably because highly conscientious people learn more (a review of 138 studies revealed conscientiousness was rather strongly related to grade point average [GPA]).[12] Higher levels of job knowledge then contribute to higher levels of job performance.

Conscientiousness is as important for managers as for front-line employees. A study of the personality scores of 313 CEO candidates in private equity companies (of whom 225 were hired, and their company's performance later correlated with their personality scores) found conscientiousness—in the form of persistence, attention to detail, and setting of high standards—was more important than other traits. The results might surprise you, but they attest to the importance of conscientiousness to organizational success.

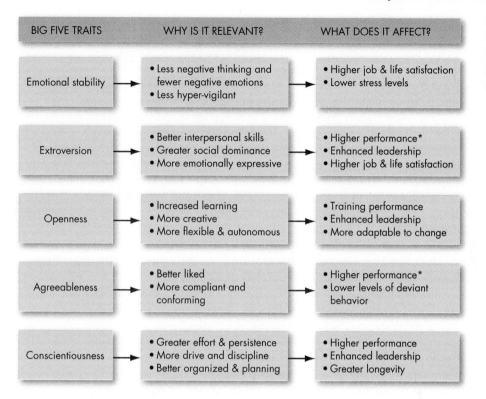

EXHIBIT 4.1
**Model of How
Big Five Traits
Influence OB
Criteria**

Although conscientiousness is the Big Five trait most consistently related to job performance, the other traits are related to aspects of performance in some situations. All five traits also have other implications for work and for life. Let's look at these one at a time. Exhibit 4.1 summarizes the discussion.

People who score high on emotional stability are happier than those who score low. Of the Big Five traits, emotional stability is most strongly related to life satisfaction, job satisfaction, and low stress levels. This is probably true because high scorers are more likely to be positive and optimistic in their thinking and experience fewer negative emotions. People low on emotional stability are hypervigilant (looking for problems or impending signs of danger) and are especially vulnerable to the physical and psychological effects of stress. Extraverts tend to be happier in their jobs and in their lives as a whole. They experience more positive emotions than do introverts, and they more freely express these feelings. They also tend to perform better in jobs that require significant interpersonal interaction, perhaps because they have more social skills—they usually have more friends and spend more time in social situations than introverts. Finally, extraversion is a relatively strong predictor of leadership emergence in groups; extraverts are more socially dominant, "take charge" sorts of people, and they are generally more assertive than introverts.[13] One downside of extraversion is that extraverts are more impulsive than introverts; they are more likely to be absent from work and engage in risky behavior such as unprotected sex, drinking, and other impulsive or sensation-seeking acts.[14]

Individuals who score high on openness to experience are more creative in science and art than those who score low. Because creativity is important to leadership, open people are more likely to be effective leaders. They also are more comfortable with ambiguity and change than those who score lower on this trait. As a result, open people cope better with organizational change and are more adaptable in changing contexts. Recent evidence also suggests, however, that they are especially susceptible to workplace accidents.[15]

You might expect agreeable people to be happier than disagreeable people. And they are, but only slightly. When people choose romantic partners, friends, or organizational team members, agreeable individuals are usually their first choice. Agreeable individuals are better liked than disagreeable people, which explains why they tend to do better in interpersonally oriented jobs such as customer service. They also are more compliant and rule abiding and less likely to get into accidents as a result. Agreeable children do better in school and as adults are less likely to get involved in drugs or excessive drinking.[16] They are also less likely to engage in organizational deviance. One downside of agreeableness is that it is associated with lower levels of career success (especially earnings). Agreeable individuals may be poorer negotiators; they are so concerned with pleasing others that they often don't negotiate as much for themselves as they might.[17]

Interestingly, conscientious people live longer because they take better care of themselves (they eat better and exercise more) and engage in fewer risky behaviors like smoking, drinking and drugs, and risky sexual or driving behavior.[18] Still, probably because they're so organized and structured, conscientious people don't adapt as well to changing contexts. They are generally performance oriented and have more trouble learning complex skills early in the training process because their focus is on performing well rather than on learning. Finally, they are often less creative than less conscientious people, especially artistically.[19]

Other Personality Traits Relevant to OB

Although the Big Five traits have proven highly relevant to OB, they don't exhaust the range of traits that can describe someone's personality. Now we'll look at other, more specific, attributes that are powerful predictors of behavior in organizations. The first relates to our core self-evaluation. The others are Machiavellianism, narcissism, self-monitoring, propensity for risk taking, and the Type A and proactive personalities.

CORE SELF-EVALUATION   People who have positive **core self-evaluations** like themselves and see themselves as effective, capable, and in control of their environment. Those with negative core self-evaluations tend to dislike themselves, question their capabilities, and view themselves as powerless over their environment.[20] We discussed in Chapter 3 that core self-evaluations relate to job satisfaction because people positive on this trait see more challenge in their job and actually attain more complex jobs.

But what about job performance? People with positive core self-evaluations perform better than others because they set more ambitious goals, are more committed to their goals, and persist longer in attempting to reach these goals. One study of life insurance agents found core self-evaluations were critical predictors of performance. Ninety percent of life insurance sales calls end in rejection, so an agent has to believe in him-or herself to persist. In fact, this study showed the majority of successful salespersons did have positive core self-evaluations.[21] Such people also provide better customer service, are more popular co-workers, and have careers that both begin on better footing and ascend more rapidly over time.[22]

You might wonder whether someone can be *too* positive. What happens when someone thinks he is capable, but he is actually incompetent? One study of *Fortune 500* CEOs, for example, showed that many are overconfident, and their perceived infallibility often causes them to make bad decisions.[23] One might say these CEOs are overconfident, but very often we humans sell ourselves short and are less happy and effective than we could be because of it. If we decide we can't do something, for example, we won't try, and not doing it only reinforces our self-doubts.

MACHIAVELLIANISM   Kuzi is a young bank manager in Taiwan. He's had three promotions in the past 4 years and makes no apologies for the aggressive tactics he's used to propel his career upward. "I'm prepared to do whatever I have to do to get ahead," he says. Kuzi would properly be called Machiavellian. Shawna led her St. Louis–based company last year in sales performance. She's assertive and persuasive, and she's effective at manipulating customers to buy her product line. Many of her colleagues, including her boss, consider Shawna Machiavellian.

The personality characteristic of **Machiavellianism** (often abbreviated *Mach*) is named after Niccolo Machiavelli, who wrote in the sixteenth century on how to gain and use power. An individual high in Machiavellianism is pragmatic, maintains emotional distance, and believes ends can justify means. "If it works, use it" is consistent with a high-Mach perspective. A considerable amount of research has related high- and low-Mach personalities to behavioral outcomes. High Machs manipulate more, win more, are persuaded less, and persuade others more than do low Machs.[24] Yet high-Mach outcomes are moderated by situational factors. High Machs flourish (1) when they interact face to face with others rather than indirectly; (2) when the situation has a minimal number of rules and regulations, allowing latitude for improvisation; and (3) when emotional involvement with details irrelevant to winning distracts low Machs.[25] Thus, whether high Machs make good employees depends on the type of job. In jobs that require bargaining skills (such as labor negotiation) or that offer substantial rewards for winning (such as commissioned sales), high Machs will be productive. But if ends can't justify the means, there are absolute standards of behavior, or the three situational factors we noted are not in evidence, our ability to predict a high Mach's performance will be severely curtailed.

NARCISSISM   Hans likes to be the center of attention. He looks at himself in the mirror a lot, has extravagant dreams, and considers himself a person of many talents. Hans is a narcissist. The term is from the Greek myth of Narcissus, a man so vain and proud he fell in love with his own image. In psychology, **narcissism** describes a person who has a grandiose sense of self-importance, requires excessive admiration, has a sense of entitlement, and is arrogant.

Narcissism can have pretty toxic consequences. A study found that although narcissists thought they were *better* leaders than their colleagues, their supervisors actually rated them as *worse*. For example, an Oracle executive described that company's CEO Larry Ellison as follows: "The difference between God and Larry is that God does not believe he is Larry."[26] Because narcissists often want to gain the admiration of others and receive affirmation of their superiority, they tend to "talk down" to those who threaten them, treating others as if they were inferior. Narcissists also tend to be selfish and exploitive and believe others exist for their benefit.[27] Their bosses rate them as less effective at their jobs than others, particularly when it comes to helping other people.[28]

SELF-MONITORING   Joyce is always in trouble at work. Though she's competent, hard-working, and productive, in performance reviews she is rated no better than average, and she seems to have made a career of irritating bosses. Joyce's problem is that she's politically inept. She's unable to adjust her behavior to fit changing situations. As she puts it, "I'm true to my-self. I don't remake myself to please others." We would describe Joyce as a low self-monitor.

Self-monitoring refers to an individual's ability to adjust his or her behavior to external, situational factors.[29] Individuals high in self-monitoring show considerable adaptability in adjusting their behavior to external situational factors. They are highly sensitive to external cues and can behave differently in different situations. High self-monitors are capable of presenting striking contradictions between their public persona and their private self. Low self-monitors, like Joyce, can't disguise themselves in that way. They tend to display their true dispositions and attitudes in every situation; hence, there is high behavioral consistency between who they are and what they do.

Evidence indicates high self-monitors pay closer attention to the behavior of others and are more capable of conforming than are low self-monitors.[30] They also receive bet-ter performance ratings, are more likely to emerge as leaders, and show less commitment to their organizations.[31] In addition, high self-monitoring managers tend to be more mobile in their careers, receive more promotions (both internal and cross-organizational), and are more likely to occupy central positions in an organization.[32]

RISK TAKING   Donald Trump stands out for his willingness to take risks. He started with almost nothing in the 1960s. By the mid-1980s, he had made a fortune by betting on a resurgent New York City real estate market. Then, trying to capitalize on his successes, Trump overextended himself. By 1994, he had a *negative* net worth of $850 million. Never fearful of taking chances, "The Donald" leveraged the few assets he had left on several New York, New Jersey, and Caribbean real estate ventures. He hit it big again. In 2007, *Forbes* estimated his net worth at $2.9 billion.

People differ in their willingness to take chances, a quality that affects how much time and information managers need to make a decision. For instance, 79 managers worked on simulated personnel exercises that required them to make hiring decisions.[33] High risk-taking managers made more rapid decisions and used less information than did the low risk-taking managers. Interestingly, decision accuracy was the same for both groups.

Although previous studies have shown managers in large organizations to be more risk averse than growth-oriented entrepreneurs who actively manage small businesses, recent findings suggest managers in large organizations may actually be more willing to take risks than entrepreneurs.[34] The work population as a whole also differs in risk propensity.[35] It makes sense to recognize these differences and even consider aligning them with specific job demands. A high risk-taking propensity may lead to more effective performance for a stock trader in a brokerage firm because that type of job demands rapid decision making. On the other hand, a willingness to take risks might prove a major obstacle to an accountant who performs auditing activities. The latter job might be better filled by someone with a low risk-taking propensity.

TYPE A PERSONALITY   Do you know people who are excessively competitive and always seem to be experiencing a sense of time urgency? If you do, it's a good bet those people have Type A personalities. A person with a **Type A personality** is "aggressively involved in a chronic, incessant struggle to achieve more and more in less and less time, and, if required to do so, against the opposing efforts of other things or other persons."[36]

In the North American culture, such characteristics tend to be highly prized and positively associated with ambition and the successful acquisition of material goods. Type A's exhibit the following characteristics:

- Are always moving, walking, and eating rapidly
- Feel impatient with the rate at which most events take place
- Strive to think or do two or more things at once
- Cannot cope with leisure time
- Are obsessed with numbers, measuring their success in terms of how many or how much of everything they acquire

The Type B is exactly the opposite, "rarely harried by the desire to obtain a wildly increasing number of things or participate in an endless growing series of events in an ever-decreasing amount of time."[37] Type B's never suffer from a sense of time urgency with its accompanying impatience, can relax without guilt, and so on.

Type A's operate under moderate to high levels of stress. They subject themselves to more or less continuous time pressure, creating a life of deadlines. These characteristics result in some rather specific behavioral outcomes. Type A's are fast workers because they emphasize quantity over quality. In managerial positions, they demonstrate their competitiveness by working long hours and, not infrequently, making poor decisions to new problems. They rarely vary in their responses to specific challenges in their milieu; hence, their behavior is easier to predict than that of Type B's.

PROACTIVE PERSONALITY   Did you ever notice that some people actively take the initiative to improve their current circumstances or create new ones? These are proactive personalities.[38] Those with a **proactive personality** identify opportunities, show initiative, take action, and persevere until meaningful change occurs, compared to others who passively react to situations. Proactives create positive change in their environment, regardless of, or even in spite of, constraints or obstacles. Not surprisingly, they have many desirable behaviors that organizations covet. They are more likely than others to be seen as leaders and to act as change agents within an organization.[39]

Other actions of proactives can be positive or negative, depending on the organization and the situation. Proactives are more likely to challenge the status quo or voice their displeasure when situations aren't to their liking.[40] If an organization requires people with entrepreneurial initiative, proactives make good candidates; however, they're also more likely to leave an organization to start their own business.[41] As individuals, proactives are more likely than others to achieve career success.[42] They select, create, and influence work situations in their favor. They seek out job and organizational information, develop contacts in high places, engage in career planning, and demonstrate persistence in the face of career obstacles.

Having discussed personality traits—the enduring characteristics that describe a person's behavior—we now turn to values. Although personality and values are related, values are often very specific and describe belief systems rather than behavioral tendencies. Some beliefs or values don't say much about a person's personality, and we don't always act consistently with our values.

VALUES

Is capital punishment right or wrong? If a person likes power, is that good or bad? The answers to these questions are value laden. Some might argue capital punishment is right because it is an appropriate retribution for crimes such as murder and treason. Others might argue, just as strongly, that no government has the right to take anyone's life.

Values represent basic convictions that "a specific mode of conduct or end-state of existence is personally or socially preferable to an opposite or converse mode of conduct or end-state of existence."[43] They contain a judgmental element in that they carry an individual's ideas as to what is right, good, or desirable. Values have both content and intensity attributes. The content attribute says a mode of conduct or end-state of existence is *important*. The intensity attribute specifies *how important* it is. When we rank an individual's values in terms of their intensity, we obtain that person's **value system**. All of us have a hierarchy of values that forms our value system. We find it in the relative importance we assign to values such as freedom, pleasure, self-respect, honesty, obedience, and equality.

Are values fluid and flexible? Generally speaking, no. They tend to be relatively stable and enduring.[44] A significant portion of the values we hold is established in our early years—by parents, teachers, friends, and others. As children, we are told certain behaviors or outcomes are *always* desirable or *always* undesirable, with few gray areas. You were never taught to be just a little bit honest or a little bit responsible, for example. It is this absolute, or "black-or-white," learning of values that ensures their stability and endurance. If we question our values, of course, they may change, but more often it reinforces them. There is also evidence linking personality to values, implying our values may be partly determined by our genetically transmitted traits.[45]

The Importance of Values

Values lay the foundation for our understanding of people's attitudes and motivation and influence our perceptions. We enter an organization with preconceived notions of what "ought" and "ought not" to be. These notions are not value free; on the contrary, they contain our interpretations of right and wrong. Furthermore, they imply we prefer certain behaviors or outcomes over others. As a result, values cloud objectivity and rationality; they influence attitudes and behavior.

Suppose you enter an organization with the view that allocating pay on the basis of performance is right, whereas allocating pay on the basis of seniority is wrong. How will you react if you find the organization you've just joined rewards seniority and not performance? You're likely to be disappointed—and this can lead to job dissatisfaction and a decision not to exert a high level of effort because "It's probably not going to lead to more money anyway." Would your attitudes and behavior be different if your values aligned with the organization's pay policies? Most likely.

Terminal versus Instrumental Values

Can we classify values? Yes. In this section, we review two approaches to developing value typologies.

ROKEACH VALUE SURVEY   Milton Rokeach created the Rokeach Value Survey (RVS).[46] It consists of two sets of values, each containing 18 individual value items. One set, called **terminal values**, refers to desirable end-states. These are the goals a person would like to achieve during his or her lifetime. The other set, called **instrumental values**, refers to preferable modes of behavior, or means of achieving the terminal values. Exhibit 4.2 gives common examples for each of these sets.

Terminal Values	Instrumental Values
Prosperity and economic success	Self-improvement
Freedom	Autonomy and self-reliance
Health and well-being	Personal discipline
World peace	Kindness
Social recognition	Ambition
Meaning in life	Goal-orientation

EXHIBIT 4.2
Terminal and Instrumental Values in the Rokeach Value Survey

Several studies confirm that RVS values vary among groups.[47] People in the same occupations or categories (corporate managers, union members, parents, students) tend to hold similar values. One study compared corporate executives, members of the steelworkers' union, and members of a community activist group. Although there was a good deal of overlap among them,[48] there were also significant differences. The activists ranked "equality" as their most important terminal value; executives and union members ranked this value 12 and 13, respectively. Activists ranked "helpful" as their second-highest instrumental value. The other two groups both ranked it 14. Because executives, union members, and activists all have a vested interest in what corporations do, these differences can create serious conflicts when groups contend with each other over an organization's economic and social policies.

LINKING AN INDIVIDUAL'S PERSONALITY AND VALUES TO THE WORKPLACE

Thirty years ago, organizations were concerned only with personality because their primary focus was to match individuals to specific jobs. That concern still exists, but it has expanded to include how well the individual's personality *and* values match the organization. Why? Because managers today are less interested in an applicant's ability to perform a *specific* job than with his or her *flexibility* to meet changing situations and commitment to the organization.

We'll now discuss person–job fit and person–organization fit in more detail.

Person–Job Fit

The effort to match job requirements with personality characteristics is best articulated in John Holland's **personality–job fit theory**.[49] Holland presents six personality types and proposes that satisfaction and the propensity to leave a position depend on how well individuals match their personalities to a job. Exhibit 4.3 describes the six types, their personality characteristics, and examples of the congruent occupations for each.

Holland developed the Vocational Preference Inventory questionnaire, which contains 160 occupational titles. Respondents indicate which they like or dislike, and their answers form personality profiles. Research strongly supports the resulting hexagonal diagram shown in Exhibit 4.4.[50] The closer two fields or orientations are in the hexagon, the more compatible they are. Adjacent categories are quite similar, whereas diagonally opposite ones are highly dissimilar.

What does all this mean? The theory argues that satisfaction is highest and turnover lowest when personality and occupation are in agreement. A realistic person in a realistic job is in a more congruent situation than a realistic person in an investigative job. A realistic

Type	Personality Characteristics	Congruent Occupations
Realistic: Prefers physical activities that require skill, strength, and coordination	Shy, genuine, persistent, stable, conforming, practical	Mechanic, drill press operator, assembly-line worker, farmer
Investigative: Prefers activities that involve thinking, organizing, and understanding	Analytical, original, curious, independent	Biologist, economist, mathematician, news reporter
Social: Prefers activities that involve helping and developing others	Sociable, friendly, cooperative, understanding	Social worker, teacher, counselor, clinical psychologist
Conventional: Prefers rule-regulated, orderly, and unambiguous activities	Conforming, efficient, practical, unimaginative, inflexible	Accountant, corporate manager, bank teller, file clerk
Enterprising: Prefers verbal activities in which there are opportunities to influence others and attain power	Self-confident, ambitious, energetic, domineering	Lawyer, real estate agent, public relations specialist, small business manager
Artistic: Prefers ambiguous and unsystematic activities that allow creative expression	Imaginative, disorderly, idealistic, emotional, impractical	Painter, musician, writer, interior decorator

EXHIBIT 4.3 Holland's Typology of Personality and Congruent Occupations

person in a social job is in the most incongruent situation possible. The key points of this model are that (1) there do appear to be intrinsic differences in personality among individuals, (2) there are different types of jobs, and (3) people in jobs congruent with their personality should be more satisfied and less likely to voluntarily resign than people in incongruent jobs.

Person–Organization Fit

We've noted that researchers in recent years have looked at matching people to organizations as well as to jobs. If an organization faces a dynamic and changing environment and

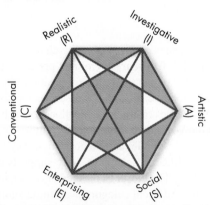

EXHIBIT 4.4 Relationships Among Occupational Personality Types

Source: Reprinted by special permission of the publisher, Psychological Assessment Resources, Inc., from *Making Vocational Choices,* copyright 1973, 1985, 1992 by Psychological Assessment Resources, Inc. All rights reserved.

requires employees able to readily change tasks and move easily between teams, it's more important that employees' personalities fit with the overall organization's culture than with the characteristics of any specific job.

The person–organization fit essentially argues that people are attracted to and selected by organizations that match their values, and they leave organizations that are not compatible with their personalities.[51] Using the Big Five terminology, for instance, we could expect that people high on extraversion fit well with aggressive and team-oriented cultures, that people high on agreeableness match up better with a supportive organizational climate than one focused on aggressiveness, and that people high on openness to experience fit better in organizations that emphasize innovation rather than standardization. Following these guidelines at the time of hiring should identify new employees who fit better with the organization's culture, which should, in turn, result in higher employee satisfaction and reduced turnover. Research on person–organization fit has also looked at whether people's values match the organization's culture. This match predicts job satisfaction, commitment to the organization, and low turnover.[52]

> Values do appear to vary across cultures, meaning that, on average, people's values in one nation tend to differ from those in another; however, there is substantial variability in values within a culture.

Global Implications

Personality

Do personality frameworks, such as the Big Five model, transfer across cultures? Are dimensions such as the Type A personality relevant in all cultures? Let's try to answer these questions.

The five personality factors identified in the Big Five model appear in almost all cross-cultural studies.[53] These studies have included a wide variety of diverse cultures—such as China, Israel, Germany, Japan, Spain, Nigeria, Norway, Pakistan, and the United States. Differences tend to be in the emphasis on dimensions and whether countries are predominantly individualistic or collectivistic. Chinese managers use the category of conscientiousness more often and agreeableness less often than do U.S. managers. And the Big Five appear to predict a bit better in individualistic than in collectivist cultures.[54] But there is a surprisingly high amount of agreement, especially among individuals from developed countries. A comprehensive review of studies covering people from what was then the 15-nation European Community found conscientiousness a valid predictor of performance across jobs and occupational groups.[55] This is exactly what U.S. studies have found.

Values

An understanding of how values differ across cultures should help explain and predict behavior of employees from different countries.

Hofstede's Framework for Assessing Cultures

One of the most widely referenced approaches for analyzing variations among cultures was done in the late 1970s by Geert Hofstede.[56] He surveyed more than 116,000 IBM employees in 40 countries about their work-related values and found that managers and employees vary on five value dimensions of national culture:

- *Power distance.* **Power distance** describes the degree to which people in a country accept that power in institutions and organizations is distributed unequally. A high rating on power distance means that large inequalities of power and wealth exist and are tolerated in the culture, as in a class or caste system that discourages upward mobility. A low power distance rating characterizes societies that stress equality and opportunity.
- *Individualism versus collectivism.* **Individualism** is the degree to which people prefer to act as individuals rather than as members of groups and believe in individual rights above all else. **Collectivism** emphasizes a tight social framework in which people expect others in groups of which they are a part to look after them and protect them.
- *Masculinity versus femininity.* Hofstede's construct of **masculinity** is the degree to which the culture favors traditional masculine roles such as

(continued)

achievement, power, and control, as opposed to viewing men and women as equals. A high masculinity rating indicates the culture has separate roles for men and women, with men dominating the society. A high **femininity** rating means the culture sees little differentiation between male and female roles and treats women as the equals of men in all respects.

• *Uncertainty avoidance.* The degree to which people in a country prefer structured over unstructured situations defines their **uncertainty avoidance.** In cultures that score high on uncertainty avoidance, people have an increased level of anxiety about uncertainty and ambiguity and use laws and controls to reduce uncertainty. Cultures low on uncertainty avoidance are more accepting of ambiguity, are less rule oriented, take more risks, and more readily accept change.

• *Long-term versus short-term orientation.* This newest addition to Hofstede's typology measures a society's devotion to traditional values. People in a culture with **long-term orientation** look to the future and value thrift, persistence, and tradition. In a **short-term orientation,** people value the here and now; they accept change more readily and don't see commitments as impediments to change.

How do different countries score on Hofstede's dimensions? Exhibit 4.5 shows the ratings for the countries for which data are available. For example, power distance is higher in Malaysia than in any other country. The United States is very individualistic; in fact, it's the most individualistic nation of all (closely followed by Australia and Great Britain). The United States also tends to be short term in orientation and low in power distance (people in the United States tend not to accept built-in class differences between people). It is also relatively low on uncertainty avoidance, meaning most adults are relatively tolerant of uncertainty and ambiguity. The United States scores relatively high on masculinity; most people emphasize traditional gender roles (at least relative to countries such as Denmark, Finland, Norway, and Sweden).

You'll notice regional differences. Western and northern nations such as Canada and the Netherlands tend to be more individualistic. Poorer countries such as Mexico and the Philippines tend to be higher on power distance. South American nations tend to be higher than other countries on uncertainty avoidance, and Asian countries tend to have a long-term orientation.

Hofstede's culture dimensions have been enormously influential on OB researchers and managers. Nevertheless, his research has been criticized. First, although the data have since been updated, the original work is more than 30 years old and was based on a single company (IBM). A lot has happened on the world scene since then. Some of the most obvious changes include the fall of the Soviet Union, the transformation of central and eastern Europe, the end of apartheid in South Africa, the spread of Islam throughout the world, and the rise of China as a global power. Second, few researchers have read the details of Hofstede's methodology closely and are therefore unaware of the many decisions and judgment calls he had to make (for example, reducing the number of cultural values to just five). Some results are unexpected. Japan, which is often considered a highly collectivist nation, is considered only average on collectivism under Hofstede's dimensions.[57] Despite these concerns, Hofstede has been one of the most widely cited social scientists ever, and his framework has left a lasting mark on OB.

The GLOBE Framework for Assessing Cultures

Begun in 1993, the Global Leadership and Organizational Behavior Effectiveness (GLOBE) research program is an ongoing cross-cultural investigation of leadership and national culture. Using data from 825 organizations in 62 countries, the GLOBE team identified nine dimensions on which national cultures differ.[58] Some—such as power distance, individualism/collectivism, uncertainty avoidance, gender differentiation (similar to masculinity versus femininity), and future orientation (similar to long-term versus short-term orientation)—resemble the Hofstede dimensions. The main difference is that the GLOBE framework added dimensions, such as humane orientation (the degree to which a society rewards individuals for being altruistic, generous, and kind to others) and performance orientation (the degree to which a society encourages and rewards group members for performance improvement and excellence).

Which framework is better? That's hard to say, and each has its adherents. We give more emphasis to Hofstede's dimensions here because they have stood the test of time and the GLOBE study confirmed them. However, researchers continue to debate the differences between these frameworks, and future studies may, in time, favor the more nuanced perspective of the GLOBE study.

Country	Power Distance		Individualism versus Collectivism		Masculinity versus Femininity		Uncertainty Avoidance		Long- versus Short-Term Orientation	
	Index	Rank	Index	Rank	Index	Rank	Index	Rank	Index	Rank
Argentina	49	35–36	46	22–23	56	20–21	86	10–15		
Australia	36	41	90	2	61	16	51	37	31	22–24
Austria	11	53	55	18	79	2	70	24–25	31	22–24
Belgium	65	20	75	8	54	22	94	5–6	38	18
Brazil	69	14	38	26–27	49	27	76	21–22	65	6
Canada	39	39	80	4–5	52	24	48	41–42	23	30
Chile	63	24–25	23	38	28	46	86	10–15		
Colombia	67	17	13	49	64	11–12	80	20		
Costa Rica	35	42–44	15	46	21	48–49	86	10–15		
Denmark	18	51	74	9	16	50	23	51	46	10
Ecuador	78	8–9	8	52	63	13–14	67	28		
El Salvador	66	18–19	19	42	40	40	94	5–6		
Finland	33	46	63	17	26	47	59	31–32	41	14
France	68	15–16	71	10–11	43	35–36	86	10–15	39	17
Germany	35	42–44	67	15	66	9–10	65	29	31	22–24
Great Britain	35	42–44	89	3	66	9–10	35	47–48	25	28–29
Greece	60	27–28	35	30	57	18–19	112	1		
Guatemala	95	2–3	6	53	37	43	101	3		
Hong Kong	68	15–16	25	37	57	18–19	29	49–50	96	2
India	77	10–11	48	21	56	20–21	40	45	61	7
Indonesia	78	8–9	14	47–48	46	30–31	48	41–42		
Iran	58	29–30	41	24	43	35–36	59	31–32		
Ireland	28	49	70	12	68	7–8	35	47–48	43	13
Israel	13	52	54	19	47	29	81	19		
Italy	50	34	76	7	70	4–5	75	23	34	19
Jamaica	45	37	39	25	68	7–8	13	52		
Japan	54	33	46	22–23	95	1	92	7	80	4
Korea (South)	60	27–28	18	43	39	41	85	16–17	75	5
Malaysia	104	1	26	36	50	25–26	36	46		
Mexico	81	5–6	30	32	69	6	82	18		
The Netherlands	38	40	80	4–5	14	51	53	35	44	11–12
New Zealand	22	50	79	6	58	17	49	39–40	30	25–26
Norway	31	47–48	69	13	8	52	50	38	44	11–12
Pakistan	55	32	14	47–48	50	25–26	70	24–25	0	34
Panama	95	2–3	11	51	44	34	86	10–15		
Peru	64	21–23	16	45	42	37–38	87	9		
Philippines	94	4	32	31	64	11–12	44	44	19	31–32
Portugal	63	24–25	27	33–35	31	45	104	2	30	25–26
Singapore	74	13	20	39–41	48	28	8	53	48	9
South Africa	49	35–36	65	16	63	13–14	49	39–40		
Spain	57	31	51	20	42	37–38	86	10–15	19	31–32
Sweden	31	47–48	71	10–11	5	53	29	49–50	33	20
Switzerland	34	45	68	14	70	4–5	58	33	40	15–16

EXHIBIT 4.5 Hofstede's Cultural Values by Nation

(continued)

Source: Copyright Geert Hofstede BV, hofstede@bovt.nl. Reprinted with permission.

Country	Power Distance Index	Power Distance Rank	Individualism versus Collectivism Index	Individualism versus Collectivism Rank	Masculinity versus Femininity Index	Masculinity versus Femininity Rank	Uncertainty Avoidance Index	Uncertainty Avoidance Rank	Long- versus Short-Term Orientation Index	Long- versus Short-Term Orientation Rank
Taiwan	58	29–30	17	44	45	32–33	69	26	87	3
Thailand	64	21–23	20	39–41	34	44	64	30	56	8
Turkey	66	18–19	37	28	45	32–33	85	16–17		
United States	40	38	91	1	62	15	46	43	29	27
Uruguay	61	26	36	29	38	42	100	4		
Venezuela	81	5–6	12	50	73	3	76	21–22		
Yugoslavia	76	12	27	33–35	21	48–49	88	8		
Regions:										
Arab countries	80	7	38	26–27	53	23	68	27		
East Africa	64	21–23	27	33–35	41	39	52	36	25	28–29
West Africa	77	10–11	20	39–41	46	30–31	54	34	16	33

EXHIBIT 4.5 (Continued)

Implications for Managers

Personality

What value, if any, does the Big Five model provide to managers? From the early 1900s through the mid-1980s, researchers unsuccessfully sought a link between personality and job performance. However, the past 20 years have been more promising, largely due to the findings about the Big Five.

Screening job candidates for high conscientiousness—as well as the other Big Five traits, depending on the criteria an organization finds most important—should pay dividends. Of course, managers still need to take situational factors into consideration. Factors such as job demands, the degree of required interaction with others, and the organization's culture are examples of situational variables that moderate the personality–job performance relationship. You need to evaluate the job, the work group, and the organization to determine the optimal personality fit. Other traits, such as core self-evaluation or narcissism, may be relevant in certain situations, too.

Although the MBTI has been widely criticized, it may have a place in organizations. In training and development, it can help employees to better under-stand themselves, and it can help team members to better understand each other. And it can open up communication in work groups and possibly reduce conflicts.

Values

Why is it important to know an individual's values? Values often underlie and explain attitudes, behaviors, and perceptions. So knowledge of an individual's value system can provide insight into what makes the person "tick."

Employees' performance and satisfaction are likely to be higher if their values fit well with the organization. The person who places great importance on imagination, independence, and freedom is likely to be poorly matched with an organization that seeks conformity from its employees. Managers are more likely to appreciate, evaluate positively, and allocate rewards to employees who fit in, and employees are more likely to be satisfied if they perceive they do fit in. This argues for management to seek job candidates who have not only the ability, experience, and motivation to perform but also a value system compatible with the organization's.

CHAPTER 5

Perception and Individual Decision Making

After studying this chapter, you should be able to:

■ Define *perception* and explain the factors that influence it.

■ Identify the shortcuts individuals use in making judgments about others.

■ Explain the link between perception and decision making.

■ List and explain the common decision biases or errors.

■ Contrast the three ethical decision criteria.

■ Define *creativity* and discuss the three-component model of creativity.

WHAT IS PERCEPTION?

Perception is a process by which individuals organize and interpret their sensory impressions in order to give meaning to their environment. However, what we perceive can be substantially different from objective reality. For example, all employees in a firm may view it as a great place to work—favorable working conditions, interesting job assignments, good pay, excellent benefits, understanding and responsible management—but, as most of us know, it's very unusual to find such agreement.

Why is perception important in the study of OB? Simply because people's behavior is based on their perception of what reality is, not on reality itself. *The world as it is perceived is the world that is behaviorally important.*

Factors That Influence Perception

How do we explain the fact that individuals may look at the same thing yet perceive it differently? A number of factors operate to shape and sometimes distort perception.

These factors can reside in the *perceiver;* in the object, or *target,* being perceived; or in the context of the *situation* in which the perception is made.

- *Perceiver.* When you look at a target and attempt to interpret what you see, your interpretation is heavily influenced by your personal characteristics. Characteristics that affect perception include

People have inherent biases in how they see others (perception) and in how they make decisions (decision making). We can better understand people by understanding these biases.

your attitudes, personality, motives, interests, past experiences, and expectations. For instance, if you expect police officers to be authoritative, young people to be lazy, or individuals holding public office to be unscrupulous, you may perceive them as such, regardless of their actual traits.

- **Target.** Characteristics of the target we observe can affect what we perceive. Loud people are more likely to be noticed in a group than quiet ones. So, too, are extremely attractive or unattractive individuals. Because we don't look at targets in isolation, the relationship of a target to its background also influences perception, as does our tendency to group close things and similar things together. For instance, we often perceive women, men, Whites, African Americans, Asians, or members of any other group that has clearly distinguishable characteristics as alike in other, unrelated ways as well.
- **Situation.** Context is also important. The time at which we see an object or event can influence our attention, as can location, light, heat, or any number of situational factors. At a nightclub on Saturday night, you may not notice a young guest "dressed to the nines." Yet that same person so attired for your Monday morning management class would certainly catch your attention (and that of the rest of the class). Neither the perceiver nor the target has changed between Saturday night and Monday morning, but the situation is different.

PERSON PERCEPTION: MAKING JUDGMENTS ABOUT OTHERS

Now we turn to the application of perception concepts most relevant to OB—*person perception,* or the perceptions people form about each other.

Attribution Theory

Nonliving objects such as desks, machines, and buildings are subject to the laws of nature, but they have no beliefs, motives, or intentions. People do. That's why when we observe people, we attempt to explain why they behave in certain ways. Our perception and judgment of a person's actions, therefore, will be significantly influenced by the assumptions we make about that person's internal state.

Attribution theory tries to explain the ways in which we judge people differently, depending on the meaning we attribute to a given behavior.[1] It suggests that when we observe an individual's behavior, we attempt to determine whether it was internally or externally caused. That determination, however, depends largely on three factors: (1) distinctiveness, (2) consensus, and (3) consistency. First, let's clarify the differences between internal and external causation, and then we'll elaborate on each of the three determining factors.

Internally caused behaviors are those we believe to be under the personal control of the individual. *Externally* caused behavior is what we imagine the situation forced the individual to do. If one of your employees is late for work, you might attribute that to his partying into the wee hours and then oversleeping. This is an internal attribution. But if you attribute his arriving late to an automobile accident that tied up traffic, then you are making an external attribution.

Now let's discuss each of the three determining factors.

1. **Distinctiveness.** *Distinctiveness* refers to whether an individual displays different behaviors in different situations. Is the employee who arrives late today also the

one co-workers say regularly "blows off" commitments? What we want to know is whether this behavior is unusual. If it is, we are likely to give it an external attribution. If it's not, we will probably judge the behavior to be internal.

2. **Consensus.** If everyone who faces a similar situation responds in the same way, we can say the behavior shows *consensus*. The behavior of our tardy employee meets this criterion if all employees who took the same route to work were also late. From an attribution perspective, if consensus is high, you would probably give an external attribution to the employee's tardiness, whereas if other employees who took the same route made it to work on time, you would attribute his lateness to an internal cause.

3. **Consistency.** Finally, an observer looks for *consistency* in a person's actions. Does the person respond the same way over time? Coming in 10 minutes late for work is not perceived in the same way for an employee who hasn't been late for several months as it is for an employee who is late two or three times a week. The more consistent the behavior, the more we are inclined to attribute it to internal causes.

Exhibit 5.1 summarizes the key elements in attribution theory. It tells us, for instance, that if an employee, Kim Randolph, generally performs at about the same level on other related tasks as she does on her current task (low distinctiveness), other employees frequently perform differently—better or worse—than Kim does on that current task (low consensus), and Kim's performance on this current task is consistent over time (high consistency), anyone judging Kim's work will likely hold her primarily responsible for her task performance (internal attribution).

One of the most interesting findings from attribution theory research is that errors or biases distort attributions. When we make judgments about the behavior of other people, we tend to underestimate the influence of external factors and overestimate the influence of internal or personal factors.[2] This **fundamental attribution error** can explain why a sales manager is prone to attribute the poor performance of her sales agents to laziness rather than to the innovative product line introduced by a competitor. Individuals and organizations also tend to attribute their own successes to internal factors such as

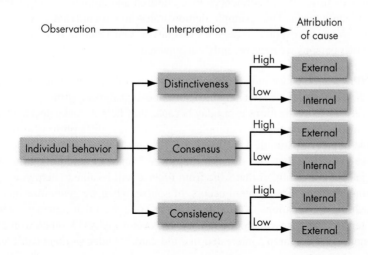

EXHIBIT 5.1
Attribution Theory

ability or effort, while putting the blame for failure on external factors such as bad luck or unproductive co-workers. This is the **self-serving bias.**[3]

Common Shortcuts in Judging Others

We use a number of shortcuts when we judge others. These techniques are frequently valuable: they allow us to make accurate perceptions rapidly and provide valid data for making predictions. However, they are not foolproof. They can and do get us into trouble. Understanding these shortcuts can help you recognize when they can result in significant distortions.

SELECTIVE PERCEPTION   Any characteristic that makes a person, an object, or an event stand out will increase the probability that we will perceive it. Why? Because it is impossible for us to assimilate everything we see; we can take in only certain stimuli. This tendency explains why you're more likely to notice cars like your own or why a boss may reprimand some people and not others who are doing the same thing. Because we can't observe everything going on about us, we engage in selective perception. **Selective perception** allows us to "speed-read" others, but not without the risk of drawing an inaccurate picture. Because we see what we want to see, we can draw unwarranted conclusions from an ambiguous situation.

HALO EFFECT   When we draw a general impression about an individual on the basis of a single characteristic, such as intelligence, sociability, or appearance, a **halo effect** is operating. The reality of the halo effect was confirmed in a classic study in which subjects were given a list of traits such as intelligent, skillful, practical, industrious, determined, and warm and asked to evaluate the person to whom those traits applied.[4] Subjects judged the person to be wise, humorous, popular, and imaginative. When the same list was modified to include "cold" instead of "warm," a completely different picture emerged. Clearly, the subjects were allowing a single trait to influence their overall impression of the person they were judging.

CONTRAST EFFECTS   An old adage among entertainers is "Never follow an act that has kids or animals in it." Why? Audiences love children and animals so much that you'll look bad in comparison. This example demonstrates how a **contrast effect** can distort perceptions. We don't evaluate a person in isolation. Our reaction to a person is influenced by other persons we have recently encountered.

STEREOTYPING   When we judge someone on the basis of our perception of the group to which he or she belongs, we are using the shortcut called **stereotyping**.

We rely on generalizations every day because they help us make decisions quickly; they are a means of simplifying a complex world. It's less difficult to deal with an unmanageable number of stimuli if we use *heuristics* or stereotypes. For example, it does make sense to assume that Tre, the new employee from accounting, is going to know something about budgeting, or that Allie from finance will be able to help you figure out a forecasting problem. The problem occurs, of course, when we generalize inaccurately or too much. In organizations, we frequently hear comments that represent stereotypes based on gender, age, race, religion, ethnicity, and even weight:[5] "Women won't relocate for a promotion," "Men aren't interested in child care," "Older workers can't learn new skills," "Asian immigrants are hardworking and conscientious," "Overweight people lack discipline." Stereotypes can be deeply ingrained and powerful enough to influence life-and-death decisions. One study, controlling for a wide array of factors (such as aggravating or mitigating circumstances), showed that the degree to which black defendants in murder trials looked "stereotypically black" essentially doubled their odds of receiving a death sentence if convicted.[6]

One of the problems of stereotypes is that they *are* widespread and often useful generalizations, despite the fact that they may not contain a shred of truth when applied to a particular person or situation. Thus, we constantly have to check ourselves to make sure we're not unfairly or inaccurately applying a stereotype in our evaluations and decisions. Stereotypes are an example of the warning "The more useful, the more danger from misuse."

THE LINK BETWEEN PERCEPTION AND INDIVIDUAL DECISION MAKING

Individuals in organizations make **decisions**, choices from among two or more alternatives. Top managers determine their organization's goals, what products or services to offer, how best to finance operations, or where to locate a new manufacturing plant. Middle- and lower-level managers set production schedules, select new employees, and decide how to allocate pay raises. Nonmanagerial employees decide how much effort to put forth at work and whether to comply with a request by the boss. In recent years, organizations have been empowering their nonmanagerial employees with decision-making authority historically reserved for managers alone. Individual decision making is thus an important part of organizational behavior. But how individuals make decisions and the quality of their choices are largely influenced by their perceptions.

Decision making occurs as a reaction to a **problem**.[7] That is, a discrepancy exists between the current state of affairs and some desired state, requiring us to consider alternative courses of action. If your car breaks down and you rely on it to get to work, you have a problem that requires a decision on your part. Unfortunately, most problems don't come neatly labeled "problem." One person's *problem* is another person's *satisfactory state of affairs.* One manager may view her division's 2 percent decline in quarterly sales to be a serious problem requiring immediate action on her part. In contrast, her counterpart in another division, who also had a 2 percent sales decrease, might consider that quite acceptable. So awareness that a problem exists and that a decision might or might not be needed is a perceptual issue.

Every decision requires us to interpret and evaluate information. We typically receive data from multiple sources and need to screen, process, and interpret it. Which data are relevant to the decision, and which are not? The decision maker's perceptions will answer that question. We also need to develop alternatives and evaluate their strengths and weaknesses. Again, the individual's perceptual process will affect the final outcome. Finally, throughout the entire decision-making process, **perceptual distortions** often surface that can bias analysis and conclusions.

DECISION MAKING IN ORGANIZATIONS

Business schools generally train students to follow rational decision-making models. Although these models have considerable merit, they don't always describe how people actually make decisions. This is where OB enters the picture: to improve how we make decisions in organizations, we must understand the decision-making errors people commit (in addition to the perception errors we've discussed). Next we describe these errors, beginning with a brief overview of the rational decision-making model.

The Rational Model, Bounded Rationality, and Intuition

RATIONAL DECISION MAKING   We often think the best decision maker is **rational** and makes consistent, value-maximizing choices within specified constraints. These decisions follow a six-step **rational decision-making model**.[8] The six steps are listed in Exhibit 5.2.

The rational decision-making model relies on a number of assumptions, including that the decision maker has complete information, is able to identify all the relevant options in an unbiased manner, and chooses the option with the highest utility. As you might imagine, most decisions in the real world don't follow the rational model. People are usually content to find an acceptable or reasonable solution to a problem rather than an optimal one. Choices tend to be limited to the neighborhood of the problem symptom and the current alternative. As one expert in decision making put it, "Most significant decisions are made by judgment, rather than by a defined prescriptive model."[9] What's more, people are remarkably unaware of making suboptimal decisions.[10]

BOUNDED RATIONALITY   The limited information-processing capability of human beings makes it impossible to assimilate and understand all the information necessary to optimize.[11] So most people respond to a complex problem by reducing it to a level at which they can readily understand it. Also many problems likely don't have an optimal solution because they are too complicated to be broken down into the parameters of the rational decision-making model. So people *satisfice;* that is, they seek solutions that are satisfactory and sufficient.

Because the human mind cannot formulate and solve complex problems with full rationality, we operate within the confines of **bounded rationality**. We construct simplified models that extract the essential features from problems without capturing all their complexity.[12] We can then behave rationally within the limits of the simple model.

How does bounded rationality work for the typical individual? Once we've identified a problem, we begin to search for criteria and alternatives. But the list of criteria is likely to be far from exhaustive. We identify a limited list of the most conspicuous choices, both easy to find and highly visible, that usually represent familiar criteria and

1. Define the problem.
2. Identify the decision criteria.
3. Allocate weights to the criteria.
4. Develop the alternatives.
5. Evaluate the alternatives.
6. Select the best alternative.

EXHIBIT 5.2 Steps in the Rational Decision-Making Model

Source: For a review of the rational decision-making model, see E. F. Harrison, *The Managerial Decision-Making Process,* 5th ed. (Boston: Houghton Mifflin, 1999), pp. 75–102.

tried-and-true solutions. Next, we begin reviewing them, but our review will not be comprehensive. Instead, we focus on alternatives that differ only in a relatively small degree from the choice currently in effect. Following familiar and well-worn paths, we review alternatives only until we identify one that is "good enough"—that meets an acceptable level of performance. That ends our search. So the solution represents a satisficing choice—the first *acceptable* one we encounter—rather than an optimal one.

Perceptual and decision-making biases and heuristics are not necessarily bad. They allow us to process information more quickly and efficiently. The key is to be self-aware enough to see when a bias or shortcut may be counterproductive.

This process of satisficing is not always a bad idea—using a simple process may frequently be more sensible than the traditional rational decision-making model.[13] To use the rational model in the real world, you need to gather a great deal of information about all the options, compute applicable weights, and then calculate values across a huge number of criteria. All these processes can cost you time, energy, and money. And if there are a great number of unknowns when it comes to weights and preferences, the fully rational model may not be any more accurate than a best guess. Sometimes a fast-and-frugal process of solving problems might be your best option.

INTUITION   Perhaps the least rational way of making decisions is to rely on intuition. **Intuitive decision making** is an unconscious process created from distilled experience. Its defining qualities are that it occurs outside conscious thought; it relies on holistic associations, or links between disparate pieces of information; it's fast; and it's *affectively charged,* meaning it usually engages the emotions.[14]

Although intuition isn't rational, it isn't necessarily wrong. Nor does it always operate in opposition to rational analysis; rather, the two can complement each other. But intuition is not superstition, or the product of some magical or paranormal sixth sense. As one recent review noted, "Intuition is a highly complex and highly developed form of reasoning that is based on years of experience and learning."[15] It appears that rational analysis has been overemphasized and, in certain instances, relying on intuition can improve decision making.

Common Biases and Errors in Decision Making

Decision makers engage in bounded rationality, but they also allow systematic biases and errors to creep into their judgments.[16] To minimize effort and avoid difficult trade-offs, people tend to rely too heavily on experience, impulses, gut feelings, and convenient rules of thumb. In many instances, these shortcuts are helpful. However, they can lead to severe distortions of rationality. Following are the most common biases in decision making.

OVERCONFIDENCE BIAS   It's been said that "no problem in judgment and decision making is more prevalent and more potentially catastrophic than over-confidence."[17] When we're given factual questions and asked to judge the probability that our answers are correct, we tend to be far too optimistic, which is called an **overconfidence bias**. When people say they're 65 to 70 percent confident they're right, they are actually correct only about 50 percent of the time.[18] When they say they're 100 percent sure, they tend to be 70 to 85 percent correct.[19]

From an organizational standpoint, one of the most interesting findings related to overconfidence is that individuals whose intellectual and interpersonal abilities are *weakest* are most likely to overestimate their performance and ability. As managers and employees become more knowledgeable about an issue, they become less likely to display overconfidence.[20] There's also a negative relationship between entrepreneurs' optimism and the performance of their new ventures: the more optimistic, the less successful.[21] The tendency for some entrepreneurs to be too confident about their ideas might keep them from planning how to avoid problems that arise.

ANCHORING BIAS   The **anchoring bias** is a tendency to fixate on initial information and fail to adequately adjust for subsequent information.[22] Anchors are widely used by people in professions in which persuasion skills are important—such as advertising, management, politics, real estate, and law. Anytime a negotiation takes place, so does anchoring. As soon as someone states a number, it compromises your ability to ignore that number. When a prospective employer asks how much you made in your prior job, your answer typically anchors the employer's offer. (Remember this when you negotiate your salary, but set the anchor only as high as you realistically can.) Finally, the more precise your anchor, the smaller the adjustment. Some research suggests people think of adjustment after an anchor is set as rounding off a number. If you suggest an initial target salary of $55,000, your boss will consider $50,000 to $60,000 a reasonable range for negotiation, but if you mention $55,650, your boss is more likely to consider $55,000 to $56,000 the range of likely values for negotiation.[23]

CONFIRMATION BIAS   The rational decision-making process assumes that we objectively gather information. But we don't. We *selectively* gather it. The **confirmation bias** represents a specific case of selective perception: we seek out information that reaffirms our past choices, and we discount information that contradicts them. We also tend to accept at face value information that confirms our preconceived views, while we are critical and skeptical of information that challenges these views. Therefore, the information we gather is typically biased toward supporting views we already hold. We even tend to seek out sources most likely to tell us what we want to hear, and we give too much weight to supporting information and too little to contradictory.

AVAILABILITY BIAS   More people fear flying than fear driving in a car. But if flying on a commercial airline really were as dangerous as driving, the equivalent of two 747s filled to capacity would crash every week, killing all aboard. Yet the media give much more attention to air accidents, so we tend to overstate the risk of flying and understate the risk of driving.

The **availability bias** is our tendency to base judgments on information readily available.[24] Events that evoke emotions, are particularly vivid, or are more recent tend to be more available in our memory, leading us to overestimate the chances of unlikely events such as an airplane crash. The availability bias can also explain why managers doing performance appraisals give more weight to recent employee behaviors than to behaviors of 6 or 9 months earlier or why credit-rating agencies such as Moody's or Standard & Poor's may issue overly positive ratings by relying on information presented by debt issuers, who have an incentive to offer data favorable to their case.[25]

ESCALATION OF COMMITMENT   Another distortion that creeps into decisions is a tendency to escalate commitment.[26] **Escalation of commitment** refers to staying with a decision even when there is clear evidence it's wrong. Consider a friend who has been dating someone for several years. Although he admits things aren't going too well, he says he is still going to marry her. His justification: "I have a lot invested in the relationship!"

Individuals escalate commitment to a failing course of action when they view themselves as responsible for the failure. They "throw good money after bad" to demonstrate their initial decision wasn't wrong and to avoid admitting they made a mistake. In fact, people who carefully gather and consider information consistent with the rational decision-making model are *more* likely to engage in escalation of commitment than those who spend less time thinking about their choices.[27] Perhaps they have invested so much time and energy into making their decisions that they have convinced themselves they're taking the right course of action and don't update their knowledge in the face of new information. Many an organization has suffered because a manager was determined to prove his or her original decision right by continuing to commit resources to a lost cause.

RISK AVERSION   Mathematically, we should find a 50–50 flip of the coin for $100 to be worth as much as a sure promise of $50. After all, the expected value of the gamble over a number of trials is $50. However, most people don't consider these options equally valuable. Rather, nearly everyone but committed gamblers would rather have the sure thing than a risky prospect.[28] For many people, a 50–50 flip of a coin even for $200 might not be worth as much as a sure promise of $50, even though the gamble is mathematically worth twice as much as the sure thing! This tendency to prefer a sure thing over a risky outcome is **risk aversion**.

Risk aversion has important implications. To offset the risks inherent in a commission-based wage, companies pay commissioned employees considerably more than they do those on straight salaries. Risk-averse employees will stick with the established way of doing their jobs, rather than taking a chance on innovative or creative methods. Sticking with a strategy that has worked in the past does minimize risk, but in the long run it will lead to stagnation. Ambitious people with power that can be taken away (most managers) appear to be especially risk averse, perhaps because they don't want to lose on a gamble everything they've worked so hard to achieve.[29] CEOs at risk of being terminated are also exceptionally risk averse, even when a riskier investment strategy is in their firms' best interests.[30]

HINDSIGHT BIAS   The **hindsight bias** is the tendency to believe falsely, after the outcome is known, that we'd have accurately predicted it. When we have accurate feedback on the outcome, we seem pretty good at concluding it was obvious.

In late 2007, when former Citigroup CEO Charles O. Prince III asked Thomas Maheras, who oversaw lending at the bank, whether everything was okay, Maheras reportedly told his boss that no big losses were looming. Maheras continued to calm concerns over the bank's risks and vulnerabilities, and Prince and other Citigroup executives relied on his word. Everything was not okay, of course, and it now seems all too clear Prince should not have taken Maheras at his word. Citigroup lost billions in its mortgage-related holdings, and Prince's job went with it.

Experts faulted Prince for relying on Maheras, Maheras for relying on credit-rating agencies, and credit-rating agencies for trusting debt issuers. Former Merrill Lynch CEO John Thain—and many other Wall Street executives—took similar blame for supposedly failing to see what now seems obvious (that housing prices were inflated, too many risk loans were made, and the values of many "securities" were based on fragile assumptions). Though the criticisms may have merit, things are often all too clear in hindsight.

ORGANIZATIONAL CONSTRAINTS ON DECISION MAKING

Having examined the rational decision-making model, bounded rationality, and some of the most salient biases and errors in decision making, we turn here to a discussion of organizational constraints. Organizations can constrain decision makers, creating deviations from the rational model. For instance, managers shape their decisions to reflect the organization's performance evaluation and reward system, to comply with its formal regulations, and to meet organizationally imposed time constraints. Precedent can also limit decisions.

PERFORMANCE EVALUATION   Managers are strongly influenced by the criteria on which they are evaluated. If a division manager believes the manufacturing plants under his responsibility are operating best when he hears nothing negative, we shouldn't be surprised to find his plant managers spending a good part of their time ensuring that negative information doesn't reach him.

REWARD SYSTEMS   The organization's reward system influences decision makers by suggesting what choices have better personal payoffs. If the organization rewards risk aversion, managers are more likely to make conservative decisions. From the 1930s through the mid-1980s, General Motors consistently gave promotions and bonuses to managers who kept a low profile and avoided controversy. They became very adept at dodging tough issues and passing controversial decisions on to committees.

FORMAL REGULATIONS   David Gonzalez, a shift manager at a Taco Bell restaurant in San Antonio, Texas, describes constraints he faces on his job: "I've got rules and regulations covering almost every decision I make—from how to make a burrito to how often I need to clean the restrooms. My job doesn't come with much freedom of choice." David's situation is not unique. All but the smallest organizations create rules and policies to program decisions and get individuals to act in the intended manner. And of course, in so doing, they limit decision choices.

SYSTEM-IMPOSED TIME CONSTRAINTS   Almost all important decisions come with explicit deadlines. A report on new-product development may have to be ready for executive committee review by the first of the month. Such conditions often make it difficult, if not impossible, for managers to gather all the information they might like before making a final choice.

HISTORICAL PRECEDENTS   Decisions aren't made in a vacuum; they have a context. In fact, individual decisions are points in a stream of choice. Those made in the past are like ghosts that haunt and constrain current choices. It's common knowledge that the largest determinant of the size of any given year's budget is last year's budget.[31] Choices made today are largely a result of choices made over the years.

WHAT ABOUT ETHICS AND CREATIVITY IN DECISION MAKING?

Ethical considerations should be an important criterion in all organizational decision making. In this section, we present three ways to frame decisions ethically.[32]

Three Ethical Decision Criteria

The first ethical yardstick is **utilitarianism**, in which decisions are made solely on the basis of their *outcomes,* ideally to provide the greatest good for the greatest number. This view dominates business decision making. It is consistent with goals such as efficiency, productivity, and high profits.

Another ethical criterion is to make decisions consistent with fundamental liberties and privileges, as set forth in documents such as the Bill of Rights. An emphasis on *rights* in decision making means respecting and protecting the basic rights of individuals, such as the right to privacy, free speech, and due process. This criterion protects **whistle-blowers** when they reveal an organization's unethical practices to the press or government agencies, using their right to free speech.

A third criterion is to impose and enforce rules fairly and impartially to ensure *justice* or an equitable distribution of benefits and costs. Union members typically favor this view. It justifies paying people the same wage for a given job regardless of performance differences and using seniority as the primary determination in layoff decisions.

Each criterion has advantages and liabilities. A focus on utilitarianism promotes efficiency and productivity, but it can sideline the rights of some individuals, particularly those with minority representation. The use of rights protects individuals from injury and is consistent with freedom and privacy, but it can create a legalistic environment that hinders productivity and efficiency. A focus on justice protects the interests of the underrepresented and less powerful, but it can encourage a sense of entitlement that reduces risk taking, innovation, and productivity.

Decision makers, particularly in for-profit organizations, feel comfortable with utilitarianism. The "best interests" of the organization and its stockholders can justify a lot of questionable actions, such as large layoffs. But many critics feel this perspective needs to change.[33] Public concern about individual rights and social justice suggests managers should develop ethical standards based on nonutilitarian criteria. This presents a challenge because satisfying individual rights and social justice creates far more ambiguities than utilitarian effects on efficiency and profits. This helps explain why managers are increasingly criticized for their actions. Raising prices, selling products with questionable effects on consumer health, closing down inefficient plants, laying off large numbers of employees, moving production overseas to cut costs, and similar decisions can be justified in utilitarian terms. But that may no longer be the single measure by which good decisions are judged.

Improving Creativity in Decision Making

Although the rational decision-making model will often improve decisions, a rational decision maker also needs **creativity**, the ability to produce novel and useful ideas. These are different from what's been done before but appropriate to the problem presented.

Why is creativity valuable in decision making? It allows the decision maker to more fully appraise and understand the problem, including seeing problems others can't see. L'Oréal puts its managers through creative exercises such as cooking or making music, and the University of Chicago requires MBA students to make short movies about their experiences.

Creativity allows the decision maker to more fully appraise and understand the problem, including seeing problems others can't see.

CREATIVE POTENTIAL   Most people have useful creative potential. But to unleash it, they have to escape the psychological ruts many of us fall into and to learn how to think about a problem in divergent ways.

Exceptional creativity is scarce. We all know of creative geniuses in science (Albert Einstein), art (Pablo Picasso), and business (Steve Jobs). But what about the typical individual? Intelligent people and those who score high on openness to experience are more likely to be creative.[34] Other traits of creative people are independence, self-confidence, risk taking, an internal locus of control, tolerance for ambiguity, a low need for structure, and perseverance.[35] Exposure to a variety of cultures can also improve creativity.[36] Those who spend extensive periods of time in other cultures generate more innovative solutions to problems. It may be that taking an international assignment, or even an international vacation, could jump-start your creative process.

THREE-COMPONENT MODEL OF CREATIVITY   What can individuals and organizations do to stimulate employee creativity? The best answer lies in the **three-component model of creativity**,[37] which proposes that individual creativity essentially requires expertise, creative thinking skills, and intrinsic task motivation. Studies confirm that the higher the level of each, the higher the creativity.

Expertise is the foundation for all creative work. The film writer, producer, and director Quentin Tarantino spent his youth working in a video rental store, where he built up an encyclopedic knowledge of movies. The potential for creativity is enhanced when individuals have abilities, knowledge, proficiencies, and similar expertise in their field of endeavor. You wouldn't expect someone with minimal knowledge of programming to be very creative as a software engineer.

The second component is *creative-thinking skills*. This encompasses personality characteristics associated with creativity, the ability to use analogies, and the talent to see the familiar in a different light.

A meta-analysis of 102 studies found positive moods increase creativity, but it depends on what sort of positive mood was considered.[38] Moods such as happiness that encourage interaction with the world are more conducive to creativity than passive moods such as calm. This means the common advice to relax and clear your mind to develop creative ideas may be misplaced. It would be better to get in an upbeat mood and then frame your work as an opportunity to have fun and experiment. Negative moods also don't always have the same effects on creativity. Passive negative moods such as sadness doesn't seem to have much effect, but avoidance-oriented negative moods such as fear and anxiety decrease creativity. Feeling threatened reduces your desire to try new activities; risk aversion increases when you're scared. Active negative moods, such as anger, however, do appear to enhance creativity, especially if you are taking your task seriously.

Being around creative others can make us more inspired, especially if we're creatively "stuck."[39] One study found that having "weak ties" to creative people—knowing them but not well—facilitates creativity because the people are there as a resource if we need them but not so close as to stunt our own independent thinking.[40]

Analogies allow decision makers to apply an idea from one context to another. One of the most famous examples was Alexander Graham Bell's observation that it might be possible to apply the way the ear operates to his "talking box." Bell noticed the bones in the ear are operated by a delicate, thin membrane. He wondered why, then, a thicker and stronger piece of membrane shouldn't be able to move a piece of steel. From that analogy, the telephone was conceived. Thinking in terms of analogies is a complex intellectual skill, which helps explain why cognitive ability is related to creativity. Demonstrating this effect, one study found children who got high scores on cognitive ability tests at age 13 were significantly more likely to have made creative achievements in their professional lives 25 years later.[41]

The final component in the three-component model of creativity is *intrinsic task motivation.* This is the desire to work on something because it's interesting, involving, exciting, satisfying, or personally challenging. It's what turns creativity *potential* into *actual* creative ideas. Environmental stimulants that foster creativity include a culture that encourages the flow of ideas; fair and constructive judgment of ideas; rewards and recognition for creative work; sufficient financial, material, and information resources; freedom to decide what work is to be done and how to do it; a supervisor who communicates effectively, shows confidence in others, and supports the work group; and work group members who support and trust each other.[42]

Global Implications

In considering potential global differences in this chapter's concepts, let's consider the three areas that have attracted the most research: (1) attributions, (2) decision making, and (3) ethics.

Attributions

The evidence on cultural differences in perception is mixed, but most suggest there *are* differences across cultures in the attributions people make.[43] We noted earlier the tendency for Asians (Japanese) to be less susceptible to the fundamental attribution error. Another study found Korean managers less likely to use the self-serving bias—they tended to accept responsibility for group failure "because I was not a capable leader" instead of attributing failure to group members.[44] On the other hand, Asian managers are more likely to lay blame on institutions or whole organizations, whereas Western observers are more likely to believe individual managers should be the focus of blame or praise.[45] That probably explains why U.S. newspapers prominently report the names of individual executives when firms do poorly, whereas Asian media provide more coverage of how the firm as a whole has failed. This tendency to make group-based attributions also explains why individuals from Asian cultures are more likely to make group-based stereotypes.[46] Attribution theory was developed largely based on experiments with U.S. and western European workers. But these studies suggest caution in making attribution theory predictions in non-Western societies, especially in countries with strong collectivist traditions.

Decision Making

The rational model makes no acknowledgment of cultural differences, nor does the bulk of OB research literature on decision making. A 2007 review of cross-cultural OB research covered 25 areas, but cultural influence on decision making was not among them. Another 2007 review identified 15 topics, but the result was the same: no research on culture and decision making.[47]

But Indonesians, for instance, don't necessarily make decisions the same way Australians do. Therefore, we need to recognize that the cultural background of a decision maker can have a significant influence on the selection of problems, the depth of analysis, the importance placed on logic and rationality, and whether organizational decisions should be made autocratically by an individual manager or collectively in groups.[48]

Cultures differ in their time orientation, the importance of rationality, their belief in the ability of people to solve problems, and their preference for collective decision making. Differences in time orientation help us understand why managers in Egypt make decisions at a much slower and more deliberate pace than their U.S. counterparts. Although rationality is valued in North America, that's not true elsewhere in the world. A North American manager might make an important decision intuitively but know it's important to appear to proceed in a rational fashion because rationality is highly valued in the West. In countries such as Iran, where rationality is not as paramount as other factors, efforts to appear rational are not necessary.

(continued)

Some cultures emphasize solving problems, whereas others focus on accepting situations as they are. The United States falls in the first category; Thailand and Indonesia are examples of the second. Because problem-solving managers believe they can and should change situations to their benefit, U.S. managers might identify a problem long before their Thai or Indonesian counterparts would choose to recognize it as such. Decision making by Japanese managers is much more group-oriented than in the United States. The Japanese value conformity and cooperation. So before Japanese CEOs make an important decision, they collect a large amount of information, which they use in consensus-forming group decisions.

Ethics

There are few global ethical standards, as contrasts between Asia and the West illustrate.[49] Because bribery is commonplace in countries such as China, a Canadian working in China might face a dilemma: Should I pay a bribe to secure business if it is an accepted part of that country's culture? A manager of a large U.S. company operating in China caught an employee stealing. Following company policy, she fired him and turned him over to the local authorities. Later, she was horrified to learn the employee had been summarily executed.[50]

Although ethical standards may seem ambiguous in the West, criteria defining right and wrong are actually much clearer there than in Asia, where few issues are black and white and most are gray. Global organizations must establish ethical principles for decision makers in countries such as India and China and modify them to reflect cultural norms if they want to uphold high standards and consistent practices.

Implications for Managers

Perception

Individuals base their behavior not on the way their external environment actually is but rather on what they see or believe it to be. Whether a manager successfully plans and organizes the work of employees and actually helps them to structure their work more efficiently and effectively is far less important than how employees perceive the manager's efforts. Similarly, employees judge issues such as fair pay, performance appraisals, and working conditions in very individual ways; we cannot be assured they will interpret conditions about their jobs in a favorable light. To influence productivity, we need to assess how workers perceive their jobs.

Absenteeism, turnover, and job satisfaction are also reactions to an individual's perceptions. Dissatisfaction with working conditions and the belief that an organization lacks promotion opportunities are judgments based on attempts to create meaning in the job. The employee's conclusion that a job is good or bad is an interpretation. Managers must spend time understanding how each individual interprets reality and, when there is a significant difference between what someone sees and what exists, try to eliminate the distortions.

Individual Decision Making

Individuals think and reason before they act. This is why an understanding of how people make decisions can be helpful for explaining and predicting their behavior.

In some decision situations, people follow the rational decision-making model. But few important decisions are simple or unambiguous enough for the rational model's assumptions to apply. Thus, we find individuals looking for solutions that satisfice rather than optimize, injecting biases and prejudices into the decision process, and relying on intuition.

What can managers do to improve their decision making? We offer four suggestions.

First, analyze the situation. Adjust your decision-making approach to the national culture you're operating in and to the criteria your organization evaluates and rewards. If you're in a country that doesn't value rationality, don't feel compelled to follow the rational decision-making model or to try to make your decisions appear rational. Similarly, organizations differ in terms of the importance they place on risk, the use of groups, and the like. Adjust your decision approach to ensure it's compatible with the organization's culture.

Second, be aware of biases. Then try to minimize their impact. Exhibit 5.3 offers some suggestions.

Third, combine rational analysis with intuition. These are not conflicting approaches to decision making. By using both, you can actually improve your decision-making effectiveness. As you gain managerial

experience, you should feel increasingly confident in imposing your intuitive processes on top of your rational analysis.

Finally, try to enhance your creativity. Actively look for novel solutions to problems, attempt to see problems in new ways, and use analogies. Try to remove work and organizational barriers that might impede your creativity.

Focus on Goals. Without goals, you can't be rational, you don't know what information you need, you don't know which information is relevant and which is irrelevant, you'll find it difficult to choose between alternatives, and you're far more likely to experience regret over the choices you make. Clear goals make decision making easier and help you eliminate options that are inconsistent with your interests.

Look for Information That Disconfirms Your Beliefs. One of the most effective means for counteracting overconfidence and the confirmation and hindsight biases is to actively look for information that contradicts your beliefs and assumptions. When we overtly consider various ways we could be wrong, we challenge our tendencies to think we're smarter than we actually are.

Don't Try to Create Meaning out of Random Events. The educated mind has been trained to look for cause-and-effect relationships. When something happens, we ask why. And when we can't find reasons, we often invent them. You have to accept that there are events in life that are outside your control. Ask yourself if patterns can be meaningfully explained or whether they are merely coincidence. Don't attempt to create meaning out of coincidence.

Increase Your Options. No matter how many options you've identified, your final choice can be no better than the best of the option set you've selected. This argues for increasing your decision alternatives and for using creativity in developing a wide range of diverse choices. The more alternatives you can generate, and the more diverse those alternatives, the greater your chance of finding an outstanding one.

**EXHIBIT 5.3
Reducing Biases
and Errors**

CHAPTER 6

Motivation Concepts

After studying this chapter, you should be able to:

- Describe the three key elements of motivation.
- Identify early theories of motivation and evaluate their applicability today.
- Contrast goal-setting theory and management by objectives.
- Demonstrate how organizational justice is a refinement of equity theory.
- Apply the key tenets of expectancy theory to motivating employees.
- Show how motivation theories are culture bound.

Motivation is one of the most frequently researched topics in OB. One reason for its popularity is revealed in a recent Gallup poll, which found that a majority of U.S. employees—55 percent—have no enthusiasm for their work.[1] Moreover, another study suggested that, by workers' own reports, they waste roughly 2 hours per day, not counting lunch and scheduled breaks (the biggest time-wasters were Internet surfing and talking with co-workers).[2] Clearly, motivation seems to be an issue. The good news is that all this research provides us with considerable insights into how to improve motivation.

In this chapter, we'll review the basics of motivation, assess a number of motivation theories, and provide an integrative model that shows how the best of these theories fit together.

DEFINING MOTIVATION

We define **motivation** as the processes that account for an individual's intensity, direction, and persistence of effort toward attaining a goal.[3] Although general motivation is concerned with effort toward *any* goal, we'll narrow the focus to *organizational* goals in order to reflect our singular interest in work-related behavior.

The three key elements in our definition are intensity, direction, and persistence. *Intensity* describes how hard a person tries. This is the element most of us focus on when we talk about motivation. However, high intensity is unlikely to lead to favorable job-performance outcomes unless the effort is channeled in a *direction* that benefits the organization. Therefore, we consider the quality of effort as well as its intensity. Effort directed toward, and consistent with, the organization's goals is the kind of effort we should be seeking. Finally, motivation has a *persistence* dimension. This measures how long a person can maintain effort. Motivated individuals stay with a task long enough to achieve their goal.

EARLY THEORIES OF MOTIVATION

The 1950s were a fruitful period in the development of motivation concepts. Four specific theories formulated during this period, although heavily attacked and now questionable in terms of validity, are probably still the best-known explanations for employee motivation. As you'll see later in this chapter, we have since developed more valid explanations of motivation, but you should know these early theories for at least two reasons: (1) They represent a foundation from which contemporary theories have grown, and (2) practicing managers still regularly use them and their terminology in explaining employee motivation.

Hierarchy of Needs Theory

It's probably safe to say the best-known theory of motivation is Abraham Maslow's **hierarchy of needs.**[4] Maslow hypothesized that within every human being, there exists a hierarchy of five needs:

1. *Physiological.* Includes hunger, thirst, shelter, sex, and other bodily needs.
2. *Safety.* Security and protection from physical and emotional harm.
3. *Social.* Affection, belongingness, acceptance, and friendship.
4. *Esteem.* Internal factors such as self-respect, autonomy, and achievement, and external factors such as status, recognition, and attention.
5. *Self-actualization.* Drive to become what we are capable of becoming; includes growth, achieving our potential, and self-fulfillment.

   Although no need is ever fully gratified, a substantially satisfied need no longer motivates. Thus as each of these needs becomes substantially satisfied, the next one becomes dominant. In terms of Exhibit 6.1, we move up the steps of the hierarchy. So if you want to motivate someone, according to Maslow, you need to understand what level of the hierarchy that person is currently on and focus on satisfying the needs at or above that level.

   Maslow separated the five needs into higher and lower orders. Physiological and safety needs were **lower-order needs** and social, esteem, and **self-actualization** were **higher-order needs**. The difference is that higher-order needs are satisfied internally

EXHIBIT 6.1 Maslow's Hierarchy of Needs
Source: A. H. Maslow, *Motivation and Personality,* 3rd ed., R. D. Frager and J. Fadiman (eds.). © 1997. Adapted by permission of Pearson Education, Inc., Upper Saddle River, New Jersey.

(within the person), whereas lower-order needs are predominantly satisfied externally (by things such as pay, union contracts, and tenure).

Maslow's needs theory has received wide recognition, particularly among practicing managers. It is intuitively logical and easy to understand. Unfortunately, however, research does not validate it. Maslow provided no empirical substantiation, and several studies that sought to validate the theory found no support for it.[5] There is little evidence that need structures are organized along the dimensions proposed by Maslow, that unsatisfied needs motivate, or that a satisfied need activates movement to a new need level.[6] But old theories, especially intuitively logical ones, apparently die hard.

Theory X and Theory Y

Douglas McGregor proposed two distinct views of human beings: one basically negative, labeled Theory X, and the other basically positive, labeled Theory Y.[7] After viewing the way in which managers dealt with employees, McGregor concluded that managers' views of the nature of human beings are based on a certain grouping of assumptions, and that managers tend to mold their behavior toward employees according to these assumptions.

Under **Theory X**, managers believe employees inherently dislike work and must therefore be directed or even coerced into performing it. Under **Theory Y**, in contrast, managers assume employees can view work as being as natural as rest or play, and therefore the average person can learn to accept, and even seek, responsibility.

To understand Theory X and Theory Y more fully, think in terms of Maslow's hierarchy. Theory Y assumes higher-order needs dominate individuals. McGregor himself held to the belief that Theory Y assumptions were more valid than Theory X. Therefore, he proposed such ideas as participative decision making, responsible and challenging jobs, and good group relations as approaches to maximize an employee's job motivation.

Unfortunately, there is no evidence to confirm that *either* set of assumptions is valid, or that accepting Theory Y assumptions and altering our actions accordingly will lead to more motivated workers. OB theories need empirical support before we can accept them. Theory X and Theory Y lack such support as much as the hierarchy of needs theories.

Two-Factor Theory

Psychologist Frederick Herzberg proposed the **two-factor theory**—also called *motivation-hygiene theory*.[8] Believing an individual's relationship to work is basic and that attitude toward work can very well determine success or failure, Herzberg investigated the question "What do people want from their jobs?" He asked people to describe, in detail, situations in which they felt exceptionally *good* or *bad* about their jobs. He then tabulated and categorized the responses.

Herzberg concluded that the replies people gave when they felt good about their jobs differed significantly from the replies given when they felt bad. As shown in Exhibit 6.2, intrinsic factors such as advancement, recognition, responsibility, and achievement seem related to job satisfaction. Respondents who felt good about their work tended to attribute these factors to themselves. On the other hand, dissatisfied respondents tended to cite extrinsic factors, such as supervision, pay, company policies, and working conditions.

The data suggest, said Herzberg, that the opposite of satisfaction is not dissatisfaction, as was traditionally believed. Removing dissatisfying characteristics from a job does

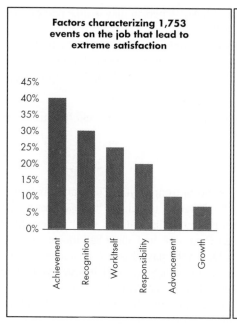

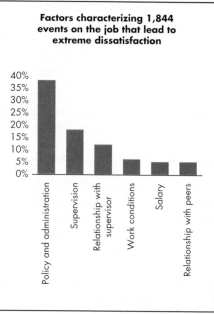

not necessarily make the job satisfying. Herzberg proposed that his findings indicated the existence of a dual continuum: The opposite of "satisfaction" is "no satisfaction," and the opposite of "dissatisfaction" is "no dissatisfaction."

According to Herzberg, the factors that lead to job satisfaction are separate and distinct from those that lead to job dissatisfaction. Therefore, managers who seek to eliminate factors that can create job dissatisfaction may bring about peace but not necessarily motivation. They will be placating rather than motivating their workers. As a result, Herzberg characterized conditions such as quality of supervision, pay, company policies, physical working conditions, relationships with others, and job security as **hygiene factors**. When they're adequate, people will not be dissatisfied; neither will they be satisfied. If we want to motivate people on their jobs, Herzberg suggested emphasizing factors associated with the work itself or with outcomes directly derived from it, such as promotional opportunities, personal growth opportunities, recognition, responsibility, and achievement. These are the characteristics people find intrinsically rewarding.

The two-factor theory has not been well supported in the literature, and it has many detractors.[9] Criticisms include the following:

1. The procedure Herzberg used is limited by its methodology. When things are going well, people tend to take credit themselves. Contrarily, they blame failure on the extrinsic environment.
2. The reliability of Herzberg's methodology is questionable. Raters have to make interpretations, so they may contaminate the findings by interpreting one response in one manner while treating a similar response differently.

3. No overall measure of satisfaction was utilized. A person may dislike part of a job yet still think the job is acceptable overall.

4. Herzberg assumed a relationship between satisfaction and productivity, but the research methodology he used looked only at satisfaction and not at productivity. To make such research relevant, we must assume a strong relationship between satisfaction and productivity.

Regardless of the criticisms, Herzberg's theory has been widely read, and few managers are unfamiliar with its recommendations.

McClelland's Theory of Needs

You have one beanbag, and five targets are set up in front of you. Each target is farther away than the last and thus more difficult to hit. Target A is a cinch. It sits almost within arm's reach. If you hit it, you get $2. Target B is a bit farther out, but about 80 percent of the people who try can hit it. It pays $4. Target C pays $8, and about half the people who try can hit it. Very few people can hit Target D, but the payoff is $16 for those who do. Finally, Target E pays $32, but it's almost impossible to achieve. Which target would you try for? If you selected C, you're likely to be a high achiever. Why? Read on.

McClelland's theory of needs was developed by David McClelland and his associates.[10] The theory focuses on three needs, defined as follows:

- **Need for achievement (nAch)** is the drive to excel, to achieve in relation to a set of standards, to strive to succeed.
- **Need for power (nPow)** is the need to make others behave in a way in which they would not have behaved otherwise.
- **Need for affiliation (nAff)** is the desire for friendly and close interpersonal relationships.

Of the three needs, McClelland and subsequent researchers focused most of their attention on nAch. High achievers perform best when they perceive their probability of success as 0.5—that is, a 50–50 chance of success. They dislike gambling with high odds because they get no achievement satisfaction from success that comes by pure chance. Similarly, they dislike low odds (high probability of success) because then there is no challenge to their skills. They like to set goals that require stretching themselves a little.

Relying on an extensive amount of research, we can make some reasonably well-supported predictions of the relationship between achievement need and job performance. Although less research has been done on power and affiliation needs, findings are consistent there, too. First, when jobs have a high degree of personal responsibility and feedback and an intermediate degree of risk, high achievers are strongly motivated. They are successful in entrepreneurial activities such as running their own businesses, for example, and managing self-contained units within large organizations.[11] Second, a high need to achieve does not necessarily make someone a good manager, especially in large organizations. People with a high achievement need are interested in how well they do personally and not in influencing others to do well. High-nAch salespeople do not necessarily make good sales managers, and the good general manager in a large organization does not typically have a high need to achieve.[12] Third, needs for affiliation and power tend to be closely related to managerial success. The best managers are high in their need for power and low in their need for affiliation.[13] In fact, a high power motive may be a requirement for managerial effectiveness.[14]

As you might have gathered, among the early theories of motivation McClelland's has had the best research support. Unfortunately, it has less practical effect than the others. Because McClelland argued that the three needs are subconscious—meaning we may be high on them but not know it—measuring them is not easy. In the most common approach, a trained expert presents pictures to individuals, asks them to tell a story about each, and then scores their responses in terms of the three needs. However, the process is time consuming and expensive, and few organizations have been willing to invest time and resources in measuring McClelland's concept.

CONTEMPORARY THEORIES OF MOTIVATION

Early theories of motivation either have not held up under close examination or have fallen out of favor. In contrast, contemporary theories have one thing in common: Each has a reasonable degree of valid supporting documentation. This doesn't mean they are unquestionably right. We call them "contemporary theories" because they represent the current state of thinking in explaining employee motivation.

Self-Determination Theory

"It's strange," said Marcia. "I started work at the Humane Society as a volunteer. I put in fifteen hours a week helping people adopt pets. And I loved coming to work. Then, three months ago, they hired me full-time at eleven dollars an hour. I'm doing the same work I did before. But I'm not finding it near as much fun."

Does Marcia's reaction seem counterintuitive? There's an explanation for it. It's called **self-determination theory**, which proposes that people prefer to feel they have control over their actions, so anything that makes a previously enjoyed task feel more like an obligation than a freely chosen activity will undermine motivation.[15] Much research on self-determination theory in OB has focused on **cognitive evaluation theory**, which hypothesizes that extrinsic rewards will reduce intrinsic interest in a task. When people are paid for work, it feels less like something they *want* to do and more like something they *have* to do. Self-determination theory also proposes that in addition to being driven by a need for autonomy, people seek ways to achieve competence and positive connections to others. A large number of studies support self-determination theory.[16] As we'll show, its major implications relate to work rewards.

When organizations use extrinsic rewards as payoffs for superior performance, employees feel less like they are doing a good job because of their own intrinsic desire to excel and more like they are doing a good job because that's what the organization wants. Eliminating extrinsic rewards can also shift from an external to an internal explanation of an individual's perception of why she works on a task. If you're reading a novel a week because your English literature instructor requires you to, you can attribute your reading behavior to an external source. However, if you find yourself continuing to read a novel a week after the course is over, your natural inclination is to say, "I must enjoy reading novels because I'm still reading one a week."

Recent studies examining how extrinsic rewards increased motivation for some creative tasks suggests we might need to place cognitive evaluation theory's predictions in a broader context.[17] Goal setting is more effective in improving motivation, for instance, when we provide rewards for achieving the goals. The original authors of self-determination theory acknowledge that extrinsic rewards such as verbal praise and feedback about competence can improve even intrinsic motivation under specific circumstances. Deadlines and specific work standards do, too, if people believe they are in control of their behavior.[18] This is consistent with the central theme of self-determination theory: rewards and deadlines diminish motivation if people see them as coercive.

What does self-determination theory suggest for providing rewards? Consider two situations. If a senior sales representative really enjoys selling and making the deal, a commission indicates she's been doing a good job at this valued task. The reward will increase her sense of competence by providing feedback that could improve intrinsic motivation. On the other hand, if a computer programmer values writing code because she likes to solve problems, a reward for working to an externally imposed standard she does not accept could feel coercive, and her intrinsic motivation would suffer. She would be less interested in the task and might reduce her effort.

A recent outgrowth of self-determination theory is **self-concordance**, which considers how strongly peoples' reasons for pursuing goals are consistent with their interests and core values. If individuals pursue goals because of an intrinsic interest, they are more likely to attain their goals and are happy even if they do not. Why? Because the process of striving toward them is fun. In contrast, people who pursue goals for extrinsic reasons (money, status, or other benefits) are less likely to attain their goals and less happy even when they do achieve them. Why? Because the goals are less meaningful to them.[19] OB research suggests that people who pursue work goals for intrinsic reasons are more satisfied with their jobs, feel like they fit into their organizations better, and may perform better.[20]

What does all this mean? It means choose your job for reasons other than extrinsic rewards. For organizations, it means managers should provide intrinsic as well as extrinsic incentives. They need to make the work interesting, provide recognition, and support employee growth and development. Employees who feel what they do is within their control and a result of free choice are likely to be more motivated by their work and committed to their employers.[21]

Goal-Setting Theory

Gene Broadwater, coach of the Hamilton High School cross-country team, gave his squad these last words before they approached the starting line for the league championship race: "Each one of you is physically ready. Now, get out there and do your best. No one can ever ask more of you than that."

In general, managers should make goals specific and difficult— managers should set the highest goals to which employees will commit.

You've heard the sentiment a number of times yourself: "Just do your best. That's all anyone can ask for." But what does "do your best" mean? Do we ever know if we've achieved that vague goal? Would the cross-country runners have recorded faster times if Coach Broadwater had given each a specific goal? Might you have done better in your high school English class if your parents had said, "You should strive for 85 percent or higher on all your work in English" rather than telling you to "do your best"? The research on **goal-setting theory** addresses these issues, and the findings, as you'll see, are impressive in terms of the effect that goal specificity, challenge, and feedback have on performance.

In the late 1960s, Edwin Locke proposed that intentions to work toward a goal are a major source of work motivation.[22] That is, goals tell an employee what needs to be done and how much effort will need to be expended. The evidence strongly supports the value of goals. More to the point, we can say that specific goals increase performance;

that difficult goals, when accepted, result in higher performance than do easy goals; and that feedback leads to higher performance than does nonfeedback.[23]

Specific goals produce a higher level of output than does the generalized goal of "do your best." Why? The specificity of the goal itself seems to act as an internal stimulus. For instance, when a trucker commits to making 12 round-trip hauls between Toronto and Buffalo, New York, each week, this intention gives him a specific objective to try to attain. All things being equal, the trucker with a specific goal will outperform a counterpart with no goals or the generalized goal of "do your best."

If factors such as acceptance of the goals are held constant, the more difficult the goal, the higher the level of performance. Of course, it's logical to assume easier goals are more likely to be accepted. But once a hard task is accepted, we can expect the employee to exert a high level of effort to try to achieve it.

But why are people motivated by difficult goals?[24] First, challenging goals get our attention and thus tend to help us focus. Second, difficult goals energize us because we have to work harder to attain them. Do you study as hard for an easy exam as you do for a difficult one? Probably not. Third, when goals are difficult, people persist in trying to attain them. Finally, difficult goals lead us to discover strategies that help us perform the job or task more effectively. If we have to struggle to solve a difficult problem, we often think of a better way to go about it.

People do better when they get feedback on how well they are progressing toward their goals, because feedback helps to identify discrepancies between what they have done and what they want to do—that is, feedback acts to guide behavior. But all feedback is not equally potent. Self-generated feedback—with which employees are able to monitor their own progress—has been shown to be a more powerful motivator than externally generated feedback.[25]

If employees can participate in the setting of their own goals, will they try harder? The evidence is mixed.[26] In some cases, participatively set goals yielded superior performance; in others, individuals performed best when assigned goals by their boss. But a major advantage of participation may be that it increases acceptance of the goal as a desirable one toward which to work. Commitment is important. If participation isn't used, then the individual assigning the goal needs to clearly explain its purpose and importance.

Are there any contingencies in goal-setting theory, or will difficult and specific goals *always* lead to higher performance? In addition to feedback, three other factors have been found to influence the goals–performance relationship: goal commitment, task characteristics, and national culture.

Goal-setting theory assumes an individual is committed to the goal and is determined not to lower or abandon it. In terms of behavior, the individual (1) believes he or she can achieve the goal and (2) wants to achieve it. Goal commitment is most likely to occur when goals are made public, when the individual has an internal locus of control, and when the goals are self-set rather than assigned.[27] Goal-setting theory doesn't work equally well on all tasks. The evidence suggests goals seem to have a more substantial effect on performance when tasks are simple rather than complex, well learned rather than novel, and independent rather than interdependent.[28] On interdependent tasks, group goals are preferable.

Finally, setting specific, difficult, individual goals may have different effects in different cultures. Most goal-setting research has been done in the United States and Canada, where individual achievement and performance are most highly valued. To date, research has not shown that group-based goals are more effective in collectivist than in individualist cultures.

There is evidence that in collectivistic and highpower-distance cultures, achievable moderate goals can be more highly motivating than difficult ones.[29] Finally, assigned goals appear to generate greater goal commitment in high rather than low power-distance cultures.[30] Much more research is needed to assess how goal constructs might differ across cultures.

Although goal setting has positive outcomes, some goals may be *too* effective.[31] When learning something is important, goals related to performance undermine adaptation and creativity because people become too focused on outcomes and ignore changing conditions. In this case, a goal to learn and generate alternative solutions will be more effective than a goal to perform. Some authors have also argued that goals can lead employees to be too focused on a single standard to the exclusion of all others. Consider the narrow focus on short-term stock prices in many businesses—so much attention to this one standard for performance may have led organizations to ignore long-term success, and even to engage in such unethical behavior as accounting fraud or excessively risky investments. Of course, it is possible for organizations to establish goals for ethical performance. Despite differences of opinion, most researchers do agree that goals are powerful in shaping behavior. Managers should make sure they are actually aligned with the company's objectives.

IMPLEMENTING GOAL SETTING   Goal-setting theory has an impressive base of research support. But as a manager, how do you make it operational? That's often left up to the individual manager or leader. Some managers set aggressive performance targets—what General Electric called "stretch goals." Some CEOs, such as Procter & Gamble's A. G. Lafley and SAP AG's Hasso Plattner, are known for the demanding performance goals they set. The problem with leaving it up to the individual manager is that many managers don't set goals. A recent survey revealed that when asked whether their job had clearly defined goals, only a minority of employees said "yes."[32]

A more systematic way to utilize goal setting is with a management by objectives program. **Management by objectives (MBO)** emphasizes participatively set goals that are tangible, verifiable, and measurable. As depicted in Exhibit 6.3, the organization's overall objectives are translated into specific objectives for each succeeding level in the organization (divisional, departmental, individual). But because lower-unit managers

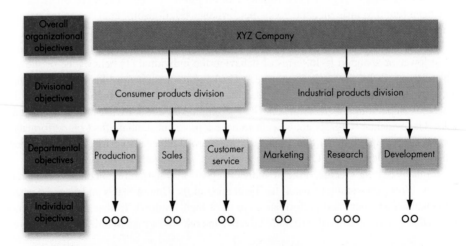

EXHIBIT 6.3
Cascading of Objectives

jointly participate in setting their own goals, MBO works from the bottom-up as well as from the top-down. The result is a hierarchy that links objectives at one level to those at the next. And for the individual employee, MBO provides specific personal performance objectives.

Four ingredients are common to MBO programs: goal specificity, participation in decision making (including participation in the setting of goals or objectives), an explicit time period, and performance feedback.[33] Many elements in MBO programs match propositions of goal-setting theory. For example, having an explicit time period to accomplish objectives matches goal-setting theory's emphasis on goal specificity. Similarly, we noted earlier that feedback about goal progress is a critical element of goal-setting theory. The only area of possible disagreement between MBO and goal-setting theory is participation: MBO strongly advocates it, whereas goal-setting theory demonstrates that managers assigning goals is usually just as effective.

Self-Efficacy Theory

Self-efficacy (also known as *social cognitive theory* or *social learning theory*) refers to an individual's belief that he or she is capable of performing a task.[34] The higher your self-efficacy, the more confidence you have in your ability to succeed. So, in difficult situations, people with low self-efficacy are more likely to lessen their effort or give up altogether, whereas those with high self-efficacy will try harder to master the challenge.

Managers will increase employees' motivation by increasing their confidence in successfully completing the task (self-efficacy).

In addition, individuals high in self-efficacy seem to respond to negative feedback with increased effort and motivation, whereas those low in self-efficacy are likely to lessen their effort when given negative feedback. How can managers help their employees achieve high levels of self- efficacy? By bringing together goal-setting theory and self-efficacy theory.

Goal-setting theory and self-efficacy theory don't compete with one another; rather, they complement each other. As Exhibit 6.4 shows, when a manager sets difficult goals for employees, they will have a higher level of self-efficacy and set higher goals for their own performance. Why? Research shows setting difficult goals for

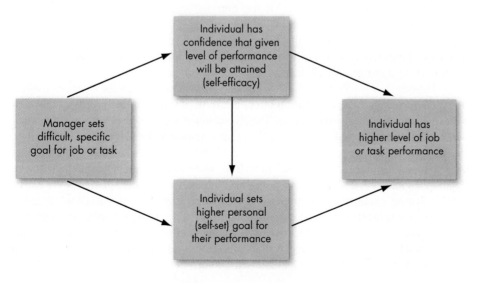

EXHIBIT 6.4 **Joint Effects of Goals and Self-Efficacy on Performance**
Source: Based on E. A. Locke and G. P. Latham, "Building a Practically Useful Theory of Goal Setting and Task Motivation: A 35-Year Odyssey," *American Psychologist,* September 2002, pp. 705–717.

people communicates your confidence in them. Imagine you learn your boss sets a higher goal for you than for your co-workers. How would you interpret this? As long as you didn't feel you were being picked on, you would probably think, "Well, I guess my boss thinks I'm capable of performing better than others." This sets in motion a psychological process in which you're more confident in yourself (higher self-efficacy) and you set higher personal goals, causing you to perform better both inside and outside the workplace.

Source: A. Bandura, *Self-Efficacy: The Exercise of Control* (New York: Freeman, 1997).

The researcher who developed self-efficacy theory, Albert Bandura, proposes four ways self-efficacy can be increased:

1. Enactive mastery
2. Vicarious modeling
3. Verbal persuasion
4. Arousal

According to Bandura, the most important source of increasing self-efficacy is *enactive mastery*—that is, gaining relevant experience with the task or job. If you've been able to do the job successfully in the past, then you're more confident you'll be able to do it in the future.

The second source is *vicarious modeling*—or becoming more confident because you see someone else doing the task. For example, if your friend slims down, it increases your confidence that you can lose weight, too. Vicarious modeling is most effective when you see yourself as similar to the person you are observing. Watching Tiger Woods play a difficult golf shot might not increase your confidence in being able to play the shot yourself, but if you watch a golfer with a handicap similar to yours, it's persuasive.

The third source is *verbal persuasion:* becoming more confident because someone convinces you that you have the skills necessary to be successful. Motivational speakers use this tactic a lot.

Finally, Bandura argues that *arousal* increases self-efficacy. Arousal leads to an energized state, which drives a person to complete a task. The person gets "psyched up" and performs better. But if the task requires a steady, lower-key perspective (say, carefully editing a manuscript), arousal may in fact hurt performance.

What are the OB implications of self-efficacy theory? Well, it's a matter of applying Bandura's sources of self-efficacy to the work setting. Training programs often make use of enactive mastery by having people practice and build their skills. In fact, one of the reasons training works is that it increases self-efficacy.[35]

The best way for a manager to use verbal persuasion is through the *Pygmalion effect* or the *Galatea effect*. The **Pygmalion effect** is a form of self-fulfilling prophecy in which believing something can make it true. The Pygmalion effect increases self-efficacy when we communicate to an individual's teacher or supervisor that the person is of high ability. In some studies, teachers were told their students had very high IQ scores when in fact they spanned a range—some high, some low, some in between. Consistent with the Pygmalion effect, the teachers spent more time with the students they *thought* were smart, gave them more challenging assignments, and expected more of them—all of which led to higher student self-efficacy and better student grades.[36] This strategy also has been used in the workplace.[37] The Galatea effect occurs when high performance expectations are communicated directly to an employee. Sailors who were told convincingly that they would not get seasick in fact were much less likely to do so.

Note that intelligence and personality are absent from Bandura's list. Much research shows that intelligence and personality (especially conscientiousness and emotional stability) can increase self-efficacy.[38] Those individual traits are so strongly related to self-efficacy (people who are intelligent, conscientiousness, and emotionally stable are much more likely to have high self-efficacy than those who score low on these characteristics) that some researchers would argue self-efficacy does not exist. They believe it is simply a by-product in a smart person with a confident personality. Although Bandura strongly disagrees with this conclusion, more research is needed.

Equity Theory/Organizational Justice

Jane Pearson graduated last year from State University with a degree in accounting. After interviews with a number of organizations on campus, she accepted a position with a top public accounting firm and was assigned to the firm's Boston office. Jane was very pleased with the offer she received: challenging work with a prestigious firm, an excellent opportunity to gain valuable experience, and the highest salary any accounting major at State was offered last year—$4,550 per month—but Jane was the top student in her class, she was articulate and mature, and she fully expected to receive a commensurate salary.

Twelve months have passed since Jane joined her employer. The work has proved to be as challenging and satisfying as she had hoped. Her employer is extremely pleased with her performance; in fact, Jane recently received a $200-per-month raise. However, Jane's motivational level has dropped dramatically in the past few weeks. Why? Her employer has just hired a fresh graduate out of State University who lacks the year of experience Jane has gained, for $4,800 per month—$50 more than Jane now makes! Jane is irate. She is even talking about looking for another job.

Jane's situation illustrates the role equity plays in motivation. Employees perceive what they get from a job situation (salary levels, raises, recognition) in relationship to what they put into it (effort, experience, education, competence) and then compare their outcome–input ratio with that of relevant others. This is shown in Exhibit 6.5. If we perceive our ratio to be equal to that of the relevant others with whom we compare ourselves, a state of equity exists; we perceive that our situation is fair and justice prevails. When we see the ratio as unequal, we experience equity tension. When we see ourselves as underrewarded, the tension creates anger; when we see ourselves as

Ratio Comparisons*	Perception
$\dfrac{O}{I} < \dfrac{O}{I_B}$	Inequity due to being underrewarded
$\dfrac{O}{I} = \dfrac{O}{I_B}$	Equity
$\dfrac{O}{I} > \dfrac{O}{I_B}$	Inequity due to being overrewarded

*Where $\dfrac{O}{I}$ represents the employee; and $\dfrac{O}{I_B}$ represents relevant others

EXHIBIT 6.5
Equity Theory

overrewarded, it creates guilt. J. Stacy Adams has proposed that this negative state of tension provides the motivation to do something to correct it.[39]

The referent an employee selects adds to the complexity of **equity theory**.[40] There are four referent comparisons:

1. *Self–inside.* An employee's experiences in a different position inside the employee's current organization.
2. *Self–outside.* An employee's experiences in a situation or position outside the employee's current organization.
3. *Other–inside.* Another individual or group of individuals inside the employee's organization.
4. *Other–outside.* Another individual or group of individuals outside the employee's organization.

Employees might compare themselves to friends, neighbors, co-workers, or colleagues in other organizations or compare their present job with past jobs they themselves have had. Which referent an employee chooses will be influenced by the information the employee holds about referents as well as by the attractiveness of the referent. Four moderating variables are gender, length of tenure, level in the organization, and amount of education or professionalism.[41]

Based on the theory, employees who perceive inequity will make one of six choices:[42]

1. Change their inputs (exert less effort if underpaid, or more if overpaid)
2. Change their outcomes (individuals paid on a piece-rate basis can increase their pay by producing a higher quantity of units of lower quality)
3. Distort perceptions of self ("I used to think I worked at a moderate pace, but now I realize I work a lot harder than everyone else.")
4. Distort perceptions of others ("Mike's job isn't as desirable as I thought.")
5. Choose a different referent ("I may not make as much as my brother-in-law, but I'm doing a lot better than my Dad did when he was my age.")
6. Leave the field (quit the job)

Some of these propositions have been supported, but others haven't.[43] First, inequities created by overpayment do not seem to have a very significant impact on behavior in most work situations. Apparently, people have a great deal more tolerance of overpayment inequities than of underpayment inequities or are better able to rationalize them. It's pretty damaging to a theory when half the equation (how people respond to overreward) falls apart. Second, not all people are equity sensitive.[44] A small part of the working population actually prefers outcome–input ratios less than the referent comparisons. Predictions from equity theory are not likely to be very accurate with these "benevolent types."

Finally, recent research has expanded the meaning of *equity,* or *fairness.*[45] Historically, equity theory focused on **distributive justice**, the employee's perceived fairness of the *amount and allocation* of rewards among individuals. But increasingly we think of equity from the standpoint of **organizational justice**, a larger perception of what is fair in the workplace. Employees perceive their organizations as just when they believe the outcomes they have received and the way they received them are fair. One key element of organizational justice is an individual's *perception* of justice. In other words, fairness or equity can be subjective, residing in our perception. What one person sees as unfair, another may see as perfectly appropriate. In general, people have an egocentric, or self-serving, bias. They see allocations or procedure favoring themselves as fair.[46]

Beyond its focus on perceptions of fairness, the other key element of organizational justice is the view that justice is multidimensional. How much we get paid relative to what we think we should be paid (distributive justice) is obviously important. But, according to researchers, *how* we get paid, is just as important. Thus the model of organizational justice in Exhibit 6.6 includes **procedural justice**—the perceived fairness of the *process* used to determine the distribution of rewards. Two key elements of procedural justice are process control and explanations. *Process control* is the opportunity to present your point of view about desired outcomes to decision makers. *Explanations* are clear reasons management gives for the outcome. Thus, for employees to see a process as fair, they need to feel they have some control over the outcome and that they were given an adequate explanation about why the outcome occurred. It's also important that a manager is *consistent* (across people and over time), is *unbiased,* makes decisions based on *accurate information,* and is *open to appeals.*[47]

The effects of procedural justice become more important when distributive justice is lacking. This makes sense. If we don't get what we want, we tend to focus on *why*. If your supervisor gives a cushy office to a co-worker instead of to you, you're much more focused on your supervisor's treatment of you than if you had gotten the office. Explanations are beneficial when they take the form of post hoc excuses ("I know this is bad, and I wanted to give you the office, but it wasn't my decision") rather than justifications ("I decided to give the office to Sam, but having it isn't a big deal.").[48]

> To promote fairness in the workplace, managers should consider openly sharing information on how allocation decisions are made. Fair and open procedures are especially important when the outcome is likely to be viewed negatively by some or all employees.

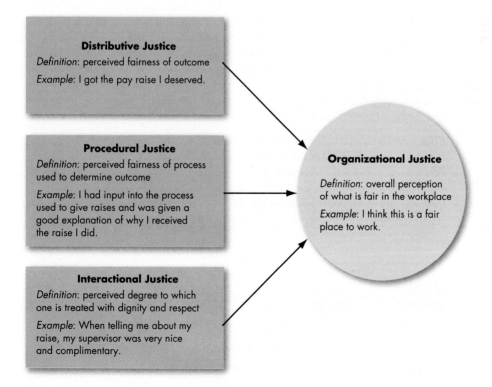

Distributive Justice

Definition: perceived fairness of outcome

Example: I got the pay raise I deserved.

Procedural Justice

Definition: perceived fairness of process used to determine outcome

Example: I had input into the process used to give raises and was given a good explanation of why I received the raise I did.

Interactional Justice

Definition: perceived degree to which one is treated with dignity and respect

Example: When telling me about my raise, my supervisor was very nice and complimentary.

Organizational Justice

Definition: overall perception of what is fair in the workplace

Example: I think this is a fair place to work.

EXHIBIT 6.6
Model of Organizational Justice

A recent addition to research on organizational justice is **interactional justice**, an individual's perception of the degree to which she is treated with dignity, concern, and respect. When people are treated in an unjust manner (at least in their own eyes), they retaliate (for example, badmouthing a supervisor). Because people intimately connect interactional justice or injustice to the conveyer of the information, we would expect perceptions of injustice to be more closely related to the supervisor. Generally, that's what the evidence suggests.[49]

Of these three forms of justice, distributive justice is most strongly related to organizational commitment and satisfaction with outcomes such as pay. Procedural justice relates most strongly to job satisfaction, employee trust, withdrawal from the organization, job performance, and citizenship behaviors. There is less evidence about interactional justice.[50]

Managers can help foster employees' perceptions of fairness. First, they should realize that employees are especially sensitive to unfairness in procedures when bad news has to be communicated (that is, when distributive justice is low). Thus, it's especially important to openly share information about how allocation decisions are made, follow consistent and unbiased procedures, and engage in similar practices to increase the perception of procedural justice. Second, when addressing perceived injustices, managers need to focus their actions on the source of the problem.

Expectancy Theory

Currently, one of the most widely accepted explanations of motivation is Victor Vroom's **expectancy theory**.[51] Although it has its critics, most of the evidence supports the theory.[52]

Expectancy theory argues that the strength of a tendency to act in a certain way depends on the strength of our expectation of a given outcome and its attractiveness. In more practical terms, employees will be motivated to exert a high level of effort when they believe it will lead to a good performance appraisal; that a good appraisal will lead to organizational rewards such as bonuses, salary increases, or promotions; and that the rewards will satisfy the employees' personal goals. The theory, therefore, focuses on three relationships (see Exhibit 6.7):

1. ***Effort–performance relationship.*** The probability perceived by the individual that exerting a given amount of effort will lead to performance.
2. ***Performance–reward relationship.*** The degree to which the individual believes performing at a particular level will lead to the attainment of a desired outcome.
3. ***Rewards–personal goals relationship.*** The degree to which organizational rewards satisfy an individual's personal goals or needs and the attractiveness of those potential rewards for the individual.

EXHIBIT 6.7
Expectancy Theory

Expectancy theory helps explain why a lot of workers aren't motivated on their jobs and do only the minimum necessary to get by. Let's frame the theory's three relationships as questions employees need to answer in the affirmative if their motivation is to be maximized.

First, *if I give a maximum effort, will it be recognized in my performance appraisal?* For many employees, the answer is "no." Why? Their skill level may be deficient, which means that no matter how hard they try, they're not likely to be high performers. The organization's performance appraisal system may be designed to assess nonperformance factors such as loyalty, initiative, or courage, which means more effort won't necessarily result in a higher evaluation. Another possibility is that employees, rightly or wrongly, perceive the boss doesn't like them. As a result, they expect to get a poor appraisal, regardless of level of effort. These examples suggest one possible source of low motivation is employees' belief that, no matter how hard they work, the likelihood of getting a good performance appraisal is low.

Second, *if I get a good performance appraisal, will it lead to organizational rewards?* Many organizations reward a lot of things besides performance. When pay is based on factors such as having seniority, being cooperative, or "kissing up" to the boss, employees are likely to see the performance–reward relationship as weak and demotivating.

Finally, *if I'm rewarded, are the rewards attractive to me?* The employee works hard in the hope of getting a promotion but gets a pay raise instead. Or the employee wants a more interesting and challenging job but receives only a few words of praise. Or the employee puts in extra effort to be relocated to the Paris office but instead is transferred to Singapore. It's important to tailor rewards to individual employee needs. Unfortunately, many managers are limited in the rewards they can distribute, which makes this difficult. Some incorrectly assume all employees want the same thing, thus overlooking the motivational effects of differentiating rewards. In either case, employee motivation is submaximized.

As a vivid example of how expectancy theory can work, consider stock analysts. They make their living by trying to forecast the future of a stock's price; the accuracy of their buy, sell, or hold recommendations is what keeps them in work or gets them fired. But it's not quite that simple. Analysts place few sell ratings on stocks, although in a steady market, by definition, as many stocks are falling as are rising. Expectancy theory provides an explanation: analysts who place a sell rating on a company's stock have to balance the benefits they receive by being accurate against the risks they run by drawing the company's ire. What are these risks? They include public rebuke, professional blackballing, and exclusion from information. When analysts place a buy rating on a stock, they face no such trade-off because, obviously, companies love that they are recommending that investors buy their stock. So, the incentive structure suggests the expected outcome of buy ratings is higher than the expected outcome of sell ratings, and that's why buy ratings vastly outnumber sell ratings.[53]

Does expectancy theory work? Some critics suggest it has only limited use and is more valid where individuals clearly perceive effort–performance and performance–reward linkages.[54] Because few individuals do perceive these links, the theory tends to be idealistic. If organizations actually rewarded individuals for performance rather than according to criteria such as seniority, effort, skill level, and job difficulty, expectancy theory might be much more valid. However, rather than invalidating it, this criticism can explain why a significant segment of the workforce exerts low levels of effort on the job.

Global Implications

Most current motivation theories were developed in the United States by and about U.S. adults. Goal-setting and expectancy theories emphasize goal accomplishment as well as rational and individual thought—characteristics consistent with U.S. culture. Let's look at several motivation theories and consider their cross-cultural transferability.

Maslow's needs hierarchy says people start at the physiological level and progress up the hierarchy to safety, social, esteem, and self-actualization needs. This hierarchy, if it applies at all, aligns with U.S. culture. In Japan, Greece, and Mexico, where uncertainty-avoidance characteristics are strong, security needs would be on top of the hierarchy. Countries that score high on nurturing characteristics—Denmark, Sweden, Norway, the Netherlands, and Finland—would have social needs on top.[55] Group work will motivate employees more when the country's culture scores high on the nurturing criterion.

The view that a high achievement need acts as an internal motivator presupposes two U.S. cultural characteristics—willingness to accept a moderate degree of risk (which excludes countries with strong uncertainty avoidance characteristics) and concern with performance (which applies to countries with strong achievement characteristics). This combination is found in Anglo-American countries such as the United States, Canada, and Great Britain[56] and much less so in Chile and Portugal.

Equity theory has gained a strong following in the United States because U.S.-style reward systems assume workers are highly sensitive to equity in reward allocations. And in the United States equity is meant to closely tie pay to performance. However, in collectivist cultures, especially the former socialist countries of central and eastern Europe, employees expect rewards to reflect their individual needs as well as their performance. Consistent with a legacy of communism and centrally planned economies, employees exhibited an entitlement attitude—that is, they expected outcomes to be *greater* than their inputs.[57] These findings suggest that U.S.-style pay practices may need modification, especially in Russia and former communist countries, to be perceived as fair by employees.

But don't assume there are *no* cross-cultural consistencies. The desire for interesting work seems important to almost all workers, regardless of their national culture. In a study of seven countries, employees in Belgium, Britain, Israel, and the United States ranked work first among 11 work goals, and workers in Japan, the Netherlands, and Germany ranked it either second or third.[58] In a study comparing job-preference outcomes among graduate students in the United States, Canada, Australia, and Singapore, growth, achievement, and responsibility had identical rankings as the top three.[59] Meta-analytic evidence shows individuals in both individualistic and collectivistic cultures prefer an equitable distribution of rewards (the most effective workers get paid the most) over an equal division (everyone gets paid the same regardless of performance).[60] Across nations, the same basic principles of procedural justice are respected, and workers around the world prefer rewards based on performance and skills over rewards based on seniority.

Implications for Managers

Some theories in this chapter address turnover, whereas others emphasize productivity. They also differ in their predictive strength. In this section, we (1) review the most established motivation theories to determine their relevance in explaining the dependent variables and (2) assess the predictive power of each.

Need Theories

Maslow's hierarchy, McClelland's needs, and the two-factor theory focus on needs. None has found widespread support, although McClelland's is the strongest, particularly regarding the relationship between achievement and productivity. In general, need theories are not very valid explanations of motivation.

Self-Determination Theory and Cognitive Evaluation Theory

As research on the motivational effects of rewards has accumulated, it increasingly appears extrinsic rewards can undermine motivation if they are seen as coercive. They can increase motivation if they provide information about competence and relatedness.

Goal-Setting Theory

Clear and difficult goals lead to higher levels of employee productivity, supporting goal-setting theory's explanation of this dependent variable. The theory does not address absenteeism, turnover, or satisfaction, however.

Equity Theory/Organizational Justice

Equity theory deals with productivity, satisfaction, absence, and turnover variables. However, its strongest legacy is that it provided the spark for research on organizational justice, which has more support in the literature.

Expectancy Theory

Expectancy theory offers a powerful explanation of performance variables such as employee productivity, absenteeism, and turnover. But it assumes employees have few constraints on decision making, such as bias or incomplete information, and this limits its applicability. Expectancy theory has some validity because for many behaviors people consider expected outcomes. However, it goes only so far in explaining behavior.

CHAPTER 7

Motivation: From Concepts to Applications

After studying this chapter, you should be able to:

- Describe the job characteristics model and evaluate the way it motivates by changing the work environment.
- Compare and contrast the main ways jobs can be redesigned.
- Give examples of employee involvement measures and show how they can motivate employees.
- Demonstrate how the different types of variable-pay programs can increase employee motivation.
- Show how flexible benefits turn benefits into motivators.
- Identify the motivational benefits of intrinsic rewards.

MOTIVATING BY CHANGING THE NATURE OF THE WORK ENVIRONMENT

Increasingly, research on motivation is focused on approaches that link motivational concepts to changes in the way work is structured. Research in **job design** suggests the way the elements in a job are organized can act to increase or decrease effort and also suggests what those elements are. We'll first review the job characteristics model and then discuss some ways jobs can be redesigned. Finally, we'll explore some alternative work arrangements.

The Job Characteristics Model

Developed by J. Richard Hackman and Greg Oldham, the **job characteristics model (JCM)** says we can describe any job in terms of five core job dimensions:[1]

1. *Skill variety.* **Skill variety** is the degree to which a job requires a variety of different activities so the worker can use a number of different skills and talent. For instance, the work of a garage owner-operator who does electrical repairs, rebuilds engines, does bodywork, and interacts with customers scores high on skill variety. The job of a bodyshop worker who sprays paint 8 hours a day scores low on this dimension.
2. *Task identity.* **Task identity** is the degree to which a job requires completion of a whole and identifiable piece of work. A cabinetmaker who designs a piece of furniture, selects the wood, builds the

object, and finishes it to perfection has a job that scores high on task identity. A job scoring low on this dimension is operating a factory lathe solely to make table legs.

3. *Task significance.* **Task significance** is the degree to which a job has an impact on the lives or work of other people. The job of a nurse handling the diverse needs of patients in a hospital intensive care unit scores high on task significance; sweeping floors in a hospital scores low.

4. *Autonomy.* **Autonomy** is the degree to which a job provides the worker freedom, independence, and discretion in scheduling the work and determining the procedures in carrying it out. A salesperson who schedules his or her own work each day and decides on the most effective sales approach for each customer without supervision has a highly autonomous job. A salesperson who is given a set of leads each day and is required to follow a standardized sales script with each potential customer has a job low on autonomy.

5. *Feedback.* **Feedback** is the degree to which carrying out work activities generates direct and clear information about your own performance. A job with high feedback is assembling iPods and testing them to see whether they operate properly. A factory worker who assembles iPods but then routes them to a quality-control inspector for testing and adjustments receives low feedback from his or her activities.

Exhibit 7.1 presents the job characteristics model. Note how the first three dimensions—skill variety, task identity, and task significance—combine to create meaningful work the incumbent will view as important, valuable, and worthwhile. Note, too, that jobs with high autonomy give incumbents a feeling of personal responsibility for the results and that, if a job provides feedback, employees will know how effectively they are performing. From a motivational standpoint, the JCM proposes that individuals obtain internal rewards when they learn (knowledge of results) that they personally (experienced responsibility) have performed well on a task they care about (experienced meaningfulness).[2] The more these three psychological states are present, the greater will be employees' motivation, performance, and satisfaction and the lower their absenteeism and likelihood of leaving. As Exhibit 7.1 shows, individuals with a high growth need are more

Though there are individual differences, most people respond well to intrinsic job characteristics; the job characteristics model does a good job of summarizing what intrinsic job characteristics might be altered to make the work more interesting and intrinsically motivating for employees.

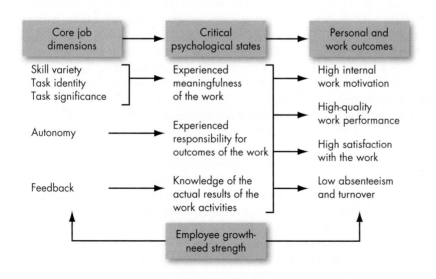

EXHIBIT 7.1
The Job Characteristics Model

Source: J.R. Hackman and G.R. Oldham, *Work Redesign* © 1980; pp. 78–80. Adapted by permission of Pearson Education, Inc., Upper Saddle River, New Jersey.

likely to experience the critical psychological states when their jobs are enriched—and respond to them more positively—than are their counterparts with low growth need.

Much evidence supports the JCM concept that the presence of a set of job characteristics—variety, identity, significance, autonomy, and feedback—does generate higher and more satisfying job performance.[3] Take some time to think about your job. Do you have the opportunity to work on different tasks, or is your day pretty routine? Are you able to work independently, or do you constantly have a supervisor or co-worker looking over your shoulder? What do you think your answers to these questions say about your job's motivating potential?

How Can Jobs Be Redesigned?

"Every day was the same thing," Frank Greer said. "Stand on that assembly line. Wait for an instrument panel to be moved into place. Unlock the mechanism and drop the panel into the Jeep Liberty as it moved by on the line. Then I plugged in the harnessing wires. I repeated that for eight hours a day. I don't care that they were paying me twenty-four dollars an hour. I was going crazy. I did it for almost a year and a half. Finally, I just said to my wife that this isn't going to be the way I'm going to spend the rest of my life. My brain was turning to JELL-O on that Jeep assembly line. So I quit. Now I work in a print shop and I make less than fifteen dollars an hour. But let me tell you, the work I do is really interesting. The job changes all the time, I'm continually learning new things, and the work really challenges me! I look forward every morning to going to work again."

The repetitive tasks in Frank Greer's job at the Jeep plant provided little variety, autonomy, or motivation. In contrast, his job in the print shop is challenging and stimulating. Let's look at some of the ways to put JCM into practice to make jobs more motivating.

JOB ROTATION   If employees suffer from overroutinization of their work, one alternative is **job rotation**, or the periodic shifting of an employee from one task to another with similar skill requirements at the same organizational level (also called *cross-training*). At Singapore Airlines, a ticket agent may take on the duties of a baggage handler. Extensive job rotation is one of the reasons Singapore Airlines is rated one of the best airlines in the world and is a highly desirable place to work. Many manufacturing firms have adopted job rotation as a means of increasing flexibility and avoiding layoffs. Managers at Apex Precision Technologies, a custom-machine shop in Indiana, train workers on all the company's equipment so they can move around as needed in response to incoming orders. During the 2001 recession, Cleveland-based Lincoln Electric moved some salaried workers to hourly clerical jobs and rotated production workers among various machines. This manufacturer of welding and cutting parts was able to minimize layoffs because of its commitment to continually cross-training and moving workers wherever they're needed.

The strengths of job rotation are that it reduces boredom, increases motivation, and helps employees better understand how their work contributes to the organization. An indirect benefit is that employees with a wider range of skills give management more flexibility in scheduling work, adapting to changes, and filling vacancies.[4] However, job rotation is not without drawbacks. Training costs increase, and productivity is reduced by moving a worker into a new position just when efficiency at the prior job is creating organizational economies. Job rotation also creates disruptions when members of the work group have to adjust to the new employee. And supervisors may also have to spend more time answering questions and monitoring the work of recently rotated employees.

JOB ENRICHMENT   Job enrichment expands jobs by increasing the degree to which the worker controls the planning, execution, and evaluation of the work. An enriched job organizes tasks to allow the worker to do a complete activity, increases the employee's freedom and independence, increases responsibility, and provides feedback so individuals can assess and correct their own performance.[5]

How does management enrich an employee's job? Exhibit 7.2 offers suggested guidelines based on the job characteristics model. *Combining tasks* puts fractionalized tasks back together to form a new and larger module of work. *Forming natural work units* makes an employee's tasks create an identifiable and meaningful whole. *Establishing client relationships* increases the direct relationships between workers and their clients (clients can be internal as well as outside the organization). *Expanding jobs vertically* gives employees responsibilities and control formerly reserved for management. *Opening feedback channels* lets employees know how well they are doing and whether their performance is improving, deteriorating, or remaining constant.

Some newer versions of job enrichment concentrate more specifically on improving the meaningfulness of work. One significant method is to relate employee experiences to customer outcomes, simply by providing employees with stories from customers who benefited from the company's products or services. The medical device manufacturer Medtronic invites people to describe how Medtronic products have improved, or even saved, their lives and shares these stories with employees during annual meetings, providing a powerful reminder of the impact of their work. Researchers recently found that when university fund-raisers briefly interacted with the undergraduates who would receive the scholarships they raised, they persisted 42 percent longer, and raised nearly twice as much money, as those who didn't interact with potential recipients.[6]

Another method for improving the meaningfulness of work is providing employees with mutual assistance programs.[7] Employees who can help each other directly through their work come to see themselves, and the organizations for which they work, in more positive, pro-social terms. This, in turn, can increase employee affective commitment.

The University of New Mexico provides job enrichment through cross-training to learn new skills and job rotation to perform new tasks in another position. To participate,

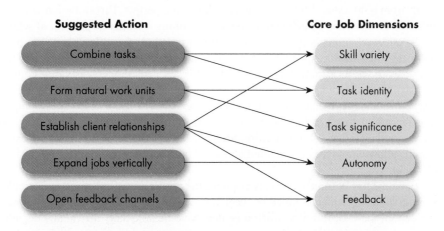

Suggested Action   **Core Job Dimensions**

Combine tasks   Skill variety

Form natural work units   Task identity

Establish client relationships   Task significance

Expand jobs vertically   Autonomy

Open feedback channels   Feedback

EXHIBIT 7.2
Guidelines for Enriching a Job

Source: J.R. Hackman and J.L. Suttle (eds.), *Improving Life at Work* (Glenview, Il: Scott Foresman, 1977), p. 138. Reprinted by permission of Richard Hackman and J. Lloyd Suttle.

employees work with their manager to set a job enrichment goal, identify desired competencies, and find an appropriate placement. Participation typically lasts 90 days, after which employees either return to their former position or obtain a new position that leverages their newfound skills.

Two university employees held administrative positions in the same academic department. One specialized in handling student records, and the other processed tuition payments. Through the enrichment program, the student-records assistant received cross-training in human resources (HR) classes to learn about purchasing and the accounting system. The accounting assistant worked with the student-records assistant 2 hours per week learning about that job. The two then proposed rotating their jobs for a summer. As a result, both expanded their repertoire of skills and experiences to enable them to cover for or help the other employee, and to better prepare for future promotions.[8]

The evidence on job enrichment shows it reduces absenteeism and turnover costs and increases satisfaction, but not all job enrichment programs are equally effective. A review of 83 organizational interventions designed to improve performance management showed that frequent, specific feedback related to solving problems was linked to consistently higher performance, but infrequent feedback that focused more on past problems than future solutions was much less effective.[9] Some recent evidence suggests job enrichment works best when it compensates for poor feedback and reward systems.[10]

Alternative Work Arrangements

Beyond redesigning work itself and including employees in decisions, another approach to motivation is to alter work arrangements with flextime, job sharing, or telecommuting. These arrangements are likely to be especially important for a diverse workforce of dual-earner couples, single parents, and employees caring for a sick or aging relative.

FLEXTIME   Susan Ross is the classic "morning person." She rises each day at 5:00 AM sharp and full of energy. However, as she puts it, "I'm usually ready for bed right after the 7:00 PM news."

Susan's work schedule as a claims processor at The Hartford Financial Services Group is flexible. Her office opens at 6:00 AM and closes at 7:00 PM. It's up to her how she schedules her 8-hour day within this 13-hour period. Because Susan is a morning person and also has a 7-year-old son who gets out of school at 3:00 PM every day, she opts to work from 6:00 AM to 3:00 PM. "My work hours are perfect. I'm at the job when I'm mentally most alert, and I can be home to take care of my son after he gets out of school."

Susan's schedule is an example of **flextime**, short for "flexible work time." Employees must work a specific number of hours per week but are free to vary their hours of work within certain limits. As in Exhibit 7.3, each day consists of a common core, usually 6 hours, with a flexibility band surrounding it. The core may be 9:00 AM to 3:00 PM, with the office actually opening at 6:00 AM and closing at 6:00 PM. All employees are required to be at their jobs during the common core period, but they may accumulate their other 2 hours before, after, or before and after that. Some flextime programs allow employees to accumulate extra hours and turn them into a free day off each month.

Flextime has become extremely popular; the proportion of full-time U.S. employees on flextime more than doubled between the late 1980s and 2005, and approximately 43 percent of the U.S. full-time workforce now have flexible daily arrival and departure

EXHIBIT 7.3
Examples of
Flextime
Schedules

Schedule 1

Percent Time:	100% = 40 hours per week
Core Hours:	9:00 AM–5:00 PM, Monday through Friday (1 hour lunch)
Work Start Time:	Between 8:00 AM and 9:00 AM
Work End Time:	Between 5:00 PM and 6:00 PM

Schedule 2

Percent Time:	100% = 40 hours per week
Work Hours:	8:00 AM–6:30 PM, Monday through Thursday (1/2 hour lunch)
	Friday off
Work Start Time:	8:00 AM
Work End Time:	6:30 PM

Schedule 3

Percent Time:	90% = 36 hours per week
Work Hours:	8:30 AM–5:00 PM, Monday through Thursday (1/2 hour lunch)
	8:00 AM–Noon Friday (no lunch)
Work Start Time:	8:30 AM (Monday–Thursday); 8:00 AM (Friday)
Work End Time:	5:00 PM (Monday–Thursday); Noon (Friday)

Schedule 4

Percent Time:	80% = 32 hours per week
	8:00 AM–6:00 PM, Monday through Wednesday (1/2 hour lunch)
Work Hours:	8:00 AM–11:30 AM Thursday (no lunch)
	Friday off
Work Start Time:	Between 8:00 AM and 9:00 AM
Work End Time:	Between 5:00 PM and 6:00 PM

times.[11] And this is not just a U.S. phenomenon. In Germany, for instance, 29 percent of businesses offer flextime.[12]

The claimed benefits are numerous. They include reduced absenteeism, increased productivity, reduced overtime expenses, reduced hostility toward management, reduced traffic congestion around work sites, elimination of tardiness, and increased autonomy and responsibility for employees, any of which may increase employee job satisfaction. But what's flextime's actual record?

Most of the performance evidence stacks up favorably. Flextime tends to reduce absenteeism and frequently improves worker productivity,[13] probably for several reasons. Employees can schedule their work hours to align with personal demands, reducing tardiness and absences, and they can work when they are most productive. Flextime can also help employees balance work and family lives; it is a popular criterion for judging how "family friendly" a workplace is.

Flextime's major drawback is that it's not applicable to every job. It works well with clerical tasks for which an employee's interaction with people outside his or her department is limited. It is not a viable option for receptionists, sales personnel in retail stores, or similar jobs for which comprehensive service demands that people be at their workstations at predetermined times.

JOB SHARING   **Job sharing** allows two or more individuals to split a traditional 40-hour-a-week job. One might perform the job from 8:00 AM to noon and the other from 1:00 PM to 5:00 PM, or the two could work full, but alternate, days. Sue Manix and Charlotte Schutzman share the title of vice president of employee communications in the Philadelphia office of Verizon.[14] Schutzman works Monday and Tuesday, Manix Thursday and Friday, and they alternate Wednesdays. The two women have job-shared for 10 years, acquiring promotions, numerous bonuses, and a 20-person staff and better balancing their work and family responsibilities.

Approximately 19 percent of large organizations now offer job sharing.[15] Reasons it is not more widely adopted are likely the difficulty of finding compatible partners to share a job and the historically negative perceptions of individuals not completely committed to their job and employer.

Job sharing allows an organization to draw on the talents of more than one individual in a given job. A bank manager who oversees two job sharers describes it as an opportunity to get two heads but "pay for one."[16] It also opens up the opportunity to acquire skilled workers—for instance, women with young children and retirees—who might not be available on a full-time basis. Many Japanese firms are increasingly considering job sharing—but for a very different reason.[17] Because Japanese executives are extremely reluctant to fire people, job sharing is seen as a potentially humanitarian means of avoiding layoffs due to overstaffing.

From the employee's perspective, job sharing increases flexibility and can increase motivation and satisfaction when a 40-hour-a-week job is just not practical. But the major drawback from management's perspective is finding compatible pairs of employees who can successfully coordinate the intricacies of one job.

TELECOMMUTING   It might be close to the ideal job for many people. No commuting, flexible hours, freedom to dress as you please, and few or no interruptions from colleagues. It's called **telecommuting**, and it refers to working at home at least 2 days a week on a computer linked to the employer's office. (A closely related term—the *virtual office*—describes working from home on a relatively permanent basis.)

The U.S. Department of the Census estimated that in 2002 approximately 15 percent of the workforce worked from home at least one day a week.[18] One recent survey of more than 5,000 HR professionals found that 35 percent of organizations allowed employees to telecommute at least part of the time, and 21 percent allowed employees to telecommute full-time.[19] Well-known organizations that actively encourage telecommuting include AT&T, IBM, American Express, Sun Microsystems, and a number of U.S. government agencies.[20] In Finland, Sweden, Britain, and Germany, telecommuters represent 17, 15, 8, and 6 percent of the workforce, respectively.[21]

What kinds of jobs lend themselves to telecommuting? There are three categories: routine information-handling tasks, mobile activities, and professional and other knowledge-related tasks.[22] Writers, attorneys, analysts, and employees who spend the majority of their time on computers or the telephone—such as telemarketers, customer-service representatives, reservation agents, and product-support specialists—are natural candidates. As telecommuters, they can access information on their computers at home as easily as in the company's office.

There are numerous stories of telecommuting's success.[23] Putnam Investments, in Boston, has made telecommuting an attractive recruitment tool that increased the number of applicants 20-fold. Putnam's management calculates that the 12 percent of its employees who telecommute have substantially higher productivity than in-office staff and about one-tenth the attrition rate.

The potential pluses of telecommuting for management include a larger labor pool from which to select, higher productivity, less turnover, improved morale, and reduced office space costs. A positive relationship exists between telecommuting and supervisor performance ratings, but the relationship between telecommuting and turnover intentions has not been substantiated in research to date.[24] The major downside for management is less direct supervision of employees. In addition, in today's team-focused workplace, telecommuting may make it more difficult for management to coordinate teamwork. From the employee's standpoint, telecommuting offers a considerable increase in flexibility—but not without costs. For employees with a high social need, telecommuting can increase feelings of isolation and reduce job satisfaction. And all telecommuters are vulnerable to the "out of sight, out of mind" effect. Employees who aren't at their desks, who miss meetings, and who don't share in day-to-day informal workplace interactions may be at a disadvantage when it comes to raises and promotions.

The Social and Physical Context of Work

Robin and Chris both graduated from college a couple years ago with degrees in elementary education. They took jobs as first-grade teachers in different school districts. Robin immediately confronted a number of obstacles on the job: a large class (42 students), a small and dingy classroom, and inadequate supplies. Chris's situation couldn't have been more different. He had only 15 students in his class, plus a teaching aide 15 hours each week, a modern and well-lighted room, a well-stocked supply cabinet, an iMac for every student, and a highly supportive principal. Not surprisingly, at the end of the first year, Chris had been a considerably more effective teacher than Robin.

The job characteristics model shows most employees are more motivated and satisfied when their intrinsic work tasks are engaging. However, having the most interesting workplace characteristics in the world may not always lead to satisfaction if you feel isolated from your co-workers, and having good social relationships can make even the most boring and onerous tasks more fulfilling. Research demonstrates that social aspects and work context are as important as other job design features.[25] Policies such as job rotation, worker empowerment, and employee participation have positive effects on productivity, at least partially because they encourage more communication and a positive social environment.

Some social characteristics that improve job performance include interdependence, social support, and interactions with other people outside work. Social interactions are strongly related to positive moods and give employees more opportunities to clarify their work role and how well they are performing. Social support gives employees greater opportunities to obtain assistance with their work. Constructive social relationships can bring about a positive feedback loop as employees assist one another in a "virtuous circle."

The work context is also likely to affect employee satisfaction. Work that is hot, loud, and dangerous is less satisfying than work conducted in climate-controlled, relatively quiet, and safe environments. This is probably why most people would rather work in a coffee shop than a metalworking foundry. Physical demands make people physically uncomfortable, which is likely to show up in lower levels of job satisfaction.

To assess why an employee is not performing to her or his best level, look at the work environment to see whether it's supportive. Does the employee have adequate tools, equipment, materials, and supplies? Does the employee have favorable working conditions, helpful co-workers, supportive work rules and procedures, sufficient information to make job-related decisions, adequate time to do a good job, and the like? If not, performance will suffer.

EMPLOYEE INVOLVEMENT

What is **employee involvement?** It's a participative process that uses employees' input to increase their commitment to the organization's success. The logic is that if we engage workers in decisions that affect them and increase their autonomy and control over their work lives, they will become more motivated, more committed to the organization, more productive, and more satisfied with their jobs.[26]

Examples of Employee Involvement Programs

Let's look at two major forms of employee involvement—participative management and representative participation—in more detail.

PARTICIPATIVE MANAGEMENT   The distinct characteristic common to all **participative management** programs is joint decision making, in which subordinates share a significant degree of decision-making power with their immediate superiors. Participative management has, at times, been promoted as a panacea for poor morale and low productivity. But for it to work, the issues in which employees are engaged must be relevant to their interests so they'll be motivated, employees must have the competence and knowledge to make a useful contribution, and trust and confidence must exist among all parties.

Dozens of studies have been conducted on the participation–performance relationship. The findings, however, are mixed.[27] Organizations that institute participative management do have higher stock returns, lower turnover rates, and higher estimated labor productivity, although these effects are typically not large.[28] A careful review of the research at the individual level shows participation typically has only a modest influence on variables such as employee productivity, motivation, and job satisfaction. Of course, this doesn't mean participative management can't be beneficial under the right conditions. What it says, however, is that it is not a sure means for improving employee performance.

REPRESENTATIVE PARTICIPATION   Almost every country in western Europe requires companies to practice **representative participation**, called "the most widely legislated form of employee involvement around the world."[29] Its goal is to redistribute power within an organization, putting labor on a more equal footing with the interests of management and stockholders by letting workers be represented by a small group of employees who actually participate.

The two most common forms are works councils and board representatives. Works councils are groups of nominated or elected employees who must be consulted when management makes decisions about employees. Board representatives are employees who sit on a company's board of directors and represent the interests of the firm's employees.

The influence of representative participation on working employees seems to be minimal.[30] Works councils are dominated by management and have little impact on employees or the organization. Although participation might increase the motivation and satisfaction of employee representatives, there is little evidence this trickles down to the operating employees they represent. Overall, "the greatest value of representative participation is symbolic. If one is interested in changing employee attitudes or in improving organizational performance, representative participation would be a poor choice."[31]

Linking Employee Involvement Programs and Motivation Theories

Employee involvement draws on a number of the motivation theories we discussed in Chapter 7. Theory Y is consistent with participative management and Theory X with the more traditional autocratic style of managing people. In terms of two-factor theory, employee involvement programs could provide intrinsic motivation by increasing opportunities for growth, responsibility, and involvement in the work itself. The opportunity to make and implement decisions—and then see them work out—can help satisfy an employee's needs for responsibility, achievement, recognition, growth, and enhanced self-esteem. And extensive employee involvement programs clearly have the potential to increase employee intrinsic motivation in work tasks.

USING REWARDS TO MOTIVATE EMPLOYEES

As we saw in Chapter 2, pay is not a primary factor driving job satisfaction. However, it does motivate people, and companies often under-estimate its importance in keeping top talent. A 2006 study found that while 45 percent of employers thought pay was a key factor in losing top talent, 71 percent of top performers indicated it was a top reason.[32]

Given that pay is so important, management must make some strategic decisions. Will the organization lead, match, or lag the market in pay? How will individual contributions be recognized? In this section, we consider (1) what to pay employees (decided by establishing a pay structure), (2) how to pay individual employees (decided through variable pay plans and skill-based pay plans), (3) what benefits and choices to offer (such as flexible benefits), and (4) how to construct employee recognition programs.

What to Pay: Establishing a Pay Structure

There are many ways to pay employees. The process of initially setting pay levels can be complex and entails balancing *internal equity*—the worth of the job to the organization (usually established through a technical process called job evaluation)—and *external equity*—the external competitiveness of an organization's pay relative to pay elsewhere in its industry (usually established through pay surveys). Obviously, the best pay system pays what the job is worth (internal equity) while also paying competitively relative to the labor market.

Some organizations prefer to be pay leaders by paying above the market, whereas some may lag the market because they can't afford to pay market rates, or they are willing to bear

As opposed to research on the job characteristics model and work redesign, which is mostly favorable, the research evidence on employee involvement programs is decidedly mixed. It is not clear that employee involvement programs have fulfilled their promise.

the costs of paying below market (namely, higher turnover as people are lured to better-paying jobs). Walmart, for example, pays less than its competitors and often outsources jobs overseas. Chinese workers in Shenzhen earn $120 a month (that's $1,440 per year) to make stereos for Walmart. Of the 6,000 factories that are worldwide suppliers to Walmart, 80 percent are located in China. In fact, one-eighth of all Chinese exports to the United States go to Walmart.[33]

Pay more, and you may get better-qualified, more highly motivated employees who will stay with the organization longer. A study covering 126 large organizations found employees who believed they were receiving a competitive pay level had higher morale and were more productive, and customers were more satisfied as well.[34] But pay is often the highest single operating cost for an organization, which means paying too much can make the organization's products or services too expensive. It's a strategic decision an organization must make, with clear trade-offs.

How to Pay: Rewarding Individual Employees Through Variable-Pay Programs

"Why should I put any extra effort into this job?" asked Anne Garcia, a fourth-grade elementary schoolteacher in Denver, Colorado. "I can excel or I can do the bare minimum. It makes no difference. I get paid the same. Why do anything above the minimum to get by?"

Comments like Anne's have been voiced by schoolteachers for decades because pay increases were tied to seniority. Recently, however, a number of states have revamped their compensation systems to motivate people like Anne to strive for excellence in their jobs. Arizona, Florida, Iowa, and Kentucky tie teacher pay to the performance of the students in their classrooms.[35] In California, some teachers can earn performance bonuses as high as $25,000 per year.[36]

Variable-pay plans, when properly designed and administered, do appear to enhance employee motivation.

A number of organizations—business firms as well as school districts and other government agencies—are moving away from paying solely on credentials or length of service. Piece-rate plans, merit-based pay, bonuses, profit sharing, gainsharing, and employee stock ownership plans are all a form of a **variable-pay program**, which bases a portion of an employee's pay on some individual and/or organizational measure of performance. Earnings, therefore, fluctuate up and down.

The fluctuation in variable pay is what makes these programs attractive to management. It turns part of an organization's fixed labor costs into a variable cost, thus reducing expenses when performance declines. When the U.S. economy encountered a recession in 2001 and 2008, companies with variable pay were able to reduce their labor costs much faster than others.[37] When pay is tied to performance, the employee's earnings also recognize contribution rather than being a form of entitlement. Over time, low performers' pay stagnates, whereas high performers enjoy pay increases commensurate with their contributions.

Let's examine the different types of variable-pay programs in more detail.

1. *Piece-rate pay.* The **piece-rate pay plan** has long been popular as a means of compensating production workers by paying a fixed sum for each unit of production completed. A pure piece-rate plan provides no base salary and pays the employee only for what he or she produces. Ballpark workers selling peanuts and soda are frequently paid this way. If they sell 40 bags of peanuts at $1 each, their

take is $40. The harder they work and the more peanuts they sell, the more they earn. The limitation of these plans is that they're not feasible for many jobs. Alabama college football coach Nick Saban earns $4 million per year regardless of how many games he wins. Would it be better to pay him $400,000 for each win? It seems unlikely he would accept such a deal, and it may cause unanticipated consequences as well (such as cheating). So, although incentives are motivating and relevant for some jobs, it is unrealistic to think they can constitute the only piece of some employees' pay.

2. *Merit-based pay.* A **merit-based pay plan** pays for individual performance based on performance appraisal ratings. A main advantage is that people thought to be high performers can be given bigger raises. If they are designed correctly, merit-based plans let individuals perceive a strong relationship between their performance and the rewards they receive.[38] Despite the intuitive appeal of paying for performance, merit pay plans have several limitations. One is that they are typically based on an annual performance appraisal and thus are only as valid as the performance ratings. Another limitation is that the pay-raise pool fluctuates on economic or other conditions that have little to do with individual performance. One year, a colleague at a top university who performed very well in teaching and research was given a pay raise of $300. Why? Because the pay-raise pool was very small. Yet that is hardly pay-for-performance. Finally, unions typically resist merit pay plans. Relatively few teachers are covered by merit pay for this reason. Instead, seniority-based pay, where all employees get the same raises, predominates.

3. *Bonuses.* An annual **bonus** is a significant component of total compensation for many jobs. The incentive effects of performance bonuses should be higher than those of merit pay because, rather than paying for performance years ago (that was rolled into base pay), bonuses reward recent performance. Moreover, when times are bad, firms can cut bonuses to reduce compensation costs. Steel company Nucor, for example, guarantees its employees only about $10 per hour, but bonuses can be substantial. In 2006, the average Nucor worker made roughly $91,000. When the recession hit, bonuses were cut dramatically: in 2009, total pay had dropped 40 percent.[39] This example also highlights the downside of bonuses: employees' pay is more vulnerable to cuts. This is particularly problematic when bonuses are a large percentage of total pay or when employees come to take bonuses for granted.

4. *Skill-based pay.* **Skill-based pay** (also called *competency-based* or *knowledge-based pay*) is an alternative to job-based pay that bases pay levels on how many skills employees have or how many jobs they can do.[40] For employers, the lure of skill-based pay plans is that they increase the flexibility of the workforce: filling staffing needs is easier when employee skills are interchangeable. Skill-based pay also facilitates communication across the organization because people gain a better understanding of each others' jobs. What about the downsides? People can "top out"—that is, they can learn all the skills the program calls for them to learn. This can frustrate employees after they've been challenged by an environment of learning, growth, and continual pay raises. Finally, skill-based plans don't address level of performance. They deal only with whether someone can perform the skill.

5. *Profit-sharing plans.* A **profit-sharing plan** is an organization-wide program that distributes compensation based on some established formula designed around a company's profitability. Compensation can be direct cash outlays or, particularly for top managers, allocations of stock options. When you read about executives like Oracle's Larry Ellison earning $75.33 million in pay, it almost all (88.8 percent in Ellison's case) comes from cashing in stock options previously granted based on company profit performance. Not all profit-sharing plans need be so grand in scale. Jacob Luke, age 13, started his own lawn-mowing business after getting a mower from his uncle. Jacob employs his brother, Isaiah, and friend, Marcel Monroe, and pays them each 25 percent of the profits he makes on each yard. Profit-sharing plans at the organizational level appear to have positive impacts on employee attitudes; employees working under profit-sharing plans have a greater feeling of psychological ownership.[41]

6. *Gainsharing.* **Gainsharing** is a formula-based group incentive plan that uses improvements in group productivity from one period to another determine the total amount of money allocated. Approximately 45 percent of *Fortune* 1000 firms have implemented gainsharing plans;[42] its popularity seems narrowly focused among large manufacturing companies such as Champion Spark Plug and Mead Paper. Gainsharing is different from profit sharing in that it ties rewards to productivity gains rather than profits. Employees in a gainsharing plan can receive incentive awards even when the organization isn't profitable. Because the benefits accrue to groups of workers, high-performing workers pressure weaker performers to work harder, improving performance for the group as a whole.

7. *Employee stock ownership plans.* An **employee stock ownership plan (ESOP)** is a company-established benefit plan in which employees acquire stock, often at below-market prices, as part of their benefits. Research on ESOPs indicates they increase employee satisfaction.[43] But their impact on performance is less clear. ESOPs have the potential to increase employee job satisfaction and work motivation. But for this potential to be realized, employees need to psychologically experience ownership. That is, in addition to their financial stake in the company, they need to be kept regularly informed of the status of the business and have the opportunity to exercise influence over it to achieve significant improvements in the organization's performance.[44] ESOPs for top management can reduce unethical behavior. CEOs are more likely to manipulate firm earnings reports to make themselves look good in the short run when they don't have an ownership share, even though this manipulation will eventually lead to lower stock prices. However, when CEOs own a large value of stock they report earnings accurately because they don't want the negative consequences of declining stock prices.[45]

EVALUATION OF VARIABLE PAY   Do variable-pay programs increase motivation and productivity? The answer is a qualified "yes." Studies generally support the idea that organizations with profit-sharing plans have higher levels of profitability than those without them.[46] Similarly, gainsharing has been found to improve productivity in a majority of cases and often has a positive impact on employee attitudes.[47] Another study found that whereas piece-rate pay-for-performance plans stimulated higher levels of productivity, this positive affect was not observed for risk-averse employees. Thus, economist Ed Lazear seems generally right when he says, "Workers respond to prices just as economic theory predicts. Claims by sociologists and others that monetizing incentives may actually reduce output are unambiguously refuted by the data." But that doesn't mean everyone responds positively to variable-pay plans.[48]

Flexible Benefits: Developing a Benefits Package

Consistent with expectancy theory's thesis that organizational rewards should be linked to each individual employee's goals, **flexible benefits** individualize rewards by allowing each employee to choose the compensation package that best satisfies his or her current needs and situation. These plans replace the "one-benefit-plan-fits-all" programs designed for a male with a wife and two children at home that dominated organizations for more than 50 years.[49] Fewer than 10 percent of employees now fit this image: About 25 percent are single, and one-third are part of two-income families with no children. Flexible benefits can accommodate differences in employee needs based on age, marital status, spouses' benefit status, number and age of dependents, and the like.

Intrinsic Rewards: Employee Recognition Programs

Laura Schendell makes only $8.50 per hour working at her fast-food job in Pensacola, Florida, and the job isn't very challenging or interesting. Yet Laura talks enthusiastically about the job, her boss, and the company that employs her. "What I like is the fact that Guy [her supervisor] appreciates the effort I make. He compliments me regularly in front of the other people on my shift, and I've been chosen Employee of the Month twice in the past six months. Did you see my picture on that plaque on the wall?"

Organizations are increasingly recognizing what Laura Schendell knows: Important work rewards can be both intrinsic and extrinsic. Rewards are intrinsic in the form of employee recognition programs and extrinsic in the form of compensation systems. In this section, we deal with ways in which managers can reward and motivate employee performance.

Employee recognition programs range from a spontaneous and private thank-you to widely publicized formal programs in which specific types of behavior are encouraged and the procedures for attaining recognition are clearly identified. Some research suggests financial incentives may be more motivating in the short term, but in the long run it's nonfinancial incentives.[50]

A few years ago, 1,500 employees were surveyed in a variety of work settings to find out what they considered the most powerful workplace motivator. Their response? Recognition, recognition, and more recognition.

An obvious advantage of recognition programs is that they are inexpensive because praise is free! It shouldn't be surprising then that they've grown in popularity. A 2002 survey of 391 companies found 84 percent had some program to recognize worker achievements, and 4 in 10 said they were doing more to foster employee recognition than they had just a year earlier.[51]

Despite the increased popularity of employee recognition programs, critics argue they are highly susceptible to political manipulation by management.[52] When applied to jobs for which performance factors are relatively objective, such as sales, recognition programs are likely to be perceived by employees as fair. However, in most jobs, the criteria for good performance aren't self-evident, which allows managers to manipulate the system and recognize their favorites. Abuse can undermine the value of recognition programs and demoralize employees.

Global Implications

Do the motivational approaches we've discussed vary by culture? Because we've covered some very different approaches in this chapter, let's break down our analysis by approach. Not every approach has been studied by cross-cultural researchers, so we consider cross-cultural differences in (1) job characteristics and job enrichment, (2) telecommuting, (3) variable pay, (4) flexible benefits, and (5) employee involvement.

Job Characteristics and Job Enrichment

A few studies have tested the job characteristics model in different cultures, but the results aren't very consistent. One study suggested that when employees are "other oriented" (concerned with the welfare of others at work), the relationship between intrinsic job characteristics and job satisfaction was weaker. The fact that the job characteristics model is relatively individualistic (considering the relationship between the employee and his or her work) suggests job enrichment strategies may not have the same effects in collectivistic cultures as in individualistic cultures (such as the United States).[53] However, another study suggested the degree to which jobs had intrinsic job characteristics predicted job satisfaction and job involvement equally well for U.S., Japanese, and Hungarian employees.[54]

Telecommuting

Does the degree to which employees telecommute vary by nation? Does its effectiveness depend on culture? First, one study suggests that telecommuting is more common in the United States than in all the European Union (EU) nations except the Netherlands. In the study, 24.6 percent of U.S. employees engaged in telecommuting, compared to only 13.0 percent of EU employees. Of the EU countries, the Netherlands had the highest rate of telecommuting (26.4 percent); the lowest rates were in Spain (4.9 percent) and Portugal (3.4 percent). What about the rest of the world? Unfortunately, there are few data comparing telecommuting rates in other parts of the world. Similarly, we don't really know whether telecommuting works better in the United States than in other countries. However, the same study that compared telework rates between the United States and the EU determined that employees in Europe appeared to have the same level of interest in telework: regardless of country, interest is higher among employees than among employers.[55]

Variable Pay

You'd probably think individual pay systems (such as merit pay or pay-for-performance) work better in individualistic cultures such as the United States than in collectivistic cultures such as China or Venezuela. Similarly, you'd probably hypothesize that group-based rewards such as gainsharing or profit sharing work better in collectivistic cultures than in individualistic cultures. Unfortunately, there isn't much research on the issue. One recent study did suggest, though, that beliefs about the fairness of a group incentive plan were more predictive of pay satisfaction for employees in the United States than for employees in Hong Kong. One interpretation of these findings is that U.S. employees are more critical in appraising a group pay plan, and therefore it's more critical that the plan be communicated clearly and administered fairly.

Flexible Benefits

Today, almost all major corporations in the United States offer flexible benefits. And they're becoming the norm in other countries, too. A recent survey of 136 Canadian organizations found that 93 percent have adopted or will adopt flexible benefits in the near term.[56] And a similar survey of 307 firms in the United Kingdom found that although only 16 percent have flexible benefits programs in place, another 60 percent are either in the process of implementing them or are seriously considering it.[57]

Employee Involvement

Employee involvement programs differ among countries. A study comparing the acceptance of employee involvement programs in four countries, including the United States and India, confirmed the importance of modifying practices to reflect national culture.[58] Specifically, while U.S. employees readily accepted these programs, managers in India who tried to empower their employees through employee involvement programs were rated low by those employees. These reactions are consistent with India's high power–distance culture, which accepts and expects differences in authority. Similarly, Chinese workers who were very accepting of traditional Chinese values showed few benefits from participative decision making, but workers who were less traditional were more satisfied and had higher performance ratings under participative management.[59] This study illustrates

the substantial differences in how management practices are perceived by individuals within as well as between countries.

Implications for Managers

We've presented a number of motivation theories and applications in Chapter 6 and in this chapter. Although it's always dangerous to synthesize a large number of complex ideas, the following suggestions summarize what we know about motivating employees in organizations.

Recognize Individual Differences

Managers should be sensitive to individual differences. For example, employees from Asian cultures prefer not to be singled out as special because it makes them uncomfortable. Spend the time necessary to understand what's important to each employee. This allows you to individualize goals, level of involvement, and rewards to align with individual needs. Design jobs to align with individual needs and maximize their motivation potential.

Use Goals and Feedback

Employees should have firm, specific goals, and they should get feedback on how well they are faring in pursuit of those goals.

Allow Employees to Participate in Decisions That Affect Them

Employees can contribute to setting work goals, choosing their own benefits packages, and solving productivity and quality problems. Participation can increase employee productivity, commitment to work goals, motivation, and job satisfaction.

Link Rewards to Performance

Rewards should be contingent on performance, and employees must perceive the link between the two. Regardless of how strong the relationship is, if individuals perceive it to be weak, the results will be low performance, a decrease in job satisfaction, and an increase in turnover and absenteeism.

Check the System for Equity

Employees should perceive that experience, skills, abilities, effort, and other obvious inputs explain differences in performance and hence in pay, job assignments, and other obvious rewards.

CHAPTER **8**

Foundations of Group Behavior

After studying this chapter, you should be able to:

- Define *group* and distinguish the different types of groups.
- Identify the five stages of group development.
- Show how role requirements change in different situations.
- Demonstrate how norms and status exert influence on an individual's behavior.
- Contrast the strengths and weaknesses of group decision making.
- Evaluate evidence for cultural differences in group status and social loafing as well as the effects of diversity in groups.

DEFINING AND CLASSIFYING GROUPS

We define a **group** as two or more individuals, interacting and interdependent, who have come together to achieve particular objectives. Groups can be either formal or informal.

By a **formal group**, we mean one defined by the organization's structure, with designated work assignments establishing tasks. In formal groups, the behaviors team members should engage in are stipulated by and directed toward organizational goals. The six members of an airline flight crew are a formal group. In contrast, an **informal group** is neither formally structured nor organizationally determined. Informal groups are natural formations in the work environment that appear in response to the need for social contact. Three employees from different departments who regularly have lunch or coffee together are an informal group. These types of interactions among individuals, though informal, deeply affect their behavior and performance.

Security.   By joining a group, individuals can reduce the insecurity of "standing alone." People feel stronger, have fewer self-doubts, and are more resistant to threats when they are part of a group.

Status.   Inclusion in a group that is viewed as important by others provides recognition and status for its members.

Self-esteem.   Groups can provide people with feelings of self-worth. That is, in addition to con-veying status to those outside the group, membership can also give increased feelings of worth to the group members themselves.

Affiliation.   Groups can fulfill social needs. People enjoy the regular interaction that comes with group membership. For many people, these on-the-job interactions are their primary source for fulfilling their needs for affiliation.

Power.   What cannot be achieved individually often becomes possible through group action. There is power in numbers.

Goal achievement.   There are times when it takes more than one person to accomplish a particular task—there is a need to pool talents, knowledge, or power in order to complete a job. In such instances, management will rely on the use of a formal group.

EXHIBIT 8.1
Why Do People Join Groups

It's possible to further subclassify groups as command, task, interest, or friendship groups.[1] Command and task groups are dictated by formal organization, whereas interest and friendship groups are informal alliances.

A **command group** is determined by the organization chart. It is composed of the individuals who report directly to a given manager. An elementary school principal and her 18 teachers form a command group, as do a director of postal audits and his five inspectors.

A **task group**, also organizationally determined, represents individuals working together to complete a job task. However, a task group's boundaries are not limited to its immediate hierarchical superior; the group can cross command relationships. If a college student is accused of a campus crime, dealing with the problem might require coordination among the dean of academic affairs, the dean of students, the registrar, the director of security, and the student's advisor. Such a formation constitutes a task group. All command groups are also task groups. But because task groups can cut across the organization, they are not always command groups.

Whether they are in command or task groups together or not, people may affiliate to attain a specific objective with which each individual is concerned. This creates an **interest group**. Employees who band together to have their vacation schedules altered, to support a peer who has been fired, or to seek improved working conditions have formed a united body to further their common interest.

Groups often develop because individual members have one or more common characteristics. We call these formations **friendship groups**. Social alliances, which frequently extend outside the work situation, can be based on common age or ethnic heritage, support for Notre Dame football, interest in the same alternative rock band, or similar political views, to name just a few such characteristics.

There is no single reason individuals join groups. Because most people belong to a number of groups, it's obvious that different groups provide different benefits to their members. Exhibit 8.1 summarizes the most popular reasons people have for joining groups.

Groups can be formal as well as informal; regardless of the type of group, group norms, roles, and identities have powerful effects on individuals' behavior.

STAGES OF GROUP DEVELOPMENT

Groups generally pass through a predictable sequence in their evolution, which we call the five-stage model of group development. Although not all groups follow this pattern,[2] it is a useful framework for understanding group development. In this section, we describe the five-stage general model and an alternative model for temporary groups with deadlines.

The Five-Stage Model

As shown in Exhibit 8.2, the **five-stage group-development model** characterizes groups as proceeding through the distinct stages of forming, storming, norming, performing, and adjourning.[3]

The first stage, **forming**, is characterized by a great deal of uncertainty about the group's purpose, structure, and leadership. Members "test the waters" to determine what types of behaviors are acceptable. This stage is complete when members have begun to think of themselves as part of a group.

The **storming stage** is one of intragroup conflict. Members accept the existence of the group but resist the constraints it imposes on individuality. Furthermore, there is conflict over who will control the group. When this stage is complete, there will be a relatively clear hierarchy of leadership within the group.

In the third stage, close relationships develop and the group demonstrates cohesiveness. There is now a strong sense of group identity and camaraderie. This **norming stage** is complete when the group structure solidifies and the group has assimilated a common set of expectations of what defines correct member behavior.

The fourth stage is **performing**. The structure at this point is fully functional and accepted. Group energy has moved from getting to know and understand each other to performing the task at hand.

For permanent work groups, performing is the last stage in development. However, for temporary committees, teams, task forces, and similar groups that have a limited task to perform, the **adjourning stage** is a preparation for disbanding. Wrapping up activities is the focus rather than high task performance. Some group members are upbeat, basking in the group's accomplishments. Others may be depressed over the loss of camaraderie and friendships gained during the work group's life.

Many interpreters of the five-stage model have assumed a group becomes more effective as it progresses through the first four stages. Although this may be generally true, what makes a group effective is actually more complex.[4] Under some conditions, high levels of conflict may be conducive to high group performance. So we might expect to find situations in which groups in stage II outperform those in stage III or IV. Nor do groups always proceed clearly from one stage to the next. Sometimes, in fact, several

EXHIBIT 8.2
Stages of Group Development

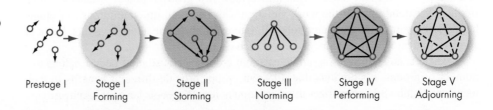

Prestage I   Stage I   Stage II   Stage III   Stage IV   Stage V
              Forming   Storming   Norming   Performing   Adjourning

stages go on simultaneously, as when groups are storming and performing at the same time. Groups even occasionally regress to previous stages. Therefore, even the strongest proponents of this model do not assume all groups follow its five-stage process precisely or that Stage IV is always preferable.

GROUP PROPERTIES: ROLES, NORMS, STATUS, SIZE, AND COHESIVENESS

Work groups are not unorganized mobs; they have properties that shape members' behavior and help explain and predict individual behavior within the group as well as the performance of the group itself. Some of these properties are roles, norms, status, size, and cohesiveness.

Group Property 1: Roles

Shakespeare said, "All the world's a stage, and all the men and women merely players." Using the same metaphor, all group members are actors, each playing a **role**. By this term, we mean a set of expected behavior patterns attributed to someone occupying a given position in a social unit. Our understanding of role behavior would be dramatically simplified if each of us chose one role and "played it out" regularly and consistently. Unfortunately, we are required to play a number of diverse roles, both on and off our jobs. As we'll see, one of the tasks in understanding behavior is grasping the role a person is currently playing.

Bill Patterson is a plant manager with EMM Industries, a large electrical equipment manufacturer in Phoenix. He fulfills a number of roles—EMM employee, member of middle management, electrical engineer, and primary company spokesperson in the community. Off the job, Bill Patterson finds himself in still more roles: husband, father, Catholic, Rotarian, tennis player, member of the Thunderbird Country Club, and president of his homeowners' association. Many of these roles are compatible; some create conflicts. How does Bill's religious commitment influence his managerial decisions regarding layoffs, expense account padding, and provision of accurate information to government agencies? A recent offer of promotion requires Bill to relocate, yet his family wants to stay in Phoenix. Can the role demands of his job be reconciled with the demands of his husband and father roles?

Like Bill Patterson, we are all required to play a number of roles, and our behavior varies with each. Bill's behavior when he attends church on Sunday morning is different from his behavior on the golf course later that same day. So different groups impose different role requirements on individuals.

ROLE PERCEPTION   Our view of how we're supposed to act in a given situation is a **role perception**. We engage in certain types of behavior based on how we believe we are supposed to behave. We get these perceptions from stimuli all around us—for example, friends, books, films, television, as when we form an impression of the work of doctors from watching *Grey's Anatomy*. Of course, the primary reason apprenticeship programs exist in many trades and professions is to allow beginners to watch an expert so they can learn to act as they should.

ROLE EXPECTATIONS   **Role expectations** are the way others believe you should act in a given context. The role of a U.S. federal judge is viewed as having propriety and dignity, whereas a football coach is seen as aggressive, dynamic, and inspiring to his players.

ROLE CONFLICT   When compliance with one role requirement may make it difficult to comply with another, the result is **role conflict**.[5] At the extreme, two or more role expectations are mutually contradictory.

Group Property 2: Norms

Did you ever notice that golfers don't speak while their partners are putting on the green or that employees don't criticize their bosses in public? Why not? The answer is norms.

All groups have established **norms**—acceptable standards of behavior shared by their members that express what they ought and ought not to do under certain circumstances. When agreed to and accepted by the group, norms influence members' behavior with a minimum of external controls. Different groups, communities, and societies have different norms, but they all have them.

Norms can cover virtually any aspect of group behavior.[6] Probably the most common is a *performance norm,* providing explicit cues about how hard members should work, what the level of output should be, how to get the job done, what level of tardiness is appropriate, and the like. These norms are extremely powerful in affecting an individual's performance—they are capable of significantly modifying a performance prediction based solely on ability and level of personal motivation. Although arguably the most important, performance norms aren't the only kind. Other types include *appearance norms* (dress codes, unspoken rules about when to look busy), *social arrangement norms* (with whom to eat lunch, whether to form friendships on and off the job), and *resource allocation norms* (assignment of difficult jobs, distribution of resources like pay or equipment).

THE HAWTHORNE STUDIES   Full-scale appreciation of the influence of norms on worker behavior did not occur until the early 1930s, following studies undertaken between 1924 and 1932 at the Western Electric Company's Hawthorne Works in Chicago.[7] Originally initiated by Western Electric officials and later overseen by Harvard professor Elton Mayo, the Hawthorne studies concluded that a worker's behavior and sentiments were closely related, that group influences were significant in affecting individual behavior, and that group standards were highly effective in establishing individual worker output.

The Hawthorne researchers began by examining the relationship between the physical environment and productivity. Illumination and other working conditions were selected to represent this physical environment. The researchers' initial findings contradicted their anticipated results. To the surprise of the researchers, as the light level was dropped in the experimental group, productivity continued to increase in both groups. In fact, productivity decreased in the experimental group only when the light intensity had been reduced to that of moonlight. As a follow-up, the researchers began a second set of experiments in the relay assembly test room at Western Electric. A small group of women assembling small telephone relays was isolated from the main work group so their behavior could be more carefully observed. Observations covering a multiyear period found this small group's output increased steadily. The number of personal and out-sick absences was approximately one-third that recorded by women in the regular production department. It became evident this group's performance was significantly influenced by its status as "special." In essence, workers in both the illumination and assembly-test-room experiments were reacting to the increased attention they received.

A third study, in the bank wiring observation room, was introduced to ascertain the effect of a sophisticated wage incentive plan. The assumption was that individual workers would maximize their productivity when they saw it was directly related to economic rewards. The most important finding of this study was that employees did not individually maximize their outputs. Rather, their output became controlled by a group norm that determined what was a proper day's work. Output was not only being restricted, but individual workers were giving erroneous reports. The total for a week would check with the total week's output, but the daily reports showed a steady level of output, regardless of actual daily production. What was going on?

Interviews determined the group was operating well below its capability and was leveling output to protect itself. Members were afraid that if they significantly increased their output, the unit incentive rate would be cut, the expected daily output would be increased, layoffs might occur, or slower workers would be reprimanded. So the group established its idea of a fair output—neither too much nor too little. They helped each other ensure their reports were nearly level.

The norms the group established included a number of "don'ts." *Don't* be a rate-buster, turning out too much work. *Don't* be a chiseler, turning out too little work. *Don't* squeal on any of your peers. How did the group enforce these norms? The methods included sarcasm, name-calling, ridicule, and even punches to the upper arm of any member who violated the group's norms. Members also ostracized individuals whose behavior was against the group's interest.

The Hawthorne studies made an important contribution to our understanding of the significant place that norms have in determining individual work behavior.

CONFORMITY   As a member of a group, you desire acceptance by the group. Thus you are susceptible to conforming to the group's norms. There is considerable evidence that groups can place strong pressures on individual members to change their attitudes and behaviors to conform to the group's standard.

> Conformity is a problem with groups; managers should encourage group leaders to actively seek input from all members and avoid expressing their own opinions, especially in the early stages of deliberation.

Do individuals conform to the pressures of all the groups to which they belong? Obviously not, because people belong to many groups, and their norms vary and are sometimes contradictory. So what do people do? They conform to the important groups to which they belong or hope to belong. These important groups are **reference groups**, in which a person is aware of other members, defines himself or herself as a member or would like to be a member, and feels group members are significant to him or her.[8] The implication, then, is that all groups do not impose equal conformity pressures on their members.

The impact that group pressures for **conformity** can have on an individual member's judgment was demonstrated in now-classic studies by Solomon Asch.[9] Asch made up groups of seven or eight people who were asked to compare two cards held by the experimenter. One card had one line, and the other had three lines of varying length, one of which was identical to the line on the one-line card, as Exhibit 8.3 shows. The difference in line length was quite obvious; in fact, under ordinary conditions, subjects made fewer than 1 percent errors in announcing aloud which of the three lines matched the single line. But what happens if members of the group begin giving incorrect answers? Will pressure to conform cause an unsuspecting subject (USS) to alter an answer? Asch arranged the group so only the USS was unaware the experiment was rigged. The seating was prearranged so the USS was one of the last to announce a decision.

EXHIBIT 8.3
Example of Cards
Used in Asch's
Study

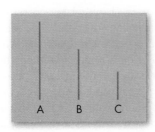

The experiment began with several sets of matching exercises. All the subjects gave the right answers. On the third set, however, the first subject gave an obviously wrong answer—for example, saying "C" in Exhibit 8.3. The next subject gave the same wrong answer, and so did the others. Now the dilemma confronting the USS was this: publicly state a perception that differs from the announced position of the others in the group, or give an incorrect answer in order to agree with the others?

The results over many experiments and trials showed 75 percent of subjects gave at least one answer that conformed—that they knew was wrong but was consistent with the replies of other group members—and the average conformer gave wrong answers 37 percent of the time. What meaning can we draw from these results? They suggest group norms press us toward conformity. We desire to be one of the group and therefore avoid being visibly different.

This research was conducted more than 50 years ago. Has time altered the conclusions' validity? And should we consider them generalizable across cultures? Evidence indicates levels of conformity have steadily declined since Asch's studies in the early 1950s, and his findings *are* culture-bound.[10] Conformity to social norms is higher in collectivist cultures, but it is still a powerful force in groups in individualistic countries.

DEVIANT WORKPLACE BEHAVIOR   LeBron Hunt is frustrated by a co-worker who constantly spreads malicious and unsubstantiated rumors about him. Debra Hundley is tired of a member of her work team who, when confronted with a problem, takes out his frustration by yelling and screaming at her and other members. And Hae-sook Kim recently quit her job as a dental hygienist after being constantly sexually harassed by her employer.

What do these three episodes have in common? They represent employees exposed to acts of *deviant workplace behavior.*[11] **Deviant workplace behavior** (also called *antisocial behavior* or *workplace incivility*) is voluntary behavior that violates significant organizational norms and, in doing so, threatens the well-being of the organization or its members.

Few organizations will admit to creating or condoning conditions that encourage and maintain deviant norms. Yet they exist. Employees report an increase in rudeness and disregard toward others by bosses and co-workers in recent years. And nearly half of employees who have suffered this incivility say it has led them to think about changing jobs, with 12 percent actually quitting because of it.[12] A study of nearly 1,500 respondents found that in addition to increasing turnover intentions, incivility at work increased reports of psychological stress and physical illness.[13]

Like norms in general, individual employees' antisocial actions are shaped by the group context within which they work. Evidence demonstrates that antisocial behavior exhibited by a work group is a significant predictor of an individual's antisocial behavior at work.[14] In other words, deviant workplace behavior is likely to flourish where it's supported by group norms. Workers who socialize either at or outside work with people who are frequently absent from work are more likely to be absent themselves.[15] What this means for managers is that when deviant workplace norms surface, employee cooperation, commitment, and motivation are likely to suffer. This, in turn, can reduce employee productivity and job satisfaction and increase turnover.

Someone who ordinarily wouldn't engage in deviant behavior might be more likely to do so when working in a group. A recent study suggests those working in a group were more likely to lie, cheat, and steal than individuals working alone. As shown in Exhibit 8.4, in this study, no individual working alone lied, but 22 percent of those working in groups did. Those working in groups also were more likely to cheat on a task (55 percent versus 23 percent of individuals working alone) and steal (29 percent compared to 10 percent working alone).[16] Groups provide a shield of anonymity, so someone who might ordinarily be afraid of getting caught can rely on the fact that other group members had the same opportunity, creating a false sense of confidence that may result in more aggressive behavior. Thus, deviant behavior depends on the accepted norms of the group—or even whether an individual is part of a group.

Group Property 3: Status

STATUS   A socially defined position or rank given to groups or group members by others—permeates every society. Even the smallest group will develop roles, rights, and rituals to differentiate its members. **Status** is a significant motivator and has major behavioral consequences when individuals perceive a disparity between what they believe their status is and what others perceive it to be.

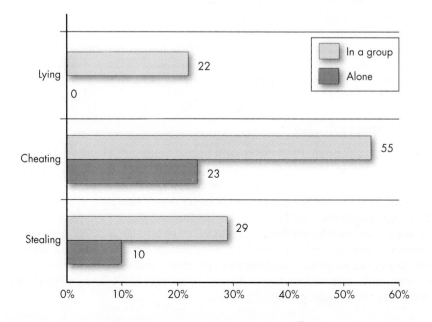

EXHIBIT 8.4
Groups and Deviant Behavior

Source: A. Erez, H. Elms, and E. Fong, "Lying, Cheating, Stealing: Groups and the Ring of Gyges," paper presented at the Academy of Management Annual Meeting, Honolulu, HI, August 8, 2005. Reprinted by permission of the authors.

WHAT DETERMINES STATUS?   According to **status characteristics theory**, status tends to derive from one of three sources:[17]

1. *The power a person wields over others.* Because they likely control the group's resources, people who control the outcomes tend to be perceived as high status.
2. *A person's ability to contribute to a group's goals.* People whose contributions are critical to the group's success tend to have high status. Some thought NBA star Kobe Bryant had more say over player decisions than his coaches (though not as much as Bryant wanted!).
3. *An individual's personal characteristics.* Someone whose personal characteristics are positively valued by the group (good looks, intelligence, money, or a friendly personality) typically has higher status than someone with fewer valued attributes.

STATUS AND NORMS   Status has some interesting effects on the power of norms and pressures to conform. High-status individuals are often given more freedom to deviate from norms than are other group members. People in high-status jobs (such as physicians, lawyers, or executives) have especially negative reactions to social pressure exerted by people in low-status jobs. Physicians actively resist administrative decisions made by lower-ranking insurance company employees.[18] High-status people are also better able to resist conformity pressures than their lower-status peers. An individual who is highly valued by a group but doesn't need or care about the group's social rewards is particularly able to disregard conformity norms.[19]

These findings explain why many star athletes, celebrities, top-performing salespeople, and outstanding academics seem oblivious to appearance and social norms that constrain their peers. As high-status individuals, they're given a wider range of discretion as long as their activities aren't severely detrimental to group goal achievement.

STATUS AND GROUP INTERACTION   High-status people tend to be more assertive group members.[20] They speak out more often, criticize more, state more commands, and interrupt others more often. But status differences actually inhibit diversity of ideas and creativity in groups, because lower-status members tend to participate less actively in group discussions. When lower-status members possess expertise and insights that could aid the group, they are not likely to be fully utilized, thus reducing the group's overall performance.

Group Property 4: Size

Does the size of a group affect the group's overall behavior? The answer is a definite "yes," but the effect depends on what dependent variables you look at. The evidence indicates smaller groups are faster at completing tasks than larger ones and that individuals perform better in smaller groups than in larger ones.[21] However, in problem solving, large groups consistently get better marks than their smaller counterparts.[22] Translating these results into specific numbers is a bit more hazardous, but large groups—those with a dozen or more members—are good for gaining diverse input. So if the goal of the group is fact-finding, larger groups should be more effective. Smaller groups are better at doing something productive with that input. Groups of approximately seven members tend to be more effective for taking action.

One of the most important findings about the size of a group concerns **social loafing**, the tendency for individuals to expend less effort when working collectively than alone.[23] It directly challenges the logic that the productivity of the group as a whole should at least equal the sum of the productivity of the individuals in that group.

A common stereotype about groups is that team spirit spurs individual effort and enhances the group's overall productivity. But that stereotype may be wrong. In the late 1920s, German psychologist Max Ringelmann compared the results of individual and group performance on a rope-pulling task.[24] He expected that three people pulling together should exert three times as much pull on the rope as one person, and eight people eight times as much. Ringelmann's results, however, didn't confirm his expectations. One person pulling on a rope alone exerted an average of 63 kilograms of force. In groups of three, the per-person force dropped to 53 kilograms. And in groups of eight, it fell to only 31 kilograms per person.

Replications of Ringelmann's research with similar tasks have generally supported his findings.[25] Group performance increases with group size, but the addition of new members has diminishing returns on productivity. So more may be better in that total productivity of a group of four is greater than that of three, but the individual productivity of each member declines.

What causes social loafing? It may be a belief that others in the group are not carrying their fair share. If you see others as lazy or inept, you can reestablish equity by reducing your effort. Another explanation is the dispersion of responsibility. Because group results cannot be attributed to any single person, the relationship between an individual's input and the group's output is clouded. Individuals may then be tempted to become free riders and coast on the group's efforts. The implications for OB are significant. When managers use collective work situations to enhance morale and teamwork, they must also be able to identify individual efforts. Otherwise, they must weigh the potential losses in productivity from using groups against possible gains in worker satisfaction.

There are several ways to prevent social loafing: (1) Set group goals, so the group has a common purpose to strive toward; (2) increase intergroup competition, which again focuses on the shared outcome; (3) engage in peer evaluation so each person evaluates each other person's contribution; (4) select members who have high motivation and prefer to work in groups, and (5) if possible, base group rewards in part on each member's unique contributions.[26] Although none of these is a magic bullet that will prevent social loafing in all cases, they should help minimize its effect.

Group Property 5: Cohesiveness

Groups differ in their **cohesiveness**—the degree to which members are attracted to each other and motivated to stay in the group. Some work groups are cohesive because the members have spent a great deal of time together, or the group's small size facilitates high interaction, or external threats have brought members close together. Cohesiveness is important because it affects group productivity.[27]

Studies consistently show that the relationship between cohesiveness and productivity depends on the group's performance-related norms.[28] If performance-related norms for quality, output, and cooperation with outsiders, for instance, are high, a cohesive group will be more productive than will a less cohesive group. But if cohesiveness is high and performance norms are low, productivity will be low. If cohesiveness is low and performance norms are high, productivity increases, but less than in the high-cohesiveness/high-norms situation. When cohesiveness and performance-related norms are both low, productivity tends to fall into the low-to-moderate range.

What can you do to encourage group cohesiveness? (1) Make the group smaller, (2) encourage agreement with group goals, (3) increase the time members spend together, (4) increase the group's status and the perceived difficulty of attaining membership, (5) stimulate competition with other groups, (6) give rewards to the group rather than to individual members, and (7) physically isolate the group.[29]

GROUP DECISION MAKING

The belief—characterized by juries—that two heads are better than one has long been accepted as a basic component of the U.S. legal system and those of many other countries. Today, many decisions in organizations are made by groups, teams, or committees. In this section, we discuss group decision making.

Groups Versus the Individual

Decision-making groups may be widely used in organizations, but are group decisions preferable to those made by an individual alone? The answer depends on a number of factors. Let's begin by looking at the strengths and weaknesses of group decision making.[30]

STRENGTHS OF GROUP DECISION MAKING   Groups generate *more complete information and knowledge.* By aggregating the resources of several individuals, groups bring more input as well as heterogeneity into the decision process. They offer *increased diversity of views.* This opens up the opportunity to consider more approaches and alternatives. Finally, groups lead to increased *acceptance of a solution.* Many decisions fail because people don't accept the solution. Group members who participated in making a decision are more likely to enthusiastically support the decision and encourage others to accept it.

WEAKNESSES OF GROUP DECISION MAKING   Group decisions have their drawbacks. They're time consuming because groups typically take more time to reach a solution. There are *conformity pressures.* The desire by group members to be accepted and considered an asset to the group can squash any overt disagreement. Group discussion can be *dominated by one or a few members.* If they're low- and medium-ability members, the group's overall effectiveness will suffer. Finally, group decisions suffer from *ambiguous responsibility.* In an individual decision, it's clear who is accountable for the final outcome. In a group decision, the responsibility of any single member is diluted.

EFFECTIVENESS AND EFFICIENCY   Whether groups are more effective than individuals depends on how you define effectiveness. Group decisions are generally more *accurate* than the decisions of the average individual in a group but less accurate than the judgments of the most accurate.[31] In terms of *speed,* individuals are superior. If *creativity* is important, groups tend to be more effective. And if effectiveness means the degree of *acceptance* the final solution achieves, the nod again goes to the group.[32]

But we cannot consider effectiveness without also assessing efficiency. Groups almost always stack up a poor second to the individual decision maker. With few exceptions, group decision making consumes more work hours than if an individual were to tackle the same problem alone. The exceptions tend to be the instances in which, to achieve comparable quantities of diverse input, the single decision maker must spend a great deal of time reviewing files and talking to people. Because groups can include members from diverse areas, the time spent searching for information can be reduced. However, as we noted, these advantages in efficiency tend to be the exception. Groups are generally less efficient than individuals. In deciding whether to use groups, then, managers must assess whether increases in effectiveness are more than enough to offset the reductions in efficiency.

Groupthink and Groupshift

Two by-products of group decision making have the potential to affect a group's ability to appraise alternatives objectively and arrive at high-quality solutions.

> Group decision making is not always better than individual decision making.

The first phenomenon, called **groupthink**, relates to norms. It describes situations in which group pressures for conformity deter the group from critically appraising unusual, minority, or unpopular views. Groupthink is a disease that attacks many groups and can dramatically hinder their performance. The second phenomenon is **groupshift**, which describes the way, in discussing a given set of alternatives and arriving at a solution, group members tend to exaggerate the initial positions they hold. In some situations, caution dominates and there is a conservative shift. More often, however, groups tend toward a risky shift. Let's look at each of these phenomena in more detail.

GROUPTHINK Have you ever felt like speaking up in a meeting, a classroom, or an informal group but decided against it? One reason may have been shyness. Or you may have been a victim of groupthink, which occurs when the norm for consensus overrides the realistic appraisal of alternative courses and the full expression of deviant, minority, or unpopular views. The individual's mental efficiency, reality testing, and moral judgment deteriorate as a result of group pressures.[33]

We have all seen the symptoms of the groupthink phenomenon:

1. Group members rationalize any resistance to the assumptions they have made. No matter how strongly the evidence may contradict their basic assumptions, members behave so as to reinforce them.
2. Members apply direct pressures on those who momentarily express doubts about any of the group's shared views, or who question the validity of arguments supporting the alternative favored by the majority.
3. Members who have doubts or differing points of view seek to avoid deviating from what appears to be group consensus by keeping silent about misgivings and even minimizing to themselves the importance of their doubts.
4. There is an illusion of unanimity. If someone doesn't speak, it's assumed he or she is in full accord. In other words, abstention becomes a "yes" vote.

Groupthink appears closely aligned with the conclusions Asch drew in his experiments with a lone dissenter. Individuals who hold a position different from that of the dominant majority are under pressure to suppress, withhold, or modify their true feelings and beliefs. As members of a group, we find it more pleasant to be in agreement—to be a positive part of the group—than to be a disruptive force, even if disruption is necessary to improve the effectiveness of the group's decisions.

Does groupthink attack all groups? No. It seems to occur most often when there is a clear group identity, when members hold a positive image of their group that they want to protect, and when the group perceives a collective threat to this positive image.[34] So groupthink is not a dissenter-suppression mechanism as much as it's a means for a group to protect its positive image. For NASA, groupthink's problems stem from its attempt to confirm its identity as "the elite organization that could do no wrong."[35]

What can managers do to minimize groupthink?[36] First, they can monitor group size. People grow more intimidated and hesitant as group size increases, and, although there is no magic number that will eliminate groupthink, individuals are likely to feel less personal responsibility when groups get larger than about ten members. Managers should also encourage group leaders to play an impartial role. Leaders should actively seek input from all members and avoid expressing their own opinions, especially in the early stages of deliberation. In addition, managers should appoint one group member to play the role of devil's advocate; this member's role is to overtly challenge the majority position and offer divergent perspectives. Still another suggestion is to use exercises that stimulate active discussion of diverse alternatives without threatening the group and intensifying identity protection. One such exercise is to have group members delay discussion of possible gains so they can first talk about the dangers or risks inherent in a decision. Requiring members to first focus on the negatives of an alternative makes the group less likely to stifle dissenting views and more likely to gain an objective evaluation.

GROUP SHIFT OR GROUP POLARIZATION   There are differences between group decisions and the individual decisions of group members.[37] Sometimes group decisions are more conservative. More often, they lean toward greater risk.[38]

What appears to happen in groups is that the discussion leads members toward a more extreme view of the position they already held. Conservatives become more cautious, and more aggressive types take on more risk. The group discussion tends to exaggerate the initial position of the group.

We can view group polarization as a special case of groupthink. The group's decision reflects the dominant decision-making norm that develops during discussion. Whether the shift in the group's decision is toward greater caution or more risk depends on the dominant pre-discussion norm.

The shift toward risk has generated several explanations.[39] It's been argued, for instance, that discussion makes the members more comfortable with each other and, thus, more bold and daring. Another argument is that the group diffuses responsibility. Group decisions free any single member from accountability for the group's final choice, so greater risks can be taken. It's also likely that people take on extreme positions because they want to demonstrate how different they are from the outgroup.[40] People on the fringes of political or social movements take on more and more extreme positions just to prove they are really committed to the cause.

So how should you use the findings on groupshift? Recognize that group decisions exaggerate the initial position of the individual members, that the shift has been shown more often to be toward greater risk, and that which way a group will shift is a function of the members' pre-discussion inclinations.

We now turn to the techniques by which groups make decisions. These reduce some of the dysfunctional aspects of group decision making.

Group Decision-Making Techniques

The most common form of group decision making takes place in **interacting groups**. Members meet face to face and rely on both verbal and nonverbal interaction to communicate. But as our discussion of groupthink demonstrated, interacting groups often censor themselves and pressure individual members toward conformity of opinion. Brainstorming and the nominal group technique have been proposed as ways to reduce problems inherent in the traditional interacting group.

Brainstorming can overcome the pressures for conformity that dampen creativity[41] by encouraging any and all alternatives while withholding criticism.

In a typical brainstorming session, a half dozen to a dozen people sit around a table. The group leader states the problem in a clear manner so all participants understand. Members then freewheel as many alternatives as they can in a given length of time. No criticism is allowed, and all alternatives are recorded for later discussion and analysis. One idea stimulates others, and judgments of even the most bizarre suggestions are withheld until later to encourage group members to "think the unusual."

Brainstorming may indeed generate ideas—but not in a very efficient manner. Research consistently shows individuals working alone generate more ideas than a group in a brainstorming session. One reason for this is "production blocking." When people are generating ideas in a group, many are talking at once, which blocks the thought process and eventually impedes the sharing of ideas. The following technique goes further than brainstorming by helping groups arrive at a preferred solution.[42]

The **nominal group technique** restricts discussion or interpersonal communication during the decision-making process, hence the term *nominal*. Group members are all physically present, as in a traditional committee meeting, but they operate independently. Specifically, a problem is presented and then the group takes the following steps:

1. Members meet as a group, but before any discussion takes place, each independently writes down ideas on the problem.
2. After this silent period, each member presents one idea to the group. No discussion takes place until all ideas have been presented and recorded.
3. The group discusses the ideas for clarity and evaluates them.
4. Each group member silently and independently rank-orders the ideas. The idea with the highest aggregate ranking determines the final decision.

The chief advantage of the nominal group technique is that it permits a group to meet formally but does not restrict independent thinking, as does an interacting group. Research generally shows nominal groups outperform brainstorming groups.[43]

Each of the three group-decision techniques has its own set of strengths and weaknesses. The choice depends on what criteria you want to emphasize and the cost–benefit trade-off. An interacting group is good for achieving commitment to a solution, brainstorming develops group cohesiveness, and the nominal group technique is an inexpensive means for generating a large number of ideas.

Global Implications

Most research on groups has been conducted in North America, but that situation is changing quickly. Cross-cultural issues are particularly important in three areas.

Status and Culture

Do cultural differences affect status? The answer is a resounding "yes."[44]

The importance of status does vary among cultures. The French are highly status conscious. Countries also differ on the criteria that create status. Latin Americans and Asians derive status from family position and formal roles in organizations. In the United States and Australia, in contrast, status is more often conferred for accomplishments than for titles or family trees.[45]

Thus it is important to understand who and what holds status when interacting with people from a culture different from one's own. A U.S. manager who doesn't know that office size is not a measure of a Japanese executive's position is likely to unintentionally offend his overseas counterparts and lessen his interpersonal effectiveness, as is someone who fails to grasp the importance the British place on family genealogy and social class.

Social Loafing

Social loafing appears to have a Western bias. It's consistent with individualistic cultures, such as the United States and Canada, that are dominated by self-interest. It is *not* consistent with collective societies, in which individuals are motivated by in-group goals. In studies comparing U.S. employees with employees from the People's Republic of China and Israel (both collectivist societies), the Chinese and Israelis showed no propensity to engage in social loafing and actually performed better in a group than alone.

Group Diversity

More research is being done on how diversity influences group performance. Some research looks at cultural diversity and some at racial, gender, and other differences. Overall, studies identify both benefits and costs from group diversity.

Diversity appears to increase group conflict, especially in the early stages of a group's tenure, which often lowers group morale and raises dropout rates. One study compared groups that were culturally diverse (composed of people from different countries) and homogeneous (composed of people from the same country). On a wilderness survival exercise the groups performed equally well, but the diverse groups were less satisfied with their groups, were less cohesive, and had more conflict.[46]

However, evidence is accumulating that, over time, culturally and demographically diverse groups may perform better, if they can get over their initial conflicts. Why might this be so?

Surface-level diversity—observable characteristics such as national origin, race, and gender—alerts people to possible differences in deep-level diversity—underlying attitudes, values, and opinions. Although those differences can lead to conflict, they also provide an opportunity to solve problems in unique ways.

One study of jury behavior found diverse juries more likely to deliberate longer, share more information, and make fewer factual errors when discussing evidence. Two studies of MBA student groups found surface-level diversity led to greater openness even when there was no deep-level diversity. In such cases, the surface-level diversity of a group may subconsciously cue team members to be more open-minded in their views.[47]

In summary, the impact of cultural diversity on groups is mixed. It is difficult to be in a diverse group in the short term. However, if members can weather their differences, over time diversity may help them be more open-minded and creative, allowing them to do better in the long run. But even positive effects are unlikely to be especially strong. As one review stated, "The business case (in terms of demonstrable financial results) for diversity remains hard to support based on the extant research."[48]

Implications for Managers

Performance

Among the most prominent properties related to group performance are role perception, norms, status differences, size of the group, and cohesiveness.

Role perception and an employee's performance evaluation are positively related.[49] The degree of congruence between the employee's and the boss's perception of the employee's job influences the degree to which the boss will judge that employee effective. An employee whose role perception fulfills the boss's role expectations will receive a higher performance evaluation.

Norms control behavior by establishing standards of right and wrong. The norms of a given group can help explain members' behaviors for managers. When norms support high output, managers can expect markedly higher individual performance than when they aim to restrict output. Norms that support antisocial behavior increase the likelihood that individuals will engage in deviant workplace activities.

Status inequities create frustration and can adversely influence productivity and willingness to remain with an organization. Incongruence is likely to reduce motivation and motivate a search for ways to bring about fairness (say, by taking another job). Because lower-status people tend to participate less in group discussions, groups with high status differences are likely to inhibit input from lower-status members and reduce their potential.

The impact of size on a group's performance depends on the type of task. Larger groups are more effective at fact-finding activities, smaller groups at action-taking tasks. Our knowledge of social loafing suggests that managers using larger groups should also provide measures of individual performance.

Cohesiveness can influence a group's level of productivity or not, depending on the group's performance-related norms.

Satisfaction

High congruence between a boss's and an employee's perception of the employee's job correlates strongly with high employee satisfaction.[50] Role conflict is associated with job-induced tension and job dissatisfaction.[51]

Most people prefer to communicate with others at their own status level or a higher one rather than with those below them.[52] As a result, we should expect satisfaction to be greater among employees whose job minimizes interaction with individuals lower in status than themselves.

The group size–satisfaction relationship is what we would intuitively expect: Larger groups are associated with lower satisfaction.[53] As size increases, opportunities for participation and social interaction decrease, as does the ability of members to identify with the group's accomplishments. At the same time, having more members also prompts dissension, conflict, and the formation of subgroups, which all act to make the group a less pleasant entity of which to be a part.

CHAPTER 9

Understanding Work Teams

After studying this chapter, you should be able to:

- Contrast groups and teams and analyze the growing popularity of teams in organizations.
- Compare and contrast four types of teams.
- Identify the characteristics of effective teams.
- Show how organizations can create team players.
- Decide when to use individuals instead of teams.
- Show how our understanding of teams differs in a global context.

WHY HAVE TEAMS BECOME SO POPULAR?

Decades ago, when companies such as W. L. Gore, Volvo, and General Foods introduced teams into their production processes, it made news because no one else was doing it. Today, it's just the opposite. The organization that *doesn't* use teams has become newsworthy. Teams are everywhere.

How do we explain the current popularity of teams? As organizations have restructured themselves to compete more effectively and efficiently, they have turned to teams as a better way to use employee talents. Teams are more flexible and responsive to changing events than traditional departments or other forms of permanent groupings. They can quickly assemble, deploy, refocus, and disband. But don't overlook the motivational properties of teams. Consistent with our discussion of employee involvement as a motivator, teams facilitate employee participation in operating decisions. So another explanation for their popularity is that they are an effective means for management to democratize organizations and increase employee motivation.

The fact that organizations have turned to teams doesn't necessarily mean they're always effective. Decision makers, as humans, can be swayed by fads and herd mentality. Are teams truly effective? What conditions affect their potential? How do members work together? These are some of the questions we'll answer in this chapter.

DIFFERENCES BETWEEN GROUPS AND TEAMS

Groups and teams are not the same thing. In this section, we define and clarify the difference between work groups and work teams.[1]

In Chapter 8, we defined a *group* as two or more individuals, interacting and interdependent, who have come together to achieve particular objectives. A **work group** is a group that interacts primarily to share information and make decisions to help each member perform within his or her area of responsibility.

Work groups have no need or opportunity to engage in collective work that requires joint effort. So their performance is merely the summation of each group member's individual contribution. There is no positive synergy that would create an overall level of performance greater than the sum of the inputs.

A **work team,** on the other hand, generates positive synergy through coordinated effort. The individual efforts result in a level of performance greater than the sum of those individual inputs. Exhibit 9.1 highlights the differences between work groups and work teams.

These definitions help clarify why so many organizations have recently restructured work processes around teams. Management is looking for positive synergy that will allow the organizations to increase performance. The extensive use of teams creates the *potential* for an organization to generate greater outputs with no increase in inputs. Notice, however, that we said *potential*. There is nothing inherently magical that ensures the achievement of positive synergy in the creation of teams. Merely calling a *group* a *team* doesn't automatically improve its performance. As we show later in this chapter, effective teams have certain common characteristics. If management hopes to gain increases in organizational performance through the use of teams, its teams must possess these.

TYPES OF TEAMS

Teams can make products, provide services, negotiate deals, coordinate projects, offer advice, and make decisions. In this section, we describe the four most common types of teams in an organization: *problem-solving teams, self-managed work teams, cross-functional teams,* and *virtual teams* (see Exhibit 9.2).

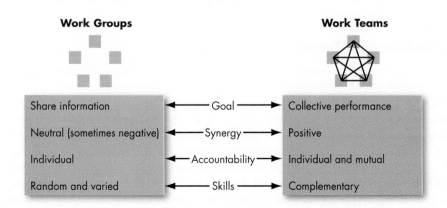

EXHIBIT 9.1
Comparing Work Groups and Work Teams

EXHIBIT 9.2
Four Types
of Teams

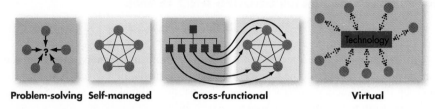

Problem-solving   Self-managed   Cross-functional   Virtual

Problem-Solving Teams

In the past, teams were typically composed of 5 to 12 hourly employees from the same department who met for a few hours each week to discuss ways of improving quality, efficiency, and the work environment.[2] In these **problem-solving team,** members share ideas or suggest how work processes and methods can be improved; they rarely have the authority to unilaterally implement any of their suggestions. Merrill Lynch created a problem-solving team to figure out ways to reduce the number of days it took to open a new cash management account.[3] By suggesting cutting the number of steps from 46 to 36, the team reduced the average number of days from 15 to 8.

Self-Managed Work Teams

Problem-solving teams only make recommendations. Some organizations have gone further and created teams that not only solve problems but implement solutions and take responsibility for outcomes.

Self-managed work teams are groups of employees (typically 10 to 15 in number) who perform highly related or interdependent jobs and take on many of the responsibilities of their former supervisors.[4] Typically, these tasks are planning and scheduling work, assigning tasks to members, making operating decisions, taking action on problems, and working with suppliers and customers. Fully self-managed work teams even select their own members and evaluate each other's performance. Supervisory positions take on decreased importance and are sometimes even eliminated.

But research on the effectiveness of self-managed work teams has not been uniformly positive.[5] Self-managed teams do not typically manage conflicts well. When disputes arise, members stop cooperating and power struggles ensue, which leads to lower group performance.[6] Moreover, although individuals on these teams report higher levels of job satisfaction than other individuals, they also sometimes have higher absenteeism and turnover rates.

Cross-Functional Teams

The Boeing Company created a team made up of employees from production, planning, quality control, tooling, design engineering, and information systems to automate shims on the company's C-17 program. The team's suggestions resulted in drastically reduced cycle time and cost as well as improved quality.[7] This example illustrates the use of **cross-functional teams,** made up of employees from about the same hierarchical level but different work areas, who come together to accomplish a task.

Many organizations have used horizontal, boundary-spanning groups for decades. In the 1960s, IBM created a large task force of employees from across departments to develop its highly successful System 360. Today, cross-functional teams are so widely used it is hard to imagine a major organizational undertaking without one. All the major automobile manufacturers—Toyota, Honda, Nissan, BMW, GM, Ford, and Chrysler—currently use this form of team to coordinate complex projects. Harley-Davidson relies on specific cross-functional teams to manage each line of its motorcycles. The teams include employees from design, manufacturing, and purchasing as well as representatives from key outside suppliers.[8]

Cross-functional teams are an effective means of allowing people from diverse areas within or even between organizations to exchange information, develop new ideas, solve problems, and coordinate complex projects. Of course, cross-functional teams are no picnic to manage. Their early stages of development are often long, as members learn to work with diversity and complexity. It takes time to build trust and teamwork, especially among people from different backgrounds with different experiences and perspectives.

Virtual Teams

The teams described in the preceding section do their work face to face. **Virtual teams** use computer technology to unite physically dispersed members and achieve a common goal.[9] They allow people to collaborate online—using communication links such as wide-area networks, video conferencing, or e-mail—whether they're a room away or continents apart. Virtual teams are so pervasive, and technology has advanced so far, that it's probably a bit of a misnomer to call them "virtual." Nearly all teams today do at least some of their work remotely.

Despite their ubiquity, virtual teams face special challenges. They may suffer because there is less social rapport and direct interaction among members. They aren't able to duplicate the normal give-and-take of face-to-face discussion. Especially when members haven't personally met, virtual teams tend to be more task oriented and exchange less social–emotional information than face-to-face teams do. Not surprisingly, their members report less satisfaction with the group interaction process than do face-to-face teams. For virtual teams to be effective, management should ensure that (1) trust is established among members (one inflammatory remark in a team member e-mail can severely undermine team trust), (2) team progress is monitored closely (so the team doesn't lose sight of its goals and no team member "disappears"), and (3) the efforts and products of the team are publicized throughout the organization (so the team does not become invisible).[10]

CREATING EFFECTIVE TEAMS

Many have tried to identify factors related to team effectiveness. However, some studies have organized what was once a "veritable laundry list of characteristics"[11] into a relatively focused model.[12] Exhibit 9.3 summarizes what we currently know about what makes teams effective. As you'll see, it builds on many of the group concepts introduced in Chapter 8.

The following discussion is based on the model in Exhibit 9.3. Keep in mind two points. First, teams differ in form and structure. Because the model attempts to generalize across all varieties of teams, avoid rigidly applying its predictions to all teams. Use it as a guide. Second, the model assumes teamwork is preferable to individual work. Creating "effective" teams when individuals can do the job better is like solving the wrong problem perfectly.

EXHIBIT 9.3
Team Effectiveness
Model

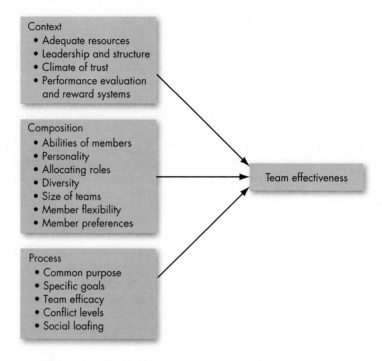

We can organize the key components of effective teams into three general categories. First are the resources and other *contextual* influences that make teams effective. The second relates to the team's *composition*. Finally, *process* variables are events within the team that influence effectiveness. What does *team effectiveness* mean in this model? Typically, it has included objective measures of the team's productivity, managers' ratings of the team's performance, and aggregate measures of member satisfaction.

Context: What Factors Determine Whether Teams Are Successful?

The four contextual factors most significantly related to team performance are adequate resources, effective leadership, a climate of trust, and a performance evaluation and reward system that reflects team contributions.

ADEQUATE RESOURCES   Teams are part of a larger organization system; every work team relies on resources outside the group to sustain it. A scarcity of resources directly reduces the ability of a team to perform its job effectively and achieve its goals. As one study concluded, after looking at 13 factors related to group performance, "perhaps one of the most important characteristics of an effective work group is the support the group receives from the organization."[13] This support includes timely information, proper equipment, adequate staffing, encouragement, and administrative assistance.

LEADERSHIP AND STRUCTURE   Teams can't function if they can't agree on who is to do what and ensure all members share the workload. Agreeing on the specifics of work and how they fit together to integrate individual skills requires leadership and structure, either from management or from the team members themselves. It's true in self-managed teams that team members absorb many of the duties typically assumed by managers. However, a manager's job then becomes managing *outside* (rather than inside) the team.

Leadership is especially important in **multi-team systems,** in which different teams coordinate their efforts to produce a desired outcome. Here, leaders need to empower teams by delegating responsibility to them, and they play the role of facilitator, making sure the teams work together rather than against one another.[14] Teams that establish shared leadership by effectively delegating it are more effective than teams with a traditional single-leader structure.[15]

CLIMATE OF TRUST   Members of effective teams trust each other. They also exhibit trust in their leaders.[16] Interpersonal trust among team members facilitates cooperation, reduces the need to monitor each others' behavior, and bonds members around the belief that others on the team won't take advantage of them. Team members are more likely to take risks and expose vulnerabilities when they believe they can trust others on their team. And, as we will discuss later in the book, trust is the foundation of leadership. It allows a team to accept and commit to its leader's goals and decisions.

PERFORMANCE EVALUATION AND REWARD SYSTEMS   How do you get team members to be both individually and jointly accountable? Individual performance evaluations and incentives may interfere with the development of high-performance teams. So, in addition to evaluating and rewarding employees for their individual contributions, management should modify the traditional, individually oriented evaluation and reward system to reflect team performance.[17] Group-based appraisals, profit sharing, gainsharing, small-group incentives, and other system modifications can reinforce team effort and commitment.

Team Composition

The team composition category includes variables that relate to how teams should be staffed—the ability and personality of team members, allocation of roles and diversity, size of the team, and members' preference for teamwork.

Team composition matters—the optimal way to construct teams depends on the ability, skill, or trait under consideration.

ABILITIES OF MEMBERS   Part of a team's performance depends on the knowledge, skills, and abilities of its individual members.[18] It's true we occasionally read about an athletic team of mediocre players who, because of excellent coaching, determination, and precision teamwork, beat a far more talented group. But such cases make the news precisely because they are unusual. A team's performance is not merely the summation of its individual members' abilities. However, these abilities set limits on what members can do and how effectively they will perform on a team.

A team requires three different types of skills. First, it needs people who have *technical expertise*. Second, it needs people who have the *problem-solving and decision-making skills* to identify problems, generate and evaluate alternatives, and make competent choices. Finally, teams need people with good listening, feedback, conflict resolution, and other *interpersonal skills*.[19] The right mix of these skills is crucial, but they don't all have to be in place at the beginning. It's not uncommon for one or more members to take responsibility for learning the skills in which the group is deficient, thus allowing the team to reach its full potential.

Research reveals some insights into team composition and performance. First, when the task entails considerable thought (solving a complex problem such as reengineering an assembly line), high-ability teams (composed of mostly intelligent members) do better than lower-ability teams, especially when the workload is distributed evenly. That way, team performance does not depend on the weakest link. High-ability teams are also more adaptable to changing situations; they can more effectively apply existing knowledge to new problems.

Second, when tasks are simple, high-ability teams do not perform as well, perhaps because members become bored and turn their attention to other activities that are more stimulating, whereas low-ability teams stay on task. High-ability teams should be reserved for tackling the tough problems. So matching team ability to the task is important.

Finally, the ability of the team's leader also matters. Smart team leaders help less intelligent team members when they struggle with a task. But a less intelligent leader can neutralize the effect of a high-ability team.[20]

PERSONALITY OF MEMBERS   We demonstrated earlier that personality significantly influences individual employee behavior. Many of the dimensions identified in the Big Five personality model are also relevant to team effectiveness; a recent review of the literature identified three.[21] Specifically, teams that rate higher on mean levels of conscientiousness and openness to experience tend to perform better, and the minimum level of team member agreeableness also matters: teams did worse when they had one or more highly disagreeable members. Perhaps one bad apple *can* spoil the whole bunch!

Research has also provided us with a good idea about why these personality traits are important to teams. Conscientious people are valuable in teams because they're good at backing up other team members, and they're also good at sensing when that support is truly needed. Open team members communicate better with one another and throw out more ideas, which makes teams composed of open people more creative and innovative.[22]

Suppose an organization needs to create 20 teams of 4 people each and has 40 highly conscientious people and 40 who score low on conscientiousness. Would the organization be better off (1) forming 10 teams of highly conscientious people and 10 teams of members low on conscientiousness, or (2) "seeding" each team with 2 people who scored high and 2 who scored low on conscientiousness?

By matching individual preferences with team role demands, managers increase the likelihood that the team members will work well together.

Perhaps surprisingly, evidence suggests option 1 is the best choice; performance across the teams will be higher if the organization forms 10 highly conscientious teams and 10 teams low in conscientiousness. "This may be because, in such teams, members who are highly conscientious not only must perform their own tasks but also must perform or re-do the tasks of low-conscientious members. It may also be because such diversity leads to feelings of contribution inequity."[23]

ALLOCATION OF ROLES   Teams have different needs, and members should be selected to ensure all the various roles are filled. A study of 778 major league baseball teams over a 21-year period highlights the importance of assigning roles appropriately.[24] As you might expect, teams with more experienced and skilled members performed better. However, the experience and skill of those in core roles who handle more of the workflow of the team, and who are central to all work processes (in this case, pitchers and catchers), were especially vital. In other words, put your most able, experienced, and conscientious workers in the most central roles in a team.

We can identify nine potential team roles. Successful work teams have selected people to play all these roles based on their skills and preferences.[25] (On many teams, individuals will play multiple roles.) To increase the likelihood the team members will work well together, managers need to understand the individual strengths each person can bring to a team, select members with their strengths in mind, and allocate work assignments that fit with members' preferred styles.

DIVERSITY OF MEMBERS   There is a great deal of discussion and research on the effect of diversity on groups. How does *team* diversity affect *team* performance?

Many of us hold the optimistic view that diversity should be a good thing—diverse teams should benefit from differing perspectives and do better. Two meta-analytic reviews of the research literature show, however, that demographic diversity is essentially unrelated to team performance overall.[26] One qualifier is that gender and ethnic diversity have more negative effects in occupations dominated by white or male employees, but in more demographically balanced occupations diversity is less of a problem. Diversity in function and expertise are positively related to group performance, but these effects are quite small and depend on the situation.

One of the pervasive challenges with teams is that although diversity may have real potential benefits, a team is deeply focused on commonly held information. But to realize their creative potential, diverse teams need to focus not on their similarities but on their differences. Some evidence suggests that when team members believe others have more expertise, they will work to support those members, leading to higher levels of effectiveness.[27] The key is for members of diverse teams to communicate what they uniquely know and also what they don't know. Proper leadership can also improve the performance of diverse teams.[28] When leaders provide an inspirational common goal for members with varying types of education and knowledge, teams are very creative. When leaders don't provide such goals, diverse teams fail to take advantage of their unique skills and are actually *less* creative than teams with homogeneous skills.

The degree to which members of a work unit (group, team, or department) share a common demographic attribute, such as age, sex, race, educational level, or length of service in the organization, is the subject of **organizational demography.** Organizational demography suggests that attributes such as age or the date of joining should help us predict turnover. The logic goes like this: Turnover will be greater among those with dissimilar experiences because communication is more difficult. Conflict and power struggles are more likely and are more severe when they occur. Increased conflict makes membership less attractive, so employees are more likely to quit.

SIZE OF TEAMS   The president of AOL Technologies says the secret to a great team is to "think small. Ideally, your team should have seven to nine people."[29] His advice is supported by evidence.[30] Generally speaking, the most effective teams have five to nine members. And experts suggest using the smallest number of people who can do the task. Unfortunately, managers often err by making teams too large. It may require only four or five members to develop diversity of views and skills, while coordination problems can increase exponentially as team members are added. When teams have excess members, cohesiveness and mutual accountability decline, social loafing increases, and more people communicate less. Members of large teams have trouble coordinating with one another, especially under time pressure. Keep teams at nine or fewer members. If a natural working unit is larger and you want a team effort, consider breaking the group into subteams.

MEMBER PREFERENCES   Not every employee is a team player. Given the option, many employees will select themselves *out* of team participation. When people who would prefer to work alone are required to team up, there is a direct threat to the team's morale and to individual member satisfaction.[31] This suggests that when selecting team members, managers should consider individual preferences along with abilities, personalities, and skills. High-performing teams are likely to be composed of people who prefer working as part of a group.

Team Processes

The final category related to team effectiveness is process variables such as member commitment to a common purpose, establishment of specific team goals, team efficacy, a managed level of conflict, and minimized social loafing. These will be especially important in larger teams and in teams that are highly interdependent.[32]

> Effective teams maintain a common plan and purpose to their actions that guides their actions and concentrates their energies.

Why are processes important to team effectiveness? Let's return to the topic of social loafing. We found that $1 + 1 + 1$ doesn't necessarily add up to 3. When each member's contribution is not clearly visible, individuals tend to decrease their effort. Social loafing, in other words, illustrates a process loss from using teams. But teams should create outputs greater than the sum of their inputs, as when a diverse group develops creative alternatives. Exhibit 9.4 illustrates how group processes can have an impact on a group's actual effectiveness.[33]

Teams are often used in research laboratories because they can draw on the diverse skills of various individuals to produce more meaningful research than could be generated by all the researchers working independently—that is, they produce positive synergy, and their process gains exceed their process losses.

COMMON PLAN AND PURPOSE   Effective teams begin by analyzing the team's mission, developing goals to achieve that mission, and creating strategies for achieving the goals. Teams that establish a clear sense of what needs to be done and how consistently perform better.[34]

Members of successful teams put a tremendous amount of time and effort into discussing, shaping, and agreeing on a purpose that belongs to them both collectively and individually. This common purpose, when accepted by the team, becomes what celestial navigation is to a ship captain: It provides direction and guidance under any and all conditions. Like a ship following the wrong course, teams that don't have good planning skills are doomed; perfectly executing the wrong plan is a lost cause. Effective teams also show **reflexivity,** meaning they reflect on and adjust their master plan when necessary. A team has to have a good plan, but it also has to be willing and able to adapt when conditions call for it.[35]

SPECIFIC GOALS   Successful teams translate their common purpose into specific, measurable, and realistic performance goals. Specific goals facilitate clear communication. They also help teams maintain their focus on getting results.

**EXHIBIT 9.4
Effects of Group
Processes**

Consistent with the research on individual goals, team goals should also be challenging. Difficult goals raise team performance on those criteria for which they're set. So, for instance, goals for quantity tend to raise quantity, goals for accuracy raise accuracy, and so on.[36]

TEAM EFFICACY   Effective teams have confidence in themselves; they believe they can succeed. We call this *team efficacy*.[37] Teams that have been successful raise their beliefs about future success, which, in turn, motivates them to work harder. What can management do to increase team efficacy? Two options are helping the team achieve small successes that build confidence and providing training to improve members' technical and interpersonal skills. The greater the abilities of team members, the more likely the team will develop confidence and the ability to deliver on that confidence.

MENTAL MODELS   Effective teams share accurate **mental models**—knowledge and beliefs (a "psychological map") about how the work gets done. If team members have the wrong mental models, which is particularly likely with teams under acute stress, their performance suffers. In the Iraq War, many military leaders said they underestimated the power of the insurgency and the infighting among Iraqi religious sects. The similarity of team members' mental models matters, too. If team members have different ideas about how to do things, the team will fight over how to do things rather than focus on what needs to be done.[38]

CONFLICT LEVELS   Conflict on a team isn't necessarily bad. Teams completely devoid of conflict are likely to become apathetic and stagnant. Thus, conflict—but not all types—can actually improve team effectiveness.[39] *Relationship conflicts*—those based on interpersonal incompatibilities, tension, and animosity toward others—are almost always dysfunctional. However, on teams performing nonroutine activities, disagreements among members about task content (called *task conflicts*) stimulate discussion, promote critical assessment of problems and options, and can lead to better team decisions. The way conflicts are resolved can also make the difference between effective and ineffective teams. A study of ongoing comments made by 37 autonomous work groups showed that effective teams resolved conflicts by explicitly discussing the issues, whereas ineffective teams had conflicts focused more on personalities and the way things were said.[40]

SOCIAL LOAFING   Individuals can engage in social loafing and coast on the group's effort because their particular contributions can't be identified. Effective teams undermine this tendency by making members individually and jointly accountable for the team's purpose, goals, and approach.[41] Therefore, members should be clear on what they are individually responsible for and what they are jointly responsible for on the team.

TURNING INDIVIDUALS INTO TEAM PLAYERS

We've made a strong case for the value and growing popularity of teams. But many people are not inherently team players, and many organizations have historically nurtured individual accomplishments. Finally, teams fit well in countries that score high on collectivism. But what if an organization wants to introduce teams into a work population of individuals born and raised in an individualistic society? A veteran employee of a large company, who had done well working in an individualistic company in an individualist country, described the experience of joining a team: "I'm learning my lesson. I just had my first negative performance appraisal in 20 years."[42]

So what can organizations do to enhance team effectiveness—to turn individual contributors into team members? Here are options for managers trying to turn individuals into team players.

Selecting: Hiring Team Players

Some people already possess the interpersonal skills to be effective team players. When hiring team members, be sure candidates can fulfill their team roles as well as technical requirements.

When faced with candidates who lack team skills, managers have three options. The candidates can undergo training to make them into team players. If this isn't possible or doesn't work, the other two options are to transfer them to another unit that does not have teams (if possible) or not to hire them. In established organizations that decide to redesign jobs around teams, some employees will resist being team players and may be untrainable. Unfortunately, they typically become casualties of the team approach. Creating teams often means resisting the urge to hire the best talent no matter what.

Training: Creating Team Players

Training specialists conduct exercises that allow employees to experience the satisfaction teamwork can provide. Workshops help employees improve their problem-solving, communication, negotiation, conflict-management, and coaching skills. L'Oréal, for example, found that successful sales teams required much more than being staffed with high-ability salespeople; management had to focus much of its efforts on team building. "What we didn't account for was that many members of our top team in sales had been promoted because they had excellent technical and executional skills," said L'Oréal's senior VP of sales, David Waldock. As a result of the focus on team training, Waldock says, "We are no longer a team just on paper, working independently. We have a real group dynamic now, and it's a good one."[43] Employees also learn the five-stage group development model described in the previous chapter. Developing an effective team doesn't happen overnight—it takes time.

Rewarding: Providing Incentives to Be a Good Team Player

An organization's reward system must be reworked to encourage cooperative efforts rather than competitive ones. Hallmark Cards Inc. added to its basic individual-incentive system an annual bonus based on achievement of team goals. Whole Foods directs most of its performance-based rewards toward team performance. As a result, teams select new members carefully so they will contribute to team effectiveness (and thus team bonuses).[44] It is usually best to set a cooperative tone as soon as possible in the life of a team. As we already noted, teams that switch from a competitive to a cooperative system do not share information and make rushed, poor-quality decisions.[45] Apparently, the low trust typical of the competitive group will not be readily replaced by high trust with a quick change in reward systems. These problems are not seen in teams that have consistently cooperative systems.

Promotions, pay raises, and other forms of recognition should be given to individuals who work effectively as team members by training new colleagues, sharing information, helping resolve team conflicts, and mastering needed new skills. This doesn't mean individual contributions should be ignored; rather, they should be balanced with selfless contributions to the team.

Finally, don't forget the intrinsic rewards, such as camaraderie, that employees can receive from teamwork. It's exciting and satisfying to be part of a successful team. The opportunity for personal development of self and teammates can be a very satisfying and rewarding experience.

BEWARE! TEAMS AREN'T ALWAYS THE ANSWER

Teamwork takes more time and often more resources than individual work. Teams have increased communication demands, conflicts to manage, and meetings to run. So the benefits of using teams have to exceed the costs, and that's not always the case. Before you rush to implement teams, carefully assess whether the work requires or will benefit from a collective effort.

How do you know whether the work of your group would be better done in teams? You can apply three tests to see whether a team fits your situation. First, can the work be done better by more than one person? A good indicator is the complexity of the work and the need for different perspectives. Simple tasks that don't require diverse input are probably better left to individuals. Second, does the work create a common purpose or set of goals for the people in the group that is more than the aggregate of individual goals? Many service departments of new-vehicle dealers have introduced teams that link customer-service people, mechanics, parts specialists, and sales representatives. Such teams can better manage collective responsibility for ensuring customer needs are properly met. The final test is to determine whether the members of the group are interdependent. Using teams makes sense when there is interdependence between tasks—the success of the whole depends on the success of each one, *and* the success of each one depends on the success of the others. Soccer, for instance, is an obvious *team* sport. Success requires a great deal of coordination between interdependent players. Conversely, except possibly for relays, swim teams are not really teams. They're groups of individuals performing individually, whose total performance is merely the aggregate summation of their individual performances.

Global Implications

Research on global considerations in the use of teams is just beginning, but three areas are particularly worth mentioning: the extent of teamwork, self-managed teams, and team cultural diversity.

Extent of Teamwork

Although work teams are pervasive in the United States, some evidence suggests the degree to which teams affect the way work is done is not as significant in the United States as in other countries. One study comparing U.S. workers to Canadian and Asian workers revealed that 51 percent of workers in Asian-Pacific countries and 48 percent of Canadian employees report high levels of teamwork. But only 32 percent of U.S. employees say their organization has a high level of teamwork.[46] Thus, there still is a heavy role for individual contributions in the United States. Given that U.S. culture is highly individualistic, that may continue to be true for quite some time.

Self-Managed Teams

Evidence suggests self-managed teams have not fared well in Mexico, largely due to that culture's low

(continued)

tolerance of ambiguity and uncertainty and employees' strong respect for hierarchical authority.[47] Thus, in countries relatively high in power distance—where roles of leaders and followers are clearly delineated—a team may need to be structured so leadership roles are spelled out and power relationships identified.

Team Cultural Diversity and Team Performance

We have discussed research on team diversity in race or gender. But what about diversity created by national differences? Like the earlier research, evidence here indicates these elements of diversity interfere with team processes, at least in the short term. Cultural diversity does seem to be an asset for tasks that call for a variety of viewpoints. But culturally heterogeneous teams have more difficulty learning to work with each other and solving problems. The good news is that these difficulties seem to dissipate with time. Although newly formed culturally diverse teams underperform newly formed culturally homogeneous teams, the differences disappear after about 3 months.[48] Fortunately, some team performance–enhancing strategies seem to work well in many cultures. One study found that teams in the European Union made up of members from collectivist and individualist countries benefited equally from group goals.[49]

Implications for Managers

Few trends have influenced jobs as much as the massive movement to introduce teams into the workplace. The shift from working alone to working on teams requires employees to cooperate with others, share information, confront differences, and sublimate personal interests for the greater good of the team.

Effective teams have common characteristics. They have adequate resources, effective leadership, a climate of trust, and a performance evaluation and reward system that reflects team contributions. These teams have individuals with technical expertise as well as problem-solving, decision-making, and interpersonal skills and the right traits, especially conscientiousness and openness. Effective teams also tend to be small—with fewer than ten people, preferably of diverse backgrounds. They have members who fill role demands and who prefer to be part of a group. And the work that members do provides freedom and autonomy, the opportunity to use different skills and talents, the ability to complete a whole and identifiable task or product, and work that has a substantial impact on others. Finally, effective teams have members who believe in the team's capabilities and are committed to a common plan and purpose, an accurate shared mental model of what is to be accomplished, specific team goals, a manageable level of conflict, and a minimal degree of social loafing.

Because individualistic organizations and societies attract and reward individual accomplishments, it can be difficult to create team players in these environments. To make the conversion, management should try to select individuals who have the interpersonal skills to be effective team players, provide training to develop teamwork skills, and reward individuals for cooperative efforts.

CHAPTER 10

Communication

After studying this chapter, you should be able to:

- Describe the communication process and distinguish between formal and informal communication.
- Contrast downward, upward, and lateral communication and provide examples of each.
- Contrast oral, written, and nonverbal communication.
- Contrast formal communication networks and the grapevine.
- Identify common barriers to effective communication.
- Show how to overcome the potential problems in cross-cultural communication.

No individual, group, or organization can exist without communication: the transfer of meaning among its members. It is only through transmitting meaning from one person to another that information and ideas can be conveyed. Communication, however, is more than merely imparting meaning. It must also be understood. In a group in which one member speaks only German and the others do not know German, the individual speaking German will not be fully understood. Therefore, **communication** must include both *the transfer and the understanding of meaning.*

Before making too many generalizations concerning communication and problems in communicating effectively, we need to describe the communication process.

THE COMMUNICATION PROCESS

Before communication can take place it needs a purpose, a message to be conveyed between a sender and a receiver. The sender encodes the message (converts it to a symbolic form) and passes it through a medium (channel) to the receiver, who decodes it. The result is transfer of meaning from one person to another.[1]

Exhibit 10.1 depicts this **communication process.** The key parts of this model are (1) the sender, (2) encoding, (3) the message, (4) the channel, (5) decoding, (6) the receiver, (7) noise, and (8) feedback.

The *sender* initiates a message by encoding a thought. The *message* is the actual physical product of the sender's *encoding.* When we speak, the speech is the message. When we write, the writing is the message. When we gesture, the movements of our arms and the expressions on our faces are the message.

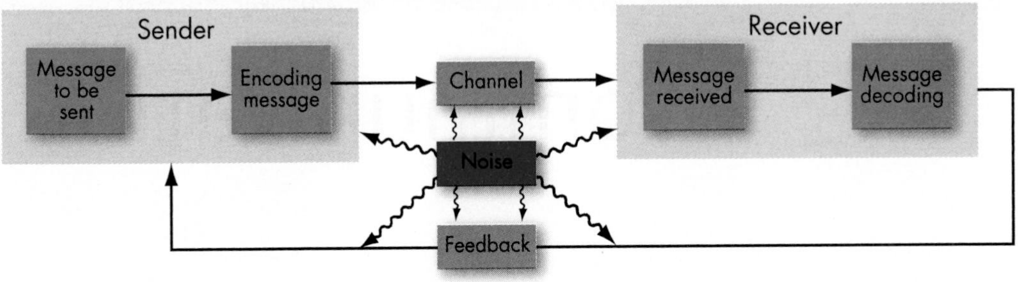

EXHIBIT 10.1 The Communication Process

The *channel* is the medium through which the message travels. The sender selects it, determining whether to use a formal or informal channel. **Formal channels** are established by the organization and transmit messages related to the professional activities of members. They traditionally follow the authority chain within the organization. Other forms of messages, such as personal or social, follow **informal channels,** which are spontaneous and emerge as a response to individual choices.[2] The *receiver* is the person(s) to whom the message is directed, who must first translate the symbols into understandable form. This step is the *decoding* of the message. *Noise* represents communication barriers that distort the clarity of the message, such as perceptual problems, information overload, semantic difficulties, or cultural differences. The final link in the communication process is a feedback loop. *Feedback* is the check on how successful we have been in transferring our messages as originally intended. It determines whether understanding has been achieved.

DIRECTION OF COMMUNICATION

Communication can flow vertically or laterally. We further subdivide the vertical dimension into downward and upward directions.[3]

Downward Communication

Downward, upward, and lateral directions of communication have their own challenges; understand and manage these unique challenges.

Communication that flows from one level of a group or organization to a lower level is *downward communication*. It's used by group leaders and managers communicating with employees to assign goals, provide job instructions, explain policies and procedures, point out problems that need attention, and offer feedback about performance. But downward communication doesn't have to be oral or face to face. When management sends letters to employees' homes to advise them of the organization's new sick-leave policy, it's using downward communication. A team leader e-mailing members of her team about an upcoming deadline uses downward communication.

When engaging in downward communication, managers must explain the reasons *why* a decision was made. One study found employees were twice as likely to be committed to changes when the reasons behind them were fully explained. Although this may seem like common sense, many managers feel they are too busy to explain things or that explanations will "open up a big can of worms." Evidence clearly indicates, though, that explanations increase employee commitment and support of decisions.[4]

Another problem in downward communication is its one-way nature; generally, managers inform employees but rarely solicit their advice or opinions. Many employees say that their boss rarely or never asks for their advice. Companies like cell phone maker

Nokia actively listen to employee's suggestions, a practice the company thinks is especially important to innovation.[5]

The best communicators explain the reasons behind their downward communications but also solicit communication from the employees they supervise. That leads us to the next direction: upward communication.

Upward Communication

Upward communication flows to a higher level in the group or organization. It's used to provide feedback to higher-ups, inform them of progress toward goals, and relay current problems. Upward communication keeps managers aware of how employees feel about their jobs, co-workers, and the organization in general. Managers also rely on upward communication for ideas on how conditions can be improved.

Given that most managers' job responsibilities have expanded, upward communication is increasingly difficult because managers are overwhelmed and easily distracted. To engage in effective upward communication, try to reduce distractions (meet in a conference room if you can, rather than your boss's office or cubicle), communicate in headlines not paragraphs (your goal is to get your boss's attention, not to engage in a meandering discussion), support your headlines with actionable items (what you believe should happen), and prepare an agenda to make sure you use your boss's attention well.[6]

Lateral Communication

When communication takes place among members of the same work group, members of work groups at the same level, managers at the same level, or any other horizontally equivalent workers, we describe it as *lateral communication*.

Why are horizontal communications needed if a group or an organization's vertical communications are effective? Horizontal communication saves time and facilitates coordination. Some lateral relationships are formally sanctioned. More often, they are informally created to short-circuit the vertical hierarchy and expedite action. So from management's viewpoint, lateral communications can be good or bad. Because strictly adhering to the formal vertical structure for all communications can be inefficient, lateral communication occurring with management's knowledge and support can be beneficial. But it can create dysfunctional conflicts when the formal vertical channels are breached, when members go above or around their superiors to get things done, or when bosses find actions have been taken or decisions made without their knowledge.

INTERPERSONAL COMMUNICATION

How do group members transfer meaning between and among each other? They essentially rely on oral, written, and nonverbal communication.

Oral, written, and nonverbal communication forms or mediums of communication have their unique purposes, and specific limitations; utilize each medium when optimal, and try to avoid their limitations.

Oral Communication

The chief means of conveying messages is oral communication. Speeches, formal one-on-one and group discussions, and the informal rumor mill or grapevine are popular forms of oral communication.

The advantages of oral communication are speed and feedback. We can convey a verbal message and receive a response in minimal time. If the receiver is unsure of the message, rapid feedback allows the sender to quickly detect and correct it. As one professional put it, "Face-to-face communication on a consistent basis is still the best way to get information to and from employees."[7]

The major disadvantage of oral communication surfaces whenever a message has to pass through a number of people: the more people, the greater the potential distortion. If you've ever played the game "Telephone," you know the problem. Each person interprets the message in his or her own way. The message's content, when it reaches its destination, is often very different from the original. In an organization, where decisions and other communiqués are verbally passed up and down the authority hierarchy, considerable opportunities arise for messages to become distorted.

Written Communication

Written communications include memos, letters, fax transmissions, e-mail, instant messaging, organizational periodicals, notices placed on bulletin boards (including electronic ones), and any other device that transmits via written words or symbols.

Why would a sender choose written communication? It's often tangible and verifiable. When it's printed, both the sender and receiver have a record of the communication; and the message can be stored for an indefinite period. If there are questions about its content, the message is physically available for later reference. This feature is particularly important for complex and lengthy communications. The marketing plan for a new product, for instance, is likely to contain a number of tasks spread out over several months. By putting it in writing, those who have to initiate the plan can readily refer to it over its lifespan. A final benefit of all written communication comes from the process itself. People are usually forced to think more thoroughly about what they want to convey in a written message than in a spoken one. Thus, written communications are more likely to be well thought out, logical, and clear.

Of course, written messages have drawbacks. They're time consuming. You could convey far more information to a college instructor in a 1-hour oral exam than in a 1-hour written exam. In fact, what you can say in 10 to 15 minutes might take you an hour to write. The other major disadvantage is lack of a built-in feedback mechanism. Oral communication allows the receiver to respond rapidly to what he thinks he hears. But mailing a memo provides no assurance it has been received or that the recipient will interpret it as the sender intended.

Nonverbal Communication

Every time we deliver a verbal message, we also impart a nonverbal message.[8] Sometimes the nonverbal component may stand alone. In a singles bar, a glance, a stare, a smile, a frown, and a provocative body movement all convey meaning. No discussion of communication would thus be complete without consideration of *nonverbal communication*—which includes body movements, the intonations or emphasis we give to words, facial expressions, and the physical distance between the sender and receiver.

We could argue that every *body movement* has a meaning, and no movement is accidental (though some are unconscious). Through body language, we say, "Help me, I'm lonely"; "Take me, I'm available"; and "Leave me alone, I'm depressed." We act out our state of being with nonverbal body language. We lift one eyebrow for disbelief. We rub our noses for puzzlement. We clasp our arms to isolate ourselves or to protect ourselves. We shrug our shoulders for indifference, wink for intimacy, tap our fingers for impatience, slap our forehead for forgetfulness.

The two most important messages body language conveys are (1) the extent to which we like another and are interested in his or her views and (2) the perceived status between a sender and receiver. We're more likely to position ourselves closer to people we like and touch them more often. Similarly, if you feel you're of higher status than another, you're more likely to display body movements—such as crossed legs or a slouched seated position—that reflect a casual and relaxed manner.[9]

Body language adds to, and often complicates, verbal communication. A body position or movement does not by itself have a precise or universal meaning, but when it is linked with spoken language, it gives fuller meaning to a sender's message.

If you read the verbatim minutes of a meeting, you wouldn't grasp the impact of what was said the same way as if you had been there or saw the meeting on video. Why? There is no record of nonverbal communication. The emphasis given to words or phrases is missing. Exhibit 10.2 illustrates how *intonations* can change the meaning of a message. *Facial expressions* also convey meaning. A snarling face says something different from a smile. Facial expressions, along with intonations, can show arrogance, aggressiveness, fear, shyness, and other characteristics.

Physical distance also has meaning. What is considered proper spacing between people largely depends on cultural norms. A businesslike distance in some European countries feels intimate in many parts of North America. If someone stands closer to you than is considered appropriate, it may indicate aggressiveness or sexual interest; if farther away than usual, it may mean disinterest or displeasure with what is being said.

It's important to be alert to these nonverbal aspects of communication and look for nonverbal cues as well as the literal meaning of a sender's words. You should particularly be aware of contradictions between the messages. Someone who frequently glances at her wristwatch is giving the message that she would prefer to terminate the conversation no matter what she actually says. We misinform others when we express one message verbally, such as trust, but nonverbally communicate a contradictory message that reads, "I don't have confidence in you."

Change your tone and you change your meaning:

Placement of the emphasis	What it means
Why don't I take **you** to dinner tonight?	I was going to take someone else.
Why don't **I** take you to dinner tonight?	Instead of the guy you were going with.
Why **don't** I take you to dinner tonight?	I'm trying to find a reason why I **shouldn't** take you.
Why don't I take you to dinner tonight?	Do you have a problem with me?
Why don't I **take** you to dinner tonight?	Instead of going on your own.
Why don't I take you to **dinner** tonight?	Instead of lunch tomorrow.
Why don't I take you to dinner **tonight**?	Not tomorrow night.

EXHIBIT 10.2
Intonations: It's the Way You Say It!

Source: Based on Kiely, "When 'No' Means 'Yes,'" Marketing, October 1993, pp. 7–9. Reproduced in A. Huczynski and D. Buchanan, *Organizational Behavior*, 4th ed. (Essex, UK: Pearson Education, 2001), p. 194.

ORGANIZATIONAL COMMUNICATION

In this section, we move from interpersonal communication to organizational communication. Our first focus will be to describe and distinguish formal networks and the grapevine. Then we discuss technological innovations in communication.

Formal Small-Group Networks

Formal organizational networks can be very complicated, including hundreds of people and a half-dozen or more hierarchical levels. To simplify our discussion, we've condensed these networks into three common small groups of five people each (see Exhibit 10.3): chain, wheel, and all channel.

The *chain* rigidly follows the formal chain of command; this network approximates the communication channels you might find in a rigid three-level organization. The *wheel* relies on a central figure to act as the conduit for all the group's communication; it simulates the communication network you would find on a team with a strong leader. The *all-channel* network permits all group members to actively communicate with each other; it's most often characterized in practice by self-managed teams, in which all group members are free to contribute and no one person takes on a leadership role.

EXHIBIT 10.3
Three Common Small-Group Networks

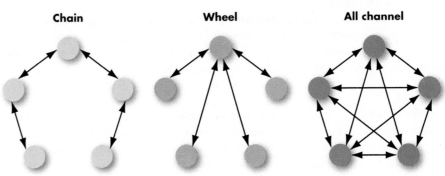

Chain   **Wheel**   **All channel**

As Exhibit 10.4 demonstrates, the effectiveness of each network depends on the dependent variable that concerns you. The structure of the wheel facilitates the emergence of a leader, the all-channel network is best if you desire high member satisfaction, and the chain is best if accuracy is most important. Exhibit 10.4 leads us to the conclusion that no single network will be best for all occasions.

EXHIBIT 10.4
Small-Group Networks and Effective Criteria

Criteria	Chain	Networks Wheel	All Channel
Speed	Moderate	Fast	Fast
Accuracy	High	High	Moderate
Emergence of a leader	Moderate	High	None
Member satisfaction	Moderate	Low	High

The Grapevine

The informal communication network in a group or organization is called the **grapevine.**[10] Although the grapevine may be informal, it's still an important source of information.

A recent study shows that grapevine or word-of-mouth information from peers about a company has important effects on whether job applicants join an organization.[11]

The grapevine has three main characteristics.[12] First, it is not controlled by management. Second, most employees perceive it as more believable and reliable than formal communiqués issued by top management. Finally, it is largely used to serve the interests of the people within it.

One of the most famous studies of the grapevine investigated communication patterns among 67 managers in a small manufacturing firm.[13] The study asked each communication recipient how he or she first received a given piece of information and then traced it back to its source. Although the grapevine was an important source, only 10 percent of the executives acted as liaison individuals (that is, passed the information on to more than one other person). When one executive decided to resign to enter the insurance business, 81 percent of the others knew about it, but only 11 percent transmitted this information to someone else.

Is the information that flows along the grapevine accurate? About 75 percent of it is.[14] But what conditions foster an active grapevine? What gets the rumor mill rolling?

It's frequently assumed rumors start because they make good gossip. This is rarely the case. Rumors emerge as a response to situations that are *important* to us, when there is *ambiguity,* and under conditions that arouse *anxiety.*[15] The fact that work situations frequently contain these three elements explains why rumors flourish in organizations. The secrecy and competition that typically prevail in large organizations—around the appointment of new bosses, the relocation of offices, downsizing decisions, or the realignment of work assignments—encourage and sustain rumors on the grapevine. A rumor will persist either until the wants and expectations creating the uncertainty are fulfilled or the anxiety has been reduced.

What can we conclude about the grapevine? Certainly it's an important part of any group or organization communication network and is well worth understanding. It gives managers a feel for the morale of their organization, identifies issues employees consider important, and helps tap into employee anxieties. The grapevine also serves employees' needs: Small talk creates a sense of closeness and friendship among those who share information, although research suggests it often does so at the expense of those in the "out-group."[16]

Can managers entirely eliminate rumors? No. What they should do, however, is minimize the negative consequences of rumors by limiting their range and impact. Exhibit 10.5 offers a few suggestions.

1. **Provide** information—in the long run, the best defense against rumors is a good offense (in other words, rumors tend to thrive in the absence of formal communication).
2. **Explain** actions and decisions that may appear inconsistent, unfair, or secretive.
3. **Refrain** from shooting the messenger—rumors are a natural fact of organizational life, so respond to them calmly, rationally, and respectfully.
4. **Maintain** open communication channels—constantly encourage employees to come to you with concerns, suggestions, and ideas.

EXHIBIT 10.5 Suggestions for Reducing the Negative Consequences of Rumors

Source: Based on L. Hirschhorn, "Managing Rumors," in L. Hirschhorn (ed.), *Cutting Back* (San Francisco: Jossey-Bass, 1983), pp. 54–56.

Electronic Communications

An indispensable—and in about 71 percent of cases, the primary—medium of communication in today's organizations is electronic. Electronic communications include e-mail, text messaging, networking software, blogs, and video conferencing. Let's discuss each.

E-MAIL E-mail uses the Internet to transmit and receive computer-generated text and documents. Its growth has been spectacular, and its use is now so pervasive it's hard to imagine life without it.

E-mail messages can be quickly written, edited, and stored. They can be distributed to one person or thousands with a click of a mouse. Recipients can read them at their own convenience. And the cost of sending formal e-mail messages to employees is a fraction of the cost of printing, duplicating, and distributing a comparable letter or brochure.[17]

E-mail is not without drawbacks. The following are some of the most significant limitations and what organizations should do to reduce or eliminate them:

- *Misinterpreting the message.* It's true we often misinterpret verbal messages, but the potential to misinterpret e-mail is even greater. One research team at New York University found we can accurately decode an e-mail's intent and tone only 50 percent of the time, yet most of us vastly overestimate our ability to send and interpret clear messages. If you're sending an important message, make sure you reread it for clarity.[18]
- *Communicating negative messages.* E-mail may not be the best way to communicate negative information. When Radio Shack decided to lay off 400 employees, it drew an avalanche of scorn inside and outside the company by doing it via e-mail. Employees need to be careful communicating negative messages via e-mail, too. Justen Deal, age 22, wrote an e-mail critical of some strategic decisions made by his employer, pharmaceutical giant Kaiser Permanente, questioning the financing of several information technology projects. Within hours, Deal's computer was seized; he was later fired.[19]
- *Time-consuming nature of e-mail.* An estimated 62 trillion e-mails are sent every year, of which approximately 60 percent, or 36 trillion, are non-spam messages,[20] and someone has to answer all those non-spam messages! A survey of Canadian managers revealed 58 percent spent 2 to 4 hours per day reading and responding to e-mails. The average worker checks his or her e-mail 50 times a day. Some people, such as venture capitalist and Dallas Mavericks owner Mark Cuban, receive more than a thousand messages a day (Cuban says 10 percent are of the "I want" variety). Although you probably don't receive *that* many, most of us have trouble keeping up with e-mail, especially as we advance in our career. Experts suggest the following strategies:
  - *Don't check e-mail in the morning.* Take care of important tasks before getting ensnared in e-mails. Otherwise, you may never get to those tasks.
  - *Check e-mail in batches.* Don't check e-mail continually throughout the day. Some experts suggest twice a day. "You wouldn't want to do a new load of laundry every time you have a dirty pair of socks," says one expert.
  - *Unsubscribe.* Stop newsletters and other subscriptions you don't really need.
  - *Stop sending e-mail.* The best way to receive lots of e-mail is to send lots of e-mail, so send less. Shorter e-mails garner shorter responses. "A well-written message can and should be as concise as possible," says one expert.

- *Declare e-mail bankruptcy.* Some people, like recording artist Moby and venture capitalist Fred Wilson, become so overwhelmed by e-mail they declare "e-mail bankruptcy." They wipe out their entire inbox and start over.

    Although some of these steps may not work for you, keep in mind that e-mail can be less productive than it seems: We often seem busy but get less accomplished through e-mail than we might think.[21]

- *E-mail emotions.* We tend to think of e-mail as a sort of sterile, faceless form of communication. Some researchers say the lack of visual and vocal cues means emotionally positive messages, like those including praise, will be seen as more emotionally neutral than the sender intended.[22] But as you no doubt know, e-mails are often highly emotional. One CEO said, "I've seen people not talk to each other, turf wars break out and people quit their jobs as a result of e-mails." E-mail tends to have a disinhibiting effect on people; without the recipient's facial expression to temper their emotional expression, senders write things they'd never be comfortable saying in person. If you find yourself angry or upset as you write an e-mail, save it as a draft, and look at it again once you are on a more even keel. When others send flaming messages, remain calm and try not to respond in kind. And, as hard as it might sometimes be, try to see the flaming message from the other party's point of view. That in itself may calm your nerves.

- *Privacy concerns.* There are two privacy issues with e-mail. First, your e-mails may be, and often are, monitored. You can't always trust the recipient of your e-mail to keep it confidential, either. For these reasons, you shouldn't write anything you wouldn't want made public. Before Walmart fired marketing VP Julie Roehm, its managers examined her e-mails for evidence of an inappropriate romantic relationship. Second, you need to exercise caution in forwarding e-mail from your company's e-mail account to a personal, or "public" (for example, Gmail, Yahoo!, MSN), e-mail account. These accounts often aren't as secure as corporate accounts, so when you forward a company e-mail to them, you may be violating your organization's policy or unintentionally disclosing confidential data. Many employers hire vendors to sift through e-mails, using software to catch not only the obvious key words ("insider trading") but the vague ("that thing we talked about") or guilt ridden ("regret"). Another survey revealed nearly 40 percent of companies have employees whose only job is to read other employees' e-mail. You are being watched—so be careful what you e-mail![23]

INSTANT MESSAGING AND TEXT MESSAGING   Like e-mail, instant messaging (IM) and text messaging (TM) use electronic media. Unlike e-mail, though, IM and TM either occur in real time (IM) or use portable communication devices (TM). In just a few years, IM and TM have become pervasive. As you no doubt know from experience, IM is usually sent via desktop or laptop computer, whereas TM is transmitted via cell phones or handheld devices such as BlackBerrys.

The growth of TM has been spectacular. In 2001, for instance, just 8 percent of U.S. employees were using it. Now that number is more than 50 percent[24] because IM and TM represent fast and inexpensive means for managers to stay in touch with employees and for employees to stay in touch with each other. In an increasing number of cases, this isn't just a luxury, it's a business imperative. Bill Green, CEO of the consulting firm Accenture, doesn't have a permanent office. Because he's on the road all the time, visiting Accenture's 100 locations scattered across the globe, TM is essential for him to keep in touch. Although there aren't many other examples so dramatic, the great advantage of TM is that it is flexible; with it, you can be reached almost anywhere, anytime.[25]

Despite their advantages, IM and TM aren't going to replace e-mail. E-mail is still probably a better device for conveying long messages that must be saved. IM is preferable for one- or two-line messages that would just clutter up an e-mail inbox. On the downside, some IM and TM users find the technology intrusive and distracting. Their continual presence can make it hard for employees to concentrate and stay focused. A survey of managers revealed that in 86 percent of meetings, at least some participants checked TM, and another survey revealed 20 percent of managers report having been castigated for using wireless devices during meetings.[26] Finally, because instant messages can be intercepted easily, many organizations are concerned about the security of IM and TM.

One other point: It's important to not let the informality of text messaging ("omg! r u serious? brb") spill over into business e-mails. Many prefer to keep business communication relatively formal. A survey of employers revealed that 58 percent rate grammar, spelling, and punctuation as "very important" in e-mail messages.[27] By making sure your professional communications are, well, professional, you'll show yourself to be mature and serious. Avoid jargon and slang, use formal titles, use formal e-mail addresses for yourself (lose that partygirl@yahoo.com), take care to make your message concise and well written. None of this means, of course, that you have to give up TM or IM; you just need to maintain the boundaries between how you communicate with your friends and how you communicate professionally.

VIDEO CONFERENCING   *Video conferencing* permits employees in an organization to have meetings with people at different locations. Live audio and video images of members allow them to see, hear, and talk with each other. Video conferencing technology, in effect, allows employees to conduct interactive meetings without the necessity of being physically in the same location.

Peter Quirk, a program manager with EMC Corporation, uses video conferencing to hold monthly meetings of employees at various locations and many other meetings as well. Doing so saves travel expenses and time. However, Quirk notes it's especially important to stimulate questions and involve all participants in order to avoid someone who is linked in but disengaged. Sun Microsystem's Karen Rhode agrees special efforts must be made to engage remote participants, suggesting "You can poll people, people can ask questions, you can do an engaging presentation."[28]

Managing Information

We all have more information at our disposal than ever. It brings us many benefits, but also two important challenges: information overload and information security. We consider each in turn.

DEALING WITH INFORMATION OVERLOAD   Do you find yourself bombarded with information—from e-mail, blogs, Internet surfing, IMs, cell phones, and televisions? You're not alone. Basex, a company that looks at worker efficiency, found the largest part of an average worker's day—43 percent—is spent on matters that are neither important nor urgent, such as responding to non-crucial e-mails and surfing the Web. (In fairness to e-mail, Basex also found 25 percent of an employee's time was spent composing and responding to important e-mail.)

Intel designed an 8-month experiment to see how limiting **information overload** might aid productivity. One group of employees was told to limit both digital and in-person contact for 4 hours on Tuesdays, while another group followed its usual routine. The first group was more productive, and 75 percent of its members suggested the program be expanded. "It's huge. We were expecting less," remarked Nathan Zeldes, an Intel engineer who led the experiments. "When people are uninterrupted they can sit back and design chips and really think."

Some of the biggest technologies companies, including Microsoft, Intel, Google, and IBM, are banding together to study the issue more systematically. As one of the team members, IBM's John Tang, noted, "There's a competitive advantage to figuring out how to address this problem."

We have already reviewed some ways of reducing the time sunk into e-mails. More generally, as the Intel study shows, it may make sense to connect to technology less frequently, to, in the words of one article, "avoid letting the drumbeat of digital missives constantly shake up and reorder to-do lists." Lynaia Lutes, an account supervisor for a small Texas company, was able to think much more strategically by taking a break from digital information each day. In the past, she said, "I basically completed an assignment" but didn't approach it strategically. By creating such breaks for yourself, you may be better able to prioritize and think about the big picture and, thereby, be more effective.[29]

BARRIERS TO EFFECTIVE COMMUNICATION

A number of barriers can retard or distort effective communication. In this section, we highlight the most important of these barriers.

Filtering

Filtering refers to how a sender purposely manipulates information so the receiver will see it more favorably. A manager who tells his boss what he feels the boss wants to hear is filtering information.

The more vertical levels in the organization's hierarchy, the more opportunities there are for filtering. But some filtering will occur wherever there are status differences. Factors such as fear of conveying bad news and the desire to please the boss often lead employees to tell their superiors what they think they want to hear, thus distorting upward communications.

Selective Perception

We have mentioned selective perception before in this book. It appears again here because the receivers in the communication process selectively see and hear based on their needs, motivations, experience, background, and other personal characteristics. Receivers also project their interests and expectations into communications as they decode them. An employment interviewer who expects a female job applicant to put her family ahead of her career is likely to see that in all female applicants, regardless of whether they actually feel that way. As we said in the chapter on perception, we don't see reality; we interpret what we see and call it reality.

Information Overload

Individuals have a finite capacity for processing data. When the information we have to work with exceeds our processing capacity, the result is information overload. We've seen that dealing with it has become a huge challenge for individuals and for organizations. It's a barrier to communication that you can manage—to some degree—by following the steps outlined previously in this chapter.

What happens when individuals have more information than they can sort and use? They tend to select, ignore, pass over, or forget information. Or they may put off further processing until the overload situation is over. In any case, the result is lost information and less effective communication. This makes it all the more important to deal with information overload.

Emotions

You may interpret the same message differently when you're angry or distraught than when you're happy. Extreme emotions such as jubilation or depression are most likely to hinder effective communication. In such instances, we are most prone to disregard our rational and objective thinking processes and substitute emotional judgments.

Language

Even when we're communicating in the same language, words mean different things to different people. Age and context are two of the biggest factors that influence such differences.

When Michael Schiller, a business consultant, was talking with his 15-year-old daughter about where she was going with her friends, he told her, "You need to recognize your ARAs and measure against them." Schiller said that in response, his daughter "looked at him like he was from outer space." (For the record, ARA stands for accountability, responsibility, and authority.) Those new to corporate lingo may find acronyms such as *ARA,* words such as *skeds* (schedules), and phrases such as *bake your noodle* (provide a service) bewildering, in the same way parents may be mystified by teen slang.[30]

In short, our use of language is far from uniform. If we knew how each of us modified the language, we could minimize communication difficulties, but we usually don't know. Senders tend to assume the words and terms they use mean the same to the receiver as to them. This assumption is often incorrect.

Silence

It's easy to ignore silence or lack of communication, precisely because it is defined by the absence of information. However, research suggests silence and withholding communication are both common and problematic. One survey found that more than 85 percent of managers reported remaining silent about at least one issue of significant concern.[31] Employee silence means managers lack information about ongoing operational problems. And silence regarding discrimination, harassment, corruption, and misconduct means top management cannot take action to eliminate this behavior. Finally, employees who are silent about important issues may also experience psychological stress.

Silence is less likely where minority opinions are treated with respect, workgroup identification is high, and high procedural justice prevails.[32] Practically, this means managers must make sure they behave in a supportive manner when employees voice divergent opinions or express concerns, and they must take these concerns under advisement. One act of ignoring or belittling an employee for expressing concerns may well lead the employee to withhold important future communication.

Communication Apprehension

An estimated 5 to 20 percent of the population[33] suffers debilitating **communication apprehension,** or social anxiety. These people experience undue tension and anxiety in oral communication, written communication, or both. They may find it extremely difficult to talk with others face to face or may become extremely anxious when they have to use the telephone, relying instead on memos or faxes when a phone call would be faster and more appropriate.

Studies show oral-communication apprehensives avoid situations, such as teaching, for which oral communication is a dominant requirement.[34] But almost all jobs require *some* oral communication. Of greater concern is evidence that high oral-communication apprehensives distort the communication demands of their jobs in order to minimize the need for communication.[35] So be aware some people severely limit their oral communication and rationalize this practice by telling themselves it isn't necessary for them to do their job effectively.

A number of barriers—such as culture—often retard or distort effective communication; understand these barriers as a means of overcoming them.

Global Implications

Effective communication is difficult under the best of conditions. Cross-cultural factors clearly create the potential for increased communication problems. For example, the thumbs up hand gesture in America signals an affirmative response to a questions but in Australia and Saudia Arabia, this is considered a rude gesture. A gesture that is well understood and acceptable in one culture can be meaningless or lewd in another. Only 18 percent of companies have documented strategies for communicating with employees across cultures, and only 31 percent require that corporate messages be customized for consumption in other cultures. Procter & Gamble seems to be an exception; more than half of the company's employees don't speak English as their first language, so the company focuses on simple messages to make sure everyone knows what's important.[36]

Cultural Barriers

Researchers have identified a number of problems related to language difficulties in cross-cultural communications.[37]

First are *barriers caused by semantics*. Words mean different things to different people, particularly people from different national cultures. Some words don't translate between cultures. The Finnish word *sisu* means something akin to "guts" or "dogged persistence" but is essentially untranslatable into English. The new capitalists in Russia may have difficulty communicating with British or Canadian counterparts because English terms such as *efficiency, free market,* and *regulation* have no direct Russian equivalents.

Second are *barriers caused by word connotations*. Words imply different things in different languages. Negotiations between U.S. and Japanese executives can be difficult because the Japanese word *hai* translates as "yes," but its connotation is "Yes, I'm listening" rather than "Yes, I agree."

Third are *barriers caused by tone differences*. In some cultures, language is formal; in others, it's informal. In some cultures, the tone changes depending on the context: People speak differently at home, in social situations, and at work. Using a personal, informal style when a more formal style is expected can be embarrassing.

(continued)

Fourth are *differences in tolerance for conflict and methods for resolving conflicts.* Individuals from individualist cultures tend to be more comfortable with direct conflicts and will make the source of their disagreements overt. Collectivists are more likely to acknowledge conflict only implicitly and avoid emotionally charged disputes. They may attribute conflicts to the situation more than to the individuals and therefore may not require explicit apologies to repair relationships, whereas individualists prefer explicit statements accepting responsibility for conflicts and public apologies to restore relationships.

Cultural Context

Cultures tend to differ in the degree to which context influences the meaning individuals take from communication.[38] In **high-context cultures** such as China, Korea, Japan, and Vietnam, people rely heavily on nonverbal and subtle situational cues in communicating with others, and a person's official status, place in society, and reputation carry considerable weight. What is *not* said may be more significant than what *is* said. In contrast, people from Europe and North America reflect their **low-context cultures.** They rely essentially on spoken and written words to convey meaning; body language and formal titles are secondary.

These contextual differences actually mean quite a lot in terms of communication. Communication in high-context cultures implies considerably more trust by both parties. What may appear to be casual and insignificant conversation in fact reflects the desire to build a relationship and create trust. Oral agreements imply strong commitments in high-context cultures. And who you are—your age, seniority, rank in the organization—is highly valued and heavily influences your credibility. But in low-context cultures, enforceable contracts tend to be in writing, precisely worded, and highly legalistic. Similarly, low-context cultures value directness. Managers are expected to be explicit and precise in conveying intended meaning. It's quite different in high-context cultures,

in which managers tend to "make suggestions" rather than give orders.

A Cultural Guide

When communicating with people from a different culture, what can you do to reduce misinterpretations? Begin by trying to assess the cultural context. You're likely to have fewer difficulties if it's similar to yours. The following rules can be helpful:[39]

1. *Assume differences until similarity is proven.* Most of us assume others are more similar to us than they actually are. You are less likely to err if you assume they are different from you until proven otherwise.

2. *Emphasize description rather than interpretation or evaluation.* Interpreting or evaluating what someone has said or done draws more on your own culture and background than on the observed situation. So delay judgment until you've had sufficient time to observe and interpret the situation from the differing perspectives of all concerned.

3. *Practice empathy.* Before sending a message, put yourself in the recipient's shoes. What are his or her values, experiences, and frames of reference? What do you know about his or her education, upbringing, and background that can give you added insight? Try to see the other person as he or she really is.

4. *Treat your interpretations as a working hypothesis.* Once you've developed an explanation for a new situation or think you empathize with someone from a foreign culture, treat your interpretation as a hypothesis that needs further testing rather than as a certainty. Carefully assess the feedback recipients provide you, to see whether it confirms your hypothesis. For important decisions or communiqués, check with other foreign and home-country colleagues to make sure your interpretations are on target.

Implications for Managers

You've probably discovered the link between communication and employee satisfaction in this chapter: the less uncertainty, the greater the satisfaction. Distortions, ambiguities, and incongruities between verbal and nonverbal messages all increase uncertainty and reduce satisfaction.

The less distortion, the more employees will receive goals, feedback, and other management messages as intended.[40] This, in turn, should reduce ambiguities and clarify the group's task. Extensive use of vertical, lateral, and informal channels also increase communication flow, reduce uncertainty, and improve group performance and satisfaction.

Perfect communication is unattainable. Yet a positive relationship exists between effective communication (which includes perceived trust, perceived accuracy, desire for interaction, top-management receptiveness, and upward information requirements) and worker productivity.[41] Choosing the correct channel, being an effective listener, and using feedback can make for more effective communication. But the human factor generates distortions we can never fully eliminate. Whatever the sender's expectations, the message as decoded in the receiver's mind represents his or her reality. And this reality will determine performance, along with the individual's level of motivation and degree of satisfaction.

Despite the great advantages of electronic communication, its pitfalls are also numerous. Because we gather so much meaning from the way a message is communicated (voice tone, facial expressions, body language), the potential for misunderstandings in electronic communication is great. We need to use e-mail, IM, TM, and networking software wisely, or we'll not be as effective as we might.

Finally, by keeping in mind communication barriers such as gender and culture, we can overcome them and increase our communication effectiveness.

CHAPTER 11

Leadership

After studying this chapter, you should be able to:

- Define *leadership* and contrast leadership and management.
- Summarize the conclusions of trait theories of leadership.
- Assess contingency theories of leadership by their level of support.
- Compare and contrast *charismatic, transformational,* and *authentic leadership.*
- Address challenges to the effectiveness of leadership.
- Assess whether charismatic and transformational leadership generalize across cultures.

In this chapter, we'll look at the basic approaches to determining what makes an effective leader and what differentiates leaders from nonleaders. First, we'll present theories of leadership. Then, we'll discuss challenges to the meaning and importance of leadership. But before we review these approaches, let's first clarify what we mean by the term *leadership*.

WHAT IS LEADERSHIP?

Leadership and *management* are often confused. What's the difference?

John Kotter of the Harvard Business School argues that management is about coping with complexity.[1] Good management brings about order and consistency by drawing up formal plans, designing rigid organization structures, and monitoring results against the plans. Leadership, in contrast, is about coping with change. Leaders establish direction by developing a vision of the future; then they align people by communicating this vision and inspiring them to overcome hurdles.

Although Kotter provides separate definitions of the two terms, both researchers and practicing managers frequently make no such distinctions. So we need to present leadership in a way that can capture how it is used in theory and practice.

We define **leadership** as the ability to influence a group toward the achievement of a vision or set of goals. The source of this influence may be formal, such as that provided by managerial rank in an organization. But not all leaders are managers, nor, for that matter, are all managers leaders. Just because an organization provides its managers with certain formal rights is no assurance they will lead effectively. Nonsanctioned leadership—the ability to influence that arises outside the formal structure of the organization—is often as important or more important than formal influence. In other words, leaders can emerge from within a group as well as by formal appointment.

In today's dynamic world, leadership has the ability to influence a group toward the achievement of a vision or set of goals.

Organizations need strong leadership *and* strong management for optimal effectiveness. We need leaders today to challenge the status quo, create visions of the future, and inspire organizational members to want to achieve the visions. We also need managers to formulate detailed plans, create efficient organizational structures, and oversee day-to-day operations.

TRAIT THEORIES

Throughout history, strong leaders—Buddha, Napoleon, Mao, Churchill, Roosevelt, Reagan—have been described in terms of their traits. **Trait theories of leadership** thus focus on personal qualities and characteristics. We recognize leaders like South Africa's Nelson Mandela, Virgin Group CEO Richard Branson, Apple co-founder Steve Jobs, and American Express chairman Ken Chenault as *charismatic, enthusiastic,* and *courageous.* The search for personality, social, physical, or intellectual attributes that differentiate leaders from nonleaders goes back to the earliest stages of leadership research.

Early research efforts at isolating leadership traits resulted in a number of dead ends. A review in the late 1960s of 20 different studies identified nearly 80 leadership traits, but only 5 were common to 4 or more of the investigations.[2] By the 1990s, after numerous studies and analyses, about the best we could say was that most leaders "are not like other people," but the particular traits that characterized them varied a great deal from review to review.[3] It was a pretty confusing state of affairs.

A breakthrough, of sorts, came when researchers began organizing traits around the Big Five personality framework. Most of the dozens of traits in various leadership reviews fit under one of the Big Five (ambition and energy are part of extraversion, for instance), giving strong support to traits as predictors of leadership.

A comprehensive review of the leadership literature, when organized around the Big Five, has found extraversion to be the most important trait of effective leaders[4] but more strongly related to leader emergence than to leader effectiveness. Sociable and dominant people are more likely to assert themselves in group situations, but leaders need to make sure they're not too assertive—one study found leaders who scored very high on assertiveness were less effective than those who were moderately high.[5]

Unlike agreeableness and emotional stability, conscientiousness and openness to experience also showed strong relationships to leadership, though not quite as strong as extraversion. Overall, the trait approach does have something to offer. Leaders who like being around people and are able to assert themselves (extraverted), disciplined and able to keep commitments they make (conscientious), and creative and flexible (open) do have an apparent advantage when it comes to leadership, suggesting good leaders do have key traits in common.

One reason is that conscientiousness and extraversion are positively related to leaders' self-efficacy, which explained most of the variance in subordinates' ratings of leader performance.[6] People are more likely to follow someone who is confident she's going in the right direction.

Another trait that may indicate effective leadership is emotional intelligence (EI), discussed in Chapter 3. Advocates of EI argue that without it, a person can have outstanding training, a highly analytical mind, a compelling vision, and an endless supply of terrific ideas but still not make a great leader. This may be especially true as individuals move up in an organization.[7] Why is EI so critical to effective leadership? A core component of EI is empathy. Empathetic leaders can sense others' needs, listen to what followers say (and don't say), and read the reactions of others. As one leader noted, "The caring part of empathy, especially for the people with whom you work, is what inspires people to stay with a leader when the going gets rough. The mere fact that someone cares is more often than not rewarded with loyalty."[8]

The link between EI and leadership effectiveness is still much less investigated than other traits. One reviewer noted, "Speculating about the practical utility of the EI construct might be premature. Despite such warnings, EI is being viewed as a panacea for many organizational malaises with recent suggestions that EI is essential for leadership effectiveness."[9] But until more rigorous evidence accumulates, we can't be confident about the connection.

Based on the latest findings, we offer two conclusions. First, traits can predict leadership. Twenty years ago, the evidence suggested otherwise. But this was probably due to the lack of a valid framework for classifying and organizing traits. The Big Five seem to have rectified that. Second, traits do a better job predicting the emergence of leaders and the appearance of leadership than actually distinguishing between *effective* and *ineffective* leaders. The fact that an individual exhibits the traits and others consider that person to be a leader does not necessarily mean the leader is successful at getting his or her group to achieve its goals.

BEHAVIORAL THEORIES

The failures of early trait studies led researchers in the late 1940s through the 1960s to go in a different direction. They wondered whether there was something unique in the way effective leaders *behave*. Trait research provides a basis for *selecting* the right people for leadership. In contrast, behavioral studies implied we could *train* people to be leaders. Many argued that **behavioral theories of leadership** had advantages over trait theories.

The most comprehensive and replicated behavioral theories resulted from the Ohio State Studies in the late 1940s,[10] which sought to identify independent dimensions of leader behavior. Beginning with more than a thousand dimensions, the studies narrowed the list to two that substantially accounted for most of the leadership behavior described by employees. Researchers called these *initiating structure* and *consideration*.

Initiating structure is the extent to which a leader is likely to define and structure his or her role and those of employees in the search for goal attainment. It includes behavior that attempts to organize work, work relationships, and goals. A leader high in initiating structure is someone who "assigns group members to particular tasks," "expects workers to maintain definite standards of performance," and "emphasizes the meeting of deadlines."

Consideration is the extent to which a person's job relationships are characterized by mutual trust, respect for employees' ideas, and regard for their feelings. A leader high in consideration helps employees with personal problems, is friendly and approachable, treats all employees as equals, and expresses appreciation and support. In a recent survey, when asked to indicate the factors that most motivated them at work, 66 percent of employees mentioned appreciation.[11]

Leadership studies at the University of Michigan's Survey Research Center had similar objectives: to locate behavioral characteristics of leaders that appeared related to performance effectiveness. The Michigan group also came up with two behavioral dimensions: the **employee-oriented leader** emphasized interpersonal relationships by taking a personal interest in the needs of employees and accepting individual differences among them; the **production-oriented leader** emphasized the technical or task aspects of the job—concern focused on accomplishing the group's tasks. These dimensions are closely related to the Ohio State dimensions. Employee-oriented leadership is similar to consideration, and production-oriented leadership is similar to initiating structure. In fact, most leadership researchers use the terms synonymously.

At one time, the results of testing behavioral theories were thought to be disappointing. One 1992 review concluded, "Overall, the research based on a two-factor conceptualization of leadership behavior has added little to our knowledge about effective leadership."[12] However, a more recent review of 160 studies found the followers of leaders high in consideration were more satisfied with their jobs, were more motivated, and had more respect for their leader. Initiating structure was more strongly related to higher levels of group and organization productivity and more positive performance evaluations.

Summary of Trait Theories and Behavioral Theories

Leaders who have certain traits and who display consideration and structuring behaviors do appear to be more effective. Perhaps you're wondering whether conscientious leaders (trait) are more likely to be structuring (behavior), and extraverted leaders (trait) to be considerate (behavior). Unfortunately, we can't be sure there is a connection. Future research is needed to integrate these approaches.

Some leaders may have the right traits or display the right behaviors and still fail. And many leaders who leave while their organizations are still successful—GE's Jack Welch or Procter & Gamble's A. G. Lafley—have their legacies clouded by events after their departure. As important as traits and behaviors are in identifying effective or ineffective leaders, they do not guarantee success. The context matters, too.

CONTINGENCY THEORIES

Some tough-minded leaders seem to gain a lot of admirers when they take over struggling companies and help lead them out of the doldrums. Home Depot and Chrysler didn't hire former CEO Bob Nardelli for his winning personality. However, such leaders also seem to be quickly dismissed when the situation stabilizes.

The rise and fall of leaders like Bob Nardelli illustrate that predicting leadership success is more complex than isolating a few traits or behaviors. In their cases, what worked in very bad times and in very good times didn't seem to translate into long-term success. The failure by researchers in the mid-twentieth century to obtain consistent results led to a focus on situational influences. The relationship between leadership style and effectiveness suggested that under condition a, style X would be appropriate, whereas style Y was more suitable for condition B, and style Z for condition C. But what *were* conditions A, B, C? It was one thing to say leadership effectiveness depends on them and another to be able to identify them. We next consider the Fiedler model approach to isolating situational variables.

The Fiedler Model

The first comprehensive contingency model for leadership was developed by Fred Fiedler.[13] The **Fiedler contingency model** proposes that effective group performance depends on the proper match between the leader's style and the degree to which the situation gives the leader control.

IDENTIFYING LEADERSHIP STYLE   Fiedler believes a key factor in leadership success is the individual's basic leadership style. He created the **least preferred co-worker (LPC) questionnaire** to identify that style by measuring whether a person is task or relationship oriented. The LPC questionnaire asks respondents to think of all the co-workers they have ever had and describe the one person they *least enjoyed* working with by rating that person on a scale of 1 to 8 for each of 16 sets of contrasting adjectives (such as pleasant–unpleasant, efficient–inefficient, open–guarded, supportive–hostile). If you describe the person you are least able to work with in favorable terms (a high LPC score), Fiedler would label you *relationship oriented.* In contrast, if you see your least preferred co-worker in relatively unfavorable terms (a low LPC score), you are primarily interested in productivity and are *task oriented.* About 16 percent of respondents score in the middle range[14] and thus fall outside the theory's predictions. The rest of our discussion relates to the 84 percent who score in either the high or low range of the LPC questionnaire.

Fiedler assumes an individual's leadership style is fixed. This means if a situation requires a task-oriented leader and the person in the leadership position is relationship oriented, either the situation has to be modified or the leader has to be replaced to achieve optimal effectiveness.

DEFINING THE SITUATION   After assessing an individual's basic leadership style through the LPC questionnaire, we match the leader with the situation. Fiedler has identified three contingency or situational dimensions:

1. **Leader–member relations** is the degree of confidence, trust, and respect members have in their leader.
2. **Task structure** is the degree to which the job assignments are procedurized (that is, structured or unstructured).
3. **Position power** is the degree of influence a leader has over power variables such as hiring, firing, discipline, promotions, and salary increases.

The next step is to evaluate the situation in terms of these three variables. Fiedler states that the better the leader–member relations, the more highly structured the job, and the stronger the position power, the more control the leader has. A very favorable situation (in which the leader has a great deal of control) might include a payroll manager who is well respected and whose employees have confidence in her (good leader–member relations); activities to be done—such as wage computation, check writing, and report filing—that are specific and clear (high task structure); and provision of considerable freedom to reward and punish employees (strong position power). An unfavorable situation might be that of the disliked chairperson of a volunteer United Way fund-raising team. In this job, the leader has very little control.

MATCHING LEADERS AND SITUATIONS   Combining the three contingency dimensions yields eight possible situations in which leaders can find themselves (Exhibit 11.1). The Fiedler model proposes matching an individual's LPC score and these eight situations to achieve maximum leadership effectiveness.[15] Fiedler concluded that task-oriented leaders perform better in situations very favorable to them and very unfavorable. So when faced with a category I, II, III, VII, or VIII situation, task-oriented leaders perform better. Relationship-oriented leaders, however, perform better in moderately favorable situations—categories IV through VI. In recent years, Fiedler has condensed these eight situations down to three. He now says task-oriented leaders perform best in situations of high and low control, while relationship-oriented leaders perform best in moderate control situations.

How would you apply Fiedler's findings? You would match leaders—in terms of their LPC scores—with the type of situation—in terms of leader–member relationships, task structure, and position power—for which they were best suited. But remember that Fiedler views an individual's leadership style as fixed. Therefore, there are only two ways to improve leader effectiveness.

First, you can change the leader to fit the situation—as a baseball manager puts a right- or left-handed pitcher into the game depending on the hitter. If a group situation rates highly unfavorable but is currently led by a relationship-oriented manager, the group's performance could be improved under a manager who is task oriented. The second alternative is to change the situation to fit the leader, by restructuring tasks or increasing or decreasing the leader's power to control factors such as salary increases, promotions, and disciplinary actions.

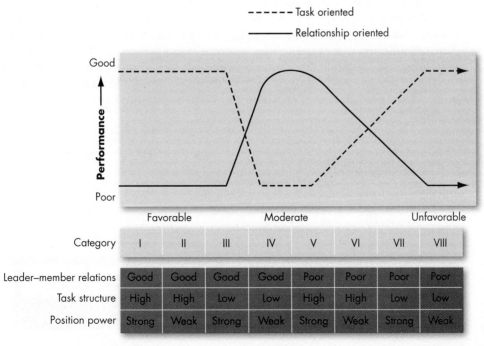

EXHIBIT 11.1
Findings from the Fiedler Model

EVALUATION   Studies testing the overall validity of the Fiedler model find considerable evidence to support substantial parts of it.[16] If we use only three categories rather than the original eight, there is ample evidence to support Fiedler's conclusions. But the logic underlying the LPC questionnaire is not well understood, and respondents' scores are not stable. The contingency variables are also complex and difficult for practitioners to assess.

LEADER–MEMBER EXCHANGE (LMX) THEORY

Think of a leader you know. Did this leader have favorites who made up his or her in-group? If you answered "yes," you're acknowledging the foundation of leader–member exchange theory. **Leader–member exchange (LMX) theory** argues that, because of time pressures, leaders establish a special relationship with a small group of their followers. These individuals make up the in-group—they are trusted, get a disproportionate amount of the leader's attention, and are more likely to receive special privileges. Other followers fall into the out-group.

The theory proposes that early in the history of the interaction between a leader and a given follower, the leader implicitly categorizes the follower as an "in" or an "out," and that relationship is relatively stable over time. Leaders induce LMX by rewarding those employees with whom they want a closer linkage and punishing those with whom they do not.[17] But for the LMX relationship to remain intact, the leader and the follower must invest in the relationship.

Just how the leader chooses who falls into each category is unclear, but there is evidence in-group members have demographic, attitude, and personality characteristics similar to those of their leader or a higher level of competence than out-group members[18] (see Exhibit 11.2). Leaders and followers of the same gender tend to have closer (higher LMX) relationships than those of different genders.[19] Even though the leader does the choosing, the follower's characteristics drive the categorizing decision.

Research to test LMX theory has been generally supportive, with substantive evidence that leaders do differentiate among followers; these disparities are far from random; and followers with in-group status will have higher performance ratings, engage in more helping or "citizenship" behaviors at work, and report greater satisfaction with their superior.[20] These positive findings for in-group members shouldn't be surprising, given our

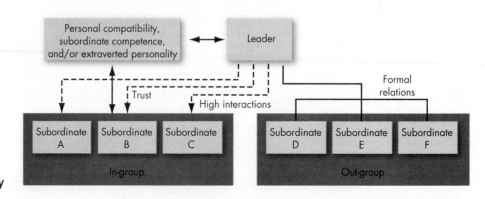

EXHIBIT 11.2

Leader-Member Exchange Theory

knowledge of self-fulfilling prophecy (see Chapter 6). Leaders invest their resources with those they expect to perform best. And believing in-group members are the most competent, leaders treat them as such and unwittingly fulfill their prophecy.[21] These relationships may be stronger when followers have a more active role in shaping their own job performance. Research on 287 software developers and 164 supervisors showed leader–member relationships have a stronger impact on employee performance and attitudes when employees have higher levels of autonomy and a more internal locus of control.[22]

CHARISMATIC LEADERSHIP AND TRANSFORMATIONAL LEADERSHIP

In this section, we present two contemporary leadership theories—charismatic leadership and transformational leadership—which have a common theme: they view leaders as individuals who inspire followers through their words, ideas, and behaviors.

Charismatic Leadership

John F. Kennedy, Martin Luther King Jr., Ronald Reagan, Bill Clinton, Mary Kay Ash (founder of Mary Kay Cosmetics), and Steve Jobs (co-founder of Apple Computer) are frequently cited as charismatic leaders. What do they have in common?

WHAT IS CHARISMATIC LEADERSHIP?   Max Weber, a sociologist, defined *charisma* (from the Greek for "gift") more than a century ago as "a certain quality of an individual personality, by virtue of which he or she is set apart from ordinary people and treated as endowed with supernatural, superhuman, or at least specifically exceptional powers or qualities. These are not accessible to the ordinary person and are regarded as of divine origin or as exemplary, and on the basis of them the individual concerned is treated as a leader."[23] Weber argued that charismatic leadership was one of several ideal types of authority.

The first researcher to consider charismatic leadership in terms of organizational behavior was Robert House. According to House's **charismatic leadership theory,** followers attribute heroic or extraordinary leadership abilities when they observe certain behaviors. A number of studies have attempted to identify the characteristics of charismatic leaders: they have a vision, they are willing to take personal risks to achieve that vision, they are sensitive to follower needs, and they exhibit extraordinary behaviors[24] (see Exhibit 11.3).

---

1. *Vision and articulation.* Has a vision—expressed as an idealized goal—that proposes a future better than the status quo; and is able to clarify the importance of the vision in terms that are understandable to others.
2. *Personal risk.* Willing to take on high personal risk, incur high costs, and engage in self-sacrifice to achieve the vision.
3. *Sensitivity to follower needs.* Perceptive of others' abilities and responsive to their needs and feelings.
4. *Unconventional behavior.* Engages in behaviors that are perceived as novel and counter to norms.

EXHIBIT 11.3 Key Characteristics of Charismatic Leaders
Source: Based on J. A. Conger and R. N. Kanungo, *Charismatic Leadership in Organizations* (Thousand Oaks, CA: Sage, 1998), p. 94.

ARE CHARISMATIC LEADERS BORN OR MADE?   Are charismatic leaders born with their qualities? Or can people actually learn to be charismatic leaders? Yes, and yes.

Individuals *are* born with traits that make them charismatic. In fact, studies of identical twins have found they score similarly on charismatic leadership measures, even if they were raised in different households and had never met. Personality is also related to charismatic leadership; charismatic leaders are likely to be extraverted, self-confident, and achievement oriented.[25] Consider Presidents Barack Obama and Ronald Reagan: Like them or not, they are often compared because both possess the qualities of charismatic leaders.

Although a small minority thinks charisma is inherited and cannot be learned, most experts believe individuals can be trained to exhibit charismatic behaviors. After all, just because we inherit certain tendencies doesn't mean we can't learn to change. One set of authors proposes a three-step process.[26] First, develop an aura of charisma by maintaining an optimistic view; using passion as a catalyst for generating enthusiasm; and communicating with the whole body, not just with words. Second, draw others in by creating a bond that inspires them to follow. Third, bring out the potential in followers by tapping into their emotions.

The approach seems to work, according to researchers who have scripted undergraduate business students to "play" charismatic.[27] The students were taught to articulate an overarching goal, communicate high performance expectations, exhibit confidence in the ability of followers to meet these expectations, and empathize with the needs of their followers; they learned to project a powerful, confident, and dynamic presence; and they practiced using a captivating and engaging voice. They were also trained to evoke charismatic nonverbal characteristics: They alternated between pacing and sitting on the edges of their desks, leaned toward the subjects, maintained direct eye contact, and had relaxed postures and animated facial expressions. Their followers had higher task performance, task adjustment, and adjustment to the leader and the group than did followers of noncharismatic leaders.

HOW CHARISMATIC LEADERS INFLUENCE FOLLOWERS   How do charismatic leaders actually influence followers? Evidence suggests a four-step process.[28] It begins with articulating an appealing **vision,** a long-term strategy for attaining a goal by linking the present with a better future for the organization. Desirable visions fit the times and circumstances and reflect the uniqueness of the organization. Steve Jobs championed the iPod at Apple, noting, "It's as Apple as anything Apple has ever done." People in the organization must also believe the vision is challenging yet attainable. The iPod achieved Apple's goal of offering groundbreaking and easy-to-use-technology.

Second, a vision is incomplete without an accompanying **vision statement,** a formal articulation of an organization's vision or mission. Charismatic leaders may use vision statements to imprint on followers an overarching goal and purpose. They then communicate high performance expectations and express confidence that followers can attain them. This enhances follower self-esteem and self-confidence.

Next, through words and actions the leader conveys a new set of values and sets an example for followers to imitate. One study of Israeli bank employees showed charismatic leaders were more effective because their employees personally identified with them. Charismatic leaders also set a tone of cooperation and mutual support. A study of 115 government employees found they had a stronger sense of personal belonging at work when they had charismatic leaders, increasing their willingness to engage in helping and compliance-oriented behavior.[29]

Finally, the charismatic leader engages in emotion-inducing and often unconventional behavior to demonstrate courage and conviction about the vision. Followers "catch" the emotions their leader is conveying.[30]

DOES EFFECTIVE CHARISMATIC LEADERSHIP DEPEND ON THE SITUATION? Research shows impressive correlations between charismatic leadership and high performance and satisfaction among followers. People working for charismatic leaders are motivated to exert extra effort and, because they like and respect their leader, express greater satisfaction. Organizations with charismatic CEOs are also more profitable, and charismatic college professors enjoy higher course evaluations.[31] However, charisma may not always be generalizable; its effectiveness may depend on the situation. Charisma appears most successful when the follower's task has an ideological component or the environment includes a high degree of stress and uncertainty.[32] Even in laboratory studies, when people are psychologically aroused, they are more likely to respond to charismatic leaders.[33] This may explain why, when charismatic leaders surface, it's likely to be in politics or religion, or during wartime or when a business is in its infancy or facing a life-threatening crisis. Franklin D. Roosevelt offered a vision to get the United States out of the Great Depression in the 1930s. In the early 1970s, on the brink of bankruptcy, Chrysler Corporation needed a leader with unconventional ideas to reinvent it, and Lee Iacocca fulfilled that need. In 1997, when Apple Computer was floundering and lacking direction, the board persuaded charismatic co-founder Steve Jobs to return as interim CEO and return the company to its innovative roots.

Another situational factor apparently limiting charisma is level in the organization. Top executives create vision, and charisma probably better explains their successes and failures than those of lower-level managers. It's more difficult to utilize a person's charismatic leadership qualities in lower-level management jobs or to align his or her visions with the larger goals of the organization as a whole.

Finally, people are especially receptive to charismatic leadership when they sense a crisis, when they are under stress, or when they fear for their lives. And some people's personalities are especially susceptible to charismatic leadership.[34] Consider self-esteem. An individual who lacks self-esteem and questions his or her self-worth is more likely to absorb a leader's direction rather than establish his or her own way of leading or thinking.

THE DARK SIDE OF CHARISMATIC LEADERSHIP   Charismatic business leaders like AIG's Hank Greenberg, GE's Jack Welch, Tyco's Dennis Kozlowski, Southwest Airlines' Herb Kelleher, Disney's Michael Eisner, and HP's Carly Fiorina became celebrities on the order of David Beckham and Madonna. Every company wanted a charismatic CEO, and to attract them boards of directors gave them unprecedented autonomy and resources—the use of private jets and multi-million-dollar penthouses, interest-free loans to buy beach homes and artwork, security staffs, and similar benefits befitting royalty. One study showed charismatic CEOs were able to leverage higher salaries even when their performance was mediocre.[35]

Unfortunately, charismatic leaders who are larger than life don't necessarily act in the best interests of their organizations. Many used their power to remake companies in their own image and allowed their own interest and personal goals to override the goals of the organization. The results at companies such as Enron, Tyco, WorldCom, and HealthSouth were leaders who recklessly used organizational resources for their personal benefit, and executives who violated laws and ethical boundaries to inflate stock prices and allow leaders to cash in millions of dollars in stock options.

We don't mean to suggest charismatic leadership isn't effective; overall it is. But a charismatic leader isn't always the answer. Success depends, to some extent, on the situation and on the leader's vision. Some charismatic leaders—Hitler, for example—are all too successful at convincing their followers to pursue a vision that can be disastrous.

Transformational Leadership

A stream of research has focused on differentiating transformational from transactional leaders.[36] The Ohio State Studies, and Fiedler's model describe **transactional leaders,** who guide their followers toward established goals by clarifying role and task requirements. **Transformational leaders** inspire followers to transcend their self-interests for the good of the organization and can have an extraordinary effect on their followers. Andrea Jung at Avon, Richard Branson of the Virgin Group, and Jim McNerney of Boeing are all transformational leaders. They pay attention to the concerns and needs of individual followers, they change followers' awareness of issues by helping them look at old problems in new ways, and they excite and inspire followers to put out extra effort to achieve group goals. Exhibit 11.4 briefly identifies and defines the characteristics that differentiate these two types of leaders.

Transactional and transformational leadership aren't opposing approaches to getting things done. They complement each other, though they're not equally important. Transformational leadership *builds on* transactional leadership and produces levels of follower effort and performance beyond what transactional leadership alone can do. But the reverse isn't true. So if you are a good transactional leader but do not have

---

Transactional Leader

Contingent Reward: Contracts exchange of rewards for effort, promises rewards for good performance, recognizes accomplishments.

Management by Exception (active): Watches and searches for deviations from rules and standards, takes correct action.

Management by Exception (passive): Intervenes only if standards are not met.

Laissez-Faire: Abdicates responsibilities, avoids making decisions.

Transformational Leader

Idealized Influence: Provides vision and sense of mission, instills pride, gains respect and trust.

Inspirational Motivation: Communicates high expectations, uses symbols to focus efforts, expresses important purposes in simple ways.

Intellectual Stimulation: Promotes intelligence, rationality, and careful problem solving.

Individualized Consideration: Gives personal attention, treats each employee individually, coaches, advises.

EXHIBIT 11.4   Characteristics of Transactional and Transformational Leaders

Source: Based on B. M. Bass, "From Transactional to Transformational Leadership: Learning to Share the Vision." *Organizational Dynamics,* Winter 1990, p. 22; Eagly, A. H., Johannesen-Schmidt, M. C., & Van Engen, M. L. (2003). "Transformational, Transactional, and Laissez-Faire Leadership Styles: A Meta-Analysis Comparing Women and Men." *Psychological Bulletin,* 129, 569–591; and Judge, T. A., & Bono, J. E. (2000). "Five Factor Model of Personality and Transformational Leadership." *Journal of Applied Psychology,* 85, 751–765.

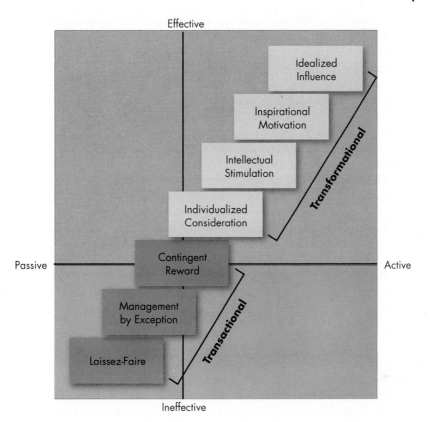

EXHIBIT 11.5
Full Range of
Leadership
Model

transformational qualities, you'll likely only be a mediocre leader. The best leaders are transactional *and* transformational.

FULL RANGE OF LEADERSHIP MODEL   Exhibit 11.5 shows the **full range of leadership model.** Laissez-faire is the most passive and therefore least effective of leader behaviors.[37] Management by exception—active or passive—is slightly better than laissez-faire, but it's still considered ineffective. Management-by-exception leaders tend to be available only when there is a problem, which is often too late. Contingent reward leadership can be an effective style of leadership but will not get employees to go above and beyond the call of duty.

Only with the four remaining styles—all aspects of transformational leadership—are leaders able to motivate followers to perform above expectations and transcend their self-interest for the sake of the organization. Individualized consideration, intellectual stimulation, inspirational motivation, and idealized influence all result in extra effort from workers, higher productivity, higher morale and satisfaction, higher organizational effectiveness, lower turnover, lower absenteeism, and greater organizational adaptability. Based on this model, leaders are generally most effective when they regularly use each of the four transformational behaviors.

HOW TRANSFORMATIONAL LEADERSHIP WORKS   Transformational leaders are more effective because they are more creative but also because they encourage those who follow them to be creative, too.[38] In companies with transformational leaders, there is greater decentralization of responsibility, managers have more propensity to take risks, and compensation plans are geared toward long-term results, all of which facilitate corporate entrepreneurship.[39]

Companies with transformational leaders also show greater agreement among top managers about the organization's goals, which yields superior organizational performance.[40] Similar results, showing that transformational leaders improve performance by building consensus among group members, have been demonstrated in the Israeli military.[41] Transformational leaders are able to increase follower self-efficacy, giving the group a "can do" spirit. Followers are more likely to pursue ambitious goals, agree on the strategic goals of the organization, and believe the goals they are pursuing are personally important.[42] VeriSign's CEO, Stratton Sclavos, says, "It comes down to charting a course—having the ability to articulate for your employees where you're headed and how you're going to get there. Even more important is choosing people to work with who have that same level of passion, commitment, fear, and competitiveness to drive toward those same goals."[43]

Sclavos' remark about goals brings up vision. Just as vision helps explain how charismatic leadership works, vision explains part of the effect of transformational leadership. One study found vision was even more important than a charismatic (effusive, dynamic, lively) communication style in explaining the success of entrepreneurial firms.[44] Finally, transformational leadership engenders commitment on the part of followers and instills greater trust in the leader.[45]

EVALUATION OF TRANSFORMATIONAL LEADERSHIP   Transformational leadership has been impressively supported at various job levels and in disparate occupations (school principals, teachers, marine commanders, ministers, presidents of MBA associations, military cadets, union shop stewards, sales reps). One recent study of research and development (R&D) firms found teams whose project leaders scored high on transformational leadership produced better-quality products as judged 1 year later and were more profitable 5 years later.[46] A review of 87 studies testing transformational leadership found it was related to the motivation and satisfaction of followers and the higher performance and perceived effectiveness of leaders.[47]

Transformational leadership isn't equally effective in all situations, however. It has a greater impact on the bottom line in smaller, privately held firms than in more complicated organizations.[48] The personal nature of transformational leadership may be most effective when leaders can directly interact with the workforce and make decisions than when they report to an external board of directors or deal with a complex bureaucratic structure. Another study showed transformational leaders were more effective in improving group potency in teams higher in power distance and collectivism.[49] Where group members are highly individualistic and don't readily cede decision-making authority, transformational leadership might not have much impact.

Transformational leadership theory is not perfect. There are concerns about whether contingent reward leadership is strictly a characteristic of transactional leaders only. And contrary to the full range of leadership model, the 4 I's in transformational leadership are not always superior in effectiveness to transactional leadership (contingent reward leadership sometimes works as well as transformational leadership).

In summary, transformational leadership is more strongly correlated than transactional leadership with lower turnover rates, higher productivity, lower employee stress and burnout, and higher employee satisfaction.[50] Like charisma, it can be learned. One study of Canadian bank managers found branches managed by those who underwent transformational leadership training performed significantly better than branches whose managers did not receive training. Other studies show similar results.[51]

TRANSFORMATIONAL LEADERSHIP VERSUS CHARISMATIC LEADERSHIP   Are transformational leadership and charismatic leadership the same? Researcher Robert House considers them synonymous, calling the differences "modest" and "minor." However, one researcher who disagrees says, "The purely charismatic [leader] may want followers to adopt the charismatic's world view and go no further; the transformational leader will attempt to instill in followers the ability to question not only established views but eventually those established by the leader."[52] Although many researchers believe transformational is broader than charismatic leadership, a leader who scores high on transformational leadership is also likely to score high on charisma. Therefore, in practice, they may be roughly equivalent.

AUTHENTIC LEADERSHIP: ETHICS AND TRUST ARE THE FOUNDATION OF LEADERSHIP

Although theories have increased our understanding of effective leadership, they do not explicitly deal with the role of ethics and trust, which some argue is essential to complete the picture. Here we consider these two concepts under the rubric of authentic leadership.

If we're looking for the best possible leader, it is not enough to be charismatic or visionary—one must also be ethical and authentic.

What Is Authentic Leadership?

Mike Ullman, JCPenney CEO, argues that leaders have to be selfless, listen well, and be honest. Campbell Soup's CEO Douglas R. Conant is decidedly understated. When asked to reflect on the strong performance of Campbell Soup, he demurs, "We're hitting our stride a little bit more (than our peers)." He regularly admits mistakes and often says, "I can do better." Ullman and Conant appear to be good exemplars of authentic leadership.[53]

Authentic leaders know who they are, know what they believe in and value, and act on those values and beliefs openly and candidly. Their followers consider them ethical people. The primary quality produced by authentic leadership, therefore, is trust. Authentic leaders share information, encourage open communication, and stick to their ideals. The result: People come to have faith in them.

Because the concept is new, there has been little research on authentic leadership. However, it's a promising way to think about ethics and trust in leadership because it focuses on the moral aspects of being a leader. Transformational or charismatic leaders can have a vision, and communicate it persuasively, but sometimes the vision is wrong (as in the case of Hitler), or the leader is more concerned with his or her own needs or pleasures, as were Dennis Kozlowski (ex-CEO of Tyco) and Jeff Skilling (ex-CEO of Enron).

Ethics and Leadership

Only recently have researchers begun to consider the ethical implications in leadership. Why now? One reason may be the growing interest in ethics throughout the field of management. Another may be the discovery that many past leaders—such as Martin Luther King Jr., John F. Kennedy, and Thomas Jefferson—suffered ethical shortcomings. Some companies, like Boeing, are tying executive compensation to ethics to reinforce the idea that, in CEO Jim McNerney's words, "There's no compromise between doing things the right way and performance."[54]

Ethics and leadership intersect at a number of junctures. Transformational leaders have been described as fostering moral virtue when they try to change the attitudes and behaviors of followers. Charisma, too, has an ethical component. Unethical leaders use their charisma to enhance *power over* followers, directed toward self-serving ends. Ethical leaders use it in a socially constructive way to serve others. Leaders who treat their followers with fairness, especially by providing honest, frequent, and accurate information, are seen as more effective.[55] Because top executives set the moral tone for an organization, they need to set high ethical standards; demonstrate those standards through their own behavior; and encourage and reward integrity in others while avoiding abuses of power, such as giving themselves large raises and bonuses while seeking to cut costs by laying off longtime employees.

Leadership is not value-free. In assessing its effectiveness, we need to address the *means* a leader uses in trying to achieve goals, as well as the content of those goals. Scholars have tried to integrate ethical and charismatic leadership by advancing the idea of **socialized charismatic leadership**—leadership that conveys other-centered (not self-centered) values by leaders who model ethical conduct.[56] Socialized charismatic leaders are able to bring employee values in line with their own values through their words and actions.

Trust and Leadership

Trust is a psychological state that exists when you agree to make yourself vulnerable to another because you have positive expectations about how things are going to turn out.[57] Even though you aren't completely in control of the situation, you are willing to take a chance that the other person will come through for you.

Trust is a primary attribute associated with leadership; breaking it can have serious adverse effects on a group's performance. As one author noted, "Part of the leader's task has been, and continues to be, working with people to find and solve problems, but whether leaders gain access to the knowledge and creative thinking they need to solve problems depends on how much people trust them. Trust and trust-worthiness modulate the leader's access to knowledge and cooperation."[58]

Followers who trust a leader are willing to be vulnerable to the leader's actions, confident their rights and interests will not be abused. Transformational leaders create support for their ideas in part by arguing that their direction will be in everyone's best interests. People are unlikely to look up to or follow someone they perceive as dishonest or likely to take advantage of them. "Honesty is absolutely essential to leadership. If people are going to follow someone willingly, whether it be into battle or into the boardroom, they first want to assure themselves that the person is worthy of their trust."[59]

In a simple contractual exchange of goods and services, your employer is legally bound to pay you for fulfilling your job description. But today's rapid reorganizations, diffusion of responsibility, and collaborative team-based work style mean employment relationships are not stable long-term contracts with explicit terms. Rather, they are more fundamentally based on trusting relationships than ever before. You have to trust that if you show your supervisor a creative project you've been working on, she won't steal the credit behind your back. You have to trust that extra work you've been doing will be recognized in your performance appraisal. In contemporary organizations, where less work is closely documented and specified, voluntary employee contribution based on trust is absolutely necessary. And only a trusted leader will be able to encourage employees to reach beyond themselves to a transformational goal.

What Are the Consequences of Trust?

Trust between supervisors and employees is related to a number of positive employment outcomes. Here are just a few of the most important that research has shown:

- *Trust encourages taking risks.* Whenever employees decide to deviate from the usual way of doing things, or to take their supervisors' word on a new direction, they are taking a risk. In both cases, a trusting relationship can facilitate that leap.
- *Trust facilitates information sharing.* One big reason employees fail to express concerns at work is that they don't feel psychologically safe revealing their views. When managers demonstrate they will give employees' ideas a fair hearing and show they are concerned enough to actively make changes, employees are more willing to speak out.[60]
- *Trusting groups are more effective.* When a leader sets a trusting tone in a group, members are more willing to help each other and exert extra effort for one another, which further increases trust. Conversely, members of mistrusting groups tend to be suspicious of each other, are constantly on guard against exploitation, and restrict communication with others in the group. These actions tend to undermine and eventually destroy the group.
- *Trust enhances productivity.* The bottom-line interest of companies also appears positively influenced by trust. Employees who trust their supervisors tend to receive higher performance ratings.[61] Mistrust focuses attention on the differences in member interests, making it difficult for people to visualize common goals. People respond by concealing information and secretly pursuing their own interests. A climate of mistrust tends to stimulate dysfunctional forms of conflict and retard cooperation.

CHALLENGES TO THE LEADERSHIP CONSTRUCT

"In the 1500s, people ascribed all events they didn't understand to God. Why did the crops fail? God. Why did someone die? God. Now our all-purpose explanation is leadership."[62] But much of an organization's success or failure is due to factors outside the influence of leadership. Sometimes it's just a matter of being in the right or wrong place at a given time. In this section, we present two perspectives and one technological change that challenge accepted beliefs about the value of leadership.

Leadership as an Attribution

As you may remember from Chapter 5, attribution theory examines how people try to make sense of cause-and-effect relationships. The **attribution theory of leadership** says leadership is merely an attribution people make about other individuals.[63] Thus we attribute to leaders intelligence, outgoing personality, strong verbal skills, aggressiveness, understanding, and industriousness. At the organizational level, we tend to see leaders, rightly or wrongly, as responsible for extremely negative or extremely positive performance.

One longitudinal study of 128 major U.S. corporations found that, whereas perceptions of CEO charisma did not lead to objective company performance, company performance did lead to perceptions of charisma.[64] Employee perceptions of their leaders' behaviors are significant predictors of leader blame for failure, even after taking leaders' self-assessments into account.[65] A study of more than 3,000 employees from western Europe, the United States, and the Middle East found people who tended to "romanticize" leadership in general were more likely to believe their own leaders were transformational.[66]

When Merrill Lynch began to lose billions in 2008 as a result of its investments in mortgage securities, it wasn't long before CEO Stan O'Neal lost his job. He appeared before the House Oversight and Government Reform Committee of the U.S. Congress for what one committee member termed "a public flogging." CNBC's Jim Cramer called him "Wall Street's Wicked Witch." Others criticized O'Neal's golf handicap, some called him a "criminal," and others suggested Merrill's losses represented "attempted destruction."[67]

Whether O'Neal was responsible for the losses at Merrill or deserved his nine-figure severance package are difficult questions to answer. However, it is not difficult to argue that he probably changed very little between 2004 when *Fortune* described him as a "turnaround genius" and 2009 when he was fired. What did change was the performance of the organization he led. It's not necessarily wrong to terminate a CEO for failing or flagging financial performance. However, O'Neal's story illustrates the power of the attribution approach to leadership: hero and genius when things are going well, villain when they aren't.

We also make demographic assumptions about leaders. Respondents in a study assumed a leader described with no identifying racial information was white at a rate beyond the base rate of white employees in a company. In scenarios where identical leadership situations are described but the leaders' race is manipulated, white leaders are rated as more effective than leaders of other racial groups.[68] Other data suggest women's perceived success as transformational leaders may be based on demographic characteristics. Teams prefer male leaders when aggressively competing against other teams, but they prefer female leaders when the competition is within teams and calls for improving positive relationships within the group.[69]

Attribution theory suggests what's important is projecting the *appearance* of being a leader rather than focusing on *actual accomplishments*. Leader-wannabes who can shape the perception that they're smart, personable, verbally adept, aggressive, hardworking, and consistent in their style can increase the probability their bosses, colleagues, and employees will view them as effective leaders.

Substitutes for and Neutralizers of Leadership

One theory of leadership suggests that in many situations leaders' actions are irrelevant.[70] Experience and training are among the **substitutes** that can replace the need for a leader's support or ability to create structure. Organizational characteristics such as explicit formalized goals, rigid rules and procedures, and cohesive work groups can also replace formal leadership, while indifference to organizational rewards can neutralize its effects. **Neutralizers** make it impossible for leader behavior to make any difference to follower outcomes (see Exhibit 11.6).

This observation shouldn't be too surprising. After all, we've introduced a number of variables—such as attitudes, personality, ability, and group norms—that affect employee performance and satisfaction. It's simplistic to think employees are guided to goal accomplishments solely by the actions of their leader. Leadership is simply another independent variable in our overall OB model.

There are many possible substitutes for and neutralizers of many different types of leader behaviors across many different situations. Moreover, sometimes the difference

Defining Characteristics	Relationship-Oriented Leadership	Task-Oriented Leadership
Individual		
Experience/training	No effect on	Substitutes for
Professionalism	Substitutes for	Substitutes for
Indifference to rewards	Neutralizes	Neutralizes
Job		
Highly structured task	No effect on	Substitutes for
Provides its own feedback	No effect on	Substitutes for
Intrinsically satisfying	Substitutes for	No effect on
Organization		
Explicit formalized goals	No effect on	Substitutes for
Rigid rules and procedures	No effect on	Substitutes for
Cohesive work groups	Substitutes for	Substitutes for

**EXHIBIT 11.6
Substitutes for and Neutralizers of Leadership**

Source: Based on S. Kerr and J.M. Jermier, "Substitutes for Leadership: Their Meaning and Measurement," *Organizational Behavior and Human Performance,* December 1978, p. 378.

between substitutes and neutralizers is fuzzy. If I'm working on a task that's intrinsically enjoyable, theory predicts leadership will be less important because the task itself provides enough motivation. But does that mean intrinsically enjoyable tasks neutralize leadership effects, or substitute for them, or both? Another problem is that although substitutes for leadership (such as employee characteristics, the nature of the task, and so forth) matter to performance, that doesn't necessarily mean that leadership doesn't.[71]

Online Leadership

How do you lead people who are physically separated from you and with whom you communicate electronically? This question has so far received minimal attention from OB researchers.[72] But today's managers and their employees are increasingly linked by networks rather than geographic proximity. Obvious examples include managers who regularly use e-mail to communicate with their staff, managers who oversee virtual projects or teams, and managers whose telecommuting employees are linked to the office by an Internet connection.

Networked communication is a powerful channel that can build and enhance leadership effectiveness. But when misused, it can undermine much of what a leader has achieved through verbal communication. We propose that online leaders have to think carefully about what actions they want their digital messages to initiate.

Online leaders also confront unique challenges, the greatest of which appears to be developing and maintaining trust. **Identification-based trust**, based on a mutual understanding of each other's intentions and appreciation of the others wants and desires, is particularly difficult to achieve without face-to-face interaction. It's not yet clear whether it's even possible for employees to identify with or trust leaders with whom they communicate only electronically.[73] And online negotiations can also be hindered because parties express lower levels of trust.[74]

This discussion leads us to the tentative conclusion that, for an increasing number of managers, good leadership skills may include the abilities to communicate support, trust, and inspiration through keyboarded words and accurately read emotions in others' messages. In electronic communication, writing skills are likely to become an extension of interpersonal skills.

Although the proper leadership style does, to some degree, vary by culture, there are also commonalities across cultures—charismatic/visionary leadership matters in most countries, even if the particular way it is expressed does vary across cultures.

Global Implications

Most of the research discussed in this chapter was conducted in English-speaking countries. We know very little about how culture might influence the validity of the theories, particularly in Eastern cultures. However, a recent analysis of the Global Leadership and Organizational Behavior Effectiveness (GLOBE) research project (see Chapter 4 for more details) has produced some useful preliminary insights.[75]

The study sought to address how culture might affect a U.S. manager given 2 years to lead a project in four prototypical countries whose cultures diverged in different ways: Brazil, France, Egypt, and China. Let's consider each.

- *Brazil.* Based on the values of Brazilian employees, a U.S. manager leading a team in Brazil would need to be team oriented, participative, and humane. Leaders high on consideration who emphasize participative decision making and have high LPC scores would be best suited to managing employees in this culture. As one Brazilian manager said in the study, "We do not prefer leaders who take self-governing decisions and act alone without engaging the group. That's part of who we are."
- *France.* Compared to U.S. employees, the French have a more bureaucratic view of leaders and are less likely to expect them to be humane and considerate. A leader high on initiating structure (relatively task oriented) will do best and can make decisions in a relatively autocratic manner. A manager who scores high on consideration (people oriented) may find that style backfiring in France.
- *Egypt.* Employees in Egypt are more likely to value team-oriented and participative leadership than U.S. employees. However, Egypt is also a relatively high-power-distance culture, meaning status differences between leaders and followers are expected. How would a U.S. manager be participative yet demonstrate his or her high level of status? The leader should ask employees for their opinions, try to minimize conflicts, but not be afraid to take charge and make the final decision (after consulting team members).
- *China.* According to the GLOBE study, Chinese culture emphasizes being polite, considerate,

and unselfish, but it also has a high performance orientation. These two factors suggest consideration and initiating structure may both be important. Although Chinese culture is relatively participative compared to that of the United States, there are also status differences between leaders and employees. This suggests a moderately participative style may work best.

Though we have little research to confirm these conclusions, and there will always be variation across employees (not every Brazilian is more collective than every U.S. employee), the GLOBE study suggests leaders need to take culture into account whenever managing employees from different cultures.

More generally, the GLOBE study—of 18,000 leaders from 825 organizations in 62 countries—reveals there *are* some universal aspects to leadership. A number of elements making up transformational leadership appear associated with effective leadership, regardless of the country.[76] This conclusion is very important because it disputes the contingency view that leadership style needs to adapt to cultural differences.

What elements of transformational leadership appear universal? Vision, foresight, providing encouragement, trustworthiness, dynamism, positiveness, and proactiveness. Two members of the GLOBE team concluded that "effective business leaders in any country are expected by their subordinates to provide a powerful and proactive vision to guide the company into the future, strong motivational skills to stimulate all employees to fulfill the vision, and excellent planning skills to assist in implementing the vision."[77]

A vision is important in any culture, then, but how it is formed and communicated may still need to vary by culture. A GE executive who used his U.S. leadership style in Japan recalls, "Nothing happened. I quickly realized that I had to adapt my approach, to act more as a consultant to my colleagues and to adopt a team-based motivational decision-making process rather than the more vocal style which tends to be common in the West. In Japan the silence of a leader means far more than a thousand words uttered by somebody else."[78]

Implications for Managers

Leadership plays a central part in understanding group behavior, because it's the leader who usually directs us toward our goals. Knowing what makes a good leader should thus be valuable in improving group performance.

The early search for a set of universal leadership traits failed. However, recent efforts using the Big Five personality framework have generated much more encouraging results. Extraversion, conscientiousness, and openness to experience show strong and consistent relationships to leadership.

The behavioral approach's major contribution was narrowing leadership into task-oriented (initiating structure) and people-oriented (consideration) styles. By considering the situation in which the leader operates, contingency theories promised to improve on the behavioral approach, but, with the exception of LPC theory, they have not fared well in leadership research.

Research on charismatic and transformational leadership has made major contributions to our understanding of leadership effectiveness. Organizations are increasingly searching for managers who can exhibit transformational leadership qualities. They want leaders with vision and the charisma to carry out their vision.

Effective managers today must also be authentic and develop trusting relationships with those they seek to lead because, as organizations have become less stable and predictable, strong bonds of trust are replacing bureaucratic rules in defining expectations and relationships. Managers who aren't trusted aren't likely to be effective leaders.

For managers who must fill key positions in their organization with effective leaders, we have shown that tests and interviews help identify people with leadership qualities. Managers should also consider investing in leadership training such as formal courses, workshops, rotating job responsibilities, coaching, and mentoring.

CHAPTER 12

Power and Politics

After studying this chapter, you should be able to:

- Define *power* and contrast leadership and power.
- Contrast the five bases of power.
- Identify nine power or influence tactics and their contingencies.
- Identify the causes and consequences of political behavior.
- Apply impression management techniques.
- Show the influence of culture on the uses and perceptions of politics.

Power and *politics* have been described as the last dirty words. It is easier for most of us to talk about sex or money than it is to talk about power or political behavior. People who have power deny it, people who want it try not to look like they're seeking it, and those who are good at getting it are secretive about how they do so.

In this chapter, we show that power determines what goals a group will pursue and how the group's resources will be distributed among its members. Further, we show how group members with good political skills use their power to influence the distribution of resources in their favor.

A DEFINITION OF *POWER*

Power refers to a capacity that *A* has to influence the behavior of *B* so *B* acts in accordance with *A*'s wishes.[1]

Someone can thus have power but not use it; it is a capacity or potential. Probably the most important aspect of power is that it is a function of **dependency.** The greater *B*'s dependence on *A,* the greater *A*'s power in the relationship. Dependence, in turn, is based on alternatives that *B* perceives, and the importance *B* places on the alternative(s) *A* controls. A person can have power over you only if he or she controls something you desire. If you want a college degree and have to pass a certain course to get it, and your current instructor is the only faculty member in the college who teaches that course, he or she has power over you. Your alternatives are highly limited, and you place a high degree of importance on obtaining a passing grade. Similarly, if you're attending college on funds totally provided by your parents, you probably recognize the power they hold over you. You're dependent on them for financial support. But once you're out of school, have a job, and are making a good income, your parents' power is reduced significantly. Who among us, though, has not known or heard of a rich relative who is able to control a large number of family members merely through the implicit or explicit threat of "writing them out of the will"?

CONTRASTING LEADERSHIP AND POWER

A careful comparison of our description of power with our description of leadership in Chapter 11 reveals the concepts are closely intertwined. Leaders use power as a means of attaining group goals.

How are the two terms different? *Power* does not require goal compatibility, merely dependence. *Leadership,* on the other hand, requires some congruence between the goals of the leader and those being led. A second difference relates to the direction of influence. Leadership focuses on the downward influence on followers. It minimizes the importance of lateral and upward influence patterns. Power does not. In still another difference, leadership research, for the most part, emphasizes style. It seeks answers to questions such as these: How supportive should a leader be? How much decision making should be shared with followers? In contrast, the research on power focuses on tactics for gaining compliance. It goes beyond the individual as the exerciser of power because groups as well as individuals can use power to control other individuals or groups.

BASES OF POWER

Where does power come from? What gives an individual or a group influence over others? We answer by dividing the bases or sources of power into two general groupings—formal and personal—and then breaking each of these down into more specific categories.[2]

Formal Power

Formal power is based on an individual's position in an organization. It can come from the ability to coerce or reward, or from formal authority.

COERCIVE POWER   The **coercive power** base depends on fear of the negative results from failing to comply. It rests on the application, or the threat of application, of physical sanctions such as the infliction of pain, frustration through restriction of movement, or the controlling by force of basic physiological or safety needs.

At the organizational level, *A* has coercive power over *B* if *A* can dismiss, suspend, or demote *B,* assuming *B* values his or her job. If *A* can assign *B* work activities *B* finds unpleasant or treat *B* in a manner *B* finds embarrassing, *A* possesses coercive power over *B.* Coercive power can also come from withholding key information. People in an organization who have data or knowledge others need can make those others dependent on them.

REWARD POWER   The opposite of coercive power is **reward power,** with which people comply because it produces positive benefits; someone who can distribute rewards others view as valuable will have power over them. These rewards can be either financial—such as controlling pay rates, raises, and bonuses—or nonfinancial, including recognition, promotions, interesting work assignments, friendly colleagues, and preferred work shifts or sales territories.[3]

LEGITIMATE POWER   In formal groups and organizations, probably the most common access to one or more of the power bases is through **legitimate power.** It represents the formal authority to control and use organizational resources based on structural position in the organization.

Legitimate power is broader than the power to coerce and reward. Specifically, it includes members' acceptance of the authority of a position. We associate power so closely associated with the concept of hierarchy that just drawing longer lines in an organization chart leads people to infer the leaders are especially powerful, and when a powerful executive is described, people tend to put the person at a higher position when drawing an organization chart.[4] When school principals, bank presidents, or army captains speak (assuming their directives are viewed as within the authority of their positions), teachers, tellers, and first lieutenants listen and usually comply.

Personal Power

Formal power can come from the ability to coerce or reward, or it can come from formal authority. However, evidence suggests that informal power, expert and reference power, *are* the most important to acquire.

Many of the most competent and productive chip designers at Intel have power, but they aren't managers and have no formal power.

What they have is **personal power,** which comes from an individual's unique characteristics. There are two bases of personal power: expertise and the respect and admiration of others.

EXPERT POWER   **Expert power** is influence wielded as a result of expertise, special skill, or knowledge. As jobs become more specialized, we become increasingly dependent on experts to achieve goals. It is generally acknowledged that physicians have expertise and hence expert power: Most of us follow our doctor's advice. Computer specialists, tax accountants, economists, industrial psychologists, and other specialists wield power as a result of their expertise.

REFERENT POWER   **Referent power** is based on identification with a person who has desirable resources or personal traits. If I like, respect, and admire you, you can exercise power over me because I want to please you.

Referent power develops out of admiration of another and a desire to be like that person. It helps explain, for instance, why celebrities are paid millions of dollars to endorse products in commercials. Marketing research shows people such as LeBron James and Tom Brady have the power to influence your choice of athletic shoes and credit cards. With a little practice, you and I could probably deliver as smooth a sales pitch as these celebrities, but the buying public doesn't identify with you and me. Some people who are not in formal leadership positions nonetheless have referent power and exert influence over others because of their charismatic dynamism, likability, and emotional effects on us.

Which Bases of Power Are Most Effective?

Of the three bases of formal power (coercive, reward, legitimate) and two bases of personal power (expert, referent), which is most important to have? Research suggests pretty clearly that the personal sources of power are most effective. Both expert and referent power are positively related to employees' satisfaction with supervision, their organizational commitment, and their performance, whereas reward and legitimate power seem to be unrelated to these outcomes. One source of formal power—coercive power—actually can backfire in that it is negatively related to employee satisfaction and commitment.[5]

Consider Steve Stoute's company, Translation, which matches pop-star spokespersons with corporations that want to promote their brands. Stoute has paired Gwen Stefani with Hewlett-Packard, Justin Timberlake with McDonald's, Beyoncé Knowles with Tommy Hilfiger, and Jay-Z with Reebok. Stoute's business seems to be all about referent power. As one record company executive commented when reflecting on Stoute's successes, "He's the right guy for guiding brands in using the record industry to reach youth culture in a credible way."[6] In other words, people buy products associated with cool figures because they wish to identify with and emulate them.

POWER TACTICS

What **power tactics** do people use to translate power bases into specific action? What options do they have for influencing their bosses, co-workers, or employees? In this section, we review popular tactical options and the conditions that may make one more effective than another.

Research has identified nine distinct influence tactics:[7]

- *Legitimacy.* Relying on your authority position or saying a request accords with organizational policies or rules.
- *Rational persuasion.* Presenting logical arguments and factual evidence to demonstrate a request is reasonable.
- *Inspirational appeals.* Developing emotional commitment by appealing to a target's values, needs, hopes, and aspirations.
- *Consultation.* Increasing the target's support by involving him or her in deciding how you will accomplish your plan.
- *Exchange.* Rewarding the target with benefits or favors in exchange for following a request.
- *Personal appeals.* Asking for compliance based on friendship or loyalty.
- *Ingratiation.* Using flattery, praise, or friendly behavior prior to making a request.
- *Pressure.* Using warnings, repeated demands, and threats.
- *Coalitions.* Enlisting the aid or support of others to persuade the target to agree.

Some tactics are more effective than others. Rational persuasion, inspirational appeals, and consultation tend to be the most effective, especially when the audience is highly interested in the outcomes of a decision process. Pressure tends to backfire and is typically the least effective of the nine tactics.[8] You can also increase your chance of success by using more than one type of tactic at the same time or sequentially, as long as your choices are compatible.[9] Using both ingratiation and legitimacy can lessen the negative reactions from appearing to "dictate" outcomes, but only when the audience does not really care about the outcomes of a decision process or the policy is routine.[10]

Let's consider the most effective way of getting a raise. You can start with rational persuasion. That means doing your homework and carefully thinking through the best way to build your case: figure out how your pay compares to that of peers, or land a competing job offer, or show objective results that testify to your performance. Kitty Dunning, a vice

Political influence behaviors are one important means of gaining power and influence. The most effective influence behaviors—consultation and inspirational appeal—tend to be the least widely used. You should make these influence tactics part of your repertoire.

EXHIBIT 12.1

Preferred
Power Tactics
by Influence
Direction

Upward Influence	Downward Influence	Lateral Influence
Rational persuasion	Rational persuasion	Rational persuasion
	Inspirational appeals	Consultation
	Pressure	Ingratiation
	Consultation	Exchange
	Ingratiation	Legitimacy
	Exchange	Personal appeals
	Legitimacy	Coalitions

president at Don Jagoda Associates, landed a 16 percent raise when she e-mailed her boss numbers showing she had increased sales.[11] You can also make good use of salary calculators such as Salary.com to compare your pay with others.

But the effectiveness of some influence tactics depends on the direction of influence.[12] As Exhibit 12.1 shows, rational persuasion is the only tactic effective across organizational levels. Inspirational appeals work best as a downward-influencing tactic with subordinates. When pressure works, it's generally downward only. Personal appeals and coalitions are most effective as lateral influence. Other factors that affect the effectiveness of influence include the sequencing of tactics, a person's skill in using the tactic, and the organizational culture.

You're more likely to be effective if you begin with "softer" tactics that rely on personal power, such as personal and inspirational appeals, rational persuasion, and consultation. If these fail, you can move to "harder" tactics, such as exchange, coalitions, and pressure, which emphasize formal power and incur greater costs and risks.[13] Interestingly, a single soft tactic is more effective than a single hard tactic, and combining two soft tactics or a soft tactic and rational persuasion is more effective than any single tactic or combination of hard tactics.[14] The effectiveness of tactics depends on the audience.[15] People especially likely to comply with soft power tactics tend to be more reflective, are intrinsically motivated, have high self-esteem, and have greater desire for control. People likely to comply with hard power tactics are more action oriented and extrinsically motivated and are more focused on getting along with others than with getting their own way.

People differ in their **political skill,** or their ability to influence others to enhance their own objectives. The politically skilled are more effective users of all of the influence tactics. Political skill also appears more effective when the stakes are high—such as when the individual is accountable for important organizational outcomes. Finally, the politically skilled are able to exert their influence without others detecting it, a key element in being effective (it's damaging to be labeled political).[16]

Finally, we know cultures within organizations differ markedly—some are warm, relaxed, and supportive; others are formal and conservative. The organizational culture in which a person works will have a bearing on which tactics are considered appropriate. Some cultures encourage participation and consultation, some encourage reason, and still others rely on pressure. People who fit the culture of the organization tend to obtain more influence.[17] Specifically, extraverts tend to be more influential in team-oriented organizations, and highly conscientious people are more influential in organizations that value working alone on technical tasks. Part of the reason people who fit the culture are influential is that they are able to perform especially well in the domains deemed most important for success. In other words, they are influential because they are competent. So the organization itself will influence which subset of power tactics is viewed as acceptable for use.

POLITICS: POWER IN ACTION

When people get together in groups, power will be exerted. People want to carve out a niche from which to exert influence, earn rewards, and advance their careers.[18] When employees in organizations convert their power into action, we describe them as being engaged in **politics.** Those with good political skills have the ability to use their bases of power effectively.[19]

Definition of *Organizational Politics*

There is no shortage of definitions of *organizational politics.* Essentially they focus on the use of power to affect decision making in an organization or on self-serving and organizationally unsanctioned behaviors.[20] For our purposes, **political behavior** in organizations consists of activities that are not required as part of an individual's formal role but that influence, or attempt to influence, the distribution of advantages and disad-vantages within the organization.[21]

This definition encompasses what most people mean when they talk about organizational politics. Political behavior is outside specified job requirements. It requires some attempt to use power bases. It includes efforts to influence the goals, criteria, or processes used for decision making. Our definition is broad enough to include varied political behaviors such as withholding key information from decision makers, joining a coalition, whistle-blowing, spreading rumors, leaking confidential information to the media, exchanging favors with others in the organization for mutual benefit, and lobbying on behalf of or against a particular individual or decision alternative.

Is there a "legitimate" dimension in political behavior?[22] **Legitimate political behavior** refers to normal everyday politics—complaining to your supervisor, bypassing the chain of command, forming coalitions, obstructing organizational policies or decisions through inaction or excessive adherence to rules, and developing contacts outside the organization through professional activities. Different from these, **illegitimate political behavior** violates the implied rules of the game. Illegitimate activities include sabotage, whistle-blowing, and symbolic protests such as wearing unorthodox dress or protest buttons and calling in sick as a group. Those who pursue such extreme activities are often said to "play hardball."

The vast majority of all organizational political actions are of the legitimate variety. The reasons are pragmatic: Extreme forms of illegitimate political behavior pose a very real risk of losing organizational membership or incurring extreme sanctions, particularly if those who use these tactics don't have enough power to ensure they work.

The Reality of Politics

Interviews with experienced managers show that most believe political behavior is a major part of organizational life.[23] Many managers report some use of political behavior is both ethical and necessary, as long as it doesn't directly harm anyone else. They describe politics as a necessary evil and believe someone who *never* uses political behavior will have a hard time getting things done. Most also indicate they had never been trained to use political behavior effectively. But why, you may wonder, must politics exist? Isn't it possible for an organization to be politics free? It's *possible* but unlikely.

Organizations are made up of individuals and groups with different values, goals, and interests.[24] This sets up the potential for conflict over the allocation of limited resources, such as departmental budgets, space, project responsibilities, and salary adjustments.[25] If resources were abundant, then all constituencies within the organization could satisfy their goals. But because they are limited, not everyone's interests can be satisfied. Furthermore, gains by one individual or group are often *perceived* as coming at the expense of others within the organization (whether they are or not). These forces create real competition among members for the organization's limited resources.

Maybe the most important factor leading to politics within organizations is the realization that most of the "facts" used to allocate the limited resources are open to interpretation. What, for instance, is *good* performance? What's an *adequate* improvement? What constitutes an *unsatisfactory* job? One person's "selfless effort to benefit the organization" is seen by another as a "blatant attempt to further one's interest."[26] The manager of any major league baseball team knows a .400 hitter is a high performer and a .125 hitter is a poor performer. You don't need to be a baseball genius to know you should play your .400 hitter and send the .125 hitter back to the minors. But what if you have to choose between players who hit .280 and .290? Then less objective factors come into play: fielding expertise, attitude, potential, ability to perform in a clutch, loyalty to the team, and so on. More managerial decisions resemble the choice between a .280 and a .290 hitter than between a .125 hitter and a .400 hitter. It is in this large and ambiguous middle ground of organizational life—where the facts *don't* speak for themselves—that politics flourish.

Finally, because most decisions have to be made in a climate of ambiguity—where facts are rarely fully objective and thus are open to interpretation—people within organizations will use whatever influence they can to taint the facts to support their goals and interests. That, of course, creates the activities we call ***politicking.***

Therefore, to answer the question of whether it is possible for an organization to be politics free, we can say "yes"—if all members of that organization hold the same goals and interests, if organizational resources are not scarce, and if performance outcomes are completely clear and objective. But that doesn't describe the organizational world in which most of us live.

CAUSES AND CONSEQUENCES OF POLITICAL BEHAVIOR

Factors Contributing to Political Behavior

Not all groups or organizations are equally political. In some organizations, for instance, politicking is overt and rampant, whereas in others politics plays a small role in influencing outcomes. Why this variation? Recent research and observation have identified a number of factors that appear to encourage political behavior. Some are individual characteristics, derived from the unique qualities of the people the organization employs; others are a result of the organization's culture or internal environment. Both individual and organizational factors can increase political behavior and provide favorable outcomes (increased rewards and averted punishments) for both individuals and groups in the organization.

INDIVIDUAL FACTORS   At the individual level, researchers have identified certain personality traits, needs, and other factors likely to be related to political behavior. In terms of traits, we find that employees who are high self-monitors, possess an internal locus of control, and have a high need for power are more likely to engage in political behavior.[27] The high self-monitor is more sensitive to social cues, exhibits higher levels of social conformity, and is more likely to be skilled in political behavior than the low self-monitor. Because they believe they can control their environment, individuals with an internal locus of control are more prone to take a proactive stance and attempt to manipulate situations in their favor. Not surprisingly, the Machiavellian personality— characterized by the will to manipulate and the desire for power—is comfortable using politics as a means to further his or her self-interest.

In addition, an individual's investment in the organization, perceived alternatives, and expectations of success influence the degree to which he or she will pursue illegitimate means of political action.[28] The more a person expects increased future benefits from the organization, the more that person has to lose if forced out and the less likely he or she is to use illegitimate means. The more alternative job opportunities an individual has—due to a favorable job market or the possession of scarce skills or knowledge, a prominent reputation, or influential contacts outside the organization—the more likely that individual is to risk illegitimate political actions. Finally, if an individual has a low expectation of success in using illegitimate means, it is unlikely he or she will attempt to do so. High expectations of success in the use of illegitimate means are most likely to be the province of both experienced and powerful individuals with polished political skills and inexperienced and naïve employees who misjudge their chances.

ORGANIZATIONAL FACTORS   Political activity is probably more a function of an organization's characteristics than of individual difference variables. Why? It is so because many organizations have a large number of employees with the individual characteristics we listed, yet the extent of political behavior varies widely.

Although we acknowledge the role individual differences can play in fostering politicking, the evidence more strongly supports the idea that certain situations and cultures promote politics. Specifically, when an organization's resources are declining, when the existing pattern of resources is changing, and when there is opportunity for promotions, politicking is more likely to surface.[29] Cultures characterized by low trust, role ambiguity, unclear performance evaluation systems, zero-sum reward allocation practices, democratic decision making, high pressures for performance, and self-serving senior managers will create breeding grounds for politicking.[30]

When organizations downsize to improve efficiency, reductions in resources have to be made. Threatened with the loss of resources, people may engage in political actions to safeguard what they have. But any changes, especially those that imply significant reallocation of resources within the organization, are likely to stimulate conflict and increase politicking.

Promotion decisions have consistently been found to be one of the most political actions in organizations. The opportunity for promotions or advancement encourages people to compete for a limited resource and to try to positively influence the decision outcome.

The less trust within the organization, the higher the level of political behavior and the more likely it will be of the illegitimate kind. So high trust should suppress the level of political behavior in general and inhibit illegitimate actions in particular.

Role ambiguity means the prescribed employee behaviors are not clear. There are therefore fewer limits to the scope and functions of the employee's political actions. Because political activities are defined as those not required as part of the employee's formal role, the greater the role ambiguity, the more he or she can engage in unnoticed political activity.

Performance evaluation is far from a perfect science. The more organizations use subjective criteria in the appraisal, emphasize a single outcome measure, or allow significant time to pass between the time of an action and its appraisal, the greater the likelihood that an employee can get away with politicking. Subjective performance criteria create ambiguity. The use of a single outcome measure encourages individuals to do whatever is necessary to "look good" on that measure, but that often occurs at the expense of good performance on other important parts of the job that are not being appraised. The time lapse between an action and its appraisal is also a relevant factor. The longer the time, the more unlikely it is that the employee will be held accountable for political behaviors.

The more an organization's culture emphasizes the zero-sum or win–lose approach to reward allocations, the more employees will be motivated to engage in politicking. The **zero-sum approach** treats the reward "pie" as fixed, so any gain one person or group achieves has to come at the expense of another person or group. If I win, you must lose! If $15,000 in annual raises is to be distributed among five employees, any employee who gets more than $3,000 takes money away from one or more of the others. Such a practice encourages making others look bad and increasing the visibility of what you do.

The more pressure employees feel to perform well, the more likely they are to engage in politicking. Being held strictly accountable for outcomes puts great pressure on people to "look good." A person who perceives that his or her entire career is riding on next quarter's sales figures or next month's plant productivity report is motivated to do whatever is necessary to make sure the numbers come out favorably.

Finally, when employees see the people on top engaging in political behavior, especially when they do so successfully and are rewarded for it, a climate is created that supports politicking. Politicking by top management, in a sense, gives permission to those lower in the organization to play politics by implying that such behavior is acceptable.

How Do People Respond to Organizational Politics?

Trish O'Donnell loves her job as a writer on a weekly television comedy series but hates the internal politics. "A couple of the writers here spend more time kissing up to the executive producer than doing any work. And our head writer clearly has his favorites. Although they pay me a lot and I get to really use my creativity, I'm sick of having to be on alert for backstabbers and constantly having to self-promote my contributions. I'm tired of doing most of the work and getting little of the credit." Are Trish O'Donnell's comments typical of people who work in highly politicized workplaces? We all know friends or relatives who regularly complain about the politics at their job. But how do people in general react to organizational politics? Let's look at the evidence.

In our previous discussion in this chapter of factors that contribute to political behavior, we focused on the favorable outcomes. But for most people—who have modest political skills or are unwilling to play the politics game—outcomes tend to be predominantly negative. Exhibit 12.2 summarizes the extensive research on the relationship

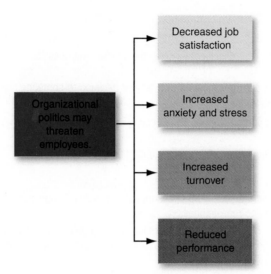

EXHIBIT 12.2

Employee Responses to Organizational Politics

between organizational politics and individual outcomes.[31] Very strong evidence indicates, for instance, that perceptions of organizational politics are negatively related to job satisfaction.[32] The perception of politics also tends to increase job anxiety and stress. This seems due to the perception that, by not engaging in politics, a person may be losing ground to others who are active politickers or, conversely, to the additional pressures felt from having entered into and competing in the political arena.[33] Not surprisingly, when politicking becomes too much to handle, it can lead employees to quit.[34] Finally, preliminary evidence suggests that politics leads to self-reported declines in employee performance, perhaps because employees perceive political environments to be unfair, which demotivates them.[35]

Researchers have also noted several interesting qualifiers. First, the politics–performance relationship appears to be moderated by an individual's understanding of the "hows" and "whys" of organizational politics. "An individual who has a clear understanding of who is responsible for making decisions and why they were selected to be the decision makers would have a better understanding of how and why things happen the way they do than someone who does not understand the decision-making process in the organization."[36] When both politics and understanding are high, performance is likely to increase because the individual will see political actions as an opportunity. This is consistent with what you might expect among individuals with well-honed political skills. But when understanding is low, individuals are more likely to see politics as a threat, which would have a negative effect on job performance.[37]

Second, when employees see politics as a threat, they often respond with **defensive behaviors**—reactive and protective behaviors to avoid action, blame, or change.[38] (Exhibit 12.3 provides some examples of these behaviors.) And defensive behaviors are often associated with negative feelings toward the job and work environment.[39] In the short run, employees may find that defensiveness protects their self-interest, but in the long run it wears them down. People who consistently rely on defensiveness find that, eventually, it is the only way they know how to behave. At that point, they lose the trust and support of their peers, bosses, employees, and clients.

Avoiding Action

Overconforming. Strictly interpreting your responsibility by saying things like "The rules clearly state . . ." or "This is the way we've always done it."

Buck passing. Transferring responsibility for the execution of a task or decision to someone else.

Playing dumb. Avoiding an unwanted task by falsely pleading ignorance or inability.

Stretching. Prolonging a task so that one person appears to be occupied—for example, turning a two-week task into a 4-month job.

Stalling. Appearing to be more or less supportive publicly while doing little or nothing privately.

Avoiding Blame

Buffing. This is a nice way to refer to "covering your rear." It describes the practice of rigorously documenting activity to project an image of competence and thoroughness.

Playing safe. Evading situations that may reflect unfavorably. It includes taking on only projects with a high probability of success, having risky decisions approved by superiors, qualifying expressions of judgment, and taking neutral positions in conflicts.

Justifying. Developing explanations that lessen one's responsibility for a negative outcome and/or apologizing to demonstrate remorse, or both.

Scapegoating. Placing the blame for a negative outcome on external factors that are not entirely blameworthy.

Misrepresenting. Manipulation of information by distortion, embellishment, deception, selective presentation, or obfuscation.

Avoiding Change

Prevention. Trying to prevent a threatening change from occurring.

Self-protection. Acting in ways to protect one's self-interest during change by guarding information or other resources.

EXHIBIT 12.3 Defensive Behaviors

Impression Management

Impression management is a specific type of political behavior, designed to alter other's immediate perceptions of us; evidence suggests that the effectiveness of impression management techniques depends on the setting (i.e., self-promotion works better in the interview than for performance evaluation).

We know people have an ongoing interest in how others perceive and evaluate them. For example, North Americans spend billions of dollars on diets, health club memberships, cosmetics, and plastic surgery—all intended to make them more attractive to others.[40] Being perceived positively by others should have benefits for people in organizations. It might, for instance, help them initially to get the jobs they want in an organization and, once hired, to get favorable evaluations, superior salary increases, and more rapid promotions. In a political context, it might help sway the distribution of advantages in their favor. The process by which individuals attempt to control the impression others form of them is called **impression management (IM).**[41]

Is everyone concerned with IM? No! Who, then, might we predict will engage in IM? No surprise here. It's our old friend, the high self-monitor.[42] Low self-monitors tend to present images of themselves that are consistent with their personalities, regardless of the beneficial or detrimental effects for them. In contrast, high self-monitors are good at reading situations and molding their appearances and behavior to fit each situation. If you want to control the impression others form of you, what IM techniques can you use? Exhibit 12.4 summarizes some of the most popular and provides an example of each.

Conformity

Agreeing with someone else's opinion to gain his or her approval is a *form of ingratiation.*

Example: A manager tells his boss, "You're absolutely right on your reorganization plan for the western regional office. I couldn't agree with you more."

Favors

Doing something nice for someone to gain that person's approval is a *form of ingratiation.*

Example: A salesperson says to a prospective client, "I've got two tickets to the theater tonight that I can't use. Take them. Consider it a thank-you for taking the time to talk with me."

Excuses

Explanations of a predicament-creating event aimed at minimizing the apparent severity of the predicament is a *defensive IM technique.*

Example: A sales manager says to her boss, "We failed to get the ad in the paper on time, but no one responds to those ads anyway."

Apologies

Admitting responsibility for an undesirable event and simultaneously seeking to get a pardon for the action is a *defensive IM technique.*

Example: An employee says to his boss, "I'm sorry I made a mistake on the report. Please forgive me."

Self-Promotion

Highlighting one's best qualities, downplaying one's deficits, and calling attention to one's achievements is a *self-focused IM technique.*

Example: A salesperson tells his boss, "Matt worked unsuccessfully for three years to try to get that account. I sewed it up in six weeks. I'm the best closer this company has."

Enhancement

Claiming that something you did is more valuable than most other members of the organizations would think is a *self-focused IM technique.*

Example: A journalist tells his editor, "My work on this celebrity divorce story was really a major boost to our sales" (even though the story only made it to page 3 in the entertainment section).

Flattery

Complimenting others about their virtues in an effort to make oneself appear perceptive and likeable is an *assertive IM technique.*

Example: A new sales trainee says to her peer, "You handled that client's complaint so tactfully! I could never have handled that as well as you did."

Exemplification

Doing more than you need to in an effort to show how dedicated and hard working you are is an *assertive IM technique.*

Example: An employee sends e-mails from his work computer when he works late so that his supervisor will know how long he's been working.

EXHIBIT 12.4 Impression Management Techniques

Source: Based on B.R. Schlenker, Impression Management (Monterey, CA: Brooks/Cole, 1980); W. L. Gardner and M.J. Martinko, "Impression Management in Organizations," Journal of Management, June 1988, p. 332; and R.B. Cialdini, "Indirect Tactics of Image Management Beyond Basking." in R.A. Giacalone and P. Rosenfeld (eds.), Impression Management in the Organization (Hillsdale, NJ: Lawrence Erlbaum, 1989), pp. 45–71.

Keep in mind that the impressions people use IM to convey are necessarily false (although, of course, they sometimes are true).[43] Excuses, for instance, may be offered with sincerity. Referring to the example in Exhibit 12.4, you can *actually* believe that ads contribute little to sales in your region. But misrepresentation can have a high cost. If you "cry wolf" once too often, no one is likely to believe you when the wolf really comes. So the impression manager must be cautious not to be perceived as insincere or manipulative.[44] As an amusing example of this principle, participants in a study in Switzerland disliked an experimental confederate who claimed to be a personal friend of the well-liked Swiss tennis star Roger Federer, but they generally liked confederates who just said they were fans.[45] Implausible name-dropping like this can harm people's first impression of you.

Are there *situations* in which individuals are more likely to misrepresent themselves or more likely to get away with it? Yes—situations characterized by high uncertainty or ambiguity provide relatively little information for challenging a fraudulent claim and reduce the risks associated with misrepresentation.[46] The increasing use of telework may be increasing the use of IM. Individuals who work remotely from their supervisors engage in high levels of IM relative to those who work closely with their supervisors.[47]

Most of the studies undertaken to test the effectiveness of IM techniques have related it to two criteria: interview success and performance evaluations. Let's consider each of these.

The evidence indicates most job applicants use IM techniques in interviews[48] and that it works.[49] In one study, for instance, interviewers felt applicants for a position as a customer service representative who used IM techniques performed better in the interview, and they seemed somewhat more inclined to hire these people.[50] Moreover, when the researchers considered applicants' credentials, they concluded it was the IM techniques alone that influenced the interviewers—that is, it didn't seem to matter whether applicants were well or poorly qualified. If they used IM techniques, they did better in the interview.

Some IM techniques work better than others in the interview. Researchers have compared applicants whose IM techniques focused on promoting their accomplishments (called *self-promotion*) to those who focused on complimenting the interviewer and finding areas of agreement (referred to as *ingratiation*). In general, applicants appear to use self-promotion more than ingratiation.[51] What's more, self-promotion tactics may be more important to interviewing success. Applicants who work to create an appearance of competence by enhancing their accomplishments, taking credit for successes, and explaining away failures do better in interviews. These effects reach beyond the interview: Applicants who use more self-promotion tactics also seem to get more follow-up job-site visits, even after adjusting for grade-point average, gender, and job type. Ingratiation also works well in interviews; applicants who compliment the interviewer, agree with his or her opinions, and emphasize areas of fit do better than those who don't.[52]

In terms of performance ratings, the picture is quite different. Ingratiation is positively related to performance ratings, meaning those who ingratiate with their supervisors get higher performance evaluations. However, self-promotion appears to backfire: Those who self-promote actually seem to receive *lower* performance evaluations.[53] There is an important qualifier to this general result. It appears that individuals high in political skill are able to translate IM into higher performance appraisals, whereas those lower in political skill are more likely to be hurt by their IM attempts.[54] Another study of 760 boards of directors found that individuals who ingratiate themselves to current board members (express agreement with the director, point out shared attitudes and opinions, compliment the director) increase their chances of landing on a board.[55]

What explains these results? If you think about them, they make sense. Ingratiating always works because everyone—both interviewers and supervisors—likes to be treated nicely. However, self-promotion may work only in interviews and backfire on the job because, whereas the interviewer has little idea whether you're blowing smoke about your accomplishments, the supervisor knows because it's his or her job to observe you. Thus, if you're going to self-promote, remember that what works in an interview won't always work once you're on the job.

THE ETHICS OF BEHAVING POLITICALLY

Although there are no clear-cut ways to differentiate ethical from unethical politicking, there are some questions you should consider. For example, what is the utility of engaging in politicking? Sometimes we engage in political behavior for little good reason. Major league baseball player Al Martin claimed he played football at USC when in fact he never did. As a baseball player, he had little to gain by pretending to have played football. Outright lies like this may be a rather extreme example of impression management, but many of us have distorted information to make a favorable impression. One thing to keep in mind is whether it's really worth the risk. Another question to ask is this: How does the utility of engaging in the political behavior balance out any harm (or potential harm) it will do to others? Complimenting a supervisor on his or her appearance in order to curry favor is probably much less harmful than grabbing credit for a project that others deserve.

Finally, does the political activity conform to standards of equity and justice? Sometimes it is difficult to weigh the costs and benefits of a political action, but its ethicality is clear. The department head who inflates the performance evaluation of a favored employee and deflates the evaluation of a disfavored employee—and then uses these evaluations to justify giving the former a big raise and nothing to the latter—has treated the disfavored employee unfairly.

Unfortunately, powerful people can become very good at explaining self-serving behaviors in terms of the organization's best interests. They can persuasively argue that unfair actions are really fair and just. Our point is that immoral people can justify almost any behavior. Those who are powerful, articulate, and persuasive are most vulnerable to ethical lapses because they are likely to be able to get away with unethical practices successfully. When faced with an ethical dilemma regarding organizational politics, try to consider whether playing politics is worth the risk and whether others might be harmed in the process. If you have a strong power base, recognize the ability of power to corrupt. Remember that it's a lot easier for the powerless to act ethically, if for no other reason than they typically have very little political discretion to exploit.

Global Implications

Although culture might enter any of the topics we've covered to this point, three questions are particularly important: (1) Does culture influence perceptions of politics? (2) Does culture affect the power of influence tactics people prefer to use? and (3) Does culture influence the effectiveness of different tactics?

Perceptions of Politics

We have already noted that (based on research conducted mostly in the United States) when people see their work environment as political, the effect on their overall work attitudes and behaviors is usually negative. When employees of two agencies in a recent study in Nigeria viewed their work environments as political, they reported higher levels of job distress and were less likely to help their co-workers. Thus, although developing countries such as Nigeria are perhaps more ambiguous and more political environments in which to work, the negative consequences appear to be the same as in the United States.[56]

Preference for Power Tactics

Evidence indicates people in different countries tend to prefer different power tactics.[57] A study comparing managers in the United States and China found that U.S. managers prefer rational appeal, whereas Chinese managers preferred coalition tactics.[58] These differences tend to be consistent with the values in these two countries. Reason is consistent with the U.S. preference for direct confrontation and the use of rational persuasion to influence others and resolve differences. Similarly, coalition tactics are consistent with the Chinese preference for using indirect approaches for difficult or controversial requests. Research also has shown that individuals in Western, individualistic cultures tend to engage in more self-enhancement (such as self-promotion) behaviors than individuals in Eastern, more collectivistic cultures.[59]

Effectiveness of Power Tactics

Are our conclusions about responses to politics globally valid? Should we expect employees in Israel, for instance, to respond the same way to workplace politics that employees in the United States do? Almost all our conclusions on employee reactions to organizational politics are based on studies conducted in North America. The few studies that have included other countries suggest some minor modifications.[60] One study of managers in U.S. culture and three Chinese cultures (People's Republic of China, Hong Kong, Taiwan) found U.S. managers evaluated "gentle persuasion" tactics such as consultation and inspirational appeal as more effective than did their Chinese counterparts.[61] As another example, Israelis and the British seem to generally respond as do North Americans—that is, their perception of organizational politics relates to decreased job satisfaction and increased turnover.[62] But in countries that are more politically unstable, such as Israel, employees seem to demonstrate greater tolerance of intense political processes in the workplace, perhaps because they are used to power struggles and have more experience in coping with them.[63] This suggests that people from politically turbulent countries in the Middle East or Latin America might be more accepting of organizational politics, and even more willing to use aggressive political tactics in the workplace, than people from countries such as Great Britain or Switzerland.

Implications for Managers

If you want to get things done in a group or an organization, it helps to have power. As a manager who wants to maximize your power, you will want to increase others' dependence on you. You can, for instance, increase your power in relation to your boss by developing knowledge or a skill she needs and for which she perceives no ready substitute. But you will not be alone in attempting to build your power bases. Others, particularly employees and peers, will be seeking to increase your dependence on them, while you are trying to minimize it and increase their dependence on you. The result is a continual battle.

Few employees relish being powerless in their job and organization. It's been argued, for instance, that when people in organizations are difficult, argumentative, and temperamental, it may be that the performance expectations placed on them exceed their resources and capabilities, making them feel powerless.[64]

People respond differently to the various power bases.[65] Expert and referent power are derived from an individual's personal qualities. In contrast, coercion, reward, and legitimate power are essentially organizationally derived. Because people are more likely to enthusiastically accept and commit to an individual they admire or whose knowledge they respect (rather than someone who relies on his or her position for influence), the effective use of expert and referent power should lead to higher employee motivation, performance, commitment, and satisfaction.[66] Competence especially appears to offer wide appeal, and its use as a power base results in high performance by group members. The message for managers seems to be "Develop and use your expert power base!"

The power of your boss may also play a role in determining your job satisfaction. "One of the reasons many of us like to work for and with people who are powerful is that they are generally more pleasant—not because it is their native disposition, but because the reputation and reality of being powerful permits them more discretion and more ability to delegate to others."[67]

An effective manager accepts the political nature of organizations. By assessing behavior in a political framework, you can better predict the actions of others and use that information to formulate political strategies that will gain advantages for you and your work unit.

Some people are significantly more politically astute than others, meaning that they are aware of the underlying politics and can manage impressions. Those who are good at playing politics can be expected to get higher performance evaluations and, hence, larger salary increases and more promotions than the politically naïve or inept.[68] The politically astute are also likely to exhibit higher job satisfaction and be better able to neutralize job stressors.[69] Employees who have poor political skills or are unwilling to play the politics game generally relate perceived organizational politics to lower job satisfaction and self-reported performance, increased anxiety, and higher turnover.

CHAPTER 13

Conflict and Negotiation

After studying this chapter, you should be able to:

▪ Define *conflict* and differentiate between the traditional, interactionist, and managed-conflict views of conflict.

▪ Outline the conflict process.

▪ Contrast distributive and integrative bargaining.

▪ Apply the five steps of the negotiation process.

▪ Show how individual differences influence negotiations.

▪ Describe cultural differences in negotiations.

Conflict can often turn personal. It can create chaotic conditions that make it nearly impossible for employees to work as a team. However, conflict also has a less well-known positive side. We'll explain the difference between negative and positive conflicts in this chapter and provide a guide to help you understand how conflicts develop. We'll also present a topic closely akin to conflict: negotiation.

A DEFINITION OF *CONFLICT*

We can define **conflict,** then, as a process that begins when one party perceives another party has or is about to negatively affect something the first party cares about.[1] This definition is purposely broad. It describes that point in any ongoing activity when an interaction crosses over to become an interparty conflict. It encompasses the wide range of conflicts people experience in organizations: incompatibility of goals, differences over interpretations of facts, disagreements based on behavioral expectations, and the like. Finally, our definition is flexible enough to cover the full range of conflict levels—from overt and violent acts to subtle forms of disagreement.

TRANSITIONS IN CONFLICT THOUGHT

It is entirely appropriate to say there has been conflict over the role of conflict in groups and organizations.

One school of thought has argued that conflict must be avoided—that it indicates a malfunctioning within the group. We call this the *traditional* view. Another perspective proposes not only that conflict can be a positive force in a group but that some conflict is absolutely necessary for a group to perform effectively. We label this the *interactionist* view. Finally, recent research argues that instead of encouraging "good" or discouraging "bad" conflict, it's more important to resolve naturally occurring conflicts productively. This perspective is the *managed conflict* view. Let's take a closer look at each view.

Conflict is an inherent part of organizational life. Indeed, some level of conflict is probably necessary for optimal organizational functioning.

The Traditional View of Conflict

The early approach to conflict assumed all conflict was bad and to be avoided. It was viewed negatively and discussed with such terms as *violence, destruction,* and *irrationality* to reinforce its negative connotation. This **traditional view of conflict** was consistent with attitudes about group behavior that prevailed in the 1930s and 1940s. Conflict was a dysfunctional outcome resulting from poor communication, a lack of openness and trust between people, and the failure of managers to be responsive to the needs and aspirations of their employees.

   The view that all conflict is bad certainly offers a simple approach to looking at the behavior of people who create conflict. We need merely direct our attention to the causes of conflict and correct those malfunctions to improve group and organizational performance. This view of conflict fell out of favor for a long time as researchers came to realize that some level of conflict was inevitable.

The Interactionist View of Conflict

The **interactionist view of conflict** encourages conflict on the grounds that a harmonious, peaceful, tranquil, and cooperative group is prone to becoming static, apathetic, and unresponsive to needs for change and innovation.[2] The major contribution of this view is recognizing that a minimal level of conflict can help keep a group viable, self-critical, and creative.

   The interactionist view does not propose that all conflicts are good. Rather, **functional conflict** supports the goals of the group and improves its performance and is, thus, a constructive form of conflict. A conflict that hinders group performance is a destructive or **dysfunctional conflict.** What differentiates functional from dysfunctional conflict? The evidence indicates we need to look at the *type* of conflict—task, relationship, and process.[3]

   Task conflict relates to the content and goals of the work. **Relationship conflict** focuses on interpersonal relationships. **Process conflict** relates to how the work gets done. Studies demonstrate that relationship conflicts are almost always dysfunctional.[4] Why? It appears that the friction and interpersonal hostilities inherent in relationship conflicts increase personality clashes and decrease mutual understanding, which hinders the completion of organizational tasks. Unfortunately, managers spend a lot of effort resolving personality conflicts among staff members; one survey indicated this task consumes 18 percent of their time.[5]

Task conflict is more constructive than process or, especially, relationship conflict.

   In contrast, low levels of process conflict and low to moderate levels of task conflict can be functional, but only in very specific cases. Recent reviews have shown that task conflicts are usually just as disruptive as relationship conflicts.[6] For process conflict to be productive, it must be kept low. Intense arguments about who should do what become dysfunctional when they create uncertainty about task roles, increase the time to complete tasks, and lead to members working at cross-purposes. Low to moderate levels of task conflict stimulate discussion of ideas. This means task conflicts relate

positively to creativity and innovation, but they are not related to routine task performance. Groups performing routine tasks that don't require creativity won't benefit from
task conflict. Moreover, if the group is already engaged in active discussion of ideas in a
nonconfrontational way, adding conflict will not help generate more ideas. Task conflict
is also related to these positive outcomes only when all members share the same goals
and have high levels of trust.[7]

Resolution Focused View of Conflict

Researchers, including those who had strongly advocated the interactionist view, have
begun to recognize some problems with encouraging conflict. As we will see, there are
some very specific cases in which conflict can be beneficial. However, workplace
conflicts are not productive; they take time away from job tasks or interacting with
customers, and hurt feelings and anger often linger after conflicts appear to be over.
People seldom can wall off their feelings into neat categories of "task" or "relationship"
disagreements, so task conflicts sometimes escalate into relationship conflicts.[8] Conflicts
produce stress, which may lead people to become more close minded and adversarial.
Studies of conflict in laboratories also fail to take account of the reductions in trust and
cooperation that occur even with relationship conflicts. Longer-term studies show that all
conflicts reduce trust, respect, and cohesion in groups, which reduces their long-term
viability.[9]

  In sum, the traditional view took a shortsighted view in assuming all conflict
should be eliminated. The interactionist view that conflict can stimulate active discussion
without spilling over into negative, disruptive emotions is incomplete. The managed
conflict perspective does recognize that conflict is probably inevitable in most organizations, and it focuses more on productive conflict resolution. The research pendulum has
swung from eliminating conflict, to encouraging limited levels of conflict, and now to
finding constructive methods for resolving conflicts productively so their disruptive
influence can be minimized.

THE CONFLICT PROCESS

The **conflict process** has five stages: potential opposition or incompatibility, cognition
and personalization, intentions, behavior, and outcomes. The process is diagrammed in
Exhibit 13.1.

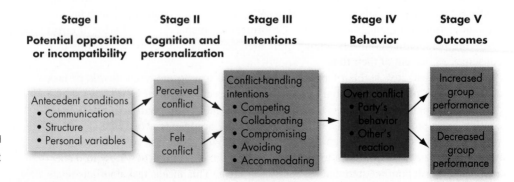

EXHIBIT 13.1
The Conflict
Process

Stage I: Potential Opposition or Incompatibility

The first step in the conflict process is the appearance of conditions that create opportunities for conflict to arise. They *need not* lead directly to conflict, but one of these
conditions is necessary if conflict is to surface. For simplicity's sake, these conditions
(which we can also look at as causes or sources of conflict) have been condensed into
three general categories: communication, structure, and personal variables.

COMMUNICATION   Communication can be a source of conflict. Opposing forces arise
from semantic difficulties, misunderstandings, and "noise" in the communication
channels. A review of the research suggests that differing word connotations, jargon,
insufficient exchange of information, and noise in the communication channel are all
barriers to communication and potential antecedent conditions to conflict. Research has
further demonstrated a surprising finding: The potential for conflict increases when either
too little or *too much* communication takes place. Apparently, an increase in
communication is functional up to a point, after which it is possible to overcommunicate,
with a resultant increase in the potential for conflict.

STRUCTURE   The term *structure* in this context includes variables such as size, degree
of specialization in the tasks assigned to group members, jurisdictional clarity,
member–goal compatibility, leadership styles, reward systems, and the degree of dependence between groups. The larger the group and the more specialized its activities, the
greater the likelihood of conflict. Tenure and conflict have been found to be inversely
related; the potential for conflict is greatest when group members are younger and when
turnover is high. The greater the ambiguity about where responsibility for actions lies, the
greater the potential for conflict to emerge. Such jurisdictional ambiguities increase
intergroup fighting for control of resources and territory. Diversity of goals among
groups is also a major source of conflict. Reward systems, too, create conflict when one
member's gain comes at another's expense. Finally, if a group is dependent on another
group (in contrast to the two being mutually independent), or if interdependence allows
one group to gain at another's expense, opposing forces are stimulated.

PERSONAL VARIABLES   Our last category of potential sources of conflict is personal
variables, which include personality, emotions, and values. Personality does appear to play
a role in the conflict process: some people just tend to get in conflicts a lot. In particular,
people high in the personality traits of disagreeableness, neuroticism, or self-monitoring are
prone to tangle with other people more often, and to react poorly when conflicts occur.[10]
Emotions can also cause conflict. An employee who shows up to work irate from her hectic
morning commute may carry that anger with her to her 9:00 AM meeting. The problem? Her
anger can annoy her colleagues, which can result in a tension-filled meeting.

Stage II: Cognition and Personalization

If the conditions cited in stage I negatively affect something one party cares about, then
the potential for opposition or incompatibility becomes actualized in the second stage.

As we noted in our definition of conflict, one or more of the parties must be aware
that antecedent conditions exist. However, because a conflict is a **perceived conflict**
does not mean it is personalized. In other words, "*A* may be aware that *B* and *A* are in

serious disagreement . . . but it may not make *A* tense or anxious, and it may have no effect whatsoever on *A*'s affection toward *B*."[11] It is at the **felt conflict** level, when individuals become emotionally involved, that parties experience anxiety, tension, frustration, or hostility.

Keep in mind two points. First, stage II is important because it's where conflict issues tend to be defined. This is the point when the parties decide what the conflict is about. The definition of a conflict is important because it typically delineates the set of possible settlements. Second, emotions play a major role in shaping perceptions. Negative emotions allow us to oversimplify issues, lose trust, and put negative interpretations on the other party's behavior.[12] In contrast, positive feelings increase our tendency to see potential relationships among the elements of a problem, take a broader view of the situation, and develop more innovative solutions.[13]

Stage III: Intentions

Intentions intervene between people's perceptions and emotions and their overt behavior. They are decisions to act in a given way.

We separate out intentions as a distinct stage because we have to infer the other's intent to know how to respond to his or her behavior. A lot of conflicts are escalated simply because one party attributes the wrong intentions to the other. There is also typically a great deal of slippage between intentions and behavior, so behavior does not always accurately reflect a person's intentions.

Using two dimensions—*cooperativeness* (the degree to which one party attempts to satisfy the other party's concerns) and *assertiveness* (the degree to which one party attempts to satisfy his or her own concerns)—we can identify five conflict-handling intentions: *competing* (assertive and uncooperative), *collaborating* (assertive and cooperative), *avoiding* (unassertive and uncooperative), *accommodating* (unassertive and cooperative), and *compromising* (midrange on both assertiveness and cooperativeness).

1. *Competing.* When one person seeks to satisfy his or her own interests regardless of the impact on the other parties to the conflict, that person is **competing.** You compete when you place a bet that only one person can win, for example.
2. *Collaborating.* When parties in conflict each desire to fully satisfy the concerns of all parties, there is cooperation and a search for a mutually beneficial outcome. In **collaborating,** the parties intend to solve a problem by clarifying differences rather than by accommodating various points of view. If you attempt to find a win–win solution that allows both parties' goals to be completely achieved, that's collaborating.
3. *Avoiding.* A person may recognize a conflict exists and want to withdraw from or suppress it. Examples of **avoiding** include trying to ignore a conflict and avoiding others with whom you disagree.
4. *Accommodating.* A party who seeks to appease an opponent may be willing to place the opponent's interests above his or her own, sacrificing to maintain the relationship. We refer to this intention as **accommodating.** Supporting someone else's opinion despite your reservations about it, for example, is accommodating.
5. *Compromising.* In **compromising,** there is no clear winner or loser. Rather, there is a willingness to ration the object of the conflict and accept a solution that provides incomplete satisfaction of both parties' concerns. The distinguishing characteristic of compromising, therefore, is that each party intends to give up something.

Intentions are not always fixed. During the course of a conflict, they might change if the parties are able to see the other's point of view or respond emotionally to the other's behavior. However, research indicates people have preferences among the five conflict-handling intentions we just described[14] and tend to rely on them quite consistently. We can predict a person's intentions rather well from a combination of intellectual and personality characteristics.

Stage IV: Behavior

When most people think of conflict situations, they tend to focus on stage IV because this is where conflicts become visible. The behavior stage includes the statements, actions, and reactions made by the conflicting parties, usually as overt attempts to implement their own intentions. As a result of miscalculations or unskilled enactments, overt behaviors sometimes deviate from these original intentions.

It helps to think of stage IV as a dynamic process of interaction. For example, you make a demand on me, I respond by arguing, you threaten me, I threaten you back, and so on. Exhibit 13.2 provides a way of visualizing conflict behavior. All conflicts exist somewhere along this continuum. At the lower part are conflicts characterized by subtle, indirect, and highly controlled forms of tension, such as a student questioning in class a point the instructor has just made. Conflict intensities escalate as they move upward along the continuum until they become highly destructive. Strikes, riots, and wars clearly fall in this upper range. For the most part, you should assume conflicts that reach the upper ranges of the continuum are almost always dysfunctional. Functional conflicts are typically confined to the lower range of the continuum.

If a conflict is dysfunctional, what can the parties do to de-escalate it? Or, conversely, what options exist if conflict is too low and needs to be increased? This brings us to techniques of **conflict management.** We have already described several as conflict-handling intentions. This shouldn't be surprising. Under ideal conditions, a person's intentions should translate into comparable behaviors.

Stage V: Outcomes

The action–reaction interplay between the conflicting parties results in consequences. As our model demonstrates (see Exhibit 13.1), these outcomes may be functional, if the conflict improves the group's performance, or dysfunctional, if it hinders performance.

EXHIBIT 13.2 Conflict-Intensity Continuum

Source: Based on S.P. Robbins, *Managing Organizational Conflict: A Nontraditional Approach* (Upper Saddle River, NJ: Prentice Hall, 1974), pp. 93–97, and R. Glasi, "The Process of Conflict Escalation and the Roles of Third Parties," in G.B.J. Bomers and R. Peterson (eds.), Conflict Management and Industrial Relations (Boston: Kluwer-Nijhoff, 1982), pp. 119–140.

FUNCTIONAL OUTCOMES   How might conflict act as a force to increase group performance? It is hard to visualize a situation in which open or violent aggression could be functional. But it's possible to see how low or moderate levels of conflict could improve the effectiveness of a group. Let's consider some examples and then review the research evidence. Note that all our examples focus on task and process conflicts and exclude the relationship variety.

Conflict is constructive when it improves the quality of decisions, stimulates creativity and innovation, encourages interest and curiosity among group members, provides the medium through which problems can be aired and tensions released, and fosters an environment of self-evaluation and change. The evidence suggests conflict can improve the quality of decision making by allowing all points to be weighed, particularly those that are unusual or held by a minority.[15] Conflict is an antidote for groupthink. It doesn't allow the group to passively rubber-stamp decisions that may be based on weak assumptions, inadequate consideration of relevant alternatives, or other debilities. Conflict challenges the status quo and therefore furthers the creation of new ideas, promotes reassessment of group goals and activities, and increases the probability that the group will respond to change. An open discussion focused on higher-order goals can make these functional outcomes more likely. Groups that are extremely polarized do not manage their underlying disagreements effectively and tend to accept suboptimal solutions, or they tend to avoid making decisions altogether rather than working out the conflict.[16]

Research studies in diverse settings confirm the functionality of active discussion. One study found that when groups analyzed decisions made by individual members of the group, the average improvement among groups that discussed differences of opinion frequently was 73 percent higher than in groups characterized by low-conflict conditions.[17] Teams members with greater differences in work styles and experience tend to share more information with one another.[18]

DYSFUNCTIONAL OUTCOMES   The destructive consequences of conflict on the performance of a group or an organization are generally well known: uncontrolled opposition breeds discontent, which acts to dissolve common ties and eventually leads to the destruction of the group. And, of course, a substantial body of literature documents how dysfunctional conflicts can reduce group effectiveness.[19] Among the more undesirable consequences are hampered communication, reductions in group cohesiveness, and subordination of group goals to the primacy of infighting among members. All forms of conflict—even the functional varieties—appear to reduce group member satisfaction and reduce trust. When active discussions turn into open conflicts between members, information sharing between members has been shown to decrease significantly.[20] At the extreme, conflict can bring group functioning to a halt and threaten the group's survival.

MANAGING FUNCTIONAL CONFLICT   If managers recognize that in some situations conflict can be beneficial, what can they do to manage conflict effectively in their organizations?[21]

One common ingredient in organizations that successfully manage functional conflict is that they reward dissent and punish conflict avoiders. This is easier said than done. It takes discipline and patience to accept news you don't wish to hear (from dissenters) and to force avoiders to speak up. Groups that resolve conflicts successfully discuss differences of opinion openly and are prepared to manage conflict when it arises.[22] The most disruptive conflicts are those that are never addressed directly. An open discussion makes it much easier to develop a shared perception of the problems at hand; it also allows groups to work toward a mutually acceptable solution. Managers need to emphasize shared interests in resolving conflicts, so groups that disagree with one another don't become too entrenched in their points of view and start to take the conflicts personally. Groups with cooperative conflict styles and a strong underlying identification to the overall group goals are more effective than groups with a more competitive style.[23]

NEGOTIATION

Negotiation permeates the interactions of almost everyone in groups and organizations.

> The most effective negotiators utilize different tactics for distributive and integrative bargaining; the chapter provides clear ways in order for you to improve each type of bargaining.

There's the obvious: Labor bargains with management. There's the not-so-obvious: Managers negotiate with employees, peers, and bosses; salespeople negotiate with customers; purchasing agents negotiate with suppliers. And there's the subtle: An employee agrees to cover for a colleague for a few minutes in exchange for some past or future benefit. In today's loosely structured organizations, in which members work with colleagues over whom they have no direct authority and with whom they may not even share a common boss, negotiation skills become critical.

We can define **negotiation** as a process that occurs when two or more parties decide how to allocate scarce resources. Although we commonly think of the outcomes of negotiation in one-shot economic terms, like negotiating over the price of a car, every negotiation in organizations also affects the relationship between the negotiators and the way the negotiators feel about themselves. Depending on how much the parties are going to interact with one another, sometimes maintaining the social relationship and behaving ethically will be just as important as the immediate outcome of each bargain. Note that we use the terms *negotiation* and *bargaining* interchangeably. In this section, we contrast two bargaining strategies, provide a model of the negotiation process, ascertain the role of moods and personality traits on bargaining, review gender and cultural differences in negotiation, and take a brief look at third-party negotiations.

Bargaining Strategies

There are two general approaches to negotiation—*distributive bargaining* and *integrative bargaining.*[24] As Exhibit 13.3 shows, they differ in their goal and motivation, focus, interests, information sharing, and duration of relationship. Let's define each and illustrate the differences.

DISTRIBUTIVE BARGAINING   You see a used car advertised for sale online. It appears to be just what you've been looking to buy. You go out to see the car. It's great, and you want it. The owner tells you the asking price. You don't want to pay that much. The two of you then negotiate over the price. The negotiating strategy you're engaging in is called **distributive bargaining.** Its most identifying feature is that it operates under zero-sum conditions—that is, any gain I make is at your expense and vice versa. Every dollar you can get the seller to cut from the car's price is a dollar you save, and every dollar more the seller can get from you comes at your expense. So the essence of distributive bargaining is negotiating over who gets

Bargaining Characteristic	Distributive Bargaining	Integrative Bargaining
Goal	Get as much of the pie as possible	Expand the pie so that both parties are satisfied
Motivation	Win-lose	Win-win
Focus	Positions ("I can't go beyond this point on this issue.")	Interests ("Can you explain why this issue is so important to you?")
Interests	Opposed	Congruent
Information sharing	Low (Sharing information will only allow other party to take advantage)	High (Sharing information will allow each party to find ways to satisfy interests of each party)
Duration of relationship	Short term	Long term

EXHIBIT 13.3 Distributive Versus Integrative Bargaining

what share of a fixed pie. By **fixed pie,** we mean a set amount of goods or services to be divvied up. When the pie is fixed, or parties believe it is, they tend to bargain distributively.

Probably the most widely cited example of distributive bargaining is labor–management negotiations over wages. Typically, labor's representatives come to the bargaining table determined to get as much money as possible out of management. Because every cent labor negotiates increases management's costs, each party bargains aggressively and treats the other as an opponent who must be defeated.

The essence of distributive bargaining is depicted in Exhibit 13.4. Parties A and B represent two negotiators. Each has a *target point* that defines what he or she would like to achieve. Each also has a *resistance point,* which marks the lowest outcome that is acceptable—the point below which the party would break off negotiations rather than accept a less favorable settlement. The area between these two points makes up each one's aspiration range. As long as there is some overlap between A's and B's aspiration ranges, there exists a settlement range in which each one's aspirations can be met.

When you are engaged in distributive bargaining, research consistently shows one of the best things you can do is make the first offer—and make it an aggressive one. One

EXHIBIT 13.4

Staking Out the Bargaining Zone

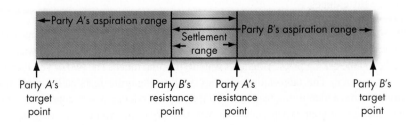

reason for this is that making the first offer shows power; individuals in power are much more likely to make initial offers, speak first at meetings, and thereby gain the advantage. Another reason is the anchoring bias. People tend to fixate on initial information. Once that anchoring point is set, they fail to adequately adjust it based on subsequent information. A savvy negotiator sets an anchor with the initial offer, and scores of negotiation studies show that such anchors greatly favor the person who sets it.[25]

INTEGRATIVE BARGAINING   Jake is a 5-year-old Chicago luxury boutique owned by Jim Wetzel and Lance Lawson. In the early days of the business, Wetzel and Lawson had no trouble moving millions of dollars of merchandise from many up-and-coming designers. They developed such a good rapport that many designers would send allotments to Jake without requiring advance payment. When the economy soured in 2008, Jake had trouble selling inventory, and the designers found they were not being paid for what they had shipped to the store. Despite the fact that many designers were willing to work with the store on a delayed payment plan, Wetzel and Lawson stopped returning their calls. Lamented one designer, Doo-Ri Chung, "You kind of feel this familiarity with people who supported you for so long. When they have cash-flow issues, you want to make sure you are there for them as well."[26] Ms. Chung's attitude shows the promise of **integrative bargaining.** In contrast to distributive bargaining, integrative bargaining operates under the assumption that one or more settlements can create a win–win solution. Of course, as the Jake example shows and as we'll highlight later, integrative bargaining takes "two to tango"—both parties must be engaged for it to work.

In terms of intraorganizational behavior, all things being equal, integrative bargaining is preferable to distributive bargaining because the former builds long-term relationships. Integrative bargaining bonds negotiators and allows them to leave the bargaining table feeling they have achieved a victory. Distributive bargaining, however, leaves one party a loser. It tends to build animosities and deepen divisions when people have to work together on an ongoing basis. Research shows that over repeated bargaining episodes, when the "losing" party feels positive about the negotiation outcome, he is much more likely to bargain cooperatively in subsequent negotiations. This points to an important advantage of integrative negotiations: even when you "win," you want your opponent to feel good about the negotiation.[27]

Why, then, don't we see more integrative bargaining in organizations? The answer lies in the conditions necessary for this type of negotiation to succeed. These include parties who are open with information and candid about their concerns, a sensitivity in both parties to the other's needs and trust, and a willingness by both parties to maintain flexibility.[28] Because these conditions seldom exist in organizations, it isn't surprising that negotiations often take on a win-at-any-cost dynamic.

There are ways to achieve more integrative outcomes. Individuals who bargain in teams reach more integrative agreements than those who bargain individually. This happens because more ideas are generated when more people are at the bargaining table. So try bargaining in teams. Another way to achieve higher joint-gain settlements is to put more issues on the table. The more negotiable issues introduced into a negotiation, the more opportunity for "logrolling," where issues are traded off because people have different preferences. This creates better outcomes for each side than if they negotiated each issue individually.

Finally, you should realize that compromise may be your worst enemy in negotiating a win–win agreement. The reason is that compromising reduces the pressure to bargain integratively. After all, if you or your opponent caves in easily, it doesn't require anyone to be creative to reach a settlement. Thus, people end up settling for less than they could have obtained if they had been forced to consider the other party's interests, trade-off issues, and be creative. Think of the classic example in which two sisters are arguing over who gets an orange. Unknown to them, one sister wants the orange to drink the juice, whereas the other wants the orange peel to bake a cake. If one sister simply capitulates and gives the other sister the orange, they will not be forced to explore their reasons for wanting the orange, and thus they will never find the win–win solution: They could *each* have the orange because they want different parts of it!

The Negotiation Process

Exhibit 13.5 provides a simplified model of the negotiation process. It views negotiation as made up of five steps: (1) preparation and planning, (2) definition of ground rules, (3) clarification and justification, (4) bargaining and problem solving, and (5) closure and implementation.[29]

PREPARATION AND PLANNING   Before you start negotiating, you need to do your homework. What's the nature of the conflict? What's the history leading up to this negotiation? Who's involved and what are their perceptions of the conflict? What do you want from the negotiation? What are *your* goals? It often helps to put your goals in writing and develop a range of outcomes—from "most hopeful" to "minimally acceptable"—to keep your attention focused.

You also want to assess what you think are the other party's goals. What are they likely to ask/request? How entrenched is their position likely to be? What intangible or hidden interests may be important to them? On what might they be willing to settle? When you can anticipate your opponent's position, you are better equipped to counter arguments with the facts and figures that support your position.

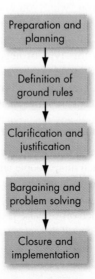

EXHIBIT 13.5

The Negotiation

Relationships will change as a result of a negotiation, so that's another outcome to take into consideration. If you could "win" a negotiation but push the other side into resentment or animosity, it might be wiser to pursue a more compromising style. If preserving the relationship will make you seem weak and easily exploited, you may want to consider a more aggressive style. As an example of how the tone of a relationship set in negotiations matters, consider that people who feel good about the *process* of a job offer negotiation are more satisfied with their jobs and less likely to turn over a year later regardless of their actual *outcomes* from these negotiations.[30] A company that is very successful in negotiating terms of employment that satisfy it but not the new hire pays a price in its long-term relationship with the employee.

Once you've gathered your information, use it to develop a strategy. For example, expert chess players know ahead of time how they will respond to any given situation. As part of your strategy, you should determine your and the other side's **b**est **a**lternative **t**o a **n**egotiated **a**greement (**BATNA**).[31] Your BATNA determines the lowest value acceptable to you for a negotiated agreement. Any offer you receive that is higher than your BATNA is better than an impasse. Conversely, you shouldn't expect success in your negotiation effort unless you're able to make the other side an offer it finds more attractive than its BATNA. If you go into your negotiation having a good idea of what the other party's BATNA is, even if you're not able to meet it you might be able to elicit a change. Think carefully about what the other side is willing to give up. People who underestimate their opponent's willingness to give on key issues before the negotiation even starts end up with lower outcomes from a negotiation.[32]

DEFINITION OF GROUND RULES   Once you've done your planning and developed a strategy, you're ready to begin defining with the other party the ground rules and procedures of the negotiation itself. Who will do the negotiating? Where will it take place? What time constraints, if any, will apply? To what issues will negotiation be limited? Will you follow a specific procedure if an impasse is reached? During this phase, the parties will also exchange their initial proposals or demands.

CLARIFICATION AND JUSTIFICATION   When you have exchanged initial positions, both you and the other party will explain, amplify, clarify, bolster, and justify your original demands. This needn't be confrontational. Rather, it's an opportunity for educating and informing each other on the issues, why they are important, and how you arrived at your initial demands. Provide the other party with any documentation that helps support your position.

BARGAINING AND PROBLEM SOLVING   The essence of the negotiation process is the actual give-and-take in trying to hash out an agreement. This is where both parties will undoubtedly need to make concessions.

CLOSURE AND IMPLEMENTATION   The final step in the negotiation process is formalizing the agreement that has been worked out and developing any procedures necessary for implementation and monitoring. For major negotiations—from labor–management negotiations to bargaining over lease terms to buying a piece of real estate to negotiating a job offer for a senior management position—this requires hammering out the specifics in a formal contract. For most cases, however, closure of the negotiation process is nothing more formal than a handshake.

Individual Differences in Negotiation Effectiveness

Are some people better negotiators than others? The answer is more complex than you might think. Three factors influence how effectively individuals negotiate: personality, mood/emotions, and gender.

PERSONALITY TRAITS IN NEGOTIATION   Can you predict an opponent's negotiating tactics if you know something about his or her personality? Because personality and negotiation outcomes are related but only weakly, the answer is, at best, "sort of." Negotiators who are agreeable or extraverted are not very successful in distributive bargaining. Why? Because extraverts are outgoing and friendly, they tend to share more information than they should. And agreeable people are more interested in finding ways to cooperate rather than to butt heads. These traits, although slightly helpful in integrative negotiations, are liabilities when interests are opposed. So the best distributive bargainer appears to be a disagreeable introvert—someone more interested in his or her own outcomes than in pleasing the other party and having a pleasant social exchange. People who are highly interested in having positive relationships with other people, and who are not very concerned about their own outcomes, are especially poor negotiators. These people tend to be very anxious about disagreements and plan to give in quickly to avoid unpleasant conflicts even before negotiations start.[33]

MOODS/EMOTIONS IN NEGOTIATION   Do moods and emotions influence negotiation? They do, but the way they do appears to depend on the type of negotiation. In distributive negotiations, it appears that negotiators in a position of power or equal status who show anger negotiate better outcomes because their anger induces concessions from their opponents. This appears to hold true even when the negotiators are instructed to show anger despite not being truly angry. On the other hand, for those in a less powerful position, displaying anger leads to worse outcomes. So if you're a boss negotiating with a peer or a subordinate, displaying anger may help you, but if you're an employee negotiating with a boss, it might hurt you.

In integrative negotiations, in contrast, positive moods and emotions appear to lead to more integrative agreements (higher levels of joint gain). This may happen because, as we noted in a previous chapter, positive mood is related to creativity.

GENDER DIFFERENCES IN NEGOTIATIONS   Do men and women negotiate differently? And does gender affect negotiation outcomes? The answer to the first question appears to be no.[34] The answer to the second is a qualified yes.[35]

A popular stereotype is that women are more cooperative and pleasant in negotiations than are men. The evidence doesn't support this belief. However, men have been found to negotiate better outcomes than women, although the difference is relatively small. It's been postulated that men and women place divergent values on outcomes. "It is possible that a few hundred dollars more in salary or the corner office is less important to women than forming and maintaining an interpersonal relationship."[36]

The belief that women are "nicer" than men in negotiations is probably due to a confusion between gender and the lower degree of power women typically hold in most large organizations. Because women are expected to be "nice" and men "tough," research shows women are penalized when they initiate negotiations.[37] What's more, when women and men actually do conform to these stereotypes—women act "nice" and men "tough"—it becomes a self-fulfilling prophecy, reinforcing the stereotypical gender differences between male and female negotiators.[38] Thus, one of the reasons negotiations favor men is that women are "damned if they do, damned if they don't." Negotiate tough and they are penalized for violating a gender stereotype. Negotiate nice and it only reinforces and lets others take advantage of the stereotype.

Global Implications

Conflict and Culture

Research suggests that differences across countries in conflict resolution strategies may be based on collectivistic tendencies and motives.[39] Collectivist cultures see people as deeply embedded in social situations, whereas individualist cultures see people as autonomous. As a result, collectivists are more likely to seek to preserve relationships and promote the good of the group as a whole than individualists. To preserve peaceful relationships, collectivists will avoid direct expression of conflicts, preferring to use more indirect methods for resolving differences of opinion. Collectivists may also be more interested in demonstrations of concern and working through third parties to resolve disputes, whereas individualists will be more likely to confront differences of opinion directly and openly.

Some research does support this theory. Compared to collectivist Japanese negotiators, their more individualist U.S. counterparts are more likely to see offers from their counterparts as unfair and to reject them. Another study revealed that whereas U.S. managers were more likely to use competing tactics in the face of conflicts, compromising and avoiding are the most preferred methods of conflict management in China.[40] Interview data, however, suggests top management teams in Chinese high-technology firms preferred integration even more than compromising and avoiding.[41]

Cultural Differences in Negotiations

Compared with the research on conflict, there is more research on how negotiating styles vary across national cultures.[42] One study compared U.S. and Japanese negotiators and found the generally conflict-avoidant Japanese negotiators tended to communicate indirectly and adapt their behaviors to the situation. A follow-up study showed that whereas among U.S. managers making early offers led to the anchoring effect we noted when discussing distributive negotiation, for Japanese negotiators early offers led to more information sharing and better integrative outcomes.[43] In another study, managers with high levels of economic power from Hong Kong, which is a high power-distance country, were more cooperative in negotiations over a shared resource than German and U.S. managers, who were lower in power distance.[44] This suggests that in high power-distance countries, those in positions of power might exercise more restraint.

Another study looked at verbal and nonverbal negotiation tactics exhibited by North Americans, Japanese, and Brazilians during half-hour bargaining sessions.[45] Some of the differences were particularly interesting. The Brazilians on average said "no" 83 times, compared to 5 times for the Japanese and 9 times for the North Americans. The Japanese displayed more than 5 periods of silence lasting longer than 10 seconds during the 30-minute sessions. North Americans averaged 3.5 such periods; the Brazilians had none. The Japanese and North Americans interrupted their opponent about the same number of times, but the Brazilians interrupted 2.5 to 3 times more often than either. Finally, the Japanese and the North Americans had no physical contact with their opponents during negotiations except for handshaking, but the Brazilians touched each other almost 5 times every half hour.

Implications for Managers

Although many people assume conflict lowers group and organizational performance, this assumption is frequently incorrect. Conflict can be either constructive or destructive to the functioning of a group or unit. As shown in Exhibit 13.6, levels of conflict can be either too high or too low. Either extreme hinders performance. An optimal level is one that prevents stagnation, stimulates creativity, allows tensions to be released, and initiates the seeds of change, without being disruptive or preventing coordination of activities.

What advice can we give managers faced with excessive conflict and the need to reduce it? Don't assume one conflict-handling intention will always be best! Select an intention appropriate for the situation. Here are some guidelines:[46]

• Use *competition* when quick, decisive action is vital (in emergencies) on important issues, when unpopular actions need to be implemented (in cost cutting, enforcement of unpopular rules, discipline), on issues vital to the organization's welfare when you know you're right, and against people who take advantage of noncompetitive behavior.

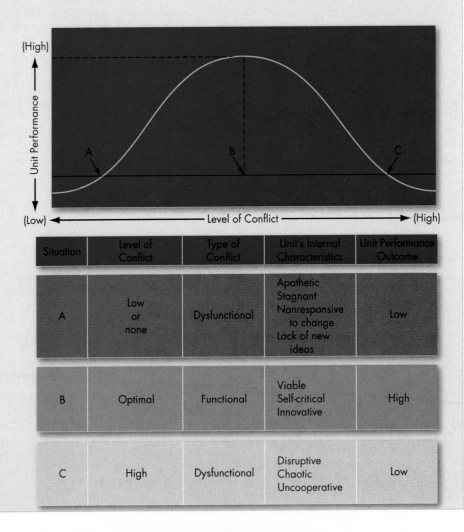

Situation	Level of Conflict	Type of Conflict	Unit's Internal Characteristics	Unit Performance Outcome
A	Low or none	Dysfunctional	Apathetic Stagnant Nonresponsive to change Lack of new ideas	Low
B	Optimal	Functional	Viable Self-critical Innovative	High
C	High	Dysfunctional	Disruptive Chaotic Uncooperative	Low

EXHIBIT 13.6

Conflict and Unit Performance

- Use *collaboration* to find an integrative solution when both sets of concerns are too important to be compromised, when your objective is to learn, when you want to merge insights from people with different perspectives or gain commitment by incorporating concerns into a consensus, and when you need to work through feelings that have interfered with a relationship.
- Use *avoidance* when an issue is trivial or symptomatic of other issues, when more important issues are pressing, when you perceive no chance of satisfying your concerns, when potential disruption outweighs the benefits of resolution, to let people cool down and regain perspective, when gathering information supersedes immediate decision, and when others can resolve the conflict more effectively.
- Use *accommodation* when you find you're wrong and to allow a better position to be heard, to learn, to show your reasonableness, when issues are more important to others than to yourself and to satisfy others and maintain cooperation, to build social credits for later issues, to minimize loss when you are outmatched and losing, when harmony and stability are especially important, and to allow employees to develop by learning from mistakes.
- Use *compromise* when goals are important but not worth the effort of potential disruption of more assertive approaches, when opponents with equal power are committed to mutually exclusive goals, to achieve temporary settlements to complex issues, to arrive at expedient solutions under time pressure, and as a backup when collaboration or competition is unsuccessful.

Negotiation is an ongoing activity in groups and organizations. Distributive bargaining can resolve disputes, but it often negatively affects the satisfaction of one or more negotiators because it is focused on the short term and because it is confrontational. Integrative bargaining, in contrast, tends to provide outcomes that satisfy all parties and that build lasting relationships. When engaged in negotiation, make sure you set aggressive goals and try to find creative ways to achieve the goals of both parties, especially when you value the long-term relationship with the other party. That doesn't mean sacrificing your self-interest; rather, it means trying to find creative solutions that give both parties what they really want.

CHAPTER 14

Foundations of Organization Structure

After studying this chapter, you should be able to:

- Identify the six elements of an organization's structure.
- Describe the common organizational designs.
- Compare and contrast the virtual and boundaryless organizations.
- Demonstrate how organizational structures differ.
- Analyze the behavioral implications of different organizational designs.
- Show how globalization affects organizational structure.

The theme of this chapter is that organizations have different structures and that these structures have a bearing on employee attitudes and behavior. More specifically, in the following pages, we'll define the key components that make up an organization's structure, present half a dozen or so structural design options, identify the contingency factors that make certain structural designs preferable in different situations, and conclude by considering the different effects that various organizational structures have on employee behavior.

WHAT IS ORGANIZATIONAL STRUCTURE?

An **organizational structure** defines how job tasks are formally divided, grouped, and coordinated. Managers need to address six key elements when they design their organization's structure: work specialization, departmentalization, chain of command, span of control, centralization and decentralization, and formalization.[1] Exhibit 14.1 presents each of these elements as answers to an important structural question, and the following sections describe them.

The Key Question	The Answer Is Provided By
1. To what degree are activities subdivided into separate jobs?	Work specialization
2. On what basis will jobs be grouped together?	Departmentalization
3. To whom do individuals and groups report?	Chain of command
4. How many individuals can a manager efficiently and effectively direct?	Span of control
5. Where does decision-making authority lie?	Centralization and decentralization
6. To what degree will there be rules and regulations to direct employees and managers?	Formalization

EXHIBIT 14.1

Key Design Questions and Answers for Designing the Proper Organizational Structure

Work Specialization

Early in the twentieth century, Henry Ford became rich by building automobiles on an assembly line. Every Ford worker was assigned a specific, repetitive task such as putting on the right-front wheel or installing the right-front door. By dividing jobs into small standardized tasks that could be performed over and over, Ford was able to produce a car every 10 seconds, using employees who had relatively limited skills.

Ford demonstrated that work can be performed more efficiently if employees are allowed to specialize. Today we use the term **work specialization,** or *division of labor,* to describe the degree to which activities in the organization are subdivided into separate jobs. The essence of work specialization is to divide a job into a number of steps, each completed by a separate individual. In essence, individuals specialize in doing part of an activity rather than the entirety.

By the late 1940s, most manufacturing jobs in industrialized countries featured high work specialization. Because not all employees in an organization have the same skills, management saw specialization as a means of making the most efficient use of its employees' skills and even successfully improving them through repetition. Less time is spent in changing tasks, putting away tools and equipment from a prior step, and getting ready for another. Equally important, it's easier and less costly to find and train workers to do specific and repetitive tasks, especially in highly sophisticated and complex operations. Could Cessna produce one Citation jet a year if one person had to build the entire plane alone? Not likely! Finally, work specialization increases efficiency and productivity by encouraging the creation of special inventions and machinery.

For much of the first half of the twentieth century, managers thus viewed work specialization as an unending source of increased productivity. And they were probably right. When specialization was not widely practiced, its introduction almost always generated higher productivity. But by the 1960s, it increasingly seemed a good thing can be carried too far. Human diseconomies from specialization began to surface as boredom, fatigue, stress, low productivity, poor quality, increased absenteeism, and high turnover, which more than offset the economic advantages (see Exhibit 14.2). Managers could increase productivity now by enlarging, rather than narrowing, the scope of job activities. Giving employees a variety of activities to do, allowing them to do a whole and complete job, and

EXHIBIT 14.2

Economies and Diseconomies of Work Specialization

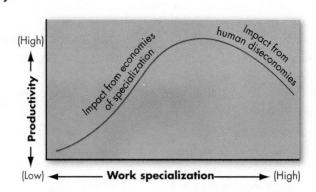

putting them into teams with interchangeable skills often achieved significantly higher output, with increased employee satisfaction.

Departmentalization

Once jobs are divided through work specialization, they must be grouped so common tasks can be coordinated. The basis by which jobs are grouped is called **departmentalization.**

One of the most popular ways to group activities is by *functions* performed. A manufacturing manager might organize a plant into engineering, accounting, manufacturing, personnel, and supply specialists departments. A hospital might have departments devoted to research, surgery, intensive care, accounting, and so forth. A professional football franchise might have departments entitled Player Personnel, Ticket Sales, and Travel and Accommodations. The major advantage of this type of functional departmentalization is efficiencies gained from putting like specialists together.

We can also departmentalize jobs by the type of *product* or *service* the organization produces. Procter & Gamble places each major product—such as Tide, Pampers, Charmin, and Pringles—under an executive who has complete global responsibility for it. The major advantage here is increased accountability for performance, because all activities related to a specific product or service are under the direction of a single manager.

When a firm is departmentalized on the basis of *geography,* or territory, the sales function, for instance, may have western, southern, midwestern, and eastern regions, each, in effect, a department organized around geography. This form is valuable when an organization's customers are scattered over a large geographic area and have similar needs based on their location.

Process departmentalization works for processing customers as well as products. If you've ever been to a state motor vehicle office to get a driver's license, you probably went through several departments before receiving your license. In one typical state, applicants go through three steps, each handled by a separate department: (1) validation by motor vehicles division, (2) processing by the licensing department, and (3) payment collection by the treasury department.

A final category of departmentalization uses the particular type of *customer* the organization seeks to reach. Microsoft, for example, is organized around four customer markets: consumers, large corporations, software developers, and small businesses. Customers in each department have a common set of problems and needs best met by having specialists for each.

Large organizations may use all the forms of departmentalization we've described. A major Japanese electronics firm organizes each of its divisions along functional lines, its manufacturing units around processes, sales around seven geographic regions, and each sales region into four customer groupings. In a strong recent trend among organizations of all sizes, rigid functional departmentalization is increasingly complemented by teams that cross traditional departmental lines. As we described in Chapter 9, as tasks have become more complex and more diverse skills are needed to accomplish them, management has turned to cross-functional teams.

As tasks have become more complex and more diverse skills have been needed to accomplish those tasks, management has turned to cross-functional teams.

Chain of Command

Although the chain of command was once a basic cornerstone in the design of organizations, it has far less importance today. But contemporary managers should still consider its implications. The **chain of command** is an unbroken line of authority that extends from the top of the organization to the lowest echelon and clarifies who reports to whom. It answers questions such as "To whom do I go if I have a problem?" and "To whom am I responsible?"

We can't discuss the chain of command without also discussing *authority* and *unity of command*. **Authority** refers to the rights inherent in a managerial position to give orders and expect them to be obeyed. To facilitate coordination, each managerial position is given a place in the chain of command, and each manager is given a degree of authority in order to meet his or her responsibilities. The principle of **unity of command** helps preserve the concept of an unbroken line of authority. It says a person should have one and only one superior to whom he or she is directly responsible. If the unity of command is broken, an employee might have to cope with conflicting demands or priorities from several superiors.

Times change, and so do the basic tenets of organizational design. A low-level employee today can access information in seconds that was available only to top managers a generation ago. Networked computers allow employees anywhere in an organization to communicate with anyone else without going through formal channels. Operating employees are empowered to make decisions previously reserved for management. Add the popularity of self-managed and cross-functional teams and the creation of new structural designs that include multiple bosses, and you can see why authority and unity of command hold less relevance. Many organizations still find they can be most productive by enforcing the chain of command. There just seem to be fewer of them today.

Span of Control

How many employees can a manager efficiently and effectively direct? This question of **span of control** is important because it largely determines the number of levels and managers an organization has. All things being equal, the wider or larger the span, the more efficient the organization.

Assume two organizations each have about 4,100 operative-level employees. One has a uniform span of four and the other a span of eight. As Exhibit 14.3 illustrates, the wider span will have two fewer levels and approximately 800 fewer managers. If the average manager makes $50,000 a year, the wider span will save $40 million a year in management salaries! Obviously, wider spans are more efficient in terms of cost. However, at some point when supervisors no longer have time to provide the necessary leadership and support, they reduce effectiveness and employee performance suffers.

Narrow or small spans have their advocates. By keeping the span of control to five or six employees, a manager can maintain close control.[2] But narrow spans have three major drawbacks. First, they're expensive because they add levels of management. Second, they

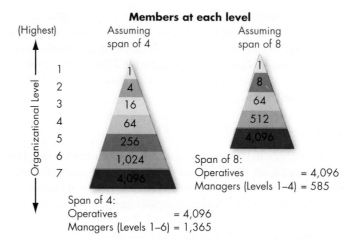

EXHIBIT 14.3
Contrasting
Spans of Control

Members at each level

(Highest)   Assuming span of 4   Assuming span of 8

Organizational Level

1   1
2   4
3   16
4   64
5   256
6   1,024
7   4,096

1
8
64
512
4,096

Span of 8:
Operatives   = 4,096
Managers (Levels 1–4) = 585

Span of 4:
Operatives   = 4,096
Managers (Levels 1–6) = 1,365

make vertical communication in the organization more complex. The added levels of hierarchy slow down decision making and tend to isolate upper management. Third, narrow spans encourage overly tight supervision and discourage employee autonomy.

The trend in recent years has been toward wider spans of control.[3] They're consistent with firms' efforts to reduce costs, cut overhead, speed decision making, increase flexibility, get closer to customers, and empower employees. However, to ensure performance doesn't suffer because of these wider spans, organizations have been investing heavily in employee training. Managers recognize they can handle a wider span when employees know their jobs inside and out or can turn to co-workers when they have questions.

Centralization and Decentralization

Centralization refers to the degree to which decision making is concentrated at a single point in the organization. In *centralized* organizations, top managers make all the decisions, and lower-level managers merely carry out their directives. In organizations at the other extreme, *decentralized* decision making is pushed down to the managers closest to the action.

The concept of centralization includes only formal authority—that is, the rights inherent in a position. An organization characterized by centralization is inherently different structurally from one that's decentralized. A decentralized organization can act more quickly to solve problems, more people provide input into decisions, and employees are less likely to feel alienated from those who make decisions that affect their work lives.

Management efforts to make organizations more flexible and responsive have produced a recent trend toward decentralized decision making by lower-level managers, who are closer to the action and typically have more detailed knowledge about problems than top managers. Sears and JCPenney have given their store managers considerably more discretion in choosing what merchandise to stock. This allows those stores to compete more effectively against local merchants.

Formalization

Formalization refers to the degree to which jobs within the organization are standardized. If a job is highly formalized, the incumbent has a minimum amount of discretion over what, when, and how to do it. Employees can be expected always to handle the same input in exactly the same way, resulting in a consistent and uniform output. There are explicit job descriptions, lots of organizational rules, and clearly defined procedures covering work processes in organizations in which there is high formalization. Where formalization is low, job behaviors are relatively unprogrammed, and employees have a great deal of freedom to exercise discretion in their work. Standardization not only eliminates the possibility of employees engaging in alternative behaviors, but it even removes the need for employees to consider alternatives.

The degree of formalization can vary widely between and within organizations. Certain jobs are well known to have little formalization. Publishing representatives who call on college professors to inform them of their company's new publications have a great deal of freedom in their jobs. They have only a general sales pitch, which they tailor as needed, and rules and procedures governing their behavior may be little more than the requirement to submit a weekly sales report and suggestions on what to emphasize in forthcoming titles. At the other extreme, clerical and editorial employees in the same publishing houses may need to be at their desks by 8:00 AM and follow a set of precise procedures dictated by management.

COMMON ORGANIZATIONAL DESIGNS

We now turn to three of the more common organizational designs: the *simple structure,* the *bureaucracy,* and the *matrix structure.*

The Simple Structure

What do a small retail store, an electronics firm run by a hard-driving entrepreneur, and an airline's "war room" in the midst of a pilot's strike have in common? They probably all use the **simple structure.**

We can think of the simple structure in terms of what it is *not* rather than what it is. The simple structure is not elaborate.[4] It has a low degree of departmentalization, wide spans of control, authority centralized in a single person, and little formalization. It is a "flat" organization; it usually has only two or three vertical levels, a loose body of employees, and one individual in whom the decision-making authority is centralized.

The simple structure is most widely practiced in small businesses in which the manager and owner are one and the same. Consider a retail men's store owned and managed by Jack Gold. Although he employs five full-time salespeople, a cashier, and extra personnel for weekends and holidays, Jack "runs the show." Large companies, in times of crisis, often simplify their structures as a means of focusing their resources.

The strength of the simple structure lies in its simplicity. It's fast, flexible, and inexpensive to operate, and accountability is clear. One major weakness is that it's difficult to maintain in anything other than small organizations. It becomes increasingly inadequate as an organization grows because its low formalization and high centralization tend to create information overload at the top. As size increases, decision making typically becomes slower and can eventually come to a standstill as the single executive tries to continue making all the decisions. This proves the undoing of many small businesses. When an organization begins to employ 50 or 100 people, it's very difficult for the owner-manager to make all the choices. If the structure isn't changed and made more elaborate, the firm often loses momentum and can eventually fail. The simple structure's other weakness is that it's risky—everything depends on one person. One illness can literally destroy the organization's information and decision-making center.

The simple structure has a low degree of departmentalization, wide spans of control, authority centralized in a single person, and little formalization.

The Bureaucracy

Standardization! That's the key concept that underlies all bureaucracies. Consider the bank where you keep your checking account, the department store where you buy clothes, or the government offices that collect your taxes, enforce health regulations, or provide local fire protection. They all rely on standardized work processes for coordination and control.

The **bureaucracy** is characterized by highly routine operating tasks achieved through specialization, very formalized rules and regulations, tasks grouped into functional departments, centralized authority, narrow spans of control, and decision making that follows the chain of command. *Bureaucracy* is a dirty word in many people's minds. However, it does have advantages. Its primary strength is its ability to perform standardized activities in a highly efficient manner. Putting like specialties together in functional departments results in economies of scale, minimum duplication of personnel and equipment, and employees who have the opportunity to talk "the same language" among their peers. Bureaucracies can get by with less talented—and, hence, less costly—middle- and lower-level managers. Rules and regulations substitute for managerial discretion. Standardized operations and high formalization allow decision making to be centralized. There is little need for innovative and experienced decision makers below the level of senior executives.

The other major weakness of a bureaucracy is something we've all witnessed: obsessive concern with following the rules. When cases don't precisely fit the rules, there is no room for modification. The bureaucracy is efficient only as long as employees confront familiar problems with programmed decision rules.

The Matrix Structure

Another popular organizational design option is the **matrix structure.** You'll find it in advertising agencies, aerospace firms, research and development laboratories, construction companies, hospitals, government agencies, universities, management consulting firms, and entertainment companies.[5] It combines two forms of departmentalization: functional and product.

The strength of functional departmentalization is putting like specialists together, which minimizes the number necessary while allowing the pooling and sharing of specialized resources across products. Its major disadvantage is the difficulty of coordinating the tasks of diverse functional specialists on time and within budget. Product departmentalization has exactly the opposite benefits and disadvantages. It facilitates coordination among specialties to achieve on-time completion and meet budget targets. It provides clear responsibility for all activities related to a product but with duplication of activities and costs. The matrix attempts to gain the strengths of each, while avoiding their weaknesses.

The most obvious structural characteristic of the matrix is that it breaks the unity-of-command concept. Employees in the matrix have two bosses: their functional department managers and their product managers.

Exhibit 14.4 shows the matrix form in a college of business administration. The academic departments of accounting, decision and information systems, marketing, and so forth are functional units. Overlaid on them are specific programs (that is, products). Thus, members in a matrix structure have a dual chain of command: to their functional department and to their product groups. A professor of accounting teaching an undergraduate course may report to the director of undergraduate programs as well as to the chairperson of the accounting department.

Academic Departments \ Programs	Undergraduate	Master's	Ph.D.	Research	Executive Development	Community Service
Accounting						
Finance						
Decision and Information Systems						
Management						
Marketing						

EXHIBIT 14.4

Matrix Structure for a College of Business Administration

The strength of the matrix is its ability to facilitate coordination when the organization has a number of complex and interdependent activities. Direct and frequent contacts between different specialties in the matrix can let information permeate the organization and more quickly reach the people who need it. The matrix reduces "bureaupathologies"—the dual lines of authority reduce people's tendency to become so busy protecting their little worlds that the organization's goals become secondary. A matrix also achieves economics of scale and facilitates the allocation of specialists by providing both the best resources and an effective way of ensuring their efficient deployment.

The major disadvantages of the matrix lie in the confusion it creates, its propensity to foster power struggles, and the stress it places on individuals.[6] Without the unity-of-command concept, ambiguity about who reports to whom is significantly increased and often leads to conflict. It's not unusual for product managers to fight over getting the best specialists assigned to their products. Bureaucracy reduces the potential for power grabs by defining the rules of the game. When those rules are "up for grabs" in a matrix, power struggles between functional and product managers result. For individuals who desire security and absence from ambiguity, this work climate can be stressful. Reporting to more than one boss introduces role conflict, and unclear expectations introduce role ambiguity. The comfort of bureaucracy's predictability is replaced by insecurity and stress.

NEW DESIGN OPTIONS

Senior managers in a number of organizations have been working to develop new structural options that can better help their firms to compete effectively. Many result in fewer layers of hierarchy and more emphasis on opening the boundaries of the organization.[7] In this section, we describe two such structural designs: the *virtual organization* and the *boundaryless organization.* We'll also discuss how efforts to reduce bureaucracy and increase strategic focus have made downsizing routine.

The Virtual Organization

Why own when you can rent? That question captures the essence of the **virtual organization** (also sometimes called the *network,* or *modular,* organization), typically a small, core organization that outsources major business functions.[8] In structural terms, the virtual organization is highly centralized, with little or no departmentalization.

The prototype of the virtual structure is today's movie-making organization. In Hollywood's golden era, movies were made by huge, vertically integrated corporations. Studios such as MGM, Warner Brothers, and 20th Century Fox owned large movie lots and employed thousands of full-time specialists—set designers, camera people, film editors, directors, and even actors. Today, most movies are made by a collection of individuals and small companies who come together and make films project by project. This structural form allows each project to be staffed with the talent best suited to its demands, rather than just the people employed by the studio. It minimizes bureaucratic overhead because there is no lasting organization to maintain. And it lessens long-term risks and their costs because there is no long term—a team is assembled for a finite period and then disbanded.

Ancle Hsu and David Ji run a virtual organization. Their firm, California-based Apex Digital, is one of the world's largest producers of DVD players, yet the company neither owns a factory nor employs an engineer. It contracts out everything to firms in China. With minimal investment, Apex has grown from nothing to annual sales of more than $500 million in just 3 years. Similarly, Newman's Own, the food products company founded by Paul Newman, sells more than $120 million in food every year yet employs only 19 people. This is possible because it outsources almost everything: manufacturing, procurement, shipping, and quality control.

What's going on here? A quest for maximum flexibility. These virtual organizations have created networks of relationships that allow them to contract out manufacturing, distribution, marketing, or any other business function management feels others can do better or more cheaply. The virtual organization stands in sharp contrast to the typical bureaucracy and concentrates on what it does best. For most U.S. firms, that means design or marketing.

Exhibit 14.5 shows a virtual organization in which management outsources all the primary functions of the business. The core of the organization is a small group of executives whose job is to oversee directly any activities done in house and to coordinate relationships with the other organizations that manufacture, distribute, and perform other crucial functions for the virtual organization. The dotted lines represent the relationships

EXHIBIT 14.5

A Virtual Organization

typically maintained under contracts. In essence, managers in virtual structures spend most of their time coordinating and controlling external relations, typically by way of computer-network links.

The major advantage of the virtual organization is its flexibility, which allows individuals with an innovative idea and little money, such as Ancle Hsu and David Ji, to successfully compete against the likes of Sony, Hitachi, and Sharp Electronics.

Virtual organizations' drawbacks have become increasingly clear as their popularity has grown.[9] They are in a state of perpetual flux and reorganization, which means roles, goals, and responsibilities are unclear: This sets the stage for political behavior. Those who work frequently with virtual organizations also note cultural alignment and shared goals can be lost because of the low degree of interaction among members. Team members who are geographically dispersed and communicate only intermittently find it difficult to share information and knowledge, which can limit innovation and slow response time. Ironically, some virtual organizations are less adaptable and innovative than those with well-established communication and collaboration networks. A leadership presence that reinforces the organization's purpose and facilitates communication is thus especially valuable.

The Boundaryless Organization

General Electric's former chairman, Jack Welch, coined the term **boundaryless organization** to describe what he wanted GE to become: a "family grocery store."[10] That is, in spite of GE's monstrous size (2009 revenues were $156 billion), Welch wanted to eliminate *vertical* and *horizontal* boundaries within it and break down *external* barriers between the company and its customers and suppliers. The boundaryless organization seeks to eliminate the chain of command, have limitless spans of control, and replace departments with empowered teams. Although GE has not yet achieved this boundaryless state—and probably never will—it has made significant progress toward that end. So have other companies, such as Hewlett-Packard, AT&T, Motorola, and 3M.

By removing vertical boundaries, management flattens the hierarchy and minimizes status and rank. Cross-hierarchical teams (which include top executives, middle managers, supervisors, and operative employees), participative decision-making practices, and the use of 360-degree performance appraisals (in which peers and others above and below the employee evaluate performance) are examples of what GE is doing to break down vertical boundaries. At Oticon A/S, a $160-million-per-year Danish hearing aid manufacturer, all traces of hierarchy have disappeared. Everyone works at uniform mobile workstations, and project teams, not functions or departments, coordinate work.

Functional departments create horizontal boundaries that stifle interaction among functions, product lines, and units. The way to reduce them is to replace functional departments with cross-functional teams and organize activities around processes. Xerox now develops new products through multidisciplinary teams that work in a single process instead of around narrow functional tasks. Some AT&T units are now doing annual budgets based not on functions or departments but on processes, such as the maintenance of a worldwide telecommunications network. Another way management can cut through horizontal barriers is to use lateral transfers, rotating people into and out of different functional areas. This approach turns specialists into generalists.

The Leaner Organization: Organization Downsizing

The goal of the new organizational forms we've described is to improve agility by creating a lean, focused, and flexible organization. Companies may need to cut divisions that aren't adding value. *Downsizing* is a systematic effort to make an organization leaner by selling off business units, closing locations, or reducing staff. It has been very controversial because of its potential negative impacts on employees.

The radical shrinking of Chrysler and General Motors in recent years was a case of downsizing due to loss of market share and changes in consumer demand. These companies probably needed to downsize just to survive. Others downsize to direct all their efforts toward their core competencies.

Despite the advantages of being a lean organization, the impact of downsizing on organizational performance has been very controversial.[11] Reducing the size of the workforce has an immediately positive outcome in the huge reduction in wage costs. Companies downsizing to improve strategic focus often see positive effects on stock prices after the announcement. On the other hand, among companies that only cut employees but don't restructure, profits and stock prices usually decline. Part of the problem is the effect of downsizing on employee attitudes. Those who remain often feel worried about future layoffs and may be less committed to the organization.[12] Stress reactions can lead to increased sickness absences, lower concentration on the job, and lower creativity. In companies that don't invest much in their employees, downsizing can also lead to more voluntary turnover, so vital human capital is lost. The result is a company that is more anemic than lean.

Companies can reduce negative impacts by preparing for the post-downsizing environment in advance, thus alleviating some employee stress and strengthening support for the new strategic direction.[13] The following are some effective strategies for downsizing and suggestions for implementing them. Most are closely linked to the principles for organizational justice we've discussed previously:

- *Investment.* Companies that downsize to focus on core competencies are more effective when they invest in high-involvement work practices afterward.
- *Communication.* When employers make efforts to discuss downsizing with employees early, employees are less worried about the outcomes and feel the company is taking their perspective into account.
- *Participation.* Employees worry less if they can participate in the process in some way. In some companies, voluntary early retirement programs or severance packages can help achieve leanness without layoffs.
- *Assistance.* Providing severance, extended health care benefits, and job search assistance demonstrates a company does really care about its employees and honors their contributions.

Companies that make themselves lean can be more agile, efficient, and productive—but only if they make cuts carefully and help employees through the process.

WHY DO STRUCTURES DIFFER?

We've described organizational designs ranging from the highly structured bureaucracy to the amorphous boundaryless organization. The other designs we discussed exist somewhere between these extremes.

The Mechanistic Model

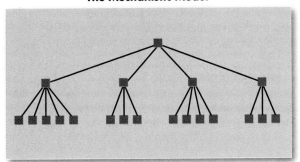

The Organic Model

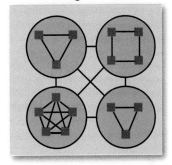

- High specialization
- Rigid departmentalization
- Clear chain of command
- Narrow spans of control
- Centralization
- High formalization

- Cross-functional teams
- Cross-hierarchical teams
- Free flow of information
- Wide spans of control
- Decentralization
- Low formalization

EXHIBIT 14.6 Mechanistic Versus Organic Models

Exhibit 14.6 recaps our discussions by presenting two extreme models of organizational design. One we'll call the **mechanistic model.** It's generally synonymous with the bureaucracy in that it has highly standardized processes for work, high formalization, and more managerial hierarchy. The other extreme, the **organic model,** looks a lot like the boundaryless organization. It's flat, has fewer formal procedures for making decisions, has multiple decision makers, and favors flexible practices.[14]

With these two models in mind, let's ask a few questions: Why are some organizations structured along more mechanistic lines, whereas others follow organic characteristics? What forces influence the choice of design? In this section we present the major causes or determinants of an organization's structure.[15]

Strategy

Because structure is a means to achieve objectives, and objectives derive from the organization's overall strategy, it's only logical that strategy and structure should be closely linked. In fact, structure should follow strategy. If management significantly changes the organization's strategy, the structure must change to accommodate.[16]

Most current strategy frameworks focus on three strategy dimensions—innovation, cost minimization, and imitation—and the structural design that works best with each.[17]

To what degree does an organization introduce major new products or services? An **innovation strategy** strives to achieve meaningful and unique innovations. Obviously, not all firms pursue innovation. Apple and 3M do, but conservative retailer Marks & Spencer doesn't. Innovative firms will use competitive pay and benefits to attract top candidates and motivate employees to take risks. Some degree of mechanistic structure can actually benefit innovation. Well-developed communication channels, policies for enhancing long-term commitment, and clear channels of authority all may make it easier to make rapid changes smoothly.

An organization pursuing a **cost-minimization strategy** tightly controls costs, refrains from incurring unnecessary expenses, and cuts prices in selling a basic product. This describes the strategy pursued by Walmart and the makers of generic or store-label grocery products. Cost-minimizing organizations pursue fewer policies meant to develop commitment among their workforce.

Organizations following an **imitation strategy** try to both minimize risk and maximize opportunity for profit, moving new products or new markets only after innovators have proven their viability. Mass-market fashion manufacturers that copy designer styles follow this strategy, as do firms such as Hewlett-Packard and Caterpillar. They follow smaller and more innovative competitors with superior products, but only after competitors have demonstrated the market is there.

Organization Size

An organization's size significantly affects its structure. Organizations that employ 2,000 or more people tend to have more specialization, more departmentalization, more vertical levels, and more rules and regulations than do small organizations. However, size becomes less important as an organization expands. Why? At around 2,000 employees, an organization is already fairly mechanistic; 500 more employees won't have much impact. But adding 500 employees to an organization of only 300 is likely to significantly shift it toward a more mechanistic structure.

Technology

Technology describes the way an organization transfers inputs into outputs. Every organization has at least one technology for converting financial, human, and physical resources into products or services. Ford Motor Company uses an assembly-line process to make its products. Colleges may use a number of instructional technologies—the ever-popular lecture method, the case-analysis method, the experiential exercise method, and the programmed learning method. Regardless, organizational structures adapt to their technology.

Numerous studies have examined the technology–structure relationship.[18] The common theme that differentiates technologies is their *degree of routineness*. Routine activities are characterized by automated and standardized operations. Nonroutine activities are customized. Examples of routine activities are injection-mold production of plastic knobs, automated transaction processing of sales transactions, and printing and binding of this book. Nonroutine activities are customized. They include varied operations such as furniture restoring, custom shoemaking, and genetic research. Nonroutine activities are customized and require frequent revision and updating. Examples of nonroutine activities are furniture restoring, genetic research, and the writing and editing of this book.

Environment

An organization's **environment** includes outside institutions or forces that can affect its performance, such as suppliers, customers, competitors, government regulatory agencies, and public pressure groups. And an organization's structure can be affected by environmental uncertainty. Static environments create significantly less uncertainty for managers than do dynamic ones. And because uncertainty is a threat to an organization's effectiveness, management will try to minimize it through adjustments in the organization's structure. They may, for example, broaden their structure to sense and respond to threats. Most companies, including Pepsi and Southwest Airlines, have added social networking departments to their structure so as to respond to negative information posted on blogs. Or companies may form strategic alliances with other companies.

Any organization's environment has three dimensions: capacity, volatility, and complexity.[19] *Capacity* refers to the degree to which the environment can support growth. Rich and growing environments generate excess resources, which can buffer the organization in times of relative scarcity.

Volatility describes the degree of instability in the environment. A dynamic environment with a high degree of unpredictable change makes it difficult for management to make accurate predictions. Because information technology changes at such a rapid pace, for instance, more organizations' environments are becoming volatile.

Finally, *complexity* is the degree of heterogeneity and concentration among environmental elements. Simple environments—like in the tobacco industry—are homogeneous and concentrated. Environments characterized by heterogeneity and dispersion—like the broadband industry—are complex and diverse, with numerous competitors.

Organizations that operate in environments characterized as scarce, dynamic, and complex face the greatest degree of uncertainty because they have high unpredictability, little room for error, and a diverse set of elements in the environment to monitor constantly. Given this three-dimensional definition of *environment,* we can offer some general conclusions about environmental uncertainty and structural arrangements. The more scarce, dynamic, and complex the environment, the more organic a structure should be. The more abundant, stable, and simple the environment, the more the mechanistic structure will be preferred.

ORGANIZATIONAL DESIGNS AND EMPLOYEE BEHAVIOR

We opened this chapter by implying that an organization's structure can have significant effects on its members. What might those effects be?

A review of the evidence leads to a pretty clear conclusion: You can't generalize! Not everyone prefers the freedom and flexibility of organic structures. Different factors stand out in different structures as well. In highly formalized, heavily structured, mechanistic organizations, the level of fairness in formal policies and procedures is a very important predictor of satisfaction. In more personal, individually adaptive organic organizations, employees value interpersonal justice more.[20] Some people are most productive and satisfied when work tasks are standardized and ambiguity minimized—that is, in mechanistic structures. So any discussion of the effect of organizational design on employee behavior has to address individual differences. To do so, let's consider employee preferences for work specialization, span of control, and centralization.[21]

The evidence generally indicates that *work specialization* contributes to higher employee productivity—but at the price of reduced job satisfaction. However, work specialization is not an unending source of higher productivity. Problems start to surface, and productivity begins to suffer, when the human diseconomies of doing repetitive and narrow tasks overtake the economies of specialization. As the workforce has become more highly educated and desirous of jobs that are intrinsically rewarding, we seem to reach the point at which productivity begins to decline more quickly than in the past.

There is still a segment of the workforce that prefers the routine and repetitiveness of highly specialized jobs. Some individuals want work that makes minimal intellectual demands and provides the security of routine; for them, high work specialization is a source of job satisfaction. The question, of course, is whether they represent 2 percent of the workforce or 52 percent. Given that some self-selection operates in the choice of careers, we might conclude that negative behavioral outcomes from high specialization are most likely to surface in professional jobs occupied by individuals with high needs for personal growth and diversity.

It is probably safe to say no evidence supports a relationship between *span of control* and employee performance. Although it is intuitively attractive to argue that large spans might lead to higher employee performance because they provide more distant supervision and more opportunity for personal initiative, the research fails to support this notion. At this point it's impossible to state that any particular span of control is best for producing high performance or high satisfaction among employees. Some people like to be left alone; others prefer the security of a boss who is quickly available at all times. Consistent with several of the contingency theories of leadership discussed in Chapter 11, we would expect factors such as employees' experiences and abilities and the degree of structure in their tasks to explain when wide or narrow spans of control are likely to contribute to their performance and job satisfaction. However, some evidence indicates that a *manager's* job satisfaction increases as the number of employees supervised increases.

We find fairly strong evidence linking *centralization* and job satisfaction. In general, organizations that are less centralized have a greater amount of autonomy. And autonomy appears positively related to job satisfaction. But, again, individual differences surface. Whereas one employee may value freedom, another may find autonomous environments frustratingly ambiguous.

Our conclusion: To maximize employee performance and satisfaction, managers must take individual differences, such as experience, personality, and the work task, into account. Culture should factor in, too.

We can draw one obvious insight: People don't select employers randomly. They are attracted to, are selected by, and stay with organizations that suit their personal characteristics.[22] Job candidates who prefer predictability are likely to seek out and take employment in mechanistic structures, and those who want autonomy are more likely to end up in an organic structure. So the effect of structure on employee behavior is undoubtedly reduced when the selection process facilitates proper matching of individual characteristics with organizational characteristics.

Globalization, strategic alliances, customer-organization links, and telecommuting are all examples of practices that reduce external boundaries.

Global Implications

When we think about how culture influences how organizations are to be structured, several questions come to mind. First, does culture really matter to organizational structure? Second, do employees in different countries vary in their perceptions of different types of organizational structures? Finally, how do cultural considerations fit with our discussion of the boundaryless organization? Let's tackle each question in turn.

Culture and Organizational Structure

Does culture really affect organizational structure? The answer might seem obvious—yes!—but there are reasons it may not matter as much as you think. The U.S. model of business has been very influential on organizational structures in other countries. Moreover, U.S. structures themselves have been influenced by structures in other countries (especially Japan, Great Britain, and Germany). However, cultural concerns still might be important. Bureaucratic structures still dominate in many parts of Europe and Asia. One management expert argues that U.S. management often places too much emphasis on individual leadership, which may be jarring in countries where decision making is more decentralized.[23]

Culture and Employee Structure Preferences

Although research is slim, it does suggest national culture influences the preference for structure.[24] Organizations that operate with people from high power-distance cultures, such as Greece, France, and most of Latin America, find that their employees are much more accepting of mechanistic structures than are employees from low power-distance countries. So consider cultural differences along with individual differences when predicting how structure will affect employee performance and satisfaction.

Culture and the Boundaryless Organization

When fully operational, the boundaryless organization also breaks down barriers created by geography.

Today, most large U.S. companies see themselves as global corporations and may well do as much business overseas as in the United States (as does Coca-Cola, for example). As a result, many companies struggle with the problem of how to incorporate geographic regions into their structure. The boundaryless organization provides one solution because it considers geography more of a tactical, logistical issue than a structural one. In short, the goal of the boundaryless organization is to break down cultural barriers.

One way to do so is through strategic alliances. Firms such as NEC Corporation, Boeing, and Apple each have strategic alliances or joint partnerships with dozens of companies. These alliances blur the distinction between one organization and another as employees work on joint projects. And some companies allow customers to perform functions previously done by management. Some AT&T units receive bonuses based on customer evaluations of the teams that serve them. Finally, telecommuting is blurring organizational boundaries. The security analyst with Merrill Lynch who does his job from his ranch in Montana or the software designer in Boulder, Colorado, who works for a San Francisco firm are just two of the millions of workers doing their jobs outside the physical boundaries of their employers' premises.

Implications for Managers

The theme of this chapter is that an organization's internal structure contributes to explaining and predicting behavior. That is, in addition to individual and group factors, the structural relationships in which people work has a bearing on employee attitudes and behavior.

What's the basis for this argument? To the degree that an organization's structure reduces ambiguity for employees and clarifies concerns such as "What am I supposed to do?" "How am I supposed to do it?" "To whom do I report?" and "To whom do I go if I have a problem?" it shapes their attitudes and facilitates and motivates them to higher levels of performance.

Of course, structure also constrains employees to the extent that it limits and controls what they do. Organizations structured around high levels of formalization and specialization, strict adherence to the chain of command, limited delegation of authority, and narrow spans of control give employees little autonomy. Controls in such organizations are tight, and behavior tends to vary within a narrow range. Structures with limited specialization, low formalization, and wide spans of control provide employees greater freedom and thus are characterized by greater behavioral diversity.

Strategy, size, technology, and environment determine the type of structure an organization will have. For simplicity's sake, we can classify structural designs as either mechanistic or organic. The specific effect of structural designs on performance and satisfaction is moderated by employees' individual preferences and cultural norms.

Finally, technology makes some organizational structures increasingly amorphous. This allows a manager the flexibility to take employee preferences, experience, and culture into account and design work systems that truly motivate.

CHAPTER 15

Organizational Culture

After studying this chapter, you should be able to:

▪ Define *organizational culture* and describe its common characteristics.

▪ Compare the functional and dysfunctional effects of organizational culture on people and the organization.

▪ Identify the factors that create and sustain an organization's culture.

▪ Show how culture is transmitted to employees.

▪ Demonstrate how an ethical culture can be created.

▪ Show how national culture may affect the way organizational culture is transported to a different country.

Just as individuals have personalities, so, too, do organizations. In Chapter 4, we found that individuals have relatively enduring and stable traits that help us predict their attitudes and behaviors. In this chapter, we propose that organizations, like people, can be characterized as, for example, rigid, friendly, warm, innovative, or conservative. These traits, in turn, can then be used to predict attitudes and behaviors of the people within these organizations.

The culture of any organization, although it may be hard to measure precisely, nevertheless exists and is generally recognized by its employees. We call this variable *organizational culture*. Just as tribal cultures have totems and taboos that dictate how each member will act toward fellow members and outsiders, organizations have cultures that govern how members behave. In this chapter, we'll discuss just what organizational culture is, how it affects employee attitudes and behavior, where it comes from, and whether it can be managed.

WHAT IS ORGANIZATIONAL CULTURE?

An executive once was asked what he thought *organizational culture* meant. He gave essentially the same answer a U.S. Supreme Court justice once gave in attempting to define pornography: "I can't define it, but I know it when I see it." We, however, need a basic definition of organizational culture to better understand the phenomenon. In this section we propose one and review several related ideas.

A Definition of *Organizational Culture*

Organizational culture refers to a system of shared meaning held by members that distinguishes the organization from other organizations. Seven primary characteristics seem to capture the essence of an organization's culture:[1]

1. *Innovation and risk taking.* The degree to which employees are encouraged to be innovative and take risks.
2. *Attention to detail.* The degree to which employees are expected to exhibit precision, analysis, and attention to detail.
3. *Outcome orientation.* The degree to which management focuses on results or outcomes rather than on the techniques and processes used to achieve them.
4. *People orientation.* The degree to which management decisions take into consideration the effect of outcomes on people within the organization.
5. *Team orientation.* The degree to which work activities are organized around teams rather than individuals.
6. *Aggressiveness.* The degree to which people are aggressive and competitive rather than easygoing.
7. *Stability.* The degree to which organizational activities emphasize maintaining the status quo in contrast to growth.

An organization's culture develops over many years and is rooted in deeply held values to which employees are strongly committed.

Each of these characteristics exists on a continuum from low to high. Appraising the organization on these seven characteristics, then, gives a composite picture of the organization's culture. This picture becomes the basis for feelings of shared understanding members have about the organization, how things are done in it, and the way members are supposed to behave.

Culture Is a Descriptive Term

Organizational culture is concerned with how employees perceive the characteristics of an organization's culture, not with whether they like them—that is, it's a descriptive term. This is important because it differentiates this concept from job satisfaction.

Research on organizational culture has sought to measure how employees see their organization: Does it encourage teamwork? Does it reward innovation? Does it stifle initiative? In contrast, *job satisfaction* seeks to measure how employees feel about the organization's expectations, reward practices, and the like. Although the two terms undoubtedly have overlapping characteristics, keep in mind that *organizational culture* is descriptive, whereas *job satisfaction* is evaluative.

Do Organizations Have Uniform Cultures?

Organizational culture represents a common perception the organization's members hold. We should expect, therefore, that individuals with different backgrounds or at different levels in the organization will tend to describe its culture in similar terms.

That doesn't mean, however, that there are no subcultures within any given culture. Most large organizations have a dominant culture and numerous subcultures.[2] A **dominant culture** expresses the core values shared by a majority of the organization's members. When we talk about an organization's culture, we are referring to its dominant culture, which gives an organization its distinct personality.[3] **Subcultures** tend to develop in large organizations to reflect common problems, situations, or experiences faced by groups of members in the same department or location. The purchasing department can have a subculture that includes the **core values** of the dominant culture plus additional values unique to members of the purchasing department.

If organizations were composed only of numerous subcultures, organizational culture as an independent variable would be significantly less powerful. It is the "shared meaning" aspect of culture that makes it such a potent device for guiding and shaping behavior. That's what allows us to say, for example, that Microsoft's culture values aggressiveness and risk taking[4] and to use that information to better understand the behavior of Microsoft executives and employees. But many organizations also have subcultures that can influence members' behavior.

Strong Versus Weak Cultures

It's possible to differentiate between strong and weak cultures.[5] If most employees (responding to management surveys) have the same opinions about the organization's mission and values, the culture is strong; if opinions vary widely, the culture is weak.

In a **strong culture,** the organization's core values are both intensely held and widely shared.[6] The more members who accept the core values and the greater their commitment, the stronger the culture and the greater its influence on member behavior because the high degree of sharedness and intensity creates an internal climate of high behavioral control. Nordstrom employees know in no uncertain terms what is expected of them, and these expectations go a long way in shaping their behavior. In contrast, Nordstrom competitor Macy's, which has struggled through an identity crisis, is working to remake its culture.

A strong culture should reduce employee turnover, because it demonstrates high agreement about what the organization represents. Such unanimity of purpose builds cohesiveness, loyalty, and organizational commitment. These qualities, in turn, lessen employees' propensity to leave.[7]

Culture Versus Formalization

We've seen that high formalization creates predictability, orderliness, and consistency. A strong culture achieves the same end without the need for written documentation.[8] Therefore, we should view formalization and culture as two different roads to a common destination. The stronger an organization's culture, the less management need be concerned with developing formal rules and regulations to guide employee behavior. Those guides will be internalized in employees when they accept the organization's culture.

WHAT DO CULTURES DO?

Let's more carefully review the role culture performs and whether it can ever be a liability for an organization.

Culture's Functions

First, culture has a boundary-defining role: it creates distinctions between one organization and others. Second, it conveys a sense of identity for organization members. Third, culture facilitates the generation of commitment to something larger than individual self-interest.

Fourth, it enhances the stability of the social system. Culture is the social glue that helps hold the organization together by providing appropriate standards for what employees should say and do. Finally, it is a sense-making and control mechanism that guides and shapes employees' attitudes and behavior. This last function is of particular interest to us. Culture defines the rules of the game:

> Culture by definition is elusive, intangible, implicit, and taken for granted. But every organization develops a core set of assumptions, understandings, and implicit rules that govern day-to-day behavior in the workplace. . . . Until newcomers learn the rules, they are not accepted as full-fledged members of the organization. Transgressions of the rules on the part of high-level executives or front-line employees result in universal disapproval and powerful penalties. Conformity to the rules becomes the primary basis for reward and upward mobility.[9]

Source: T. E. Deal and A. A. Kennedy, "Culture: A New Look Through Old Lenses," *Journal of Applied Behavioral Sciences,* November 1983, p. 501.

Today's trend toward decentralized organizations makes culture more important than ever, but ironically it also makes establishing a strong culture more difficult. When formal authority and control systems are reduced, culture's *shared meaning* points everyone in the same direction. However, employees organized in teams may show greater allegiance to their team and its values than to the values of the organization as a whole. In virtual organizations, the lack of frequent face-to-face contact makes establishing a common set of norms very difficult. Strong leadership that communicates frequently about common goals and priorities is especially important in innovative organizations.[10]

Individual–organization "fit"—that is, whether the applicant's or employee's attitudes and behavior are compatible with the culture—strongly influences who gets a job offer, a favorable performance review, or a promotion. It's no coincidence that Disney theme park employees appear almost universally attractive, clean, and wholesome with bright smiles. The company selects employees who will maintain that image. On the job, a strong culture, supported by formal rules and regulations, ensures they will act in a relatively uniform and predictable way.

Culture Creates Climate

If you've worked with someone whose positive attitude inspired you to do your best, or with a lackluster team that drained your motivation, you've experienced the effects of climate. **Organizational climate** refers to the shared perceptions organizational members have about their organization and work environment. This aspect of culture is like team spirit at the organizational level. When everyone has the same general feelings about what's important or how well things are working, the effect of these attitudes will be more than the sum of the individual parts. The same appears true for organizations. One meta-analysis found that across dozens of different samples, psychological climate was strongly related to individuals' level of job satisfaction, involvement, commitment, and motivation.[11] A positive overall workplace climate has been linked to higher customer satisfaction and financial performance as well.[12]

Dozens of dimensions of climate have been studied, including safety, justice, diversity, and customer service, to name a few.[13] A person who encounters a positive climate for performance will think about doing a good job more often and will believe others support his or her success. Someone who encounters a positive climate for diversity will feel more comfortable collaborating with co-workers regardless of their demographic background. Climate also influences the habits people adopt. If the climate for safety is positive, everyone wears safety gear and follows safety procedures even if individually they wouldn't normally think very often about being safe.

Culture as a Liability

Culture enhances organizational commitment and increases the consistency of employee behavior. These are clearly benefits to an organization. From an employee's standpoint, culture is valuable because it spells out how things are done and what's important. But we shouldn't ignore the potentially dysfunctional aspects of culture, especially a strong one, on an organization's effectiveness.

INSTITUTIONALIZATION   When an organization undergoes **institutionalization** and becomes *institutionalized*—that is, it is valued for itself and not for the goods or services it produces—it takes on a life of its own, apart from its founders or members.[14] It doesn't go out of business even if its original goals are no longer relevant. Acceptable modes of behavior become largely self-evident to members, and although this isn't entirely nega- tive, it does mean behaviors and habits that should be questioned and analyzed become taken for granted, which can stifle innovation and make maintaining the organization's culture an end in itself.

BARRIERS TO CHANGE   Culture is a liability when the shared values are not in agreement with those that further the organization's effectiveness. This is most likely when an organi- zation's environment is undergoing rapid change and its entrenched culture may no longer be appropriate.[15] Consistency of behavior, an asset in a stable environment, may then bur- den the organization and make it difficult to respond to changes. This helps explain the challenges executives have recently faced at Citigroup, Eastman Kodak, Yahoo!, Airbus, and the U.S. Federal Bureau of Investigation.[16] Strong cultures worked well for them in the past but become barriers to change when "business as usual" is no longer effective.

BARRIERS TO DIVERSITY   Hiring new employees who differ from the majority in race, age, gender, disability, or other characteristics creates a paradox:[17] Management wants to demonstrate support for the differences these employees bring to the workplace, but new- comers who wish to fit in must accept the organization's core cultural values. Because diverse behaviors and unique strengths are likely to diminish as people attempt to assimilate, strong cultures can become liabilities when they effectively eliminate these advantages.

By limiting the range of acceptable values and styles, strong cultures put consider- able pressure on employees to conform. In some instances, such as the widely publicized Texaco case in which senior managers made disparaging remarks about minorities (settled on behalf of 1,400 employees for $176 million), a strong culture that condones prejudice can even undermine formal corporate diversity policies.[18] Strong cultures can also be liabil- ities when they support institutional bias or become insensitive to people who are different.

BARRIERS TO ACQUISITIONS AND MERGERS   Historically, when management looked at acquisition or merger decisions, the key factors were financial advantage and product synergy. In recent years, cultural compatibility has become the primary concern. All things being equal, whether the acquisition actually works seems to have more to do with how well the two organizations' cultures match up.

A survey by consulting firm A. T. Kearney revealed that 58 percent of mergers failed to reach the value goals set by top managers.[19] The primary cause of failure is conflicting organizational cultures. As one expert commented, "Mergers have an unusually high failure rate, and it's always because of people issues." The $183 billion merger between America Online (AOL) and Time Warner in 2001 was the largest in U.S. corporate history. It was also a disaster. Only 2 years later, the stock had fallen an astounding 90 percent, and the new company reported what was then the largest financial loss in U.S. history. To this day, Time Warner stock—trading around $25 per share in late 2009—remains at a fraction of its former price (around $200 per share before the merger). Culture clash is commonly argued to be one of the causes of AOL Time Warner's problems. As one expert noted, "In some ways the merger of AOL and Time Warner was like the marriage of a teenager to a middle-aged banker. The cultures were vastly different. There were open collars and jeans at AOL. Time Warner was more buttoned-down."[20]

CREATING AND SUSTAINING CULTURE

An organization's culture doesn't pop out of thin air, and once established it rarely fades away. What forces influence the creation of a culture? What reinforces and sustains them once they're in place?

How a Culture Begins

An organization's current customs, traditions, and general way of doing things are largely due to what it has done before and how successful it was in doing it. This leads us to the ultimate source of an organization's culture: its founders.[21] Founders traditionally have a major impact on an organization's early culture. Free of previous customs or ideologies, they have a vision of what the organization should be, and its small size makes it easy to impose that vision on all members.

Culture creation occurs in three ways.[22] First, founders hire and keep only employees who think and feel the same way they do. Second, they indoctrinate and socialize these employees to their way of thinking and feeling. And finally, the founders' own behavior encourages employees to identify with them and internalize their beliefs, values, and assumptions. When the organization succeeds, the founders' personality becomes embedded in the culture.

The fierce, competitive style and disciplined, authoritarian nature of Hyundai, the giant Korean conglomerate, are the same characteristics often used to describe founder Chung Ju-Yung. Other founders with immeasurable impact on their organization's culture include Bill Gates at Microsoft, Ingvar Kamprad at IKEA, Herb Kelleher at Southwest Airlines, Fred Smith at FedEx, and Richard Branson at the Virgin Group.

Keeping a Culture Alive

Once a culture is in place, practices within the organization maintain it by giving employees a set of similar experiences. The selection process, performance evaluation criteria, training and development activities, and promotion procedures ensure those hired fit in with the culture, reward those who support it, and penalize (and even expel) those who challenge it. Three forces play a particularly important part in sustaining a culture: selection practices, the actions of top management, and socialization methods. Let's take a closer look at each.

SELECTION   The explicit goal of the selection process is to identify and hire individuals with the knowledge, skills, and abilities to perform successfully. The final decision, because it's significantly influenced by the decision maker's judgment of how well the candidates will fit into the organization, identifies people whose values are essentially consistent with at least a good portion of the organization's.[23] Selection also provides information to applicants. Those who perceive a conflict between their values and those of the organization can remove themselves from the applicant pool. Selection thus becomes a two-way street, allowing employer or applicant to avoid a mismatch and sustaining an organization's culture by selecting out those who might attack or undermine its core values.

W. L. Gore & Associates, the maker of Gore-Tex fabric used in outerwear, prides itself on its democratic culture and teamwork. There are no job titles at Gore, nor bosses nor chains of command. All work is done in teams. In Gore's selection process, teams of employees put job applicants through extensive interviews to ensure they can deal with the level of uncertainty, flexibility, and teamwork that's normal in Gore plants. Not surprisingly, W. L. Gore appears regularly on *Fortune*'s list of "100 Best Companies to Work For" (#15 in 2009).[24]

TOP MANAGEMENT   The actions of top management also have a major impact on the organization's culture.[25] Through words and behavior, senior executives establish norms that filter through the organization about, for instance, whether risk taking is desirable, how much freedom managers should give employees, what is appropriate dress, and what actions pay off in terms of pay raises, promotions, and other rewards.

The culture of supermarket chain Wegmans—which believes driven, happy, and loyal employees are more eager to help one another and provide exemplary customer service—is a direct result of the beliefs of the Wegman family. The chain began in 1930 when brothers John and Walter Wegman opened their first grocery store in Rochester, New York. Its focus on fine foods quickly separated it from other grocers— a focus maintained by the company's employees, many of whom are hired based on their interest in food. In 1950, Walter's son, Robert, became president and immediately added a generous number of employee benefits such as profit sharing and medical coverage, completely paid for by the company. Now Robert's son, Danny, is president of the company, and he has continued the Wegmans tradition of taking care of employees. To date, Wegmans has paid more than $54 million in college scholarships for its employees, both full-time and part-time. Pay is well above the market average, making annual turnover for full-time employees a mere 6 percent, according to the Food Marketing Institute. The industry average is 24 percent. Wegman's regularly appears on *Fortune*'s list as well (#5 in 2009).

SOCIALIZATION   No matter how good a job the organization does in recruiting and selection, new employees are not fully indoctrinated in the organization's culture and can disrupt beliefs and customs already in place. The process that helps new employees adapt to the prevailing culture is **socialization.**[26]

For example, all Marines must go through boot camp, where they "prove" their commitment. At the same time, the Marine trainers are indoctrinating new recruits in the "Marine way." All new employees at Neumann Homes in Warrenville, Illinois, go through a 40-hour orientation program.[27] They're introduced to the company's values and culture through a variety of activities, including a customer service lunch, an interactive departmental roundtable fair, and presentations about the company's core values that new hires make to the CEO. For incoming employees in the upper ranks, companies often put considerably more time and effort into the socialization process. As an example of the dark side of socialization, German giant Siemens used bribes so widely that a German government official said, "Bribery was Siemens' business model. Siemens had institutionalized corruption." Managers were frequently socialized on how to bribe officials, where to obtain the money (bribes were referred to as "NA" for *nützliche Aufwendungen* or "useful money"), and how to hide it in a sham accounting system. In the end, 2,700 of Siemens' contracts were found to be won through bribes, and when they were discovered, the company and its managers faced myriad penalties.[28]

We can think of socialization as a process with three stages: prearrival, encounter, and metamorphosis.[29] This process, shown in Exhibit 15.1, has an impact on the new employee's work productivity, commitment to the organization's objectives, and eventual decision to stay with the organization.

The **prearrival stage** explicitly recognizes that each individual arrives with a set of values, attitudes, and expectations about both the work to be done and the organization. One major purpose of a business school, for example, is to socialize business students to the attitudes and behaviors business firms want. Newcomers to high-profile organizations with a strong market position will make their own assumptions about what it must be like to work there.[30] Most new recruits will expect Nike to be dynamic and exciting, a prestigious law firm to be high in pressure and rewards, and the Marine Corps to require both discipline and courage. No matter how well managers think they can socialize newcomers, however, the most important predictor of future behavior is past behavior. What people know before they join the organization, and how proactive their personality is, are critical predictors of how well they adjust to a new culture.[31]

One way to capitalize on the importance of prehire characteristics in socialization is to use the selection process to inform prospective employees about the organization as a whole. We've also seen how the selection process ensures the inclusion of the "right type"—those who will fit in. "Indeed, the ability of the individual to present the appropriate face during the selection process determines his ability to move into the organization in the first place. Thus, success depends on the degree to which the aspiring member has correctly anticipated the expectations and desires of those in the organization in charge of selection."[32]

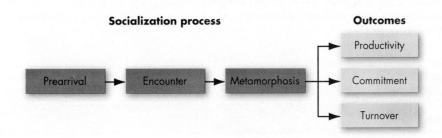

EXHIBIT 15.1

A Socialization Model

On entry into the organization, the new member enters the **encounter stage** and confronts the possibility that expectations—about the job, co-workers, the boss, and the organization in general—may differ from reality. If expectations were fairly accurate, the encounter stage merely cements earlier perceptions. However, this is often not the case. At the extreme, a new member may become disillusioned enough with the reality to resign. Proper recruiting and selection should significantly reduce that outcome, along with encouraging friendship ties in the organization—newcomers are more committed when friends and co-workers help them "learn the ropes."[33]

Finally, to work out any problems discovered during the encounter stage, the new member changes or goes through the **metamorphosis stage.** The options presented in Exhibit 15.2 are alternatives designed to bring about the desired metamorphosis. Most research suggests there are two major "bundles" of socialization practices. The more management relies on formal, collective, sequential, fixed, and serial socialization programs and emphasize divestiture, the more likely newcomers' differences will be stripped away and replaced by standardized predictable behaviors. These *institutional* practices are common in police departments, fire departments, and other organizations that value rule following and order. Programs that are informal, individual, random, variable, and disjunctive and emphasize investiture are more likely to give newcomers an innovative sense of their role and methods of working. Creative fields, such as research and development, advertising, and filmmaking, rely on these *individual* practices. Most research suggests high levels of

---

FORMAL VS. INFORMAL The more a new employee is segregated from the ongoing work setting and differentiated in some way to make explicit his or her newcomer's role, the more formal socialization is. Specific orientation and training programs are examples. Informal socialization puts the new employee directly into the job, with little or no special attention.

INDIVIDUAL VS. COLLECTIVE New members can be socialized individually. This describes how it's done in many professional offices. They can also be grouped together and processed through an identical set of experiences, as in military boot camp.

FIXED VS. VARIABLE This refers to the time schedule in which newcomers make the transition from outsider to insider. A fixed schedule establishes standardized stages of transition. This characterizes rotational training programs. It also includes probationary periods, such as the 8- to 10-year "associate" status used by accounting and law firms before deciding on whether or not a candidate is made a partner. Variable schedules give no advance notice of their transition timetable. Variable schedules describe the typical promotion system, in which one is not advanced to the next stage until one is "ready."

SERIAL VS. RANDOM Serial socialization is characterized by the use of role models who train and encourage the newcomer. Apprenticeship and mentoring programs are examples. In random socialization, role models are deliberately withheld. New employees are left on their own to figure things out.

INVESTITURE VS. DIVESTITURE Investiture socialization assumes that the newcomer's qualities and qualifications are the necessary ingredients for job success, so these qualities and qualifications are confirmed and supported. Divestiture socialization tries to strip away certain characteristics of the recruit. Fraternity and sorority "pledges" go through divestiture socialization to shape them into the proper role.

EXHIBIT 15.2

Entry
Socialization
Options

EXHIBIT 15.3

How Organization Cultures Form

institutional practices encourage person–organization fit and high levels of commitment, whereas individual practices produce more role innovation.[34]

The three-part entry socialization process is complete when new members have become comfortable with the organization and their job. They have internalized and accepted the norms of the organization and their work group, are confident in their competence, and feel trusted and valued by their peers. They understand the system—not only their own tasks but the rules, procedures, and informally accepted practices as well. Finally, they know what is expected of them and what criteria will be used to measure and evaluate their work. As Exhibit 15.1 showed, successful metamorphosis should have a positive impact on new employees' productivity and their commitment to the organization and reduce their propensity to leave the organization.

Summary: How Cultures Form

Exhibit 15.3 summarizes how an organization's culture is established and sustained. The original culture derives from the founder's philosophy and strongly influences hiring criteria as the firm grows. Top managers' actions set the general climate, including what is acceptable behavior and what is not. The way employees are socialized will depend both on the degree of success achieved in matching new employees' values to those of the organization in the selection process, and on top management's preference for socialization methods.

HOW EMPLOYEES LEARN CULTURE

Culture is transmitted to employees in a number of forms, the most potent being stories, rituals, material symbols, and language.

Stories

When Henry Ford II was chairman of Ford Motor Company, you would have been hard-pressed to find a manager who hadn't heard how he reminded his executives, when they got too arrogant, "It's my name that's on the building." The message was clear: Henry Ford II ran the company.

A number of senior Nike executives spend much of their time serving as corporate storytellers. And the stories they tell are meant to convey what Nike is about.[35] When they tell how co-founder (and Oregon track coach) Bill Bowerman went to his workshop and poured rubber into his wife's waffle iron to create a better running shoe, they're talking about Nike's spirit of innovation. When new hires hear tales of Oregon running star Steve Prefontaine's battles to make running a professional sport and attain better-performance equipment, they learn of Nike's commitment to helping athletes.

Stories such as these circulate through many organizations. They typically contain a narrative of events about the organization's founders, rule breaking, rags-to-riches successes, reductions in the workforce, relocation of employees, reactions to past mistakes, and organizational coping.[36] These stories anchor the present in the past and explain and legitimate current practices.

Rituals

Rituals are repetitive sequences of activities that express and reinforce the key values of the organization—what goals are most important, which people are important, and which people are expendable.[37] One of the better-known is Walmart's company chant. Begun by the company's founder, Sam Walton, as a way to motivate and unite his workforce, "Gimme a W, gimme an A, gimme an L, gimme a squiggle, give me an M, A, R, T!" has become a ritual that bonds workers and reinforces Walton's belief in the value of his employees to the company's success. Similar corporate chants are used by IBM, Ericsson, Novell, Deutsche Bank, and PricewaterhouseCoopers.[38]

Material Symbols

Alcoa headquarters doesn't look like your typical head-office operation. There are few individual offices, even for senior executives. The space is essentially made up of cubicles, common areas, and meeting rooms. This informality conveys to employees that Alcoa values openness, equality, creativity, and flexibility. Some corporations provide their top executives with chauffeur-driven limousines and a corporate jet. Others drive the company car themselves and travel in the economy section.

The layout of corporate headquarters, the types of automobiles top executives are given, and the presence or absence of corporate aircraft are a few examples of **material symbols.** Others include the size of offices, the elegance of furnishings, executive perks, and attire.[39] These convey to employees who is important, the degree of egalitarianism top management desires, and the kinds of behavior that are appropriate, such as risk taking, conservative, authoritarian, participative, individualistic, or social.

Language

Many organizations and subunits within them use language to help members identify with the culture, attest to their acceptance of it, and help preserve it. Unique terms describe equipment, officers, key individuals, suppliers, customers, or products that relate to the business. New employees may at first be overwhelmed by acronyms and jargon, that, once assimilated, act as a common denominator to unite members of a given culture or subculture. If you're a new employee at Boeing, you'll find yourself learning a unique vocabulary, including *BOLD* (Boeing online data), *CATIA* (computer-graphics-aided three-dimensional interactive application), *MAIDS* (manufacturing assembly and installation data system), *POP* (purchased outside production), and *SLO* (service-level objectives).[40]

CREATING AN ETHICAL ORGANIZATIONAL CULTURE

The organizational culture most likely to shape high ethical standards among its members is one that's high in risk tolerance, low to moderate in aggressiveness, and focused on means as well as outcomes.[41] This type of culture also takes a long-term perspective and balances the rights of multiple stakeholders, including the communities in which the business operates, its employees, and its stockholders. Managers are supported for taking risks and innovating, discouraged from engaging in unbridled competition, and guided to pay attention not just to *what* goals are achieved but also to *how.*

If the culture is strong and supports high ethical standards, it should have a very powerful and positive influence on employee behavior. Johnson & Johnson has a strong culture that has long stressed corporate obligations to customers, employees, the community, and shareholders, in that order. When poisoned bottles of Tylenol (a Johnson & Johnson product) were found in stores some years ago, company employees independently pulled the product from shelves across the United States before management had even issued a statement about the tampering. No one had to tell these individuals what was morally right; they knew what Johnson & Johnson would expect them to do. On the other hand, a strong culture that encourages pushing the limits can be a powerful force in shaping unethical behavior. Enron's aggressive culture, with its unrelenting pressure on executives to rapidly expand earnings, encouraged ethical lapses and eventually contributed to the company's downfall.[42]

What can management do to create a more ethical culture? Research suggests managers can have an effect on the ethical behavior of employees by adhering to the following principles:[43]

- *Be a visible role model.* Employees will look to the actions of top management as a benchmark for appropriate behavior. Senior managers taking the ethical high road send a positive message to all employees.
- *Communicate ethical expectations.* Minimize ethical ambiguities by creating and disseminating an organizational code of ethics. The code should state the organization's primary values and the ethical rules employees are expected to follow.
- *Provide ethical training.* Set up seminars, workshops, and similar ethical training programs. Use these to reinforce the organization's standards of conduct, clarify what practices are and are not permissible, and address potential ethical dilemmas.
- *Visibly reward ethical acts and punish unethical ones.* Include in managers' performance appraisals a point-by-point evaluation of how their decisions measure up against the organization's code of ethics. Review the means taken to achieve goals as well as the ends themselves. Visibly reward those who act ethically. Just as important, unethical acts should be conspicuously punished.
- *Provide protective mechanisms.* Provide formal mechanisms so employees can discuss ethical dilemmas and report unethical behavior without fear of reprimand. These might include ethical counselors, ombudsmen, or ethical officers.

Setting a positive ethical climate has to start at the top of the organization.[44] A study of 195 managers demonstrated that when top management emphasizes strong ethical values, supervisors are more likely to practice ethical leadership. This positive ethical attitude transfers down to line employees, who show lower levels of deviant behavior and higher levels of cooperation and assistance. The general ethical behavior and attitudes of other members of the department matter too for shaping individual ethical behavior. Finally, employees whose ethical values are similar to those of their department are more likely to be promoted, so we can think of ethical culture as flowing from the bottom up as well.[45]

CREATING A POSITIVE ORGANIZATIONAL CULTURE

It is possible to form ethical cultures and positive organizational cultures, but the means by which such cultures are attained are quite different.

At first blush, creating a positive culture may sound hopelessly naïve or like a Dilbert-style conspiracy. The one thing that makes us believe this trend is here to stay, however, are signs that management practice and OB research are converging.

A **positive organizational culture** emphasizes building on employee strengths, rewards more than it punishes, and emphasizes individual vitality and growth.[46] Let's consider each of these areas.

BUILDING ON EMPLOYEE STRENGTHS　A lot of OB, and of management practice, considers how to fix employee problems. Although a positive organizational culture does not ignore problems, it does emphasize showing workers how they can capitalize on their strengths. Do you know what your strengths are? Wouldn't it be better to be in an organizational culture that helped you discover them, and learn ways to make the most of them?

Larry Hammond used this approach—finding and exploiting employee strengths—when you'd least expect it: during his firm's darkest days. Hammond is CEO of Auglaize Provico, an agribusiness company based in Ohio. The company was in the midst of its worst financial struggles and had to lay off one-quarter of its workforce. At that nadir, Hammond decided to try a different approach. Rather than dwell on what was wrong, he took advantage of what was right. "If you really want to [excel], you have to know yourself—you have to know what you're good at, and you have to know what you're not so good at," says Hammond. With the help of Gallup consultant Barry Conchie, Hammond focused on discovering and using employee strengths and helped the company turn itself around. "You ask Larry [Hammond] what the difference is, and he'll say that it's individuals using their natural talents," says Conchie.[47] One employee may be strong in ideation (the ability to find connections between seemingly disparate phenomena) and learn to use that strength more often and effectively, whereas another may discover and develop the skill of consistency (the ability to set clear rules and adhere to them).

REWARDING MORE THAN PUNISHING　Although most organizations are sufficiently focused on extrinsic rewards such as pay and promotions, they often forget about the power of smaller (and cheaper) rewards such as praise. Part of creating a positive organizational culture is "catching employees doing something right." Another part is articulating praise. Many managers withhold praise either because they're afraid employees will coast or because they think praise is not valued. Because employees generally don't ask for praise, managers usually don't realize the costs of failing to do it. Failing to praise can become a silent killer, like escalating blood pressure.

Consider El'zbieta Górska-Kolodziejczyk, a plant manager for International Paper's facility in Kwidzyn, Poland. The job environment at the plant is bleak and difficult. Employees work in a windowless basement. Staffing is roughly one-third its prior level, while production has tripled. These challenges had done in the previous three managers. So, when Górska-Kolodziejczyk took over, she knew she had her work cut out for her. Although she had many items on her list of ways to transform the organization, at the top were recognition and praise. She initially found it difficult to give praise to those who weren't used to it, especially men. "They were like cement at the beginning," she said. "Like cement." Over time, however, she found they valued and even reciprocated praise. One day a department supervisor pulled her over to tell her she was doing a good job. "This I do remember, yes," she said.[48]

EMPHASIZING VITALITY AND GROWTH   A positive organizational culture emphasizes not only organizational effectiveness but also individuals' growth. No organization will get the best from employees who see themselves as mere tools or parts of the organization. A positive culture recognizes the difference between a job and a career and supports not only what the employee does to contribute to organizational effectiveness but also what the organization can do to make the employee more effective (personally and professionally).

Although it may take more creativity to encourage employee growth in some types of industries, consider the fast-paced food industry. Philippe Lescornez leads a team of employees at Masterfoods in Belgium. One of his team members is Didier Brynaert, who works in Luxembourg, nearly 150 miles from the Masterfoods Belgian headquarters. Brynaert was considered a good sales promoter who was meeting expectations. Lescornez decided Brynaert's job could be made more important if he were seen less as just another sales promoter and more as an expert on the unique features of the Luxembourg market. So Lescornez asked Brynaert for information he could share with the home office. He hoped that by raising Brynaert's profile in Brussels, he could create in him a greater sense of ownership for his remote sales territory. "I started to communicate much more what he did to other people [within the company], because there's quite some distance between the Brussels office and the section he's working in. So I started to communicate, communicate, communicate. The more I communicated, the more he started to provide material," says Lescornez. As a result, "Now he's recognized as the specialist for Luxembourg—the guy who is able to build a strong relationship with the Luxembourg clients," says Lescornez. What's good for Brynaert is, of course, also good for Lescornez, who gets credit for helping Brynaert grow and develop.[49]

LIMITS OF POSITIVE CULTURE   Is a positive culture a panacea? Though companies such as GE, Xerox, Boeing, and 3M have embraced aspects of a positive organizational culture, it is a new enough idea for us to be uncertain about how and when it works best.

Not all cultures value being positive as much as U.S. culture does, and, even within U.S. culture, there surely are limits to how far we should go to preserve a positive culture. For example, Admiral, a British insurance company, has established a Ministry of Fun in its call centers to organize such events as poem writings, foosball, conker (a British game involving chestnuts) competitions, and fancy dress days. When does the pursuit of a positive culture start to seem coercive or even Orwellian? As one critic notes, "Promoting a social orthodoxy of positiveness focuses on a particular constellation of desirable states and traits but, in so doing, can stigmatize those who fail to fit the template."[50]

Our point is that there may be benefits to establishing a positive culture, but an organization also needs to be careful to be objective and not pursue it past the point of effectiveness.

Organizational culture and national culture are not the same thing, though to some degree, an organization's culture reflects the dominant values of its host country.

Global Implications

We considered global cultural values (collectivism–individualism, power distance, and so on) in Chapter 4. Here our focus is a bit narrower: How is organizational culture affected by a global context? Organizational cultures are so powerful they often transcend national boundaries. But that doesn't mean organizations should, or could, be blissfully ignorant of local culture.

Organizational cultures often reflect national culture. The culture at AirAsia, a Malaysian-based airline, emphasizes informal dress so as not to create status differences. The carrier has lots of parties, participative management, and no private offices, reflecting Malaysia's relatively collectivistic culture. However, the culture of US Airways does not reflect the same degree of informality. If US Airways were to set up operations in Malaysia or merge with AirAsia, it would need to take these cultural differences into account. So when an organization opens up operations in another country, it ignores the local culture at its own risk.

One of the primary things U.S. managers can do is to be culturally sensitive. The United States is a dominant force in business and in culture, and with that influence comes a reputation. "We are broadly seen throughout the world as arrogant people, totally self-absorbed and loud," says one U.S. executive. Companies such as American Airlines, Lowe's, Novell, ExxonMobil, and Microsoft have implemented training programs to sensitize their managers to cultural differences. Some ways in which U.S. managers can be culturally sensitive include talking in a low tone of voice, speaking slowly, listening more, and avoiding discussions of religion and politics.

The management of ethical behavior is one area where national culture can rub up against corporate culture.[51] Many strategies for improving ethical behavior are based on the values and beliefs of the host country. U.S. managers endorse the supremacy of anonymous market forces and implicitly or explicitly view profit maximization as a moral obligation for business organizations. This worldview sees bribery, nepotism, and favoring personal contacts as highly unethical. Any action that deviates from profit maximization may indicate that inappropriate or corrupt behavior may be occurring. In contrast, managers in developing economies are more likely to see ethical decisions as embedded in a social environment. That means doing special favors for family and friends is not only appropriate but may even be an ethical responsibility. Managers in many nations also view capitalism skeptically and believe the interests of workers should be put on a par with the interests of shareholders.

U.S. employees are not the only ones who need to be culturally sensitive. Three times a week, employees at the Canadian unit of Japanese video game maker Koei begin the day by standing next to their desks, facing their boss, and saying "Good morning" in unison. Employees then deliver short speeches on topics that range from corporate principles to three-dimensional game engines. Koei also has employees punch a time clock and asks women to serve tea to top executive guests. Although these practices are consistent with Koei's culture, they do not fit Canadian culture very well. "It's kind of like school," says one Canadian employee.[52]

Implications for Managers

Employees form an overall subjective perception of the organization based on factors such as degree of risk tolerance, team emphasis, and support of people. This overall perception becomes, in effect, the organization's culture or personality and affects employee performance and satisfaction, with stronger cultures having greater impact.

Just as people's personalities tend to be stable over time, so too do strong cultures. This makes a strong culture difficult for managers to change if it becomes mismatched to its environment. Changing an organization's culture is a long and difficult process. Thus, at least in the short term, managers should treat their organization's culture as relatively fixed.

One of the most important managerial implications of organizational culture relates to selection decisions. Hiring individuals whose values don't align with those of the organization is likely to yield employees who lack motivation and commitment and are dissatisfied with their jobs and the organization.[53] Not surprisingly, employee "misfits" have considerably higher turnover rates.[54]

An employee's performance also depends to a considerable degree on knowing what to do and not do. Understanding the right way to do a job indicates proper socialization.

As a manager, you can shape the culture of your work environment. All managers can especially do their part to create an ethical culture and to consider spirituality and its role in creating a positive organizational culture. Often, you can do as much to shape your organizational culture as the culture of the organization shapes you.

CHAPTER 16

Organizational Change and Stress Management

After studying this chapter, you should be able to:

- Identify forces that act as stimulants to change.
- List the sources for resistance to change.
- Compare the four main approaches to managing organizational change.
- Demonstrate two ways of creating a culture for change.
- Describe the causes and consequences of work stress.
- Explain global differences in organizational change and work stress.

This chapter is about change. We describe environmental forces that require managers to implement comprehensive change programs. We also consider why people and organizations often resist change and how this resistance can be overcome. We review various processes for managing organizational change. We also discuss contemporary work stress issues for today's managers.

FORCES FOR CHANGE

No company today is in a particularly stable environment. Even those with dominant market share must change, sometimes radically. While Microsoft struggled with its controversial operating system Vista, it has also been trying to outflank rivals such as Google and smaller companies offering free, Web-based software. How well Microsoft performs is a function not of managing one change but of weathering both short- and long-term changes.

Thus, "Change or die!" is the rallying cry among today's managers worldwide. In a number of places in this book, we've discussed the *changing nature of the workforce*. Almost every organization must adjust to a multicultural environment, demographic changes, immigration, and outsourcing. *Technology* is continually changing jobs and organizations. It is not hard to imagine the very idea of an office becoming an antiquated concept in the near future.

The housing and financial sectors recently have experienced extraordinary *economic shocks*, leading to the elimination, bankruptcy, or acquisition of some of the best-known U.S. companies, including Bear Stearns, Merrill Lynch, Lehman Brothers, Countrywide Financial, Washington Mutual, and Ameriquest. Tens of thousands of jobs were lost and may never return. After years of declining bankruptcies, the global recession caused the bankruptcy of auto manufacturers General Motors and Chrysler, retailers Circuit City and Eddie Bauer, and myriad other organizations.

Competition is changing. Competitors are as likely to come from across the ocean as from across town. Successful organizations will be fast on their feet, capable of developing new products rapidly and getting them to market quickly. In other words, they'll be flexible and will require an equally flexible and responsive workforce. Increasingly, in the United States and Europe, the government regulates business practices, including executive pay. Employment rights have been extended to gay, lesbian, and transgender employees.

Social trends don't remain static. Consumers now meet and share information in chat rooms and blogs. Companies must continually adjust product and marketing strategies to be sensitive to changing social trends, as Liz Claiborne did when it sold off brands (such as Ellen Tracy), de-emphasized large vendors such as Macy's, and streamlined operations and cut staff. Consumers, employees, and organizational leaders are more sensitive to environmental concerns. "Green" practices are quickly becoming expected rather than optional.

Not even globalization's strongest proponents could have imagined how *world politics* would change in recent years. We've seen the breakup of the Soviet Union, the opening of China and Southeast Asia, and the rise of Muslim fundamentalism. Through the industrialized world, businesses—particularly in the banking and financial sectors—have come under new scrutiny.

RESISTANCE TO CHANGE

Our egos are fragile, and we often see change as threatening. One recent study showed that even when employees are shown data that suggest they need to change, they latch onto whatever data they can find that suggests they are okay and don't need to change.[1] Employees who have negative feelings about a change cope by not thinking about it, increasing their use of sick time, and quitting. All these reactions can sap the organization of vital energy when it is most needed.[2]

Resistance to change can be positive if it leads to open discussion and debate. These responses are usually preferable to apathy or silence and can indicate that members of the organization are engaged in the process, providing change agents an opportunity to explain the change effort. Change agents can also use resistance to modify the change to fit the preferences of other members of the organization. When they treat resistance only as a threat, rather than a point of view to be discussed, they may increase dysfunctional conflict.

> One of the most well-documented findings from studies of individual and organizational behavior is that organizations and their members resist change.

Resistance doesn't necessarily surface in standardized ways. It can be overt, implicit, immediate, or deferred. It's easiest for management to deal with overt and immediate resistance, such as complaints, a work slowdown, or a strike threat. The greater challenge is managing resistance that is implicit or deferred. These responses—loss of loyalty or motivation, increased errors or absenteeism—are more subtle and more difficult to recognize for what they are. Deferred actions also cloud the link between the change and the reaction to it and may surface weeks, months, or even years later. Or a single change of little inherent impact may be the straw that breaks the camel's back because resistance to earlier changes has been deferred and stockpiled.

Exhibit 16.1 summarizes major forces for resistance to change, categorized by their sources. Individual sources reside in human characteristics such as perceptions, personalities, and needs. Organizational sources reside in the structural makeup of organizations themselves.

It's worth noting that not all change is good. Speed can lead to bad decisions, and sometimes those initiating change fail to realize the full magnitude of the effects or their true costs. Rapid, transformational change is risky, and some organizations, such as Baring Brothers Bank in the United Kingdom, have collapsed for this reason.[3] Change agents need to carefully think through the full implications.

Overcoming Resistance to Change

Eight tactics can help change agents deal with resistance to change.[4] Let's review them briefly.

Individual Sources

Habit—To cope with life's complexities, we rely on habits or programmed responses. But when confronted with change, this tendency to respond in our accustomed ways becomes a source of resistance.

Security—People with a high need for security are likely to resist change because it threatens feelings of safety.

Economic factors—Changes in job tasks or established work routines can arouse economic fears if people are concerned that they won't be able to perform the new tasks or routines to their previous standards, especially when pay is closely tied to productivity.

Fear of the unknown—Change substitutes ambiguity and uncertainty for the unknown.

Selective information processing—Individuals are guilty of selectively processing information in order to keep their perceptions intact. They hear what they want to hear and they ignore information that challenges the world they've created.

Organizational Sources

Structural inertia—Organizations have built-in mechanisms—like their selection processes and formalized regulations—to produce stability. When an organization is confronted with change, this structural inertia acts as a counterbalance to sustain stability.

Limited focus of change—Organizations are made up of a number of interdependent subsystems. One can't be changed without affecting the others. So limited changes in subsystems tend to be nullified by the larger system.

Group inertia—Even if individuals want to change their behavior, group norms may act as a constraint.

Threat to expertise—Changes in organizational patterns may threaten the expertise of specialized groups.

Threat to established power relationships—Any redistribution of decision-making authority can threaten long-established power relationships within the organization.

Threat to established resource allocations—Groups in the organization that control sizable resources often see change as a threat. They tend to be content with the way things are.

EXHIBIT 16.1
Sources of Resistance to Change

EDUCATION AND COMMUNICATION   Communicating the logic of a change can reduce employee resistance on two levels. First, it fights the effects of misinformation and poor communication: If employees receive the full facts and clear up misunderstandings, resistance should subside. Second, communication can help "sell" the need for change by packaging it properly. A study of German companies revealed changes are most effective when a company communicates a rationale that balances the interests of various stakeholders (shareholders, employees, community, customers) rather than those of shareholders only.[5]

PARTICIPATION   It's difficult to resist a change decision in which we've participated. Assuming participants have the expertise to make a meaningful contribution, their involvement can reduce resistance, obtain commitment, and increase the quality of the change decision. However, against these advantages are the negatives: potential for a poor solution and great consumption of time.

BUILDING SUPPORT AND COMMITMENT   When employees' fear and anxiety are high, counseling and therapy, new-skills training, or a short paid leave of absence may facilitate adjustment. When managers or employees have low emotional commitment to change, they favor the status quo and resist it.[6] Thus, firing up employees can also help them emotionally commit to the change rather than embrace the status quo.

DEVELOP POSITIVE RELATIONSHIPS   People are more willing to accept changes if they trust the managers implementing them. One study surveyed 235 employees from a large housing corporation in the Netherlands that was experiencing a merger. Those who had a more positive relationship with their supervisors, and who felt that the work environment supported development, were much more positive about the change process.[7]

IMPLEMENTING CHANGES FAIRLY   One way organizations can minimize negative impact is to make sure change is implemented fairly. As we saw in Chapter 6, procedural fairness is especially important when employees perceive an outcome as negative, so it's crucial that employees see the reason for the change and perceive its implementation as consistent and fair.[8]

MANIPULATION AND COOPTATION   *Manipulation* refers to covert influence attempts. Twisting facts to make them more attractive, withholding information, and creating false rumors to get employees to accept change are all examples of manipulation. If management threatens to close a manufacturing plant whose employees are resisting an across-the-board pay cut, and if the threat is actually untrue, management is using manipulation. *Cooptation,* on the other hand, combines manipulation and participation. It seeks to "buy off" the leaders of a resistance group by giving them a key role, seeking their advice not to find a better solution but to get their endorsement. Both manipulation and cooptation are relatively inexpensive ways to gain the support of adversaries, but they can backfire if the targets become aware they are being tricked or used. Once that's discovered, the change agent's credibility may drop to zero.

SELECTING PEOPLE WHO ACCEPT CHANGE   Research suggests the ability to easily accept and adapt to *change* is related to personality—some people simply have more positive attitudes about change than others. Such individuals are open to experience, take a positive attitude toward change, are willing to take risks, and are flexible in their behavior. One study of managers in the United States, Europe, and Asia found those with a positive self-concept and high risk tolerance coped better with organizational change. A study of 258 police officers found those higher in growth-needs strength, internal locus of control, and internal work motivation had more positive attitudes about organizational change efforts.[9] Another study found that selecting people based on a resistance-to-change scale worked well in winnowing out those who tended to be rigid or react emotionally to change.[10] Individuals higher in general mental ability are also better able to learn and adapt to changes in the workplace.[11] In sum, an impressive body of evidence shows organizations can facilitate change by selecting people predisposed to accept it.

COERCION   Last on the list of tactics is *coercion,* the application of direct threats or force on the resisters. If management really is determined to close a manufacturing plant whose employees don't acquiesce to a pay cut, the company is using coercion. Other examples are threats of transfer, loss of promotions, negative performance evaluations, and a poor letter of recommendation. The advantages and drawbacks of coercion are approximately the same as for manipulation and cooptation.

APPROACHES TO MANAGING ORGANIZATIONAL CHANGE

Now we turn to several approaches to managing change: Lewin's classic three-step model of the change process, Kotter's eight-step plan, action research, and organizational development.

Lewin's Three-Step Model

Kurt Lewin argued that successful change in organizations should follow three steps: **unfreezing** the status quo, **movement** to a desired end state, and **refreezing** the new change to make it permanent[12] (see Exhibit 16.2).

   This status quo is an equilibrium state. To move from equilibrium—to overcome the pressures of both individual resistance and group conformity—unfreezing must happen in one of three ways (see Exhibit 16.3). The **driving forces,** which direct behavior away from the status quo, can be increased. The **restraining forces,** which hinder

EXHIBIT 16.2

Lewin's Three-Step Change Model

EXHIBIT 16.3

Unfreezing the Status Quo

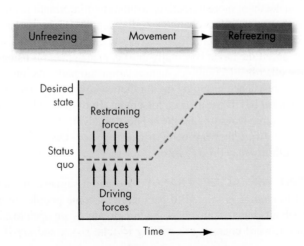

movement away from equilibrium, can be decreased. A third alternative is to combine the first two approaches. Companies that have been successful in the past are likely to encounter restraining forces because people question the need for change. Similarly, research shows that companies with strong cultures excel at incremental change but are overcome by restraining forces against radical change.[13]

Research on organizational change has shown that, to be effective, change has to happen quickly.[14] Organizations that build up to change do less well than those that get to and through the movement stage quickly.

Once change has been implemented, to be successful the new situation must be refrozen so it can be sustained over time. Without this last step, change will likely be short-lived and employees will attempt to revert to the previous equilibrium state. The objective of refreezing, then, is to stabilize the new situation by balancing the driving and restraining forces.

Kotter's Eight-Step Plan for Implementing Change

John Kotter built on Lewin's three-step model to create a more detailed approach for implementing change.[15] Kotter began by listing common mistakes managers make when trying to initiate change. They may fail to create a sense of urgency about the need for change, to create a coalition for managing the change process, to have a vision for change and effectively communicate it, to remove obstacles that could impede the vision's achievement, to provide short-term and achievable goals, and to anchor the changes into the organization's culture. They may also declare victory too soon.

Kotter then established eight sequential steps to overcome these problems. They're listed in Exhibit 16.4. Notice how Kotter's first four steps essentially extrapolate Lewin's "unfreezing" stage. Steps 5 through 7 represent "movement," and the final step works on "refreezing." So Kotter's contribution lies in providing managers and change agents with a more detailed guide for successfully implementing change.

Organizational Development

Organizational development (OD) is a collection of change methods that try to improve organizational effectiveness and employee well-being.[16]

OD methods value human and organizational growth, collaborative and participative processes, and a spirit of inquiry.[17] Contemporary OD borrows heavily from

1. Establish a sense of urgency by creating a compelling reason for why change is needed.
2. Form a coalition with enough power to lead the change.
3. Create a new vision to direct the change and strategies for achieving the vision.
4. Communicate the vision throughout the organization.
5. Empower others to act on the vision by removing barriers to change and encouraging risk taking and creative problem solving.
6. Plan for, create, and reward short-term "wins" that move the organization toward the new vision.
7. Consolidate improvements, reassess changes, and make necessary adjustments in the new programs.
8. Reinforce the changes by demonstrating the relationship between new behaviors and organizational success.

EXHIBIT 16.4

Kotter's Eight-Step Plan for Implementing Change

Source: Based on J. P. Kotter, *Leading Change* (Boston: Harvard Business School Press, 1996).

postmodern philosophy in placing heavy emphasis on the subjective ways in which people see their environment. The focus is on how individuals make sense of their work environment. The change agent may take the lead in OD, but there is a strong emphasis on collaboration. These are the underlying values in most OD efforts:

1. *Respect for people.* Individuals are perceived as responsible, conscientious, and caring. They should be treated with dignity and respect.
2. *Trust and support.* An effective and healthy organization is characterized by trust, authenticity, openness, and a supportive climate.
3. *Power equalization.* Effective organizations de-emphasize hierarchical authority and control.
4. *Confrontation.* Problems should be openly confronted, not swept under the rug.
5. *Participation.* The more engaged in the decisions they are, the more people affected by a change will be committed to implementing them.

What are some OD techniques or interventions for bringing about change? Here are five.

1. *Survey feedback.* One tool for assessing attitudes held by organizational members, identifying discrepancies among member perceptions, and solving these differences is the **survey feedback** approach.[18] A questionnaire, usually completed by all members of the organization or unit, typically asks about their perceptions and attitudes on a range of topics, including decision-making practices; communication effectiveness; coordination among units; and satisfaction with the organization, job, peers, and immediate supervisor. These data become the springboard for identifying problems and clarifying issues that may be creating difficulties for people. Particular attention is given to encouraging discussion and ensuring it focuses on issues and ideas and not on attacking individuals. For instance, are people listening? Are new ideas being generated? Can decision making, interpersonal relations, or job assignments be improved? Answers should lead the group to commit to various remedies for the problems identified.
2. *Process consultation.* Managers often sense their unit's performance can be improved but are unable to identify what to improve and how. The purpose of **process consultation (PC)** is for an outside consultant to assist a client, usually a manager, "to perceive, understand, and act upon process events" with which the manager must deal.[19] PC is similar to sensitivity training in assuming we can improve organizational effectiveness by dealing with interpersonal problems and in emphasizing involvement. But PC is more task directed, and consultants are there to "give the client 'insight' into what is going on around him, within him, and between him and other people."[20] They do not solve the organization's problems but rather guide or coach the client to solve his or her own problems after *jointly* diagnosing what needs improvement. The client develops the skill to analyze processes within his or her unit and can continue to call on it long after the consultant is gone.
3. *Team building.* We've noted throughout this book that organizations increasingly rely on teams to accomplish work tasks. **Team building** uses high-interaction group activities to increase trust and openness among team members, improve coordinative efforts, and increase team performance.[21] Team building typically includes goal setting, development of interpersonal relations among team

members, role analysis to clarify each member's role and responsibilities, and team process analysis. It may emphasize or exclude certain activities, depending on the purpose of the development effort and the specific problems with which the team is confronted.

4. *Intergroup development.* A major area of concern in OD is dysfunctional conflict between groups. **Intergroup development** seeks to change groups' attitudes, stereotypes, and perceptions about each other. Here, training sessions closely resemble diversity training (in fact, diversity training largely evolved from intergroup development in OD), except rather than focusing on demographic differences, they focus on differences among occupations, departments, or divisions within an organization. Among several approaches for improving intergroup relations, a popular one emphasizes problem solving.[22] Each group meets independently to list its perceptions of itself and of the other group, and how it believes the other group perceives it. The groups share their lists, discuss similarities and differences, and look for the causes of disparities. Once they have identified the causes of the difficulty, the groups move to the integration phase—developing solutions to improve relations between them. Subgroups can be formed of members from each of the conflicting groups to conduct further diagnosis and formulate alternative solutions.

5. *Appreciative inquiry.* Most OD approaches are problem centered. They identify a problem or set of problems, and then look for a solution. **Appreciative inquiry (AI)** instead accentuates the positive;[23] that is, AI focuses on an organization's successes rather than its problems. The AI process consists of four steps—discovery, dreaming, design, and discovery—often played out in a large-group meeting over a 2- or 3-day time period and overseen by a trained change agent. *Discovery* sets out to identify what people think are the organization's strengths. Employees recount times they felt the organization worked best or when they specifically felt most satisfied with their jobs. In *dreaming,* employees use information from the discovery phase to speculate on possible futures, such as what the organization will be like in 5 years. In *design,* participants find a common vision of how the organization will look in the future and agree on its unique qualities. For the fourth step, participants seek to define the organization's *destiny* or how to fulfill their dream, and they typically write action plans and develop implementation strategies.

CREATING A CULTURE FOR CHANGE

We've considered how organizations can *adapt* to change. But recently, some OB scholars have focused on a more proactive approach—how organizations can *embrace* change by transforming their cultures. In this section we review two such approaches: stimulating an innovative culture and creating a learning organization.

There are various approaches that can be used to manage organizational change and for developing a culture for change; it is unlikely one approach is always best in every situation.

Stimulating a Culture of Innovation

How can an organization become more innovative? An excellent model is W. L. Gore, the $1.4-billion-per-year company best known as the maker of Gore-Tex fabric.[24] Gore has developed a reputation as one of the most innovative U.S. companies by developing a stream of diverse products—including guitar strings, dental floss, medical devices, and fuel cells.

What's the secret of Gore's success? What can other organizations do to duplicate its track record for innovation? Although there is no guaranteed formula, certain characteristics surface repeatedly when researchers study innovative organizations. We've grouped them into structural, cultural, and human resource categories. Change agents should consider introducing these characteristics into their organization to create an innovative climate. Before we look at these characteristics, however, let's clarify what we mean by innovation.

DEFINITION OF *INNOVATION*   We said change refers to making things different. **Innovation,** a more specialized kind of change, is a new idea applied to initiating or improving a product, process, or service.[25] Thus, all innovations imply change, but not all changes necessarily introduce new ideas or lead to significant improvements. Innovations can range from small incremental improvements, such as netbook computers, to radical breakthroughs, such as Toyota's battery-powered Prius.

SOURCES OF INNOVATION   *Structural variables* have been the most studied potential source of innovation. A comprehensive review of the structure–innovation relationship leads to the following conclusions.[26] First, organic structures positively influence innovation. Because they're lower in vertical differentiation, formalization, and centralization, organic organizations facilitate the flexibility, adaptation, and cross-fertilization that make the adoption of innovations easier. Second, long tenure in management is associated with innovation. Managerial tenure apparently provides legitimacy and knowledge of how to accomplish tasks and obtain desired outcomes. Third, innovation is nurtured when there are slack resources. Having an abundance of resources allows an organization to afford to purchase innovations, bear the cost of instituting them, and absorb failures. Finally, interunit communication is high in innovative organizations.[27] These organizations are high users of committees, task forces, cross-functional teams, and other mechanisms that facilitate interaction across departmental lines.

Innovative organizations tend to have similar *cultures*. They encourage experimentation. They reward both successes and failures. They celebrate mistakes. Unfortunately, in too many organizations, people are rewarded for the absence of failures rather than for the presence of successes. Such cultures extinguish risk taking and innovation. People will suggest and try new ideas only when they feel such behaviors exact no penalties. Managers in innovative organizations recognize that failures are a natural by-product of venturing into the unknown. Alex Rodriguez is one of baseball's best players still playing, yet in his career he has more strikeouts (1,702) than home runs (574) or runs batted in (1,669). And he is remembered (and paid $27.5 million per year) for the latter two, not the former one (though, sadly, he'll also be remembered for his admitted steroid use).

Within the *human resources* category, innovative organizations actively promote the training and development of their members so they keep current, offer high job security so employees don't fear getting fired for making mistakes, and encourage individuals to become champions of change. Once a new idea is developed, **idea champions** actively and enthusiastically promote it, build support, overcome resistance, and ensure it's implemented.[28] Champions have common personality characteristics: extremely high self-confidence, persistence, energy, and a tendency to take risks. They also display characteristics associated with transformational leadership—they inspire and energize others with their vision of an innovation's potential and their strong personal conviction about their mission. They are also good at gaining the commitment of others. Idea champions have jobs that provide considerable decision-making discretion; this autonomy helps them introduce and implement innovations.[29]

WORK STRESS AND ITS MANAGEMENT

Friends say they're stressed from greater workloads and longer hours because of downsizing at their companies. Parents worry about the lack of job stability and reminisce about a time when a job with a large company implied lifetime security. We read surveys in which employees complain about the stress of trying to balance work and family responsibilities.[30] Indeed, work is, for most people, the most important source of stress in life. What are the causes and consequences of stress, and what can individuals and organizations do to reduce it?

What Is Stress?

Stress is a dynamic condition in which an individual is confronted with an opportunity, demand, or resource related to what the individual desires and for which the outcome is perceived to be both uncertain and important.[31] This is a complicated definition. Let's look at its components more closely.

Although stress is typically discussed in a negative context, it is not necessarily bad in and of itself; it also has a positive value. It's an opportunity when it offers potential gain. Consider, for example, the superior performance an athlete or stage performer gives in a "clutch" situation. Such individuals often use stress positively to rise to the occasion and perform at their maximum. Similarly, many professionals see the pressures of heavy workloads and deadlines as positive challenges that enhance the quality of their work and the satisfaction they get from their job.

Recently, researchers have argued that **challenge stressors**—or stressors associated with workload, pressure to complete tasks, and time urgency—operate quite differently from **hindrance stressors**—or stressors that keep you from reaching your goals (for example, red tape, office politics, confusion over job responsibilities).

Although research is just starting to accumulate, early evidence suggests challenge stressors produce less strain than hindrance stressors.[32] A meta-analysis of responses from more than 35,000 individuals showed role ambiguity, role conflict, role overload, job insecurity, environmental uncertainty, and situational constraints were all consistently negatively related to job performance.[33] There is also evidence that challenge stress improves job performance in a supportive work environment, whereas hindrance stress reduces job performance in all work environments.[34]

> Change is often stressful to individuals, but, like change, researchers are beginning to accept that not all stress is harmful.

Researchers have sought to clarify the conditions under which each type of stress exists. It appears that employees who have a stronger affective commitment to their organization can transfer psychological stress into greater focus and higher sales performance, whereas employees with low levels of commitment perform worse under stress.[35] And when challenge stress increases, those with high levels of organizational support have higher role-based performance, but those with low levels of organizational support do not.[36]

More typically, stress is associated with **demands** and **resources**. Demands are responsibilities, pressures, obligations, and uncertainties individuals face in the workplace.

Resources are things within an individual's control that he or she can use to resolve the demands. Let's discuss what this demands–resources model means.[37]

When you take a test at school or you undergo your annual performance review at work, you feel stress because you confront opportunities and performance pressures. A good performance review may lead to a promotion, greater responsibilities, and a higher salary. A poor review may prevent you from getting a promotion. An extremely poor review might even result in your being fired. To the extent you can apply resources to the demands on you—such as being prepared, placing the exam or review in perspective, or obtaining social support—you will feel less stress.

Research suggests adequate resources help reduce the stressful nature of demands when demands and resources match. If emotional demands are stressing you, having emotional resources in the form of social support is especially important. If the demands are cognitive—say, information overload—then job resources in the form of computer support or information are more important. Thus, under the demands–resources perspective, having resources to cope with stress is just as important in offsetting it as demands are in increasing it.[38]

Consequences of Stress

Stress shows itself in a number of ways, such as high blood pressure, ulcers, irritability, difficulty making routine decisions, loss of appetite, accident proneness, and the like. These symptoms fit under three general categories: physiological, psychological, and behavioral symptoms.[39]

PHYSIOLOGICAL SYMPTOMS   Most early concern with stress was directed at physiological symptoms because most researchers were specialists in the health and medical sciences. Their work led to the conclusion that stress could create changes in metabolism, increase heart and breathing rates and blood pressure, bring on headaches, and induce heart attacks.

Because symptoms are complex and difficult to measure objectively, the link between stress and particular physiological effects is not clear. Traditionally, researchers concluded there were few, if any, consistent relationships.[40] More recently, some evidence suggests stress may have harmful physiological effects. One study linked stressful job demands increase susceptibility to upper respiratory illnesses and poor immune system functioning, especially for individuals with low self-efficacy.[41]

PSYCHOLOGICAL SYMPTOMS   Job dissatisfaction is "the simplest and most obvious psychological effect" of stress.[42] But stress shows itself in other psychological states—for instance, tension, anxiety, irritability, boredom, and procrastination.

Jobs that make multiple and conflicting demands or that lack clarity about the incumbent's duties, authority, and responsibilities increase both stress and dissatisfaction.[43] Similarly, the less control people have over the pace of their work, the greater the stress and dissatisfaction. Although more research is needed to clarify the relationship, jobs that provide a low level of variety, significance, autonomy, feedback, and identity appear to create stress and reduce satisfaction and involvement in the job.[44] Not everyone reacts to autonomy in the same way, however. For those who have an external locus of control, increased job control increases the tendency to experience stress and exhaustion.[45]

BEHAVIORAL SYMPTOMS   Behavior-related stress symptoms include changes in productivity, absence, and turnover, as well as changes in eating habits, increased smoking or consumption of alcohol, rapid speech, fidgeting, and sleep disorders.[46]

Managing Stress

Because low to moderate levels of stress can be functional and lead to higher performance, management may not be concerned when employees experience them. Employees, however, are likely to perceive even low levels of stress as undesirable. It's not unlikely, therefore, for employees and management to have different notions of what constitutes an acceptable level of stress on the job. What management may consider to be "a positive stimulus that keeps the adrenaline running" is very likely to be seen as "excessive pressure" by the employee. Keep this in mind as we discuss individual and organizational approaches toward managing stress.[47]

INDIVIDUAL APPROACHES   An employee can take personal responsibility for reducing stress levels. Individual strategies that have proven effective include time-management techniques, increased physical exercise, relaxation training, and expanded social support networks.

Many people manage their time poorly. The well-organized employee, like the well-organized student, can often accomplish twice as much as the person who is poorly organized. So an understanding and utilization of basic time-management principles can help individuals better cope with tensions created by job demands.[48] A few of the best-known time-management principles are (1) making daily lists of activities to be accomplished, (2) prioritizing activities by importance and urgency, (3) scheduling activities according to the priorities set, and (4) knowing your daily cycle and handling the most demanding parts of your job when you are most alert and productive.[49]

Physicians have recommended noncompetitive physical exercise, such as aerobics, walking, jogging, swimming, and riding a bicycle, as a way to deal with excessive stress levels. These forms of *physical exercise* increase heart capacity, lower the at-rest heart rate, provide a mental diversion from work pressures, and even slow the physical and mental effects of aging.[50]

Individuals can teach themselves to reduce tension through *relaxation techniques* such as meditation, hypnosis, and biofeedback. The objective is to reach a state of deep physical relaxation, in which you feel somewhat detached from the immediate environment and from body sensations.[51] Deep relaxation for 15 or 20 minutes a day releases tension and provides a pronounced sense of peacefulness, as well as significant changes in heart rate, blood pressure, and other physiological factors.

As we have noted, friends, family, or work colleagues talk to provide an outlet when stress levels become excessive. Expanding your *social support network* provides someone to hear your problems and offer a more objective perspective on the situation than your own.

ORGANIZATIONAL APPROACHES   Several factors that cause stress—particularly task and role demands—are controlled by management and thus can be modified or changed. Strategies to consider include improved personnel selection and job placement, training, realistic goal setting, redesign of jobs, increased employee involvement, improved organizational communication, employee sabbaticals, and corporate wellness programs.

Certain jobs are more stressful than others but, as already noted, individuals differ in their response to stressful situations. We know individuals with little experience or an external locus of control tend to be more prone to stress. *Selection and placement* decisions should take these facts into consideration. Obviously, management shouldn't restrict hiring to only experienced individuals with an internal locus, but such individuals may adapt better to high-stress jobs and perform those jobs more effectively. Similarly, *training* can increase an individual's self-efficacy and thus lessen job strain.

We discussed *goal setting* in Chapter 6. Individuals perform better when they have specific and challenging goals and receive feedback on their progress toward these goals. Goals can reduce stress as well as provide motivation.[52] Employees who are highly committed to their goals and see purpose in their jobs experience less stress because they are more likely to perceive stressors as challenges rather than hindrances. Specific goals perceived as attainable clarify performance expectations. In addition, goal feedback reduces uncertainties about actual job performance. The result is less employee frustration, role ambiguity, and stress.

Redesigning jobs to give employees more responsibility, more meaningful work, more autonomy, and increased feedback can reduce stress because these factors give employees greater control over work activities and lessen dependence on others. But as we noted in our discussion of work design, not all employees want enriched jobs. The right redesign for employees with a low need for growth might be less responsibility and increased specialization. If individuals prefer structure and routine, reducing skill variety should also reduce uncertainties and stress levels.

Role stress is detrimental to a large extent because employees feel uncertain about goals, expectations, how they'll be evaluated, and the like. By giving these employees a voice in the decisions that directly affect their job performance, management can increase employee control and reduce role stress. So managers should consider *increasing employee involvement* in decision making.[53]

Increasing formal *organizational communication* with employees reduces uncertainty by lessening role ambiguity and role conflict. Given the importance that perceptions play in moderating the stress–response relationship, management can also use effective communications as a means to shape employee perceptions. Remember that what employees categorize as demands, threats, or opportunities is an interpretation and that interpretation can be affected by the symbols and actions communicated by management.

Our final suggestion is organizationally supported **wellness programs.** These typically provide workshops to help people quit smoking, control alcohol use, lose weight, eat better, and develop a regular exercise program; they focus on the employee's total physical and mental condition. Some help employees improve their psychological health as well. A meta-analysis of 36 programs designed to reduce stress (including wellness programs) showed that interventions to help employees reframe stressful situations and use active coping strategies led to an appreciable reduction in stress levels.[54] Most wellness programs assume employees need to take personal responsibility for their physical and mental health and that the organization is merely a means to that end.

Global Implications

Organizational Change

A number of change issues we've discussed in this chapter are culture bound. To illustrate, let's briefly look at five questions: (1) Do people believe change is possible? (2) If it's possible, how long will it take to bring it about? (3) Is resistance to change greater in some cultures than in others? (4) Does culture influence how change efforts will be implemented? (5) Do successful idea champions do things differently in different cultures?

Do people believe change is possible? Remember that cultures vary in terms of beliefs about their ability to control their environment. In cultures in which people believe that they can dominate their environment, individuals will take a proactive view of change. This, for example, would describe the United States and Canada. In many other countries, such as Iran and Saudi Arabia, people see themselves as subjugated to their environment and thus will tend to take a passive approach toward change.

If change is possible, how long will it take to bring it about? A culture's time orientation can help us answer this question. Societies that focus on the long term, such as Japan, will demonstrate considerable patience while waiting for positive outcomes from change efforts. In societies with a short-term focus, such as the United States and Canada, people expect quick improvements and will seek change programs that promise fast results.

Is resistance to change greater in some cultures than in others? Resistance to change will be influenced by a society's reliance on tradition. Italians, as an example, focus on the past, whereas U.S. adults emphasize the present. Italians, therefore, should generally be more resistant to change efforts than their U.S. counterparts.

Does culture influence how change efforts will be implemented? Power distance can help with this issue. In high power-distance cultures, such as Spain or Thailand, change efforts will tend to be autocratically implemented by top management. In contrast, low power-distance cultures value democratic methods. We'd predict, therefore, a greater use of participation in countries such as Denmark and the Netherlands.

Finally, do successful idea champions do things differently in different cultures? Yes.[55] People in collectivist cultures prefer appeals for cross-functional support for innovation efforts; people in high power-distance cultures prefer champions to work closely with those in authority to approve innovative activities before work is begun; and the higher the uncertainty avoidance of a society, the more champions should work within the organization's rules and procedures to develop the innovation. These findings suggest that effective managers will alter their organization's championing strategies to reflect cultural values. So, for instance, although idea champions in Russia might succeed by ignoring budgetary limitations and working around confining procedures, champions in Austria, Denmark, Germany, or other cultures high in uncertainty avoidance will be more effective by closely following budgets and procedures.

Stress

In considering global differences in stress, there are three questions to answer: (1) Do the causes of stress vary across countries? (2) Do the outcomes of stress vary across cultures? and (3) Do the factors that lessen the effects of stress vary by culture? Let's deal with each of these questions in turn.

First, research suggests the job conditions that cause stress show some differences across cultures. One study of U.S. and Chinese employees revealed that whereas U.S. employees were stressed by a lack of control, Chinese employees were stressed by job evaluations and lack of training. Although the job conditions that lead to stress may differ across countries, it doesn't appear that personality effects on stress are different across cultures. One study of employees in Hungary, Italy, the United Kingdom, Israel, and the United States found Type A personality traits predicted stress equally well across countries.[56] A study of 5,270 managers from 20 countries found individuals from individualistic countries such as the United States, Canada, and the United Kingdom experienced higher levels of stress due to work interfering with family than did individuals from collectivist countries in Asia and Latin America.[57] The authors proposed that this may occur because in collectivist cultures working extra hours is seen as a sacrifice to help the family, whereas in individualistic cultures work is seen as a means to personal achievement that takes away from the family.

(continued)

Second, evidence tends to suggest that stressors are associated with perceived stress and strains among employees in different countries. In other words, stress is equally bad for employees of all cultures.[58]

Third, although not all factors that reduce stress have been compared across cultures, research does suggest that, whereas the demand to work long hours leads to stress, this stress can be reduced by such resources of social support as having friends or family with whom to talk. A recent study found this to be true of workers in a diverse set of countries (Australia, Canada, England, New Zealand, the United States, China, Taiwan, Argentina, Brazil, Colombia, Ecuador, Mexico, Peru, and Uruguay).[59]

Implications for Managers

The need for change has been implied throughout this text. "A casual reflection on change should indicate that it encompasses almost all of our concepts in the organizational behavior literature."[60] For instance, think about attitudes, motivation, work teams, communication, leadership, organizational structures, human resource practices, and organizational cultures. Change was an integral part in our discussion of each.

If environments were perfectly static, if employees' skills and abilities were always up to date and incapable of deteriorating, and if tomorrow were always exactly the same as today, organizational change would have little or no relevance to managers. But the real world is turbulent, requiring organizations and their members to undergo dynamic change if they are to perform at competitive levels.

Managers are the primary change agents in most organizations. By the decisions they make and their role-modeling behaviors, they shape the organization's change culture. Management decisions related to structural design, cultural factors, and human resource policies largely determine the level of innovation within the organization. Management policies and practices will determine the degree to which the organization learns and adapts to changing environmental factors.

We found that the existence of work stress, in and of itself, need not imply lower performance. The evidence indicates that stress can be either a positive or a negative influence on employee performance. Low to moderate amounts of stress enable many people to perform their jobs better by increasing their work intensity, alertness, and ability to react. However, a high level of stress, or even a moderate amount sustained over a long period, eventually takes its toll, and performance declines. The impact of stress on satisfaction is far more straightforward. Job-related tension tends to decrease general job satisfaction.[61] Even though low to moderate levels of stress may improve job performance, employees find stress dissatisfying.

Epilogue

The end of a book typically has the same meaning to an author that it has to the reader: It generates feelings of both accomplishment and relief. As both of us rejoice at having completed our tour of the essential concepts in organizational behavior, this is a good time to examine where we've been and what it all means.

The underlying theme of this book has been that the behavior of people at work is not a random phenomenon. Employees are complex entities, but their attitudes and behavior can nevertheless be explained and predicted with a reasonable degree of accuracy. Our approach has been to look at organizational behavior at three levels: the individual, the group, and the organization system.

We started with the individual and reviewed the major psychological contributions to understanding why individuals act as they do. We found that many of the individual differences among employees can be systematically labeled and categorized, and therefore generalizations can be made. For example, we know that individuals with a conventional type of personality are better matched to certain jobs in corporate management than are people with investigative personalities. So placing people into jobs that are compatible with their personality types should result in higher-performing and more satisfied employees.

Next, our analysis moved to the group level. We argued that the understanding of group behavior is more complex than merely multiplying what we know about individuals by the number of members in the group, because people act differently in a group than when they are alone. We demonstrated how roles, norms, leadership styles, power relationships, and other similar group factors affect the behavior of employees.

Finally, we overlaid system-wide variables on our knowledge of individual and group behavior to further improve our understanding of organizational behavior. Major emphasis was given to showing how an organization's structure, design, and culture affect both the attitudes and the behavior of employees.

It may be tempting to criticize the stress this book placed on theoretical concepts, but as noted psychologist Kurt Lewin is purported to have said, "There is nothing so practical as a good theory." Of course, it's also true that there is nothing so impractical as a good theory that leads nowhere. To avoid presenting theories that lead nowhere, this book included a wealth of examples and illustrations. And we regularly stopped to inquire about the implications of theory for the practice of management. The result has been the presentation of numerous concepts that, individually, offer some insights into behavior, but which, when taken together, provide a complex system to help you explain, predict, and control organizational behavior.

ENDNOTES

Chapter 1

1. S. E. Humphrey, J. D. Nahrgang, and F. P. Morgeson, "Integrating Motivational, Social, and Contextual Work Design Features: A Meta-Analytic Summary and Theoretical Extension of the Work Design Literature," *Journal of Applied Psychology* 92, no. 5 (2007), pp. 1332–1356.

2. I. S. Fulmer, B. Gerhart, and K. S. Scott, "Are the 100 Best Better? An Empirical Investigation of the Relationship Between Being a 'Great Place to Work' and Firm Performance," *Personnel Psychology,* Winter 2003, pp. 965–993.

3. See, for instance, C. Heath and S. B. Sitkin, "Big-B Versus Big-O: What Is *Organizational* about Organizational Behavior?" *Journal of Organizational Behavior,* February 2001, pp. 43–58.

4. D. M. Rousseau and S. McCarthy, "Educating Managers from an Evidence-Based Perspective," *Academy of Management Learning & Education* 6, no. 1 (2007), pp. 84–101; and S. L. Rynes, T. L. Giluk, and K. G. Brown, "The Very Separate Worlds of Academic and Practitioner Periodicals in Human Resource Management: Implications for Evidence-Based Management," *Academy of Management Journal* 50, no. 5 (2007), pp. 987–1008.

5. See, for instance, M. Workman and W. Bommer, "Redesigning Computer Call Center Work: A Longitudinal Field Experiment," *Journal of Organizational Behavior,* May 2004, pp. 317–337.

6. See, for instance, V. S. Major, K. J. Klein, and M. G. Ehrhart, "Work Time, Work Interference with Family, and Psychological Distress," *Journal of Applied Psychology,* June 2002, pp. 427–436.

7. See, for instance, *The 2002 National Study of the Changing Workforce* (New York: Families and Work Institute, 2002); and W. J. Casper and L. C. Buffardi, "Work–Life Benefits and Job Pursuit Intentions: The Role of Anticipated Organizational Support," *Journal of Vocational Behavior* 65, no. 3 (2004), pp. 391–410.

8. Cited in S. Armour, "Workers Put Family First Despite Slow Economy, Jobless Fears." USA Today, June 6, 2002, Section 3B.

9. S. Shellenbarger, "What Job Candidates Really Want to Know: Will I Have a Life?" *Wall Street Journal,* November 17, 1999, p. B1; and "U.S. Employers Polish Image to Woo a Demanding New Generation," *Manpower Argus,* February 2000, p. 2.

10. W. Bailey and A. Spicer, "When Does National Identity Matter? Convergence and Divergence in International Business Ethics," *Academy of Management Journal* 50, no. 6, pp. 1462–1480; and A. B. Oumlil and J. L. Balloun, "Ethical Decision-Making Differences Between American and Moroccan Managers," *Journal of Business Ethics* 84, no. 4 (2009), pp. 457–478.

11. J. Merritt, "For MBAs, Soul-Searching 101," *BusinessWeek,* September 16, 2002, pp. 64–66; and S. Greenhouse, "The Mood at Work: Anger and Anxiety," *New York Times,* October 29, 2002, p. E1.

12. See, for instance, G. R. Weaver, L. K. Trevino, and P. L. Cochran, "Corporate Ethics Practices in the Mid-1990's: An Empirical Study of the Fortune 1000," *Journal of Business Ethics,* February 1999, pp. 283–294; and C. De Mesa Graziano, "Promoting Ethical Conduct: A Review of Corporate Practices," *Strategic Investor Relations,* Fall 2002, pp. 29–35.

13. D. M. Mayer, M. Kuenzi, R. Greenbaum, M. Bardes, and R. Salvador, "How Low Does Ethical Leadership Flow? Test of a Trickle-Down Model," *Organizational Behavior and Human Decision Processes* 108, no. 1 (2009), pp. 1–13; and A. Ardichvili, J. A. Mitchell, and D. Jondle, "Characteristics of Ethical Business Cultures," *Journal of Business Ethics* 85, no. 4 (2009), pp. 445–451.

Chapter 2

1. S. J. Breckler, "Empirical Validation of Affect, Behavior, and Cognition as Distinct Components of Attitude," *Journal of Personality and Social Psychology,* May 1984, pp. 1191–1205.

2. L. Festinger, *A Theory of Cognitive Dissonance* (Stanford, CA: Stanford University Press, 1957).

3. See, for instance, L. R. Fabrigar, R. E. Petty, S. M. Smith, and S. L. Crites, "Understanding Knowledge Effects on Attitude–Behavior Consistency: The Role of Relevance, Complexity, and Amount of Knowledge," *Journal of Personality and Social Psychology* 90, no. 4 (2006), pp. 556–577; and D. J. Schleicher, J. D. Watt, and G. J. Greguras, "Reexamining the Job Satisfaction-Performance Relationship: The Complexity of Attitudes," *Journal of Applied Psychology* 89, no. 1 (2004), pp. 165–177.

4. See, for instance, J. Nocera, "If It's Good for Philip Morris, Can It Also Be Good for Public Health?" *New York Times,* June 18, 2006.

5. See L. R. Glasman and D. Albarracín, "Forming Attitudes That Predict Future Behavior: A Meta-analysis

of the Attitude–Behavior Relation," *Psychological Bulletin,* September 2006, pp. 778–822; and M. Riketta, "The Causal Relation Between Job Attitudes and Performance: A Meta-analysis of Panel Studies," *Journal of Applied Psychology* 93, no. 2 (2008), pp. 472–481.

6. Ibid.

7. D. A. Harrison, D. A. Newman, and P. L. Roth, "How Important Are Job Attitudes? Meta-analytic Comparisons of Integrative Behavioral Outcomes and Time Sequences," *Academy of Management Journal* 49, no. 2 (2006), pp. 305–325.

8. D. P. Moynihan and S. K. Pandey, "Finding Workable Levers Over Work Motivation: Comparing Job Satisfaction, Job Involvement, and Organizational Commitment," *Administration & Society* 39, no. 7 (2007), pp. 803–832.

9. See, for example, J. M. Diefendorff, D. J. Brown, and A. M. Kamin, "Examining the Roles of Job Involvement and Work Centrality in Predicting Organizational Citizenship Behaviors and Job Performance," *Journal of Organizational Behavior,* February 2002, pp. 93–108.

10. A. Ergeneli, G. Saglam, and S. Metin, "Psychological Empowerment and Its Relationship to Trust in Immediate Managers," *Journal of Business Research,* January 2007, pp. 41–49; and S. E. Seibert, S. R. Silver, and W. A. Randolph, "Taking Empowerment to the Next Level: A Multiple-Level Model of Empowerment, Performance, and Satisfaction," *Academy of Management Journal* 47, no. 3 (2004), pp. 332–349.

11. B. J. Avolio, W. Zhu, W. Koh, and P. Bhatia, "Transformational Leadership and Organizational Commitment: Mediating Role of Psychological Empowerment and Moderating Role of Structural Distance," *Journal of Organizational Behavior* 25, no. 8, 2004, pp. 951–968.

12. J. M. Diefendorff, D. J. Brown, A. M. Kamin, and R. G. Lord, "Examining the Roles of Job Involvement and Work Centrality in Predicting Organizational Citizenship Behaviors and Job Performance," *Journal of Organizational Behavior,* February 2002, pp. 93–108.

13. M. R. Barrick, M. K. Mount, and J. P. Strauss, "Antecedents of Involuntary Turnover Due to a Reduction in Force," *Personnel Psychology* 47, no. 3 (1994), pp. 515–535.

14. J. P. Meyer, N. J. Allen, and C. A. Smith, "Commitment to Organizations and Occupations: Extension and Test of a Three-Component Conceptualization," *Journal of Applied Psychology* 78, no. 4 (1993), pp. 538–551.

15. T. A. Wright and D. G. Bonett, "The Moderating Effects of Employee Tenure on the Relation Between Organizational Commitment and Job Performance: A Meta-analysis," *Journal of Applied Psychology,* December 2002, pp. 1183–1190.

16. See, for instance, T. Simons and Q. Roberson, "Why Managers Should Care About Fairness: The Effects of Aggregate Justice Perceptions on Organizational Outcomes," *Journal of Applied Psychology* 88, no. 3 (2003), pp. 432–443.

17. Y. Gong, K. S. Law, S. Chang, and K. R. Xin, "Human Resources Management and Firm Performance: The Differential Role of Managerial Affective and Continuance Commitment," *Journal of Applied Psychology* 94, no. 1 (2009), pp. 263–275.

18. A. A. Luchak and I. R. Gellatly, "A Comparison of Linear and Nonlinear Relations Between Organizational Commitment and Work Outcomes," *Journal of Applied Psychology* 92, no. 3 (2007), pp. 786–793.

19. L. Rhoades, R. Eisenberger, and S. Armeli, "Affective Commitment to the Organization: The Contribution of Perceived Organizational Support," *Journal of Applied Psychology* 86, no. 5 (2001), pp. 825–836.

20. C. Vandenberghe, K. Bentein, R. Michon, J. Chebat, M. Tremblay, and J. Fils, "An Examination of the Role of Perceived Support and Employee Commitment in Employee–Customer Encounters," *Journal of Applied Psychology* 92, no. 4 (2007), pp. 1177–1187; and P. Eder and R. Eisenberger, "Perceived Organizational Support: Reducing the Negative Influence of Coworker Withdrawal Behavior," *Journal of Management* 34, no. 1 (2008), pp. 55–68.

21. J. Farh, R. D. Hackett, and J. Liang, "Individual-Level Cultural Values as Moderators of Perceived Organizational Support—Employee Outcome Relationships in China: Comparing the Effects of Power Distance and Traditionality," *Academy of Management Journal* 50, no. 3 (2007), pp. 715–729.

22. D. R. May, R. L. Gilson, and L. M. Harter, "The Psychological Conditions of Meaningfulness, Safety and Availability and the Engagement of the Human Spirit at Work," *Journal of Occupational and Organizational Psychology* 77, no. 1 (2004), pp. 11–37.

23. J. K. Harter, F. L. Schmidt, and T. L. Hayes, "Business-Unit-Level Relationship Between Employee Satisfaction, Employee Engagement, and Business Outcomes: A Meta-analysis," *Journal of Applied Psychology* 87, no. 2 (2002), pp. 268–279.

24. N. R. Lockwood, *Leveraging Employee Engagement for Competitive Advantage* (Alexandria, VA: Society for Human Resource Management, 2007); and R. J. Vance, *Employee Engagement and Commitment* (Alexandria, VA: Society for Human Resource Management, 2006).

25. W. H. Macey and B. Schneider, "The Meaning of Employee Engagement," *Industrial and Organizational Psychology* 1 (2008), pp. 3–30; and A. Saks, "The Meaning and Bleeding of Employee Engagement: How Muddy Is the Water?" *Industrial and Organizational Psychology* 1 (2008), pp. 40–43.

26. L. Rhoades and R. Eisenberger, "Perceived Organizational Support: A Review of the Literature," *Journal of Applied Psychology* 87, no. 4 (2002), pp. 698–714; and R. L. Payne and D. Morrison, "The Differential Effects of Negative Affectivity on Measures of Well-Being Versus Job Satisfaction and Organizational Commitment," *Anxiety, Stress & Coping: An International Journal* 15, no. 3 (2002), pp. 231–244.

27. For problems with the concept of job satisfaction, see R. Hodson, "Workplace Behaviors," *Work and Occupations,* August 1991, pp. 271–290; and H. M. Weiss and R. Cropanzano, "Affective Events Theory: A Theoretical Discussion of the Structure, Causes and Consequences of Affective Experiences at Work," in B. M. Staw and L. L. Cummings (eds.), *Research in Organizational Behavior,* vol. 18 (Greenwich, CT: JAI Press, 1996), pp. 1–3.

28. The Wyatt Company's 1989 national WorkAmerica study identified 12 dimensions of satisfaction: work organization, working conditions, communications, job performance and performance review, co-workers, supervision, company management, pay, benefits, career development and training, job content and satisfaction, and company image and change.

29. See E. Spector, *Job Satisfaction: Application, Assessment, Causes, and Consequences* (Thousand Oaks, CA: Sage, 1997), p. 3.

30. J. Wanous, A. E. Reichers, and M. J. Hudy, "Overall Job Satisfaction: How Good Are Single-Item Measures?" *Journal of Applied Psychology,* April 1997, pp. 247–252.

31. "Job Satisfaction High in America, Says Conference Board Study," *Monthly Labor Review,* February 1985, p. 52; E. Graham, "Work May Be a Rat Race, but It's Not a Daily Grind," *Wall Street Journal,* September 19, 1997, p. R1; and K. Bowman, "Attitudes About Work, Chores, and Leisure in America," *AEI Opinion Studies,* August 25, 2003.

32. J. Barling, E. K. Kelloway, and R. D. Iverson, "High-Quality Work, Job Satisfaction, and Occupational Injuries," *Journal of Applied Psychology* 88, no. 2 (2003), pp. 276–283; and F. W. Bond and D. Bunce, "The Role of Acceptance and Job Control in Mental Health, Job Satisfaction, and Work Performance," *Journal of Applied Psychology* 88, no. 6 (2003), pp. 1057–1067.

33. S. E. Humphrey, J. D. Nahrgang, and F. P. Morgeson, "Integrating Motivational, Social, and Contextual Work Design Features: A Meta-analytic Summary and Theoretical Extension of the Work Design Literature," *Journal of Applied Psychology* 92, no. 5 (2007), pp. 1332–1356; and D. S. Chiaburu and D. A. Harrison, "Do Peers Make the Place? Conceptual Synthesis and Meta-analysis of Coworker Effect on Perceptions, Attitudes, OCBs, and Performance," *Journal of Applied Psychology* 93, no. 5 (2008), pp. 1082–1103.

34. E. Diener, E. Sandvik, L. Seidlitz, and M. Diener, "The Relationship Between Income and Subjective Well-Being: Relative or Absolute?" *Social Indicators Research* 28 (1993), pp. 195–223.

35. E. Diener and M. E. P. Seligman, "Beyond Money: Toward an Economy of Well-Being," *Psychological Science in the Public Interest* 5, no. 1 (2004), pp. 1–31; and A. Grant, "Money = Happiness? That's Rich: Here's the Science Behind the Axiom," *The (South Mississippi) Sun Herald,* January 8, 2005.

36. T. A. Judge and C. Hurst, "The Benefits and Possible Costs of Positive Core Self-Evaluations: A Review and Agenda for Future Research," in D. Nelson and C. L. Cooper (eds.), *Positive Organizational Behavior* (London, UK: Sage Publications, 2007), pp. 159–174.

37. See D. Farrell, "Exit, Voice, Loyalty, and Neglect as Responses to Job Dissatisfaction: A Multidimensional Scaling Study," *Academy of Management Journal,* December 1983, pp. 596–606; M. J. Withey and W. H. Cooper, "Predicting Exit, Voice, Loyalty, and Neglect," *Administrative Science Quarterly,* December 1989, pp. 521–539.

38. R. B. Freeman, "Job Satisfaction as an Economic Variable," *American Economic Review,* January 1978, pp. 135–141.

39. T. A. Judge, C. J. Thoresen, J. E. Bono, and G. K. Patton, "The Job Satisfaction–Job Performance Relationship: A Qualitative and Quantitative Review," *Psychological Bulletin,* May 2001, pp. 376–407.

40. C. Ostroff, "The Relationship Between Satisfaction, Attitudes, and Performance: An Organizational Level Analysis," *Journal of Applied Psychology,* December 1992, pp. 963–974; and J. K. Harter, F. L. Schmidt, and T. L. Hayes, "Business-Unit Level Relationship Between Employee Satisfaction, Employee Engagement, and Business Outcomes: A Meta-analysis," *Journal of Applied Psychology,* April 2002, pp. 268–279.

41. See P. Podsakoff, S. B. MacKenzie, J. B. Paine, and D. G. Bachrach, "Organizational Citizenship Behaviors: A Critical Review of the Theoretical and Empirical Literature and Suggestions for Future Research," *Journal of Management* 26, no. 3 (2000), pp. 513–563.

42. B. J. Hoffman, C. A. Blair, J. P. Maeriac, and D. J. Woehr, "Expanding the Criterion Domain? A Quantitative Review of the OCB Literature," *Journal of Applied Psychology* 92, no. 2 (2007), pp. 555–566; and J. A. LePine, A. Erez, and D. E. Johnson, "The Nature and Dimensionality of Organizational Citizenship Behavior: A Critical Review and Meta-analysis," *Journal of Applied Psychology,* February 2002, pp. 52–65.

43. S. L. Blader and T. R. Tyler, "Testing and Extending the Group Engagement Model: Linkages Between Social Identity, Procedural Justice, Economic Outcomes, and

Extrarole Behavior," *Journal of Applied Psychology* 94, no. 2 (2009), pp. 445–464; and M. A. Konovsky and D. W. Organ, "Dispositional and Contextual Determinants of Organizational Citizenship Behavior," *Journal of Organizational Behavior,* May 1996, pp. 253–266.

44. D. S. Chiaburu and D. A. Harrison, "Do Peers Make the Place? Conceptual Synthesis and Meta-analysis of Coworker Effect on Perceptions, Attitudes, OCBs, and Performance," *Journal of Applied Psychology* 93, no. 5 (2008), pp. 1082–1103.

45. See, for instance, D. J. Koys, "The Effects of Employee Satisfaction, Organizational Citizenship Behavior, and Turnover on Organizational Effectiveness: A Unit-Level, Longitudinal Study," *Personnel Psychology,* Spring 2001, pp. 101–114; J. Griffith, "Do Satisfied Employees Satisfy Customers? Support-Services Staff Morale and Satisfaction Among Public School Administrators, Students, and Parents," *Journal of Applied Social Psychology,* August 2001, pp. 1627–1658.

46. J. M. O'Brien, "Zappos Knows How to Kick It," *Fortune,* February 2, 2009, pp. 55–60.

47. T. Frank, "Report: Low Morale May Hurt Airport Security," *USA Today,* June 25, 2008, p. 3A; and J. Bailey, "Fliers Fed Up? The Employees Feel the Same," *New York Times,* December 22, 2007, pp. A1, A18.

48. E. A. Locke, "The Nature and Causes of Job Satisfaction," in M. D. Dunnette (ed.), *Handbook of Industrial and Organizational Psychology* (Chicago: Rand McNally, 1976), p. 1331; K. D. Scott and G. S. Taylor, "An Examination of Conflicting Findings on the Relationship Between Job Satisfaction and Absenteeism: A Meta-analysis," *Academy of Management Journal,* September 1985, pp. 599–612; and R. Steel and J. R. Rentsch, "Influence of Cumulation Strategies on the Long-Range Prediction of Absenteeism," *Academy of Management Journal,* December 1995, pp. 1616–1634.

49. J. P. Hausknecht, N. J. Hiller, and R. J. Vance, "Work-Unit Absenteeism: Effects of Satisfaction, Commitment, Labor Market Conditions, and Time," *Academy of Management Journal* 51, no. 6 (2008), pp. 1123–1245.

50. W. Hom and R. W. Griffeth, *Employee Turnover* (Cincinnati, OH: South-Western Publishing, 1995); and R. W. Griffeth, P. W. Hom, and S. Gaertner, "A Meta-analysis of Antecedents and Correlates of Employee Turnover: Update, Moderator Tests, and Research Implications for the Next Millennium," *Journal of Management* 26, no. 3 (2000), p. 479.

51. T. H. Lee, B. Gerhart, I. Weller, and C. O. Trevor, "Understanding Voluntary Turnover: Path-Specific Job Satisfaction Effects and the Importance of Unsolicited Job Offers," *Academy of Management Journal* 51, no. 4 (2008), pp. 651–671.

52. P. E. Spector, S. Fox, L. M. Penney, K. Bruursema, A. Goh, and S. Kessler, "The Dimensionality of Counterproductivity: Are All Counterproductive Behaviors Created Equal?" *Journal of Vocational Behavior* 68, no. 3 (2006), pp. 446–460; and D. S. Chiaburu and D. A. Harrison, "Do Peers Make the Place? Conceptual Synthesis and Meta-analysis of Coworker Effect on Perceptions, Attitudes, OCBs, and Performance," *Journal of Applied Psychology* 93, no. 5 (2008), pp. 1082–1103.

53. K. Holland, "Inside the Minds of Your Employees," *New York Times,* January 28, 2007, p. B1; "Study Sees Link Between Morale and Stock Price," *Workforce Management,* February 27, 2006, p. 15; and "The Workplace as a Solar System," *New York Times,* October 28, 2006, p. B5.

54. E. White, "How Surveying Workers Can Pay Off," *Wall Street Journal,* June 18, 2007, p. B3.

55. M. J. Gelfand, M. Erez, and Z. Aycan, "Cross-Cultural Organizational Behavior," *Annual Review of Psychology* 58 (2007), pp. 479–514; and A. S. Tsui, S. S. Nifadkar, and A. Y. Ou, "Cross-National, Cross-Cultural Organizational Behavior Research: Advances, Gaps, and Recommendations," *Journal of Management,* June 2007, pp. 426–478.

56. M. Benz and B. S. Frey, "The Value of Autonomy: Evidence from the Self-Employed in 23 Countries," working paper 173, Institute for Empirical Research in Economics, University of Zurich, November 2003 (ssrn.com/abstract=475140); and P. Warr, *Work, Happiness, and Unhappiness* (Mahwah, NJ: Laurence Erlbaum, 2007).

57. Harrison, Newman, and Roth, "How Important Are Job Attitudes?" pp. 320–321.

Chapter 3

1. S. G. Barsade and D. E. Gibson, "Why Does Affect Matter in Organizations?" *Academy of Management Perspectives,* February 2007, pp. 36–59.

2. See N. H. Frijda, "Moods, Emotion Episodes and Emotions," in M. Lewis and J. M. Haviland (eds.), *Handbook of Emotions* (New York: Guilford Press, 1993), pp. 381–403.

3. H. M. Weiss and R. Cropanzano, "Affective Events Theory: A Theoretical Discussion of the Structure, Causes and Consequences of Affective Experiences at Work," in B. M. Staw and L. L. Cummings (eds.), *Research in Organizational Behavior,* vol. 18 (Greenwich, CT: JAI Press, 1996), pp. 17–19.

4. See P. Ekman and R. J. Davidson (eds.), *The Nature of Emotions: Fundamental Questions* (Oxford, UK: Oxford University Press, 1994).

5. Frijda, "Moods, Emotion Episodes and Emotions," p. 381.

6. See Ekman and Davidson, *The Nature of Emotions.*

7. See, for example, P. Ekman, "An Argument for Basic Emotions," *Cognition and Emotion,* May/July 1992, pp. 169–200; C. E. Izard, "Basic Emotions, Relations

Among Emotions, and Emotion–Cognition Relations," *Psychological Bulletin,* November 1992, pp. 561–565; and J. L. Tracy and R. W. Robins, "Emerging Insights into the Nature and Function of Pride," *Current Directions in Psychological Science* 16, no. 3 (2007), pp. 147–150.

8. R. C. Solomon, "Back to Basics: On the Very Idea of 'Basic Emotions,'" *Journal for the Theory of Social Behaviour* 32, no. 2 (June 2002), pp. 115–144.

9. Weiss and Cropanzano, "Affective Events Theory," pp. 20–22.

10. Cited in R. D. Woodworth, *Experimental Psychology* (New York: Holt, 1938).

11. D. Watson, L. A. Clark, and A. Tellegen, "Development and Validation of Brief Measures of Positive and Negative Affect: The PANAS Scales," *Journal of Personality and Social Psychology,* 1988, pp. 1063–1070.

12. J. T. Cacioppo and W. L. Gardner, "Emotion," in *Annual Review of Psychology,* vol. 50 (Palo Alto, CA: Annual Reviews, 1999), pp. 191–214.

13. L. M. Poverny and S. Picascia, "There Is No Crying in Business," *Womensmedia.com,* www.womensmedia.com/new/Crying-at-Work.shtml.

14. A. R. Damasio, *Descartes' Error: Emotion, Reason, and the Human Brain* (New York: Quill, 1994).

15. Ibid.

16. R. J. Larsen and E. Diener, "Affect Intensity as an Individual Difference Characteristic: A Review," *Journal of Research in Personality* 21 (1987), pp. 1–39.

17. D. Watson, *Mood and Temperament* (New York: Guilford Press, 2000).

18. J. J. A. Denissen, L. Butalid, L. Penke, and M. A. G. van Aken, "The Effects of Weather on Daily Mood: A Multilevel Approach," *Emotion* 8, no. 5, pp. 662–667; M. C. Keller, B. L. Fredrickson, O. Ybarra, S. Côté, K. Johnson, J. Mikels, A. Conway, and T. Wagner (2005), "A Warm Heart and a Clear Head: The Contingent Effects of Weather on Mood and Cognition," *Psychological Science* 16, (2005) pp. 724–731; and Watson, *Mood and Temperament.*

19. Watson, *Mood and Temperament,* p. 100.

20. J. A. Fuller, J. M. Stanton, G. G. Fisher, C. Spitzmüller, S. S. Russell, and P. C. Smith, "A Lengthy Look at the Daily Grind: Time Series Analysis of Events, Mood, Stress, and Satisfaction," *Journal of Applied Psychology* 88, no. 6 (December 2003), pp. 1019–1033.

21. A. M. Isen, "Positive Affect as a Source of Human Strength," in L. G. Aspinwall and U. Staudinger (eds.), *The Psychology of Human Strengths* (Washington, DC: American Psychological Association, 2003), pp. 179–195.

22. Watson, *Mood and Temperament.*

23. M. Lavidor, A. Weller, and H. Babkoff, "How Sleep Is Related to Fatigue," *British Journal of Health Psychology* 8 (2003), pp. 95–105; and J. J. Pilcher and E. Ott, "The Relationships Between Sleep and Measures of Health and Well-Being in College Students: A Repeated Measures Approach," *Behavioral Medicine* 23 (1998), pp. 170–178.

24. E. K. Miller and J. D. Cohen, "An Integrative Theory of Prefrontal Cortex Function," *Annual Review of Neuroscience* 24 (2001), pp. 167–202.

25. B. A. Scott and T. A. Judge, "Insomnia, Emotions, and Job Satisfaction: A Multilevel Study," *Journal of Management* 32, no. 5 (2006), pp. 622–645.

26. P. R. Giacobbi, H. A. Hausenblas, and N. Frye, "A Naturalistic Assessment of the Relationship Between Personality, Daily Life Events, Leisure-Time Exercise, and Mood," *Psychology of Sport & Exercise* 6, no. 1 (January 2005), pp. 67–81.

27. L. L. Carstensen, M. Pasupathi, M. Ulrich, and J. R. Nesselroade, "Emotional Experience in Everyday Life Across the Adult Life Span," *Journal of Personality and Social Psychology* 79, no. 4 (2000), pp. 644–655.

28. M. LaFrance and M. Banaji, "Toward a Reconsideration of the Gender–Emotion Relationship," in M. Clark (ed.), *Review of Personality and Social Psychology,* vol. 14 (Newbury Park, CA: Sage, 1992), pp. 178–197; and A. M. Kring and A. H. Gordon, "Sex Differences in Emotion: Expression, Experience, and Physiology," *Journal of Personality and Social Psychology,* March 1998, pp. 686–703.

29. L. R. Brody and J. A. Hall, "Gender and Emotion," in M. Lewis and J. M. Haviland (eds.), *Handbook of Emotions* (New York: Guilford Press, 1993), pp. 447–460; M. G. Gard and A. M. Kring, "Sex Differences in the Time Course of Emotion," *Emotion* 7, no. 2 (2007), pp. 429–437; and M. Grossman and W. Wood, "Sex Differences in Intensity of Emotional Experience: A Social Role Interpretation," *Journal of Personality and Social Psychology,* November 1992, pp. 1010–1022.

30. P. Ekman, W. V. Friesen, and M. O'Sullivan, "Smiles When Lying," in P. Ekman and E. L. Rosenberg (eds.), *What the Face Reveals: Basic and Applied Studies of Spontaneous Expression Using the Facial Action Coding System (FACS)* (London: Oxford University Press, 1997), pp. 201–216.

31. A. Grandey, "Emotion Regulation in the Workplace: A New Way to Conceptualize Emotional Labor," *Journal of Occupational Health Psychology* 5, no. 1 (2000), pp. 95–110; and R. Cropanzano, D. E. Rupp, and Z. S. Byrne, "The Relationship of Emotional Exhaustion to Work Attitudes, Job Performance, and Organizational Citizenship Behavior," *Journal of Applied Psychology,* February 2003, pp. 160–169.

32. A. R. Hochschild, "Emotion Work, Feeling Rules, and Social Structure," *American Journal of Sociology,* November 1979,

pp. 551–575; M. W. Kramer and J. A. Hess, "Communication Rules for the Display of Emotions in Organizational Settings," *Management Communication Quarterly,* August 2002, pp. 66–80; and J. M. Diefendorff and E. M. Richard, "Antecedents and Consequences of Emotional Display Rule Perceptions," *Journal of Applied Psychology,* April 2003, pp. 284–294.

33. B. M. DePaulo, "Nonverbal Behavior and Self-Presentation," *Psychological Bulletin,* March 1992, pp. 203–243.

34. C. M. Brotheridge and R. T. Lee, "Development and Validation of the Emotional Labour Scale," *Journal of Occupational & Organizational Psychology* 76, no. 3 (September 2003), pp. 365–379.

35. A. A. Grandey, "When 'The Show Must Go On': Surface Acting and Deep Acting as Determinants of Emotional Exhaustion and Peer-Rated Service Delivery," *Academy of Management Journal,* February 2003, pp. 86–96; and A. A. Grandey, D. N. Dickter, and H. Sin, "The Customer Is Not Always Right: Customer Aggression and Emotion Regulation of Service Employees," *Journal of Organizational Behavior* 25, no. 3 (May 2004), pp. 397–418.

36. J. P. Trougakos, D. J. Beal, S. G. Green, and H. M. Weiss, "Making the Break Count: An Episodic Examination of Recovery Activities, Emotional Experiences, and Positive Affective Displays," *Academy of Management Journal* 51, no. 1 (2008), pp. 131–146.

37. Daniel Goleman, *Emotional Intelligence* (New York: Bantam, 1995); P. Salovey and D. Grewal, "The Science of Emotional Intelligence," *Current Directions in Psychological Science* 14, no. 6 (2005), pp. 281–285; M. Davies, L. Stankov, and R. D. Roberts, "Emotional Intelligence: In Search of an Elusive Construct," *Journal of Personality and Social Psychology,* October 1998, pp. 989–1015; D. Geddes and R. R. Callister, "Crossing the Line(s): A Dual Threshold Model of Anger in Organizations," *Academy of Management Review* 32, no. 3 (2007), pp. 721–746; and J. Ciarrochi, J. P. Forgas, and J. D. Mayer (eds.), *Emotional Intelligence in Everyday Life* (Philadelphia: Psychology Press, 2001).

38. M. Seo and L. F. Barrett, "Being Emotional During Decision Making—Good or Bad? An Empirical Investigation," *Academy of Management Journal* 50, no. 4 (2007), pp. 923–940.

39. C. Cherniss, "The Business Case for Emotional Intelligence," *Consortium for Research on Emotional Intelligence in Organizations*, 1999, www.eiconsortium.org/reports/business_case_for_ei.html.

40. K. S. Law, C. Wong, and L. J. Song, "The Construct and Criterion Validity of Emotional Intelligence and Its Potential Utility for Management Studies," *Journal of Applied Psychology* 89, no. 3 (2004), pp. 483–496.

41. H. A. Elfenbein and N. Ambady, "Predicting Workplace Outcomes from the Ability to Eavesdrop on Feelings," *Journal of Applied Psychology* 87, no. 5 (October 2002), pp. 963–971.

42. D. L. Van Rooy and C. Viswesvaran, "Emotional Intelligence: A Meta-analytic Investigation of Predictive Validity and Nomological Net," *Journal of Vocational Behavior* 65, no. 1 (August 2004), pp. 71–95.

43. R. Bar-On, D. Tranel, N. L. Denburg, and A. Bechara, "Exploring the Neurological Substrate of Emotional and Social Intelligence," *Brain* 126, no. 8 (August 2003), pp. 1790–1800.

44. P. A. Vernon, K. V. Petrides, D. Bratko, J. A. Schermer, "A Behavioral Genetic Study of Trait Emotional Intelligence," *Emotion* 8, no. 5 (2008), pp. 635–642.

45. E. A. Locke, "Why Emotional Intelligence Is an Invalid Concept," *Journal of Organizational Behavior* 26, no. 4 (June 2005), pp. 425–431.

46. J. M. Conte, "A Review and Critique of Emotional Intelligence Measures," *Journal of Organizational Behavior* 26, no. 4 (June 2005), pp. 433–440; and Davies, Stankov, and Roberts, "Emotional Intelligence," pp. 989–1015.

47. T. Decker, "Is Emotional Intelligence a Viable Concept?" *Academy of Management Review* 28, no. 2 (April 2003), pp. 433–440; and Davies, Stankov, and Roberts, "Emotional Intelligence."

48. F. J. Landy, "Some Historical and Scientific Issues Related to Research on Emotional Intelligence," *Journal of Organizational Behavior* 26, no. 4 (June 2005), pp. 411–424.

49. J. Park and M. R. Banaji, "Mood and Heuristics: The Influence of Happy and Sad States on Sensitivity and Bias in Stereotyping," *Journal of Personality and Social Psychology* 78, no. 6 (2000), pp. 1005–1023.

50. See A. M. Isen, "Positive Affect and Decision Making," in M. Lewis and J. M. Haviland-Jones (eds.), *Handbook of Emotions,* 2nd ed. (New York: Guilford, 2000), pp. 261–277.

51. L. B. Alloy and L. Y. Abramson, "Judgement of Contingency in Depressed and Nondepressed Students: Sadder but Wiser?" *Journal of Experimental Psychology: General* 108 (1979), pp. 441–485.

52. N. Ambady and H. M. Gray, "On Being Sad and Mistaken: Mood Effects on the Accuracy of Thin-Slice Judgments," *Journal of Personality and Social Psychology* 83, no. 4 (2002), pp. 947–961.

53. A. M. Isen, "On the Relationship Between Affect and Creative Problem Solving," in S. W. Russ (ed.), *Affect, Creative Experience and Psychological Adjustment* (Philadelphia, PA: Brunner/Mazel, 1999), pp. 3–17; and S. Lyubomirsky, L. King, and E. Diener, "The Benefits of Frequent Positive Affect: Does Happiness Lead to Success?" *Psychological Bulletin* 131, no. 6 (2005), pp. 803–855.

54. M. J. Grawitch, D. C. Munz, and E. K. Elliott, "Promoting Creativity in Temporary Problem-Solving Groups: The Effects of Positive Mood and Autonomy in Problem Definition on Idea-Generating Performance," *Group Dynamics* 7, no. 3 (September 2003), pp. 200–213.

55. S. Lyubomirsky, L. King, and E. Diener, "The Benefits of Frequent Positive Affect: Does Happiness Lead to Success?" *Psychological Bulletin* 131, no. 6 (2005), pp. 803–855.

56. J. M. George and J. Zhou, "Understanding When Bad Moods Foster Creativity and Good Ones Don't: The Role of Context and Clarity of Feelings," *Journal of Applied Psychology* 87, no. 4 (August 2002), pp. 687–697; and J. P. Forgas and J. M. George, "Affective Influences on Judgments and Behavior in Organizations: An Information Processing Perspective," *Organizational Behavior and Human Decision Processes* 86, no. 1 (2001), pp. 3–34.

57. C. K. W. De Dreu, M. Baas, and B. A. Nijstad, "Hedonic Tone and Activation Level in the Mood-Creativity Link: Toward a Dual Pathway to Creativity Model," *Journal of Personality and Social Psychology* 94, no. 5 (2008), pp. 739–756; and J. M. George and J. Zhou, "Dual Tuning in a Supportive Context: Joint Contributions of Positive Mood, Negative Mood, and Supervisory Behaviors to Employee Creativity," *Academy of Management Journal* 50, no. 3 (2007), pp. 605–622.

58. A. Erez and A. M. Isen, "The Influence of Positive Affect on the Components of Expectancy Motivation," *Journal of Applied Psychology* 87, no. 6 (2002), pp. 1055–1067.

59. R. Ilies and T. A. Judge, "Goal Regulation Across Time: The Effect of Feedback and Affect," *Journal of Applied Psychology* 90, no. 3 (May 2005), pp. 453–467.

60. W. Tsai, C. Chen, and H. Liu, "Test of a Model Linking Employee Positive Moods and Task Performance," *Journal of Applied Psychology* 92, no. 6 (2007), pp. 1570–1583.

61. K. M. Lewis, "When Leaders Display Emotion: How Followers Respond to Negative Emotional Expression of Male and Female Leaders," *Journal of Organizational Behavior,* March 2000, pp. 221–234; and J. M. George, "Emotions and Leadership: The Role of Emotional Intelligence," *Human Relations,* August 2000, pp. 1027–1055.

62. Ashforth, B.E. and Humphrey, R. H. "Emotion in the Workplace: A Reappraisal," Human Relations 48, (1995), pp. 97–125.

63. J. E. Bono, H. J. Foldes, G. Vinson, and J. P. Muros, "Workplace Emotions: The Role of Supervision and Leadership," *Journal of Applied Psychology* 92, no. 5 (2007), pp. 1357–1367.

64. G. A. Van Kleef, C. K. W. De Dreu, and A. S. R. Manstead, "The Interpersonal Effects of Emotions in Negotiations: A Motivated Information Processing Approach," *Journal of Personality and Social Psychology* 87, no. 4 (2004),

pp. 510–528; and G. A. Van Kleef, C. K. W. De Dreu, and A. S. R. Manstead, "The Interpersonal Effects of Anger and Happiness in Negotiations," *Journal of Personality and Social Psychology* 86, no. 1 (2004), pp. 57–76.

65. E. van Dijk, G. A. van Kleef, W. Steinel, and I. van Beest, "A Social Functional Approach to Emotions in Bargaining: When Communicating Anger Pays and When It Backfires," *Journal of Personality and Social Psychology* 94, no. 4 (2008), pp. 600–614.

66. K. M. O'Connor and J. A. Arnold, "Distributive Spirals: Negotiation Impasses and the Moderating Role of Disputant Self-Efficacy," *Organizational Behavior and Human Decision Processes* 84, no. 1 (2001), pp. 148–176.

67. B. Shiv, G. Loewenstein, A. Bechara, H. Damasio, and A. R. Damasio, "Investment Behavior and the Negative Side of Emotion," *Psychological Science* 16, no. 6 (2005), pp. 435–439.

68. W.-C. Tsai and Y.-M. Huang, "Mechanisms Linking Employee Affective Delivery and Customer Behavioral Intentions," *Journal of Applied Psychology,* October 2002, pp. 1001–1008.

69. Grandey, "When 'The Show Must Go On.'"

70. See P. B. Barker and A. A. Grandey, "Service with a Smile and Encounter Satisfaction: Emotional Contagion and Appraisal Mechanisms," *Academy of Management Journal* 49, no. 6 (2006), pp. 1229–1238; and S. D. Pugh, "Service with a Smile: Emotional Contagion in the Service Encounter," *Academy of Management Journal,* October 2001, pp. 1018–1027.

71. D. E. Rupp and S. Spencer, "When Customers Lash Out: The Effects of Customer Interactional Injustice on Emotional Labor and the Mediating Role of Emotions," *Journal of Applied Psychology* 91, no. 4 (2006), pp. 971–978; and Tsai and Huang, "Mechanisms Linking Employee Affective Delivery and Customer Behavioral Intentions."

72. R. Ilies and T. A. Judge, "Understanding the Dynamic Relationships Among Personality, Mood, and Job Satisfaction: A Field Experience Sampling Study," *Organizational Behavior and Human Decision Processes* 89 (2002), pp. 1119–1139.

73. R. Rau, "Job Strain or Healthy Work: A Question of Task Design," *Journal of Occupational Health Psychology* 9, no. 4 (October 2004), pp. 322–338; and R. Rau and A. Triemer, "Overtime in Relation to Blood Pressure and Mood During Work, Leisure, and Night Time," *Social Indicators Research* 67, no. 1–2 (June 2004), pp. 51–73.

74. Z. Song, M. Foo, and M. A. Uy, "Mood Spillover and Crossover Among Dual-Earner Couples: A Cell Phone Event Sampling Study," *Journal of Applied Psychology* 93, no. 2 (2008), pp. 443–452.

75. T. A. Judge and R. Ilies, "Affect and Job Satisfaction: A Study of Their Relationship at Work and at Home," *Journal of Applied Psychology* 89 (2004), pp. 661–673.

76. A. G. Bedeian, "Workplace Envy," *Organizational Dynamics,* Spring 1995, p. 50; and Ben-Ze'ev, *The Subtlety of Emotions,* (MIT Press: Boston, 2000).

77. Bedeian, "Workplace Envy," p. 54.

78. S. C. Douglas, C. Kiewitz, M. Martinko, P. Harvey, Y. Kim, and J. U. Chun, "Cognitions, Emotions, and Evaluations: An Elaboration Likelihood Model for Workplace Aggression," *Academy of Management Review* 33, no. 2 (2008), pp. 425–451.

79. T. A. Judge, B. A. Scott, and R. Ilies, "Hostility, Job Attitudes, and Workplace Deviance: Test of a Multilevel Model," *Journal of Applied Psychology* 91, no. 1 (2006), 126–138; and S. Kaplan, J. C. Bradley, J. N. Luchman, and D. Haynes, "On the Role of Positive and Negative Affectivity in Job Performance: A Meta-analytic Investigation," *Journal of Applied Psychology* 94, no. 1 (2009), pp. 162–176.

80. R. D. Iverson and P. J. Erwin, "Predicting Occupational Injury: The Role of Affectivity," *Journal of Occupational and Organizational Psychology* 70, no. 2 (1997), pp. 113–128; and Kaplan, Bradley, Luchman, and Haynes, "On the Role of Positive and Negative Affectivity in Job Performance."

81. A. M. Isen, A. A. Labroo, and P. Durlach, "An Influence of Product and Brand Name on Positive Affect: Implicit and Explicit Measures," *Motivation & Emotion* 28, no. 1 (March 2004), pp. 43–63.

82. T. Sy, S. Côté, and R. Saavedra, "The Contagious Leader: Impact of the Leader's Mood on the Mood of Group Members, Group Affective Tone, and Group Processes," *Journal of Applied Psychology* 90, no. 2 (2005), pp. 295–305.

83. P. Totterdell, "Catching Moods and Hitting Runs: Mood Linkage and Subjective Performance in Professional Sports Teams," *Journal of Applied Psychology* 85, no. 6 (2000), pp. 848–859.

84. M. Eid and E. Diener, "Norms for Experiencing Emotions in Different Cultures: Inter- and Intranational Differences," *Journal of Personality & Social Psychology* 81, no. 5 (2001), pp. 869–885.

85. S. Oishi, E. Diener, and C. Napa Scollon, "Cross-Situational Consistency of Affective Experiences Across Cultures," *Journal of Personality & Social Psychology* 86, no. 3 (2004), pp. 460–472.

86. Eid and Diener, "Norms for Experiencing Emotions in Different Cultures."

87. Ibid.

88. Ashforth and Humphrey, "Emotion in the Workplace," p. 104; B. Plasait, "Accueil des Touristes Dans les Grands Centres de Transit Paris," *Rapport du Bernard Plasait,* October 4, 2004, www.tourisme.gouv.fr/fr/navd/presse/dossiers/att00005767/dp_plasait.pdf; B. Mesquita, "Emotions in Collectivist and Individualist Contexts," *Journal of Personality and Social Psychology* 80, no. 1 (2001), pp. 68–74; and D. Rubin, "Grumpy German Shoppers Distrust the Wal-Mart Style," *Seattle Times,* December 30, 2001, p. A15.

89. H. A. Elfenbein and N. Ambady, "When Familiarity Breeds Accuracy: Cultural Exposure and Facial Emotional Recognition," *Journal of Personality and Social Psychology* 85, no. 2 (2003), pp. 276–290.

90. B. Mesquita and N. H. Frijda, "Cultural Variations in Emotions: A Review," *Psychological Bulletin,* September 1992, pp. 179–204; and B. Mesquita, "Emotions in Collectivist and Individualist Contexts," *Journal of Personality and Social Psychology,* January 2001, pp. 68–74.

91. S. Nelton, "Emotions in the Workplace," *Nation's Business*, February 1996, p. 25.

Chapter 4

1. G. W. Allport, *Personality: A Psychological Interpretation* (New York: Holt, Rinehart & Winston, 1937), p. 48.

2. K. I. van der Zee, J. N. Zaal, and J. Piekstra, "Validation of the Multicultural Personality Questionnaire in the Context of Personnel Selection," *European Journal of Personality* 17 (2003), pp. S77–S100.

3. S. A. Birkeland, T. M. Manson, J. L. Kisamore, M. T. Brannick, and M. A. Smith, "A Meta-analytic Investigation of Job Applicant Faking on Personality Measures," *International Journal of Selection and Assessment* 14, no. 14 (2006), pp. 317–335.

4. See R. Illies, R. D. Arvey, and T. J. Bouchard, "Darwinism, Behavioral Genetics, and Organizational Behavior: A Review and Agenda for Future Research," *Journal of Organizational Behavior* 27, no. 2 (2006), pp. 121–141; and T. J. Bouchard, Jr., and J. C. Loehlin, "Genes, Evolution, and Personality," *Behavior Genetics,* May 2001, pp. 243–273.

5. S. Srivastava, O. P. John, and S. D. Gosling, "Development of Personality in Early and Middle Adulthood: Set Like Plaster or Persistent Change?" *Journal of Personality and Social Psychology,* May 2003, pp. 1041–1053; and B. W. Roberts, K. E. Walton, and W. Viechtbauer, "Patterns of Mean-Level Change in Personality Traits Across the Life Course: A Meta-analysis of Longitudinal Studies," *Psychological Bulletin* 132, no. 1 (2006), pp. 1–25.

6. S. E. Hampson and L. R. Goldberg, "A First Large Cohort Study of Personality Trait Stability Over the 40 Years Between Elementary School and Midlife," *Journal of Personality and Social Psychology* 91, no. 4 (2006), pp. 763–779.

7. R. B. Kennedy and D. A. Kennedy, "Using the Myers-Briggs Type Indicator in Career Counseling," *Journal of Employment Counseling,* March 2004, pp. 38–44.

8. See, for instance, R. M. Capraro and M. M. Capraro, "Myers-Briggs Type Indicator Score Reliability Across Studies: A Meta-analytic Reliability Generalization Study," *Educational & Psychological Measurement,* August 2002, pp. 590–602; and R. C. Arnau, B. A. Green, D. H. Rosen, D. H. Gleaves, and J. G. Melancon, "Are Jungian Preferences Really Categorical? An Empirical Investigation Using Taxometric Analysis," *Personality & Individual Differences,* January 2003, pp. 233–251.

9. See, for example, J. M. Digman, "Personality Structure: Emergence of the Five-Factor Model," in M. R. Rosenzweig and L. W. Porter (eds.), *Annual Review of Psychology,* vol. 41 (Palo Alto, CA: Annual Reviews, 1990), pp. 417–440; and M. R. Barrick and M. K. Mount, "Yes, Personality Matters: Moving On to More Important Matters," *Human Performance* 18, no. 4 (2005), pp. 359–372.

10. See, for instance, M. R. Barrick and M. K. Mount, "The Big Five Personality Dimensions and Job Performance: A Meta-analysis," *Personnel Psychology,* Spring 1991, pp. 1–26; and G. M. Hurtz and J. J. Donovan, "Personality and Job Performance: The Big Five Revisited," *Journal of Applied Psychology,* December 2000, pp. 869–879.

11. M. K. Mount, M. R. Barrick, and J. P. Strauss, "Validity of Observer Ratings of the Big Five Personality Factors," *Journal of Applied Psychology,* April 1994, p. 272; and M. R. Barrick, M. K. Mount, and T. A. Judge, "The FFM Personality Dimensions and Job Performance: Meta-analysis of Meta-analyses," *International Journal of Selection and Assessment* 9 (2001), pp. 9–30.

12. A. E. Poropat, "A Meta-Analysis of the Five-Factor Model of Personality and Academic Performance," *Psychological Bulletin* 135, no. 2 (2009), pp. 322–338.

13. R. J. Foti and M. A. Hauenstein, "Pattern and Variable Approaches in Leadership Emergence and Effectiveness," *Journal of Applied Psychology,* March 2007, pp. 347–355.

14. L. I. Spirling and R. Persaud, "Extraversion as a Risk Factor," *Journal of the American Academy of Child & Adolescent Psychiatry* 42, no. 2 (2003), p. 130.

15. S. Clarke and I. Robertson, "An Examination of the Role of Personality in Accidents Using Meta-analysis," *Applied Psychology: An International Review* 57, no. 1 (2008), pp. 94–108.

16. B. Laursen, L. Pulkkinen, and R. Adams, "The Antecedents and Correlates of Agreeableness in Adulthood," *Developmental Psychology* 38, no. 4 (2002), pp. 591–603.

17. B. Barry and R. A. Friedman, "Bargainer Characteristics in Distributive and Integrative Negotiation," *Journal of Personality and Social Psychology,* February 1998, pp. 345–359.

18. T. Bogg and B. W. Roberts, "Conscientiousness and Health-Related Behaviors: A Meta-analysis of the Leading Behavioral Contributors to Mortality," *Psychological Bulletin* 130, no. 6 (2004), pp. 887–919.

19. S. Lee and H. J. Klein, "Relationships Between Conscientiousness, Self-Efficacy, Self-Deception, and Learning over Time," *Journal of Applied Psychology* 87, no. 6 (2002), pp. 1175–1182; and G. J. Feist, "A Meta-analysis of Personality in Scientific and Artistic Creativity," *Personality and Social Psychology Review* 2, no. 4 (1998), pp. 290–309.

20. T. A. Judge and J. E. Bono, "A Rose by Any Other Name . . . Are Self-Esteem, Generalized Self-Efficacy, Neuroticism, and Locus of Control Indicators of a Common Construct?" in B. W. Roberts and R. Hogan (eds.), *Personality Psychology in the Workplace* (Washington, DC: American Psychological Association), pp. 93–118.

21. A. Erez and T. A. Judge, "Relationship of Core Self-Evaluations to Goal Setting, Motivation, and Performance," *Journal of Applied Psychology* 86, no. 6 (2001), pp. 1270–1279.

22. A. N. Salvaggio, B. Schneider, L. H. Nishi, D. M. Mayer, A. Ramesh, and J. S. Lyon, "Manager Personality, Manager Service Quality Orientation, and Service Climate: Test of a Model," *Journal of Applied Psychology* 92, no. 6 (2007), pp. 1741–1750; B. A. Scott and T. A. Judge, "The Popularity Contest at Work: Who Wins, Why, and What Do They Receive?" *Journal of Applied Psychology* 94, no. 1 (2009), pp. 20–33; and T. A. Judge and C. Hurst, "How the Rich (and Happy) Get Richer (and Happier): Relationship of Core Self-Evaluations to Trajectories in Attaining Work Success," *Journal of Applied Psychology* 93, no. 4 (2008), pp. 849–863.

23. U. Malmendier and G. Tate, "CEO Overconfidence and Corporate Investment," *Journal of Finance* 60, no. 6 (December 2005), pp. 2661–2700.

24. R. Christie and F. L. Geis, *Studies in Machiavellianism* (New York: Academic Press, 1970), p. 312; and N. V. Ramanaiah, A. Byravan, and F. R. J. Detwiler, "Revised Neo Personality Inventory Profiles of Machiavellian and Non-Machiavellian People," *Psychological Reports,* October 1994, pp. 937–938.

25. Christie and Geis, *Studies in Machiavellianism.*

26. M. Maccoby, "Narcissistic Leaders: The Incredible Pros, the Inevitable Cons," *The Harvard Business Review,* January–February 2000, pp. 69–77, www.maccoby.com/Articles/NarLeaders.shtml.

27. W. K. Campbell and C. A. Foster, "Narcissism and Commitment in Romantic Relationships: An Investment Model Analysis," *Personality and Social Psychology Bulletin* 28, no. 4 (2002), pp. 484–495.

28. T. A. Judge, J. A. LePine, and B. L. Rich, "The Narcissistic Personality: Relationship with Inflated Self-Ratings of Leadership and with Task and Contextual Performance," *Journal of Applied Psychology* 91, no. 4 (2006), pp. 762–776.

29. See M. Snyder, *Public Appearances/Private Realities: The Psychology of Self-Monitoring* (New York: W. H. Freeman, 1987); and S. W. Gangestad and M. Snyder, "Self-Monitoring: Appraisal and Reappraisal," *Psychological Bulletin,* July 2000, pp. 530–555.

30. F. J. Flynn and D. R. Ames, "What's Good for the Goose May Not Be as Good for the Gander: The Benefits of Self-Monitoring for Men and Women in Task Groups and Dyadic Conflicts," *Journal of Applied Psychology* 91, no. 2 (2006), pp. 272–281.

31. D. V. Day, D. J. Shleicher, A. L. Unckless, and N. J. Hiller, "Self-Monitoring Personality at Work: A Meta-analytic Investigation of Construct Validity," *Journal of Applied Psychology,* April 2002, pp. 390–401.

32. H. Oh and M. Kilduff, "The Ripple Effect of Personality on Social Structure: Self-monitoring Origins of Network Brokerage," *Journal of Applied Psychology* 93, no. 5 (2008), pp. 1155–1164.

33. R. N. Taylor and M. D. Dunnette, "Influence of Dogmatism, Risk-Taking Propensity, and Intelligence on Decision-Making Strategies for a Sample of Industrial Managers," *Journal of Applied Psychology,* August 1974, pp. 420–423.

34. W. H. Stewart Jr., and L. Roth, "Risk Propensity Differences Between Entrepreneurs and Managers: A Meta-analytic Review," *Journal of Applied Psychology,* February 2001, pp. 145–153; and J. B. Miner and N. S. Raju, "Risk Propensity Differences Between Managers and Entrepreneurs and Between Low- and High-Growth Entrepreneurs: A Reply in a More Conservative Vein," *Journal of Applied Psychology* 89, no. 1 (2004).

35. J. K. Maner, J. A. Richey, K. Cromer, M. Mallott, C. W. Lejuez, T. E. Joiner, and N. B. Schmidt, "Dispositional Anxiety and Risk-Avoidant Decision Making," *Personality and Individual Differences* 42, no. 4 (2007), pp. 665–675.

36. M. Friedman and R. H. Rosenman, *Type A Behavior and Your Heart* (New York: Alfred A. Knopf, 1974), p. 84.

37. Ibid., pp. 84–85.

38. J. M. Crant, "Proactive Behavior in Organizations," *Journal of Management* 26, no. 3 (2000), p. 436; S. E. Seibert, M. L. Kraimer, and J. M. Crant, "What Do Proactive People Do? A Longitudinal Model Linking Proactive Personality and Career Success," *Personnel Psychology,* Winter 2001, p. 850.

39. T. S. Bateman and J. M. Crant, "The Proactive Component of Organizational Behavior: A Measure and Correlates," *Journal of Organizational Behavior,* March 1993, pp. 103–118; and J. M. Crant and T. S. Bateman, "Charismatic Leadership Viewed from Above: The Impact of Proactive Personality," *Journal of Organizational Behavior,* February 2000, pp. 63–75.

40. Crant, "Proactive Behavior in Organizations," p. 436.

41. See, for instance, R. C. Becherer and J. G. Maurer, "The Proactive Personality Disposition and Entrepreneurial Behavior Among Small Company Presidents," *Journal of Small Business Management,* January 1999, pp. 28–36.

42. S. E. Seibert, J. M. Crant, and M. L. Kraimer, "Proactive Personality and Career Success," *Journal of Applied Psychology,* June 1999, pp. 416–427; Seibert, Kraimer, and Crant, "What Do Proactive People Do?" p. 850; and D. J. Brown, R. T. Cober, K. Kane, P. E. Levy, and J. Shalhoop, "Proactive Personality and the Successful Job Search: A Field Investigation with College Graduates," *Journal of Applied Psychology* 91, no. 3 (2006), pp. 717–726.

43. M. Rokeach, *The Nature of Human Values* (New York: The Free Press, 1973), p. 5.

44. M. Rokeach and S. J. Ball-Rokeach, "Stability and Change in American Value Priorities, 1968–1981," *American Psychologist* 44, no. 5 (1989), pp. 775–784; and B. M. Meglino and E. C. Ravlin, "Individual Values in Organizations: Concepts, Controversies, and Research," *Journal of Management* 24, no. 3 (1998), p. 355.

45. S. Roccas, L. Sagiv, S. H. Schwartz, and A. Knafo, "The Big Five Personality Factors and Personal Values," *Personality and Social Psychology Bulletin* 28, no. 6 (2002), pp. 789–801.

46. Rokeach, *The Nature of Human Values,* p. 6.

47. J. M. Munson and B. Z. Posner, "The Factorial Validity of a Modified Rokeach Value Survey for Four Diverse Samples," *Educational and Psychological Measurement,* Winter 1980, pp. 1073–1079; and W. C. Frederick and J. Weber, "The Values of Corporate Managers and Their Critics: An Empirical Description and Normative Implications," in W. C. Frederick and L. E. Preston (eds.), *Business Ethics: Research Issues and Empirical Studies* (Greenwich, CT: JAI Press, 1990), pp. 123–144.

48. Frederick and Weber, "The Values of Corporate Managers and Their Critics," pp. 123–144.

49. J. L. Holland, *Making Vocational Choices: A Theory of Vocational Personalities and Work Environments* (Odessa, FL: Psychological Assessment Resources, 1997).

50. See, for example, J. L. Holland and G. D. Gottfredson, "Studies of the Hexagonal Model: An Evaluation (or, The Perils of Stalking the Perfect Hexagon)," *Journal of Vocational Behavior,* April 1992, pp. 158–170; and T. J. Tracey and J. Rounds, "Evaluating Holland's and Gati's Vocational-Interest Models: A Structural Meta-analysis," *Psychological Bulletin,* March 1993, pp. 229–246.

51. See B. Schneider, H. W. Goldstein, and D. B. Smith, "The ASA Framework: An Update," *Personnel Psychology,* Winter 1995, pp. 747–773; W. Arthur Jr., S. T. Bell, A. J. Villado, and D. Doverspike, "The Use of Person-Organization Fit in Employment Decision-Making:

An Assessment of Its Criterion-Related Validity," *Journal of Applied Psychology* 91, no. 4 (2006), pp. 786–801; and J. R. Edwards, D. M. Cable, I. O. Williamson, L. S. Lambert, and A. J. Shipp, "The Phenomenology of Fit: Linking the Person and Environment to the Subjective Experience of Person–Environment Fit," *Journal of Applied Psychology* 91, no. 4 (2006), pp. 802–827.

52. M. L. Verquer, T. A. Beehr, and S. E. Wagner, "A Meta-analysis of Relations Between Person–Organization Fit and Work Attitudes," *Journal of Vocational Behavior* 63, no. 3 (2003), pp. 473–489; and J. C. Carr, A. W. Pearson, M. J. Vest, and S. L. Boyar, "Prior Occupational Experience, Anticipatory Socialization, and Employee Retention, *Journal of Management* 32, no. 32 (2006), pp. 343–359.

53. See, for instance, R. R. McCrae and P. T. Costa, Jr., "Personality Trait Structure as a Human Universal," *American Psychologist,* May 1997, pp. 509–516; S. Yamagata, A. Suzuki, J. Ando, Y. Ono, K. Yutaka, N. Kijima, et al., "Is the Genetic Structure of Human Personality Universal? A Cross-Cultural Twin Study from North America, Europe, and Asia," *Journal of Personality and Social Psychology* 90, no. 6 (2006), pp. 987–998.

54. A. T. Church and M. S. Katigbak, "Trait Psychology in the Philippines," *American Behavioral Scientist,* September 2000, pp. 73–94.

55. J. F. Salgado, "The Five Factor Model of Personality and Job Performance in the European Community," *Journal of Applied Psychology,* February 1997, pp. 30–43.

56. G. Hofstede, *Cultures and Organizations: Software of the Mind* (London: McGraw-Hill, 1991); G. Hofstede and M. F. Peterson, "National Values and Organizational Practices," in N. M. Ashkanasy, C. M. Wilderom, and M. F. Peterson (eds.), *Handbook of Organizational Culture and Climate* (Thousand Oaks, CA: Sage, 2000), pp. 401–416; and G. Hofstede, *Culture's Consequences: Comparing Values, Behaviors, Institutions, and Organizations Across Nations*, 2nd ed. (Thousand Oaks, CA: Sage, 2001).

57. G. Ailon, "Mirror, Mirror on the Wall: *Culture's Consequences* in a Value Test of Its Own Design," *Academy of Management Review* 33, no. 4 (2008), pp. 885–904; and M. H. Bond, "Reclaiming the Individual from Hofstede's Ecological Analysis—A 20-Year Odyssey: Comment on Oyserman et al. (2002)," *Psychological Bulletin* 128, no. 1 (2002), pp. 73–77.

58. M. Javidan and R. J. House, "Cultural Acumen for the Global Manager: Lessons from Project GLOBE," *Organizational Dynamics* 29, no. 4 (2001), pp. 289–305; and R. J. House, P. J. Hanges, M. Javidan, and P. W. Dorfman (eds.), *Leadership, Culture, and Organizations: The GLOBE Study of 62 Societies* (Thousand Oaks, CA: Sage, 2004).

Chapter 5

1. H. H. Kelley, "Attribution in Social Interaction," in E. Jones et al. (eds.), *Attribution: Perceiving the Causes of Behavior* (Morristown, NJ: General Learning Press, 1972).

2. See L. Ross, "The Intuitive Psychologist and His Shortcomings," in L. Berkowitz (ed.), *Advances in Experimental Social Psychology,* vol. 10 (Orlando, FL: Academic Press, 1977), pp. 174–220; and A. G. Miller and T. Lawson, "The Effect of an Informational Option on the Fundamental Attribution Error," *Personality and Social Psychology Bulletin,* June 1989, pp. 194–204.

3. See, for instance, N. Epley and D. Dunning, "Feeling 'Holier Than Thou': Are Self-Serving Assessments Produced by Errors in Self- or Social Prediction?" *Journal of Personality and Social Psychology,* December 2000, pp. 861–875.

4. S. E. Asch, "Forming Impressions of Personality," *Journal of Abnormal and Social Psychology,* July 1946, pp. 258–290.

5. See, for example, G. N. Powell, "The Good Manager: Business Students' Stereotypes of Japanese Managers Versus Stereotypes of American Managers," *Group & Organizational Management,* March 1992, pp. 44–56; C. Ostroff and L. E. Atwater, "Does Whom You Work with Matter? Effects of Referent Group Gender and Age Composition on Managers' Compensation," *Journal of Applied Psychology,* August 2003, pp. 725–740; and R. A. Posthuma and M. A. Campion, "Age Stereotypes in the Workplace: Common Stereotypes, Moderators, and Future Research Directions," *Journal of Management* 35, no. 1 (2009), pp. 158–188.

6. J. L. Eberhardt, P. G. Davies, V. J. Purdie-Vaughns, and S. L. Johnson, "Looking Deathworthy: Perceived Stereotypicality of Black Defendants Predicts Capital-Sentencing Outcomes," *Psychological Science* 17, no. 5 (2006), pp. 383–386.

7. R. Sanders, *The Executive Decisionmaking Process: Identifying Problems and Assessing Outcomes* (Westport, CT: Quorum, 1999).

8. For a review of the rational decision-making model, see E. F. Harrison, *The Managerial Decision-Making Process,* 5th ed. (Boston: Houghton Mifflin, 1999), pp. 75–102.

9. M. Bazerman, *Judgment in Managerial Decision Making,* 3rd ed. (New York: Wiley, 1994), p. 5.

10. J. E. Russo, K. A. Carlson, and M. G. Meloy, "Choosing an Inferior Alternative," *Psychological Science* 17, no. 10 (2006), pp. 899–904.

11. D. Kahneman, "Maps of Bounded Rationality: Psychology for Behavioral Economics," *The American Economic Review* 93, no. 5 (2003), pp. 1449–1475; and J. Zhang, C. K. Hsee, and Z. Xiao, "The Majority Rule in Individual

Decision Making," Organizational *Behavior and Human Decision Processes* 99 (2006), pp. 102–111.

12. See H. A. Simon, *Administrative Behavior,* 4th ed. (New York: The Free Press, 1997); and M. Augier, "Simon Says: Bounded Rationality Matters," *Journal of Management Inquiry,* September 2001, pp. 268–275.

13. G. Gigerenzer, "Why Heuristics Work," *Perspectives on Psychological Science* 3, no. 1 (2008), pp. 20–29; and A. K. Shah and D. M. Oppenheimer, "Heuristics Made Easy: An Effort-Reduction Framework," *Psychological Bulletin* 134, no. 2 (2008), pp. 207–222.

14. E. Dane and M. G. Pratt, "Exploring Intuition and Its Role in Managerial Decision Making," *Academy of Management Review* 32, no. 1 (2007), pp. 33–54.

15. P. D. Brown, "Some Hunches About Intuition," *New York Times,* November 17, 2007, p. B5.

16. S. P. Robbins, *Decide & Conquer: Making Winning Decisions and Taking Control of Your Life* (Upper Saddle River, NJ: Financial Times/Prentice Hall, 2004), p. 13.

17. S. Plous, *The Psychology of Judgment and Decision Making* (New York: McGraw-Hill, 1993), p. 217.

18. S. Lichtenstein and B. Fischhoff, "Do Those Who Know More Also Know More About How Much They Know?" *Organizational Behavior and Human Performance,* December 1977, pp. 159–183.

19. B. Fischhoff, P. Slovic, and S. Lichtenstein, "Knowing with Certainty: The Appropriateness of Extreme Confidence," *Journal of Experimental Psychology: Human Perception and Performance,* November 1977, pp. 552–564.

20. B. Fischhoff, P. Slovic, and S. Lichtenstein, "Knowing with Certainty: The Appropriateness of Extreme Confidence," *Journal of Experimental Psychology* 3 (1977), pp. 552–564.

21. K. M. Hmieleski and R. A. Baron, "Entrepreneurs' Optimism and New Venture Performance: A Social Cognitive Perspective," *Academy of Management Journal* 52, no. 3 (2009), pp. 473–488.

22. See, for instance, A. Tversky and D. Kahneman, "Judgment Under Uncertainty: Heuristics and Biases," *Science,* September 1974, pp. 1124–1131.

23. C. Janiszewski and D. Uy, "Precision of the Anchor Influences the Amount of Adjustment," *Psychological Science* 19, no. 2 (2008), pp. 121–127.

24. See A. Tversky and D. Kahneman, "Availability: A Heuristic for Judging Frequency and Probability," in D. Kahneman, P. Slovic, and A. Tversky (eds.), *Judgment Under Uncertainty: Heuristics and Biases* (Cambridge, UK: Cambridge University Press, 1982), pp. 163–178.

25. G. Morgenson, "Debt Watchdogs: Tamed or Caught Napping?" *New York Times,* December 7, 2009, pp. 1, 32.

26. See B. M. Staw, "The Escalation of Commitment to a Course of Action," *Academy of Management Review,* October 1981, pp. 577–587; K. Fai, E. Wong, M. Yik, and J. Y. Y. Kwong, "Understanding the Emotional Aspects of Escalation of Commitment: The Role of Negative Affect," *Journal of Applied Psychology* 91, no. 2 (2006), pp. 282–297.

27. K. F. E. Wong, J. Y. Y. Kwong, and C. K. Ng, "When Thinking Rationally Increases Biases: The Role of Rational Thinking Style in Escalation of Commitment," *Applied Psychology: An International Review* 57, no. 2 (2008), pp. 246–271.

28. See, for example, D. J. Keys and B. Schwartz, "Leaky Rationality: How Research on Behavioral Decision Making Challenges Normative Standards of Rationality," *Psychological Science* 2, no. 2 (2007), pp. 162–180; and U. Simonsohn, "Direct Risk Aversion: Evidence from Risky Prospects Valued Below Their Worst Outcome," *Psychological Science* 20, no. 6 (2009), pp. 686–692.

29. J. K. Maner, M. T. Gailliot, D. A. Butz, and B. M. Peruche, "Power, Risk, and the Status Quo: Does Power Promote Riskier or More Conservative Decision Making," *Personality and Social Psychology Bulletin* 33, no. 4 (2007), pp. 451–462.

30. Chakraborty, S. Sheikh, and N. Subramanian, "Termination Risk and Managerial Risk Taking," *Journal of Corporate Finance* 13, (2007), pp. 170–188.

31. Wildavsky, *The Politics of the Budgetary Process* (Boston: Little, Brown, 1964).

32. G. F. Cavanagh, D. J. Moberg, and M. Valasquez, "The Ethics of Organizational Politics," *Academy of Management Journal,* June 1981, pp. 363–374.

33. See, for example, T. Machan (ed.), *Commerce and Morality* (Totowa, NJ: Rowman and Littlefield, 1988).

34. G. J. Feist and F. X. Barron, "Predicting Creativity from Early to Late Adulthood: Intellect, Potential, and Personality," *Journal of Research in Personality,* April 2003, pp. 62–88.

35. R. W. Woodman, J. E. Sawyer, and R. W. Griffin, "Toward a Theory of Organizational Creativity," *Academy of Management Review,* April 1993, p. 298; and E. F. Rietzschel, C. K. W. de Dreu, and B. A. Nijstad, "Personal Need for Structure and Creative Performance: The Moderating Influence of Fear of Invalidity," *Personality and Social Psychology Bulletin,* June 2007, pp. 855–866.

36. K. Leung, W. W. Maddux, A. D. Galinsky, and C. Chiu, "Multicultural Experience Enhances Creativity," *American Psychologist* 63, no. 3 (2008), pp. 169–180.

37. This section is based on T. M. Amabile, "Motivating Creativity in Organizations: On Doing What You Love and Loving What You Do," *California Management Review* 40, no. 1 (Fall 1997), pp. 39–58.

38. M. Baas, C. K. W. De Dreu, and B. A. Nijstad, "A Meta-analysis of 25 Years of Mood-Creativity Research: Hedonic

Tone, Activation, or Regulatory Focus?" *Psychological Bulletin* 134, no. 6 (2008), pp. 779–806.

39. J. Zhou, "When the Presence of Creative Coworkers Is Related to Creativity: Role of Supervisor Close Monitoring, Developmental Feedback, and Creative Personality," *Journal of Applied Psychology* 88, no. 3 (June 2003), pp. 413–422.

40. J. E. Perry-Smith, "Social yet Creative: The Role of Social Relationships in Facilitating Individual Creativity," *Academy of Management Journal* 49, no. 1 (2006), pp. 85–101.

41. G. Park, D. Lubinski, and C. P. Benbow, "Contrasting Intellectual Patterns Predict Creativity in the Arts and Sciences," *Psychological Science* 18, no. 11 (2007), pp. 948–952.

42. G. Hirst, D. Van Knippenberg, and J. Zhou, "A Cross-Level Perspective on Employee Creativity: Goal Orientation, Team Learning Behavior, and Individual Creativity," *Academy of Management Journal* 52, no. 2 (2009), pp. 280–293; and C. E. Shalley, L. L. Gilson, and T. C. Blum, "Interactive Effects of Growth Need Strength, Work Context, and Job Complexity on Self-Reported Creative Performance," *Academy of Management Journal* 52, no. 3 (2009), pp. 489–505.

43. D. S. Krull, M. H.-M. Loy, J. Lin, C.-F. Wang, S. Chen, and X. Zhao, "The Fundamental Attribution Error: Correspondence Bias in Individualistic and Collectivist Cultures," *Personality & Social Psychology Bulletin,* October 1999, pp. 1208–1219; and F. F. T. Chiang and T. A. Birtch, "Examining the Perceived Causes of Successful Employee Performance: An East-West Comparison," *International Journal of Human Resource Management* 18, no. 2 (2007), pp. 232–248.

44. S. Nam, "Cultural and Managerial Attributions for Group Performance," unpublished doctoral dissertation, University of Oregon. Cited in R. M. Steers, S. J. Bischoff, and L. H. Higgins, "Cross-Cultural Management Research," *Journal of Management Inquiry,* December 1992, pp. 325–326.

45. T. Menon, M. W. Morris, C. Y. Chiu, and Y. Y. Hong, "Culture and the Construal of Agency: Attribution to Individual Versus Group Dispositions," *Journal of Personality and Social Psychology* 76, (1999), pp. 701–717; and R. Friedman, W. Liu, C. C. Chen, and S. S. Chi, "Causal Attribution for Interfirm Contract Violation: A Comparative Study of Chinese and American Commercial Arbitrators," *Journal of Applied Psychology* 92, no. 3 (2007), pp. 856–864.

46. J. Spencer-Rodgers, M. J. Williams, D. L. Hamilton, K. Peng, and L. Wang, "Culture and Group Perception: Dispositional and Stereotypic Inferences About Novel and National Groups," *Journal of Personality and Social Psychology* 93, no. 4 (2007), pp. 525–543.

47. M. J. Gelfand, M. Erez, and Z. Aycan, "Cross-Cultural Organizational Behavior," *Annual Review of Psychology,* January 2007, pp. 479–514; and A. S. Tsui, S. S. Nifadkar, and A. Y. Ou, "Cross-National, Cross-Cultural Organizational

Behavior Research: Advances, Gaps, and Recommendations," *Journal of Management,* June 2007, pp. 426–478.

48. N. J. Adler, *International Dimensions of Organizational Behavior,* 4th ed. (Cincinnati, OH: South-Western Publishing, 2002), pp. 182–189.

49. W. Chow Hou, "To Bribe or Not to Bribe?" *Asia, Inc.,* October 1996, p. 104.

50. P. Digh, "Shades of Gray in the Global Marketplace," *HRMagazine,* April 1997, p. 91.

Chapter 6

1. Cited in D. Jones, "Firms Spend Billions to Fire Up Workers—With Little Luck," *USA Today,* May 10, 2001, p. 1A.

2. "Wasted Time at Work Costs Employers Billions," *IPMA-HR Bulletin,* August 11, 2006, pp. 1–7.

3. See, for instance, T. R. Mitchell, "Matching Motivational Strategies with Organizational Contexts," in L. L. Cummings and B. M. Staw (eds.), *Research in Organizational Behavior,* vol. 19 (Greenwich, CT: JAI Press, 1997), pp. 60–62.

4. Maslow, *Motivation and Personality* (New York: Harper & Row, 1954).

5. See, for example, E. E. Lawler III and J. L. Suttle, "A Causal Correlation Test of the Need Hierarchy Concept," *Organizational Behavior and Human Performance,* April 1972, pp. 265–287; and A. K. Korman, J. H. Greenhaus, and I. J. Badin, "Personnel Attitudes and Motivation," in M. R. Rosenzweig and L. W. Porter (eds.), *Annual Review of Psychology* (Palo Alto, CA: Annual Reviews, 1977), pp. 178–179.

6. M. A. Wahba and L. G. Bridwell, "Maslow Reconsidered: A Review of Research on the Need Hierarchy Theory," *Organizational Behavior and Human Performance,* April 1976, pp. 212–240.

7. D. McGregor, *The Human Side of Enterprise* (New York: McGraw-Hill, 1960). For an updated analysis of Theory X and Theory Y constructs, see R. J. Summers and S. F. Cronshaw, "A Study of McGregor's Theory X, Theory Y and the Influence of Theory X, Theory Y Assumptions on Causal Attributions for Instances of Worker Poor Performance," in S. L. McShane (ed.), *Organizational Behavior, ASAC 1988 Conference Proceedings,* vol. 9, part 5 (Halifax, Nova Scotia, 1988), pp. 115–123.

8. F. Herzberg, B. Mausner, and B. Snyderman, *The Motivation to Work* (New York: Wiley, 1959).

9. R. J. House and L. A. Wigdor, "Herzberg's Dual-Factor Theory of Job Satisfaction and Motivations: A Review of the Evidence and Criticism," *Personnel Psychology,* Winter 1967, pp. 369–389.

10. D. C. McClelland, *The Achieving Society* (New York: Van Nostrand Reinhold, 1961); J. W. Atkinson and J. O. Raynor,

Motivation and Achievement (Washington, DC: Winston, 1974); D. C. McClelland, *Power: The Inner Experience* (New York: Irvington, 1975); and M. J. Stahl, *Managerial and Technical Motivation: Assessing Needs for Achievement, Power, and Affiliation* (New York: Praeger, 1986).

11. D. C. McClelland and D. G. Winter, *Motivating Economic Achievement* (New York: The Free Press, 1969); and J. B. Miner, N. R. Smith, and J. S. Bracker, "Role of Entrepreneurial Task Motivation in the Growth of Technologically Innovative Firms: Interpretations from Follow-up Data," *Journal of Applied Psychology,* October 1994, pp. 627–630.

12. D. C. McClelland, *Power*; D. C. McClelland and D. H. Burnham, "Power Is the Great Motivator," *Harvard Business Review,* March–April 1976, pp. 100–110; and R. E. Boyatzis, "The Need for Close Relationships and the Manager's Job," in D. A. Kolb, I. M. Rubin, and J. M. McIntyre, *Organizational Psychology: Readings on Human Behavior in Organizations,* 4th ed. (Upper Saddle River, NJ: Prentice Hall, 1984), pp. 81–86.

13. D. G. Winter, "The Motivational Dimensions of Leadership: Power, Achievement, and Affiliation," in R. E. Riggio, S. E. Murphy, and F. J. Pirozzolo (eds.), *Multiple Intelligences and Leadership* (Mahwah, NJ: Lawrence Erlbaum, 2002), pp. 119–138.

14. J. B. Miner, *Studies in Management Education* (New York: Springer, 1965).

15. E. Deci and R. Ryan (eds.), *Handbook of Self-Determination Research* (Rochester, NY: University of Rochester Press, 2002); R. Ryan, and E. Deci, "Self-Determination Theory and the Facilitation of Intrinsic Motivation, Social Development, and Well-Being," *American Psychologist* 55, no. 1 (2000), pp. 68–78; and M. Gagné and E. L. Deci, "Self-Determination Theory and Work Motivation," *Journal of Organizational Behavior* 26, no. 4 (2005), pp. 331–362.

16. E. L. Deci, R. Koestner, and R. M. Ryan, "A Meta-analytic Review of Experiments Examining the Effects of Extrinsic Rewards on Intrinsic Motivation," *Psychological Bulletin* 125, no. 6 (1999), pp. 627–668; and G. J. Greguras and J. M. Diefendorff, "Different Fits Satisfy Different Needs: Linking Person-Environment Fit to Employee Commitment and Performance Using Self-Determination Theory," *Journal of Applied Psychology* 94, no. 2 (2009), pp. 465–477.

17. R. Eisenberger and L. Rhoades, "Incremental Effects of Reward on Creativity," *Journal of Personality and Social Psychology* 81, no. 4 (2001), 728–741; and R. Eisenberger, W. D. Pierce, and J. Cameron, "Effects of Reward on Intrinsic Motivation—Negative, Neutral, and Positive: Comment on Deci, Koestner, and Ryan (1999)," *Psychological Bulletin* 125, no. 6 (1999), pp. 677–691.

18. M. Burgess, M. E. Enzle, and R. Schmaltz, "Defeating the Potentially Deleterious Effects of Externally Imposed Deadlines: Practitioners' Rules-of-Thumb," *Personality and Social Psychology Bulletin* 30, no. 7 (2004), pp. 868–877.

19. K. M. Sheldon, A. J. Elliot, and R. M. Ryan, "Self-Concordance and Subjective Well-being in Four Cultures," *Journal of Cross-Cultural Psychology* 35, no. 2 (2004), pp. 209–223.

20. J. E. Bono and T. A. Judge, "Self-Concordance at Work: Toward Understanding the Motivational Effects of Transformational Leaders," *Academy of Management Journal* 46, no. 5 (2003), pp. 554–571.

21. J. P. Meyer, T. E. Becker, and C. Vandenberghe, "Employee Commitment and Motivation: A Conceptual Analysis and Integrative Model," *Journal of Applied Psychology* 89, no. 6 (2004), pp. 991–1007.

22. E. A. Locke, "Toward a Theory of Task Motivation and Incentives," *Organizational Behavior and Human Performance,* May 1968, pp. 157–189.

23. See M. E. Tubbs "Goal Setting: A Meta-analytic Examination of the Empirical Evidence," *Journal of Applied Psychology,* August 1986, pp. 474–483; and E. A. Locke and G. P. Latham, "New Directions in Goal-Setting Theory," *Current Directions in Psychological Science* 15, no. 5 (2006), pp. 265–268.

24. Locke and Latham, "Building a Practically Useful Theory of Goal Setting and Task Motivation," pp. 705–717.

25. J. M. Ivancevich and J. T. McMahon, "The Effects of Goal Setting, External Feedback, and Self-Generated Feedback on Outcome Variables: A Field Experiment," *Academy of Management Journal,* June 1982, pp. 359–372; and E. A. Locke, "Motivation Through Conscious Goal Setting," *Applied and Preventive Psychology* 5 (1996), pp. 117–124.

26. See, for example, G. P. Latham, M. Erez, and E. A. Locke, "Resolving Scientific Disputes by the Joint Design of Crucial Experiments by the Antagonists: Application to the Erez-Latham Dispute Regarding Participation in Goal Setting," *Journal of Applied Psychology,* November 1988, pp. 753–772; and S. G. Harkins and M. D. Lowe, "The Effects of Self-Set Goals on Task Performance," *Journal of Applied Social Psychology,* January 2000, pp. 1–40.

27. J. R. Hollenbeck, C. R. Williams, and H. J. Klein, "An Empirical Examination of the Antecedents of Commitment to Difficult Goals," *Journal of Applied Psychology,* February 1989, pp. 18–23. See also J. C. Wofford, V. L. Goodwin, and S. Premack, "Meta-analysis of the Antecedents of Personal Goal Level and of the Antecedents and Consequences of Goal Commitment," *Journal of Management,* September 1992, pp. 595–615.

28. See R. E. Wood, A. J. Mento, and E. A. Locke, "Task Complexity as a Moderator of Goal Effects: A Meta-analysis," *Journal of Applied Psychology,* August 1987, pp. 416–425; and A. M. O'Leary-Kelly, J. J. Martocchio, and D. D. Frink,

"A Review of the Influence of Group Goals on Group Performance," *Academy of Management Journal,* October 1994, pp. 1285–1301.

29. D. F. Crown, "The Use of Group and Groupcentric Individual Goals for Culturally Heterogeneous and Homogeneous Task Groups: An Assessment of European Work Teams," *Small Group Research* 38, no. 4 (2007), pp. 489–508; and M. Erez and P. C. Earley, "Comparative Analysis of Goal-Setting Strategies Across Cultures," *Journal of Applied Psychology* 72, no. 4 (1987), pp. 658–665.

30. Sue-Chan and M. Ong, "Goal Assignment and Performance: Assessing the Mediating Roles of Goal Commitment and Self-Efficacy and the Moderating Role of Power Distance," *Organizational Behavior and Human Decision Processes* 89, no. 2 (2002), pp. 1140–1161.

31. G. P. Latham and E. A. Locke, "Enhancing the Benefits and Overcoming the Pitfalls of Goal Setting," *Organizational Dynamics* 35, no. 6, pp. 332–340; and L. D. Ordóñez, M. E. Schweitzer, A. D. Galinsky, and M. Bazerman, "Goals Gone Wild: The Systematic Side Effects of Overprescribing Goal Setting," *Academy of Management Perspectives* 23, no. 1 (2009), pp. 6–16.

32. "KEYGroup Survey Finds Nearly Half of All Employees Have No Set Performance Goals," IPMA-HR Bulletin, March 10, 2006, p. 1; "P&G CEO Wields High Expectations but No Whip," *USA Today,* February 19, 2007, p. 3B.

33. See, for instance, S. J. Carroll and H. L. Tosi, *Management by Objectives: Applications and Research* (New York: Macmillan, 1973); and R. Rodgers and J. E. Hunter, "Impact of Management by Objectives on Organizational Productivity," *Journal of Applied Psychology,* April 1991, pp. 322–336.

34. Bandura, *Self-Efficacy: The Exercise of Control* (New York: Freeman, 1997).

35. L. Holladay and M. A. Quiñones, "Practice Variability and Transfer of Training: The Role of Self-Efficacy Generality," *Journal of Applied Psychology* 88, no. 6 (2003), pp. 1094–1103.

36. R. C. Rist, "Student Social Class and Teacher Expectations: The Self-Fulfilling Prophecy in Ghetto Education," *Harvard Educational Review* 70, no. 3 (2000), pp. 266–301.

37. Eden, "Self-Fulfilling Prophecies in Organizations," in J. Greenberg (ed.), *Organizational Behavior: The State of the Science,* 2nd ed. (Mahwah, NJ: Lawrence Erlbaum, 2003), pp. 91–122.

38. T. A. Judge, C. L. Jackson, J. C. Shaw, B. Scott, and B. L. Rich, "Self-Efficacy and Work-Related Performance: The Integral Role of Individual Differences," *Journal of Applied Psychology* 92, no. 1 (2007), pp. 107–127.

39. J. S. Adams, "Inequity in Social Exchanges," in L. Berkowitz (ed.), *Advances in Experimental Social Psychology* (New York: Academic Press, 1965), pp. 267–300.

40. P. S. Goodman, "An Examination of Referents Used in the Evaluation of Pay," *Organizational Behavior and Human Performance,* October 1974, pp. 170–195; and T. P. Summers and A. S. DeNisi, "In Search of Adams' Other: Reexamination of Referents Used in the Evaluation of Pay," *Human Relations,* June 1990, pp. 497–511.

41. T. Kulik and M. L. Ambrose, "Personal and Situational Determinants of Referent Choice," *Academy of Management Review,* April 1992, pp. 212–237.

42. See, for example, E. Walster, G. W. Walster, and W. G. Scott, *Equity: Theory and Research* (Boston: Allyn & Bacon, 1978); and J. Greenberg, "Cognitive Reevaluation of Outcomes in Response to Underpayment Inequity," *Academy of Management Journal,* March 1989, pp. 174–184.

43. P. S. Goodman and A. Friedman, "An Examination of Adams' Theory of Inequity," *Administrative Science Quarterly,* September 1971, pp. 271–288; and R. T. Mowday, "Equity Theory Predictions of Behavior in Organizations," in R. Steers, L. W. Porter, and G. Bigley (eds.), *Motivation and Work Behavior,* 6th ed. (New York: McGraw-Hill, 1996), pp. 111–131.

44. See, for example, R. C. Huseman, J. D. Hatfield, and E. W. Miles, "A New Perspective on Equity Theory: The Equity Sensitivity Construct," *Academy of Management Journal,* April 1987, pp. 222–234; J. A. Colquitt, "Does the Justice of One Interact with the Justice of Many? Reactions to Procedural Justice in Teams," *Journal of Applied Psychology* 89, no. 4 (2004), pp. 633–646.

45. See, for instance, J. A. Colquitt, D. E. Conlon, M. J. Wesson, C. O. L. H. Porter, and K. Y. Ng, "Justice at the Millennium: A Meta-analytic Review of the 25 Years of Organizational Justice Research," *Journal of Applied Psychology,* June 2001, pp. 425–445; T. Simons and Q. Roberson, "Why Managers Should Care About Fairness: The Effects of Aggregate Justice Perceptions on Organizational Outcomes," *Journal of Applied Psychology,* June 2003, pp. 432–443.

46. K. Leung, K. Tong, and S. S. Ho, "Effects of Interactional Justice on Egocentric Bias in Resource Allocation Decisions," *Journal of Applied Psychology* 89, no. 3 (2004), pp. 405–415.

47. G. S. Leventhal, "What Should Be Done with Equity Theory? New Approaches to the Study of Fairness in Social Relationships," in K. Gergen, M. Greenberg, and R. Willis (eds.), *Social Exchange: Advances in Theory and Research* (New York: Plenum, 1980), pp. 27–55.

48. J. C. Shaw, E. Wild, and J. A. Colquitt, "To Justify or Excuse? A Meta-analytic Review of the Effects of Explanations," *Journal of Applied Psychology* 88, no. 3 (2003), pp. 444–458.

49. R. Cropanzano, C. A. Prehar, and P. Y. Chen, "Using Social Exchange Theory to Distinguish Procedural from Interactional Justice," *Group & Organization Management* 27, no. 3 (2002), pp. 324–351; and S. G. Roch and

L. R. Shanock, "Organizational Justice in an Exchange Framework: Clarifying Organizational Justice Dimensions," *Journal of Management,* April 2006, pp. 299–322.

50. Colquitt, Conlon, Wesson, Porter, and Ng, "Justice at the Millennium," pp. 425–445.

51. V. H. Vroom, *Work and Motivation* (New York: Wiley, 1964).

52. For criticism, see T. R. Mitchell, "Expectancy Models of Job Satisfaction, Occupational Preference and Effort: A Theoretical, Methodological and Empirical Appraisal," *Psychological Bulletin,* November 1974, pp. 1053–1077. For support, see J. J. Donovan, "Work Motivation," in N. Anderson et al (eds.), *Handbook of Industrial, Work & Organizational Psychology,* vol. 2 (Thousand Oaks, CA: Sage, 2001), pp. 56–59.

53. J. Nocera, "The Anguish of Being an Analyst," *New York Times,* March 4, 2006, pp. B1, B12.

54. R. J. House, H. J. Shapiro, and M. A. Wahba, "Expectancy Theory as a Predictor of Work Behavior and Attitudes: A Re-evaluation of Empirical Evidence," *Decision Sciences,* January 1974, pp. 481–506.

55. G. Hofstede, "Motivation, Leadership, and Organization: Do American Theories Apply Abroad?" *Organizational Dynamics,* Summer 1980, p. 55.

56. Ibid.

57. S. L. Mueller and L. D. Clarke, "Political-Economic Context and Sensitivity to Equity: Differences Between the United States and the Transition Economies of Central and Eastern Europe," *Academy of Management Journal,* June 1998, pp. 319–329.

58. Harpaz, "The Importance of Work Goals: An International Perspective," *Journal of International Business Studies,* First Quarter 1990, pp. 75–93.

59. G. E. Popp, H. J. Davis, and T. T. Herbert, "An International Study of Intrinsic Motivation Composition," *Management International Review,* January 1986, pp. 28–35.

60. R. Fischer and P. B. Smith, "Reward Allocation and Culture: A Meta-analysis," *Journal of Cross-Cultural Psychology* 34, no. 3 (2003), pp. 251–268.

Chapter 7

1. J. R. Hackman and G. R. Oldham, "Motivation Through the Design of Work: Test of a Theory," *Organizational Behavior and Human Performance,* August 1976, pp. 250–279; and J. R. Hackman and G. R. Oldham, *Work Redesign* (Reading, MA: Addison-Wesley, 1980).

2. J. R. Hackman, "Work Design," in J. R. Hackman and J. L. Suttle (eds.), *Improving Life at Work* (Santa Monica, CA: Goodyear, 1977), p. 129.

3. T. Loher, R. A. Noe, N. L. Moeller, and M. P. Fitzgerald, "A Meta-analysis of the Relation of Job Characteristics to Job Satisfaction," *Journal of Applied Psychology,* May 1985, pp. 280–289; T. A. Judge, "Promote Job Satisfaction Through Mental Challenge," in E. A. Locke (ed.), *Handbook of Principles of Organizational Behavior,* pp. 75–89 (Hoboken, NJ: Wiley-Blackwell, 2003); and S. E. Humphrey, J. D. Nahrgang, and F. P. Morgeson, "Integrating Motivational, Social, and Contextual Work Design Features: A Meta-analytic Summary and Theoretical Extension of the Work Design Literature," *Journal of Applied Psychology* 92, no. 5 (2007), pp.1332–1356.

4. J. Ortega, "Job Rotation as a Learning Mechanism," *Management Science,* October 2001, pp. 1361–1370.

5. Hackman and Oldham, *Work Redesign.*

6. M. Grant, E. M. Campbell, G. Chen, K. Cottone, D. Lapedis, and K. Lee, "Impact and the Art of Motivation Maintenance: The Effects of Contact with Beneficiaries on Persistence Behavior," *Organizational Behavior and Human Decision Processes* 103 (2007), pp. 53–67.

7. M. Grant, J. E. Dutton, and B. D. Rosso, "Giving Commitment: Employee Support Programs and the Prosocial Sensemaking Process," *Academy of Management Journal* 51, no. 5 (2008), pp. 898–918.

8. "Career Development—Job Enrichment," University of New Mexico Department of Human Resources (hr.unm.edu/compensation/jobenrichment.php).

9. R. D. Pritchard, M. M. Harrell, D. DiazGrandos, and M. J. Guzman, "The Productivity Measurement and Enhancement System: A Meta-analysis," *Journal of Applied Psychology* 93, no. 3 (2008), pp. 540–567.

10. P. Morgeson, M. D. Johnson, M. A. Campion, G. J. Medsker, and T. V. Mumford, "Understanding Reactions to Job Redesign: A Quasi-Experimental Investigation of the Moderating Effects of Organizational Contact on Perceptions of Performance Behavior," *Personnel Psychology* 39 (2006), pp. 333–363.

11. From the National Study of the Changing Workforce, cited in S. Shellenbarger, "Number of Women Managers Rise," *Wall Street Journal,* September 30, 2003, p. D2.

12. Cited in "Flextime Gains in Popularity in Germany," *Manpower Argus,* September 2000, p. 4.

13. See, for example, D. A. Ralston and M. F. Flanagan, "The Effect of Flextime on Absenteeism and Turnover for Male and Female Employees," *Journal of Vocational Behavior,* April 1985, pp. 206–217; B. B. Baltes, T. E. Briggs, J. W. Huff, J. A. Wright, and G. A. Neuman, "Flexible and Compressed Workweek Schedules: A Meta-analysis of Their Effects on Work-Related Criteria," *Journal of Applied Psychology* 84, no. 4 (1999), pp. 496–513; and

J. G. Grzywacz, D. S. Carlson, and S. Shulkin, "Schedule Flexibility and Stress: Linking Formal Flexible Arrangements and Perceived Flexibility to Employee Health." *Community, Work, and Family* 11, no. 2 (2008), pp. 199–214.

14. Cited in S. Caminiti, "Fair Shares," *Working Woman,* November 1999, pp. 52–54.

15. Society for Human Resource Management, *2008 Employee Benefits* (Alexandria, VA: Author, 2008).

16. S. Shellenbarger, "Two People, One Job: It Can Really Work," *Wall Street Journal,* December 7, 1994, p. B1.

17. Dawson, "Japan: Work-Sharing Will Prolong the Pain," *BusinessWeek,* December 24, 2001, p. 46.

18. U.S. Census Bureau, *Statistical Abstract of the United States: 2002, The National Data Book, Section 12, Labor Force, Employment, and Earnings.* (Washington, DC: Author, 2002).

19. Society for Human Resource Management, *2008 Employee Benefits.*

20. See, for instance, M. Conlin, "The Easiest Commute of All," *BusinessWeek*, December 12, 2005, p. 78; and S. Shellenbarger, "Telework Is on the Rise, but It Isn't Just Done from Home Anymore," *Wall Street Journal* (January 23, 2001), p. B1.

21. U. Huws, "Wired in the Country," *People Management,* November 1999, pp. 46–47.

22. Conlin, "The Easiest Commute of All."

23. Cited in S. J. Wells, "Making Telecommuting Work," *HRMagazine,* October 2001, pp. 34–45.

24. E. Kossek, B. A. Lautsch, S. C. Eaton, "Telecommuting, Control, and Boundary Management: Correlates of Policy Use and Practice, Job Control, and Work-Family Effectiveness," *Journal of Vocational Behavior* 68, no. 2 (2006), pp. 347–367.

25. S. E. Humphrey, J. D. Nahrgang, and F. P. Morgeson, "Integrating Motivational, Social, and Contextual Work Design Features: A Meta-analytic Summary and Theoretical Extension of the Work Design Literature," *Journal of Applied Psychology* 92, no. 5 (2007), pp. 1332–1356; and R. Takeuchi, D. P. Lepak, H. Wang, and K. Takeuchi, "An Empirical Examination of the Mechanisms Mediating Between High-Performance Work Systems and the Performance of Japanese Organizations," *Journal of Applied Psychology* 92, no. 4 (2007), pp. 1069–1083.

26. See, for example, the increasing body of literature on empowerment, such as W. A. Randolph, "Re-Thinking Empowerment: Why Is It So Hard to Achieve?" *Organizational Dynamics* 29, no. 2 (2000), pp. 94–107; and S. E. Seibert, S. R. Silver, and W. A. Randolph, "Taking Empowerment to the Next Level: A Multiple-Level Model

of Empowerment, Performance, and Satisfaction," *Academy of Management Journal* 47, no. 3 (2004), pp. 332–349.

27. See, for instance, K. L. Miller and P. R. Monge, "Participation, Satisfaction, and Productivity: A Meta-analytic Review," *Academy of Management Journal,* December 1986, pp. 727–753; C. Doucouliagos, "Worker Participation and Productivity in Labor-Managed and Participatory Capitalist Firms: A Meta-analysis," *Industrial and Labor Relations Review,* October 1995, pp. 58–77; and E. A. Locke, M. Alavi, and J. A. Wagner III, "Participation in Decision Making: An Information Exchange Perspective," in G. R. Ferris (ed.), *Research in Personnel and Human Resource Management,* vol. 15 (Greenwich, CT: JAI Press, 1997), pp. 293–331.

28. K. Datta, J. P. Guthrie, and P. M. Wright, "Human Resource Management and Labor Productivity: Does Industry Matter? *Academy of Management Journal* 48, no. 1 (2005), pp. 135–145; C. M. Riordan, R. J. Vandenberg, and H. A. Richardson, "Employee Involvement Climate and Organizational Effectiveness." *Human Resource Management* 44, no. 4 (2005), pp. 471–488.

29. J. L. Cotton, *Employee Involvement* (Newbury Park, CA: Sage, 1993), p. 114.

30. Ibid., pp. 129–130, 139–140.

31. Ibid., p. 140.

32. White, "Opportunity Knocks, and It Pays a Lot Better," *Wall Street Journal,* November 13, 2006, p. B3.

33. P. S. Goodman and P. P. Pan, "Chinese Workers Pay for Wal-Mart's Low Prices," *The Washington Post,* February 8, 2004, p. A1.

34. M. Sabramony, N. Krause, J. Norton, and G. N. Burns "The Relationship Between Human Resource Investments and Organizational Performance: A Firm-Level Examination of Equilibrium Theory," *Journal of Applied Psychology* 93, no. 4 (2008), pp. 778–788.

35. See T. Henry, "States to Tie Teacher Pay to Results," *USA Today,* September 30, 1999, p. 1A.

36. Kollars, "Some Educators Win $25,000 Bonus as Test Scores Rise*," Sacramento (California) Bee,* January 8, 2001, p. 1.

37. Wysocki, Jr., "Chilling Reality Awaits Even the Employed," *Wall Street Journal,* November 5, 2001, p. A1.

38. M. Fein, "Work Measurement and Wage Incentives," *Industrial Engineering,* September 1973, pp. 49–51. For updated reviews of the effect of pay on performance, see G. D. Jenkins, Jr., N. Gupta, A. Mitra, and J. D. Shaw, "Are Financial Incentives Related to Performance? A Meta-analytic Review of Empirical Research," *Journal of Applied Psychology,* October 1998, pp. 777–787; and S. L. Rynes,

B. Gerhart, and L. Parks, "Personnel Psychology: Performance Evaluation and Pay for Performance," *Annual Review of Psychology* 56, no. 1 (2005), pp. 571–600.

39. N. Byrnes, "Pain, But No Layoffs at Nucor," *BusinessWeek,* March 26, 2009, www.businessweek.com.

40. B. Murray and B. Gerhart, "An Empirical Analysis of a Skill-Based Pay Program and Plant Performance Outcomes," *Academy of Management Journal,* February 1998, pp. 68–78 and J. D. Shaw, N. Gupta, A. Mitra, and G. E. Ledford Jr., "Success and Survival of Skill-Based Pay Plans," *Journal of Management,* February 2005, pp. 28–49.

41. N. Chi and T. Han, "Exploring the Linkages Between Formal Ownership and Psychological Ownership for the Organization: The Mediating Role of Organizational Justice," *Journal of Occupational and Organizational Psychology* 81, no. 4 (2008), pp. 691–711.

42. Employment Policy Foundation, *U.S. Wage and Productivity Growth Attainable Through Gainsharing*, May 10, 2000.

43. A. Buchko, "The Effects of Employee Ownership on Employee Attitudes: A Test of Three Theoretical Perspectives," *Work and Occupations* 19, no. 1 (1992), 59–78.

44. See data in D. Stamps, "A Piece of the Action," *Training,* March 1996, p. 66.

45. X. Zhang, K. M. Bartol, K. G. Smith, M. D. Pfarrer, and D. M. Khanin, "CEOs on the Edge: Earnings Manipulation and Stock-Based Incentive Misalignment," *Academy of Management Journal* 51, no. 2 (2008), pp. 241–258.

46. G. Hanson and W. D. Bell, *Profit Sharing and Profitability: How Profit Sharing Promotes Business Success* (London: Kogan Page, 1987); and D. D'Art and T. Turner, "Profit Sharing, Firm Performance, and Union Influence in Selected European Countries," *Personnel Review* 33, no. 3 (2004), pp. 335–350.

47. T. M. Welbourne and L. R. Gomez-Mejia, "Gainsharing: A Critical Review and a Future Research Agenda," *Journal of Management* 21, no. 3 (1995), pp. 559–609.

48. C. B. Cadsby, F. Song, and F. Tapon, "Sorting and Incentive Effects of Pay for Performance: An Experimental Investigation," *Academy of Management Journal* 50, no. 2 (2007), pp. 387–405.

49. See, for instance, M. W. Barringer and G. T. Milkovich, "A Theoretical Exploration of the Adoption and Design of Flexible Benefit Plans: A Case of Human Resource Innovation," *Academy of Management Review,* April 1998, pp. 305–324; and N. D. Cole and D. H. Flint, "Perceptions of Distributive and Procedural Justice in Employee Benefits: Flexible Versus Traditional Benefit Plans," *Journal of Managerial Psychology* 19, no. 1 (2004), pp. 19–40.

50. S. E. Markham, K. D. Scott, and G. H. McKee, "Recognizing Good Attendance: A Longitudinal, Quasi-Experimental Field Study," *Personnel Psychology,*

Autumn 2002, p. 641; and S. J. Peterson and F. Luthans, "The Impact of Financial and Nonfinancial Incentives on Business Unit Outcomes over Time," *Journal of Applied Psychology* 91, no. 1 (2006), pp. 156–165.

51. Cited in K. J. Dunham, "Amid Shrinking Workplace Morale, Employers Turn to Recognition," *Wall Street Journal,* November 19, 2002, p. B8.

52. Ibid.

53. B. M. Meglino and A. M. Korsgaard, "The Role of Other Orientation in Reactions to Job Characteristics," *Journal of Management,* February 2007, pp. 57–83.

54. M. F. Peterson and S. A. Ruiz-Quintanilla, "Cultural Socialization as a Source of Intrinsic Work Motivation," *Group & Organization Management,* June 2003, pp. 188–216.

55. P. Peters and L. den Dulk, "Cross Cultural Differences in Managers' Support for Home-Based Telework: A Theoretical Elaboration," *International Journal of Cross Cultural Management,* December 2003, pp. 329–346.

56. Brown, "Everybody Loves Flex," *Canadian HRReporter,* November 18, 2002, p. 1.

57. Unsworth, "U.K. Employers Find Flex Benefits Helpful: Survey," *Business Insurance,* May 21, 2001, pp. 19–20.

58. C. Robert, T. M. Probst, J. J. Martocchio, R. Drasgow, and J. J. Lawler, "Empowerment and Continuous Improvement in the United States, Mexico, Poland, and India: Predicting Fit on the Basis of the Dimensions of Power Distance and Individualism," *Journal of Applied Psychology,* October 2000, pp. 643–658.

59. Z. X. Chen and S. Aryee, "Delegation and Employee Work Outcomes: An Examination of the Cultural Context of Mediating Processes in China," *Academy of Management Journal* 50, no. 1 (2007), pp. 226–238.

Chapter 8

1. L. R. Sayles, "Work Group Behavior and the Larger Organization," in C. Arensburg et al. (eds.), *Research in Industrial Relations* (New York: Harper & Row, 1957), pp. 131–145.

2. J. F. McGrew, J. G. Bilotta, and J. M. Deeney, "Software Team Formation and Decay: Extending the Standard Model for Small Groups," *Small Group Research* 30, no. 2, (1999), pp. 209–234.

3. W. Tuckman, "Developmental Sequences in Small Groups," *Psychological Bulletin,* June 1965, pp. 384–399; and B. W. Tuckman and M. C. Jensen, "Stages of Small-Group Development Revisited," *Group and Organizational Studies,* December 1977, pp. 419–427.

4. J. F. George and L. M. Jessup, "Groups Over Time: What Are We Really Studying?" *International Journal of Human-Computer Studies* 47, no. 3 (1997), pp. 497–511.

5. See M. F. Peterson et al., "Role Conflict, Ambiguity, and Overload: A 21-Nation Study," *Academy of Management Journal,* April 1995, pp. 429–452; and I. H. Settles, R. M. Sellers, and A. Damas Jr., "One Role or Two? The Function of Psychological Separation in Role Conflict," *Journal of Applied Psychology,* June 2002, pp. 574–582.

6. Adapted from P. S. Goodman, E. Ravlin, and M. Schminke, "Understanding Groups in Organizations," in L. L. Cummings and B. M. Staw (eds.), *Research in Organizational Behavior,* vol. 9 (Greenwich, CT: JAI Press, 1987), p. 159.

7. Mayo, *The Human Problems of an Industrial Civilization* (New York: Macmillan, 1933); and F. J. Roethlisberger and W. J. Dickson, *Management and the Worker* (Cambridge, MA: Harvard University Press, 1939).

8. A. Kiesler and S. B. Kiesler, *Conformity* (Reading, MA: Addison-Wesley, 1969).

9. S. E. Asch, "Effects of Group Pressure upon the Modification and Distortion of Judgments," in H. Guetzkow (ed.), *Groups, Leadership and Men* (Pittsburgh: Carnegie Press, 1951), pp. 177–190; and S. E. Asch, "Studies of Independence and Conformity: A Minority of One Against a Unanimous Majority," *Psychological Monographs: General and Applied* 70, no. 9 (1956), pp. 1–70.

10. R. Bond and P. B. Smith, "Culture and Conformity: A Meta-analysis of Studies Using Asch's (1952, 1956) Line Judgment Task," *Psychological Bulletin,* January 1996, pp. 111–137.

11. See S. L. Robinson and A. M. O'Leary-Kelly, "Monkey See, Monkey Do: The Influence of Work Groups on the Antisocial Behavior of Employees," *Academy of Management Journal,* December 1998, pp. 658–672; and C. M. Berry, D. S. Ones, and P. R. Sackett, "Interpersonal Deviance, Organizational Deviance, and Their Common Correlates: A Review and Meta-Analysis," *Journal of Applied Psychology* 92, no. 2 (2007), pp. 410–424.

12. M. Pearson, L. M. Andersson, and C. L. Porath, "Assessing and Attacking Workplace Civility," *Organizational Dynamics* 29, no. 2 (2000), p. 130; see also C. Pearson, L. M. Andersson, and C. L. Porath, "Workplace Incivility," in S. Fox and P. E. Spector (eds.), *Counterproductive Work Behavior: Investigations of Actors and Targets* (Washington, DC: American Psychological Association, 2005), pp. 177–200.

13. S. Lim, L. M. Cortina, V. J. Magley, "Personal and Workgroup Incivility: Impact on Work and Health Outcomes," *Journal of Applied Psychology* 93, no. 1 (2008), pp. 95–107.

14. Robinson and O'Leary-Kelly, "Monkey See, Monkey Do"; and T. M. Glomb and H. Liao, "Interpersonal Aggression in Workgroups: Social Influence, Reciprocal, and Individual Effects," *Academy of Management Journal* 46 (2003), pp. 486–496.

15. P. Bamberger and M. Biron, "Group Norms and Excessive Absenteeism: The Role of Peer Referent Others," *Organizational Behavior and Human Decision Processes* 103, no. 2 (2007), pp. 179–196; and A. Väänänen, N. Tordera, M. Kivimäki, A. Kouvonen, J. Pentti, A. Linna, and J. Vahtera, "The Role of Work Group in Individual Sickness Absence Behavior," *Journal of Health & Human Behavior* 49, no. 4 (2008), pp. 452–467.

16. Erez, H. Elms, and E. Fong, "Lying, Cheating, Stealing: It Happens More in Groups," paper presented at the European Business Ethics Network Annual Conference, Budapest, Hungary, August 30, 2003.

17. See R. S. Feldman, *Social Psychology,* 3rd ed. (Upper Saddle River, NJ: Prentice Hall, 2001), pp. 464–465.

18. R. R. Callister and J. A. Wall Jr., "Conflict Across Organizational Boundaries: Managed Care Organizations Versus Health Care Providers," *Journal of Applied Psychology* 86, no. 4 (2001), pp. 754–763; and P. Chattopadhyay, W. H. Glick, and G. P. Huber, "Organizational Actions in Response to Threats and Opportunities," *Academy of Management Journal* 44, no. 5 (2001), pp. 937–955.

19. O. J. Harvey and C. Consalvi, "Status and Conformity to Pressures in Informal Groups," *Journal of Abnormal and Social Psychology,* Spring 1960, pp. 182–187.

20. See J. M. Levine and R. L. Moreland, "Progress in Small Group Research," in J. T. Spence, J. M. Darley, and D. J. Foss (eds.), *Annual Review of Psychology,* vol. 41 (Palo Alto, CA: Annual Reviews, 1990), pp. 585–634; and J. M. Twenge, "Changes in Women's Assertiveness in Response to Status and Roles: A Cross-Temporal Meta-analysis, 1931–1993," *Journal of Personality and Social Psychology,* July 2001, pp. 133–145.

21. H. Seijts and G. P. Latham, "The Effects of Goal Setting and Group Size on Performance in a Social Dilemma," *Canadian Journal of Behavioural Science* 32, no. 2 (2000), pp. 104–116.

22. M. E. Shaw, *Group Dynamics: The Psychology of Small Group Behavior,* 3rd ed. (New York: McGraw-Hill, 1981).

23. See, for instance, D. R. Comer, "A Model of Social Loafing in Real Work Groups," *Human Relations,* June 1995, pp. 647–667; S. M. Murphy, S. J. Wayne, R. C. Liden, and B. Erdogan, "Understanding Social Loafing: The Role of Justice Perceptions and Exchange Relationships," *Human Relations,* January 2003, pp. 61–84; and R. C. Liden, S. J. Wayne, R. A. Jaworski, and N. Bennett, "Social Loafing: A Field Investigation," *Journal of Management,* April 2004, pp. 285–304.

24. W. Moede, "Die Richtlinien der Leistungs-Psychologie," *Industrielle Psychotechnik* 4 (1927), pp. 193–207. See also D. A. Kravitz and B. Martin, "Ringelmann Rediscovered: The Original Article," *Journal of Personality and Social Psychology,* May 1986, pp. 936–941.

25. See, for example, J. A. Shepperd, "Productivity Loss in Performance Groups: A Motivation Analysis," *Psychological Bulletin,* January 1993, pp. 67–81; and S. J. Karau and K. D. Williams, "Social Loafing: A Meta-analytic Review and Theoretical Integration," *Journal of Personality and Social Psychology,* October 1993, pp. 681–706.

26. Gunnthorsdottir and A. Rapoport, "Embedding Social Dilemmas in Intergroup Competition Reduces Free-Riding," *Organizational Behavior and Human Decision Processes* 101 (2006), pp. 184–199; and E. M. Stark, J. D. Shaw, and M. K. Duffy, "Preference for Group Work, Winning Orientation, and Social Loafing Behavior in Groups," *Group and Organization Management* 32, no. 6 (2007), pp. 699–723.

27. Mullen and C. Cooper, "The Relation Between Group Cohesiveness and Performance: An Integration," *Psychological Bulletin,* March 1994, pp. 210–227; and D. J. Beal, R. R. Cohen, M. J. Burke, and C. L. McLendon, "Cohesion and Performance in Groups: A Meta-analytic Clarification of Construct Relations," *Journal of Applied Psychology,* December 2003, pp. 989–1004.

28. Ibid.

29. Based on J. L. Gibson, J. M. Ivancevich, and J. H. Donnelly Jr., *Organizations,* 8th ed. (Burr Ridge, IL: Irwin, 1994), p. 323.

30. See N. R. F. Maier, "Assets and Liabilities in Group Problem Solving: The Need for an Integrative Function," *Psychological Review,* April 1967, pp. 239–249; and G. W. Hill, "Group Versus Individual Performance: Are N+1 Heads Better Than One?" *Psychological Bulletin,* May 1982, pp. 517–539.

31. Gigone and R. Hastie, "Proper Analysis of the Accuracy of Group Judgments," *Psychological Bulletin,* January 1997, pp. 149–167; and B. L. Bonner, S. D. Sillito, and M. R. Baumann, "Collective Estimation: Accuracy, Expertise, and Extroversion as Sources of Intra-Group Influence," *Organizational Behavior and Human Decision Processes* 103 (2007), pp. 121–133.

32. See, for example, W. C. Swap and Associates, *Group Decision Making* (Newbury Park, CA: Sage, 1984).

33. L. Janis, *Groupthink* (Boston: Houghton Mifflin, 1982); W. Park, "A Review of Research on Groupthink," *Journal of Behavioral Decision Making,* July 1990, pp. 229–245; and J. N. Choi and M. U. Kim, "The Organizational Application of Groupthink and Its Limits in Organizations," *Journal of Applied Psychology,* April 1999, pp. 297–306.

34. M. E. Turner and A. R. Pratkanis, "Mitigating Groupthink by Stimulating Constructive Conflict," in C. De Dreu and E. Van de Vliert (eds.), *Using Conflict in Organizations* (London: Sage, 1997), pp. 53–71.

35. Ibid., p. 68.

36. See N. R. F. Maier, *Principles of Human Relations* (New York: Wiley, 1952); I. L. Janis, *Groupthink: Psychological Studies of Policy Decisions and Fiascoes,* 2nd ed. (Boston: Houghton Mifflin, 1982); N. Richardson Ahlfinger and J. K. Esser, "Testing the Groupthink Model: Effects of Promotional Leadership and Conformity Predisposition," *Social Behavior & Personality* 29, no. 1 (2001), pp. 31–41; and S. Schultz-Hardt, F. C. Brodbeck, A. Mojzisch, R. Kerschreiter, and D. Frey, "Group Decision Making in Hidden Profile Situations: Dissent as a Facilitator for Decision Quality," *Journal of Personality and Social Psychology* 91, no. 6 (2006), pp. 1080–1093.

37. See D. J. Isenberg, "Group Polarization: A Critical Review and Meta-analysis," *Journal of Personality and Social Psychology,* December 1986, pp. 1141–1151; J. L. Hale and F. J. Boster, "Comparing Effect Coded Models of Choice Shifts," *Communication Research Reports,* April 1988, pp. 180–186; and P. W. Paese, M. Bieser, and M. E. Tubbs, "Framing Effects and Choice Shifts in Group Decision Making," *Organizational Behavior and Human Decision Processes,* October 1993, pp. 149–165.

38. See, for example, N. Kogan and M. A. Wallach, "Risk Taking as a Function of the Situation, the Person, and the Group," in *New Directions in Psychology,* vol. 3 (New York: Holt, Rinehart and Winston, 1967); and M. A. Wallach, N. Kogan, and D. J. Bem, "Group Influence on Individual Risk Taking," *Journal of Abnormal and Social Psychology* 65 (1962), pp. 75–86.

39. R. D. Clark III, "Group-Induced Shift Toward Risk: A Critical Appraisal," *Psychological Bulletin,* October 1971, pp. 251–270.

40. Z. Krizan and R. S. Baron, "Group Polarization and Choice-Dilemmas: How Important Is Self-Categorization?" *European Journal of Social Psychology* 37, no. 1 (2007), pp. 191–201.

41. F. Osborn, *Applied Imagination: Principles and Procedures of Creative Thinking,* 3rd ed. (New York: Scribner, 1963). See also R. P. McGlynn, D. McGurk, V. S. Effland, N. L. Johll, and D. J. Harding, "Brainstorming and Task Performance in Groups Constrained by Evidence," *Organizational Behavior and Human Decision Processes,* January 2004, pp. 75–87; and R. C. Litchfield, "Brainstorming Reconsidered: A Goal-Based View," *Academy of Management Review* 33, no. 3 (2008), pp. 649–668.

42. See A. L. Delbecq, A. H. Van deVen, and D. H. Gustafson, *Group Techniques for Program Planning: A Guide to Nominal and Delphi Processes* (Glenview, IL: Scott Foresman, 1975); and P. B. Paulus and H.-C. Yang, "Idea Generation in Groups: A Basis for Creativity in Organizations," *Organizational Behavior and Human Decision Processing,* May 2000, pp. 76–87.

43. Faure, "Beyond Brainstorming: Effects of Different Group Procedures on Selection of Ideas and Satisfaction with the Process," *Journal of Creative Behavior* 38 (2004), pp. 13–34.

44. See G. Hofstede, *Cultures and Organizations: Software of the Mind* (New York, McGraw-Hill, 1991).

45. This section is based on P. R. Harris and R. T. Moran, *Managing Cultural Differences,* 5th ed. (Houston: Gulf Publishing, 1999).

46. S. Staples and L. Zhao, "The Effects of Cultural Diversity in Virtual Teams Versus Face-to-Face Teams," *Group Decision and Negotiation,* July 2006, pp. 389–406.

47. K. W. Phillips and D. L. Loyd, "When Surface and Deep-Level Diversity Collide: The Effects on Dissenting Group Members," *Organizational Behavior and Human Decision Processes* 99 (2006), pp. 143–160; and S. R. Sommers, "On Racial Diversity and Group Decision Making: Identifying Multiple Effects of Racial Composition on Jury Deliberations," *Journal of Personality and Social Psychology,* April 2006, pp. 597–612.

48. Mannix and M. A. Neale, "What Differences Make a Difference? The Promise and Reality of Diverse Teams in Organizations," *Psychological Science in the Public Interest,* October 2005, pp. 31–55.

49. T. P. Verney, "Role Perception Congruence, Performance, and Satisfaction," in D. J. Vredenburgh and R. S. Schuler (eds.), *Effective Management: Research and Application, Proceedings of the 20th Annual Eastern Academy of Management,* Pittsburgh, PA, May 1983, pp. 24–27.

50. Ibid.

51. G. Bedeian and A. A. Armenakis, "A Path-Analytic Study of the Consequences of Role Conflict and Ambiguity," *Academy of Management Journal,* June 1981, pp. 417–424; and P. L. Perrewe, K. L. Zellars, G. R. Ferris, A. M. Rossi, C. J. Kacmar, and D. A. Ralston, "Neutralizing Job Stressors: Political Skill as an Antidote to the Dysfunctional Consequences of Role Conflict," *Academy of Management Journal,* February 2004, pp. 141–152.

52. Shaw, *Group Dynamics.*

53. Mullen, C. Symons, L. Hu, and E. Salas, "Group Size, Leadership Behavior, and Subordinate Satisfaction," *Journal of General Psychology,* April 1989, pp. 155–170.

Chapter 9

1. This section is based on J. R. Katzenbach and D. K. Smith, *The Wisdom of Teams* (Cambridge, MA: Harvard University Press, 1993), pp. 21, 45, 85; and D. C. Kinlaw, *Developing Superio r Work Teams* (Lexington, MA: Lexington Books, 1991), pp. 3–21.

2. J. H. Shonk, *Team-Based Organizations* (Homewood, IL: Business One Irwin, 1992); and M. A. Verespej, "When Workers Get New Roles," *IndustryWeek,* February 3, 1992, p. 11.

3. G. Bodinson and R. Bunch, "AQP's National Team Excellence Award: Its Purpose, Value and Process," *Journal for Quality and Participation,* Spring 2003, pp. 37–42.

4. See, for example, A. Erez, J. A. LePine, and H. Elms, "Effects of Rotated Leadership and Peer Evaluation on the Functioning and Effectiveness of Self-Managed Teams: A Quasi-experiment," *Personnel Psychology,* Winter 2002, pp. 929–948.

5. See, for instance, R. A. Cook and J. L. Goff, "Coming of Age with Self-Managed Teams: Dealing with a Problem Employee," *Journal of Business and Psychology,* Spring 2002, pp. 485–496; and C. W. Langfred, "Too Much of a Good Thing? Negative Effects of High Trust and Individual Autonomy in Self-Managing Teams," *Academy of Management Journal,* June 2004, pp. 385–399.

6. W. Langfred, "The Downside of Self-Management: A Longitudinal Study of the Effects of Conflict on Trust, Autonomy, and Task Interdependence in Self-Managing Teams," *Academy of Management Journal* 50, no. 4 (2007), pp. 885–900.

7. Bodinson and Bunch, "AQP's National Team Excellence Award."

8. M. Brunelli, "How Harley-Davidson Uses Cross-Functional Teams," *Purchasing Online,* November 4, 1999, www.purchasing.com/article/CA147865.html.

9. See, for example, J. Lipnack and J. Stamps, *Virtual Teams: People Working Across Boundaries and Technology,* 2nd ed. (New York: Wiley, 2000); C. B. Gibson and S. G. Cohen (eds.), *Virtual Teams That Work* (San Francisco: Jossey-Bass, 2003); and L. L. Martins, L. L. Gilson, and M. T. Maynard, "Virtual Teams: What Do We Know and Where Do We Go from Here?" *Journal of Management,* November 2004, pp. 805–835.

10. Malhotra, A. Majchrzak, and B. Rosen, "Leading Virtual Teams," *Academy of Management Perspectives,* February 2007, pp. 60–70; and J. M. Wilson, S. S. Straus, and B. McEvily, "All in Due Time: The Development of Trust in Computer-Mediated and Face-to-Face Teams," *Organizational Behavior and Human Decision Processes* 19 (2006), pp. 16–33.

11. E. Hyatt and T. M. Ruddy, "An Examination of the Relationship Between Work Group Characteristics and Performance: Once More into the Breech," *Personnel Psychology,* Autumn 1997, p. 555.

12. This model is based on M. A. Campion, E. M. Papper, and G. J. Medsker, "Relations Between Work Team Characteristics and Effectiveness: A Replication and Extension," *Personnel Psychology,* Summer 1996, pp. 429–452; Hyatt and Ruddy, "An Examination of the Relationship Between Work Group Characteristics and Performance," pp. 553–585; and J. R. Hackman, *Leading*

Teams: Setting the Stage for Great Performance (Boston: Harvard Business School Press, 2002).

13. Hyatt and Ruddy, "An Examination of the Relationship Between Work Group Characteristics and Performance," p. 577.

14. P. Balkundi and D. A. Harrison, "Ties, Leaders, and Time in Teams: Strong Inference About Network Structure's Effects on Team Viability and Performance," *Academy of Management Journal* 49, no. 1 (2006), pp. 49–68; G. Chen, B. L. Kirkman, R. Kanfer, D. Allen, and B. Rosen, "A Multilevel Study of Leadership, Empowerment, and Performance in Teams," *Journal of Applied Psychology* 92, no. 2 (2007), pp. 331–346; and J. E. Mathieu, K. K. Gilson, and T. M. Ruddy, "Empowerment and Team Effectiveness: An Empirical Test of an Integrated Model," *Journal of Applied Psychology* 91, no. 1 (2006), pp. 97–108.

15. J. B. Carson, P. E. Tesluk, and J. A. Marrone, "Shared Leadership in Teams: An Investigation of Antecedent Conditions and Performance," *Academy of Management Journal* 50, no. 5 (2007), pp. 1217–1234.

16. K. T. Dirks, "Trust in Leadership and Team Performance: Evidence from NCAA Basketball," *Journal of Applied Psychology,* December 2000, pp. 1004–1012; and M. Williams, "In Whom We Trust: Group Membership as an Affective Context for Trust Development," *Academy of Management Review,* July 2001, pp. 377–396.

17. See S. T. Johnson, "Work Teams: What's Ahead in Work Design and Rewards Management," *Compensation & Benefits Review,* March–April 1993, pp. 35–41; and L. N. McClurg, "Team Rewards: How Far Have We Come?" *Human Resource Management,* Spring 2001, pp. 73–86.

18. R. R. Hirschfeld, M. H. Jordan, H. S. Feild, W. F. Giles, and A. A. Armenakis, "Becoming Team Players: Team Members' Mastery of Teamwork Knowledge as a Predictor of Team Task Proficiency and Observed Teamwork Effectiveness," *Journal of Applied Psychology* 91, no. 2 (2006), pp. 467–474.

19. For a more detailed breakdown of team skills, see M. J. Stevens and M. A. Campion, "The Knowledge, Skill, and Ability Requirements for Teamwork: Implications for Human Resource Management," *Journal of Management,* Summer 1994, pp. 503–530.

20. L. Jackson and J. A. LePine, "Peer Responses to a Team's Weakest Link: A Test and Extension of LePine and Van Dyne's Model," *Journal of Applied Psychology* 88, no. 3 (June 2003), pp. 459–475; and J. A. LePine, "Team Adaptation and Postchange Performance: Effects of Team Composition in Terms of Members' Cognitive Ability and Personality," *Journal of Applied Psychology* 88, no. 1 (February 2003), pp. 27–39.

21. S. T. Bell, "Deep-Level Composition Variables as Predictors of Team Performance: A Meta-analysis," *Journal of Applied Psychology* 92, no. 3 (2007), pp. 595–615; and

M. R. Barrick, G. L. Stewart, M. J. Neubert, and M. K. Mount, "Relating Member Ability and Personality to Work-Team Processes and Team Effectiveness," *Journal of Applied Psychology,* June 1998, pp. 377–391.

22. O. L. H. Porter, J. R. Hollenbeck, and D. R. Ilgen, "Backing Up Behaviors in Teams: The Role of Personality and Legitimacy of Need," *Journal of Applied Psychology* 88, no. 3 (June 2003), pp. 391–403; J. A. Colquitt, J. R. Hollenbeck, and D. R. Ilgen, "Computer-Assisted Communication and Team Decision-Making Performance: The Moderating Effect of Openness to Experience," *Journal of Applied Psychology* 87, no. 2 (April 2002), pp. 402–410; J. A. LePine, J. R. Hollenbeck, D. R. Ilgen, and J. Hedlund, "The Effects of Individual Differences on the Performance of Hierarchical Decision Making Teams: Much More Than G," *Journal of Applied Psychology* 82 (1997), pp. 803–811.

23. Barrick, Stewart, Neubert, and Mount, "Relating Member Ability and Personality to Work-Team Processes and Team Effectiveness," p. 388; and S. E. Humphrey, J. R. Hollenbeck, C. J. Meyer, and D. R. Ilgen, "Trait Configurations in Self-Managed Teams: A Conceptual Examination of the Use of Seeding for Maximizing and Minimizing Trait Variance in Teams," *Journal of Applied Psychology* 92, no. 3 (2007), pp. 885–892.

24. S. E. Humphrey, F. P. Morgeson, and M. J. Mannor, "Developing a Theory of the Strategic Core of Teams: A Role Composition Model of Team Performance," *Journal of Applied Psychology* 94, no. 1 (2009), pp. 48–61.

25. Margerison and D. McCann, *Team Management: Practical New Approaches* (London: Mercury Books, 1990).

26. Joshi and H. Roh, "The Role of Context in Work Team Diversity Research: A Meta-analytic Review," *Academy of Management Journal* 52, no. 3 (2009), pp. 599–627; and S. K. Horwitz and I. B. Horwitz, "The Effects of Team Diversity on Team Outcomes: A Meta-analytic Review of Team Demography," *Journal of Management* 33, no. 6 (2007), pp. 987–1015.

27. G. S. Van Der Vegt, J. S. Bunderson, and A. Oosterhof, "Expertness Diversity and Interpersonal Helping in Teams: Why Those Who Need the Most Help End Up Getting the Least," *Academy of Management Journal* 49, no. 5 (2006), pp. 877–893.

28. S. J. Shin and J. Zhou, "When Is Educational Specialization Heterogeneity Related to Creativity in Research and Development Teams? Transformational Leadership as a Moderator," *Journal of Applied Psychology* 92, no. 6 (2007), pp. 1709–1721.

29. J. Katzenbach, "What Makes Teams Work?" *Fast Company,* November 2000, p. 110.

30. L. A. Curral, R. H. Forrester, and J. F. Dawson, "It's What You Do and the Way That You Do It: Team Task, Team Size, and Innovation-Related Group Processes," *European*

Journal of Work & Organizational Psychology 10, no. 2 (June 2001), pp. 187–204; R. C. Liden, S. J. Wayne, and R. A. Jaworski, "Social Loafing: A Field Investigation," *Journal of Management* 30, no. 2 (2004), pp. 285–304.

31. S. A. Kiffin-Peterson and J. L. Cordery, "Trust, Individualism, and Job Characteristics of Employee Preference for Teamwork," *International Journal of Human Resource Management,* February 2003, pp. 93–116.

32. J. A. LePine, R. F. Piccolo, C. L. Jackson, J. E. Mathieu, and J. R. Saul, "A Meta-analysis of Teamwork Processes: Tests of a Multidimensional Model and Relationships with Team Effectiveness Criteria," *Personnel Psychology* 61 (2008), pp. 273–307.

33. D. Steiner, *Group Processes and Productivity* (New York: Academic Press, 1972).

34. LePine, Piccolo, Jackson, Mathieu, and Saul, "A Meta-analysis of Teamwork Processes: Tests of a Multidimensional Model and Relationships with Team Effectiveness Criteria"; and J. E. Mathieu and T. L. Rapp, "Laying the Foundation for Successful Team Performance Trajectories: The Roles of Team Charters and Performance Strategies," *Journal of Applied Psychology* 94, no. 1 (2009), pp. 90–103.

35. S. Burke, K. C. Stagl, E. Salas, L. Pierce, and D. Kendall, "Understanding Team Adaptation: A Conceptual Analysis and Model," *Journal of Applied Psychology* 91, no. 6 (2006), pp. 1189–1207.

36. Weldon and L. R. Weingart, "Group Goals and Group Performance," *British Journal of Social Psychology,* Spring 1993, pp. 307–334. See also R. P. DeShon, S. W. J. Kozlowski, A. M. Schmidt, K. R. Milner, and D. Wiechmann, "A Multiple-Goal, Multilevel Model of Feedback Effects on the Regulation of Individual and Team Performance," *Journal of Applied Psychology,* December 2004, pp. 1035–1056.

37. K. Tasa, S. Taggar, and G. H. Seijts, "The Development of Collective Efficacy in Teams: A Multilevel and Longitudinal Perspective," *Journal of Applied Psychology* 92, no. 1 (2007), pp. 17–27; and R. R. Hirschfeld and J. B. Bernerth, "Mental Efficacy and Physical Efficacy at the Team Level: Inputs and Outcomes Among Newly Formed Action Teams," *Journal of Applied Psychology* 93, no. 6 (2008), pp. 1429–1437.

38. S. W. J. Kozlowski and D. R. Ilgen, "Enhancing the Effectiveness of Work Groups and Teams," *Psychological Science in the Public Interest,* December 2006, pp. 77–124; and B. D. Edwards, E. A. Day, W. Arthur Jr., and S. T. Bell, "Relationships Among Team Ability Composition, Team Mental Models, and Team Performance," *Journal of Applied Psychology* 91, no. 3 (2006), pp. 727–736.

39. K. A. Jehn, "A Qualitative Analysis of Conflict Types and Dimensions in Organizational Groups," *Administrative Science Quarterly,* September 1997, pp. 530–557. See also R. S. Peterson and K. J. Behfar, "The Dynamic Relationship Between Performance Feedback, Trust, and Conflict in

Groups: A Longitudinal Study," *Organizational Behavior and Human Decision Processes,* September–November 2003, pp. 102–112.

40. K. J. Behfar, R. S. Peterson, E. A. Mannix, and W. M. K. Trochim, "The Critical Role of Conflict Resolution in Teams: A Close Look at the Links Between Conflict Type, Conflict Management Strategies, and Team Outcomes," *Journal of Applied Psychology* 93, no. 1 (2008), pp. 170–188.

41. K. H. Price, D. A. Harrison, and J. H. Gavin, "Withholding Inputs in Team Contexts: Member Composition, Interaction Processes, Evaluation Structure, and Social Loafing," *Journal of Applied Psychology* 91, no. 6 (2006), pp. 1375–1384.

42. See, for instance, B. L. Kirkman and D. L. Shapiro, "The Impact of Cultural Values on Employee Resistance to Teams: Toward a Model of Globalized Self-Managing Work Team Effectiveness," *Academy of Management Review,* July 1997, pp. 730–757; and B. L. Kirkman, C. B. Gibson, and D. L. Shapiro, "'Exporting' Teams: Enhancing the Implementation and Effectiveness of Work Teams in Global Affiliates," *Organizational Dynamics* 30, no. 1 (2001), pp. 12–29.

43. H. M. Guttman, "The New High-Performance Player," *The Hollywood Reporter,* October 27, 2008, www.hollywoodreporter.com.

44. T. Erickson and L. Gratton, "What It Means to Work Here," *BusinessWeek,* January 10, 2008, www.businessweek.com.

45. M. D. Johnson, J. R. Hollenbeck, S. E. Humphrey, D. R. Ilgen, D. Jundt, and C. J. Meyer, "Cutthroat Cooperation: Asymmetrical Adaptation to Changes in Team Reward Structures," *Academy of Management Journal* 49, no. 1 (2006), pp. 103–119.

46. "Watson Wyatt's Global Work Studies," www.watsonwyatt.com/research/featured/workstudy.asp.

47. E. Nicholls, H. W. Lane, and M. Brehm Brechu, "Taking Self-Managed Teams to Mexico," *Academy of Management Executive,* August 1999, pp. 15–27.

48. W. E. Watson, K. Kumar, and L. K. Michaelsen, "Cultural Diversity's Impact on Interaction Process and Performance: Comparing Homogeneous and Diverse Task Groups," *Academy of Management Journal,* June 1993, pp. 590–602.

49. F. Crown, "The Use of Group and Groupcentric Individual Goals for Culturally Heterogeneous and Homogeneous Task Groups: An Assessment of European Work Teams," *Small Group Research* 38, no. 4 (2007), pp. 489–508.

Chapter 10

1. D. K. Berlo, *The Process of Communication* (New York: Holt, Rinehart & Winston, 1960), pp. 30–32.

2. J. Langan-Fox, "Communication in Organizations: Speed, Diversity, Networks, and Influence on Organizational

Effectiveness, Human Health, and Relationships," in N. Anderson, D. S. Ones, H. K. Sinangil, and C. Viswesvaran (eds.), *Handbook of Industrial, Work and Organizational Psychology*, vol. 2 (Thousand Oaks, CA: Sage, 2001), p. 190.

3. R. L. Simpson, "Vertical and Horizontal Communication in Formal Organizations," *Administrative Science Quarterly,* September 1959, pp. 188–196; B. Harriman, "Up and Down the Communications Ladder," *Harvard Business Review,* September–October 1974, pp. 143–151; and A. G. Walker and J. W. Smither, "A Five-Year Study of Upward Feedback: What Managers Do with Their Results Matter," *Personnel Psychology,* Summer 1999, pp. 393–424.

4. P. Dvorak, "How Understanding the 'Why' of Decisions Matters," *Wall Street Journal,* March 19, 2007, p. B3.

5. J. Ewing, "Nokia: Bring on the Employee Rants," *BusinessWeek,* June 22, 2009, p. 50.

6. E. Nichols, "Hyper-Speed Managers," *HRMagazine,* April 2007, pp. 107–110.

7. L. Dulye, "Get Out of Your Office," *HRMagazine,* July 2006, pp. 99–101.

8. L. S. Rashotte, "What Does That Smile Mean? The Meaning of Nonverbal Behaviors in Social Interaction," *Social Psychology Quarterly,* March 2002, pp. 92–102.

9. N. M. Henley, "Body Politics Revisited: What Do We Know Today?" in P. J. Kalbfleisch and M. J. Cody (eds.), *Gender, Power, and Communication in Human Relationships* (Hillsdale, NJ: Lawrence Erlbaum, 1995), pp. 27–61.

10. See, for example, N. B. Kurland and L. H. Pelled, "Passing the Word: Toward a Model of Gossip and Power in the Workplace," *Academy of Management Review,* April 2000, pp. 428–438; and N. Nicholson, "The New Word on Gossip," *Psychology Today,* June 2001, pp. 41–45.

11. G. Van Hoye and F. Lievens, "Tapping the Grapevine: A Closer Look at Word-of-Mouth as a Recruitment Source," *Journal of Applied Psychology* 94, no. 2 (2009), pp. 341–352.

12. See, for instance, J. W. Newstrom, R. E. Monczka, and W. E. Reif, "Perceptions of the Grapevine: Its Value and Influence," *Journal of Business Communication,* Spring 1974, pp. 12–20; and S. J. Modic, "Grapevine Rated Most Believable," *IndustryWeek,* May 15, 1989, p. 14.

13. K. Davis, "Management Communication and the Grapevine," *Harvard Business Review,* September–October 1953, pp. 43–49.

14. K. Davis, cited in R. Rowan, "Where Did That Rumor Come From?" *Fortune,* August 13, 1979, p. 134.

15. R. L. Rosnow and G. A. Fine, *Rumor and Gossip: The Social Psychology of Hearsay* (New York: Elsevier, 1976).

16. J. K. Bosson, A. B. Johnson, K. Niederhoffer, and W. B. Swann, Jr., "Interpersonal Chemistry Through Negativity: Bonding by Sharing Negative Attitudes About Others," *Personal Relationships* 13 (2006), pp. 135–150.

17. B. Gates, "How I Work," *Fortune,* April 17, 2006, money.cnn.com.

18. D. Brady, "*!#?@ the E-mail. Can We Talk?" *BusinessWeek,* December 4, 2006, p. 109.

19. E. Binney, "Is E-mail the New Pink Slip?" *HR Magazine,* November 2006, pp. 32–33; and R. L. Rundle, "Critical Case: How an Email Rant Jolted a Big HMO," *Wall Street Journal,* April 24, 2007, pp. A1, A16.

20. S. Hourigan, "62 Trillion Spam Emails Cause Huge Carbon Footprint," *Courier Mail,* April 17, 2009, www.news.com .au/couriermail.

21. R. Stross, "The Daily Struggle to Avoid Burial by E-Mail," *New York Times,* April 21, 2008, p. BU5; H. Rhodes, "You've Got Mail . . . Again," *Gainesville Sun,* September 29, 2008, pp. 1D, 6D.

22. C. Byron, "Carrying Too Heavy a Load? The Communication and Miscommunication of Emotion by Email," *Academy of Management Review* 33, no. 2 (2008), pp. 309–327.

23. R. Zeidner, "Keeping E-mail in Check," *HRMagazine,* June 2007, pp. 70–74; "E-mail May Be Hazardous to Your Career," *Fortune,* May 14, 2007, p. 24; J. D. Glater, "Open Secrets," *New York Times,* June 27, 2008, pp. B1, B5.

24. Cited in C. Y. Chen, "The IM Invasion," *Fortune,* May 26, 2003, pp. 135–138.

25. C. Hymowitz, "Have Advice, Will Travel," *Wall Street Journal,* June 5, 2006, pp. B1, B3.

26. A. Williams, "Mind Your BlackBerry or Mind Your Manners," *New York Times,* June 21, 2009, www.nytimes.com.

27. K. Gurchiek, "Shoddy Writing Can Trip Up Employees, Organizations," *SHRM Online,* April 27, 2006, pp. 1–2.

28. E. Agnvall, "Meetings Go Virtual," *HR Magazine,* January 2009, pp. 74–77.

29. M. Richtel, "Lost in E-mail, Tech Firms Face Self-Made Beast," *New York Times,* June 14, 2008, pp. A1, A14; and M. Johnson, "Quelling Distraction," *HR Magazine,* August 2008, pp. 43–46.

30. J. Sandberg, "The Jargon Jumble," *Wall Street Journal,* October 24, 2006, p. B1.

31. F. J. Milliken, E. W. Morrison, and P. F. Hewlin, "An Exploratory Study of Employee Silence: Issues That Employees Don't Communicate Upward and Why," *Journal of Management Studies* 40, no. 6 (2003), pp. 1453–1476.

32. S. Tangirala and R. Ramunujam, "Employee Silence on Critical Work Issues: The Cross-Level Effects of Procedural

Justice Climate," *Personnel Psychology* 61, no. 1 (2008), pp. 37–68; and F. Bowen and K. Blackmon, "Spirals of Silence: The Dynamic Effects of Diversity on Organizational Voice," *Journal of Management Studies* 40, no. 6 (2003), pp. 1393–1417.

33. B. R. Schlenker and M. R. Leary, "Social Anxiety and Self-Presentation: A Conceptualization and Model," *Psychological Bulletin* 92, (1982), pp. 641–669; and L. A. Withers, and L. L. Vernon, "To Err Is Human: Embarrassment, Attachment, and Communication Apprehension," *Personality and Individual Differences* 40, no. 1 (2006), pp. 99–110.

34. See, for example, L. Stafford and J. A. Daly, "Conversational Memory: The Effects of Instructional Set and Recall Mode on Memory for Natural Conversations," *Human Communication Research,* Spring 1984, pp. 379–402; and T. L. Rodebaugh, "I Might Look OK, But I'm Still Doubtful, Anxious, and Avoidant: The Mixed Effects of Enhanced Video Feedback on Social Anxiety Symptoms," *Behaviour Research & Therapy* 42, no. 12 (December 2004), pp. 1435–1451.

35. J. A. Daly and M. D. Miller, "The Empirical Development of an Instrument of Writing Apprehension," *Research in the Teaching of English,* Winter 1975, pp. 242–249.

36. R. E. Axtell, *Gestures: The Do's and Taboos of Body Language Around the World* (New York: Wiley, 1991); Watson Wyatt Worldwide, "Effective Communication: A Leading Indicator of Financial Performance—2005/2006 Communication ROI Study," www.watsonwyatt.com/research/resrender.asp?id=w-868; and A. Markels, "Turning the Tide at P&G," *U.S. News & World Report,* October 30, 2006, p. 69.

37. See M. Munter, "Cross-Cultural Communication for Managers," *Business Horizons,* May–June 1993, pp. 75–76; and H. Ren and B. Gray, "Repairing Relationship Conflict: How Violation Types and Culture Influence the Effectiveness of Restoration Rituals," *Academy of Management Review* 34, no. 1 (2009), pp. 105–126.

38. See E. T. Hall and M. R. Hall, *Understanding Cultural Differences* (Yarmouth, ME: Intercultural Press, 1990); W. L. Adair and J. M. Brett, "The Negotiation Dance: Time, Culture, and Behavioral Sequences in Negotiation," *Organization Science* 16, no. 1 (2005), pp. 33–51; E. Giebels and P. J. Taylor, "Interaction Patterns in Crisis Negotiations: Persuasive Arguments and Cultural Differences," *Journal of Applied Psychology* 94, no. 1 (2009), pp. 5–19.

39. N. Adler, *International Dimensions of Organizational Behavior,* 4th ed. (Cincinnati, OH: South-Western Publishing, 2002), p. 94.

40. J. P. Walsh, S. J. Ashford, and T. E. Hill, "Feedback Obstruction: The Influence of the Information Environment on Employee Turnover Intentions," *Human Relations,* January 1985, pp. 23–46.

41. S. A. Hellweg and S. L. Phillips, "Communication and Productivity in Organizations: A State-of-the-Art Review," in *Proceedings of the 40th Annual Academy of Management Conference,* Detroit, 1980, pp. 188–192. See also B. A. Bechky, "Sharing Meaning Across Occupational Communities: The Transformation of Understanding on a Production Floor," *Organization Science* 14, no. 3 (May–June 2003), pp. 312–330.

Chapter 11

1. J. P. Kotter, "What Leaders Really Do," *Harvard Business Review,* May–June 1990, pp. 103–111; and J. P. Kotter, *A Force for Change: How Leadership Differs from Management* (New York: The Free Press, 1990).

2. J. G. Geier, "A Trait Approach to the Study of Leadership in Small Groups," *Journal of Communication,* December 1967, pp. 316–323.

3. S. A. Kirkpatrick and E. A. Locke, "Leadership: Do Traits Matter?" *Academy of Management Executive,* May 1991, pp. 48–60; and S. J. Zaccaro, R. J. Foti, and D. A. Kenny, "Self-Monitoring and Trait-Based Variance in Leadership: An Investigation of Leader Flexibility Across Multiple Group Situations," *Journal of Applied Psychology,* April 1991, pp. 308–315.

4. T. A. Judge, J. E. Bono, R. Ilies, and M. W. Gerhardt, "Personality and Leadership: A Qualitative and Quantitative Review," *Journal of Applied Psychology,* August 2002, pp. 765–780.

5. R. Ames and F. J. Flynn, "What Breaks a Leader: The Curvilinear Relation Between Assertiveness and Leadership," *Journal of Personality and Social Psychology* 92, no. 2 (2007), pp. 307–324.

6. K. Ng, S. Ang, and K. Chan, "Personality and Leader Effectiveness: A Moderated Mediation Model of Leadership Self-Efficacy, Job Demands, and Job Autonomy," *Journal of Applied Psychology* 93, no. 4 (2008), pp. 733–743.

7. This section is based on D. Goleman, "What Makes a Leader?" *Harvard Business Review,* November–December 1998, pp. 93–102; and D. R. Caruso and C. J. Wolfe, "Emotional Intelligence and Leadership Development," in D. David and S. J. Zaccaro (eds.), *Leader Development for Transforming Organizations: Growing Leaders for Tomorrow* (Mahwah, NJ: Lawrence Erlbaum, 2004), pp. 237–263.

8. J. Champy, "The Hidden Qualities of Great Leaders," *Fast Company* 76 (November 2003), p. 135.

9. J. Antonakis, "Why 'Emotional Intelligence' Does Not Predict Leadership Effectiveness: A Comment on Prati, Douglas, Ferris, Ammeter, and Buckley (2003)," *International Journal of Organizational Analysis* 11 (2003), pp. 355–361.

10. A. Schriesheim, C. C. Cogliser, and L. L. Neider, "Is It 'Trustworthy'? A Multiple-Levels-of-Analysis Reexamination of an Ohio State Leadership Study, with Implications for Future Research," *Leadership Quarterly,* Summer 1995, pp. 111–145; and T. A. Judge, R. F. Piccolo, and R. Ilies, "The Forgotten Ones? The Validity of Consideration and Initiating Structure in Leadership Research," *Journal of Applied Psychology,* February 2004, pp. 36–51.

11. Akst, "The Rewards of Recognizing a Job Well Done," *Wall Street Journal,* January 31, 2007, p. D9.

12. Yukl and D. D. Van Fleet, "Theory and Research on Leadership in Organizations," in M. D. Dunnette and L. M. Hough (eds.), *Handbook of Industrial and Organizational Psychology,* vol. 2 (Palo Alto, CA: Consulting Psychologists Press, 1992), pp. 147–197.

13. E. Fiedler, *A Theory of Leadership Effectiveness* (New York: McGraw-Hill, 1967).

14. S. Shiflett, "Is There a Problem with the LPC Score in LEADER MATCH?" *Personnel Psychology,* Winter 1981, pp. 765–769.

15. F. E. Fiedler, M. M. Chemers, and L. Mahar, *Improving Leadership Effectiveness: The Leader Match Concept* (New York: Wiley, 1977).

16. L. H. Peters, D. D. Hartke, and J. T. Pohlmann, "Fiedler's Contingency Theory of Leadership: An Application of the Meta-analysis Procedures of Schmidt and Hunter," *Psychological Bulletin,* March 1985, pp. 274–285; C. A. Schriesheim, B. J. Tepper, and L. A. Tetrault, "Least Preferred Coworker Score, Situational Control, and Leadership Effectiveness: A Meta-analysis of Contingency Model Performance Predictions," *Journal of Applied Psychology,* August 1994, pp. 561–573.

17. Stilwell, "A Longitudinal Study of the Early Development of Leader–Member Exchanges," *Journal of Applied Psychology,* August 1993, pp. 662–674; and S. S. Masterson, K. Lewis, and B. M. Goldman, "Integrating Justice and Social Exchange: The Differing Effects of Fair Procedures and Treatment on Work Relationships," *Academy of Management Journal* 43, no. 4 (August 2000), pp. 738–748.

18. Duchon, S. G. Green, and T. D. Taber, "Vertical Dyad Linkage: A Longitudinal Assessment of Antecedents, Measures, and Consequences," *Journal of Applied Psychology,* February 1986, pp. 56–60; R. C. Liden, S. J. Wayne, and D. Stilwell, "A Longitudinal Study of the Early Development of Leader–Member Exchanges," *Journal of Applied Psychology,* August 1993, pp. 662–674; and M. Uhl-Bien, "Relationship Development as a Key Ingredient for Leadership Development," in S. E. Murphy and R. E. Riggio (eds.), *Future of Leadership Development* (Mahwah, NJ: Lawrence Erlbaum, 2003) pp. 129–147.

19. R. Vecchio and D. M. Brazil, "Leadership and Sex-Similarity: A Comparison in a Military Setting," *Personnel Psychology* 60 (2007), pp. 303–335.

20. See, for instance, C. R. Gerstner and D. V. Day, "Meta-analytic Review of Leader–Member Exchange Theory: Correlates and Construct Issues," *Journal of Applied Psychology,* December 1997, pp. 827–844; and R. Ilies, J. D. Nahrgang, and F. P. Morgeson, "Leader–Member Exchange and Citizenship Behaviors: A Meta-analysis," *Journal of Applied Psychology* 92, no. 1 (2007), pp. 269–277.

21. D. Eden, "Leadership and Expectations: Pygmalion Effects and Other Self-fulfilling Prophecies in Organizations," *Leadership Quarterly,* Winter 1992, pp. 278–279.

22. M. Ozer, "Personal and Task-Related Moderators of Leader-Member Exchange Among Software Developers," *Journal of Applied Psychology* 93, no. 5 (2008), pp. 1174–1182.

23. M. Weber, *The Theory of Social and Economic Organization,* A. M. Henderson and T. Parsons (trans.) (New York: The Free Press, 1947).

24. J. A. Conger and R. N. Kanungo, *Charismatic Leadership in Organizations* (Thousand Oaks, CA: Sage, 1998); and R. Awamleh and W. L. Gardner, "Perceptions of Leader Charisma and Effectiveness: The Effects of Vision Content, Delivery, and Organizational Performance," *Leadership Quarterly,* Fall 1999, pp. 345–373.

25. R. J. House and J. M. Howell, "Personality and Charismatic Leadership," *Leadership Quarterly* 3 (1992), pp. 81–108; D. N. Den Hartog and P. L. Koopman, "Leadership in Organizations," in N. Anderson and D. S. Ones (eds.), *Handbook of Industrial, Work and Organizational Psychology,* vol. 2 (Thousand Oaks, CA: Sage, 2002), pp. 166–187.

26. R. J. Richardson and S. K. Thayer, *The Charisma Factor: How to Develop Your Natural Leadership Ability* (Upper Saddle River, NJ: Prentice Hall, 1993).

27. J. M. Howell and P. J. Frost, "A Laboratory Study of Charismatic Leadership," *Organizational Behavior and Human Decision Processes,* April 1989, pp. 243–269. See also M. Frese, S. Beimel, and S. Schoenborn, "Action Training for Charismatic Leadership: Two Evaluations of Studies of a Commercial Training Module on Inspirational Communication of a Vision," *Personnel Psychology,* Autumn 2003, pp. 671–697.

28. B. Shamir, R. J. House, and M. B. Arthur, "The Motivational Effects of Charismatic Leadership: A Self-Concept Theory," *Organization Science,* November 1993, pp. 577–594.

29. D. N. Den Hartog, A. H. B. De Hoogh, and A. E. Keegan, "The Interactive Effects of Belongingness and Charisma on Helping and Compliance," *Journal of Applied Psychology* 92, no. 4 (2007), pp. 1131–1139.

30. Erez, V. F. Misangyi, D. E. Johnson, M. A. LePine, and K. C. Halverson, "Stirring the Hearts of Followers: Charismatic Leadership as the Transferal of Affect," *Journal of Applied Psychology* 93, no. 3 (2008), pp. 602–615.

31. H. B. de Hoogh, D. N. Den Hartog, P. L. Koopman, H. Thierry, P. T. van den Berg, and J. G. van der Weide, "Charismatic Leadership, Environmental Dynamism, and Performance," *European Journal of Work and Organizational Psychology,* December 2004, pp. 447–471.

32. R. J. House, "A 1976 Theory of Charismatic Leadership," in J. G. Hunt and L. L. Larson (eds.), *Leadership: The Cutting Edge* (Carbondale: Southern Illinois University Press, 1977), pp. 189–207; and Robert J. House and Ram N. Aditya, "The Social Scientific Study of Leadership," *Journal of Management* 23, no. 3 (1997), p. 441.

33. J. C. Pastor, M. Mayo, and B. Shamir, "Adding Fuel to Fire: The Impact of Followers' Arousal on Ratings of Charisma," *Journal of Applied Psychology* 92, no. 6 (2007), pp. 1584–1596.

34. Cohen, S. Solomon, M. Maxfield, T. Pyszczynski, and J. Greenberg, "Fatal Attraction: The Effects of Mortality Salience on Evaluations of Charismatic, Task-Oriented, and Relationship-Oriented Leaders," *Psychological Sciences,* December 2004, pp. 846–851.

35. L. Tosi, V. Misangyi, A. Fanelli, D. A. Waldman, and F. J. Yammarino, "CEO Charisma, Compensation, and Firm Performance," *Leadership Quarterly,* June 2004, pp. 405–420.

36. See, for instance, T. A. Judge and R. F. Piccolo, "Transformational and Transactional Leadership: A Meta-analytic Test of Their Relative Validity," *Journal of Applied Psychology,* October 2004, pp. 755–768.

37. T. R. Hinkin and C. A. Schriescheim, "An Examination of 'Nonleadership': From Laissez-Faire Leadership to Leader Reward Omission and Punishment Omission," *Journal of Applied Psychology* 93, no. 6 (2008), pp. 1234–1248.

38. S. J. Shin and J. Zhou, "Transformational Leadership, Conservation, and Creativity: Evidence from Korea," *Academy of Management Journal,* December 2003, pp. 703–714; and S. A. Eisenbeiss, D. van Knippenberg, and S. Boerner, "Transformational Leadership and Team Innovation: Integrating Team Climate Principles," *Journal of Applied Psychology* 93, no. 6 (2008), pp. 1438–1446.

39. Y. Ling, Z. Simsek, M. H. Lubatkin, and J. F. Veiga, "Transformational Leadership's Role in Promoting Corporate Entrepreneurship: Examining the CEO-TMT Interface," *Academy of Management Journal* 51, no. 3 (2008), pp. 557–576.

40. E. Colbert, A. E. Kristof-Brown, B. H. Bradley, and M. R. Barrick, "CEO Transformational Leadership: The Role of Goal Importance Congruence in Top Management Teams," *Academy of Management Journal* 51, no. 1 (2008), pp. 81–96.

41. D. Zohar and O. Tenne-Gazit, "Transformational Leadership and Group Interaction as Climate Antecedents: A Social Network Analysis," *Journal of Applied Psychology* 93, no. 4 (2008), pp. 744–757.

42. J. E. Bono and T. A. Judge, "Self-Concordance at Work: Toward Understanding the Motivational Effects of Transformational Leaders," *Academy of Management Journal,* October 2003, pp. 554–571; and J. Schaubroeck, S. S. K. Lam, and S. E. Cha, "Embracing Transformational Leadership: Team Values and the Impact of Leader Behavior on Team Performance," *Journal of Applied Psychology* 92, no. 4 (2007), pp. 1020–1030.

43. S. Shinn, "21st-Century Engineer," *BizEd,* January/February, 2005, pp. 18–23.

44. J. R. Baum, E. A. Locke, and S. A. Kirkpatrick, "A Longitudinal Study of the Relation of Vision and Vision Communication to Venture Growth in Entrepreneurial Firms," *Journal of Applied Psychology,* February 2000, pp. 43–54.

45. J. Avolio, W. Zhu, W. Koh, and P. Bhatia, "Transformational Leadership and Organizational Commitment: Mediating Role of Psychological Empowerment and Moderating Role of Structural Distance," *Journal of Organizational Behavior,* December 2004, pp. 951–968.

46. R. T. Keller, "Transformational Leadership, Initiating Structure, and Substitutes for Leadership: A Longitudinal Study of Research and Development Project Team Performance," *Journal of Applied Psychology* 91, no. 1 (2006), pp. 202–210.

47. Judge and Piccolo, "Transformational and Transactional Leadership."

48. Y. Ling, Z. Simsek, M. H. Lubatkin, and J. F. Veiga, "The Impact of Transformational CEOs on the Performance of Small- to Medium-Sized Firms: Does Organizational Context Matter?" *Journal of Applied Psychology* 93, no. 4 (2008), pp. 923–934.

49. J. Schaubroeck, S. S. K. Lam, and S. E. Cha, "Embracing Transformational Leadership."

50. Hetland, G. M. Sandal, and T. B. Johnsen, "Burnout in the Information Technology Sector: Does Leadership Matter?" *European Journal of Work and Organizational Psychology* 16, no. 1 (2007), pp. 58–75; and K. B. Lowe, K. G. Kroeck, and N. Sivasubramaniam, "Effectiveness Correlates of Transformational and Transactional Leadership: A Meta-analytic Review of the MLQ Literature," *Leadership Quarterly,* Fall 1996, pp. 385–425.

51. See, for instance, J. Barling, T. Weber, and E. K. Kelloway, "Effects of Transformational Leadership Training on Attitudinal and Financial Outcomes: A Field Experiment," *Journal of Applied Psychology,* December 1996, pp. 827–832; and T. Dvir, D. Eden, and B. J. Avolio, "Impact of Transformational Leadership on Follower Development and Performance: A Field Experiment," *Academy of Management Journal,* August 2002, pp. 735–744.

52. J. Avolio and B. M. Bass, "Transformational Leadership, Charisma and Beyond," working paper, School of

Management, State University of New York, Binghamton, 1985, p. 14.

53. Tan, "CEO Pinching Penney in a Slowing Economy," *Wall Street Journal,* January 31, 2008, pp. 1–2; and A. Carter, "Lighting a Fire Under Campbell," *BusinessWeek,* December 4, 2006, pp. 96–101.

54. L. Lunsford, "Piloting Boeing's New Course," *Wall Street Journal,* June 13, 2006, pp. B1, B3.

55. van Knippenberg, D. De Cremer, and B. van Knippenberg, "Leadership and Fairness: The State of the Art," *European Journal of Work and Organizational Psychology* 16, no. 2 (2007), pp. 113–140.

56. M. E. Brown and L. K. Treviño, "Socialized Charismatic Leadership, Values Congruence, and Deviance in Work Groups," *Journal of Applied Psychology* 91, no. 4 (2006), pp. 954–962.

57. D. M. Rousseau, S. B. Sitkin, R. S. Burt, and C. Camerer, "Not So Different After All: A Cross-Discipline View of Trust," *Academy of Management Review,* July 1998, pp. 393–404; and J. A. Simpson, "Psychological Foundations of Trust," *Current Directions in Psychological Science* 16, no. 5 (2007), pp. 264–268.

58. D. E. Zand, *The Leadership Triad: Knowledge, Trust, and Power* (New York: Oxford University Press, 1997), p. 89.

59. M. Kouzes and B. Z. Posner, *Credibility: How Leaders Gain and Lose It, and Why People Demand It* (San Francisco: Jossey-Bass, 1993), p. 14.

60. R. Detert and E. R. Burris, "Leadership Behavior and Employee Voice: Is the Door Really Open?" *Academy of Management Journal* 50, no. 4 (2007), pp. 869–884.

61. J. A. Colquitt, B. A. Scott, and J. A. LePine, "Trust, Trustworthiness, and Trust Propensity: A Meta-analytic Test of Their Unique Relationships with Risk Taking and Job Performance," *Journal of Applied Psychology* 92, no. 4 (2007), pp. 909–927.

62. Comment by Jim Collins, cited in J. Useem, "Conquering Vertical Limits," *Fortune,* February 19, 2001, p. 94.

63. See, for instance, J. R. Meindl, "The Romance of Leadership as a Follower-centric Theory: A Social Constructionist Approach," *Leadership Quarterly,* Fall 1995, pp. 329–341; and B. Schyns, J. Felfe, and H. Blank, "Is Charisma Hyper-Romanticism? Empirical Evidence from New Data and a Meta-analysis," *Applied Psychology: An International Review* 56, no. 4 (2007), pp. 505–527.

64. R. Agle, N. J. Nagarajan, J. A. Sonnenfeld, and D. Srinivasan, "Does CEO Charisma Matter?" *Academy of Management Journal* 49, no. 1 (2006), pp. 161–174.

65. C. Bligh, J. C. Kohles, C. L. Pearce, J. E. Justin, and J. F. Stovall, "When the Romance Is Over: Follower Perspectives of Aversive Leadership," *Applied Psychology: An International Review* 56, no. 4 (2007), pp. 528–557.

66. Schyns, Felfe, and Blank, "Is Charisma Hyper-Romanticism?"

67. J. Cassidy, "Subprime Suspect: The Rise and Fall of Wall Street's First Black C.E.O.," *The New Yorker,* March 31, 2008, pp. 78–91.

68. S. Rosette, G. J. Leonardelli, and K. W. Phillips, "The White Standard: Racial Bias in Leader Categorization," *Journal of Applied Psychology* 93, no. 4 (2008), pp. 758–777.

69. Van Vugt and B. R. Spisak, "Sex Differences in the Emergence of Leadership During Competitions Within and Between Groups," *Psychological Science* 19, no. 9 (2008), pp. 854–858.

70. Ibid.

71. S. D. Dionne, F. J. Yammarino, L. E. Atwater, and L. R. James, "Neutralizing Substitutes for Leadership Theory: Leadership Effects and Common-Source Bias," *Journal of Applied Psychology* 87 (2002), pp. 454–464; and J. R. Villa, J. P. Howell, P. W. Dorfman, and D. L. Daniel, "Problems with Detecting Moderators in Leadership Research Using Moderated Multiple Regression," *Leadership Quarterly* 14 (2002), pp. 3–23.

72. L. A. Hambley, T. A. O'Neill, and T. J. B. Kline, "Virtual Team Leadership: The Effects of Leadership Style and Communication Medium on Team Interaction Styles and Outcomes," *Organizational Behavior and Human Decision Processes* 103 (2007), pp. 1–20; and B. J. Avolio and S. S. Kahai, "Adding the 'E' to E-Leadership: How It May Impact Your Leadership," *Organizational Dynamics* 31, no. 4 (2003), pp. 325–338.

73. Shamir, "Leadership in Boundaryless Organizations: Disposable or Indispensable?" *European Journal of Work and Organizational Psychology* 8, no. 1 (1999), pp. 49–71.

74. E. Naquin and G. D. Paulson, "Online Bargaining and Interpersonal Trust," *Journal of Applied Psychology,* February 2003, pp. 113–120.

75. Javidan, P. W. Dorfman, M. S. de Luque, and R. J. House, "In the Eye of the Beholder: Cross Cultural Lessons in Leadership from Project GLOBE," *Academy of Management Perspectives,* February 2006, pp. 67–90.

76. R. J. House, M. Javidan, P. Hanges, and P. Dorfman, "Understanding Cultures and Implicit Leadership Theories Across the Globe: An Introduction to Project GLOBE," *Journal of World Business,* Spring 2002, pp. 3–10.

77. E. Carl and M. Javidan, "Universality of Charismatic Leadership: A Multi-Nation Study," paper presented at the National Academy of Management Conference, Washington, DC, August 2001, p. 29.

78. Beccalli, "European Business Forum Asks: Do Companies Get the Leaders They Deserve?" *European Business Forum,* 2003, www.pwcglobal.com/extweb/pwcpublications.nsf/DocID/D1EC3380F589844585256D7300346A1B.

Chapter 12

1. Based on B. M. Bass, *Bass & Stogdill's Handbook of Leadership,* 3rd ed. (New York: The Free Press, 1990).

2. J. R. P. French Jr., and B. Raven, "The Bases of Social Power," in D. Cartwright (ed.), *Studies in Social Power* (Ann Arbor, MI: University of Michigan, Institute for Social Research, 1959), pp. 150–167; B. J. Raven, "The Bases of Power: Origins and Recent Developments," *Journal of Social Issues,* Winter 1993, pp. 227–251; and G. Yukl, "Use Power Effectively," in E. A. Locke (ed.), *Handbook of Principles of Organizational Behavior* (Malden, MA: Blackwell, 2004), pp. 242–247.

3. E. A. Ward, "Social Power Bases of Managers: Emergence of a New Factor," *Journal of Social Psychology,* February 2001, pp. 144–147.

4. S. R. Giessner and T. W. Schubert, "High in the Hierarchy: How Vertical Location and Judgments of Leaders' Power Are Interrelated," *Organizational Behavior and Human Decision Processes* 104, no. 1 (2007), pp. 30–44.

5. P. M. Podsakoff and C. A. Schriesheim, "Field Studies of French and Raven's Bases of Power: Critique, Reanalysis, and Suggestions for Future Research," *Psychological Bulletin,* May 1985, pp. 387–411; T. R. Hinkin and C. A. Schriesheim, "Development and Application of New Scales to Measure the French and Raven (1959) Bases of Social Power," *Journal of Applied Psychology,* August 1989, pp. 561–567; and P. P. Carson, K. D. Carson, and C. W. Roe, "Social Power Bases: A Meta-analytic Examination of Interrelationships and Outcomes," *Journal of Applied Social Psychology* 23, no. 14 (1993), pp. 1150–1169.

6. J. L. Roberts, "Striking a Hot Match," *Newsweek,* January 24, 2005, pp. 54–55.

7. See, for example, D. Kipnis and S. M. Schmidt, "Upward-Influence Styles: Relationship with Performance Evaluations, Salary, and Stress," *Administrative Science Quarterly,* December 1988, pp. 528–542; G. Yukl and J. B. Tracey, "Consequences of Influence Tactics Used with Subordinates, Peers, and the Boss," *Journal of Applied Psychology,* August 1992, pp. 525–535; G. Blickle, "Influence Tactics Used by Subordinates: An Empirical Analysis of the Kipnis and Schmidt Subscales," *Psychological Reports,* February 2000, pp. 143–154; and Yukl, "Use Power Effectively," pp. 249–252.

8. G. Yukl, *Leadership in Organizations,* 5th ed. (Upper Saddle River, NJ: Prentice Hall, 2002), pp. 141–174; G. R. Ferris, W. A. Hochwarter, C. Douglas, F. R. Blass, R. W. Kolodinsky, and D. C. Treadway, "Social Influence Processes in Organizations and Human Resource Systems," in G. R. Ferris and J. J. Martocchio (eds.), *Research in Personnel and Human Resources Management,* vol. 21 (Oxford, UK: JAI Press/Elsevier, 2003), pp. 65–127; and C. A. Higgins, T. A. Judge, and G. R. Ferris, "Influence Tactics and Work Outcomes: A Meta-analysis," *Journal of Organizational Behavior,* March 2003, pp. 89–106.

9. C. M. Falbe and G. Yukl, "Consequences for Managers of Using Single Influence Tactics and Combinations of Tactics," *Academy of Management Journal,* July 1992, pp. 638–653.

10. R. E. Petty and P. Briñol, "Persuasion: From Single to Multiple to MetaCognitive Processes," *Perspectives on Psychological Science* 3, no. 2 (2008), pp. 137–147.

11. J. Badal, "Getting a Raise from the Boss," *Wall Street Journal,* July 8, 2006, pp. B1, B5.

12. Yukl, *Leadership in Organizations.*

13. Ibid.

14. Falbe and Yukl, "Consequences for Managers of Using Single Influence Tactics and Combinations of Tactics."

15. W. Kruglanski, A. Pierro, and E. T. Higgins, "Regulatory Mode and Preferred Leadership Styles: How Fit Increases Job Satisfaction," *Basic and Applied Social Psychology* 29, no. 2 (2007), pp. 137–149; and A. Pierro, L. Cicero, and B. H. Raven, "Motivated Compliance with Bases of Social Power," *Journal of Applied Social Psychology* 38, no. 7 (2008), pp. 1921–1944.

16. G. R. Ferris, D. C. Treadway, P. L. Perrewé, R. L. Brouer, C. Douglas, and S. Lux, "Political Skill in Organizations," *Journal of Management,* June 2007, pp. 290–320; K. J. Harris, K. M. Kacmar, S. Zivnuska, and J. D. Shaw, "The Impact of Political Skill on Impression Management Effectiveness," *Journal of Applied Psychology* 92, no. 1 (2007), pp. 278–285; W. A. Hochwarter, G. R. Ferris, M. B. Gavin, P. L. Perrewé, A. T. Hall, and D. D. Frink," Political Skill as Neutralizer of Felt Accountability–Job Tension Effects on Job Performance Ratings: A Longitudinal Investigation," *Organizational Behavior and Human Decision Processes* 102 (2007), pp. 226–239; and D. C. Treadway, G. R. Ferris, A. B. Duke, G. L. Adams, and J. B. Tatcher, "The Moderating Role of Subordinate Political Skill on Supervisors' Impressions of Subordinate Ingratiation and Ratings of Subordinate Interpersonal Facilitation," *Journal of Applied Psychology* 92, no. 3 (2007), pp. 848–855.

17. C. Anderson, S. E. Spataro, and F. J. Flynn, "Personality and Organizational Culture as Determinants of Influence," *Journal of Applied Psychology* 93, no. 3 (2008), pp. 702–710.

18. S. A. Culbert and J. J. McDonough, *The Invisible War: Pursuing Self-Interest at Work* (New York: Wiley, 1980), p. 6.

19. H. Mintzberg, *Power In and Around Organizations* (Upper Saddle River, NJ: Prentice Hall, 1983), p. 26. See also

K. M. Kacmar and R. A. Baron, "Organizational Politics: The State of the Field, Links to Related Processes, and an Agenda for Future Research," in G. R. Ferris (ed.), *Research in Personnel and Human Resources Management,* vol. 17 (Greenwich, CT: JAI Press, 1999), pp. 1–39; and G. R. Ferris, D. C. Treadway, R. W. Kolokinsky, W. A. Hochwarter, C. J. Kacmar, and D. D. Frink, "Development and Validation of the Political Skill Inventory," *Journal of Management,* February 2005, pp. 126–152.

20. S. B. Bacharach and E. J. Lawler, "Political Alignments in Organizations," in R. M. Kramer and M. A. Neale (eds.), *Power and Influence in Organizations* (Thousand Oaks, CA: Sage, 1998), pp. 68–69.

21. D. Farrell and J. C. Petersen, "Patterns of Political Behavior in Organizations," *Academy of Management Review,* July 1982, p. 405. For analyses of the controversies underlying the definition of organizational politics, see A. Drory and T. Romm, "The Definition of Organizational Politics: A Review," *Human Relations,* November 1990, pp. 1133–1154; and R. S. Cropanzano, K. M. Kacmar, and D. P. Bozeman, "Organizational Politics, Justice, and Support: Their Differences and Similarities," in R. S. Cropanzano and K. M. Kacmar (eds.), *Organizational Politics, Justice and Support: Managing Social Climate at Work* (Westport, CT: Quorum Books, 1995), pp. 1–18.

22. Farrell and Petersen, "Patterns of Political Behavior in Organizations," pp. 406–407; and A. Drory, "Politics in Organization and Its Perception Within the Organization," *Organization Studies* 9, no. 2 (1988), pp. 165–179.

23. D. A. Buchanan, "You Stab My Back, I'll Stab Yours: Management Experience and Perceptions of Organization Political Behavior," *British Journal of Management* 19, no. 1 (2008), pp. 49–64.

24. J. Pfeffer, *Power in Organizations* (Marshfield, MA: Pitman, 1981).

25. Drory and Romm, "The Definition of Organizational Politics."

26. S. M. Rioux and L. A. Penner, "The Causes of Organizational Citizenship Behavior: A Motivational Analysis," *Journal of Applied Psychology,* December 2001, pp. 1306–1314; M. A. Finkelstein and L. A. Penner, "Predicting Organizational Citizenship Behavior: Integrating the Functional and Role Identity Approaches," *Social Behavior & Personality* 32, no. 4 (2004), pp. 383–398 and J. Schwarzwald, M. Koslowsky, and M. Allouf, "Group Membership, Status, and Social Power Preference," *Journal of Applied Social Psychology* 35, no. 3 (2005), pp. 644–665.

27. See, for example, G. R. Ferris, G. S. Russ, and P. M. Fandt, "Politics in Organizations," in R. A. Giacalone and P. Rosenfeld (eds.), *Impression Management in the Organization* (Hillsdale, NJ: Lawrence Erlbaum, 1989), pp. 155–156; and W. E. O'Connor and T. G. Morrison, "A Comparison of Situational and Dispositional Predictors of Perceptions of Organizational Politics," *Journal of Psychology,* May 2001, pp. 301–312.

28. Farrell and Petersen, "Patterns of Political Behavior in Organizations," p. 408.

29. G. R. Ferris and K. M. Kacmar, "Perceptions of Organizational Politics," *Journal of Management,* March 1992, pp. 93–116.

30. See, for example, P. M. Fandt and G. R. Ferris, "The Management of Information and Impressions: When Employees Behave Opportunistically," *Organizational Behavior and Human Decision Processes,* February 1990, pp. 140–158; Ferris, Russ, and Fandt, "Politics in Organizations," p. 147; and J. M. L. Poon, "Situational Antecedents and Outcomes of Organizational Politics Perceptions," *Journal of Managerial Psychology* 18, no. 2 (2003), pp. 138–155.

31. Ferris, Russ, and Fandt, "Politics in Organizations"; and K. M. Kacmar, D. P. Bozeman, D. S. Carlson, and W. P. Anthony, "An Examination of the Perceptions of Organizational Politics Model: Replication and Extension," *Human Relations,* March 1999, pp. 383–416.

32. W. A. Hochwarter, C. Kiewitz, S. L. Castro, P. L. Perrewe, and G. R. Ferris, "Positive Affectivity and Collective Efficacy as Moderators of the Relationship Between Perceived Politics and Job Satisfaction," *Journal of Applied Social Psychology,* May 2003, pp. 1009–1035; and C. C. Rosen, P. E. Levy, and R. J. Hall, "Placing Perceptions of Politics in the Context of Feedback Environment, Employee Attitudes, and Job Performance," *Journal of Applied Psychology* 91, no. 1 (2006), pp. 211–230.

33. G. R. Ferris, D. D. Frink, M. C. Galang, J. Zhou, K. M. Kacmar, and J. L. Howard, "Perceptions of Organizational Politics: Prediction, Stress-Related Implications, and Outcomes," *Human Relations,* February 1996, pp. 233–266; and E. Vigoda, "Stress-Related Aftermaths to Workplace Politics: The Relationships Among Politics, Job Distress, and Aggressive Behavior in Organizations," *Journal of Organizational Behavior,* August 2002, pp. 571–591.

34. C. Kiewitz, W. A. Hochwarter, G. R. Ferris, and S. L. Castro, "The Role of Psychological Climate in Neutralizing the Effects of Organizational Politics on Work Outcomes," *Journal of Applied Social Psychology,* June 2002, pp. 1189–1207; and M. C. Andrews, L. A. Witt, and K. M. Kacmar, "The Interactive Effects of Organizational Politics and Exchange Ideology on Manager Ratings of Retention," *Journal of Vocational Behavior,* April 2003, pp. 357–369.

35. S. Aryee, Z. Chen, and P. S. Budhwar, "Exchange Fairness and Employee Performance: An Examination of the Relationship Between Organizational Politics and Procedural Justice," *Organizational Behavior & Human Decision Processes,* May 2004, pp. 1–14; and Kacmar, Bozeman, Carlson, and Anthony, "An Examination of the Perceptions of Organizational Politics Model."

36. Kacmar, Bozeman, Carlson, and Anthony, "An Examination of the Perceptions of Organizational Politics Model," p. 389.

37. Ibid., p. 409.

38. B. E. Ashforth and R. T. Lee, "Defensive Behavior in Organizations: A Preliminary Model," *Human Relations,* July 1990, pp. 621–648.

39. M. Valle and P. L. Perrewe, "Do Politics Perceptions Relate to Political Behaviors? Tests of an Implicit Assumption and Expanded Model," *Human Relations,* March 2000, pp. 359–386.

40. M. R. Leary and R. M. Kowalski, "Impression Management: A Literature Review and Two-Component Model," *Psychological Bulletin,* January 1990, pp. 34–47.

41. See, for instance, W. L. Gardner and M. J. Martinko, "Impression Management in Organizations," *Journal of Management,* June 1988, pp. 321–338; M. C. Bolino and W. H. Turnley, "More Than One Way to Make an Impression: Exploring Profiles of Impression Management," *Journal of Management* 29, no. 2 (2003), pp. 141–160; S. Zivnuska, K. M. Kacmar, L. A. Witt, D. S. Carlson, and V. K. Bratton, "Interactive Effects of Impression Management and Organizational Politics on Job Performance," *Journal of Organizational Behavior,* August 2004, pp. 627–640; and M. C. Bolino, K. M. Kacmar, W. H. Turnley, and J. B. Gilstrap, "A Multi-Level Review of Impression Management Motives and Behaviors," *Journal of Management* 34, no. 6 (2008), pp. 1080–1109.

42. M. Snyder and J. Copeland, "Self-monitoring Processes in Organizational Settings," in R. A. Giacalone and P. Rosenfeld (eds.), *Impression Management in the Organization* (Hillsdale, NJ: Lawrence Erlbaum, 1989), p. 11; M. C. Bolino and W. H. Turnley, "More than One Way to Make an Impression: Exploring Profiles of Impression Management," *Journal of Management* 29 (2003), pp. 141–160; and W. H. Turnley and M. C. Bolino, "Achieved Desired Images While Avoiding Undesired Images: Exploring the Role of Self-Monitoring in Impression Management," *Journal of Applied Psychology,* April 2001, pp. 351–360.

43. Leary and Kowalski, "Impression Management," p. 40.

44. R. A. Baron, "Impression Management by Applicants During Employment Interviews: The 'Too Much of a Good Thing' Effect," in R. W. Eder and G. R. Ferris (eds.), *The Employment Interview: Theory, Research, and Practice* (Newbury Park, CA: Sage, 1989), pp. 204–215.

45. C. Lebherz, K. Jonas, and B. Tomljenovic, "Are We Known by the Company We Keep? Effects of Name Dropping on First Impressions," *Social Influence* 4, no. 1 (2009), pp. 62–79.

46. Ferris, Russ, and Fandt, "Politics in Organizations."

47. Z. I. Barsness, K. A. Diekmann, and M. L. Seidel, "Motivation and Opportunity: The Role of Remote Work,

Demographic Dissimilarity, and Social Network Centrality in Impression Management," *Academy of Management Journal* 48, no. 3 (2005), pp. 401–419.

48. A. P. J. Ellis, B. J. West, A. M. Ryan, and R. P. DeShon, "The Use of Impression Management Tactics in Structural Interviews: A Function of Question Type?" *Journal of Applied Psychology,* December 2002, pp. 1200–1208.

49. C. K. Stevens and A. L. Kristof, "Making the Right Impression: A Field Study of Applicant Impression Management During Job Interviews," *Journal of Applied Psychology* 80 (1995), pp. 587–606; L. A. McFarland, A. M. Ryan, and S. D. Kriska, "Impression Management Use and Effectiveness Across Assessment Methods," *Journal of Management* 29, no. 5 (2003), pp. 641–661; C. A. Higgins and T. A. Judge, "The Effect of Applicant Influence Tactics on Recruiter Perceptions of Fit and Hiring Recommendations: A Field Study," *Journal of Applied Psychology* 89, no. 4 (2004), pp. 622–632; and W. C. Tsai, C. C. Chen, and S. F. Chiu, "Exploring Boundaries of the Effects of Applicant Impression Management Tactics in Job Interviews," *Journal of Management,* February 2005, pp. 108–125.

50. D. C. Gilmore and G. R. Ferris, "The Effects of Applicant Impression Management Tactics on Interviewer Judgments," *Journal of Management,* December 1989, pp. 557–564.

51. Stevens and Kristof, "Making the Right Impression."

52. C. A. Higgins, T. A. Judge, and G. R. Ferris, "Influence Tactics and Work Outcomes: A Meta-analysis," *Journal of Organizational Behavior,* March 2003, pp. 89–106.

53. Ibid.

54. K. J. Harris, K. M. Kacmar, S. Zivnuska, and J. D. Shaw, "The Impact of Political Skill on Impression Management Effectiveness," *Journal of Applied Psychology* 92, no. 1 (2007), pp. 278–285; and D. C. Treadway, G. R. Ferris, A. B. Duke, G. L. Adams, and J. B. Thatcher, "The Moderating Role of Subordinate Political Skill on Supervisors' Impressions of Subordinate Ingratiation and Ratings of Subordinate Interpersonal Facilitation," *Journal of Applied Psychology* 92, no. 3 (2007), pp. 848–855.

55. J. D. Westphal and I. Stern, "Flattery Will Get You Everywhere (Especially if You Are a Male Caucasian): How Ingratiation, Boardroom Behavior, and Demographic Minority Status Affect Additional Board Appointments of U.S. Companies," *Academy of Management Journal* 50, no. 2 (2007), pp. 267–288.

56. O. J. Labedo, "Perceptions of Organisational Politics: Examination of the Situational Antecedent and Consequences Among Nigeria's Extension Personnel," *Applied Psychology: An International Review* 55, no. 2 (2006), pp. 255–281.

57. P. P. Fu and G. Yukl, "Perceived Effectiveness of Influence Tactics in the United States and China," *Leadership Quarterly,* Summer 2000, pp. 251–266; O. Branzei,

"Cultural Explanations of Individual Preferences for Influence Tactics in Cross-Cultural Encounters," *International Journal of Cross Cultural Management,* August 2002, pp. 203–218; G. Yukl, P. P. Fu, and R. McDonald, "Cross-Cultural Differences in Perceived Effectiveness of Influence Tactics for Initiating or Resisting Change," *Applied Psychology: An International Review,* January 2003, pp. 66–82; and P. P. Fu, T. K. Peng, J. C. Kennedy, and G. Yukl, "Examining the Preferences of Influence Tactics in Chinese Societies: A Comparison of Chinese Managers in Hong Kong, Taiwan, and Mainland China," *Organizational Dynamics* 33, no. 1 (2004), pp. 32–46.

58. Fu and Yukl, "Perceived Effectiveness of Influence Tactics in the United States and China."

59. S. J. Heine, "Making Sense of East Asian Self-Enhancement," *Journal of Cross-Cultural Psychology,* September 2003, pp. 596–602.

60. See T. Romm and A. Drory, "Political Behavior in Organizations: A Cross-Cultural Comparison," *International Journal of Value Based Management* 1 (1988), pp. 97–113; and E. Vigoda, "Reactions to Organizational Politics: A Cross-Cultural Examination in Israel and Britain," *Human Relations,* November 2001, pp. 1483–1518.

61. J. L. T. Leong, M. H. Bond, and P. P. Fu, "Perceived Effectiveness of Influence Strategies in the United States and Three Chinese Societies," *International Journal of Cross Cultural Management,* May 2006, pp. 101–120.

62. Vigoda, "Reactions to Organizational Politics," p. 1512.

63. Ibid., p. 1510.

64. R. M. Kanter, *Men and Women of the Corporation* (New York: Basic Books, 1977).

65. See, for instance, Falbe and Yukl, "Consequences for Managers of Using Single Influence Tactics and Combinations of Tactics."

66. See M. A. Rahim, "Relationships of Leader Power to Compliance and Satisfaction with Supervision: Evidence from a National Sample of Managers," *Journal of Management,* December 1989, pp. 545–556; P. A. Wilson, "The Effects of Politics and Power on the Organizational Commitment of Federal Executives," *Journal of Management,* Spring 1995, pp. 101–118; and A. R. Elangovan and J. L. Xie, "Effects of Perceived Power of Supervisor on Subordinate Stress and Motivation: The Moderating Role of Subordinate Characteristics," *Journal of Organizational Behavior,* May 1999, pp. 359–373.

67. J. Pfeffer, *Managing with Power: Politics and Influence in Organizations* (Boston: Harvard Business School Press, 1992).

68. G. R. Ferris, P. L. Perrewé, W. P. Anthony, and D. C. Gilmore, "Political Skill at Work," *Organizational Dynamics,* Spring 2000, pp. 25–37; K. K. Ahearn, G. R. Ferris, W. A. Hochwarter, C. Douglas, and A. P. Ammeter, "Leader Political Skill and Team Performance," *Journal of Management* 30, no. 3 (2004), pp. 309–327; and S. E. Seibert, M. L. Kraimer, and J. M. Crant, "What Do Proactive People Do? A Longitudinal Model Linking Proactive Personality and Career Success," *Personnel Psychology,* Winter 2001, pp. 845–874.

69. R. W. Kolodinsky, W. A. Hochwarter, and G. R. Ferris, "Nonlinearity in the Relationship Between Political Skill and Work Outcomes: Convergent Evidence from Three Studies," *Journal of Vocational Behavior,* October 2004, pp. 294–308; W. Hochwarter, "The Interactive Effects of Pro-Political Behavior and Politics Perceptions on Job Satisfaction and Affective Commitment," *Journal of Applied Social Psychology,* July 2003, pp. 1360–1378; and P. L. Perrewé, K. L. Zellars, G. R. Ferris, A. Rossi, C. J. Kacmar, and D. A. Ralston, "Neutralizing Job Stressors: Political Skill as an Antidote to the Dysfunctional Consequences of Role Conflict," *Academy of Management Journal,* February 2004, pp. 141–152.

Chapter 13

1. K. W. Thomas, "Conflict and Negotiation Processes in Organizations," in M. D. Dunnette and L. M. Hough (eds.), *Handbook of Industrial and Organizational Psychology*, 2nd ed., vol. 3 (Palo Alto, CA: Consulting Psychologists Press, 1992), pp. 651–717.

2. For a comprehensive review of the interactionist approach, see C. De Dreu and E. Van de Vliert (eds.), *Using Conflict in Organizations* (London: Sage, 1997).

3. See K. A. Jehn, "A Multimethod Examination of the Benefits and Detriments of Intragroup Conflict," *Administrative Science Quarterly,* June 1995, pp. 256–282; K. A. Jehn, "A Qualitative Analysis of Conflict Types and Dimensions in Organizational Groups," *Administrative Science Quarterly,* September 1997, pp. 530–557; K. A. Jehn and E. A. Mannix, "The Dynamic Nature of Conflict: A Longitudinal Study of Intragroup Conflict and Group Performance," *Academy of Management Journal,* April 2001, pp. 238–251; and C. K. W. De Dreu and L. R. Weingart, "Task Versus Relationship Conflict, Team Performance, and Team Member Satisfaction: A Meta-analysis," *Journal of Applied Psychology,* August 2003, pp. 741–749.

4. J. Yang and K. W. Mossholder, "Decoupling Task and Relationship Conflict: The Role of Intragroup Emotional Processing," *Journal of Organizational Behavior* 25, no. 5 (August 2004), pp. 589–605; and N. Gamero, V. González-Romá, and J. M. Peiró, "The Influence of Intra-Team Conflict on Work Teams' Affective Climate: A Longitudinal Study," *Journal of Occupational and Organizational Psychology* 81, no. 1 (2008), pp. 47–69.

5. "Survey Shows Managers Have Their Hands Full Resolving Staff Personality Conflicts," *IPMA-HR Bulletin,* November 3, 2006.

6. C. K. W. De Dreu and L. R. Weingart, "Task Versus Relationship Conflict, Team Performance, and Team Member Satisfaction."

7. C. K.W. De Dreu and M. A. West, "Minority Dissent and Team Innovation: The Importance of Participation in Decision Making," *Journal of Applied Psychology* 86, no. 6 (2001), pp. 1191–1201.

8. R. S. Peterson and K. J. Behfar, "The Dynamic Relationship Between Performance Feedback, Trust, and Conflict in Groups: A Longitudinal Study," *Organizational Behavior and Human Decision Process* 92, no. 1–2 (2003), pp. 102–112.

9. K. A. Jehn, L. Greer, S. Levine, and G. Szulanski, "The Effects of Conflict Types, Dimensions, and Emergent States on Group Outcomes," *Group Decision and Negotiation* 17, no. 6 (2008), pp. 465–495.

10. T. M. Glomb and H. Liao, "Interpersonal Aggression in Work Groups: Social Influence, Reciprocal, and Individual Effects," *Academy of Management Journal* 46, no. 4 (2003), pp. 486–496; and V. Venkataramani and R. S. Dalal, "Who Helps and Who Harms? Relational Aspects of Interpersonal Helping and Harming in Organizations," *Journal of Applied Psychology* 92, no. 4 (2007), pp. 952–966.

11. L. R. Pondy, "Organizational Conflict: Concepts and Models," *Administrative Science Quarterly,* September 1967, p. 302.

12. Ibid.

13. P. J. D. Carnevale and A. M. Isen, "The Influence of Positive Affect and Visual Access on the Discovery of Integrative Solutions in Bilateral Negotiations," *Organizational Behavior and Human Decision Processes,* February 1986, pp. 1–13.

14. See R. A. Baron, "Personality and Organizational Conflict: Effects of the Type A Behavior Pattern and Self-monitoring," *Organizational Behavior and Human Decision Processes,* October 1989, pp. 281–296; R. J. Volkema and T. J. Bergmann, "Conflict Styles as Indicators of Behavioral Patterns in Interpersonal Conflicts," *Journal of Social Psychology,* February 1995, pp. 5–15; and J. A. Rhoades, J. Arnold, and C. Jay, "The Role of Affective Traits and Affective States in Disputants' Motivation and Behavior During Episodes of Organizational Conflict," *Journal of Organizational Behavior,* May 2001, pp. 329–345.

15. See, for instance, K. A. Jehn, "Enhancing Effectiveness: An Investigation of Advantages and Disadvantages of Value-Based Intragroup Conflict," *International Journal of Conflict Management,* July 1994, pp. 223–238; R. L. Priem, D. A. Harrison, and N. K. Muir, "Structured Conflict and Consensus Outcomes in Group Decision Making," *Journal of Management* 21, no. 4 (1995), pp. 691–710; and K. A. Jehn and E. A. Mannix, "The Dynamic Nature of Conflict: A Longitudinal Study of Intragroup Conflict and Group Performance," *Academy of Management Journal,* April 2001, pp. 238–251.

16. B. A. Nijstad and S. C. Kaps, "Taking the Easy Way Out: Preference Diversity, Decision Strategies, and Decision Refusal in Groups," *Journal of Personality and Social Psychology* 94, no. 5 (2008), pp. 860–870.

17. J. Hall and M. S. Williams, "A Comparison of Decision-Making Performances in Established and Ad-hoc Groups," *Journal of Personality and Social Psychology,* February 1966, p. 217.

18. M. E. Zellmer-Bruhn, M. M. Maloney, A. D. Bhappu, and R. Salvador, "When and How Do Differences Matter? An Exploration of Perceived Similarity in Teams," *Organizational Behavior and Human Decision Processes* 107, no. 1 (2008), pp. 41–59.

19. For example, see J. A. Wall, Jr., and R. R. Callister, "Conflict and Its Management," pp. 523–526, for evidence supporting the argument that conflict is almost uniformly dysfunctional. See also P. J. Hinds, and D. E. Bailey, "Out of Sight, Out of Sync: Understanding Conflict in Distributed Teams," *Organization Science,* November–December 2003, pp. 615–632.

20. Zellmer-Bruhn, Maloney, Bhappu, and Salvador, "When and How Do Differences Matter?"

21. This section is based on F. Sommerfield, "Paying the Troops to Buck the System," *Business Month,* May 1990, pp. 77–79; W. Kiechel III, "How to Escape the Echo Chamber," *Fortune,* June 18, 1990, pp. 129–130; E. Van de Vliert and C. De Dreu, "Optimizing Performance by Stimulating Conflict," *International Journal of Conflict Management,* July 1994, pp. 211–222; E. Van de Vliert, "Enhancing Performance by Conflict-Stimulating Intervention," in C. De Dreu and E. Van de Vliert (eds.), *Using Conflict in Organizations* (London: Sage, 1997), pp. 208–222; K. M. Eisenhardt, J. L. Kahwajy, and L. J. Bourgeois III, "How Management Teams Can Have a Good Fight," *Harvard Business Review,* July–August 1997, pp. 77–85; S. Wetlaufer, "Common Sense and Conflict," *Harvard Business Review,* January–February 2000, pp. 114–124; and G. A. Okhuysen and K. M. Eisenhardt, "Excel Through Group Process," in E. A. Locke (ed.), *Handbook of Principles of Organizational Behavior* (Malden, MA: Blackwell, 2004), pp. 216–218.

22. K. J. Behfar, R. S. Peterson, E. A. Mannix, and W. M. K. Trochim, "The Critical Role of Conflict Resolution in Teams: A Close Look at the Links Between Conflict Type, Conflict Management Strategies, and Team Outcomes," *Journal of Applied Psychology* 93, no. 1 (2008), pp. 170–188; A. G. Tekleab, N. R. Quigley, and P. E. Tesluk, "A Longitudinal Study of Team Conflict, Conflict Management, Cohesion, and Team Effectiveness," *Group and Organization Management* 34, no. 2 (2009), pp. 170–205; and E. Van de Vliert, M. C. Euwema, and S. E. Huismans, "Managing Conflict with a Subordinate or a Superior: Effectiveness of Conglomerated Behavior," *Journal of Applied Psychology* 80 (1995), pp. 271–281.

23. A. Somech, H. S. Desivilya, and H. Lidogoster, "Team Conflict Management and Team Effectiveness: The Effects of Task Interdependence and Team Identification," *Journal of Organizational Behavior* 30, no. 3 (2009), pp. 359–378.

24. R. E. Walton and R. B. McKersie, *A Behavioral Theory of Labor Negotiations: An Analysis of a Social Interaction System* (New York: McGraw-Hill, 1965).

25. J. C. Magee, A. D. Galinsky, and D. H. Gruenfeld, "Power, Propensity to Negotiate, and Moving First in Competitive Interactions," *Personality and Social Psychology Bulletin,* February 2007, pp. 200–212.

26. E. Wilson, "The Trouble with Jake," *New York Times,* July 15, 2009, www.nytimes.com.

27. J. R. Curhan, H. A. Elfenbein, and H. Xu, "What Do People Value When They Negotiate? Mapping the Domain of Subjective Value in Negotiation," *Journal of Personality and Social Psychology* 91, no. 3 (2006), pp. 493–512.

28. Thomas, "Conflict and Negotiation Processes in Organizations."

29. This model is based on R. J. Lewicki, "Bargaining and Negotiation," *Exchange: The Organizational Behavior Teaching Journal* 6, no. 2 (1981), pp. 39–40.

30. J. R. Curhan, H. A. Elfenbein, and G. J. Kilduff, "Getting Off on the Right Foot: Subjective Value Versus Economic Value in Predicting Longitudinal Job Outcomes from Job Offer Negotiations," *Journal of Applied Psychology* 94, no. 2 (2009), pp. 524–534.

31. M. H. Bazerman and M. A. Neale, *Negotiating Rationally* (New York: Free Press, 1992), pp. 67–68.

32. R. P. Larrick and G. Wu, "Claiming a Large Slice of a Small Pie: Asymmetric Disconfirmation in Negotiation," *Journal of Personality and Social Psychology* 93, no. 2 (2007), pp. 212–233.

33. E. T. Amanatullah, M. W. Morris, and J. R. Curhan, "Negotiators Who Give Too Much: Unmitigated Communion, Relational Anxieties, and Economic Costs in Distributive and Integrative Bargaining," *Journal of Personality and Social Psychology* 95, no. 3 (2008), pp. 723–738.

34. C. Watson and L. R. Hoffman, "Managers as Negotiators: A Test of Power Versus Gender as Predictors of Feelings, Behavior, and Outcomes," *Leadership Quarterly,* Spring 1996, pp. 63–85.

35. A. E. Walters, A. F. Stuhlmacher, and L. L. Meyer, "Gender and Negotiator Competitiveness: A Meta-analysis," *Organizational Behavior and Human Decision Processes,* October 1998, pp. 1–29; and A. F. Stuhlmacher and A. E. Walters, "Gender Differences in Negotiation Outcome: A Meta-analysis," *Personnel Psychology,* Autumn 1999, pp. 653–677.

36. Stuhlmacher and Walters, "Gender Differences in Negotiation Outcome," p. 655.

37. H. R. Bowles, L. Babcock, and L. Lei, "Social Incentives for Gender Differences in the Propensity to Initiative Negotiations: Sometimes It Does Hurt to Ask," *Organizational Behavior and Human Decision Processes* 103 (2007), pp. 84–103.

38. L. J. Kray, A. D. Galinsky, and L. Thompson, "Reversing the Gender Gap in Negotiations: An Exploration of Stereotype Regeneration," *Organizational Behavior & Human Decision Processes,* March 2002, pp. 386–409.

39. H. R. Markus and S. Kitayama, "Culture and the Self: Implications for Cognition, Emotion, and Motivation," *Psychological Review* 98, no. 2 (1991), pp. 224–253; and H. Ren and B. Gray, "Repairing Relationship Conflict: How Violation Types and Culture Influence the Effectiveness of Restoration Rituals," *Academy of Management Review* 34, no. 1 (2009), pp. 105–126.

40. M. J. Gelfand, M. Higgins, L. H. Nishii, J. L. Raver, A. Dominguez, F. Murakami, S. Yamaguchi, and M. Toyama, "Culture and Egocentric Perceptions of Fairness in Conflict and Negotiation," *Journal of Applied Psychology,* October 2002, pp. 833–845; and Z. Ma, "Chinese Conflict Management Styles and Negotiation Behaviours: An Empirical Test," *International Journal of Cross Cultural Management,* April 2007, pp. 101–119.

41. P. P. Fu, X. H. Yan, Y. Li, E. Wang, and S. Peng, "Examining Conflict-Handling Approaches by Chinese Top Management Teams in IT Firms," *International Journal of Conflict Management* 19, no. 3 (2008), pp. 188–209.

42. Gelfand et al., "Culture and Egocentric Perceptions of Fairness in Conflict and Negotiation," pp. 833–845; and X. Lin and S. J. Miller, "Negotiation Approaches: Direct and Indirect Effect of National Culture," *International Marketing Review* 20, no. 3 (2003), pp. 286–303.

43. W. L. Adair, T. Okumura, and J. M. Brett, "Negotiation Behavior When Cultures Collide: The United States and Japan," *Journal of Applied Psychology,* June 2001, pp. 371–385; and W. L. Adair, L. Weingart, and J. Brett, "The Timing and Function of Offers in U.S. and Japanese Negotiations," *Journal of Applied Psychology* 92, no. 4 (2007), pp. 1056–1068.

44. S. Kopelman, "The Effect of Culture and Power on Cooperation in Commons Dilemmas: Implications for Global Resource Management," *Organizational Behavior and Human Decision Processes* 108, no. 1 (2009), pp. 153–163.

45. J. Graham, "The Influence of Culture on Business Negotiations," *Journal of International Business Studies,* Spring 1985, pp. 81–96.

46. K. W. Thomas, "Toward Multidimensional Values in Teaching: The Example of Conflict Behaviors," *Academy of Management Review,* July 1977, p. 487.

Chapter 14

1. See, for instance, R. L. Daft, *Organization Theory and Design,* 10th ed. (Cincinnati, OH: South-Western Publishing, 2010).

2. See, for instance, J. H. Gittell, "Supervisory Span, Relational Coordination, and Flight Departure Performance: A Reassessment of Postbureaucracy Theory," *Organization Science,* July–August 2001, pp. 468–483.

3. J. Child and R. G. McGrath, "Organizations Unfettered: Organizational Form in an Information-Intensive Economy," *Academy of Management Journal,* December 2001, pp. 1135–1148.

4. H. Mintzberg, *Structure in Fives: Designing Effective Organizations* (Upper Saddle River, NJ: Prentice Hall, 1983), p. 157.

5. L. R. Burns and D. R. Wholey, "Adoption and Abandonment of Matrix Management Programs: Effects of Organizational Characteristics and Interorganizational Networks," *Academy of Management Journal,* February 1993, pp. 106–138.

6. See, for instance, T. Sy and L. S. D'Annunzio, "Challenges and Strategies of Matrix Organizations: Top-Level and Mid-Level Managers' Perspectives," *Human Resource Planning* 28, no. 1 (2005), pp. 39–48.

7. N. Anand and R. L. Daft, "What Is the Right Organization Design?" *Organizational Dynamics* 36, no. 4 (2007), pp. 329–344.

8. See, for instance, R. E. Miles and C. C. Snow, "The New Network Firm: A Spherical Structure Built on Human Investment Philosophy," *Organizational Dynamics,* Spring 1995, pp. 5–18; and N. S. Contractor, S. Wasserman, and K. Faust, "Testing Multitheoretical, Multilevel Hypotheses About Organizational Networks: An Analytic Framework and Empirical Example," *Academy of Management Review* 31, no. 3 (2006) pp. 681–703.

9. C. B. Gibson and J. L. Gibbs, "Unpacking the Concept of Virtuality: The Effects of Geographic Dispersion, Electronic Dependence, Dynamic Structure, and National Diversity on Team Innovation," *Administrative Science Quarterly* 51, no. 3 (2006), pp. 451–495.

10. "GE: Just Your Average Everyday $60 Billion Family Grocery Store," *IndustryWeek,* May 2, 1994, pp. 13–18.

11. See J. P. Guthrie and D. K. Datta, "Dumb and Dumber: The Impact of Downsizing on Firm Performance as Moderated by Industry Conditions," *Organization Science* 19, no. 1 (2008), pp. 108–123; and W. F. Cascio, C. E. Young, and J. R. Morris, "Financial Consequences of Employment-Change Decisions in Major U.S. Corporations," *Academy of Management Journal* 40 (1997), pp. 1175–1189.

12. See, for example, C. O. Trevor and A. J. Nyberg, "Keeping Your Headcount When All About You Are Losing Theirs: Downsizing, Voluntary Turnover Rates, and the Moderating Role of HR Practices," *Academy of Management Journal* 51, no. 2 (2008), pp. 259–276; and T. M. Probst, S. M. Stewart, M. L. Gruys, and B. W. Tierney, "Productivity, Counterproductivity and Creativity: The Ups and Downs of Job Insecurity," *Journal of Occupational and Organizational Psychology* 80, no. 3 (2007), pp. 479–497.

13. C. D. Zatzick, and R. D. Iverson, "High-Involvement Management and Workforce Reduction: Competitive Advantage or Disadvantage?" *Academy of Management Journal* 49, no. 5 (2006), pp. 999–1015; and J. D. Kammeyer-Mueller, H. Liao, and R. D. Arvey, "Downsizing and Organizational Performance: A Review of the Literature from a Stakeholder Perspective," *Research in Personnel and Human Resources Management* 20 (2001), pp. 269–329.

14. T. Burns and G. M. Stalker, *The Management of Innovation* (London: Tavistock, 1961); and J. A. Courtright, G. T. Fairhurst, and L. E. Rogers, "Interaction Patterns in Organic and Mechanistic Systems," *Academy of Management Journal,* December 1989, pp. 773–802.

15. See, for instance, J. M. Pennings, "Structural Contingency Theory: A Reappraisal," in B. M. Staw and L. L. Cummings (eds.), *Research in Organizational Behavior,* vol. 14 (Greenwich, CT: JAI Press, 1992), pp. 267–309; and A. Drach-Zahavy and A. Freund, "Team Effectiveness Under Stress: A Structural Contingency Approach," *Journal of Organizational Behavior* 28, no. 4 (2007), pp. 423–450.

16. T. L. Amburgey and T. Dacin, "As the Left Foot Follows the Right? The Dynamics of Strategic and Structural Change," *Academy of Management Journal,* December 1994, pp. 1427–1452.

17. See R. E. Miles and C. C. Snow, *Organizational Strategy, Structure, and Process* (New York: McGraw-Hill, 1978).

18. See C. Perrow, "A Framework for the Comparative Analysis of Organizations," *American Sociological Review,* April 1967, pp. 194–208; J. Hage and M. Aiken, "Routine Technology, Social Structure, and Organizational Goals," *Administrative Science Quarterly,* September 1969, pp. 366–377; C. C. Miller, W. H. Glick, Y. Wang, and G. P. Huber, "Understanding Technology-Structure Relationships: Theory Development and Meta-analytic Theory Testing," *Academy of Management Journal,* June 1991, pp. 370–399; and W. D. Sine, H. Mitsuhashi, and D. A. Kirsch, "Revisiting Burns and Stalker: Formal Structure and New Venture Performance in Emerging Economic Sectors," *Academy of Management Journal* 49, no. 1 (2006), pp. 121–132.

19. G. G. Dess and D. W. Beard, "Dimensions of Organizational Task Environments," *Administrative Science Quarterly,* March 1984, pp. 52–73; E. A. Gerloff, N. K. Muir, and W. D. Bodensteiner, "Three Components of Perceived Environmental Uncertainty: An Exploratory Analysis of the Effects of Aggregation," *Journal of Management,* December 1991, pp. 749–768.

20. C. S. Spell and T. J. Arnold, "A Multi-Level Analysis of Organizational Justice and Climate, Structure, and Employee Mental Health," *Journal of Management* 33, no. 5 (2007), pp. 724–751; and M. L. Ambrose and M. Schminke, "Organization Structure as a Moderator of the Relationship Between Procedural Justice, Interactional Justice, Perceived Organizational Support, and Supervisory Trust," *Journal of Applied Psychology* 88, no. 2 (2003), pp. 295–305.

21. See, for instance, L. W. Porter and E. E. Lawler III, "Properties of Organization Structure in Relation to Job Attitudes and Job Behavior," *Psychological Bulletin,* July 1965, pp. 23–51; C. S. Spell and T. J. Arnold, "A Multi-Level Analysis of Organizational Justice Climate, Structure, and Employee Mental Health," *Journal of Management* 33, no. 5 (2007), pp. 724–751; and J. D. Shaw and N. Gupta, "Job Complexity, Performance, and Well-Being: When Does Supplies-Values Fit Matter? *Personnel Psychology* 57, no. 4, 847–879.

22. See, for instance, B. Schneider, H. W. Goldstein, and D. B. Smith, "The ASA Framework: An Update," *Personnel Psychology* 48, no. 4 (1995), pp. 747–773; and R. E. Ployhart, J. A. Weekley, and K. Baughman, "The Structure and Function of Human Capital Emergence: A Multilevel Examination of the Attraction-Selection-Attrition Model," *Academy of Management Journal* 49, no. 4 (2006), pp. 661–677.

23. P. Dvorak, "Making U.S. Management Ideas Work Elsewhere," *Wall Street Journal,* May 22, 2006, p. B3.

24. See, for example, P. R. Harris and R. T. Moran, *Managing Cultural Differences,* 5th ed. (Houston, TX: Gulf Publishing, 1999).

Chapter 15

1. This seven-item description is based on C. A. O'Reilly III, J. Chatman, and D. F. Caldwell, "People and Organizational Culture: A Profile Comparison Approach to Assessing Person-Organization Fit," *Academy of Management Journal,* September 1991, pp. 487–516; and J. A. Chatman and K. A. Jehn, "Assessing the Relationship Between Industry Characteristics and Organizational Culture: How Different Can You Be?" *Academy of Management Journal,* June 1994, pp. 522–553.

2. See S. A. Sackmann, "Culture and Subcultures: An Analysis of Organizational Knowledge," *Administrative Science Quarterly,* March 1992, pp. 140–161; and G. Hofstede, "Identifying

Organizational Subcultures: An Empirical Approach," *Journal of Management Studies,* January 1998, pp. 1–12.

3. D. A. Hoffman and L. M. Jones, "Leadership, Collective Personality, and Performance," *Journal of Applied Psychology* 90, no. 3 (2005), pp. 509–522.

4. S. Hamm, "No Letup—And No Apologies," *BusinessWeek,* October 26, 1998, pp. 58–64; and C. Carlson, "Former Intel Exec Slams Microsoft Culture," *eWEEK.com,* March 26, 2002, www.eweek.com/article2/0,1759,94976,00.asp.

5. See, for example, J. B. Sorensen, "The Strength of Corporate Culture and the Reliability of Firm Performance," *Administrative Science Quarterly,* March 2002, pp. 70–91; and J. Rosenthal and M. A. Masarech, "High-Performance Cultures: How Values Can Drive Business Results," *Journal of Organizational Excellence,* Spring 2003, pp. 3–18.

6. Y. Wiener, "Forms of Value Systems: A Focus on Organizational Effectiveness and Cultural Change and Maintenance," *Academy of Management Review,* October 1988, p. 536; and B. Schneider, A. N. Salvaggio, and M. Subirats, "Climate Strength: A New Direction for Climate Research," *Journal of Applied Psychology* 87 (2002), pp. 220–229.

7. C. Vandenberghe, "Organizational Culture, Person-Culture Fit, and Turnover: A Replication in the Health Care Industry," *Journal of Organizational Behavior,* March 1999, pp. 175–184; and M. Schulte, C. Ostroff, S. Shmulyian, and A. Kinicki, "Organizational Climate Configurations: Relationships to Collective Attitudes, Customer Satisfaction, and Financial Performance," *Journal of Applied Psychology* 94, no. 3 (2009), pp. 618–634.

8. S. L. Dolan and S. Garcia, "Managing by Values: Cultural Redesign for Strategic Organizational Change at the Dawn of the Twenty-First Century," *Journal of Management Development* 21, no. 2 (2002), pp. 101–117.

9. T. E. Deal and A. A. Kennedy, "Culture: A New Look Through Old Lenses," *Journal of Applied Behavioral Sciences,* November 1983, p. 501.

10. Y. Ling, Z. Simsek, M. H. Lubatkin, and J. F. Veiga, "Transformational Leadership's Role in Promoting Corporate Entrepreneurship: Examining the CEO-TMT Interface," *Academy of Management Journal* 51, no. 3 (2008), pp. 557–576; and A. Malhotra, A. Majchrzak, and B. Rosen, Benson, "Leading Virtual Teams," *Academy of Management Perspectives* 21, no. 1 (2007), pp. 60–70.

11. J. Z. Carr, A. M. Schmidt, J. K. Ford, and R. P. DeShon, "Climate Perceptions Matter: A Meta-analytic Path Analysis Relating Molar Climate, Cognitive and Affective States, and Individual Level Work Outcomes," *Journal of Applied Psychology* 88, no. (2003), pp. 605–619.

12. Schulte, Ostroff, Shmulyian, and Kinicki, "Organizational Climate Configurations: Relationships to Collective Attitudes, Customer Satisfaction, and Financial Performance."

13. See, for example, D. S. Pugh, J. Dietz, A. P. Brief, and J. W. Wiley, "Looking Inside and Out: The Impact of Employee and Community Demographic Composition on Organizational Diversity Climate," *Journal of Applied Psychology* 93, no. 6 (2008), pp. 1422–1428; and J. C. Wallace, E. Popp, and S. Mondore, "Safety Climate as a Mediator Between Foundation Climates and Occupational Accidents: A Group-Level Investigation," *Journal of Applied Psychology* 91, no. 3 (2006), pp. 681–688.

14. T. B. Lawrence, M. K. Mauws, B. Dyck, and R. F. Kleysen, "The Politics of Organizational Learning: Integrating Power into the 4I Framework," *Academy of Management Review,* January 2005, pp. 180–191.

15. Sorensen, "The Strength of Corporate Culture and the Reliability of Firm Performance."

16. See, for instance, P. L. Moore, "She's Here to Fix the Xerox," *BusinessWeek,* August 6, 2001, pp. 47–48; and C. Ragavan, "FBI Inc.," *U.S. News & World Report,* June 18, 2001, pp. 15–21.

17. See T. Cox Jr., *Cultural Diversity in Organizations: Theory, Research & Practice* (San Francisco: Berrett-Koehler, 1993), pp. 162–170; and D. L. Stone, E. F. Stone-Romero, and K. M. Lukaszewski, "The Impact of Cultural Values on the Acceptance and Effectiveness of Human Resource Management Policies and Practices," *Human Resource Management Review* 17, no. 2 (2007), pp. 152–165.

18. K. Labich, "No More Crude at Texaco," *Fortune,* September 6, 1999, pp. 205–212; and "Rooting Out Racism," *BusinessWeek,* January 10, 2000, p. 66.

19. P. Gumbel, "Return of the Urge to Merge," *Time Europe Magazine,* July 13, 2003, www.time.com/time/europe/magazine/article/0,13005,901030721-464418,00.html.

20. S. F. Gale, "Memo to AOL Time Warner: Why Mergers Fail—Case Studies," *Workforce Management,* February 2003, www.workforce.com; and W. Bock, "Mergers, Bubbles, and Steve Case," *Wally Bock's Monday Memo,* January 20, 2003, www.mondaymemo.net/030120feature.htm.

21. E. H. Schein, "The Role of the Founder in Creating Organizational Culture," *Organizational Dynamics,* Summer 1983, pp. 13–28.

22. E. H. Schein, "Leadership and Organizational Culture," in F. Hesselbein, M. Goldsmith, and R. Beckhard (eds.), *The Leader of the Future* (San Francisco: Jossey-Bass, 1996), pp. 61–62.

23. B. Schneider, H. W. Goldstein, and D. B. Smith, "The ASA Framework: An Update," *Personnel Psychology,* Winter 1995, pp. 747–773; and W. Li, Y. Wang, P. Taylor, K. Shi, and D. He, "The Influence of Organizational Culture on Work-Related Personality Requirement Ratings: A Multilevel Analysis," *International Journal of Selection and Assessment* 16, no. 4 (2008), pp. 366–384.

24. R. Levering and M. Moskowitz, "And the Winners Are . . . ," *Fortune,* February 2, 2009, pp. 67–78.

25. D. C. Hambrick and P. A. Mason, "Upper Echelons: The Organization as a Reflection of Its Top Managers," *Academy of Management Review,* April 1984, pp. 193–206; and H. M. Trice and J. M. Beyer, "Cultural Leadership in Organizations," *Organization Science,* May 1991, pp. 149–169.

26. See, for instance, J. P. Wanous, *Organizational Entry,* 2nd ed. (New York: Addison-Wesley, 1992); G. T. Chao, A. M. O'Leary-Kelly, S. Wolf, H. J. Klein, and P. D. Gardner, "Organizational Socialization: Its Content and Consequences," *Journal of Applied Psychology,* October 1994, pp. 730–743; and D. M. Cable and C. K. Parsons, "Socialization Tactics and Person-Organization Fit," *Personnel Psychology,* Spring 2001, pp. 1–23.

27. S. Schubert and T. C. Miller, "Where Bribery Was Just a Line Item," *New York Times,* December 21, 2008, pp. 1, 6.

28. K. Rhodes, "Breaking in the Top Dogs," *Training,* February 2000, pp. 67–74.

29. J. Van Maanen and E. H. Schein, "Career Development," in J. R. Hackman and J. L. Suttle (eds.), *Improving Life at Work* (Santa Monica, CA: Goodyear, 1977), pp. 58–62; and D. C. Feldman, "The Multiple Socialization of Organization Members," *Academy of Management Review,* April 1981, p. 310.

30. C. J. Collins, "The Interactive Effects of Recruitment Practices and Product Awareness on Job Seekers' Employer Knowledge and Application Behaviors," *Journal of Applied Psychology* 92, no. 1 (2007), pp. 180–190.

31. G. Chen and R. J. Klimoski, "The Impact of Expectations on Newcomer Performance in Teams as Mediated by Work Characteristics, Social Exchanges, and Empowerment," *Academy of Management Journal* 46 (2003), pp. 591–607; C. R. Wanberg and J. D. Kammeyer-Mueller, "Predictors and Outcomes of Proactivity in the Socialization Process," *Journal of Applied Psychology* 85 (2000), pp. 373–385; and J. D. Kammeyer-Mueller and C. R. Wanberg, "Unwrapping the Organizational Entry Process: Disentangling Multiple Antecedents and Their Pathways to Adjustment," *Journal of Applied Psychology* 88 (2003), pp. 779–794.

32. Van Maanen and Schein, "Career Development," p. 59.

33. E. W. Morrison, "Newcomers' Relationships: The Role of Social Network Ties During Socialization," *Academy of Management Journal* 45 (2002), pp. 1149–1160.

34. T. N. Bauer, T. Bodner, B. Erdogan, D. M. Truxillo, and J. S. Tucker, "Newcomer Adjustment During Organizational Socialization: A Meta-analytic Review of Antecedents, Outcomes, and Methods," *Journal of Applied Psychology* 92, no. 3 (2007), pp. 707–721.

35. E. Ransdell, "The Nike Story? Just Tell It!" *Fast Company,* January–February 2000, pp. 44–46.

36. D. M. Boje, "The Storytelling Organization: A Study of Story Performance in an Office-Supply Firm," *Administrative Science Quarterly,* March 1991, pp. 106–126; C. H. Deutsch, "The Parables of Corporate Culture," *New York Times,* October 13, 1991, p. F25; and M. Ricketts and J. G. Seiling, "Language, Metaphors, and Stories: Catalysts for Meaning Making in Organizations," *Organization Development Journal,* Winter 2003, pp. 33–43.

37. See K. Kamoche, "Rhetoric, Ritualism, and Totemism in Human Resource Management," *Human Relations,* April 1995, pp. 367–385.

38. V. Matthews, "Starting Every Day with a Shout and a Song," *Financial Times,* May 2, 2001, p. 11; and M. Gimein, "Sam Walton Made Us a Promise," *Fortune,* March 18, 2002, pp. 121–130.

39. Rafaeli and M. G. Pratt, "Tailored Meanings: On the Meaning and Impact of Organizational Dress," *Academy of Management Review,* January 1993, pp. 32–55; and J. M. Higgins and C. McAllaster, "Want Innovation? Then Use Cultural Artifacts That Support It," *Organizational Dynamics,* August 2002, pp. 74–84.

40. *DCAcronyms* (Seattle: Boeing, April 1997).

41. See B. Victor and J. B. Cullen, "The Organizational Bases of Ethical Work Climates," *Administrative Science Quarterly,* March 1988, pp. 101–125; R. L. Dufresne, "An Action Learning Perspective on Effective Implementation of Academic Honor Codes," *Group & Organization Management,* April 2004, pp. 201–218; and A. Ardichvilli, J. A. Mitchell, and D. Jondle, "Characteristics of Ethical Business Cultures," *Journal of Business Ethics* 85, no. 4 (2009), pp. 445–451.

42. J. A. Byrne, "The Environment Was Ripe for Abuse," *BusinessWeek,* February 25, 2002, pp. 118–120; and A. Raghavan, K. Kranhold, and A. Barrionuevo, "How Enron Bosses Created a Culture of Pushing Limits," *Wall Street Journal* (August 26, 2002), p. A1.

43. J. P. Mulki, J. F. Jaramillo, and W. B. Locander, "Critical Role of Leadership on Ethical Climate and Salesperson Behaviors," *Journal of Business Ethics* 86, no. 2 (2009), pp. 125–141; and M. E. Brown, L. K. Treviño, and D. A. Harrison, "Ethical Leadership: A Social Learning Perspective for Construct Development and Testing," *Organizational Behavior and Human Decision Processes* 97, no. 2 (2005), pp. 117–134.

44. D. M. Mayer, M. Kuenzi, R. Greenbaum, M. Bardes, and S. Salvador, "How Low Does Ethical Leadership Flow? Test of a Trickle-Down Model," *Organizational Behavior and Human Decision Processes* 108, no. 1 (2009), pp. 1–13.

45. M. L. Gruys, S. M. Stewart, J. Goodstein, M. N. Bing, and A. C. Wicks, "Values Enactment in Organizations: A Multi-Level Examination," *Journal of Management* 34, no. 4 (2008), pp. 806–843.

46. D. L. Nelson and C. L. Cooper (eds.), *Positive Organizational Behavior* (London: Sage, 2007); K. S. Cameron, J. E. Dutton, and R. E. Quinn (eds.), *Positive Organizational Scholarship: Foundations of a New Discipline* (San Francisco: Berrett-Koehler, 2003); and F. Luthans and C. M. Youssef, "Emerging Positive Organizational Behavior," *Journal of Management,* June 2007, pp. 321–349.

47. J. Robison, "Great Leadership Under Fire," *Gallup Leadership Journal,* March 8, 2007, pp. 1–3.

48. R. Wagner and J. K. Harter, *12: The Elements of Great Managing* (New York: Gallup Press, 2006).

49. R. Wagner and J. K. Harter, "Performance Reviews Without the Anxiety," *Gallup Leadership Journal,* July 12, 2007, pp. 1–4; and Wagner and Harter, *12: The Elements of Great Managing.*

50. S. Fineman, "On Being Positive: Concerns and Counterpoints," *Academy of Management Review* 31, no. 2 (2006), pp. 270–291.

51. D. J. McCarthy and S. M. Puffer, "Interpreting the Ethicality of Corporate Governance Decision in Russia: Utilizing Integrative Social Contracts Theory to Evaluate the Relevance of Agency Theory Norms," *Academy of Management Review* 33, no. 1 (2008), pp. 11–31.

52. P. Dvorak, "A Firm's Culture Can Get Lost in Translation," *Wall Street Journal,* April 3, 2006, pp. B1, B3; K. Kranhold, "The Immelt Era, Five Years Old, Transforms GE," *Wall Street Journal,* September 11, 2006, pp. B1, B3; and S. McCartney, "Teaching Americans How to Behave Abroad," *Wall Street Journal,* April 11, 2006, pp. D1, D4.

53. J. A. Chatman, "Matching People and Organizations: Selection and Socialization in Public Accounting Firms," *Administrative Science Quarterly,* September 1991, pp. 459–484; and A. E. M. Van Vianen, "Person-Organization Fit: The Match Between Newcomers' and Recruiters' Preferences for Organizational Cultures," *Personnel Psychology,* Spring 2000, pp. 113–149.

54. J. E. Sheridan, "Organizational Culture and Employee Retention," *Academy of Management Journal,* December 1992, pp. 1036–1056.

Chapter 16

1. P. G. Audia and S. Brion, "Reluctant to Change: Self-Enhancing Responses to Diverging Performance Measures," *Organizational Behavior and Human Decision Processes* 102 (2007), pp. 255–269.

2. M. Fugate, A. J. Kinicki, and G. E. Prussia, "Employee Coping with Organizational Change: An Examination of Alternative Theoretical Perspectives and Models," *Personnel Psychology* 61, no. 1 (2008), pp. 1–36.

3. M. T. Hannan, L. Pólos, and G. R. Carroll, "The Fog of Change: Opacity and Asperity in Organizations," *Administrative Science Quarterly,* September 2003. pp. 399–432.

4. J. P. Kotter and L. A. Schlesinger, "Choosing Strategies for Change," *Harvard Business Review,* March–April 1979, pp. 106–114.

5. P. C. Fiss and E. J. Zajac, "The Symbolic Management of Strategic Change: Sensegiving via Framing and Decoupling," *Academy of Management Journal* 49, no. 6 (2006), pp. 1173–1193.

6. D. M. Herold, D. B. Fedor, and S. D. Caldwell, "Beyond Change Management: A Multilevel Investigation of Contextual and Personal Influences on Employees' Commitment to Change," *Journal of Applied Psychology* 92, no. 4 (2007), pp. 942–951; and G. B. Cunningham, "The Relationships Among Commitment to Change, Coping with Change, and Turnover Intentions," *European Journal of Work and Organizational Psychology* 15, no. 1 (2006), pp. 29–45.

7. K. van Dam, S. Oreg, and B. Schyns, "Daily Work Contexts and Resistance to Organisational Change: The Role of Leader-Member Exchange, Development Climate, and Change Process Characteristics," *Applied Psychology: An International Review* 57, no. 2 (2008), pp. 313–334.

8. D. B. Fedor, S. Caldwell, and D. M. Herold, "The Effects of Organizational Changes on Employee Commitment: A Multilevel Investigation," *Personnel Psychology* 59 (2006), pp. 1–29.

9. S. M. Elias, "Employee Commitment in Times of Change: Assessing the Importance of Attitudes Toward Organizational Change," *Journal of Management* 35, no. 1 (2009), pp. 37–55.

10. T. A. Judge, C. J. Thoresen, V. Pucik, and T. M. Welbourne, "Managerial Coping with Organizational Change: A Dispositional Perspective," *Journal of Applied Psychology,* February 1999, pp. 107–122; and S. Oreg, "Resistance to Change: Developing an Individual Differences Measure," *Journal of Applied Psychology,* August 2003, pp. 680–693.

11. J. W. B. Lang and P. D. Bliese, "General Mental Ability and Two Types of Adaptation to Unforseen Change: Applying Discontinuous Growth Models to the Task-Change Paradigm," *Journal of Applied Psychology* 94, no. 2 (2009), pp. 411–428.

12. K. Lewin, *Field Theory in Social Science* (New York: Harper & Row, 1951).

13. J. B. Sorensen, "The Strength of Corporate Culture and the Reliability of Firm Performance," *Administrative Science Quarterly,* March 2002, pp. 70–91.

14. J. Amis, T. Slack, and C. R. Hinings, "The Pace, Sequence, and Linearity of Radical Change," *Academy of Management Journal,* February 2004, pp. 15–39; and E. Autio, H. J. Sapienza, and J. G. Almeida, "Effects of Age at Entry, Knowledge Intensity, and Imitability on International Growth," *Academy of Management Journal,* October 2000, pp. 909–924.

15. J. P. Kotter, "Leading Changes: Why Transformation Efforts Fail," *Harvard Business Review,* March–April 1995, pp. 59–67; and J. P. Kotter, *Leading Change* (Cambridge, MA: Harvard Business School Press, 1996).

16. For a sampling of various OD definitions, see H. K. Sinangil and F. Avallone, "Organizational Development and Change," in N. Anderson, D. S. Ones, H. K. Sinangil, and C. Viswesvaran (eds.), *Handbook of Industrial, Work and Organizational Psychology*, vol. 2 (Thousand Oaks, CA: Sage, 2001), pp. 332–335; and R. J. Marshak and D. Grant, "Organizational Discourse and New Organization Development Practices," *British Journal of Management* 19, no. 1 (2008), pp. S7–S19.

17. See, for instance, R. Lines, "Influence of Participation in Strategic Change: Resistance, Organizational Commitment and Change Goal Achievement," *Journal of Change Management,* September 2004, pp. 193–215.

18. J. E. Edwards and M. D. Thomas, "The Organizational Survey Process: General Steps and Practical Considerations," in P. Rosenfeld, J. E. Edwards, and M. D. Thomas (eds.), *Improving Organizational Surveys: New Directions, Methods, and Applications* (Newbury Park, CA: Sage, 1993), pp. 3–28.

19. E. H. Schein, *Process Consultation: Its Role in Organizational Development*, 2nd ed. (Reading, MA: Addison-Wesley, 1988), p. 9. See also E. H. Schein, *Process Consultation Revisited: Building Helpful Relationships* (Reading, MA: Addison-Wesley, 1999).

20. Schein, *Process Consultation.*

21. W. Dyer, *Team Building: Issues and Alternatives* (Reading, MA: Addison-Wesley, 1994).

22. R. R. Blake, J. S. Mouton, and R. L. Sloma, "The Union–Management Intergroup Laboratory: Strategy for Resolving Intergroup Conflict," *Journal of Applied Behavioral Science,* 1 (1965), pp. 25–57.

23. See, for example, R. Fry, F. Barrett, J. Seiling, and D. Whitney (eds.), *Appreciative Inquiry & Organizational Transformation: Reports from the Field* (Westport, CT: Quorum, 2002); J. K. Barge and C. Oliver, "Working with Appreciation in Managerial Practice," *Academy of*

Management Review, January 2003, pp. 124–142; and D. van der Haar and D. M. Hosking, "Evaluating Appreciative Inquiry: A Relational Constructionist Perspective," *Human Relations,* August 2004, pp. 1017–1036.

24. D. Anfuso, "Core Values Shape W. L. Gore's Innovative Culture," *Workforce,* March 1999, pp. 48–51; and A. Harrington, "Who's Afraid of a New Product?" *Fortune,* November 10, 2003, pp. 189–192.

25. See, for instance, R. M. Kanter, "When a Thousand Flowers Bloom: Structural, Collective and Social Conditions for Innovation in Organizations," in B. M. Staw and L. L. Cummings (eds.), *Research in Organizational Behavior,* vol. 10 (Greenwich, CT: JAI Press, 1988), pp. 169–211.

26. Ibid., pp. 555–590.

27. See P. R. Monge, M. D. Cozzens, and N. S. Contractor, "Communication and Motivational Predictors of the Dynamics of Organizational Innovation," *Organization Science,* May 1992, pp. 250–274.

28. J. M. Howell and C. A. Higgins, "Champions of Change," *Business Quarterly*, Spring 1990, pp. 31–32; and D. L. Day, "Raising Radicals: Different Processes for Championing Innovative Corporate Ventures," *Organization Science,* May 1994, pp. 148–172.

29. Howell and Higgins, "Champions of Change."

30. See, for instance, S. Armour, "Rising Job Stress Could Affect Bottom Line," *USA Today,* July 29, 2003, p. 1B; J. Schramm, "Work/Life On Hold," *HRMagazine* 53, October 2008, p. 120.

31. Adapted from R. S. Schuler, "Definition and Conceptualization of Stress in Organizations," *Organizational Behavior and Human Performance,* April 1980, p. 189. For an updated review of definitions, see C. L. Cooper, P. J. Dewe, and M. P. O'Driscoll, *Organizational Stress: A Review and Critique of Theory, Research, and Applications* (Thousand Oaks, CA: Sage, 2002).

32. N. P. Podsakoff, J. A. LePine, and M. A. LePine, "Differential Challenge-Hindrance Stressor Relationships with Job Attitudes, Turnover Intentions, Turnover, and Withdrawal Behavior: A Meta-analysis," *Journal of Applied Psychology* 92, no. 2 (2007), pp. 438–454; and J. A. LePine, M. A. LePine, and C. L. Jackson, "Challenge and Hindrance Stress: Relationships with Exhaustion, Motivation to Learn, and Learning Performance," *Journal of Applied Psychology,* October 2004, pp. 883–891.

33. S. Gilboa, A. Shirom, Y. Fried, and C. Cooper, "A Meta-analysis of Work Demand Stressors and Job Performance: Examining Main and Moderating Effects," *Personnel Psychology* 61, no. 2 (2008), pp. 227–271.

34. J. C. Wallace, B. D. Edwards, T. Arnold, M. L. Frazier, and D. M. Finch, "Work Stressors, Role-Based Performance, and

the Moderating Influence of Organizational Support," *Journal of Applied Psychology* 94, no. 1 (2009), pp. 254–262.

35. L. W. Hunter and S. M. B. Thatcher, "Feeling the Heat: Effects of Stress, Commitment, and Job Experience on Job Performance," *Academy of Management Journal* 50, no. 4 (2007), pp. 953–968.

36. J. C. Wallace, B. D. Edwards, T. Arnold, M. L. Frazier, and D. M. Finch, "Work Stressors, Role-Based Performance, and the Moderating Influence of Organizational Support," *Journal of Applied Psychology* 94, no. 1 (2009), pp. 254–262.

37. N. W. Van Yperen and O. Janssen, "Fatigued and Dissatisfied or Fatigued but Satisfied? Goal Orientations and Responses to High Job Demands," *Academy of Management Journal,* December 2002, pp. 1161–1171; and N. W. Van Yperen and M. Hagedoorn, "Do High Job Demands Increase Intrinsic Motivation or Fatigue or Both? The Role of Job Control and Job Social Support," *Academy of Management Journal,* June 2003, pp. 339–348.

38. J. de Jonge and C. Dormann, "Stressors, Resources, and Strain at Work: A Longitudinal Test of the Triple-Match Principle," *Journal of Applied Psychology* 91, no. 5 (2006), pp. 1359–1374.

39. Schuler, "Definition and Conceptualization of Stress," pp. 200–205; and R. L. Kahn and M. Byosiere, "Stress in Organizations," in M. D. Dunnette and L. M. Hough (eds.), *Handbook of Industrial and Organizational Psychology,* 2nd ed., vol. 3 (Palo Alto, CA: Consulting Psychologists Press, 1992), pp. 604–610.

40. See T. A. Beehr and J. E. Newman, "Job Stress, Employee Health, and Organizational Effectiveness: A Facet Analysis, Model, and Literature Review," *Personnel Psychology,* Winter 1978, pp. 665–699; and B. D. Steffy and J. W. Jones, "Workplace Stress and Indicators of Coronary-Disease Risk," *Academy of Management Journal,* September 1988, pp. 686–698.

41. J. Schaubroeck, J. R. Jones, and J. L. Xie, "Individual Differences in Utilizing Control to Cope with Job Demands: Effects on Susceptibility to Infectious Disease," *Journal of Applied Psychology,* April 2001, pp. 265–278.

42. Steffy and Jones, "Workplace Stress and Indicators of Coronary-Disease Risk," p. 687.

43. C. L. Cooper and J. Marshall, "Occupational Sources of Stress: A Review of the Literature Relating to Coronary Heart Disease and Mental Ill Health," *Journal of Occupational Psychology* 49, no. 1 (1976), pp. 11–28.

44. J. R. Hackman and G. R. Oldham, "Development of the Job Diagnostic Survey," *Journal of Applied Psychology,* April 1975, pp. 159–170.

45. L. L. Meier, N. K. Semmer, A. Elfering, and N. Jacobshagen, "The Double Meaning of Control: Three-Way

Interactions Between Internal Resources, Job Control, and Stressors at Work," *Journal of Occupational Health Psychology* 13, no. 3 (2008), pp. 244–258.

46. E. M. de Croon, J. K. Sluiter, R. W. B. Blonk, J. P. J. Broersen, and M. H. W. Frings-Dresen, "Stressful Work, Psychological Job Strain, and Turnover: A 2-Year Prospective Cohort Study of Truck Drivers," *Journal of Applied Psychology,* June 2004, pp. 442–454; and R. Cropanzano, D. E. Rupp, and Z. S. Byrne, "The Relationship of Emotional Exhaustion to Work Attitudes, Job Performance, and Organizational Citizenship Behaviors," *Journal of Applied Psychology,* February 2003. pp. 160–169.

47. The following discussion has been influenced by J. E. Newman and T. A. Beehr, "Personal and Organizational Strategies for Handling Job Stress," *Personnel Psychology,* Spring 1979, pp. 1–38; J. M. Ivancevich and M. T. Matteson, "Organizational Level Stress Management Interventions: A Review and Recommendations," *Journal of Organizational Behavior Management,* Fall–Winter 1986, pp. 229–248; M. T. Matteson and J. M. Ivancevich, "Individual Stress Management Interventions: Evaluation of Techniques," *Journal of Management Psychology,* January 1987, pp. 24–30; J. M. Ivancevich, M. T. Matteson, S. M. Freedman, and J. S. Phillips, "Worksite Stress Management Interventions," *American Psychologist,* February 1990, pp. 252–261; and R. Schwarzer, "Manage Stress at Work Through Preventive and Proactive Coping," in E. A. Locke (ed.), *Handbook of Principles of Organizational Behavior* (Malden, MA: Blackwell, 2004), pp. 342–355.

48. T. H. Macan, "Time Management: Test of a Process Model," *Journal of Applied Psychology,* June 1994, pp. 381–391; and B. J. C. Claessens, W. Van Eerde, C. G. Rutte, and R. A. Roe, "Planning Behavior and Perceived Control of Time at Work," *Journal of Organizational Behavior,* December 2004, pp. 937–950.

49. See, for example, G. Lawrence-Ell, *The Invisible Clock: A Practical Revolution in Finding Time for Everyone and Everything* (Seaside Park, NJ: Kingsland Hall, 2002); and B. Tracy, *Time Power* (New York: AMACOM, 2004).

50. S. A. Devi, "Aging Brain: Prevention of Oxidative Stress by Vitamin E and Exercise," *Scientific World Journal* 9 (2009), pp. 366–372. See also J. Kiely and G. Hodgson, "Stress in the Prison Service: The Benefits of Exercise Programs," *Human Relations,* June 1990, pp. 551–572.

51. E. J. Forbes and R. J. Pekala, "Psychophysiological Effects of Several Stress Management Techniques," *Psychological Reports,* February 1993, pp. 19–27; and M. Der Hovanesian, "Zen and the Art of Corporate Productivity," *BusinessWeek,* July 28, 2003, p. 56.

52. E. R. Greenglass and L. Fiksenbaum, "Proactive Coping, Positive Affect, and Well-Being: Testing for Mediation Using Path Analysis," *European Psychologist* 14, no. 1 (2009), pp. 29–39; and P. Miquelon and R. J. Vallerand, "Goal Motives, Well-Being, and Physical Health: Happiness and Self-Realization as Psychological Resources under Challenge," *Motivation and Emotion* 30, no. 4 (2006), pp. 259–272.

53. S. E. Jackson, "Participation in Decision Making as a Strategy for Reducing Job-Related Strain," *Journal of Applied Psychology,* February 1983, pp. 3–19.

54. K. M. Richardson and H. R. Rothstein, "Effects of Occupational Stress Management Intervention Programs: A Meta-analysis," *Journal of Occupational Health Psychology* 13, no. 1 (2008), pp. 69–93.

55. See S. Shane, S. Venkataraman, and I. MacMillan, "Cultural Differences in Innovation Championing Strategies," *Journal of Management* 21, no. 5 (1995), pp. 931–952.

56. J. Chen, C. Silverthorne, and J. Hung, "Organization Communication, Job Stress, Organizational Commitment, and Job Performance of Accounting Professionals in Taiwan and America," *Leadership & Organization Development Journal* 27, no. 4 (2006), pp. 242–249; C. Liu, P. E. Spector, and L. Shi, "Cross-National Job Stress: A Quantitative and Qualitative Study," *Journal of Organizational Behavior,* February 2007, pp. 209–239.

57. P. E. Spector, T. D. Allen, S. A. Y. Poelmans, L. M. Lapierre, C. L. Cooper, M. O'Driscoll, et al., "Cross National Differences in Relationships of Work Demands, Job Satisfaction, and Turnover Intention with Work-Family Conflict," *Personnel Psychology* 60, no. 4 (2007), pp. 805–835.

58. H. M. Addae and X. Wang, "Stress at Work: Linear and Curvilinear Effects of Psychological-, Job-, and Organization-Related Factors: An Exploratory Study of Trinidad and Tobago," *International Journal of Stress Management,* November 2006, pp. 476–493.

59. P. E. Spector et al., "A Cross-National Comparative Study of Work-Family Stressors, Working Hours, and Well-Being: China and Latin America Versus the Anglo World," *Personnel Psychology,* Spring 2004, pp. 119–142.

60. P. S. Goodman and L. B. Kurke, "Studies of Change in Organizations: A Status Report," in P. S. Goodman (ed.), *Change in Organizations* (San Francisco: Jossey-Bass, 1982), p. 1.

61. Kahn and Byosiere, "Stress in Organizations," pp. 605–608.

GLINDEX   (Combined Glossary and Index)

Definitions are shown in italics.

A

Abilities, of team members, 127–128

Absenteeism, 22, 23, 94

Accenture, 143–144

Accessibility, of attitudes, 15–16

Accommodating, *the willingness of one party in a conflict to place the opponent's interests above his or her own,* 190, 201

Accuracy, 42

Acquisitions, organizational culture as barrier to, 222–223

Acting, 33

Adams, J. Stacy, 84

Adjourning stage, *the final stage in group development for temporary groups, characterized by concern with wrapping up activities rather than task performance,* 108

Admiral, 231

Affect, *a broad range of feelings that people experience,* 14, 27

  positive and negative, 28–29

Affect intensity, *individual differences in the strength with which individuals experience their emotions,* 30

Affective commitment, *an emotional attachment to the organization and a belief in its values,* 17

Affective component, *the emotional or feeling component of an attitude,* 14

Age, 8, 32

Agreeableness, *a personality dimension that describes someone who is good natured, cooperative, and trusting,* 44, 46

AirAsia, 232

Airbus, 222

All-channel network, 140

Allport, Gordon, 41

Amazon.com, 9

Ambiguity, 141

America Online (AOL), 223

American Airlines, 232

Ameriquest, 235

Anchoring bias, *a tendency to fixate on initial information, from which one then fails to adequately adjust for subsequent information,* 64

Anger, 28, 37

Anthropology, *the study of societies for the purpose of learning about human beings and their activities,* 5

Antisocial behavior, 112

Anxiety, 141, 147

Apex Digital, 210

Apologies, 181

Appeals, 173

Appearance norms, 110

Apple Computer, 43, 159, 213, 217

Appreciative inquiry (AI), *an approach that seeks to identify the unique qualities and special strengths of an organization, which can then be built on to improve performance,* 241

Arousal, 82

Asch, Solomon, 111, 117, 223

Ash, Mary Kay, 157

Asian-Pacific countries. *see also individual* countries listed by name

  group status, 120

  organizational structure, 217

  status, 120

  stress, 247

  teams and teamwork, 133

Assertiveness, 190

AT&T, 43, 211, 217

Attitudes, *evaluative statements, either favorable or unfavorable, concerning objects, people, or events,* 13

  behavior and, 15

  intergroup development and, 241

  job, 16–17, 38

  main components of, 14

  moderating variables of, 15–16

Attribution, 69

Attribution theory, *an attempt to determine whether an individual's behavior is internally or externally caused,* 58

Attribution theory of leadership, *leadership is merely an attribution that people make about other individuals,* 165–166

Audience, 174

Auglaize Provico, 230

Australia

  decision making, 69

  group status, 120

  hand gestures in, 147

  motivation, 88

  service industries in, 7

  status in, 120

Austria, 247

Authentic leaders, *leaders who know who they are, know what they believe in and value, and act on those values and beliefs openly and candidly; their followers would consider them to be ethical people,* 163

Authority, *rights inherent in a managerial position to give orders and expect the orders to be obeyed,* 205

Autonomy, *the degree to which a job provides substantial freedom and discretion to the individual in scheduling the work and in determining the procedure to be used in carrying it out,* 91

Availability bias, *the tendency for people to base their judgments on information that is readily available to them,* 64

Avoiding, *the desire to withdraw from or suppress a conflict,* 190, 201

Avon, 160

B

Bandura, Albert, 82, 83

Bargaining strategies, 178, 193–196

Basex, 144–145

BATNA, *the best alternative to a negotiated agreement; the least the individual should accept,* 197

Bear Stearns, 235

Behavior and attitudes, 15

Behavior stage, of conflict process, 188, 191

Behavioral component, *an intention to behave in a certain way toward someone or something,* 14

Behavioral symptoms, of stress, 245

Behavioral theories of leadership, *theories proposing that specific behaviors differentiate leaders from nonleaders,* 152–153

Benefits, 103

Best alternative to a negotiated agreement (BATNA), 197

Bethlehem Steel, 9

Biases, 59–60, 63–65, 71

Big Five Model, *a personality assessment model that taps five basic dimensions,* 44–46
  in cross-cultural studies, 53
  leadership and, 151

Blogs, 142

Board representatives, 99

Body movements, 138–139

Boeing, 9, 124, 160, 163, 217, 228

Bonus, *a way to reward employees for recent performance rather than historical performance,* 101

Boundaryless organization, *an organization that seeks to eliminate the chain of command, have limitless spans of control, and replace departments with empowered teams,* 211, 217

Bounded rationality, *a process of making decisions by constructing simplified models that extract the essential features from problems without capturing all their complexity,* 62

Bowerman, Bill, 227

Brainstorming, *an idea-generation process that specifically encourages any and all alternatives while withholding any criticism of these alternatives,* 119

Branson, Richard, 160, 223

Brazil, 168, 199

Broadwater, Gene, 78

Bryant, Kobe, 114

Brynaert, Didier, 231

Buck passing, 180

Buffing, 180

Bureaucracy, *an organization structure with highly routine operating tasks achieved through specialization, very formalized rules and regulations, tasks that are grouped into functional departments, centralized authority, narrow spans of control, and decision making that follows the chain of command,* 208

Burger King, 6

C

Campbell Soup, 169

Canada
  motivation, 88
  organizational change, 247
  organizational culture, 232
  social loafing, 120
  stress, 247
  teams and teamwork, 133

Capacity, 215

Caterpillar, 214

Centralization, *the degree to which decision making is concentrated at a single point in the organization,* 206, 216

Cessna, 203

Chain network, 140

Chain of command, *unbroken line of authority that extends from the top of the organization to its lowest echelon and clarifies who reports to whom,* 205

Challenge stressors, *stressors associated with workload, pressure to complete tasks, and time urgency,* 243

Change
  approaches for managing, 238–241
  creating a culture for, 9, 241–243
  cultural differences in organizational, 247
  forces for, 234–235
  Kotter's Eight-Step Plan for Implementing, 239
  Lewin's Three-Step Change Model, 238–239
  organizational culture as barrier to, 222
  organizational development (OD), 239–241
  resistance to, 235–238
  social psychology's study of, 4

Change agents, 235, 240, 248

Channels, 136

Charisma, 157

Charismatic leadership theory, *a leadership theory that states that followers make attributions of heroic or extraordinary leadership abilities when they observe certain behaviors,* 157–158, 163

Chile, 88

China
  conflict resolution in, 199
  emotions, 34, 39
  employee involvement, 104–105
  ethics, 70
  high-context culture, 148
  leadership, 168
  personality, 53
  power tactics in, 184
  social loafing, 120
  stress, 247
  variable-pay program, 104

Chrysler Corporation, 153, 159, 212, 235
Chung, Doo-Ri, 195
Chung Ju-Yung, 223
Circuit City, 235
Citigroup, 43, 65, 222
Clarification and justification, 196
Clinton, Bill, 157
Closure and implementation, 196
Coalitions, 173
Coca Cola, 217
Coercion, 238–241
Coercive power, *a power base that is dependent on fear of the negative results from failing to comply,* 171
Cognition, 188
Cognition and personalization stage, of conflict process, 188, 189–190
Cognitive component, *the opinion or belief segment of an attitude,* 14
Cognitive dissonance, *any incompatibility between two or more attitudes or between behavior and attitudes,* 15
Cognitive evaluation theory, 77
Cohesiveness, *the degree to which members are attracted to each other and are motivated to stay in the group,* 115–116
Collaborating, *a situation in which the parties to a conflict each desire to satisfy fully the concerns of all parties,* 190, 201
Collectivism, *a tight social framework in which people expect others in groups of which they are a part to look after them and protect them,* 53
Command group, *individuals who report directly to a given manager,* 107
Commitment
  change and, 237
  escalation of, 64–65
  goal-setting and, 79
  organizational, 17
Common plan, 130
Communication
  barriers to effective, 145–147
  change and, 237
  cross-cultural barriers to, 147–148
  cultural differences in, 147–148
  direction of, 136–137
  downward, 136–137, 246
  electronic, 142
  e-mail, 142–143
  emotions and moods and, 146
  employee satisfaction and, 149
  filtering, 145
  formal, 140
  horizontal, 137
  informal, 141
  information overload, 144–145
  instant messaging (IM), 143–144
  interpersonal, 137–139
  language in, 146
  lateral, 137
  networked, 167
  oral, 137–138
  in organizations, 140–145
  process of, 135–136
  selective perception, 145
  silence as, 146–147
  as source of conflict, 189
  text messaging (TM), *the transfer and understanding of meaning,* 143–144
  upward, 137
  video conferencing, 144
  written, 138
Communication apprehension, *undue tension and anxiety about oral communication, written communication, or both,* 147
Communication process, *the steps between a source and a receiver that result in the transfer and understanding of meaning,* 135–136
Comparisons, in equity theory, 84
Competency-based pay, 101
Competing, *a desire to satisfy one's interests, regardless of the impact on the other party to the conflict,* 190
Competition, 200, 235
Complexity, 215
Compromising, *a situation in which each party to a conflict is willing to give up something,* 190, 196
Conant, Douglas R., 163
Conchie, Barry, 230
Confirmation bias, *the tendency to seek out information that reaffirms past choices and to discount information that contradicts past judgments,* 64
Conflict, *process that begins when one party perceives that another party has negatively affected, or is about to negatively affect, something that the first party cares about,* 186
  in cross-cultural communication, 148
  cultural differences and, 199
  dysfunctional, 187, 192
  felt, 190
  interactionist view of, 187
  managed, 187
  perceived, 189
  resolution focused view of, 188
  role, 110, 121
  self-managed work teams and, 124
  task, 131, 187, 188
  traditional view of, 186–187
  work teams and, 131
Conflict management, *the use of resolution and stimulation techniques to achieve the desired level of conflict,* 191–193
Conflict process, *a process that has five stages: potential opposition or incompatibility, cognition and personalization, intentions, behavior, and outcomes,* 188–193
Conflict-intensity continuum, 191
Conformity, 111–112, 116, 181

Conscientiousness, *a personality dimension that describes someone who is responsible, dependable, persistent, and organized,* 44, 46, 151

Consensus, 59

Consideration, *the extent to which a person is likely to have job relationships that are characterized by mutual trust, respect for employees' ideas, and regard for their feelings,* 152–153

Consistency, 59

Consultation, 173

Context, in cross-cultural communication, 148

Contextual factors, for team effectiveness, 125–126

Contingency variables, *situational factors; variables that moderate the relationship between two or more other variables,* 5

Continuance commitment, *the perceived economic value of remaining with an organization compared to leaving it,* 17

Contrast effect, *evaluation of a person's characteristics that is affected by comparisons with other people recently encountered who rank higher or lower on the same characteristics,* 60

Cooperativeness, 132, 174, 190

Cooptation, 237

Coors, Molson, 18

Core self-evaluations, *the degree to which an individual likes or dislikes himself or herself, whether the person sees himself or herself as capable and effective, and whether the person feels in control of his or her environment or powerless over the environment; bottom-line conclusions individuals have about their capabilities, competence, and worth as a person,* 21, 46–47

Core values, *the primary or dominant values that are accepted throughout the organization,* 220

Correspondence to behavior and attitudes, 15–16

Cost-minimization strategy, *a strategy that emphasizes tight cost controls, avoidance of unnecessary innovation or marketing expenses, and price cutting,* 214

Countrywide Financial, 235

Cramer, Jim, 166

Creative potential, 67–68

Creative-thinking skills, 68

Creativity, *the ability to produce novel and useful ideas*
  in decision making, 67
  moods and, 36
  openness to experience and, 46
  three-component model of, 68

Cross-functional teams, *employees from about the same hierarchical level, but from different work areas, who come together to accomplish a task,* 124–125

Cross-training, 92–93

Cuban, Mark, 142

Cultural differences
  in attribution, 69
  communication, 147–148
  conflict, 199
  in conformity, 112

  in decision making, 69–70
  emotions, 39–40
  employee involvement, 104–105
  in ethics, 70
  flexible benefits and, 104
  globalized workforce and, 6–7
  goal-setting and, 79
  in group diversity, 120–121
  job satisfaction, 24
  leadership, 168
  in motivation, 88, 104
  negotiation process, 199
  organizational change, 247
  organizational culture, 232–233
  organizational structure, 216–217
  personality, 53
  social loafing, 120
  status, 120
  stress, 247–248
  teams and teamwork, 133–134
  values, 53–56

Culture
  appropriateness of power tactics and, 174
  innovation and, 242

Customer satisfaction, 22

Customer service, 7–8, 37–38

D

Day of the week, 30–31

Deadlines, 66

Deal, Justen, 142

Decentralization, 206

Decision making
  biases and errors in, 63–65, 71
  conflict and, 192
  creativity in, 67
  cultural differences in, 69–70
  emotions and moods and, 36
  ethics in, 66–67
  group, 116–119
  individual, 61
  intuitive, 63
  organizational constraints on, 66
  organizational politics and, 179
  in organizations, 61–62
  rational, 62
  sleep and, 32
  stress and, 246
  utilitarianism system for, 66–67

Decoding, 136

Deep acting, *trying to modify one's true inner feelings based on display rules,* 33

Defensive behaviors, *reactive and proactive behaviors to avoid action, blame, or change,* 179, 180

Degree of routineness, 214

Demands, *responsibilities, pressures, obligations, and even uncertainties that individuals face in the workplace,* 243

Denmark, 88, 247

Departmentalization, *basis by which jobs are grouped together,* 204–205

Dependency, *B's relationship to A when A possesses something that B requires,* 170

Design, 241

Destiny, 241

Deviant workplace behavior, *voluntary behavior that violates significant organizational norms and, in so doing, threatens the well-being of the organization or its members; also called workplace misbehavior or workplace incivility,* 12, 23, 38, 112–113

Direct experience, attitude, 15–16

Direction, 72–73

Disability, 8

Discovery, 241

Disgust, 28

Disney, 221

Displayed emotions, *the emotions that the organization requires workers to show and consider appropriate in a given job,* 33

Disruptiveness, of emotions, 26

Dissonance, 15

Distinctiveness, 58–59

Distributive bargaining, *negotiation that seeks to divide up a fixed amount of resources; a win/lose situation,* 193–195

Distributive justice, 84, 86

Diversity
    cultural differences in group, 120–121
    organizational culture as barrier to, 222
    surface-level, 120
    team member, 129, 134
    workforce, 7, 8

Division of labor, 203

Domestic partners, 8

Dominant culture, *a culture that expresses the core values that are shared by a majority of the organization's members,* 219

Domino's, 9

Downsizing, 212

Downward communication, 136–137

Dreaming, 241

Driving forces, *forces that direct behavior away from the status quo,* 238

Dunning, Kitty, 173–174

Dysfunctional conflict, *conflict that hinders group performance,* 187, 192

E

Eastman Kodak, 222

Economic pressures, 6

Economic trends, 234–235

Eddie Bauer, 235

Education, 237

Effectiveness, in group decision making, 116–117

Efficiency, in group decision making, 116–117

Egypt, 69, 168

Eisner, Michael, 159

Ellison, Larry, 47

Email, 136, 142

EMC Corporation, 144

EMM Industries, 109

Emotional contagion, *the process by which people's emotions are caused by the emotions of others,* 38

Emotional dissonance, *inconsistencies between the emotions people feel and the emotions they project,* 33, 37–38

Emotional intelligence (EI), *one's ability to be self-aware, detect emotions in others, and manage emotional cues and information,* 34–35, 152

Emotional labor, *an employee's expression of organizationally desired emotions during interpersonal transactions at work,* 32–33

Emotional stability, *a personality dimension that characterizes someone as calm, self-confident, and secure (positive) versus nervous, depressed, and insecure (negative),* 44, 45

Emotions. *see also* Moods, *intense feelings that are directed at someone or something*
    affect, 14, 27–29
    basic, 28
    cultural differences in, 39–40
    displayed, 33
    effective communication and, 146
    in email correspondence, 143
    felt, 33
    function of, 29–30
    in negotiation, 198
    rational thinking and, 30
    sources of, 30
    surface acting, 33

Empathy
    in cross-cultural communication, 148
    leadership effectiveness and, 152

Employee behavior and organizational design (OD), 215–216

Employee engagement, *individuals' involvement with, satisfaction with, and enthusiasm for, the work they do,* 17–18

Employee involvement, *a participative process that uses the input of employees and is intended to increase employee commitment to an organization's success,* 98–99, 104–105

Employee performance. *see* Job performance

Employee recognition programs, 103

Employee recognition programs. *see also* Reward systems

Employee response, to organizational politics, 178–179

Employee stock ownership plan (ESOP), *a company-established benefit plan in which employees acquire stock, often at below-market prices, as part of their benefits,* 102

Employee withdrawal, 23

Employee-oriented leaders, *leaders who emphasizes interpersonal relations, takes a personal interest in the needs of employees, and accepts individual differences among members,* 153

Enactive mastery, 82

Encoding, 135

Encounter stage, *the stage in the socialization process in which a new employee sees what the organization is really like and confronts the possibility that expectations and reality may diverge,* 226

Engagement, 18

Enhancement, 181

Enron, 159, 229

Environment, *institutions or forces outside the organization that potentially affect the organization's performance,* 98, 214–215

Envy, 38

Equity, internal versus external, 99–100

Equity theory, *a theory that says that individuals compare their job inputs and outcomes with those of others and then respond to eliminate any inequities,* 83–84, 88, 89

Escalation of commitment, *an increased commitment to a previous decision in spite of negative information,* 64–65

Ethical behavior, cultural differences in, 232

Ethical choices, *decisions made on the basis of ethical criteria, including the outcomes of the decision, the rights of those affected, and the equitable distribution of benefits and costs,* 11

Ethical dilemmas, *situations in which members of organizations are required to define right and wrong conduct,* 11

Ethics
  cultural differences in, 70
  leadership and, 163–164
  in organizational culture, 228–229

European Union, 133–134

Evaluation. *see* Performance evaluation

Evidence-based management (EBM), *the basing of managerial decisions on the best available scientific evidence,* 3

Exchange, 173

Excuses, 181

Exemplification, 181

Exercise, 32

Exit, *dissatisfaction expressed through behavior directed toward leaving the organization,* 21–22

Exit-voice-loyalty-neglect framework, 21

Expectancy theory, *a theory that says that the strength of a tendency to act in a certain way depends on the strength of the expectation that the act will be followed by a given outcome and on the attractiveness of that outcome to the individual,* 86–87, 89

Expectations, 109

Expert power, *influence based on special skills or knowledge,* 172

Expertise, 68

Explanations, 85

Extraversion, *a personality dimension describing someone who is sociable, gregarious, and assertive,* 44, 45, 151, 174

Extrinsic rewards, 77, 103

ExxonMobil, 6, 232

F

Facial expressions, 139

Fairness, 22, 84–85, 237

Favors, 181

Fear, 28

Federal Bureau of Investigation (FBI), 222

FedEx, 223

Feedback, *the degree to which carrying out the work activities required by a job results in the individual obtaining direct and clear information about the effectiveness of his or her performance*
  in communication process, 135
  in job characteristic model (JCM), 91
  job satisfaction measurement, 20
  in self-efficacy theory, 81
  self-generated, 79

Felt conflict, *emotional involvement in a conflict that creates anxiety, tenseness, frustration, or hostility,* 190

Felt emotions, *an individual's actual emotions,* 33

Femininity, *a national culture attribute that indicates little differentiation between male and female roles; a high rating indicates that women are treated as the equals of men in all aspects of the society,* 54

Festinger, Leon, 15

Fiedler, Fred, 154

Fiedler contingency model, *the theory that effective groups depend on a proper match between a leader's style of interacting with subordinates and the degree to which the situation gives control and influence to the leader,* 154–156

Filtering, *a sender's purposely manipulating information so that it will be seen more favorably by the receiver,* 145

Finland, 88

Fiorina, Carly, 159

Five-stage group-development model, *the five distinct stages groups go through: forming, storming, norming, performing, and adjourning,* 108

Fixed pie, *the belief that there is only a set amount of goods or services to be divided up between the parties,* 194

Flattery, 181

Flexibility, 9

Flexible benefits, *a benefits plan that allows each employee to put together a benefit package individually tailored to his or her own needs and situation,* 103, 104

Flextime, *flexible work hours,* 94–96

Ford, Henry, 203, 227

Ford Motor Company, 214, 227

Foreign assignments, 6

Formal channels, *communication channels established by an organization to transmit messages related to the professional activities of members,* 136

Formal groups, 106

Formal power, *a designated work group defined by an organization's structure,* 171

Formal regulations, 66

Formal small-group networks, 140

Formalization, *degree to which jobs within the organization are standardized,* 206–207

Forming stage, *the first stage in group development, characterized by much uncertainty,* 108

France, 39, 168, 217

Freezing, 238

Friendship groups, *groups that forms because the individual members have one or more common characteristics,* 107

Full range of leadership model, *describes a wide variety of possible management and leadership styles, including laissez faire, management by exception, contingent rewards, individualized consideration, intellectual stimulation, inspirational motivation, and idealized influence,* 161

Functional conflict, *conflict that supports the goals of the group and improves its performance,* 187

Fundamental attribution error, 59

G

Gage, Phineas, 29

Gainsharing, *a formula-based group incentive plan,* 102

Galatea effect, 82

Gates, Bill, 30, 223

Gender
    differences in negotiation, 198–199
    emotions and moods, 32
    workforce diversity, 8

General Electric (GE), 10, 43, 80, 153, 211

General Foods, 122

General Motors (GM), 9, 65, 212, 235

Germany, 7, 39, 88, 217, 247

Global Leadership and Organizational Behavior Effectiveness (GLOBE), 54, 168

Globalization, 6

GLOBE Framework for Assessing Cultures, 54

Goal-setting theory, *a theory that says that specific and difficult goals, with feedback, lead to higher performance,* 78–81, 89, 246

Gonzalez, David, 66

Górska-Kolodziejczyk, El'zbieta, 230–231

Grapevine, *an organization's informal communication network,* 141

Great Britain, 88, 216

Greece, 88, 217

Green, Bill, 143

Greenberg, Hank, 159

Ground rules, 197

Group behavior
    cohesiveness and, 115–116, 121
    command group, 107
    conflict and, 186–193
    conformity, 111–112
    decision making as a, 116–119
    development models for, 108–109
    deviant workplace, 112–113
    formal, 106
    friendship, 107
    Hawthorne studies, 110–111
    informal, 106
    interacting, 119
    negotiation and, 193–197
    norms in, 110–113, 121

organizational politics and, 175–180
    properties of, 109–116
    roles and, 109–110
    social loafing, 115, 130, 131
    status in, 113–114, 121
    task groups, 107

Group decision making
    brainstorming, 119
    groupshift, 117–118
    groupthink, 117
    nominal group technique, 119
    polarization, 118
    strengths and weaknesses of, 116
    techniques, 119

Group polarization, 118

Groups. *see also* Teams, *two or more individuals, interacting and interdependent, who have come together to achieve particular objectives*
    cultural differences in, 120–121
    defining and classifying, 106–107
    development models for, 108–109
    interacting, 119
    properties of, 109–116
    size of, 114–115, 121
    teams versus, 123
    trust and, 165

Groupshift, *a change in decision risk between a group's decision and an individual decision that a member within that group would make; the shift can be toward either conservatism or greater risk,* 117, 118

Groupthink, *a phenomenon in which the norm for consensus overrides the realistic appraisal of alternative courses of action,* 117–118, 192

Growth, 231

H

Hackman, J. Richard, 90–91

Hallmark Cards, Inc., 132

Halo effect, *the tendency to draw a general impression about an individual on the basis of a single characteristic,* 60

Hammond, Larry, 230

Hand gestures, 147

Happiness, 28

Harley-Davidson, 125

Hawthorne studies, 110–111

HealthSouth, 159

Heredity, *factors determined at conception; one's biological, physiological, and inherent psychological makeup,* 42–43

Herzberg, Frederick, 74–76

Heurstics, 36

Hewlett-Packard, 211, 214

Hierarchy of needs, *Abraham Maslow's hierarchy of five needs—physiological, safety, social, esteem, and self-actualization—in which, as each need is substantially satisfied, the next need becomes dominant,* 73–74, 88

High-context culture, *culture that relies heavily on nonverbal and subtle situational cues in communication,* 148

Higher-order needs, 73

Hindrance stressors, *stressors hat keep you from reaching your goals (for example, red tape, office politics, confusion over job responsibilities),* 243

Hindsight bias, *tendency for us to believe falsely, after an outcome is actually known, that we would have accurately predicted the outcome,* 65

Historical precedents, 66

Hofstede, Geert, 53–54

Hofstede's Framework for Assessing Cultures, 54
  cultural values, table of, by country, 55–56

Holland, John, 51

Home Depot, 153

Hong Kong, 104, 184

Horizontal communication, 137

House, Robert, 157, 163

Hsu, Ancle, 210

Human resources, 242

Hungary, 247

Hygiene factors, *factors—such as company policy and administration, supervision, and salary—that, when adequate in a job placate workers; when these factors are adequate, people will not be dissatisfied,* 75

Hyundai, 223

I

Iacocca, Lee, 159

IBM, 124, 145

Idea champions, *people who actively and enthusiastically promote the idea, build support, overcome resistance, and ensure that the innovation is implemented,* 242–243

Identification-based trust, 167

IKEA, 223

Illegitimate political behavior, *actions that violate the implied rules of the game,* 174

Illusory correlation, *the tendency of people to correlate two events when in reality there is no connection,* 31

Imitation strategy, *a strategy that seeks to move into new products or new markets only after their viability has already been proven,* 214

Impression management (IM), *process by which individuals attempt to control the impression others form of them,* 180–183

Incompatibility stage, of conflict process, 188, 189

India, 70, 104

Individual behavior
  attitudes and, 14–16
  creativity and, 66–69
  felt emotions, 33
  job attitudes and, 16–18
  job satisfaction, 19–21
  motivation, 72–73
  negotiation and, 37
  personality and, 41–45, 51–52
  political, 177
  safety and, 38–39

Individualism, *the degree to which people prefer to act as individuals rather than as members of groups and believe in individual rights above all else,* 53

Indonesia, 69

Influence, 171, 174

Informal channels, *communication channels that are created spontaneously and that emerge as responses to individual choices,* 136

Informal groups, 106

Information management, 144–145

Information overload, *a condition in which information inflow exceeds an individual's processing capacity,* 145, 146

Information sharing, 165

Ingratiation, 173, 182–183

In-group, 156

Initiating structure, *the extent to which a leader is likely to define and structure his or her role and those of employees in the search for goal attainment,* 152

Injuries, workplace, 38–39

Innovation, *a new idea applied to initiating or improving a product, process, or service,* 9, 241–242

Innovation strategy, *a strategy that emphasizes the introduction of major new products and services,* 213

Inspirational appeals, 173

Instant messaging (IM), 143–144

Institutionalization, *a condition that occurs when an organization takes on a life of its own, apart from any of its members, and acquires immortality,* 222

Instrumental values, *preferable codes of behavior or means of achieving one's terminal values,* 50–51

Integrative bargaining, *negotiation that seeks one or more settlements that can create a win/win solution,* 193, 195–196

Intel, 145

Intelligence, 83

Intensity, 72–73

Intentions, *decisions to act in a given way,* 191

Intentions stage, of conflict process, 188, 190

Interacting groups, *typical groups in which members interact with each other face-to-face,* 119

Interactional justice, *the perceived degree to which individual is treated with dignity, concern, and respect,* 86

Interactionist view of conflict, *the belief that conflict is not only a positive force in a group but is also an absolute necessity for a group to perform effectively,* 187

Interdependence, 20

Interest groups, *people working together to attain a specific objective with which each is concerned,* 107

Intergroup development, *OD efforts to change the attitudes, stereotypes, and perceptions that groups have of each other,* 241

Interpersonal communication, 137–139. *see also* Communication

Interviews, 182

Intonations, 139

Intrinsic task motivation, 69, 103

Intuition, *a gut feeling not necessarily supported by research,* 2–3, 63

Intuitive appeal, 34
Intuitive decision making, *an unconscious process created out of distilled experience,* 63
Iran, 247
Israel, 120, 184, 247
Italy, 247

J

Japan
  attributions, 69
  conflict resolution in, 199
  decision making, 70
  emotions, 40
  high-context culture, 148
  leadership, 168
  motivation, 88
  organizational change, 247
  organizational structure, 216
  service industries in, 7
JCPenney, 163, 206
Ji, David, 210
Job attitudes, 16–18, 38
Job characteristics model (JCM), *a model that proposes that any job can be described in terms of five core job dimensions: skill variety, task identity, task significance, autonomy, and feedback,* 90–91, 104
Job design, 90–97
Job enrichment, *the vertical expansion of jobs, which increases the degree to which the worker controls the planning, execution, and evaluation of the work,* 93–94, 104
Job fit-personality theory, 51
Job involvement, *the degree to which a person identifies with a job, actively participates in it, and considers performance important to self-worth,* 16–17
Job performance
  achievement need and, 76
  core self-evaluations and, 46
  emotional intelligence (EI) and, 34
  expectations and, 86–87
  goal-setting and, 78–79
  job satisfaction and, 18, 22
  personality and, 44, 56
  social environment and, 97
  values and, 56
Job rotation, *the periodic shifting of an employee from one task to another,* 92–93
Job satisfaction, *a positive feeling about one's job resulting from an evaluation of its characteristics,* 16, 121
  absenteeism and, 23
  causes of, 20
  centralization and, 216
  charismatic leadership and, 159
  core self-evaluations and, 21
  cultural differences in, 24
  customer satisfaction and, 22
  emotional stability and, 45
  job performance and, 18, 22

justice and, 86
  measuring, 19–20
  morale and, 23
  organizational citizenship behavior (OCB) and, 22
  organizational politics and, 179
  personality-job fit theory and, 51–52
  sleep and, 32
  turnover and, 23
  two-factor theory of, 74–76
  values and, 56
  work context and, 98
  workplace deviance and, 23
Job sharing, *an arrangement that allows two or more individuals to split a traditional 40-hour-a-week job,* 96
Jobs, movement of, 6
Jobs, Steve, 158, 159
Johnson & Johnson, 229
Judgment, of others, 60–61
Jung, Andrea, 160
Justice
  distributive, 84
  in ethical decision making, 67
  interactional, 86
  organizational, 84–86, 89
  procedural, 85
Justifying, 180

K

Kaiser Permanente, 142
Kamprad, Ingvar, 223
Kelleher, Herb, 159, 223
Kennedy, John F., 157
King, Martin Luther, Jr., 157
Knight, Bobby, 30
Knowledge-based pay, 101
Koei, 232
Korea, 69, 148
Kotter, John, 150, 239
Kotter's Eight-Step Plan for Implementing Change, 239
Kozlowski, Dennis, 159, 163

L

Labor force, diversity in. *see* Workforce diversity
Lafley, A. G., 80, 153
Laissez-faire leadership, 161
Language
  effective communication and, 146
  organizational culture and, 228
Lateral communication, 137
Latin America, 120, 217, 247
Lawson, Lance, 195
Lazear, Ed, 102
Leader–member exchange (LMX) theory, *a theory that supports leaders' creation of in-groups and out-groups; subordinates with in-group status will have higher performance ratings, less turnover, and greater job satisfaction,* 156

Leader–member relations, *the degree of confidence, trust, and respect subordinates have in their leader,* 154

Leadership, *the ability to influence a group toward the achievement of a vision or set of goals,* 37
  attribution theory of, 165–166
  authentic, 163–165
  behavioral theories of, 152–153
  Big Five Model and, 151
  challenges to the construct of, 165–167
  charismatic, 157–160
  compared to management, 150
  cultural differences in, 168
  effectiveness, 154
  ethics and, 163–164
  Fiedler's contingency theory of, 152–156
  influence and, 171
  laissez-faire, 161
  leader–member exchange (LMX) theory of, 156–157
  neutralizers for, 166
  online, 167
  versus power, 171
  socialized charismatic, 164
  structure and, 126–127
  style, 154, 171
  trait theories of, 151–152
  transformational, 157, 168
  trust and, 164

Least preferred co-worker (LPC) questionnaire, *an instrument that purports to measure whether a person is task or relationship oriented,* 154

Legitimacy, 173

Legitimate political behavior, *normal everyday politics,* 174

Legitimate power, *the power a person receives as a result of his or her position in the formal hierarchy of an organization,* 172

Lehman Brother, 235

Lescornez, Philippe, 231

Lewin, Kurt, 238

Lewin's Three-Step Change Model, 238–239

Life satisfaction, 45

Life-work conflicts, 10

Liz Clairborne, 235

Locke, Edwin, 78

Long-term orientation, *a national culture attribute that emphasizes the future, thrift, and persistence,* 54

L'Oreal, 65, 132

Low-context culture, *a culture that relies heavily on words to convey meaning in communication,* 148

Lower-order needs, 73

Lowe's, 232

Loyalty, *dissatisfaction expressed by passively waiting for conditions to improve,* 21–22

Lucent Technologies, 9

Lutes, Lynaia, 145

M

Machiavellianism, *the degree to which an individual is pragmatic, maintains emotional distance, and believes that ends can justify means,* 47

Macy's, 220, 235

Maheras, Thomas, 65

Managed conflict, 187

Management
  compared to leadership, 150
  organizational culture and, 224

Management by exception, 161

Management by objectives (MBO), *a program that encompasses specific goals, participatively set, for an explicit time period, with feedback on goal progress,* 80–81

Managers, implications for
  communication, 149
  conflict management, 200–201
  decision making, 70–71
  emotions and moods, 40
  employee motivation, 105
  groups, 121
  job satisfaction, 25
  leadership, 169
  need theories for motivation, 88–89
  negotiation, 201
  organizational behavior (OB), 12
  organizational change, 248
  organizational culture, 233
  organizational structure, 217
  perception, 70
  performance, 121
  personality, 56
  power tactics, 184–185
  satisfaction, 121
  stress, 248
  teams, 134
  values, 56

Manipulation, 237

Marks & Spencer, 213

Mary Kay Cosmetics, 157

Masculinity, *a national culture attribute describing the extent to which the culture favors traditional masculine work roles of achievement, power, and control; societal values are characterized by assertiveness and materialism,* 53

Maslow, Abraham, 73–74

Maslow's hierarchy of needs theory, 73–74, 88

Masterfoods, 231

Material symbols, *objects that serve as signals of organization's culture, including the size of offices, executive perks, and attire.,* 228

Matrix structure, *a structure that creates dual lines of authority and combine functional and product departmentalization,* 208–209

Mayo, Elton, 110

McClelland, David, 76

McClelland's theory of needs, *a theory stating that achievement, power, and affiliation are three important needs that help explain motivation,* 76–77

McDaniel, Jonathan, 23–24

McDonald's, 6

McGregor, Douglas, 74

McNerney, Jim, 160, 163

Measurements
  of emotional intelligence (EI), 35
  job satisfaction, 20–21

Mechanistic model, *a structure characterized by extensive departmentalization, high formalization, a limited information network, and centralization,* 213

Member preferences, 130

Mental models, *team members' knowledge beliefs about how the work gets done by the team,* 131

Mergers, organizational culture as barrier to, 222–223

Merit-based pay plan, *a pay plan based on performance appraisal ratings,* 101

Merrill Lynch, 166, 217, 235

Messages, 135, 143–144

Metamorphosis stage, *the stage in the socialization process in which a new employee changes and adjusts to the job, work group, and organization,* 226

Mexico, 88, 133–134

Microsoft, 204, 220, 223, 232, 234

Middle East, 39

Misrepresenting, 180

Moby, 143

Moderating variables, 15–16

Montgomery Ward, 9

Moods, *feelings that tend to be less intense than emotions and that lack a contextual stimulus,* 27–28. *see also Emotions*
  in negotiation, 198
  sources of, 30
  structure of, 28–29

Morale, 23

Motivation, *the process that accounts for an individual's intensity, direction, and persistence of effort toward attaining a goal*
  cultural differences in, 88, 104
  defining, 72–73
  employee involvement, 98–99
  equity theory, 83–86
  expectancy theory, 86–87
  goal-setting theory, 78–81
  Herzberg's two-factor theory of, 74–76
  intrinsic, 69, 103
  job design and, 90–97
  job satisfaction and, 75
  management by objectives (MBO), 80–81
  Maslow's hierarchy of needs theory, 73–74
  McClelland's theory of needs, 76–77
  moods and, 36–37
  motivation-hygiene theory, 74–76
  rewards as, 99–100

self-determination theory, 77
self-efficacy theory, 81–83
social cognitive theory, 81–83
social learning theory, 81–83
theories of, 73–87
Theory X, 74
Theory Y, 74
in the work environment, 90–103
Motivation-hygiene theory, 74–76
Motorola, 211
Movement, *a change process that transforms the organization from the status quo to a desired end-state,* 238
Mutual assistance programs, 93
Myers-Briggs Type Indicator (MBTI), *a personality test that taps four characteristics and classifies people into 1 of 16 personality types,* 43–44, 56

N

Narcissism, *the tendency to be arrogant, have a grandiose sense of self-importance, require excessive admiration, and have a sense of entitlement,* 47

Nardelli, Bob, 153

National origin, 8

NEC Corporation, 217

Need for achievement (nAch), *the drive to excel, to achieve in relationship to a set of standards, and to thrive to succeed,* 76

Need for affiliation (nAff), *the desire for friendly and close interpersonal relationships,* 76

Need for power (nPow), *the need to make others behave in a way in which they would not have behaved otherwise,* 76

Needs
  Maslow's hierarchy of, 73–74, 88
  McClelland's theory of, 76–77

Negative affect, *a mood dimension that consists of emotions such as nervousness, stress, and anxiety at the high end and relaxation, tranquility, and poise at the low end,* 29

Neglect, *dissatisfaction expressed through allowing conditions to worsen,* 21–22

Negotiation, *a process in which two or more parties exchange goods or services and attempt to agree on the exchange rate for them*
  anger and, 37
  bargaining strategies for, 196
  best alternative to a negotiated agreement (BATNA), 197
  distributive bargaining, 193–195
  effectiveness of, 198–199
  fixed pie, 194
  gender differences in, 198–199
  group behavior and, 193–197
  integrative bargaining, 195–196
  moods in, 198
  personality traits in, 198
  process, 196–199
Netherlands, The, 88, 247
Networked organizations, 10

Networks, formal small-group, 140

Neumann Homes, 225

Neutralizers, *attributes that make it impossible for leader behavior to make any difference to follower outcomes,* 166

Newman's Own, 210

Nigeria, 184

Nike, 225, 227

Noise, 136

Nokia, 6, 137

Nominal group technique, *a group decision-making method in which individuals meet face-to-face to pool their judgments in a systematic but independent fashion,* 119

Nonverbal communication, 138

Nordstrom, 220

Normative commitment, *an obligation to remain with the organization for moral or ethical reasons,* 17

Norming stage, *the third stage in group development, characterized by close relationships and cohesiveness,* 108

Norms, *acceptable standards of behavior that are shared by the group's members*
  appearance, 110
  group behavior, 110–113, 121
  groupthink and, 117
  performance, 110
  resource allocation, 110
  social arrangement, 110
  status and, 114

Norway, 88

Novell, 232

O

O'Donnell, Trish, 178

Ohio State, 152

Oldham, Greg, 90–91

O'Neal, Stan, 166

Online leadership, 167

Openness to experience, *a personality dimension that characterizes someone in terms of imagination, sensitivity, and curiosity,* 44, 46, 151

Oral communication, 137–138

Organic model, *a structure that is flat, uses cross-hierarchical and cross-functional teams, has low formalization, possesses a comprehensive information network, and relies on participative decision making,* 213

Organizational behavior (OB), *a field of study that investigates the impact that individuals, groups, and structures have on a behavior within organizations, for the purpose of applying such knowledge toward improving an organization's effectiveness*
  challenges and opportunities for, 5–6
  core topics of, 2
  levels of analysis for, 12
  managerial implications of, 12
  toward a discipline of, 4

Organizational change. *see* Change

Organizational citizenship behavior (OCB), 22

Organizational climate, *the shared perceptions organizational members have about their organization and work environment,* 221–222

Organizational commitment, *the degree to which an employee identifies with a particular organization and its goals and wishes to maintain membership in the organization,* 17

Organizational culture, *a system of shared meaning held by members that distinguishes the organization from other organizations,* 22, 218–219
  creating and sustaining, 223
  dominant, 219
  ethics in, 228–229
  formalization versus, 220
  functions of, 220–221
  job satisfaction versus, 219
  as a liability, 222–223
  material symbols, 228
  positive, creating, 230–231
  rituals, 228
  stories, 227–228
  strong versus weak, 220
  subcultures, 219–220
  transmission of, 227–228

Organizational demography, *the degree to which members of a work unit share a common demographic attribute, such as age, sex, race, educational level, or length of service in an organization, and the impact of this attribute on turnover,* 129

Organizational designs, 207–211, 215–216

Organizational development (OD), *a collection of planned change interventions, built on humanistic-democratic values, that seeks to improve organizational effectiveness and employee well-being,* 239–240

Organizational justice, *an overall perception of what is fair in the workplace, composed of distributive, procedural, and interactional justice,* 84–86, 89

Organizational politics, *the use of power to affect decision making in an organization, often based on self-serving and organizationally unsanctioned behaviors,* 174, 177–180

Organizational structure, *how job tasks are formally divided, grouped, and coordinated*
  boundaryless, 211
  bureaucracy, 208
  centralization, 206, 216
  chain of command, 205
  cultural differences and, 216–217
  departmentalization, 204–205
  determinants of, 213–215
  downsizing, 212
  formalization, 206–207
  matrix, 208
  mechanistic model, 213
  organic model, 213
  overview, 202
  simple, 207
  size of, 214

span of control, 205–206
  virtual, 209–211
Outcomes stage, of conflict process, 188, 191–192
Out-group, 156
Overconfidence bias, 63–64
Overconforming, 180

P

Participation
  change and, 237
  in decision making, 81
  representative, 98–99
Participative management, *a process in which subordinates share a significant degree of decision-making power with their immediate superiors,* 98
Patterson, Bill, 109
Pay structure
  job satisfaction measurement, 20–21
  as motivation, 99–100
  types of, 100–104
People skills, 9
Perceived conflict, *awareness by one or more parties of the existence of conditions that create opportunities for conflicts to arise,* 189
Perceived organizational support (POS), *the degree to which employees believe the organization values their contributions and cares about their well-being,* 17
Perceiver, 57
Perception, *a process by which individuals organize and interpret their sensory impressions to give meaning to their environment*
  influences on, 57–58
  of justice, 84–85
  role, 109
  selective, 145
Perceptual distortions, *errors in perceiving situations based on phenomena like overconfidence bias, anchoring bias, confirmation bias, availability bias, escalation of commitment, risk aversion, and hindsight bias,* 61
Performance. *see* Job performance
Performance evaluation
  constraints on, 66
  expectancy theory and, 86–87
  ingratiation and, 182–183
  politicking and, 178
  work teams and, 127
Performance norms, 110
Performing stage, *the fourth stage in group development, during which the group is fully functional,* 108
Persistence, 72–73
Person perception, 58
Personal appeals, 173
Personal power, *influence derived from an individual's characteristics,* 172, 173
Personal variables, as source of conflict, 189
Personality, *the sum total of ways in which an individual reacts to and interacts with others,* 41–49

Big Five model, 44–46, 53
  change and, 237–238
  core self-evaluations and, 46
  cultural differences in, 53
  determinants of, 42
  job performance and, 56
  job-fit theory, 51
  Machiavellianism, 47
  measurement of, 42
  Myers-Briggs Type Indicator (MBTI), 43–44
  narcissistic, 47
  in negotiation, 198
  occupational types, 52–53
  proactive, 49
  risk-taking, 48
  self-efficacy theory and, 83
  self-monitoring, 48
  as source of emotions and moods, 30
  of team members, 128
  Type A, 48–49
  Type B, 49
Personality traits, *Enduring characteristics that describe an individual's behavior,* 43
Personality–job fit theory, *a theory that identifies six personality types and proposes that the fit between personality type and occupational environment determines satisfaction and turnover,* 51
Personalization and cognition stage, of conflict process, 188, 189–190
Person-organization fit, 52–53
Physical distance, 139
Physical exercise, 245
Physiological symptoms, of stress, 244
Piece-rate pay plan, *plan in which employees are paid fixed sum for each unit of production completed,* 100–101
Placement process and stress, 246
Plattner, Hasso, 80
Playing dumb, 180
Playing safe, 180
Polarization, group, 118
Political behavior, *activities that are not required as part of one's formal role in the organization but that influence, or attempt to influence, the distribution of advantages and disadvantages within the organization*
  causes and consequences of, 175–183
  ethics of, 183
  legitimate and illegitimate, 174
Political skills, 174
Politicking, *when people use their influence to taint the facts in an ambiguous environment to support their goals and interests,* 176–178
Politics, *when employees convert their power into action to exert influence, earn rewards, and advance their careers.*
  cultural perception of, 184
  organizational, 174
  reality of, 175–176
Portugal, 88

Position power, *influence derived from one's formal structural position in the organization; includes power to hire, fire, discipline, promote, and give salary increases,* 154

Positive affect, *a mood dimension consisting of positive emotions such as excitement, self-assurance, and cheerfulness on the high end and boredom, sluggishness, and tiredness at the low end,* 29

Positive organizational culture, *a culture that emphasizes building on employee strengths, rewards more than it punishes, and emphasizes individual vitality and growth,* 230–231

Positivity offset, *the tendency of most individuals to experience a mildly positive mood at zero input (when nothing in particular is going on),* 29

Potential, 67–68, 123

Potential opposition stage, of conflict process, 188, 189

Power, *a capacity that A has to influence the behavior of B so that B acts in accordance with A's wishes*
   coercive, 171
   expert, 172
   formal, 171–173
   versus leadership, 171
   legitimate, 172
   personal, 172, 173
   position, 154
   referent, 172
   reward, 171–172

Power distance, *degree to which people in a country accept that power in institutions and organizations is distributed unequally,* 53

Power tactics, *ways in which individuals translate power bases into specific actions,* 173–174, 184

Praise, 230–231

Prearrival stage, *the period of learning in the socialization process that occurs before a new employee joins the organization,* 225

Precedents, 66

Predictability, 3, 16

Preferences, 130

Preparation and planning, 196

Pressure tactic, 173

Prevention, 180

Prince, Charles O., III, 65

Privacy, 143

Proactive personality, *people who identify opportunities, show initiative, take action, and persevere until meaningful change occurs,* 49

Problem-solving teams, *a group of 5 to 12 employees from the same department who meet for a few hours each week to discuss ways of improving quality, efficiency, and the work environment,* 124, 241

Procedural justice, *the perceived fairness of the process used to determine the distribution of rewards,* 85, 86

Process conflict, *conflict over how work gets done,* 187

Process consultation (PC), *a meeting in which a consultant assists a client in understanding process events with which he or she must deal and identifying processes that need improvement,* 240

Process control, 85

Proctor & Gamble, 80, 147, 153, 204

Production-oriented leader, *a leader who emphasizes technical or task aspects of the job,* 153

Productivity, 22, 115–116, 165

Profit-sharing plans, *organization-wide program that distributes compensation based on some established formula designed around a company's profitability,* 102

Promotions, 177

Protests, 175

Psychological empowerment, *employees' belief in the degree to which they affect their work environments, their competence, the meaningfulness of their jobs, and the perceived autonomy in their work,* 16

Psychological symptoms, of stress, 244

Psychology, *the science that seeks to measure, explain, and sometimes change the behavior of humans and other animals,* 3–4

Purpose, 130

Pygmalion effect, *a form of self-fulfilling prophecy in which believing something can make it true,* 82

Q

Quality, 9, 12

Quirk, Peter, 144

R

Race, 8

Radio Shack, 142

Rational decision-making model, *a decision-making model that describes how individuals should behave in order to maximize some outcome,* 62

Rational persuasion, 173

Rational thinking and emotions, 30

Rationality, 26, 62–63

Reagan, Ronald, 157

Receivers, 136

Recognition, 103, 132–133, 230–231

Redesigning jobs, 246

Referent power, *influence based on identification with a person who has desirable resources or personal traits,* 172

Reflexivity, 130

Refreezing, *stabilizing a change intervention by balancing and restraining forces,* 238

Relationship conflict, *conflict based on interpersonal relationships,* 131, 187

Relationship oriented leaders, in Fiedler contingency model, 154

Relaxation techniques, 245

Religion, 8

Representative participation, *a system in which workers participate in organizational decision making through a small group of representative employees,* 98–99

Resistance point, 194

Resistance to change, 236–238

Resolution focused view of conflict, 188

Resource allocation norms, 110

Resources, *things within an individual's control that can be used to resolve demands,* 126, 244

Responsibility, 115, 116

Restraining forces, *forces that hinder movement from the existing equilibrium,* 238–239

Reward power, *compliance achieved based on the ability to distribute rewards that others view as valuable,* 171–172

Reward systems
  as a constraint, 66
  employee recognition programs, 103
  expectancy theory and, 86–87
  extrinsic versus intrinsic, 77–78
  for motivation, 99–100
  praise as, 230–231
  for team players, 132
  work teams and, 127

Rhode, Karen, 144

Rights, in decision making, 67

Ringelmann, Max, 115

Risk
  charismatic leaders and, 157
  groupshift and, 118
  trust and, 165

Risk aversion, *the tendency to prefer a sure gain of a moderate amount over a riskier outcome, even if the riskier outcome might have a higher expected payoff,* 65

Risk-taking behavior, 48

Rituals, *repetitive sequences of activities that express and reinforce the key values of the organization,* 228

Rodriguez, Alex, 242

Roehm, Julie, 143

Rokeach, Milton, 50

Rokeach Value Survey (RVS), 50–51

Role ambiguity, 178

Role conflict, *when an individual finds that compliance with one role requirement may make it difficult to comply with another,* 110, 121

Role expectations, *how others believe a person should act in a given situation,* 109

Role perception, *an individual's view of how he or she is supposed to act in a given situation,* 109, 121

Roles, *a set of expected behavior patterns attributed to someone occupying a given position in a social unit,* 109, 128–129

Roosevelt, Franklin D., 159

Routineness, degree of, 214

Rules
  ground, 197
  of thumb, 36

Rumors, 141

Russia
  motivation, 88
  organizational change, 247

S

Sabotage, 175

Sadness, 28

Safety, 38–39

Sagan, Carl, 29

SAP AG, 80

Satisfactory state of affairs, 61

Saudi Arabia, 147, 247

Scandinavia, 24

Scapegoating, 180

Schiller, Michael, 146

Sclavos, Stratton, 162

Sears, 9, 206

Selection process
  emotional intelligence (EI) and, 35
  organizational culture and, 224–226
  stress and, 246
  for team players, 132

Selective perception, *any characteristic that makes a person, object, or event stand out will increase the probability that it will be perceived,* 60, 145

Self-actualization, *the drive to become what a person is capable of becoming,* 73

Self-concordance, *the degree to which people's reasons for pursuing goals are consistent with their interests and core values,* 78

Self-determination theory, *a theory of motivation that is concerned with the beneficial effects of intrinsic motivation and the harmful effects of extrinsic motivation,* 77, 89

Self-efficacy, *an individual's belief that he or she is capable of performing a task,* 81

Self-efficacy theory, 81–83, 151

Self-evaluations, 21, 46–47

Self-fulfilling prophecy, 82, 157

Self-managed work teams, *groups of 10-15 people who take on responsibilities of their former supervisors,* 124

Self-monitoring, *a personality trait that measures an individual's ability to adjust his or her behavior to external, situational factors,* 48, 180

Self-promotion, 181, 182–183

Self-protection, 42, 180

Self-serving bias, *the tendency for individuals to attribute their own successes to internal factors and put the blame for failures on external factors,* 59–60

Semantics, 147

Senders, 135

Sensitivity, 157

Service industries, 7–8

Short-term orientation, *a national culture attribute that emphasizes the past and present, respect for tradition, and fulfillment of social obligations,* 54

Siemens, 225

Silence, 146–147

Simple structure, *an organization structure characterized by a low degree of departmentalization, wide spans of control, authority centralized in a single person, and little formalization,* 207

Singapore, 88

Single global rating, 19

Situation
  charismatic leadership and, 159
  perception, 58
Size
  of groups, 114–115
  of organizations, 214
  of teams, 129
Skill variety, *the degree to which a job requires a variety of different activities,* 90
Skill-based pay plan, *a pay plan that sets pay levels on the basis of how many skills employees have or how many jobs they can do,* 101
Skilling, Jeff, 163
Skills, of team members, 127–128
Sleep, 32
Smith, Fred, 223
Smith Corona, 9
Social activities, 32
Social anxiety, 147
Social arrangement norms, 110
Social cognitive theory, 81
Social environment, 97
Social learning theory, 81
Social loafing, *the tendency for individuals to expend less effort when working collectively than when working individually,* 115, 120, 130, 131
Social pressures, 16
Social psychology, *focuses on people's influences on one another,* 4–5
Social support, 20, 245
Social trends, 235
Socialization, *a process that adapts employees to the organization's culture,* 224–227
Socialized charismatic leadership, *a leadership concept that states that leaders convey values that are other-centered versus self-centered and role-model ethical conduct,* 164
Sociology, *the study of people in relation to their social environment or culture,* 5
Southwest Airlines, 223
Span of control, *the number of subordinates a manager can efficiently and effectively direct,* 205–206, 216
Spontaneity, 9
Stalling, 180
Status, *a socially defined position or rank given to group or group members by others,* 113–114, 120, 121
Status characteristics theory, *a theory that states that differences in status characteristics create status hierarchies within groups,* 114
Stereotyping, *when we judge someone on the basis of our perception of the group to which he or she belongs,* 60–61
Stories, 227–228
Storming stage, *the second stage in group development, characterized by intragroup conflict,* 108
Stoute, Steve, 173
Strategic alliances, 217

Stress, *a dynamic condition in which an individual is confronted with an opportunity, a demand, or a resource related to what the individual desires and for which the outcome is perceived to be both uncertain and important,* 32, 243
  consequences of, 244–245
  emotional stability and, 45
  organizational approaches to, 245–246
Stress management, 245
Stretching, 180
Strong culture, *a culture in which the core values are intensely held and widely shared,* 220, 222
Structural variables, 242
Structure
  leadership and, 126–127
  as source of conflict, 189
Subcultures, *minicultures within an organization, typically defined by department designations and geographical separation,* 219–220
Substitutes, *attributes, such as experience and training, that can replace the need for a leader's support or ability to create structure,* 166
Summation, of job facets, 19
Sun Microsystem, 144
Surface acting, *hiding one's inner feelings and foregoing emotional expressions in response to display rules,* 33
Surprise, 28
Survey feedback, *the use of questionnaires to identify discrepancies among member perceptions; discussion follows and remedies are suggested,* 240
Sweden, 88
Systematic study, *looking at relationships, attempting to attribute causes and effects, and drawing conclusions based on scientific evidence,* 3
System-imposed time constraints, 66

T

Taco Bell, 65
Taiwan, 39, 184
Tang, John, 145
Target, 58
Target point, in distributive bargaining, 194
Task conflicts, *conflicts over content and goals of the work,* 131, 187, 188
Task groups, *individuals working together to complete a task or job,* 107
Task identity, *the degree to which job requires completion of a whole and identifiable piece of work,* 90–92
Task motivation, 69
Task significance, *the degree to which a job has a substantial impact on the lives or work of other people,* 91
Task structure, *the degree to which the job assignments are procedurized,* 154
Task-oriented leadership style, 154
Team building, *high interaction among team members to increase trust and openness,* 240–241

Team efficacy, *the degree to which the members of a team believe in their ability to achieve future success,* 131
Team processes, 130–131
Teams, 122–126, 241. *see also* Groups; Work teams
  composition of, 127
  effectiveness model for, 125–126
  groups versus, 123
  problem-solving, 124
  process, 130–131
  types of, 123–125
  virtual, 125
Technology, *the way in which an organization transfers its inputs into outputs,* 214, 234
Telecommuting, *working from home at least two days a week on a computer that is linked to the employer's office,* 96–97, 104, 217
Temperament. *see* Emotions; Moods
Temporariness, coping with, 9
Terminal values, *desirable end-states of existence; the goals a person would like to achieve during his or her lifetime,* 50–51
Text messaging (TM), 143–144
Theory X, *the assumption that employees dislike work, are lazy, dislike responsibility, and must be coerced to perform,* 74, 99
Theory Y, *the assumption that employees like work, are creative, seek responsibility, and can exercise self-direction,* 74, 99
3M Company, 43, 211, 213
Three-component model of creativity, *the proposition that individual creativity require expertise, creative thinking skills, and intrinsic task motivation,* 68
Time constraints, 66
Time management, 245
Time of the day, 30–31
Time Warner, 223
Tone differences, 147
Traditional view of conflict, *the belief that all conflict is harmful and must be avoided,* 186–187
Training process
  cross, 92–93
  stress and, 246
  for team players, 132
Trait theories of leadership, *theories that consider personal qualities and characteristics that differentiate leaders from nonleaders,* 151, 153
Traits. *see* Personality traits
Transactional leaders, *leaders who guide or motivate their followers in the direction of established goals by clarifying the role and task requirements,* 160
Transformational leaders, *leaders who inspire followers to transcend their own self-interests and who are capable of having a profound and extraordinary effect on followers,* 157, 160–163
Transformational leadership, 162–163, 168
Translation, 173

Trump, Donald, 48
Trust, *a positive expectation that another will not act opportunistically*
  climate of, 127
  consequences of, 165
  groups and, 165
  identification-based, 167
  information sharing and, 165
  leadership and, 164
  politicking and, 177
  productivity and, 165
Turnover
  job dissatisfaction and, 22
  job enrichment and, 94
  job satisfaction and, 23
  organizational culture and, 220
TWA, 9
Two-factor theory, *a theory that relates intrinsic factors to job satisfaction, while associating extrinsic factor with dissatisfaction; also called motivation-hygiene theory,* 74–76, 99
Tyco, 159
Type A personality, *aggressive involvement in a chronic, incessant struggle to achieve more and more in less and less time and, if necessary, against the opposing efforts of other things or other people,* 48–49
Type B personality, 49

U

U. S. Air Force, 35
U. S. Marine Corps, 225
Ullman, Mike, 163
Uncertainty avoidance, *a national culture attribute that describes the extent to which a society feels threatened by uncertain and ambiguous situations and tries to avoid them,* 54
Unfreezing, *changing to overcome the pressures of both individual resistance and group conformity,* 238
United Kingdom, 7, 104, 247
United States
  decision making, 69–70
  emotions, 39
  employee involvement, 104
  hand gestures in, 147
  job characteristic model (JCM), 104
  job satisfaction, 24
  motivation, 88
  organizational change, 247
  organizational culture, 232
  organizational structure, 216
  personality, 53
  social loafing, 120
  status, 120
  stress, 247
  teams, 133
  workforce diversity, 7, 8

Unity of command, *the idea that a subordinate should have only one superior to whom he or she is directly responsible,* 205

Unpredictability, 9

Upward communication, 137

US Airways, 22, 232

Utilitarianism, *a system in which decisions are made solely on the basis of their outcomes or consequences and to provide the greatest good for the greatest number,* 66–67

V

Value system, *a hierarchy based on a ranking of an individual's values in terms of their intensity,* 50

Values, *basic convictions that a specific mode of conduct or end-state of existence is personally or socially preferable to an opposite or converse mode of conduct or end-state of existence,* 49–53
  core, 220
  cultural differences in, 53–56
  employee performance and, 56
  Hofstede's Framework for Assessing Cultures, 53–54, 55–56
  importance of, 50
  instrumental, 50–51
  job satisfaction and, 56
  Rokeach Value Survey (RVS), 50–51
  terminal, 50

Variable-pay program, *a pay plan that bases a portion of an employee's pay on some individual and/or organizational measure of performance,* 100, 102–103, 104

Venezuela, 104

Verbal persuasion, 82

Verisign, 162

Vicarious modeling, 82

Video conferencing, 144

Vietnam, 148

Virgin Group, 160, 223

Virtual organization, *a small, core organization that outsources major business functions,* 209–211

Virtual teams, *teams that use computer technology to tie together physically dispersed members to achieve a common goal,* 125

Vision, *a long-term strategy for attaining a goal or goals,* 157, 158

Vision statement, *a formal articulation of an organization's vision or mission,* 158

Vitality, 231

Vocational Preference Inventory questionnaire, 51

Voice, *dissatisfaction expressed through active and constructive attempts to improve conditions,* 21–22

Volatility, 215

Volvo, 122

Vroom, Victor, 86

W

W. L. Gore & Associates, 122, 224, 241

Waldock, David, 132

Walmart, 143, 228

Walton, Sam, 228

Washington Mutual, 235

Weather, 31

Weber, Max, 157

Wegmans, 224

Welch, Jack, 3, 153, 159, 211

Wellness programs, *organizationally supported programs that focus on the employee's total physical and mental condition,* 246

Western Electric Company, 110

Wetzal, Jim, 195

Wheel network, 140

Whistle-blowers, *individuals who report unethical or illegal practices by their employers to outsiders,* 67

Whistle-blowing, 175

Whole Foods, 132

Wilson, Fred, 143

Women, in the workforce, 7

Woolworth, 9

Word connotations, in cross-cultural communication, 147

Word-of-mouth, 141

Work environment. *see* Environment

Work group, *a group that interacts primarily to share information and to make decisions to help each group member perform within his or her area of responsibility,* 123

Work specialization, *the degree to which tasks in an organization are subdivided into separate jobs,* 203, 215–216

Work teams, *a group whose individual efforts result in a performance that is greater than the sum of the individual inputs,* 122, 123
  assessment of need for, 132–133
  cultural differences of, 133–134
  self-managed, 124

Workforce diversity, *the concept that organizations are becoming more heterogeneous in terms of gender, age, race, ethnicity, sexual orientation, and inclusion of other diverse groups,* 7, 8

Work-life conflicts, 10

Workplace incivility, 112

Workplace misbehavior. *see* Deviant workplace behavior

Works councils, 99

World politics, 235

WorldCom, 9, 159

Written communication, 138

Y

Yahoo! 222

Z

Zappos, 22

Zeldes, Nathan, 145

Zero-sum approach, *an approach to bargaining in which the gains made by one side come at the expense of the other side, and vice versa,* 178